Planning for Drought

Published in cooperation with the Institute of Agriculture and Natural Resources of the University of Nebraska–Lincoln, the Illinois State Water Survey of the Illinois Department of Energy and Natural Resources, NSF, NCPO/NOAA, CSRS/USDA, U.S.AID, UCAR, IAPO/UN, UNDP, WMO, and UNEP

Planning for Drought

Toward a Reduction
of Societal Vulnerability

edited by
Donald A. Wilhite
and William E. Easterling
with Deborah A. Wood

Westview Press / Boulder and London

UNEP

Published in 1987 in the United States of America by Westview Press, Inc.; Frederick A. Praeger, Publisher; 5500 Central Avenue, Boulder, Colorado 80301

Library of Congress Cataloging-in-Publication Data
Planning for drought.
    1. Droughts.   I. Wilhite, Donald A.
II. Easterling, William E.
QC929.D8D764 1987   551.57'73   87-13968
ISBN 0-8133-7255-0

Composition for this book was provided by the editors.
This book was produced without formal editing by the publisher.

Printed and bound in the United States of America

The paper used in this publication meets the requirements of the American National Standard for Permanence of Paper for Printed Library Materials Z39.48-1984.

6   5   4   3   2   1

CONTENTS

PART 1
BACKGROUND

PART 2
PREDICTION

PART 3
MONITORING AND EARLY WARNING

FOREWORD

The single most difficult task for a representative democracy is to engage in long-range planning. If we are planning for something which, moreover, no one believes (or wants to believe) will happen and which might require us to work or restrain now to avoid a possible disaster later, the task is even more difficult.

Stated differently, if you tell me that an action today *will* harm me, I will probably avoid doing it. Tell me that a pattern of behavior together with certain external conditions *could* harm me, and I might try to beat the odds.

In short, governments of our type seem doomed to lead an existence that abhors long-range planning. The most striking example of this is the drought scenario. The day that I took office, I realized that the single most devastating event that could befall our beautiful state was a widespread drought.

Fortunately, I inherited and recruited a group of advisors that were combat veterans from the 1976-77 Great Plains drought. My friend and advisor, Jim Exon, also admonished me about the problems of dealing with the effects of a widespread and prolonged drought. We formed a small working group in the summer of 1984, and I agreed to make drought planning a high priority for the Kerrey administration. We received enthusiastic support and cooperation from the University of Nebraska and the natural resources related state agencies.

Also fortunately, an evaluation of the governmental response to the 1976-77 drought assessment and response effort had been completed at the University of Nebraska. We decided that Nebraska would be among the first states to develop a truly comprehensive state drought response plan. In a parallel effort the University of Nebraska's Center for Agricultural Meteorology and Climatology and the Illinois State Water Survey organized the International Symposium and Workshop on Drought.

As I reflect on my four years as governor and specifically my participation in the fall 1986 Symposium, I have learned many lessons.

Government can react to disasters in one of two ways. One approach is to wait until an event occurs and try to mitigate the consequences by whatever means available as quickly as possible. Alternatively, procedures may be developed before a disaster that will define mechanisms to respond to various kinds of events. The first of these approaches is crisis management and the second is risk management.

There are a number of barriers to effective risk management in general and to drought planning in particular. One obstacle is that the typical mode of operation is crisis management. The amount of resources consumed as solutions are found for consecutive crises leaves few, if any, resources for risk planning efforts.

Another barrier to drought planning is the uncertainty of drought itself. Drought prediction is a tenuous process, if not totally impossible. In addition, each drought is unique in its magnitude and duration, and thus its impacts also differ. These uncertainties increase the difficulty of effective drought planning.

Perhaps the greatest barrier is spawned by a lack of interest in risk management. Such endeavors have no visual effect and do not receive much attention from the media and, consequently, the public. Government is less likely to plan for things like drought without public interest or demand. Elected representatives would rather deal with issues that are high profile and will serve as testimony to their constituents.

However, recognition of the advantage of risk planning (in terms of time and money) may be significant enough in times of tight budgets to give it a higher profile. Nebraska has made some movement in that direction. Interest has been strong enough that a drought plan has been developed and will be maintained as part of overall risk management in state government.

Drought management and planning is certainly an important policy issue today and in the future. I applaud the efforts of the coorganizers of this symposium and workshop for undertaking this task. Perhaps the information presented on drought prediction, monitoring, impact assessment, adaptation, and response, as well as the research priorities and recommendations for future actions included in this volume, will stimulate additional intellectual activity on this important policy issue and, ultimately, reduce society's vulnerability to drought.

Robert Kerrey

PREFACE

Scientist, politician, businessman, or concerned citizen—each of us has a particular perception of drought. Even within these groups, there are significant differences in perceptions of drought, based on our experiences, training, and environment. Meteorologists and sociologists, for example, view drought as quite different problems—the former striving to predict or explain the physical causes of drought or describe the magnitude of the precipitation deficiency while the latter is more interested in the effects of the deficiency on people and their institutions.

To those who study drought, regardless of our perspective, it is clear that drought is a normal feature of climate and its recurrence is inevitable. And, the widespread occurrence of severe drought during the past decade repeatedly underscores the vulnerability of both developed and developing societies to its ravages. Whether referring to the well-documented recent tragedies of Ethiopia or the economic impacts of the 1986 drought in the southeastern United States, the message seems clear—society has typically chosen to react (i.e., employ crisis management) to drought rather than prepare (i.e., employ risk management) for it. With few exceptions this approach has been, at best, ineffective.

The International Symposium and Workshop on Drought was organized to review and assess our current knowledge of drought and to determine what research and information is needed to improve national and international capacity to cope with drought. The symposium and workshop was intended to provide a forum for discussion of the physical and societal implications of drought within the context of a variety of spatial scales, from local (i.e., farm level) to supernational regions (i.e., the Sahel), and also within the context of economically developed as well as developing nations. Discussions initiated at the symposium were to culminate in the workshop. The purpose of the workshop was to draw attention to drought as a policy issue, one that can be managed more effectively through an interdisciplinary and cooperative effort from the scientific and policy communities. The ultimate goal of the workshop was to establish the rudiments for a "plan of action" to facilitate drought preparedness on a global scale. Attendance at the symposium was open to all who wished to participate, though the number of participants in the workshop was restricted to maintain a proper working environment.

A comprehensive symposium program was organized around six principal themes: (1) prediction; (2) detection, monitoring, and early warning; (3) impact assessment; (4) technological and sociopolitical adaptation; (5) the role of government in planning for and responding to drought; and (6) the role of international and donor organizations in planning for and responding to drought. The program was carefully organized and speakers were recruited on the basis of their expertise in one or more research areas or in some aspect of drought policy.

In the papers included in this volume, many interesting and, at times, conflicting viewpoints of drought are presented. F. Kenneth Hare, a scientist with vast experience and insight into the drought condition, introduces Part 1 with a discussion of drought and desiccation, providing personal reminiscences to illustrate his points. His overview gives the reader a fascinating perspective on drought and the need to recognize its many facets and to "know one's enemy." The second and final paper in Part 1 reviews the way scientists define drought in order to achieve a better understanding of its far-reaching impacts, and concludes with several recommendations on a conceptualization that incorporates both physical and social measures of drought that have local or regional significance.

In Part 2, Eugene Rasmusson provides an overview of the global prospects for drought prediction from a meteorological perspective, giving attention to what progress has been made, what techniques are providing the most skillful predictions, and where and when we can expect the most progress in future predictability. Specific assessments of the prospects of prediction for Northeast Brazil and Australia and Indonesia follow. Vit Klemeš concludes the section with an examination of the predictability of drought from a hydrological point of view.

Part 3 presents the technology currently available to detect, monitor, and provide early warning of the onset of drought conditions using both surface and satellite networks. The overview papers were prepared by Kenneth Hubbard (surface monitoring systems) and Compton Tucker and Sam Goward (satellite systems). Examples of the application of these technologies in Australia and the semiarid regions of Africa are presented. Part 3 concludes with a discussion by Norton Strommen and Ray Motha of the operational early warning agricultural weather system developed by the World Agricultural Outlook Board of the U.S. Department of Agriculture.

Part 4 presents examples of current research on drought impact assessment methodology and the details of specific programs recently established to provide early warning of the impact of drought on various geographic scales. The overview paper on impact assessment methodology was prepared by Martin Parry and Timothy Carter. The particular programs chosen were the drought early warning program of NOAA/-NESDIS/AISC and the food shortage assessment and prediction program of the Ethiopian Relief and Rehabilitation Administration. John McIntire's paper illustrates the importance of incorporating the concept of impact assessment into an operational phase of an early warning system.

Part 5 discusses two issues of critical importance to the theme of the symposium. First, Michael Glantz examines the interrelationships between climate, particularly drought, and economic development in sub-Saharan Africa. Second, Norman Rosenberg considers the global implications of climate change, such as that brought on by carbon dioxide enrichment of the atmosphere, on the frequency and severity of drought.

In Part 6 consideration is given to the role that societal adaptation and adjustment can play in mitigating some of the worst effects of drought. In his overview, Steven Sonka argues for integrating models of the adjustment process, beginning at the farm level and aggregating to regions. This is followed by case studies from South Australia, India, and the U.S. Great Plains.

The role of government in planning for and responding to drought is the subject of Part 7. Donald Wilhite explores drought as a policy issue that governments have traditionally responded to through crisis management. The case studies that follow describe the experiences of Botswana, India, Northeast Brazil, and South Africa and provide further evidence of the need for a proactive approach to drought management.

In Part 8, Harold Dregne draws from his years of experience in international agriculture to discuss the role of international organizations in coping with famine and the effects of drought on agricultural production systems. Clifford May of the New York Times discusses the role of the media in identifying and publicizing recent droughts, particularly in Ethiopia. Dawit Giorgis, former director of the Ethiopian Relief and Rehabilitation Administration, documents the actions of the Ethiopian government and other organizations during the recent drought.

In Part 9 Tom Potter summarizes the discussions of the symposium, reflecting on the objectives of the meeting, the lessons learned, and the challenges that lie ahead. He emphasizes the need to identify data and information needs, available techniques, and ways to implement and evaluate the usefulness of those techniques. These objectives were addressed in the workshop.

The final section of the volume presents the results of the workshop discussions on how best to foster drought planning efforts in both developed and developing nations. Following the identification of the constraints to drought planning and ways to overcome these constraints, each of five task groups responded to a set of specific questions on the use of available and emerging technology in strategy formulation, research priorities to further this goal, and recommendations for further actions by governments and international and donor organizations. Part 10 concludes with a ten-step planning process, distilled from workshop discussions, that national and provincial governments could follow to facilitate the establishment of drought plans on a global basis.

Progress toward improving the drought coping capacity of national and provincial governments and international and donor organizations through better planning was the principal goal of this symposium and workshop. The information, experiences, and recommendations presented in this volume represent the collective wisdom of an interdisciplinary and international roster of scientists and policy officials. Their insights and recommendations will provide the intellectual basis for a model that can assist all drought-prone nations in achieving a more effective drought management strategy.

Donald A. Wilhite
William E. Easterling

ACKNOWLEDGMENTS

Few realize the time, energy, manpower, and financial resources required to organize and conduct an international symposium and workshop, as well as assemble and edit the proceedings. The results of such an effort are presented in the pages that follow.

Two years have elapsed since the idea for a symposium on drought preparedness first emerged at the Climate-Related Impacts Networkshop at the National Center for Atmospheric Research in Boulder, Colorado. The list of persons who have contributed to the successful completion of this project seems endless, certainly too long to mention here without fear of some omission. Their contribution is gratefully acknowledged. However, the efforts of several persons at the University of Nebraska-Lincoln must be highlighted. The editors would like to thank Sharon Kelly and Roberta Sandhorst, who provided secretarial assistance for the numerous organizational aspects of the symposium, and Nancy Brown for her patience and diligence in typing manuscripts and tables. Special thanks go to Keith Bartels for his desktop publishing expertise, patience, and persistence in preparing the manuscripts in final form.

The editors wish to express their appreciation to the contributors, who so willingly agreed to write papers for inclusion in this volume. Thanks also to the many workshop participants that shared their ideas and experiences with the hope of stimulating progress toward a "plan of action" for managing drought in a more effective manner, and to the reviewers, whose valuable suggestions added immensely to the final product.

We acknowledge the contribution of the sponsors and supporters of this symposium and workshop. The Institute of Agriculture and Natural Resources of the University of Nebraska–Lincoln and the Illinois State Water Survey of the Illinois Department of Energy and Natural Resources contributed our time and other resources for a successful meeting. The U.S. National Science Foundation, National Climate Program Office/NOAA, Cooperative State Research Service/USDA, U.S. Agency for International Development, University Corporation for Atmospheric Research, International Agricultural Programs Office of the University of Nebraska, United Nations Development Program, United Nations Environment Program, and World Meteorological Organization provided financial support and valuable advice.

We would like to thank Norman Rosenberg and Peter Lamb, who supported our involvement in this important professional endeavor and assisted us in the development of the symposium program and some organizational aspects of the meeting.

Lastly, the editors are indebted to Deborah Wood for her countless hours assisting us with the organizational aspects of the symposium and workshop and, more recently, for editing and proofreading the manuscripts. Her contribution to each of the manuscripts is clearly evident.

D.A.W. and W.E.E.

PART 1

Background

CHAPTER 1
DROUGHT AND DESICCATION:
TWIN HAZARDS OF A VARIABLE CLIMATE

F. Kenneth Hare

INTRODUCTION

My earliest recollections are of an intense drought, all of sixty-five years ago. Nineteen-twenty-one set records across much of England, and my childhood home on Salisbury Plain was in the thick of it. I remember still the midsummer dropping of the linden and copper beech leaves, the withering of the fruit, and drying up of all the wells but one, our deepest. Even the river became smelly, weed-choked and insect-laden; the trout went belly up in July, and we lost our fishing tenants, who weren't prepared to pay for lifeless putrefaction. I remember nothing before that time, and virtually nothing for two or three years on. But that drought is still vivid; it made me a climatologist for life.

In the same country, 1920 and 1922 were unremarkable. Nineteen-twenty-one experienced a drought of the classical sort—one where the rain stops falling and then starts again when the drought is over, usually within the year, as it did again in England in 1976. I suspect that 1986 will turn out to be that way in Georgia and South Carolina, where drought has already run two to three years. I don't know what causes these short-term droughts, or even whether *cause* is a useful word when you are talking about a system like climate, which is boundlessly variable, wide open to space, and utterly dependent on the oceans. Certainly, we know of nothing external to climate itself as potential causes. Climate is inclined to be manic-depressive; its moods are pathological. Yet we are aware that it gets back to normal—and we bet on it, by our economic strategies.

Contrast my experience at that time, and your own personal recollections of drought, with what Africans will remember of the 1970s and 1980s. The Sahel went through a severe drought at the outset of the 1970s. The Sahelian drought, more even than the so-called food crisis of 1973-75, put climate on the front pages of the newspapers. Then it rained again in 1974 and 1975. The drought was over, the conventional wisdom decided (as did most governments and United Nations agencies). But it wasn't. It came back, intensified, and spread—until by 1985 it was an international disaster, at its worst in Ethiopia, but wrenchingly effective over most of the tragic continent. It wasn't a drought, but a desiccation—a prolonged, gradually intensifying nightmare from 1968 until 1984. In 1985 and 1986, rains have been more abundant in many areas. The desiccation may be over. But I want to stress the difference between the two ideas—drought and desiccation. The one resembles mononucleosis: you get it, but you get over it (after examinations are over!). The other is like a chronic wasting disease. You get it, but you don't get over it. It slowly worsens.

I'll try to justify this distinction with a few personal reminiscences. What I've learned, in the course of a long professional life, is that one must add a personal sense of what matters to the insights that theory can give. I admit to being an all-out supporter of the modelers. I believe that our major thrust, as research workers, has got to be toward the mechanics of drought and desiccation—what causes them, how they evolve, and what they evolve into. Atmospheric scientists like myself pin their faith on the satellite, the supercomputer and the stray genius that knows how to model the climatic system (though not if he or she wants to spend the entire budget for drought research!). But to use such resources effectively, one must know one's enemy—how drought strikes, what it does, and how to cope with it. That's what this international symposium is about.

THE NATURE OF DROUGHT

Our institutions, it seems to me, all function on the assumption that drought will not endure. And this is what, for most of us, experience says will happen. The time and space scales of drought limit the stress it can place upon us and the damage it can do.

Climatic drought is, among other things, the failure of expected precipitation, over a period long enough for it to hurt. Abundant rainfall in the Great Basin would be accounted a dry year in the Corn Belt. Our institutions, technology, farm calendars, and assumptions about energy demand all relate to an accepted expectation of precipitation—its amount, the form it takes, the time of year at which it comes. Built into this expectation are all kinds of allowances for variability—for the usual uncertainties of runoff, snow melt, soil moisture recharge, peak transpiration demands, and so on. We expect variation in all these things as well as in the normal impact of precipitation.

I treat climatic drought as being the incidence, for a damaging period of time, of things outside this broader kind of expectation. If you accept my usage, drought is a phenomenon of the moist climates; there are no droughts in the rainless Sahara or Atacama deserts. In fact, human settlements at the oases within the deserts see floods from excessive rainfall as the chief threat to their crops and irrigation systems. Drought is a meaningless term when rain is a rare event.

Long ago we built into this notion of expected precipitation the role of soil water storage, which modulates the actual delivery of water to plants, air, ground water, and ultimately runoff. The better indices of drought that we use—those of Palmer (1965) and Bhalme and Mooley (1983) in particular—use this idea, as do the various water budget schemes used by hydrologists. Atmospheric scientists are gradually learning how to incorporate this crucial element into their models of climate over land surfaces—and even to ask whether it cannot be scanned adequately from satellite altitudes.

Behind these small advances, however, we have remained very largely in the position that we can predict neither the beginning nor the end of specific droughts; and we can say little in advance about their intensity, geographical extent, and root causes. Droughts occur on what may be the least predictable time scale of atmospheric events. We have had to treat them, as the lay world does implicitly, as stochastic in nature. There are experts here who will show that some progress is being made; but we are a long way from prediction. Moreover, we now realize the limitations of periodicities in rainfall records. Recent research has shown, via spectral analysis of current and proxy climatic records, that there is no firm twenty-or twenty-two-year Hale-related rhythm in

Great Plains rainfall, though several periods in the range of fifteen to twenty-five years show statistical significance (Stockton and Meko, 1983). Neither farmers nor governments can make much use of such vague information. Most of all we need to know, if such quasi periodicity is there, what mechanisms underlie it. We are a long way from such understanding. The climatic forecaster will get no free lunch from the statisticians.

This same research has also confirmed what we knew from experience: that severe drought in North America is quite limited in duration—it does not usually affect successive growing seasons—and is also spatially restricted. Maps of Palmer's drought index have a mesoscale look about them. Areas of severe drought usually alternate with moist areas only a few hundred kilometers away. Adjacent states or provinces may be affected (as in the 1986 southeastern drought), but this is rarely true of a large part of the continent. Even in the 1930s, severe drought extended across much of the Great Plains only in a few years. The droughts of 1983, 1984, and 1985 in the Canadian prairies affected only parts of the spring wheat belt. The economic impact of spatially extensive drought is very much greater than the patchwork quilt pattern normally displayed by the rainfall maps would indicate.

Work by Nicholson (1982) has shown, in contrast, that African rainfall displays remarkable spatial coherence. At its peak, the great desiccation of the 1960s, 1970s, and 1980s affected almost the entire continent. In 1984 no less than twenty-three contiguous countries were listed by FAO as suffering from consequent food shortages.The African desiccation was devastating partly because it was so widespread: There can be no help from your neighbor if she or he, too, is hungry.

Why does rainfall sometimes fail? Amazingly there is no clear answer. We can surmise (and in selected cases demonstrate) that the causes may include lower-than-normal precipitable water (not true in Africa in 1972); more widespread tropospheric subsidence, and hence greater stability, suppressing convection; an absence of rain-generating disturbances; complex air-sea interactions, so lovingly treated by Jerry Namias; and perhaps even microphysical variations in atmospheric aerosol. But there is still too much surmising and too little concrete knowledge.

I vividly recall the drought of 1933-34 in southern England, when front after front crossed the country dry. Was this due to reduced vertical motion, or drier mid-tropospheric air? There was no simple way of answering, because research into quantities of rainfall was not—and still is not—conducted on the relevant time scale.

Here on the Great Plains the answers will have to come from better understanding of mesoscale rainfall systems—for example, the mesoscale convective complexes (MCCs) first named by R. A. Maddox (1980) only in 1980—and their relation both to synoptic-scale control and to the remarkable diurnal effects that give a nocturnal rainfall maximum to the eastern Plains. The journals are full of good papers on these developments. But we need to apply them to the mechanics of drought, itself a large mesoscale event in most cases.

The same is true in the United Kingdom, where equally distinguished work has been done on the mesosynoptic scale linkages, and where multilevel baroclinic modeling of rainfall has achieved some spectacular successes. In the United Kingdom, drought is unmistakably related to year-to-year variations in blocking, which is not so simply true in North America. But blocking is itself a difficult event to predict.

And so, I end this part of my talk with a pessimistic conclusion: that drought is still largely unpredictable, and its causes are obscure. This may well remain so. But at least we know now what the questions are, and we are working hard to answer them. Those who are concerned to make human institutions drought-proof, or at least drought-aware, are not wasting their time. The climatologist is not on the point of making their work superfluous—or of going out of business.

WHAT OF DESICCATION?

From the standpoint of human strategy, drought is a well-understood hazard: our tactics—and strategies are compounded of tactics—are to outwait it. Nature adopts a similar approach. Natural ecosystems outlive prolonged drought with little or no change. Individual plants and animals die, but the populations to which they belong survive, and even flourish—since drought eliminates aggression from less hardy species. Xerophytic ecosystems are among the world's most patient and stable systems. Anyone who has visited a semidesert just after the rains return has seen the miracle reenact itself, as luxuriant life reassumes possession of the land.

Human society places more value on the individual than does nature, and we are disquieted when farmers are driven off their land, or when thousands of Africans are forced to migrate to escape starvation. So our ability to outwait a drought depends on who and where we are, and on how long it lasts. But always there is in our minds the conviction that the rains will, indeed, come back. Meanwhile we wait, economize, defer decisions, and watch our individual and collective bank accounts or grain stores with growing anxiety.

Vastly more demoralizing is a true desiccation—a prolonged period in which drought slowly and intermittently intensifies. Even natural ecosystems may be confounded by two or three decades of progressively decreasing rainfall. Fortunately such episodes are rare in North America, and almost unknown in western Europe. But they are a fact of life and death in Africa and Australia—and, I suspect, elsewhere.

The Sahelian drought itself exemplified the process of desiccation. Nicholson's work, supported by similar analyses by Winstanley (1974), Lamb (1982), and others, has shown that African rainfall has in recent years exhibited much spatial coherence—as I stressed earlier. But it also showed that the great drought of 1968-73 was part of a much more prolonged and profound disturbance of rainfall over much of Africa. In the Sahelian and Sudanian belts of northern and western Africa, the 1950s and early 1960s were remarkably wet, and in the early 1960s these favorable conditions spread to the plateaus and mountainsides of east Africa. It was a joyous time for the African colonies to gain their independence, as so many did at that time. It was a green, productive world that they inherited. It was easy for statesmen to assume that these lush conditions would continue—and political suicide for them to move more cautiously.

Unfortunately, the good times did not last, through no fault of the new nations. From the mid-1960s on, rainfall decreased haltingly but remorselessly over much of Africa. In Sudan and the Sahel—the semidesert scrubs and savannas of North Africa—the decline led to the great drought of 1968-73. Moderate rains returned in 1974 and 1975, but then the desiccation resumed, reaching its dreadful climax in 1984. I do not need to remind you that this further desiccation also affected East Africa, and for a time southern Africa, too. All of us still remember the faces of dying Ethiopian children, thanks to television cameras.

With the perspective of hindsight we can now see that this was indeed a desiccation—a progressive increase of drought intensity, mitigated by occasional years of relative abundance. I have not seen the consequences analyzed in quite these terms, but I imagine that the political and economic impact has been more serious than that of a severe drought alone. In particular, the periods of remission took everyone's eyes off the ball. At the United Nations Conference on Desertification in 1977, all sense of urgency had departed from the politicians present because there had been two better years (actually still subnormal) immediately before the Conference. The drought was over, in their minds. In fact, the second round, more severe than the first, had already begun.

Another desiccation of this kind was observed in central Australia between 1945 and 1972 (Hare, 1983). Locally it was perceived as a succession of dry years, which are scarcely news in the semidesert interior rangelands of the desert continent. Nevertheless, it was a true desiccation of part of the already dry interior, with a slow intensification spread over more than two decades. Alice Springs was in the midst of it. Australian pastoralists are an adaptable breed; but by 1972, when conditions were at their worst, many station holders had almost forgotten what the better years could mean to their flocks, herds, and horses (and the water in their wells).

Desiccations mean many things that short-term drought does not mean. One is the increasing strain on human institutions, and on people, none of whom is likely to perceive the situation with any accuracy. I am sure that some part of the deterioration of Africa's political life has arisen from the long desiccation, which was neither expected nor recognized by those who were trying to make new nations out of the colonies. It is one of the bitter ironies of history that nature should have turned so sour just as Africans were trying to take command of their own destinies.

And, of course, desiccation means a great drawdown of water resources. The great rivers of West Africa—Senegal, Niger, Chad—have progressively fallen, until the inland delta of the Niger and the flood-plain lands of the Senegal have become difficult or impossible to farm. The Nile at the Aswan High Dam fell to dangerously low levels. Lake Chad has all but disappeared (as it has done before in history). Ground water everywhere has been mined, as it always is under such conditions. In a drought the loses can be made good, but not so in a true desiccation. Woody vegetation, and organic content in soil, disappear and do not return for decades. Desiccation means a loss of capital stock, a writing-off of assets, perhaps also permanent impoverishment.

I have no idea why such prolonged episodes occur, though I have speculated in print about the effect of various feedbacks—albedo, soil water shortage, and perhaps others (Hare, 1983). We all wonder about the relation between rainfall in semiarid Africa, Australia, and monsoon Asia; the ENSO phenomenon; and other quasi-periodic processes. Much of the effort being put into the World Meteorological Organization's World Climate Research Program, and into ventures such as Tropical Oceans and Global Atmosphere (TOGA) and WOCE, aims at the prediction of such long-term changes. We are not yet sure that they *are* predictable, at least with present monitoring and computing facilities and present levels of theoretical understanding.

So far, during my lifetime, such desiccation has always ended with rain—for example, in Australia in 1973-74, in such abundance that Lake Eyre, nearly dry for a decade, rose to a 10,000-year maximum level within a year. So far this has not happened in Africa, where 1985 and 1986 rains have, as far as I know, been adequate rather than abundant—though experience will vary from country to country. But perhaps the African desiccation really has ended. I do not know.

WHAT OF THE FUTURE?

The whole point of my talk is the bearing these events have on the future. We are now largely convinced (not quite all of us) that a lasting climatic change is in progress, because of a greenhouse warming of the troposphere and surface. Some remain skeptical. Others prefer to wait for empirical evidence that a true warming signal is stepping out of the noise. The noise level is very high, so that signal detection is difficult. Nevertheless, the conviction is growing that a greenhouse warming is in progress and will be unmistakable within a decade or two.

Going with the model predictions of rising temperatures are less confident foreshadowings (not all models agree) of decreased moisture availability in midlatitude continental areas—most notably in the Great Plains, prairies, and Midwest (the great American granary, as Dean Abrahamson calls it). We have several drought years in the southern Canadian prairies, and I am often asked: "Is this the beginning of a greenhouse desiccation?" I can't answer the question confidently. What the Manabe-Stouffer-Wetherald modeling at the Geophysical Fluid Dynamics Laboratory at Princeton University has predicted is in any case an increase in evaporation, rather than a decrease in rainfall (Manabe and Stouffer, 1980). And people are not conscious of evaporation as a critical control. Actually the events of the past decade throughout the Plains have been unremarkable, in a statistical sense. I doubt whether the greenhouse effect has yet stepped out onto center stage.

I want to close by suggesting that this desiccation, if it happens, will show itself to the public as an intermittent and erratic increase in the duration, frequency, and extent of drought. We are all familiar with how it will feel. Many recent summers have simulated the ordinary conditions of a doubled greenhouse effect. In Canada the entire ENSO-plagued year of 1982-83 gave us a dry run for such conditions. The winter was 2–6° C above normal across the entire country (as was true also of much of the United States). The Great Lakes barely froze, and could have been navigated. Snow cover was drastically reduced in the south, but increased elsewhere. The subsequent summer was also hot (1–3° C above normal), and there was severe drought and searing late summer heat over much of the Canadian prairies and the spring wheat belt of the United States. Had we known that this was coming we could have drastically altered our economic strategy—planting winter wheat instead of spring, navigating the Great Lakes more freely, and altering our handling of water at the dams. But, of course, we did *not* know, so that considerable stresses arose, and opportunities were lost.

The trends in temperature and (possibly) available soil moisture associated with the greenhouse effect will be very slow indeed by comparison with the interannual differences that we already take in our stride—and which completely dominate public perception of climatic influences. If we are to meet these changes in a reasonable way, we shall have to deal with the same effect that showed itself in Africa in 1974 and 1975—when temporary increases of rainfall lulled the politicians into comfortable slumber. I have little hope that North American politicians will be more alert. But I am confident that people like those in this room can at least persuade engineers, farmers, and business people who make long-term investments that the present climate may *not* be the right assumption for decisions with long-term effects. A whole new generation of interpreters has grown up—social scientists who know the myths of the climatologist, and can translate them into meaning for the hard-hatted, hard-faced men who tend to run the world's business. Many of the best of these interpreters are here in this auditorium.

I appreciate being invited to open this conference, which is being held in the heart of the American granary. My own origins were in a wheat-growing area. My earliest recollections were of drought. It has fascinated me ever since. I look forward to a week of excellent discussion.

REFERENCES

Bhalme, H. N.; and D. A. Mooley. 1983. On the performance of modified Palmer index. Archiv. fur Meteorologie, Geophysik und Bioklimalogie Ser. B. 22:281-295.

Hare, F. K. 1983. Climate and Desertification: A RevisedAnalysis. WCP-44, World Climate Applications Programme, World Meteorological Organization, Geneva.

Lamb, P. J. 1982. Persistence of subsaharan drought. Nature 299:46-48.

Maddox, R. A. 1980. Mesoscale convective complexes. Bull. Am. Meteorol. Soc. 61:1374-1387.

Manabe, S.; and R.J. Stouffer. 1980. Sensitivity of a global climate model to an increase of CO_2 concentration in the atmosphere. J. Geophys. Res. 85, no. 10:5529-5554.

Nicholson, S. 1982. The climatology of sub-Saharan Africa. pp. 71-92. In Environmental Change in the West African Sahel. National Academy Press, Washington, D.C.

Palmer, W. C. 1965. Meteorological drought. U.S. Weather Bureau, Department of Commerce, Res. Paper 45, Washington, D.C.

Stockton, C. W.; and D. M. Meko. 1983. Drought recurrence in the Great Plains as reconstructed from long-term tree-ring records. J. Clim. Applied Meteorol. 22:17-29.

Winstanley, D. 1974. Seasonal rainfall forecasting in West Africa. Nature 248:464-465.

CHAPTER 2
UNDERSTANDING THE DROUGHT PHENOMENON: THE ROLE OF DEFINITIONS

Donald A. Wilhite and Michael H. Glantz

INTRODUCTION

The occurrence of widespread, severe drought in Africa, India, North America, China, the USSR, Australia, and western Europe has once again underscored the vulnerability of developed and developing societies to drought. The occurrence of severe drought during 1982-83 is shown in Fig. 1. These recent droughts have emphasized the need for more research on the causes as well as the impacts of drought and the need for additional planning to help mitigate the possible worst effects of future droughts. Drought has been the subject of a great deal of systematic study, particularly reconstructions of drought history, computations of drought frequency, and, to a lesser extent, investigations of first-, second-, and even third-order impacts of drought on society.

Considerable disagreement exists about the concept of drought. During a recent drought in the Brazilian Northeast, for example, some Brazilian scientists and policy makers suggested that the region had been affected by a five-year drought. However, Brazilian meteorologists noted that the rainfall record indicated that only two of the last five years could have been classified as experiencing drought. Similar conflicts occurred in Australia as recently as 1984 between the Bureau of Meteorology and state Department of Agriculture officials as to the existence of drought conditions at the beginning of the planting season for winter wheat.

This paper reviews numerous definitions of drought to determine those characteristics scientists consider most essential for a description and understanding of the phenomenon. It also discusses the far-reaching impacts of drought on society. The final section suggests that definitions of drought are typically simplistic and, in that way, often lead to a rather poor understanding of the dimensions of the concept. It is suggested that definitions of drought should not be formulated in a narrow sense, but rather should incorporate both physical and social measures that have a local or regional significance.

DROUGHT: AN OVERVIEW

Drought occurs in high as well as low rainfall areas. It is a condition relative to some long-term average condition of balance between rainfall and evapotranspiration in a particular area, a condition often perceived as "normal." Yet average rainfall does not

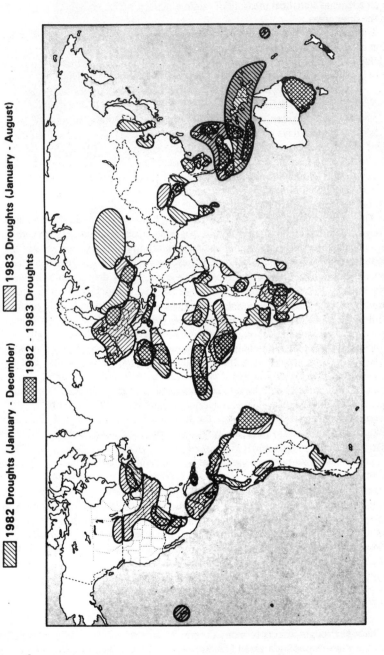

1982 Droughts (January - December)

1983 Droughts (January - August)

1982 Droughts (January - August)

1982 - 1983 Droughts

Fig. 1 The occurrence of drought, January 1982 to August 1983.

provide an adequate statistical measure of rainfall characteristics in a given region, especially in the drier areas.

Drought is a "creeping phenomenon" (Gillette, 1950), making an accurate prediction of either its onset or end a difficult task. To most observers, it seems to start with a delay in the timing (or a failure) of the rains. Others suggest that it can be identified only in retrospect. Tannehill (1947), for example, noted:

> We have no good definition of drought. We may say truthfully that we scarcely know a drought when we see one. We welcome the first clear day after a rainy spell. Rainless days continue for a time and we are pleased to have a long spell of such fine weather. It keeps on and we are a little worried. A few days more and we are really in trouble. The first rainless day in a spell of fine weather contributes as much to the drought as the last, but no one knows how serious it will be until the last dry day is gone and the rains have come again.... we are not sure about it until the crops have withered and died.

Drought severity, too, is difficult to determine. It is dependent not only on the duration, intensity, and geographical extent of a specific drought episode, but also on the demands made by human activities and by the vegetation on a region's water supplies. Drought's characteristics along with its far-reaching impacts make its effects on society, economy, and environment difficult, though not impossible, to identify and quantify. The significance of drought should not be divorced from its societal context. While a drought may take place in a season or in a run of years, its impacts on society may linger for many years. Also, the impact of a drought depends largely on society's vulnerability to drought at that particular moment. Subsequent droughts in the same region will probably have different effects, even if the droughts are identical in intensity, duration, and spatial characteristics.

Common to all types of drought is the fact that they originate from a deficiency of precipitation that results in water shortage for some activity (e.g., plant growth) or for some group (e.g., farmer). Clearly there are many natural and human factors that ultimately affect the availability of water to society. Sometimes this shortage coincides with periods of high temperature, low humidity, and/or high wind speed. Water shortages related to drought, however, must be considered a relative, rather than absolute, condition.

The lack of general acceptance of a precise and objective definition of drought, according to Yevjevich (1967), has been one of the principal obstacles to the investigation of drought. Indeed, Yevjevich's view may represent the dominant view about drought definitions. Many contend that conflicting drought definitions often lead to confusion among decision makers about what constitutes a drought (Glantz and Katz, 1977). Confusion can lead to inaction, indecision, and, in many cases, ad hoc responses with little understanding of the societal and environmental implications of those responses (Wilhite, et al., 1984). Some observers suggest that a precise and objective drought definition could, at least in theory, form the basis for the development of more appropriate drought management strategies by individual citizens and government.

Because drought affects so many economic and social sectors, scores of definitions have been developed by a variety of disciplines. In addition, because drought occurs with varying frequency in all regions of the globe, in all types of economic systems (socialist and capitalist), and in developed and less developed countries alike, the approaches taken to define drought also reflect regional differences as well as differences in ideological perspectives. Impacts also differ from one location to the next, depending on the societal context in which drought is occurring. Therefore, the search for a universally acceptable definition of drought appears to be a fruitless endeavor.

THE DEFINITION OF DROUGHT

Drought definitions might be categorized as either conceptual or operational, with *conceptual* referring to those definitions formulated in general terms to identify the boundaries of the concept of drought. For example, the American Heritage Dictionary (1976) defined drought as "a long period with no rain, especially during a planting season." As another example, Random House Dictionary (1969) defined it as "an extended period of dry weather, especially one injurious to crops." Conceptual definitions provide little guidance to those who wish to apply them to current (i.e., real-time) drought assessments.

Operational definitions attempt to identify the onset, severity, and termination of drought episodes. Estimations of potential impacts are included in some operational definitions. An operational definition, for example, would be one that compares daily precipitation values to evapotranspiration (ET) rates to determine the rate of soil moisture depletion, and expresses these relationships in terms of drought effects on plant behavior at various stages of crop development. The effects of these meteorological conditions on plant growth would be reevaluated continuously by agricultural specialists as the growing season progresses.

Operational definitions can also be used to analyze drought frequency, severity, and duration for a given historical period. Such definitions, however, require data on hourly, daily, monthly, or seasonal moisture deficiency, or yield departures from "normal" (i.e., expected) in order to identify when drought occurred. These definitions can be used to calculate the probabilities of droughts of varying intensity, duration, and spatial characteristics.

Disciplinary Views of Drought

Drought is frequently defined according to disciplinary perspective. Subrahmanyam (1967) has identified six types of drought: meteorological, climatological, atmospheric, agricultural, hydrologic, and water management. Many others have also included economic or socioeconomic factors as an essential factor in the determination of drought occurrence (Hoyt, 1942; Gibbs, 1975; Guerrero Salazar, 1975). Although it is useful to compartmentalize the various views of drought, the boundary separating these views is often vague.

The discussion of the disciplinary perspectives of drought which follows is the result of a review of more than 150 published definitions. For purposes of discussion these definitions of drought are clustered into four types—meteorological, agricultural, hydrologic, and socioeconomic.

Meteorological Drought. Meteorological definitions of drought are the most prevalent. They often define drought solely on the basis of the degree of dryness and the duration of the dry period. For example, meteorological drought has been defined as a "period of more than some particular number of days with precipitation less than some specified small amount" (Great Britain Meteorological Office, 1951). Linsley, et al. (1958), referred to it as a "sustained period of time without significant rainfall." Downer, et al. (1967), considered it to be a "deficit of water below a given reference value, with both deficit duration and deficit magnitude taken into account." Each of these definitions is vague. What is meant, for example, by *sustained* and *significant?*

Meteorological drought definitions are also often site specific, and the thresholds used to distinguish drought from nondrought periods are seldom spelled out. Some meteorological drought definitions developed for application in various countries of the world include:

1. United States: Less than 2.5 mm of rainfall in forty-eight hours (Blumenstock, 1942).
2. Britain: Fifteen days, none of which received as much as 0.25 mm of rain-fall (British Rainfall Organization, 1936).
3. Libya: When annual rainfall is less than 180 mm (Hudson, 1964).
4. India: Actual seasonal rainfall is deficient by more than twice the mean deviation (Ramdas, 1960).
5. Bali: A period of six days without rain (Hudson, 1964).

Definitions constructed for application to one region but applied to another often create problems since the meteorological conditions that result in drought are high-ly variable around the world. Perceptions of these conditions are equally variable. Both of these points must be taken into account in order to identify the characteristics of drought and make comparisons between regions.

To answer the question, What is a viable meteorological definition of drought? we must know the reason behind the choice for each of the delimiting criteria used in each definition. What, for example, is the significance of forty-eight hours with less than 2.5 mm of rainfall? Were these values arbitrarily selected, or were they chosen to coincide with a critical threshold in plant behavior or streamflow reduction? Answers to these questions are important, because they allow us to test a definition's reliability and applicability.

Other drought definitions compare the degree of dryness to a long-term average, often referred to as "normal." McGuire and Palmer (1957), for example, have referred to drought as a "period of monthly or annual precipitation less than some par-ticular percentage of normal." To some (e.g., Palmer, 1957), drought is a temporary departure from the average climate toward drier conditions.

The Palmer Drought Severity Index (PDSI), developed in 1965 by W. C. Pal-mer (1965), is probably the best-known meteorologic drought definition in the United States and is well known internationally. For example, its applicability in assessments of moisture conditions has recently been tested in South Africa, China, and Australia. The index is based on the concept of a hydrologic accounting system.

The PDSI relates drought severity to the accumulated weighted differences be-tween actual precipitation and the precipitation requirement of evapotranspiration (ET). Although commonly referred to as a drought index, the PDSI is actually used to evaluate prolonged periods of abnormally wet or abnormally dry weather. It is widely used in the

United States to evaluate long-term moisture conditions. A national map of index values is published monthly in the U.S. Department of Agriculture's Weekly Weather and Crop Bulletin.

Gibbs and Maher (1967) have applied the concept of deciles of precipitation to the study and classification of droughts in Australia. Monthly and annual precipitation totals are ranked, highest to lowest, and decile ranges are determined from the cumulative frequency of the distribution. The first decile represents the precipitation values in the lowest 10% of the distribution. The second decile represents the precipitation values falling between 10% and 20% of the distribution, and so on. The tenth decile range would represent the highest 10% of the precipitation values in the distribution.

This system has formed the basis of the Australian Drought Watch System (Lee, 1979). Severe drought is equated with a dry period not exceeding the fifth decile range over a period of three or more months. Extreme drought occurs when precipitation values do not exceed the first decile range over a period of three or more months. Severe and extreme drought occurred over all of eastern Australia during the peak of the 1982-83 drought episode (Gibbs, 1984). Meteorological droughts do not necessarily coincide with periods of agricultural drought. At times, inconsistencies of this kind result in conflicts between the agriculturist and meteorologist, as noted above.

In the United States, Changnon (1980) has attempted to link drought thresholds and impacts in Illinois. Using departure of precipitation from normal over a twelve-month period as the basis for his study, Changnon found that 75% of normal precipitation over a twelve-month period resulted in only selected economic sectors being affected, such as some agricultural activities and the water supply of a few small towns. All agricultural activities and production were affected when precipitation was 60% of normal; 50% of normal precipitation produced an impact on all agricultural activities and most urban and industrial users.

Some scientists are critical of climatically defined drought because it is expressed in terms of a thirty-year precipitation period, which has been agreed to (by international convention) as the basis for the calculation of "normal." Thirty years, however, represents only a small part of the historical record for most locations and would not be representative of the long-term climatic record. Moreover, for climatic regimes characterized by a large interannual variation of precipitation, the "normal" is less meaningful than other statistical measures such as the range, median, or mode of the precipitation distribution (Glantz and Katz, 1977).

Some meteorological definitions of drought also encompass atmospheric parameters other than precipitation, but these definitions are less common. Popov (1948) used wet-bulb depression and Ivanov (1948) incorporated humidity and temperature as an indicator of the drying power of the atmosphere. Levitt (1958) expressed atmospheric drought as proportional to the vapor pressure deficit of the air. Condra (1944) referred to drought as a "period of strong wind, low precipitation, high temperature and, usually, low relative humidity," a definition formulated for the U.S. Great Plains and reflecting drought characteristics specific to this region. These definitions, however, may not be transferable to other regions of the world.

Agricultural Drought. Agricultural drought definitions link various characteristics of meteorological drought to agricultural impacts, focusing, for example, on precipitation shortages (Humphreys, 1931; Rosenberg, 1980), departures from normal

(World Book Encyclopedia, 1975), or numerous meteorological factors such as evapotranspiration (Laikhtman and Rusin, 1957).

A plant's demand for water is dependent on prevailing meteorological conditions, biological characteristics of the specific plant, its stage of growth, and the physical and biological properties of the soil. An operational definition of agricultural drought should account for the variable susceptibility of crops at different stages of crop development. For example, deficient subsoil moisture in an early growth stage will have little impact on final crop yield if topsoil moisture is sufficient to meet early growth requirements. However, if the deficiency of subsoil moisture continues, a substantial yield loss would result. Barger and Thom (1949) have tried to link drought to its impact on a specific crop—corn.

Kulik (1958) represented drought intensity as the difference between plant water demand and available soil water. Kulik concluded that the upper 0.2 m of soil was critical to plant growth because of nutrient supplies and the root activity and activities of microorganisms that take place in that layer. Therefore, drying of this soil layer was an early indicator of yield loss (i.e., a measure of drought intensity). Kulik defined a dry period as one during which only 19 mm of available water remained in the upper 0.2 m of soil; when only 9 mm of available water remains, very dry conditions prevail.

In 1968 Palmer (1968) modified the PDSI to better reflect agricultural drought conditions. The Crop Moisture Index (CMI) defined drought in terms of the magnitude of computed abnormal ET deficit. This deficit is the difference between actual and expected weekly ET. The expected weekly ET is the normal value, adjusted up or down according to the departure of the week's temperature from normal. The CMI has been adopted by the U.S. Department of Agriculture and is published weekly in its Weekly Weather and Crop Bulletin as an indicator of the availability of moisture to meet short-term crop needs.

Hydrologic Drought. Definitions of hydrologic drought are concerned with the effects of dry spells on surface or subsurface hydrology, rather than with the meteorological explanation of the event. For example, Linsley, et al. (1975), considered hydrologic drought a "period during which streamflows are inadequate to supply established uses under a given water management system" (see also Dracup, 1980). The frequency and severity of hydrologic drought is often defined on the basis of its influence on river basins. Hydrologic droughts are often out of phase with both meteorological and agricultural drought.

Whipple (1966) defined a drought year as one in which the aggregate runoff is less than the long-term average runoff. Since low-flow frequencies have been determined for most streams, hydrologic drought periods can be of any specified length. If the actual flow for a selected period of time falls below a certain threshold, then hydrologic drought is considered to be in progress. However, the number of days and the level of probability that must be exceeded to define a hydrologic drought period is arbitrary (Matthai, 1979). These criteria are specific to individual streams or river basins.

Although the PDSI is sometimes used as an indicator of hydrologic drought, other definitions have been formulated which better serve the needs of hydrologists. For example, a definition of hydrologic drought was developed in Colorado during 1981 to provide information about drought conditions and water supply in high-elevation river basins that are dependent on snow melt as their main source of water supply (Dezman, et al., 1982). The Surface Water Supply Index (SWSI) was intended to be complementary to the PDSI, with the latter applying mainly to nonirrigated areas independent of mountain water supplies.

The SWSI integrates historical data with current figures of reservoir storage, streamflow, and precipitation at high elevation into a single index number. The SWSI scale is synonymous with the scale used for PDSI values. Colorado's Drought Assessment and Response Plan (Colorado Division of Disaster Emergency Services, 1981) is implemented when SWSI and PDSI values exceed specified thresholds. For example, a SWSI of -1.0 activates Colorado's Water Availability Task Force, which makes assessments and projections on snowpack, soil moisture, reservoir and ground-water levels, precipitation, temperature, and streamflow.

Socioeconomic Drought. Definitions that express features of the socioeconomic effects of drought can also incorporate features of meteorological, agricultural, and hydrological drought (Kifer and Stewart, 1938). They are usually associated with the supply and demand of some economic good. Yevjevich (1967) has suggested that the time and space processes of supply and demand are the two basic processes that should be considered for an objective definition of drought. Heathcote (1974), for example, defined agricultural drought as a "shortage of water harmful to man's agricultural activities. It occurs as an interaction between agricultural activity (i.e., demand) and natural events (i.e., supply), which results in a water volume or quality inadequate for plant and/or animal needs." Gibbs (1975) expanded this definition, noting that demand was "dependent upon the distribution of plant, animal and human populations, their lifestyle and their use of the land."

In some instances, land use practices can either create a drought situation (e.g., agricultural or hydrologic drought) or make an existing one worse. The Dust Bowl years in the U.S. Great Plains in the 1930s, the Sahelian drought in West Africa in the early 1970s, and the recent Ethiopian drought are often cited as examples of the symbiosis between drought and human activities.

In 1936, J. C. Hoyt (1936) referred to drought as occurring "when precipitation is not sufficient to meet the needs of established human activities." He proposed this definition in the midst of the 1930s U.S. Great Plains drought. W. G. Hoyt (1942) later expanded this concept, stating that droughts may result if "in the economic development of a region man creates a demand for more water than is normally available."

Sandford (1979) argued that drought should be linked not only to precipitation (supply) but also to trends or fluctuations in demand as well as to factors other than weather which influence supply. Sandford presents two scenarios that represent time (x axis) and supply of some economic good (y axis). In the first scenario, demand by society for an economic good is assumed to be static throughout the time period. The level of supply (livestock feed in Sandford's example) varies considerably from one year to the next as a result of shortages of rainfall and other factors influencing supply. Therefore, drought occurs when supply falls below the level of requirement. In the second scenario, the demand trend is more realistically represented as increasing with time. The trend of supply, however, is decreasing as a result of ecological changes, such as declining soil fertility. Thus the frequency with which supply falls below demand increases. We feel that the interrelationship between man and drought requires more scientific attention.

The preceding discussion illustrates several significant features of drought. First, the various approaches taken by scientists and nonscientists to define drought demonstrate its complex and interdisciplinary nature. Second, although most definitions emphasize the physical aspects of drought, the social aspects are closely related. Third, few (if any) definitions adequately address the impacts of drought. As a result, the primary, secondary, and tertiary impacts of drought are poorly understood.

THE IMPACT OF DROUGHT

Yevjevich, et al. (1978), suggested that the study of drought problems would be facilitated if drought was considered in a systems context. Figure 2 describes succinctly the interrelationships between the physical and social factors. As Yevjevich, et al., noted, the physical aspects of drought are derived from the atmosphere-ocean-continent system. Each drought is unique in its set of physical characteristics as well as in its geographic scope and location. It is interesting to note that Yevjevich considers the physical characteristics of drought to be dictated by the physical environment. Drought events are shown as inputs to a physical-environment system and a social system. The characteristics of drought events, physical-environment systems, and social systems combine and interact to produce impacts on the physical-environment and social system. The social system responds to mitigate or alleviate drought-related impacts. This view of drought reflects the focus of previous studies of drought on the physical aspects of the phenomenon. Yet the ultimate significance of drought to society lies in its impacts.

Figure 3, from a U.S. Department of Agriculture report on food problems and prospects in sub-Saharan Africa (USDA/ERS, 1981), presents a similar picture about weather (or climate), and drought as a part of it. Weather is viewed strictly as a physical phenomenon, whose origins and impacts are independent from social factors. After examining Fig. 3, it is evident that weather, or drought, affects far more than just crop yields and that social factors can be equally significant in determining society's vulnerability to drought and, thus, the type and magnitude of drought impacts. Thus, how drought is perceived, and defined, determines the likely response of societies to drought events.

The far-reaching impacts of drought in the United States (Table 1) were recently classified by the Institute for Policy Research of the Western Governors' Policy Office (WESTPO). WESTPO (1977) assembled this comprehensive listing of drought-related impacts in the economic, environmental, and social sectors in response to several consecutive years of drought. Many of these impacts are relevant to drought situations in other countries. In the United States' case, each impact cited is linked to one or more of the following five groups: municipalities, state governments, businesses and industries, agricultural enterprises, and households and individual citizens. This list suggests that droughts often have complex and long-lasting impacts. Also listed in Table 1 are constraints that inhibit responses to drought by each of these groups.

Although Table 1 appears to be a complete summary of drought impacts, at least one important group, the federal government, has been omitted. Since the 1930s drought in the United States, the federal government has become the primary, and usually only, source of assistance to the distressed area. During the mid-1970s drought, sixteen federal agencies administered forty separate assistance programs. During 1976-77, aid to water users alone, primarily in the form of loans and grants from four agencies, totaled $5 billion (General Accounting Office, 1979). The total cost to the federal govern-

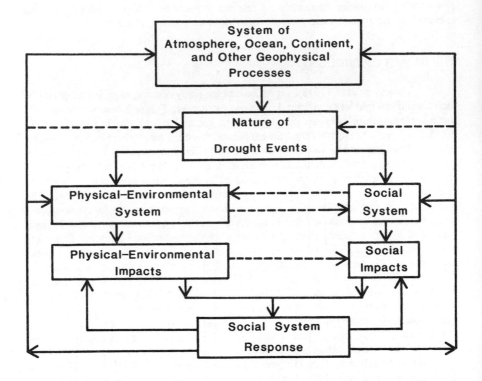

Fig. 2 Drought viewed in a systems context (Gibbs, 1975).

ment of the 1974-77 drought program probably exceeded $7 billion (Wilhite, et al., 1984). Other governments, such as Australia, South Africa, the United Kingdom, India, and Kenya, to name just a few, have responded in a similar fashion (but on a lesser scale) to recent episodes of severe drought.

Table 1 shows clearly that the potential impacts of drought in the United States, at least, are concentrated largely in the economic sector, with agriculture the most often affected of the five groups identified. Because of the diversity of these impacts and their ripple effect on the economy, they are difficult to quantify. More explicit and objective definitions, incorporating both physical and socioeconomic aspects of drought, could assist in the quantification of impacts and allow for more precise comparisons of the effects of drought within and between geographical regions.

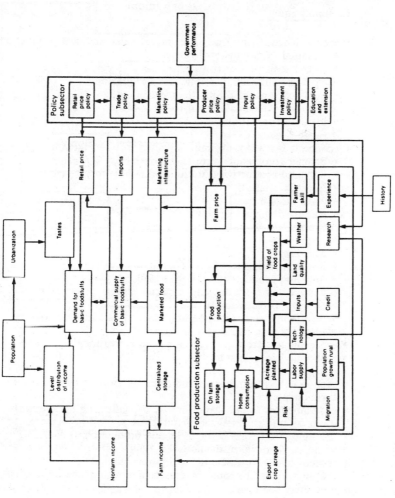

Fig. 3 Interaction among food balance factors, sub-Saharan Africa (USDA/ERS, 1981).

Table 1
Identification and Classification of Drought-Related Problems

AFFECTED GROUPS AND SECTORS[a]	PROBLEMS AND IMPACTS
	Economic Impacts
A	• economic loss from drought-impacted dairy and beef production
A	• impaired productivity of rangeland
A	• forced reduction of foundation stock
A	• closure/limitation of public lands to grazing
A	• high cost/unavailability of water for cattle
A	• high cost/unavailability of feed for cattle
A	• increased predation
AMS	• range fires
A	• economic loss from drought-impacted crop production
A	• damage to perennial crops; crop loss
A	• impaired productivity of cropland (wind erosion, etc.)
A	• insect infestation
AS	• plant disease
A	• wildlife damage to crops
B	• economic loss from drought-impacted timber production
B	• forest fires
BS	• tree disease
BS	• insect infestation
BS	• impaired productivity of forest land
AS	• economic loss from drought-impacted fishery production
HS	• damage to fish habitat
HS	• insufficient flows for anadromous and catadramous fish
HS	• loss of young fish due to decreased flows
BMS	• economic loss from drought-impacted recreational businesses
BMS	• economic loss to manufacturers and sellers of recreational equipment
BMS	• economic loss to industries impacted by drought-related power curtailments
BMS	• economic loss to industries directly dependent on agricultural production (e.g., fertilizer manufacturers, food processors, etc.)
HBS	• unemployment from drought-related production declines
SA	• strain on financial institutions
SM	• revenue losses to state and local governments
M	• revenues to water supply firms
M	• revenue shortfalls
M	• windfall profits
B	• economic loss from impaired navigability of streams, rivers, and canals
HABMS	• cost of water transport or transfer
HABMS	• cost of new or supplemental water source development

Environmental Impacts

AS	• damage to animal species
SH	• damage to wildlife habitat
AH	• lack of feed and drinking water
AS	• disease
A	• vulnerability to predation
S	• damage to fish species
S	• damage to plant species
AM	• water quality effects (e.g., salt concentration)
HS	• air quality effects (dust, pollutants)
HS	• visual and landscape quality (dust, vegetative cover, etc.)

Social Impacts

MS	• public safety from forest and range fires
MS	• health-related low flow problems (e.g., diminished sewage flows, increased pollutant concentrations, etc.)
AHBMS	• inequity in the distribution of drought impacts/relief
	• lifestyle impacts
HAS	• unemployment
A	• loss of ownership
HA	• loss of savings
H	• retirement
A	• small family farming
HABMS	• uncertainty
HBMS	• recreation
H	• personal hygiene
H	• dirty cars and streets
H	• water reuse in home
HB	• entertaining

Constraints to Implementation of Drought Mitigation Measures

MS	• legal/institutional constraints
MSA	• to water conservation/efficiency measures
MSA	• to water supply augmentation measures
HABMS	• financial constraints
ABMS	• to water conservation/efficiency measures
ABM	• to water supply augmentation measures
	• inadequate drought management capability/authority
M	• local, state, federal
MS	• inadequate understanding of drought problems and mitigation measures; public apathy
AM	• shortages of needed parts, equipment, manpower

[a]M - Municipalities   A - Agricultural enterprises
  S - State governments   H - Households and individuals
  B - Businesses and industries

Source: WESTPO, 1977.

CONCLUSION

To summarize:

1. The lack of a precise (and objective) definition of drought in a specific situation has been an obstacle to understanding drought, which has led to indecision and/or inaction on the part of managers, policy makers, and others.
2. There cannot (and should not) be a universal definition of drought.
3. Available definitions demonstrate a multidisciplinary interest in drought.
4. It is useful to subdivide definitions of drought into four types on the basis of disciplinary perspective (meteorologic, agricultural, hydrologic, and socioeconomic).
5. Drought is a complex phenomenon with pervasive societal ramifications.
6. Most scientific research related to drought has emphasized physical rather than societal aspects.
7. Drought severity is sometimes expressed by its societal impacts, although the precise nature of those impacts is difficult to quantify.
8. Secondary and tertiary effects often extend beyond the spatially defined borders of drought.
9. Drought impacts are long lasting, at times lingering for many years.
10. Human or social factors often aggravate the effects of drought.

Each of these points highlights our need to develop a better understanding of the concept of drought. The criteria selected to define drought must be stated explicitly so that the definition can be evaluated and its applicability to other locations examined.

Drought's impacts must be seen as dynamic, resulting from interactions between supply and demand. Supply can be expressed in terms of the physical subsystem and linked to concomitant impacts in the social subsystem. Demand must be viewed as interacting with supply and as continually changing. The relationships of supply and demand for the principal economic goods are highly variable from one country to another, from one region to the next, and from one period to another.

Definitions of drought should reflect a regional bias since water supply is largely a function of climatic regime. Of course, the size of the region over which any definition is applicable may vary considerably. Primary impacts will likewise be regional in character, but secondary and tertiary effects of a drought can have national and, at times, global implications. For example, droughts in Zimbabwe can adversely affect regional food supplies in southern Africa.

The inadequate understanding of the concept of drought and the lack of appreciation of its physical and social impacts by the scientific community and governments has serious worldwide implications for the future as the difference between food production and consumption narrows. Governments should prepare for droughts by developing and implementing strategies and plans that reduce associated impacts. More precise and objective definitions of drought can greatly improve the understanding of the concept and its impacts and facilitate strategy development. Otherwise, the mistakes and failures of the past will no doubt be repeated, although with the likelihood of more severe consequences.

This paper was previously published in Water International and is reprinted with their permission.

ACKNOWLEDGMENTS

The authors wish to thank Professors Norman J. Rosenberg, Albert Weiss, Gordon McKay, and Jonathan Taylor for their critical review of this paper. Deborah Wood and Steven Meyer assisted with the library research and the classification of the numerous definitions of drought, respectively. Deborah Wood, along with Maria Krenz, assisted in editing the manuscript. Sharon Kelly was responsible for the preparation of the manuscript. Their help is gratefully acknowledged.

The work was conducted under Nebraska Experiment Station Project 27-001. This material is based on work partially supported by the National Science Foundation under Grant ATM-8108447.

REFERENCES

American Heritage Dictionary. 1976. Drought. Houghton Mifflin, Boston.
Barger, G. L.; and H. C. S. Thom. 1949. Method for characterizing drought intensity in Iowa. Agron. J. 41:13-19.
Blumenstock, G., Jr. 1942. Drought in the U.S. analyzed by means of the theory of probability. USDA Tech. Bull. 819. GPO, Washington, D.C.
British Rainfall Organization. 1936. British Rainfall. Air Ministry, Meteorological Office, London. Cited in World Meteorological Organization. 1975. Drought and agriculture. Technical Note 138. WMO, Geneva.
Changnon, S. A. 1980. Removing the confusion over droughts and floods: The interface between scientists and policy makers. Water Int. 5:10-18.
Colorado Division of Disaster Emergency Services. 1981. The Colorado drought response plan. Colorado Division of Disaster Emergency Services, Denver.
Condra, G. E. 1944. Drought, its effects and measure of control in Nebraska. Conservation Bulletin 25. Conservation and Survey Division, University of Nebraska-Lincoln.
Dezman, L. E.; B. A. Shafer; H. D. Simpson; and J. A. Danielson. 1982. Development of a surface water supply index—A drought severity indicator for Colorado. In A. I. Johnson and R. A. Clark, eds. Proc. International Symposium on Hydrometeorology. American Water Resources Association, Bethesda, Maryland.
Downer, R. N.; M. M. Siddiqui; and V. Yevjevich. 1967. Applications of runs to hydrologic droughts. pp. 496-505. In Proc. International Hydrology Symposium. Colorado State University, Fort Collins.
Dracup, J. A.; K. S. Lee; and E. G. Paulson, Jr. 1980. On the definition of droughts. Water Resour. Res. 16(2):297-302.
General Accounting Office. 1979. Federal response to the 1976-77 drought: What should be done next? Report to the Comptroller General. GPO, Washington, D.C.

Gibbs, W. J. 1975. Drought—its definition, delineation, and effects. pp. 3-39. In Drought: Lectures presented at the 26th session of the WMO Executive Committee. Special Environmental Report No. 5. WMO, Geneva.

Gibbs, W. J. 1984. The great Australian drought: 1982-83. Disasters, published by the International Disaster Institute, London, August 2.

Gibbs, W. J.; and J. V. Maher. 1967. Rainfall deciles as drought indicators. Bureau of Meteorology Bulletin No. 48. Melbourne, Australia.

Gillette, H. P. 1950. A creeping drought under way. Water and Sewage Works, March, pp. 104-105.

Glantz, M. H.; and R. Katz. 1977. When is a drought a drought? Nature 267:192-193.

Great Britain Meteorological Office. 1951. The Meteorological Glossary. Chemical Publishing Co., New York.

Guerrero Salazar, P.; and V. Yevjevich. 1975. Analysis of drought characteristics by the theory of runs. Hydrology Paper No. 80, Department of Civil Engineering, Colorado State University, Fort Collins.

Heathcote, R. L. 1974. Drought in South Australia. p. 129. In G. F. White, ed. Natural Hazards: Local, National, Global. Oxford, New York.

Hoyt, J. C. 1936. Droughts of 1930-1934. USGS Water Supply Paper No. 680. USGS, Washington, D.C.

Hoyt, W. G. 1942. Droughts. p. 579. In O. E. Meinzer, ed. Hydrology. Dover Publications, New York.

Hudson, H. E.; and R. Hazen. 1964. Drought and low streamflow. Chap. 18. In V. T. Chow, ed. Handbook of Applied Hydrology. McGraw-Hill, New York.

Humphreys, W. J. 1931. How droughts occur. Bull. Am. Meteorol. Soc. 12:18-22.

Ivanov, N. N. 1948. Landscape-climatic zones of the earth surface. Proc. All Soviet Geographical Conference, New Series Vol. 1. Academy of Sciences of the U.S.S.R., Leningrad.

Kifer, R. S.; and H. L. Stewart. 1938. Farming hazards in the drought area. Works Progress Administration, Monograph XVI, Washington, D.C.

Kulik, M. S. 1958. Agroclimatic indices of drought. In F. F. Davidaya and M. S. Kulik, eds. Compendium of abridged reports to the second session of CAgM (WMO). Hydrometeorological Publishing, Moscow; trans. A. Nurlik, Meteorological Translations 7:75-81 (1962).

Laikhtman, D. L.; and N. P. Rusin. 1957. On the meteorological criterion of drought [in Russian]. Glavnaia Geofizicheskaia Observatoriia, Trudy, 69:65-70.

Lee, D. M. 1979. Australian drought watch system. In M. T. Hinchey, ed. Botswana Drought Symposium. Botswana Society, Gaborone, Botswana.

Levitt, J. 1958. Frost, drought and heat resistance. Protoplasmatologia 8(6).

Linsley, R. K.; M. A. Kohler; and J. L. H. Paulhus. 1958. Hydrology for Engineers. McGraw-Hill, New York.

Linsley, R. K., Jr.; M. A. Kohler; and J. L. H. Paulhus. 1975. Hydrology for Engineers, 2nd ed. McGraw-Hill, Kogukusha, Tokyo.

Matthai, H. F. 1979. Hydrologic and human aspects of the 1976-77 drought. USGS Survey Professional Paper 1130. GPO, Washington, D.C.

McGuire, J. K.; and W. C. Palmer. 1957. The 1957 drought in the eastern U. S. Mon. Weather Rev. 85, No. 9 (September 1957):305-314.

Palmer, W. C. 1957. Drought—A normal part of climate. In Weekly Weather and Crop Bulletin 44, No. 1a (January 10):6-8.

Palmer, W. C. 1965. Meteorological drought. Research Paper No. 45. U. S. Weather Bureau, Washington, D.C.

Palmer, W. C. 1968. Keeping track of crop moisture conditions, nationwide: The new crop moisture index. Weatherwise 21(4):156-161.

Popov, V. P. 1948. Moisture balance in the soil and the dryness indices of climate in the Ukrainian S.S.R. Sci. Rep. of the State Univ. of Kiev, Vol. 7, No. 1.

Ramdas, D. A. 1960. Crops and weather in India. ICAR, New Delhi, India.

Random House Dictionary. 1969. Drought. Random House, New York.

Rosenberg, N. J., ed. 1980. Drought in the Great Plains: Research on Impacts and Strategies. Water Resources Publications, Littleton, Colorado.

Sandford, S. 1979. Towards a definition of drought. In M. T. Hinchey, ed. Botswana Drought Symposium. Botswana Society, Gaborone, Botswana.

Subrahmanyam, V. P. 1967. Incidence and spread of continental drought. WMO/IHD Report No. 2. WMO, Geneva.

Tannehill, I. R. 1947. Drought, Its Causes and Effects. Princeton University Press, Princeton, New Jersey.

U. S. Department of Agriculture, Economic Research Service (USDA/ERS). 1981. Food problems and prospects in Sub-Saharan Africa—The decade of the 1980s. Foreign Agricultural Research Report No. 156, August. Washington, D.C.

Western Governors' Policy Office (WESTPO). 1977. Directory of Federal Drought Assistance. Prepared by the Institute for Policy Research for the Western Region Drought Action Task Force. USDA, Washington, D.C.

Whipple, W., Jr. 1966. Regional drought frequency analysis. Proc. ASCE 92, No. IR2 (June 1966):11-31.

Wilhite, D. A.; N. J. Rosenberg; and M. H. Glantz. 1984. Government response to drought in the United States. Completion Report to the National Science Foundation. CAMaC Progress Reports 84-1 to 84-4. Center for Agricultural Meteorology and Climatology, University of Nebraska-Lincoln.

World Book Encyclopedia. 1975. Drought. Field Enterprises Educational Corporation, Chicago.

Yevjevich, V. 1967. An objective approach to definitions and investigations of continental hydrologic droughts. Hydrology Papers, No. 23. Colorado State University, Fort Collins.

Yevjevich, V.; W. A. Hall; and J. D. Salas, eds. 1978. Proc. Conference on Drought Research Needs. Water Resources Publications, Fort Collins.

PART 2

Prediction

CHAPTER 3
GLOBAL PROSPECTS FOR THE PREDICTION OF DROUGHT: A METEOROLOGICAL PERSPECTIVE

Eugene M. Rasmusson

INTRODUCTION

A variety of impact-oriented indices have been developed to quantify various aspects of drought (e.g., Palmer, 1965). These indices usually involve some measure of duration and magnitude of water deficiency. Practically speaking, the prediction of drought reduces to a prediction of one or more of these indices. This requires a knowledge of antecedent conditions, reflected in the present value of the index, and future meteorological conditions, precipitation being by far the most important. This review will focus on the prospects for and limitations of monthly and seasonal precipitation forecasts.

SOURCES OF CLIMATE VARIABILITY

Day-to-day weather fluctuations are primarily controlled by internal atmospheric dynamics. They are manifestations of the growth, decay, and propagation of meteorological disturbances that derive their energy from the internal structure of the atmosphere (i.e., horizontal or vertical gradients of wind, temperature, and moisture). Using modern methods of numerical weather prediction, operational meteorological centers are now able to forecast these synoptic fluctuations several days in advance with considerable skill. However, because of the unstable nature of the fluctuations and the complexity of atmospheric dynamics, the theoretical limit of predictability does not exceed a few weeks (Shukla, 1985).

As the time scale of variability lengthens, the relative importance of external influences with longer time scales increases. Perhaps the most important of these for seasonal-interannual prediction are the surface boundary conditions: sea surface temperature (SST), snow and sea ice, soil moisture, albedo (the percentage of incoming solar radiation reflected from the earth's surface) and vegetative cover. These interface parameters govern, to a large extent, the time-averaged exchange of thermal and mechanical energy between the atmosphere and the more slowly varying land and ocean "memory components" of the climate system.

It is difficult to establish the effect of anomalous boundary conditions from observational data alone. An invaluable theoretical aid in this task is an atmospheric general circulation model (GCM). These numerical models are based on the mathematical representation of the physical laws governing large-scale atmospheric motions. They are similar to models used in day-to-day numerical weather prediction, but the atmospheric GCMs are integrated, using large computers, for long periods of simulated time. The present state-of-the-art GCMs are capable of realistic simulation of the global climate. Such models have been coupled in an interactive but admittedly crude manner with land surface processes, including hydrology, and are now beginning to be coupled with companion oceanic GCMs.

Since the oceans constitute 71% of the earth's surface, the role of upper-ocean thermal anomalies in short-term climate variability is an important area of climate research (Namias, 1965). In the temperate latitudes, pronounced anomalies in upper-ocean heat content and ocean-atmosphere heat exchange do occur seasonally, but major anomalies in the basin-scale ocean circulations evolve more slowly, over years and decades (Philander, 1979). Quite different, however, is the situation within a few degrees of the equator. At these extreme low latitudes, the ocean dynamics are relatively "fast," allowing a close coupling on the seasonal-interannual time scale between the large-scale atmospheric and oceanic circulations. The most pronounced example of coupled ocean/atmosphere interactions is the El Niño/Southern Oscillation phenomenon.

The tendency for persistence of drought regimes invites speculation about the possibility of a natural feedback between anomalous, drought-related surface conditions (albedo, evapotranspiration, and surface roughness) and the drought-sustaining atmospheric circulation. GCM experiments suggest that these processes may be an important factor in regional rainfall variability (Mintz, 1984; Sud, et al., 1986), but the results to date are not conclusive. Observations have been inadequate to ascertain the accuracy of the climatological values and variability of surface parameters used in the experiments, and the models have not been sensitive enough to allow scientists to obtain definitive answers.

The influences of volcanic eruptions and solar variability continue to be issues in climate prediction. Observational evidence of relationships between North American drought regimes and the 22-year Hale and 18.6-year lunar nodal regression cycles is discussed in the section below on decadal time-scale variations.

Anthropogenic effects (e.g., desertification, deforestation, greenhouse warming) are more closely related to questions of climate change than climate variability. Although not directly addressed in this review, the potential human effect on climate must be kept in mind when interpreting climate data, both past and present, and when projecting longer time-scale trends.

MODES OF ATMOSPHERIC VARIABILITY

The atmosphere exhibits preferred regional or even global patterns of variability. These features, usually called *teleconnections*, appear over and over again in roughly the same form, and often persist or recur throughout a month or season. They may reflect patterns of remote response to causal mechanisms. Such responses, a fundamental feature of atmosphere dynamics, dictate a global view of climate variability and prediction.

Atmospheric regimes or oscillations that are large in amplitude and global in scale, have time scales comparable to or longer than the monthly or seasonal prediction period, and exhibit a systematic and relatively predictable evolution are of fundamental importance to climate prediction. Although atmospheric circulation regimes often exhibit some of these features, only three oscillations that fully fit the description have thus far been clearly identified. The first, referred to as the quasi-biennial oscillation (QBO), is tropical and stratospheric, with an average period of a little more than two years. Its amplitude is large--in fact, comparable to the annual cycle--and its course very regular and, therefore, relatively predictable for several months in advance. QBOs have also been identified in surface data, but they are weak, irregular, and (thus far) appear to be of marginal value for predicting surface climate fluctuations.

The two other oscillations are also most pronounced in the tropics, but affect parts of the extratropics as well. The first is the El Niño/Southern Oscillation (ENSO) phenomenon, which has a lifetime of about two years and repeats at irregular intervals of two to seven years. The second is an oscillation with a predominant period of thirty to sixty days.

EL NIÑO/SOUTHERN OSCILLATION (ENSO)

El Niño is an anomalous warming of the eastern equatorial Pacific. The Southern Oscillation is a global-scale seesaw in surface pressure, with centers of action near Indonesia-North Australia and in the southeast Pacific. The two phenomena are atmospheric and oceanic parts of an elegant and pervasive global system of climate fluctuations now referred to as ENSO. (For an ENSO review and bibliography, see Rasmusson, 1985). ENSO is the most notable and pronounced example of global climate variability on the interannual time scale. It leads to massive dislocations of the rainfall regimes of the tropics, bringing drought to large areas and torrential rains to otherwise arid regions. The related atmospheric circulation anomalies extend deep into the extratropics, where they are associated with unusual wintertime conditions over regions as far apart as the United States and New Zealand (Fig. 1a). Although there is a remarkable degree of consistency in the evolution of ENSO episodes, it should be kept in mind that ENSOs' effects vary both regionally and seasonally, and the amplitude of regional anomalies varies from episode to episode. Because ENSO is global in nature, it leads to the nearly simultaneous appearance of pronounced climate anomalies around the world.

ENSO owes its existence to large-scale, ocean-atmosphere interactions in the equatorial Pacific. The world's most extensive region of warm water (SST greater than 28° C) is located in the western tropical Pacific-Indonesian region. The heavy rainfall and associated heating of the atmosphere over this huge "warm pool" represents a major source of atmospheric heating, which drives the large-scale circulation. As an ENSO episode develops, this warm pool extends eastward, resulting in increasing SST in the central equatorial Pacific and an eastward extension of the west Pacific region of heavy rainfall. With the eastward shift of this atmospheric heat source, the low-level winds back in the western equatorial Pacific take on a stronger component from the west. The enhanced eastward frictional drag on the ocean surface leads to a stronger eastward component in the upper ocean currents. This, in turn, brings warm water farther east, closing an interactive, positive feedback loop between ocean and atmosphere. ENSO episodes usually begin early in the year and most follow a rather similar evolution over a period of 18-24 months. The "mature phase" of the episode, when the global pattern of atmos-

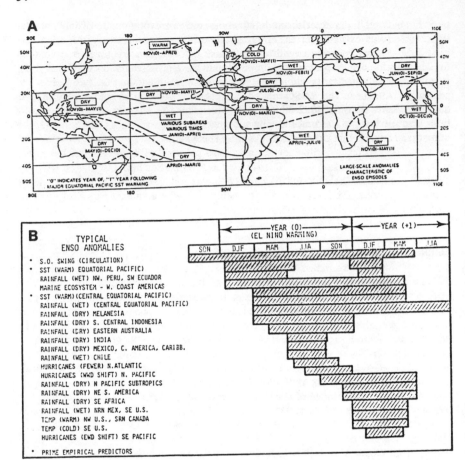

Fig. 1 (a) Schematic showing the general pattern of climate anomalies during an ENSO episode. (b) The time sequence of major anomalies during a typical ENSO episode. The pattern of lag relationships of up to three seasons offers the potential for long lead-time predictions.

pheric anomalies becomes most widespread and intense, occurs near the end of the first year and during the early months of the second year, i.e., during the Northern Hemisphere cold season (Fig. 1b). The anomaly pattern then enters a period of decay that usually spans several months.

Although the effects of ENSO are global, the most pronounced anomalies occur in the Indian Ocean-tropical Pacific sector. The west Pacific-Indian ocean monsoon region and the northeast Pacific subtropics are plagued by drought, while the eastern equatorial Pacific receives abnormally heavy rainfall (Fig. 1a). The global pattern of droughts is well illustrated by the 1982-83 episode, one of the strongest of the past century. On balance, India experienced deficient monsoon rainfall in 1982. Drought conditions, which had existed over eastern Australia and Indonesia since mid-1982, eased early in 1983, but persisted over Melanesia and spread across the north Pacific subtropics, enveloping the southern Philippines and the Hawaiian Islands. Farther east, satellite data indicated far below normal precipitation from the Amazon Basin eastward across the Atlantic. The ENSO-related drought that occurred over southeast Africa during the rainy season of 1982-83 was among the worst of the century in that region. In this case, however, it was embedded in a more pervasive and longer-lasting period of widespread drought that afflicted much of sub-Saharan Africa between 1982 and 1984.

THIRTY- TO SIXTY-DAY OSCILLATIONS

The first evidence of systematic, intraseasonal oscillations was provided by Madden and Julian (1971), who identified a global-scale oscillation with an average period between forty and fifty days which propagates eastward in the low latitudes. The oscillation is particularly evident as large amplitude rainfall and wind fluctuations over the low-latitude eastern Indian Ocean/ western Pacific sector. In many ways, it mimics the atmospheric ENSO fluctuations on a much shorter time scale. The global aspects of this phenomenon have been better defined during the past few years through the work of a number of investigators (e.g., Weickmann, et al., 1985; Knutson, et al., 1986).

Although most pronounced in the tropical belt, the thirty to sixty day oscillation also appears to be associated with wintertime weather regime "flip-flops" over parts of the Northern Hemisphere, including North America (Weickmann, et al., 1985). Thus far, there is no evidence of a significant summertime signal in the Northern Hemisphere extratropics (Knutson, et al., 1986); but in the tropics, the oscillation appears to be intimately related to the timing of the Indian monsoon's onset and withdrawal and its active and break periods (Yasunari, 1980).

DECADAL TIME-SCALE VARIATIONS

Pronounced decadal-scale fluctuations occur in many regions (Fig. 2), but the degree to which they exhibit a systematic behavior is hard to establish from the relatively short time series of precipitation measurements. Mitchell, et al. (1979), developed a proxy "Drought Area Index" (DAI) for the western United States by calibrating tree ring data (1600-1962) with 32 years of Palmer Drought Severity Index values (Palmer, 1965). They found an apparently significant phase locking between the 22-year Hale sunspot cycle and large amplitude variations in the DAI. Subsequently, Bell (1981) and Currie (1981) claimed the existence of an 18.6-year period in the DAI data, phased with the lunar nodal regression cycle. Hameed (1984) and Hameed, et al. (1983), also identified solar and lunar rhythms in the historical records of Nile floods and the semiquantitative record of Beijing rainfall.

Questions have been raised regarding the reality or persistence of these rhythms. (Following a recent reexamination of the data, Mitchell [personal communication, 1986] concluded that both signals exist in the DAI series and are of roughly equal strength. The 22-year feature is quite regular in phase, but undergoes long-term changes

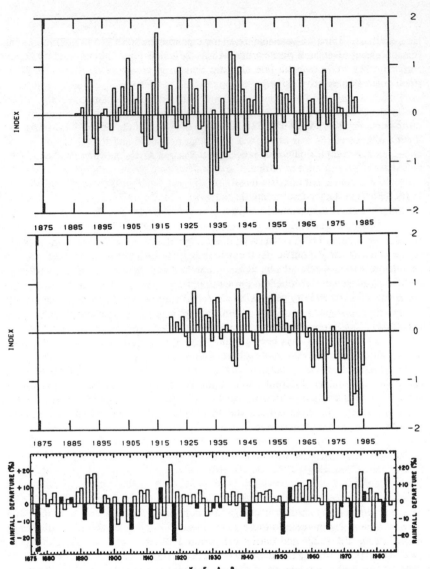

Fig. 2 Regional precipitation indices showing the relative year-to-year precipitation anomalies. The three areas shown have substantial deca-dal-scale variability. (a) October-September for the Great Plains west of approximately 95 °W. The year indicated is for the last nine months of the period. (b) June-September (rainy season) for twenty sub-Saharan stations in West Africa west of 10 °E between 11 °N and 19 °N; developed by Lamb (1985). (c) June-September (southwest monsoon) for India (provided to WMO by M. Choudry, Indian Meteorological Department). Black bars indicate years of ENSO.

in amplitude. The 18.6-year feature also varies in amplitude, but in addition exhibits a disconcerting reversal of phase around 1800. Mitchell concluded that both components merit further study as bona fide climatic signals, to clarify their physical origins and their potential predictive value.)

AFRICA: A DROUGHT-PRONE CONTINENT

The complex nature of precipitation variability and causal relationships is well illustrated by the climate of Africa. The continent spans a variety of tropical and temperature climate zones, but consists mostly of arid and semiarid regions where year-to-year variability and longer-term trends in rainfall are relatively large. The agricultural and pastoral systems of the semiarid regions are extremely sensitive to interannual variations in the already marginal rainfall.

The pattern of African precipitation anomalies typically exhibits large-scale features. Particularly notable is the extreme east-west spatial coherence of rainfall anomalies across the Sahel. In addition, anomalies of opposite sign are sometimes observed in the equatorial zone and the subtropical latitudes (Nicholson, 1986). A pattern of alternating wet and dry periods, each generally lasting for a year or two, is typical of most semiarid regions of Africa, although weaker, longer-term regimes also appear in the record. However, over the Sahel, decadal or longer regimes are a dominant feature of the variability. This has been dramatically evident during the past three decades in the catastrophic turn toward more arid conditions.

The large-scale processes associated with year-to-year rainfall variability may be quite different in different parts of the continent. A substantial fraction of the variability over southern Africa has been clearly linked to the ENSO phenomenon (Rasmusson, 1986). In West Africa, year-to-year rainfall variability appears to be more closely related to atmospheric and SST fluctuations over the tropical Atlantic (see, for example, Lough, 1986). These Atlantic SST fluctuations, however, may not be entirely independent of ENSO-related fluctuations in the Pacific. Thus, complex global linkages seem to exist. The 1950s-1980s downturn in Sahel rainfall is the most severe of the twentieth century. Reconstruction of pre-twentieth-century climate variations, before the era of instrumental records, is difficult, since they must be deduced from a variety of qualitative historical sources and archaeological and geological records. (These data indicate that conditions comparable to those of the past two decades may have prevailed in the Sahel during the 1820s and during the period 1738-56 [S. Nicholson, 1985, personal communication]. Thus, the most recent drought regime in the Sahel, while extreme, may still be within the bounds of natural variability observed during the past few centuries.)

PREDICTION: PROSPECTS AND LIMITATIONS

The theoretical framework for addressing the question of weather predictability was developed during the 1960s, and a consensus on the ultimate limits has been reached. No such framework or consensus exists for short-term climate prediction, although the past decade has witnessed considerable progress toward defining the predic-

38

tion problem and identifying promising avenues of research. The generalized nature of atmospheric predictability on time scales of one week to one year is represented in Fig. 3 for the tropics and extratropics.

It cannot be stressed too strongly that a forecast's value for a serious user depends not only on the quality of the forecast and the particular needs of that user, but also on the user's knowledge of that quality and of how the forecast should be applied (Gilman, 1985). The probabilities attached to a forecast may or may not be high enough to allow it to be used in making decisions. No forecast is complete without information on its level of confidence. It is essential that the user clearly understand the climatological background that the forecast modifies, the limitations of the forecast, and the economic or social impact of links with climate fluctuations if the forecast is to be used properly. Improper decisions may be made if a low-confidence forecast is simply used as a categorical "yes/no" statement. Without the proper background and knowledge, the user may apply a potentially useful forecast in a harmful way.

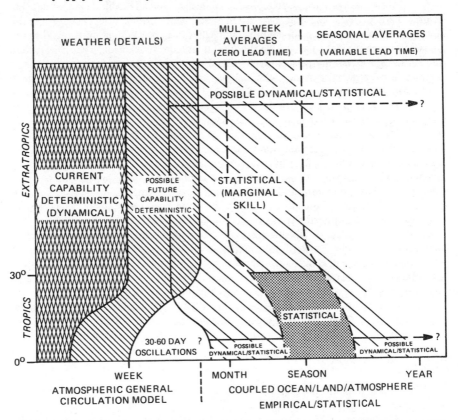

Fig. 3 Schematic representation of the nature of atmospheric predictability (suggested by Winn Neilsen, Vatican City, 1986).

Consequently, a basic distinction needs to be made between what might be called "academic prediction" and "applied prediction." The term *academic* is used in the sense of one of Webster's definitions--"Merely theoretical, no practical application"--for predictions too vague in location or timing to be useful, or for a skill level either too low for practical application or not convincingly demonstrated. *Applied prediction* refers to products whose demonstrable skill is sufficient for at least some aspects of socioeconomic planning and whose presentation is adequately quantitative and complete. The dividing line between the two categories is not always clear.

EMPIRICAL/STATISTICAL PREDICTION

The Tropics

One of the great advances in our understanding of the climate system during the past few years has been the discovery, based on observational studies and ocean and atmospheric modeling experiments, that a significant share--and in the tropics, probably a major share--of the atmospheric variability on time scales of months to a few years is associated with variations in tropical SST. This is largely the basis for increased optimism regarding the possibilities of seasonal prediction in at least some parts of the tropics.

The predictability of the onset of an ENSO episode is an unanswered question, which is being addressed as part of the ten-year Tropical Ocean Global Atmosphere Program of the World Climate Research Program (World Meteorological Organization, 1985) that began in 1986. Once an ENSO episode begins, however, its relatively consistent pattern of evolution, which is tightly locked into the annual cycle, together with its large amplitude and interannual time scale, provides potentially useful information one or more seasons in advance for the most strongly and reliably affected areas.

Empirical relationships of this type have recently been exploited in developing a number of prediction schemes for tropical and near-tropical regions (e.g., Nicholls, 1985; Shukla and Paolino, 1983). The best of those relationships typically show correlations of 0.6-0.8 between seasonally averaged conditions over large regions, such as the Indian Peninsula, and predictive parameters from the previous season. Beyond this, any real "breakthroughs," if they occur, will likely require the use of coupled ocean-atmosphere dynamical models. Prediction relationships based on slowly varying tropical parameters, such as those between Atlantic SST and west African and northeast Brazilian rainfall, offer promise, as does the possible exploitation of the thirty- to sixty-day oscillations on the shorter, monthly time scale.

THE EXTRATROPICS

Official monthly and seasonal forecasts are currently issued by the U. S. National Weather Service for an area north of 30° N, with the major effort, including the verification of the forecasts, concentrated on the United States. The current forecasts are of very limited skill, and it is unclear what further progress can be expected from empirical/statistical methodology alone.

To date, the only ENSO relationship clearly identified with extratropical North American precipitation is that with wintertime precipitation over the Gulf Coast region (Ropelewski and Halpert, 1986). With the possible exception of precipitation in the Great Basin, no warm-season relationship with ENSO has been convincingly demonstrated (Ropelewski and Halpert, 1986).

No reliable ENSO signal has been identified over extratropical Eurasia. In the Southern Hemisphere, consistent patterns of ENSO-related precipitation anomalies have been identified at latitudes equatorward of 40° in South America, Southern Africa, and Australia.

DYNAMICAL PREDICTION

Forecasts of day-to-day weather variations a month in advance are beyond the theoretical limit of predictability. If, however, we relax our objective from predicting instantaneous states to predicting time averages over a specific period, the limits of predictability may increase substantially (Shukla, 1985). This is because the large-scale, more slowly varying components of the atmospheric circulation, which primarily determine the space- and time-averaged state-of-the-atmosphere for periods longer than a few days, are potentially more predictable than the more transient synoptic features that dominate the patterns on daily weather maps.

MONTHLY MEANS

Monthly and seasonal forecasting methodology will likely diverge during the next decade. The most important development in monthly forecasting probably will be a continuation of the movement from a predominantly empirical/statistical approach to a mix of empirical and dynamical methodology that includes an increasing use of extended-range weather predictions from dynamical models. A broad range of prediction products, covering the entire world, can be produced, including confidence limits for each forecast.

By predicting at least a portion of the "weather variability" during the first part of the month, dynamical prediction may help overcome the time/space mismatch between precipitation events and the large-scale, time-average nature of climate forecasts. However, since these forecasts depend heavily on conditions at the beginning of the forecast period, they are of little value in forecasting precipitation during the second and subsequent months. Thus, the outlook for longer lead-time monthly forecasts appears dismal.

SEASONAL MEANS

Longer lead-time seasonal forecasts appear more feasible, since the weather sampling problems become less important relative to the lower-frequency, potentially more predictable climate signal. However, the extension of dynamical methodology to the prediction of seasonal means requires improved, more complex GCMs that accurately simulate both the internal dynamics of the atmosphere and the effects of surface boundary conditions. In addition, prediction of the evolution of the boundary conditions requires the development of coupled ocean/atmosphere models and better parameters for atmosphere-land surface interactions.

MULTIYEAR DRY REGIMES

Until the controlling processes are better understood, prediction of runs of predominantly dry years or multiyear trends in precipitation will continue to be hazardous and highly controversial. Although there is considerable observational evidence of systematic rainfall variability on time scales of around 22 and 18.6 years, the relationship thus far established is for average conditions over a very large area, for several seasons or even years. Therefore, the forecast skill for a particular point and season is very small; it is well to note that as yet "the connection between drought and solar behavior (also lunar tides?) is scarcely to be described as a reliable basis for operational climate prediction" (Mitchell, et al., 1979).

FINAL REMARKS

On balance, the prospects for prediction seem a bit brighter than a decade ago, when Schneider (1977) concluded that "little drought forecast skill now exists, and prospects for improved skill are hard to assess." This is due in part to developments in dynamical modeling and a better understanding of the role of the tropics in general, and the ENSO phenomenon in particular, in short-term climate variability. Nevertheless, potential predictability varies with region, season, and climatic regime. Thus, uniformly skillful seasonal forecasts one or more seasons in advance are, in all probability, an unattainable goal.

Major improvements in the spatial resolution of monthly/seasonal precipitation forecasts do not appear likely. Except for specific cases in which strong relationships can be found between mean atmospheric circulation and precipitation in particular basins, only the large-scale aspects of the anomalies can be expected to be resolved. This may be less critical during periods of drought, when widespread atmospheric subsidence tends to suppress rainfall rather uniformly over an entire region. Nevertheless, the ability to predict large-scale, seasonally-averaged patterns of precipitation anomalies, or shifts from the climatological probabilities, can be of significant value.

Lack of adequate observations is among the most important factors limiting our understanding of climate dynamics. Establishing the limits of short-term climate prediction and exploiting the predictability within the system requires not only a better monitoring of the global atmosphere, but also a far better description of variations in the temperature and currents of the the upper ocean, and a more accurate description of land surface boundary conditions. These requirements can only be met by a more comprehensive and stable global observational network, in which meteorological and oceanographic satellites play a key role.

42

ACKNOWLEDGMENTS

Thanks are due to D. L. Gilman for constructive comments on the manuscript and C. F. Ropelewski for providing the rainfall indices.

REFERENCES

Bell, P. R. 1981. The combined solar tidal influence in climate/Predominant periods in the time series of drought area index for the western High Plains AD 1700 to 1962. pp. 241-264. In S. Sofia, ed. Variations of the Solar Constant. NASA Conference Publication 2191, Washington, D. C.

Currie, R. G. 1981. Evidence for 18.6-year M_N signal in temperature and drought conditions in North America since A.D. 1800. J. Geophys. Res. 86:11055-11064.

Gilman, D. L. 1985. Long-range forecasting: the present and the future. Bull. Am. Meteorol. Soc. 66:159-164.

Hameed, S. 1984. Fourier analysis of Nile flood levels. Geophys. Res. Lett. 11:843-845.

Hameed, S.; W. M. Yeh; M. T. Li; R. D. Cess; and W. C. Wang. 1983. An analysis of periodicities in the 1470 to 1974 Beijing precipitation record. Geophys. Res. Lett. 10:436-439.

Knutson, T. R.; K. M. Weickmann; and J. E. Kutzbach. 1986. Global scale intraseasonal oscillations of outgoing longwave radiation and 250 mb zonal wind during the Northern Hemisphere summer. Mon. Weather Rev. 114:605-623.

Lamb, P. J. 1985. Rainfall in Subsaharan West Africa during 1941-83. Zeit. Gletscher. Glazialgeologie 21(1):131-139.

Lough, J. M. 1986. Tropical Atlantic sea surface temperatures and rainfall variations in Subsaharan Africa and northeast Brazil. Mon. Weather Rev. 114:561-570.

Madden, R. A.; and P. R. Julian. 1971. Detection of a 40-50 day oscillation in the zonal wind in the tropical Pacific. J. Atmos. Sci. 28:702-708.

Mintz, Y. 1984. The sensitivity of numerically simulated climate to land surface boundary conditions. pp. 79-105. In J. T. Houghton, ed. The Global Climate. Cambridge University Press, Cambridge.

Mitchell, J. M.; W. C. Stockton; and D. M. Meko. 1979. Evidence of a 22-year rhythm of drought in the western United States related to the Hale solar cycle since the 17th century. pp. 125-143. In B. M. McCormac and T. A. Seliga, eds. Solar-Terrestrial Influences on Weather and Climate. D. Reidel, Dordrecht, Holland.

Namias, J. 1965. Short period climate fluctuations. Science 147:696-706.

Nicholls, N. 1985. Toward the prediction of major Australian droughts. Aust. Met. Mag. 33:161-166.

Nicholson, S. E. 1986. The spatial coherence of African rainfall anomalies-interhemispheric teleconnections. J. Clim. Applied Meteorol. (in press).

Palmer, W. C. 1965. Meteorological drought. Research Paper No. 45, U. S. Weather Bureau, Washington, D. C.

Philander, S. G. F. 1979. Variability of the tropical oceans. pp. 191-208. Dynamics Atmos. Oceans.

Rasmusson, E. M. 1986. African drought in a global and regional context. In M. H. Glantz, ed. Drought and Hunger in Africa: Denying Famine a Future. Cambridge University Press, Cambridge (in press).

Rasmusson, E. M. 1985. El Niño and variations in climate. Am. Scientist 73:168-178.

Ropelewski, C. F.; and M. S. Halpert. 1986. North American precipitation and temperature patterns associated with the El Niño/Southern Oscillation (ENSO). Mon. Weather. Rev. (in press).

Schneider, S. H. 1977. Forecasting future droughts: Is it possible? pp. 163-171. In N. J. Rosenberg, ed. AAAS Symposium on North American Droughts. Westview Press, Boulder, Colorado.

Shukla, J. 1985. Predictability. pp. 87-122. In S. Manabe, ed. Issues in Atmospheric and Oceanic Modeling Part B: Weather Dynamics. Academic Press, New York.

Shukla, J.; and D. A. Paolino. 1983. The Southern Oscillation and long-range forecasting of the summer monsoon rainfall over India. Mon. Weather Rev. 111:1830-1837.

Sud, Y. C.; J. Shukla; and Y. Mintz. 1986. Influence of land surface roughness on atmospheric circulation and rainfall: A sensitivity study with a general circulation model (submitted to J. Atmos. Sci.)

Weickmann, K. M.; G. R. Lussky; and J. E. Kutzbach. 1985. Intraseasonal (30-60 day) fluctuations of outgoing longwave radiation and 250 mb streamfunction during northern winter. Mon. Weather Rev. 113:941-961.

World Meteorological Organization. 1985. Scientific Plan for the Tropical Ocean and Global Atmosphere Programme. WCRP-3, WMO, Geneva.

Yasunari, T. 1980. A quasistationary appearance of 30-40 day period in the cloudiness fluctuations during the summer monsoon over India. J. Meteor. Soc. Japan. 58:225-229.

CHAPTER 4
THE DROUGHTS OF NORTHEAST BRAZIL AND THEIR PREDICTION

Stefan Hastenrath

INTRODUCTION

The droughts of Northeast Brazil are among the most disastrous climatic events of the tropics. Attention to this regional example in the present symposium appears particularly pertinent, not only because of the extraordinary human impact of the *Sêcas*, or droughts, in Brazil's Nordeste, but also because they are unusually well defined in the large-scale circulation setting, and recent research indicates that their timely prediction is possible. This symposium contribution draws on various original publications in the course of the past decade (Hastenrath and Heller, 1977; Hastenrath, et al., 1984; Hastenrath, 1984; Hastenrath, 1985, pp. 339-344, 363-369; Hastenrath, 1986), which may also be consulted.

HISTORY OF HUMAN IMPACT

An extensive account of the societal consequences of the Sêcas since early colonial times is found in Hastenrath (1985, pp. 363-369), but a brief summary must suffice here. Throughout its long history, Northeast Brazil has been plagued repeatedly by drought catastrophes. Famines are recorded since the early colonial era, and emigration to other parts of Brazil began in the seventeenth century. Government drought response measures and the first famine relief organization date back to the 1700s. In the nineteenth century the government directed the drilling of artesian wells and the study of other possible measures to cope with the economic and social consequences of drought. The great famine of 1877-79 led to the recognition of the Nordeste Sêcas as a national problem. The great drought of 1958 gave the final impetus for the foundation of a specialized government agency (SUDENE) concerned with the development of the Nordeste. A variety of measures, including the construction of dams, irrigation schemes, and roads, as well as diverse emergency plans, addressed the impact of the droughts on the population of the interior Nordeste. The development of operational climate prediction remains an important task.

GENERAL CIRCULATION BACKGROUND

The annual cycle of circulation and climate in the Brazil-tropical Atlantic sector is extensively documented in various surface and upper-air atlases (Atkinson and Sadler, 1970; Hastenrath and Lamb, 1977; Chu and Hastenrath, 1982). The march of the seasons in Northeast Brazil is dominated by the latitudinal migration of the near-equatorial trough of low pressure and associated confluence zone and convergence band over the western North Atlantic, sandwiched as they are between the subtropical highs of the two hemispheres. Figures 1a and 1b illustrate the surface wind field over the tropical Atlantic around the extremes of the annual cycle, namely in April and August. The near-equatorial trough and associated confluence zone and convergence band are farthest north at the height of the boreal summer, then shift equatorward, reaching a southernmost location in March and April. The sea surface temperature pattern (Figs. 1c, d) is characterized by warmest waters in the Northern Hemisphere in a zone extending from northern South America to West Africa, and lowest temperatures to the south of the equator; meridional gradients of sea surface temperature are steepest around August and weakest around March/April.

Mean annual rainfall varies greatly throughout the Nordeste (Departamento Nacional de Obras contra as Sêcas, 1969a, 1969b; Ratisbona, 1976). In the wettest region along the east coast, annual totals exceed 1600 mm. Broadly parallel to this zone and westward of the coastal highlands lies the dry region of the Nordeste, where annual rainfall ranges from 300 to 800 mm. Proceeding farther west toward Amazonia, annual rainfall gradually increases to more than 2000 mm.

The rainy season in the northern Nordeste is narrowly concentrated in March/April. At least three concurrent seasonal features in the large-scale atmospheric and oceanic surface fields in the tropical Atlantic appear conducive to precipitation activity: (1) the near-equatorial confluence axis and associated convergence band reach their southernmost location, although they stay well to the north of the Nordeste even at this time of year; (2) the south equatorial Atlantic waters are warmest, thus enhancing the moisture and instability of atmospheric flow upstream from the Nordeste; (3) the perennial contrast between warm north equatorial waters and cold waters to the south of the equator is weakest. Moura and Shukla (1981) hypothesized that the juxtaposition of warm surface waters to the north and cold waters to the south would induce a meridional circulation cell in the atmosphere with subsidence over the Nordeste. This process is expected to be weakest in the season of weakest meridional gradients of sea surface temperature.

The annual march of rainfall shows a gradual transition from the northern to the southern Nordeste, where the maximum is found around November/December. Frontal influences from the Southern Hemisphere affect the southern Nordeste in particular (Sampaio Ferraz, 1925, 1929; Ratisbona, 1976; Kousky, 1979). The rainfall mechanisms at the eastern Nordeste coast, in particular the land-sea breeze system and westward propagating cloud clusters, have been discussed by Ramos (1975), Yamazaki and Rao (1977), and Kousky (1980).

Of particular interest in the present study is the central northern Nordeste (Figs. 2, 3), for which the average annual precipitation is low, the peak of the rainy season is narrowly confined to March/April, and both the average annual cycle and the interannual variability of rainfall are conspicuously related to the large-scale circulation.

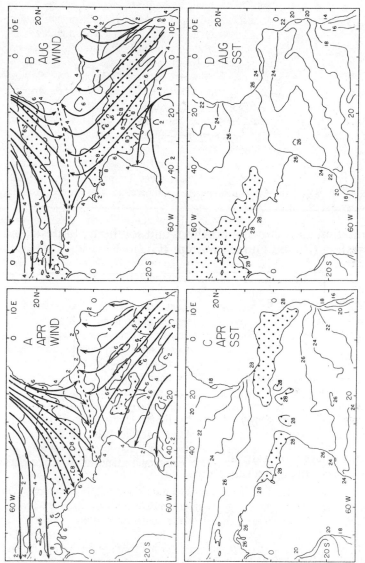

Fig. 1 Climatic mean (1911-70) maps of surface resultant streamlines and isotachs (m s^{-1}) during (a) April and (b) August, and SST (in °C) during (c) April and (d) August. Dot roster denotes, respectively, areas with wind speed larger than 6 m s^{-1} and SST larger than 28 °C.

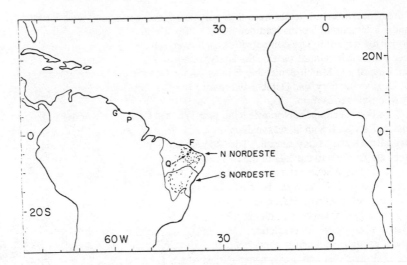

Fig. 2 Orientation map showing northern and southern Nordeste and stations Fortaleza (F) and Quixeramobim (Q).

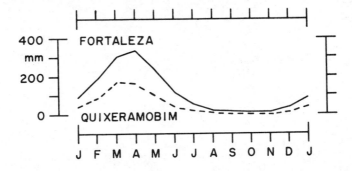

Fig. 3 Annual march of rainfall in the central northern Nordeste, stations Fortaleza and Quixeramobim.

YEAR-TO-YEAR VARIATIONS OF RAINFALL

Rainfall indices representative of large areas are constructed in order to account for the great space and time variability of tropical rainfall. For the northern Nordeste, thirty-two stations are used here that possess a correlation coefficient of at least + 0.7 with Quixeramobim in central Ceará (Fig. 2). A rainfall index was compiled from these thirty-two stations as follows. For each station, rainfall totals for the twelve-month period October to September were computed, in accordance with the rainy season centered on March/April. Mean totals, departures from the mean, and standard deviation of these twelve-month totals were then calculated, and departures were divided by the standard deviation ("normalized departure"). Finally, the thirty-two-station average of normalized departure was computed for each twelve-month period, thus yielding an October-September rainfall index. Similarly, index series were compiled for the periods March-April and March-September, as well as for October-November, October-December, October-January, and October-February. The October-September index is plotted in Fig. 4 in time series form.

For the southern Nordeste, Chu (1983) compiled a similar index based on fourteen stations and with a seasonalization from July to June, in accordance with the November-January rainy season. The index is also shown in Fig. 4. For both series, values are ascribed to the later of the two calendar years.

Figure 4 serves to show that despite some similarities, precipitation departures differ considerably between the northern and southern Nordeste. The rainfall index series for the northern Nordeste as displayed in Fig. 4 is used to identify rainfall anomalies for the purposes of diagnostics. The index series for March-April and March-September are used for prediction. In view of the temporal and spatial variability of tropical rainfall, statements concerning rainfall departures appear appropriate only for large time intervals and areas, namely most of the rainy season and the northern Nordeste as a whole.

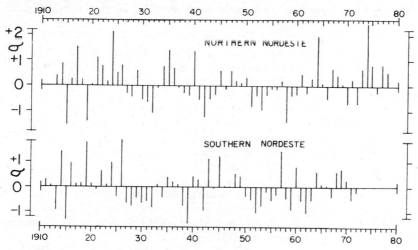

Fig. 4 Average of normalized departure of annual rainfall for all stations in the northern and southern Nordeste.

DIAGNOSTICS OF DROUGHT AND FLOOD REGIMES

The departure patterns of large-scale atmospheric and oceanic fields associated with hydrometeorological anomalies in the northern Nordeste have been studied by Hastenrath and Heller (1977); Hastenrath, et al. (1984); and Hastenrath (1984). The major departure characteristics of the pressure, wind, divergence, sea surface temperature, and cloudiness fields at the height of the March-April rainy season in the northern Nordeste are illustrated in Fig. 5, taken from Hastenrath (1984). The collection of wet and dry years used in this stratification were identified from the hydrometeorological index series for the northern Nordeste shown in Fig. 4. The departure patterns of the wet years are broadly inverse to those of the dry years. Features are enhanced in the patterns of wet versus dry.

The circulation departures of an abundant rainy season are as follows: the near-equatorial trough of low pressure is displaced southward (Fig. 5a), as is the confluence between the Northern and Southern Hemisphere trade wind airstreams (Figs. 5b, c) and the associated band of maximum convergence and cloudiness (Figs. 5e, f); surface water of the equatorial South Atlantic is anomalously warm, while negative sea surface temperature departures prevail in much of the tropical North Atlantic (Fig. 5d). During drought years in Northeast Brazil the departure patterns of the various atmospheric and oceanic fields are approximately inverse to those in the wet years. Refer to Hastenrath (1984) for the statistical significance testing of the departure pattern.

The departure characteristics of the pressure, wind, and convergence fields are internally consistent and symptomatic of an anomalous latitude position of the near-equatorial trough. The band of anomalous convergence (Fig. 5c) extending from Brazil to equatorial Africa is matched by a corresponding zone of enhanced cloudiness (Fig. 5f).

In the earlier discussion of the average annual precipitation cycle, three factors were pointed out as conducive to precipitation activity at the height of the northern Nordeste rainy season. The same mechanisms operating in the annual cycle also appear instrumental in the interannual variability of circulation and climate (Hastenrath, 1984). Thus the following three corollaries to the average annual cycle are apparent for a deficient rainy season in the northern Nordeste:

1. The near-equatorial confluence axis and associated convergence band assume a more northerly location, comparable to the drier times of the year in the average annual cycle.
2. The south equatorial Atlantic waters are cold, thus also departing toward the average dry season conditions.
3. The juxtaposition of warm waters in the North Atlantic and cold ocean surfaces in the south equatorial Atlantic--which would induce a meridional circulation cell in the atmosphere with subsidence over the Nordeste (Moura and Shukla, 1981)--is pronounced and hence similar to the dry season conditions in the average annual cycle.

The focus here is on the northern Nordeste; reference is made to Chu (1983) for the southern Nordeste.

Extreme climatic events in the Nordeste are beyond the tropical Atlantic sector further associated with circulation anomalies in more remote regions. These have been reviewed in part by Kousky and Moura (1981). As a rule, these teleconnections can be understood in terms of the circulation mechanisms operative in the tropical Atlantic domain, as described above. Thus, Namias (1972) pointed out that increased cyclonic activity in the Newfoundland area is associated with abundant rainfall in the Nordeste. There is an inverse coupling of surface pressure between the subpolar and subtropical Atlantic, as was shown by Van Loon and Rogers (1978). As explained above, the strengthened North Atlantic high is conducive to a more southerly position of quasi-per-

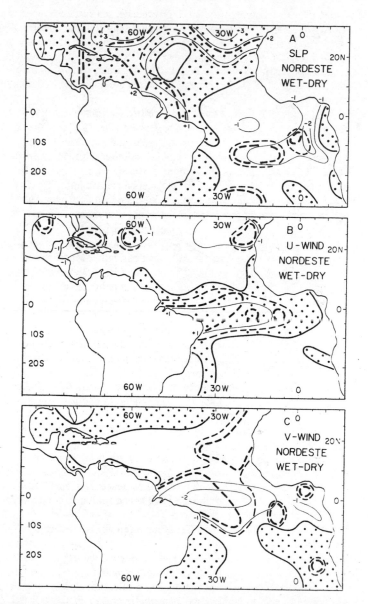

Fig. 5 Maps of March-April circulation departures associated with rainfall anomalies in the northern Nordeste. (a) Sea-level pressure; (b) zonal (u) and (c) meridional (v) component of wind; (d) sea surface temperature; (e) divergence; (f) cloudiness. The charts represent the difference of departures for the composite of wet years (1917, 1921,

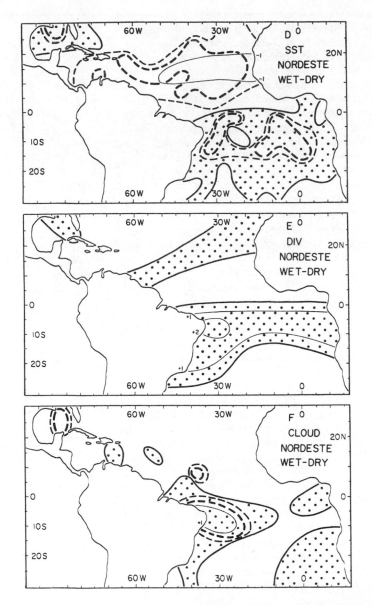

1922, 1924, 1926, 1934, 1935, 1940, 1964, 1967) minus the departures for the composite of dry years (1915, 1930, 1932, 1936, 1942, 1951, 1953, 1958). Areas significant at the 5% and 10% levels are enclosed, respectively, by heavy and thin broken lines, (e) being excepted from testing.

manent circulation features over the tropical Atlantic and rainfall in the northern Nordeste. A similar pressure seesaw is conceivable for the South Atlantic.

These analyses of departure patterns in the surface circulation are nicely complemented by Nobre and Moura's (1984) recent study of upper-air departure patterns associated with extreme rainy seasons in Northeast Brazil. Thus, Nobre and Moura find for the drought years an anomalous cyclonic circulation over the subtropical North Atlantic and an anomalous anticyclonic circulation over the subtropical North Atlantic. For the lower troposphere, these findings are consistent with the earlier work of Hastenrath and Heller (1977) and Namias (1972), but Nobre and Moura's work shows these circulation anomalies extending through the whole depth of the troposphere.

Kousky and Moura (1981) further suggest a relation of Northeast Brazil rainfall to the intensity and position of the upper-tropospheric anticyclone, which persists over the Bolivian-Peruvian Altiplano and the adjacent regions of southern Amazonia during the austral summer (Chu and Hastenrath, 1982).

Caviedes (1973), Hastenrath and Heller (1977), Hastenrath (1978), and Covey and Hastenrath (1978) have discussed the general circulation causes for coupling between Northeast Brazil droughts and the Pacific El Niño phenomenon. Both climatic disasters appear to be related to the Southern Oscillation, the pressure over the South Atlantic being of immediate relevance for the rainfall in the northern Nordeste. It is then not surprising that various departure characteristics of the Southern Oscillation in remote regions may coincide with rainfall anomalies in the Nordeste.

In efforts to predict seasonal rainfall for the northern Nordeste, the departure characteristics in the tropical Atlantic domain are regarded as the most immediately relevant. To the extent that the circulation over the Atlantic is related to processes on a much larger scale, specific predictors from more remote regions may also be pertinent.

VARIOUS PREDICTION ENDEAVORS

In the course of the twentieth century, the meteorological community has sporadically attempted to provide seasonal forecasts of drought (see also Aldaz, 1971, 1983, pp. 6-26; Carvalho, 1973, pp. 193-229). The approaches proposed include:

1. The extrapolation of presumed periodicities such as the sunspot cycle (Sampaio Ferraz, 1950; Markham, 1974; Jones and Kearns, 1976).
2. The assessment of statistical relationships with pressure and other data at distant locations (Walker, 1928; Sampaio Ferraz, 1929; Serra, 1956).
3. The relation of preseason rainfall to the precipitation amounts at the peak of the rainy season (Freise, 1938; Markham, 1967; Serra, 1973a, 1973b).

Continuing a tradition of coping with the environmental problems of the Nordeste (Carvalho, 1973; Gonçalves de Souza, 1979), the government of Brazil (Conselho Nacional de Pesquisas, 1980) is taking an active interest in the possibility of forecasting the Sêcas.

Various papers (Markham, 1974; Jones and Kearns, 1976; Kousky and Chu, 1978; Hastenrath and Kaczmarczyk, 1981; Chu, 1984) have presented evidence to the effect that rainfall variability in Northeast Brazil is concentrated with some preference in the frequency bands of somewhat more than 2 years, around 14 years, and around 28 years. Moreover, the studies of Hastenrath and Kaczmarczyk (1981) and Chu (1984) suggest that the circulation and climate anomaly mechanisms identified above are with some preference operative at the time scales of 2+ and about 14 and 28 years. It appears tempting to exploit such time series characteristics for long-range rainfall prediction (e.g., Sampaio Ferraz, 1950), especially with lead times of several years. Such endeavors hinge on two criteria: (1) the percentage of total rainfall variance explained by the particular frequency band or harmonic; and (2) the stationarity of the time series.

A limited investigation was made into the possibility of predicting rainfall from past spectral characteristics (Hastenrath, et al., 1984). The harmonics corresponding to 26 and 28 months each explain about 2% of the total variance of 12-monthly (October-September) rainfall. The pairs of harmonics corresponding to 13 and 26, or 13.5 and 27 years, explain only about 18% of the total variance of the 12-monthly rainfall. Averaging over 5-year intervals eliminates the higher harmonics, so that the aforementioned pairs of harmonics (14/28 and 13.5/27 years) account for about 40% of the 5-year average annual rainfall. Spectral and harmonic analyses for various portions of the historical record do not yield identical results, so strict stationarity is not expected for the future. Sample calculations not presented here suggest the possible usefulness of spectral extrapolation for estimating 5-year average rainfall. Spectral extrapolation yields low rainfall for the mid-1980s. However, this approach is definitely not appropriate for the prediction of individual years.

FORECASTING FROM ANTECEDENT CIRCULATION ANOMALIES

In the following discussion, a method (Hastenrath, et al., 1984) is developed for predicting northern Nordeste rainfall, in the form of March-April and March-September precipitation indices. For input, the method uses information that would exist by certain dates preceding the March/April rainy season peak in the northern Nordeste, namely through the end of October, November, January, and February. Plausible predictor candidates are identified from the diagnostic studies summarized above and input to a stepwise multiple regression model (years 1931-40, 1946-Feb. 1956). The resulting regression equations are then applied in a predictive mode on an independent data set (years 1957-72).

Concerning possible predictors, it was noted above that droughts in the northern Nordeste are heralded by an anomalously far northerly position of the near-equatorial trough and associated symptoms. Since the mechanisms of interannual circulation and climate variability in the Brazil-tropical Atlantic sector are to be regarded as modulations of the average annual cycle, departures of preseason rainfall in Northeast Brazil and northern South America may precede the precipitation anomalies around the March/April peak of the northern Nordeste rainy season. Inasmuch as the pressure distribution over the Atlantic--which is instrumental in Northeast Brazil rainfall anomalies--is related to large-scale mass redistributions of the Southern Oscillation type (Hastenrath and Heller, 1977), various indicators of the Southern Oscillation and parameters from more remote parts of the globe are of interest.

With a view toward identifying suitable predictor candidates, isocorrelate maps were constructed of the October-September Northeast Brazil rainfall index with pressure, sea surface temperature, zonal and meridional wind components, and cloudiness over the Atlantic. The regions of correlation exceeding 0.3 in absolute value were identified, and time series were compiled as input to a regression model. The screening is intended to safeguard against noise. Other predictor candidates considered include preseason rainfall in the northern Nordeste itself, rainfall at Paramaribo and Georgetown in Guyana, pressure at Port Stanley in the South Atlantic, temperature in the southeastern United States, India rainfall, and Wright's (1975, 1977) Southern Oscillation index. Of seventeen candidate series, eleven possess a correlation with Northeast Brazil exceeding 0.3 in absolute value; these were input into a stepwise multiple regression scheme with a 5% significance margin. Pressure, sea surface temperature, and zonal and meridional wind components over the tropical Atlantic were thus identified as the most important predictors. Of further use was the preseason rainfall in northern Northeast Brazil itself and the May-June-July Southern Oscillation index value.

Regression models were constructed for 1921-40 and 1946-56 for all months from October through March for two "predictands," namely the March-April and the March-September rainfall indices. Results not detailed here show for both "predictands" a general increase of the explained variance as one approaches the peak rainy season. Thus the explained variance is largest for the months January and February (respectively March). The March-April and the March-September rainfall are specified to a very high degree by the departure ensemble of the general circulation in February and March. However, February leaves no lead time for the practical use of the forecast, while November accounts only for a small percentage of the rainfall variability. Accordingly, the January models merit particular attention.

Figure 6a is a scatter plot of the regression model (years 1921-40 and 1943-46) with significance level X = 5%, for the March-September rainfall index-regressed an information through January; the correlation coefficient between "regressed" and "observed" rainfall being +0.81.

The regression models developed from the 1921-40 and 1946-56 record were used to predict the rainfall anomalies of the fifteen years from 1958 to 1972. Figure 6b is a scatter plot of the January model predicting the March-September rainfall index. Information such as that in Fig. 6a serves as background reference for rainfall index forecasts for years beyond the base period of the regression models, as presented in Fig. 6b.

As a basis for the appraisal of forecast performance, various forms of evidence are considered. The scatter diagram in Fig. 6b shows a positive relation between forecast and observed values, although the scatter is larger than for the regression model plotted in Fig. 6a. The correlation coefficient between forecast and observed values in Fig. 6b is high. In addition, skill scores (Panofsky and Brier, 1968, pp. 191-208) and stochastic joint probabilities (Preisendorfer and Mobley, 1982) were calculated. These also show appreciable forecast skill. The pertinent information is contained in Fig. 6, but details are not discussed here. In context, the various measures of prediction quality all bear out a remarkable forecast performance.

Fig. 6 shows particularly good forecasts for the extreme drought year 1958, as well as for the dry years 1959 and 1966 and the wet year 1964. By contrast, the discrepancy is worst for the January forecasts of the March-April and March-September rainfall of 1960. This is understandable because of the peculiar seasonal evolution from late 1959 into the March/April rainy season: the large-scale circulation conditions (as well as preseason rainfall) remained characteristic of droughts through February 1960, and then changed unusually abruptly to a setting typical of abundant rainfall.

56

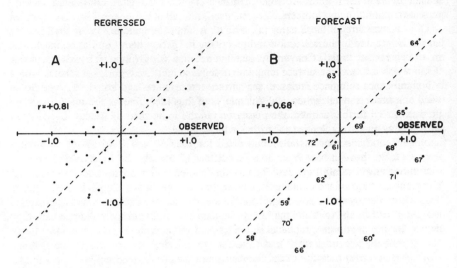

Fig. 6 Scatter diagram of March-September Nordeste rainfall index based on observations through January. (a) Regression period 1921-40, 1946-56, correlation coefficient r = +0.81. (b) Forecast period 1958-72, with numbers indicating the years, r = +0.68, significant at the 1% level. Broken lines denote 45° angle (from Hastenrath, et al, 1984).

The study (Hastenrath, et al., 1984) shows that the March-April and entire season rainfall is specified to a very high degree by the departure ensemble of the large-scale circulation, especially in the tropical Atlantic around the peak rainy season. To a lesser extent, the rainfall anomalies are presaged by the antecedent establishment of circulation anomaly patterns. The severe 1958 drought in particular was highly predictable using this methodology.

SYNTHESIS AND OUTLOOK

The development of the empirically-based forecast method outlined above demonstrates that nearly half of the interannual variance of northern Nordeste rainfall can be predicted from antecedent departures in the large-scale circulation. Ongoing basic research is directed to the issues of secular variations in predictability, optimal length of dependent record, and updating of the regression base period.

Turning to the translation of this method into operational application, the input information must satisfy the following two criteria simultaneously: (1) long (more than ten years) internally homogeneous series are needed, although absolute calibration is not essential; and (2) the information must be available on a timely basis. The information most essential for Nordeste climate prediction includes: (a) indicative atmospheric and oceanic fields in the tropical Atlantic; (b) a measure of the Southern Oscillation; and (c) preseason rainfall in the Nordeste.

For the first of these items (a), long-term ship observations have proved useful, but the long delay in the collection and processing of data presently precludes their use on an operational basis. Conversely, satellite sensing can provide information on the cloudiness, wind, and sea surface temperature fields in quasi real time, but long internally homogeneous reference series so far have not been created--a task well beyond the reach of a small research group. In principle, both ship observation and satellite sensing are potentially useful for prediction purposes, but a serious commitment is needed to satisfy, in either case, the need for timely information. Of particular interest here is the automatic wind recorder installed under the auspices of an oceanographic research program (SEQUAL) on St. Peter and Paul Rocks in the western equatorial Atlantic. Measurements are transmitted daily by satellite to the Lamont Observatory of Columbia University and are thus available on a timely basis. The short record so far shows a close relation between the zonal wind component in January at St. Peter and Paul Rocks and the subsequent Nordeste rainfall. Maintenance of this station is thus relevant beyond the original oceanographic objectives.

For the second item (b), the pressure difference between Tahiti and Darwin seems to be a useful measure of the Southern Oscillation, and it appears possible to obtain these observations on a timely basis.

The third ingredient (c) may seem trivial, but this task is the most painful. Of the forty rainfall stations originally used in the construction of a long-term rainfall index (Hastenrath and Heller, 1977), less than twenty-eight still report--an example of the alarming decay of surface (and upper-air) stations that has taken place in much of the tropics over the past fifteen years, sadly coincident with the era of GARP.

Climate prediction is one of the foremost challenges of modern low-latitude meteorology. Beyond the exclusively meteorological tasks, various issues arise: What percentage of interannual rainfall variance should be explained for the forecast to be useful? Should prediction be publicized or held confidential? What forms of forecasts and what lead times are needed for practical application? In fact, what use will be made at all of the climate predictions? The wisdom of agriculturists, economists, and other planners is needed not only in the eventual application but also in the very design of the prediction schemes. Conversely, we meteorologists should attempt to make potential users aware of the possibilities and limitations of climate prediction. This symposium may be an important step toward establishing such a dialogue.

ACKNOWLEDGMENTS

This work was supported by National Science Foundation Grant No. ATM84-13575.

58

REFERENCES

Aldaz, L. 1971. A partial characterization of the rainfall regime of Brazil. Publicacão Técnica No. 4, DINMET Vol. 1. SUDENE, Rio de Janeiro.

Aldaz, L. 1983. Aplicación del concepto de interacción de escalas temporales al fenómeno de las sequías extremas en el Nordeste del Brazil. Ph.D. dissertation, Universidad Complutense, Madrid.

Atkinson, G. D.; and J. C. Sadler. 1970. Mean-cloudiness and gradient-level wind charts over the tropics. Air Weather Service Technical Report 215, Vol. 2.

Carvalho, J. O., ed. 1973. Plano integrado para o combate preventivo aos efeitos das Sêcas do Nordeste. Ministerio do Interior, Serie Desenvolvimento Regional, 1.

Caviedes, C. N. 1973. Sêcas and El Niño: Two simultaneous climatical hazards in South America. Proc. Assoc. Am. Geogr. 5:44-49.

Chu, P. S. 1983. Diagnostic studies of rainfall anomalies in northeast Brazil. Mon. Weather Rev. 111:1655-1664.

Chu, P. S. 1984. Time and space variability of rainfall and surface circulation in the northeast Brazil-tropical Atlantic sector. J. Meteor. Soc. Japan 62:363-370.

Chu, P. S.; and S. Hastenrath. 1982. Atlas of upper-air circulation over tropical South America. Department of Meteorology, University of Wisconsin, Madison.

Conselho Nacional de Pesquisas. 1980. Workshop on drought forecasting for northeast Brazil. INPE, São José dos Campos.

Covey, D. C.; and S. Hastenrath. 1978. The Pacific El Niño phenomenon and the Atlantic circulation. Mon. Weather Rev. 106:1280-1287.

Departamento Nacional de Obras contra as Sêcas. 1969a. Observações pluviométricas no Nordeste do Brazil. 2 Vols. Fortaleza, Brazil.

Departamento Nacional de Obras contra as Sêcas. 1969b. Atlas pluviometrico do Nordeste do Brazil. Fortaleza, Brazil.

Environmental Sciences Service Administration. 1967. World weather records 1951-1960. U. S. Government Printing Office, Washington, D.C.

Freise, F. W. 1938. The drought region of northeastern Brazil. Geogr. Rev. 28:363-378.

Gonçalves de Souza, J. 1979. O Nordeste Brasileiro. Banco do Nordesto do Brasil, S. A., Fortaleza.

Hastenrath, S. 1978. On modes of tropical circulation and climate anomalies. J. Atmos. Sci. 35:2222-2231.

Hastenrath, S. 1984. Interannual variability and annual cycle: Mechanisms of circulation and climate in the tropical Atlantic sector. Mon. Weather Rev. 112:1097-1107.

Hastenrath, S. 1985. Climate and circulation of the tropics. D. Reidel, Dordrecht, Holland.

Hastenrath, S. 1986. On climate prediction in the tropics. Bull. Am. Meteorol. Soc. 67:696-702.

Hastenrath, S.; and L. Heller. 1977. Dynamics of climatic hazards in northeast Brazil. Quart. J. Roy. Meteorol. Soc. 103:77-92.

Hastenrath, S.; and E. B. Kaczmarczyk. 1981. On spectra and coherence of tropical climate anomalies. Tellus 33:453-462.

Hastenrath, S.; and P. J. Lamb. 1977. Climatic Atlas of the Tropical Atlantic and Eastern Pacific Oceans. University of Wisconsin Press, Madison.

Hastenrath, S; M.-C. Wu; and P. S. Chu. 1984. Towards the monitoring and prediction of Northeast Brazil droughts. Quart. J. Roy. Meteorol. Soc. 110:411-425.

Jones, R. H.; and J. P. Kearns. 1976. Fortaleza, Ceará, Brazil, rainfall. J. Appl. Meteorol. 15:307-308.

Kousky, V. E. 1979. Frontal influences on northeast Brazil. Mon. Weather Rev. 107:1140-1153.

Kousky, V. E. 1980. Diurnal rainfall variation in northeast Brazil. Mon. Weather Rev. 108:488-498.

Kousky, V. E.; and P. S. Chu. 1978. Fluctuations in annual rainfall for northeast Brazil. J. Meteorol. Soc. Japan 57:457-465.

Kousky, V. E.; and A. D. Moura. 1981. Previsão de precipitacão no Nordeste do Brazil: O aspecto dinâmico. IV Simposio Brasileiro de Hidrologia e Recursos Hidricos, November 1981, Fortaleza.

Markham, C. G. 1967. Climatological aspects of drought in northeast Brazil. Ph.D. dissertation, Department of Geography, University of California, Berkeley.

Markham, C. G. 1974. Apparent periodicities in rainfall at Fortaleza, Ceará, Brazil. J. Appl. Meteorol. 13:176-179.

Moura, A. D.; and J. Shukla. 1981. On the dynamics of droughts in northeast Brazil: Observations, theory, and numerical experiments with a general circulation model. J. Atmos. Sci. 38:2653-2675.

Namias, J. 1972. Influence of northern hemisphere general circulation on drought in northeast Brazil. Tellus 24:336-343.

Nobre, P.; and Moura, A. D. 1984. Large scale tropical heat sources and global atmosphere energy propagation associated with droughts in Northeast Brazil. pp. 83-86. In World Meteorological Organization. Extended Abstracts of Papers Presented at the Second WMO Symposium on Meteorological Aspects of Tropical Droughts. TMP Report Series No. 15. World Meteorological Organization, Geneva.

Panofsky, H. A.: and G. W. Brier. 1968. Some Applications of Statistics to Meteorology. Pennsylvania State University Press, State College.

Preisendorfer, R. W.; and C. D. Mobley. 1982. Climate forecast verifications, U.S. mainland, 1974-82. NOAA Technical Memorandum ERL PMEL-36, Seattle, Washington.

Ramos, R. P. L. 1975. Precipitation characteristics in the northeast Brazil dry region. J. Geophys. Res. 80:1665-1678.

Ratisbona, L. R. 1976. The climate of Brazil. In World Survey of Climatology 12:219-269. Elsevier, New York.

Sampaio Ferraz, J. de. 1925. Causas provaveis das sêcas do Nordeste Brasileiro. Ministerio da Agricultura, Directoria de Meteorologia, Rio de Janeiro.

Sampaio Ferraz, J. de. 1929. Sir Gilbert Walker's formula for Ceara droughts: Suggestion for its physical explanation. Meteor. Magazine 64:81-84.

Sampaio Ferraz, J. de. 1950. Iminencia duma "Grande" Seca Nordestina. Revista Brasileira de Geografía 12, no. 1:3-15.

Serra, A. 1956. As Sêcas do Nordeste. Boletim Geográfico 14:269-270.

Serra, A. 1973a. Previsao das sêcas Nordestinos: Testes estatististicos. Boletim Geografico 32:78-104.

Serra, A. 1973b. Previsao das sêcas nordestinas. Banco do Nordeste do Brazil, Fortaleza. 55 pp.

Superintendencia do Desenvolvimento do Nordeste. 1969. Dados pluviométricos mensais. Recife, Brazil.

Van Loon, H.; and J. C. Rogers. 1978. The seesaw in winter temperatures between Greenland and northern Europe. Part I: General description. Mon. Weather Rev. 106:296-310.

Walker, G. T. 1928. Ceará (Brazil) famines and the general air movement. Beitr. Phys. d. freien Atm. 14:88-93.

Wright, P. B. 1975. An index of the Southern Oscillation. University of East Anglia, Climatic Research Unit, Research Publication No. 4.

Wright, P. B. 1977. The Southern Oscillation--Patterns, and mechanisms of the teleconnections and the persistence. Hawaii Institute of Geophysics, HIG-77-13.

Yamazaki, Y.; and V. B. Rao. 1977. Tropical cloudiness over the South Atlantic Ocean. J. Meteor. Soc. Japan 55:205-207.

CHAPTER 5
PROSPECTS FOR DROUGHT PREDICTION IN AUSTRALIA AND INDONESIA

Neville Nicholls

IMPACT OF DROUGHT

Australia is a land of poets and droughts, and drought has always been a popular subject for poems. Many of these indicate the awe with which Australians traditionally have viewed drought.

> I am the Master, the dread King Drought,
> And the great West Land is mine!
> W. H. Ogilvie

The economic and social effects of past droughts in Australia certainly justified their label as the "dread King Drought." Even now, with agriculture declining in importance in the economy, losses resulting from droughts are still the most significant of all losses from natural hazards affecting Australia. The 1982-83 drought resulted in a drop of 18% in the volume of agricultural production and a 45% reduction in average farm cash operating surplus available for consumption and investment.

The close relationship between rainfall and agricultural production is illustrated in Fig. 1. Here values of a rainfall index for eastern Australia during winter and spring (June-November) are plotted, along with deviations (anomalies) of Australian wheat yield (in tons/ha) from the long-term trend. Wheat is Australia's major crop, with a typical yield of 1.2 tons/ha. Substantial anomalies of up to 0.5 tons/ha are observed in some years, and the years of low yield are those with drought during winter and spring (the growing season).

The loss of production is not, however, the only deleterious effect of drought. On February 16, 1983, at the end of the drought, bush fires devastated much of southeast Australia. Seventy-two lives were lost, 1700 homes were destroyed, and more than 350,000 ha of countryside were burned out (Voice and Gauntlett, 1984).

In Indonesia the effects of drought can be even more severe than in Australia. For example, in 1982-83, Indonesia experienced an unusually severe dry season (April-September) and a late start to the wet season. This led to water shortages in big cities and outbreaks of cholera and famine, which claimed hundreds of lives. Forest fires on Kalimantan damaged more than 4 million ha of forest in one of the worst environmental disasters of this century. The future loss of revenue for the Indonesian forestry sector has been estimated at more than US$6 billion (Malingreau, 1986).

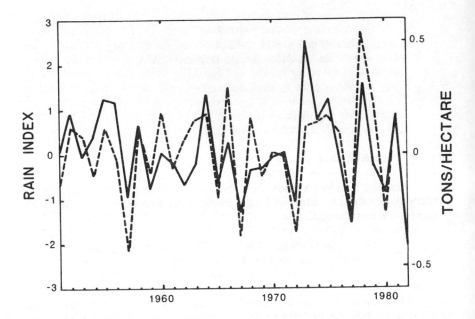

Fig. 1 Time series of east Australian winter-spring rain index (full line) and anomalies of Australian wheat yield in tons/hectare (broken line). Positive values of the rain index indicate wet periods.

DROUGHT PATTERNS

The severe impact of droughts on Australia and Indonesia has generated much interest in identifying "patterns" of drought occurrence that might be useful in drought prediction. Campbell (1973) suggested, referring to Australia, that the "opportunities of minimizing drought losses by good management which the availability of reliable long-term predictions would open up would far outweigh all the benefits of investments in agricultural research and irrigation which has been made in the past with drought mitigation as their objective." Research on the nature and predictability of rainfall fluctuations in Indonesia and Australia began more than a hundred years ago. Late last century and in the first few decades of the present century, Dutch meteorologists in Indonesia provided much of the groundwork for establishing the existence of the Southern Oscillation.

In Australia, most of the early work concentrated on searches for drought "cycles." By the time the U.S. Exploring Squadron, commanded by Charles Wilkes, visited Australia between 1838 and 1842, strong ideas about the nature of Australian droughts had already been established, even though much of the continent was still unexplored:

> Periods, or cycles, of ten or twelve years duration, distinctly mark the division of the the Australian climate into wet and dry. In the course of each cycle, there is ordinarily one year of unmitigated drought, during which no rain falls, whose effects are visible, as well in the mountains and fells of the elevated regions, as in the boggy marshes and desert flats of the interior—as well in the sandy plains along the southern coast, as in the jungles of tropical Australia. This dry season is followed by a year of freshets and floods: the rains are then incessant, but they diminish in number and quantity, in each succeeding year, until the dry epoch again recurs (Jenkins, 1850).

This early quotation postulates four "patterns" of Australian droughts:
1. They are continental in scale.
2. They last about a year.
3. They tend to be followed by very wet years.
4. They occur in a ten-to twelve-year cycle.

Most subsequent research has concentrated on whether a ten- to twelve-year cycle, or some other cycle, exists in Australian rainfall. If such a long cycle were real, it could be of great value in long-range prediction. By the end of the nineteenth century, claims had been lodged for drought cycles of two, seven, nine, eleven, twelve, and nineteen years in length. Subsequent analysis (O'Mahoney, 1961) has confirmed the existence of a two-year cycle (i.e., drier periods do tend to last about a year and do tend to be followed by wetter years). The existence of other cycles of drought occurrence has not been demonstrated despite considerable efforts. In particular, no evidence has been found for a link between Australian rainfall and the eleven-year sunspot cycle (Nicholls, 1981a).

The spatial and temporal scales of major Australian droughts are illustrated by the 1982-83 drought. Almost all of the eastern half of the continent was seriously affected, from the "jungles of tropical Australia" to the "sandy plains along the southern coast." Drought-breaking rains relieved the situation over most of the country in March 1983, about a year after the drought commenced.

Earlier droughts affecting much of the eastern half of the country also tended to last about a year. The state of New South Wales (see Fig. 2 for location), for the purposes of drought declaration, is divided into fifty-eight districts, each of which may be declared drought affected. Wilhite, et al. (1985), list the numbers of districts declared drought affected in each month from 1957 on. There were six cases of widespread drought, when more than thirty-five districts were drought affected between 1957 and 1985. The average number of districts declared drought affected for each month during these widespread droughts is shown in Fig. 3. Average numbers of declared districts have been calculated separately for each month, beginning in the January before the start of the drought and ending two years later. Although each drought is somewhat different, they all show the general pattern of Fig. 3: few areas are declared drought-affected early in the first year, but the numbers increase through winter and spring and reach a maximum near the start of the next year before falling progressively during the autumn and winter. If we define the period of widespread drought as occurring when at least twenty-

64

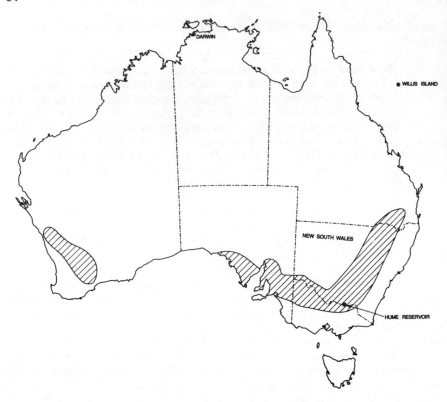

Fig. 2 Locations of Darwin, Willis Island, Hume water storage, New South Wales, and the major wheat area (hatched).

five districts are drought affected, then widespread droughts, typically, start about May or June and last about twelve months.

Thus the typical pattern of Australian drought reported by the U.S. Exploring Squadron in 1850--large-scale and lasting about a year--is confirmed. Furthermore, drought tends to start in autumn or early winter. This pattern can be used to provide a form of a drought forecast. If in June or July there is widespread drought in eastern Australia, we can assume that the drought probably will continue into the following calendar year.

This persistence of conditions into the second half of the year is evident also in streamflow. Records of inflow into the Hume water storage in southeast Australia (see Fig. 2) for the past ninety-five years are available. In Fig. 4, the inflow in July has been plotted against the inflow in August to December. There is a very strong relationship with a correlation coefficient of 0.71. The Hume storage provides water for irrigation, and the decision on how much water to allocate to each property during spring and summer is made in August. The relationship in Fig. 4 could be used to improve this allocation decision.

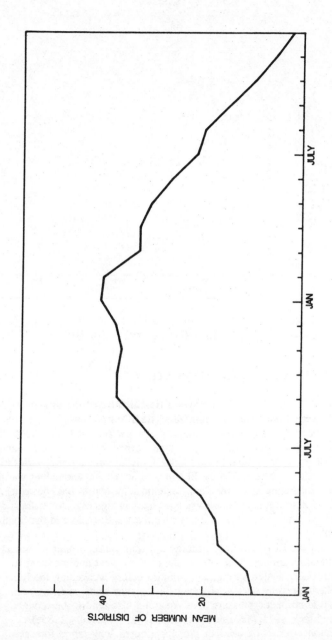

Fig. 3 Mean number of New South Wales districts declared drought-affected in each month of a two-year period encompassing each of the six widespread droughts between 1957 and 1985.

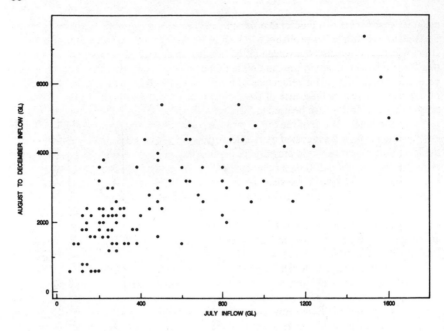

Fig. 4 Scatter diagram of July inflow into Hume water storage versus inflow for August-December. Data for period 1891-1985.

DROUGHT AND THE SOUTHERN OSCILLATION

The drought "pattern" described above arises because of the influence of the Southern Oscillation (SO) on Australia's rainfall. The SO is an out-of-phase relationship between atmospheric pressure over the southeast Pacific and the Indian Ocean, first noticed last century. When pressure is higher than normal in the Indian Ocean and across Australia, it is lower than usual in the south Pacific Ocean. Rainfall varies in the opposite direction. The SO is related to the El Niño, an occasional anomalous warming of the sea surface temperature along the Peru-Ecuador coast and in the equatorial east and central Pacific. These warmings occur when pressure is high over Australia and the Indian Ocean. Rasmusson and Wallace (1983) describe the El Niño and the Southern Oscillation in detail.

The SO and the El Niño have "patterns" of occurrence similar to Australian droughts. The El Niño warming starts early in the calendar year and increases through the Southern Hemisphere winter, spring, and summer before weakening the following autumn. Atmospheric pressure over Australia also shows the same pattern. Years with higher-than-normal atmospheric pressure over Australia also tend to be drought years (see, for example, Pittock, 1975; McBride and Nicholls, 1983; Nicholls, 1985a).

This relationship can be used to produce limited long-range forecasts. By monitoring atmospheric pressure (usually at Darwin, see Fig. 2) the phase of the SO can be determined by June or July. The SO is then unlikely to change phase until the next calendar year, so we can predict that the climatic anomalies usually associated with that particular phase of the SO probably will be present throughout the remainder of the year. If Darwin pressure is above average in the Southern Hemisphere winter, we can predict that for spring and summer, pressure will still be above average and rainfall will tend to be lower than normal. This reluctance of the SO to change phase during the second half of the calendar year is the cause of the typical drought pattern shown in Fig. 3 and the reason why July inflow can be used to forecast August-December inflow (Fig. 4).

The potential use of the SO to provide some predictability of rainfall over eastern Australia was first suggested more than fifty years ago (Quayle, 1929). In Indonesia the idea of using atmospheric pressure during the first half of the calendar year to predict rainfall in the second half (i.e., around the time of onset of the wet season) was proposed even earlier. These ideas have since been confirmed by independent data (Nicholls and Woodcock, 1981; Nicholls, 1981b) and extended to cover northern Australia, where the onset of the wet season can also be predicted (Nicholls, 1984a). Even the numbers of tropical cyclones observed around north Australia in a cyclone season (November-April) are related to the SO and are predictable also by monitoring the phase of the SO using Darwin pressure, or one of a number of other indices of the SO (Nicholls, 1984b, 1985b).

A similar approach can be used to predict yields of certain crops. Sorghum, Australia's fifth most valuable crop, is grown during the summer (planted between October and December) in eastern Australia, where rainfall is influenced by the SO. Sorghum is rainfed and yields are low when rainfall before and during the growing season is low. The yield, per hectare, is related to indices of the SO in the months before planting When Darwin pressure is high during June-August, low spring and summer rainfall can be expected in the growing area, resulting in low yields. This relationship can be used to give quite good forecasts of sorghum yield even before the crop is planted (Nicholls, 1986).

WINTER AND SPRING DROUGHTS

Sorghum is a special case, however. Most of Australia's major crops, such as wheat, are planted around June and harvested around December. They are grown mainly in that part of eastern Australia where winter and spring rainfall is strongly affected by the SO (the location of the major wheat belt is shown in Fig. 2). In Fig. 5, time series of the eastern Australian winter-spring rainfall index (previously used in Fig. 1) and Darwin pressure for the same period are shown. There is, as expected from the earlier discussion, a strong relationship between the two. When Darwin pressure, an index of the SO, is higher than normal, rainfall is low over much of eastern Australia.

This relationship indicates that if we could find an early warning of a Southern Oscillation "event," say by about May, this might be useful for predicting the major eastern Australia winter-spring droughts, which have severe impacts on agriculture. Changes in tropical sea and air temperature may provide such an "early warning." Streten (1981) demonstrated that cooler-than-normal sea surface temperatures around northern Australia tend to accompany Australian droughts. This is illustrated in Fig. 6, which shows the sea surface temperature anomalies (deviations from the 1964-82 mean) around north Australia (5°-15°S, 120°-160°E) for each month in 1981, a relatively wet year, and 1982, a drought year. In 1981 the tropical sea surface was warmer than nor-

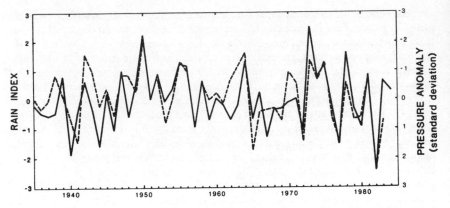

Fig. 5 Time series of east Australian winter-spring rain index (full line) and winter-spring mean sea-level pressure anomalies at Darwin (broken line, scale reversed).

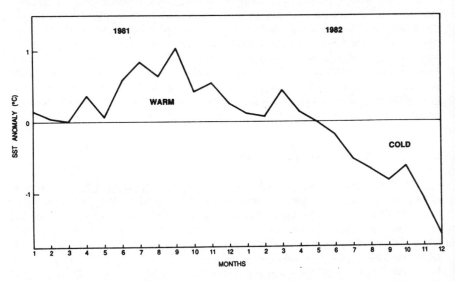

Fig. 6 Sea surface temperature anomalies (from 1964-82 mean) in the area 5-15 °S, 120-160 °E, for each month of 1981 and 1982.

mal, but from October 1981 on, the temperature dropped until by May 1982 it was colder than normal. A similar drop in the anomalies of sea surface temperature was noted by Streten (1981) across the summer between 1950 (a wet year) and 1951 (a drought year). This suggests that the change in sea surface temperature around northern Australia might provide an early warning of drought, available before the planting of the winter and spring crops.

Unfortunately, a long-enough record of good quality sea surface temperature is not available to test whether such changes routinely precede drought years. Minimum nocturnal air temperature at Willis Island, a small island off the northeast coast of Australia (see Fig. 2), however, provides a good proxy for sea surface temperature. We have air temperature records at Willis back to 1939, so we can test the hypothesis that cooling around northern Australia across the summer foreshadows drought.

A significant correlation (0.64) was found between values of the index of winter and spring rainfall in eastern Australia and the change in minimum nocturnal air temperature at Willis Island from early summer (November-January) to early autumn (February-April). The relationship is illustrated in Fig. 7, which shows a scatter diagram of the two variables. The tendency for years with low winter-spring rainfall to be preceded by a decrease in air temperature over the summer is quite strong. Drought is unlikely if the air temperature at Willis Island increases by more than 0.5°C over the summer, but a wet year is unlikely if the temperature falls by more than this amount. This relationship can therefore provide some early information, before the time of planting of Australia's major crops, on the likelihood of severe drought.

The approach described above might also be useful for forecasting the severity of the Indonesian dry season, since rainfall during this season in Indonesia is also closely related to the El Niño-Southern Oscillation. However, some caveats need to be considered before this relationship can be used in forecasting drought. First, the relationship has been developed from a relatively small amount of data and requires testing on independent data. Second, there is considerable scatter in Fig. 7--that is, the relationship is far from perfect and other mechanisms undoubtedly cause droughts in Australia and Indonesia. Finally, changes in climate might alter the relationship between Australian drought, the SO, and changes in temperature around northern Australia, invalidating this proposed method of drought prediction.

CONCLUDING REMARKS

Much of the interannual variability of Australian and Indonesian rainfall is related to the Southern Oscillation phenomenon. This applies especially to rainfall from May to December, the main growing season for the nontropical parts of Australia, and the dry season and onset of the wet season for Indonesia and northern Australia. This relationship, and the tendency for SO "events" to have a particular temporal pattern to their formation, growth, and decay, means that many droughts in this region also tend to have a similar life cycle. Severe droughts tend to start about May and last about twelve months, are continental in scale, and are often followed by wet years. This pattern can be used to provide a degree of predictability about the evolution of drought, once the drought has begun.

Better forecasts can be produced by monitoring simple indices of SO, such as Darwin pressure. Such indices can be used to forecast (during winter, spring, and early summer) eastern Australian rainfall, whether the Indonesian and northern Australian wet season will be late, the yields of some summer-grown crops, and also the number of tropical cyclones expected in the cyclone season.

Finally, some recent work suggests, tentatively, that changes in air or sea temperatures around northern Australia from early to late summer may provide an early

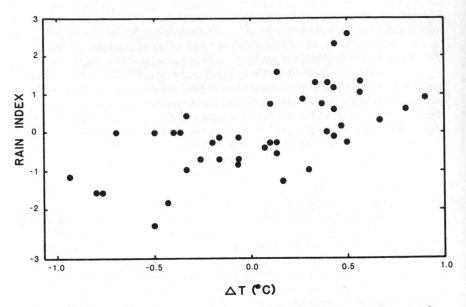

Fig. 7 Scatter diagram of values of each Australian winter-spring rainfall index versus change in Willis Island minimum air temperature from November-January to February-April. Data from 1940-83.

warning of the widespread winter and spring droughts that severely disrupt Australian and Indonesian agriculture and society.

All the methods of drought prediction discussed here use very simple statistical techniques, and small amounts of routinely observed data are all that is required to produce the forecasts. The simplicity of the techniques results from the SO's dominance of interannual rainfall variability in this area. As we learn more about the SO, our ability to predict major eastern and northern Australian droughts may improve. In other areas where the impact of the SO is less striking we are unlikely to be able to use such simple methods for drought prediction. This applies, for instance, to the southwest corner of Australia. This area is becoming more important for Australian agriculture, but rainfall there is not dominated by the SO and the prediction methods outlined in this paper cannot be applied.

One advantage of the simplicity of the drought prediction methods described here is that potential users can obtain the data and make the predictions themselves. In this way they can quickly develop an understanding of the limits of accuracy of the predictions, and they can also "tailor" the predictions to their own needs.

REFERENCES

Campbell, K. O. 1973. The future role of agriculture in the Australian economy. pp. 3-14. In J. V. Lovett, ed. The Environmental, Economic and Social Significance of Drought. Angus and Robertson, Sydney.

Jenkins, J. S. 1850. Voyage of the U. S. Exploring Squadron commanded by Captain Charles Wilkes of the United States Navy, in 1838, 1839, 1840, 1841 and 1842: Together with explorations and discoveries made by Admiral d'Urville, Captain Ross, and other navigators and travellers; and an account of the expedition to the dead sea, under Lieutenant Lynch. James M. Alden, Auburn.

Malingreau, J-P. 1986. The 1982-83 Drought in Indonesia: Assessment and Monitoring. In M. H. Glantz, ed. Report on the Workshop on the Economic and Societal Impacts of the 1982-83 Worldwide Climate Anomalies, Lugano, Switzerland, 11-13 November 1985. National Center for Atmospheric Research, Boulder, Colorado.

McBride, J. L.; and N. Nicholls. 1983. Seasonal relationships between Australian rainfall and the Southern Oscillation. Mon. Weather Rev. 111, No. 10 (October):1998-2004.

Nicholls, N. 1981a. Sunspot cycles and Australian rainfall. Search 12, Nos. 3-4 (March/April):83-85.

Nicholls, N. 1981b. Air-sea interaction and the possibility of long-range weather prediction in the Indonesian Archipelago. Mon. Weather Rev. 109, No. 12 (December): 2435-2443.

Nicholls, N. 1984a. A system for predicting the onset of the north Australian wet-season. J. Climatol. 4, No. 4 (July-August):425-435.

Nicholls, N. 1984b. The Southern Oscillation, sea surface temperature, and interannual fluctuations in Australian tropical cyclone activity. J. Climatol. 4, No. 6 (November-December):661-670.

Nicholls, N. 1985a. Towards the prediction of major Australian droughts. Australian Meteorological Magazine 33, No. 4 (December):161-166.

Nicholls, N. 1985b. Predictability of interannual variations of Australian seasonal tropical cyclone activity. Mon. Weather Rev. 113, No. 7 (July):1144-1149.

Nicholls, N. 1986. Use of the Southern Oscillation to predict Australian sorghum yield. Agric. For. Meteorol. (in press).

Nicholls, N.; and F. Woodcock. 1981. Verification of an empirical long-range weather forecasting technique. Quart. J. Royal Meteorol. Soc. 107, No. 454 (October):973-976.

O'Mahoney, G. 1961. Time series analysis of some Australian rainfall data. Commonwealth Bureau of Meteorology, Meteorological Study 14. Melbourne.

Pittock, A. B. 1975. Climatic change and patterns of variations in Australian rainfall. Search 6, No. 11-12 (November-December):498-504.

Quayle, E. T. 1929. Long-range rainfall forecasting from tropical (Darwin) air pressure. Proc. Roy. Soc. Victoria 41, Part II (April):160-164.

Rasmusson, E. M.; and J. M. Wallace. 1983. Meteorological aspects of the El Niño/Southern Oscillation. Science 222, No. 4629 (December 16):1195-1202.

Streten, N. A. 1981. Southern Hemisphere sea surface temperature variability and apparent associations with Australian rainfall. J. Geophys. Res. 86, No. C1 (April-June):485-497.

Voice, M. E.; and F. J. Gauntlett. 1984. The 1983 Ash Wednesday fires in Australia. Mon. Weather Rev. 112, No. 3 (March):584-590.

Wilhite, D. A.; N. J. Rosenberg; and M. H. Glantz. 1985. Drought response in the United States and Australia: A comparative analysis. CAMaC Progress Report 85-5. Center for Agricultural Meteorology and Climatology, University of Nebraska-Lincoln.

CHAPTER 6
FORECASTING DROUGHT PROBABILISTICALLY

Ian Cordery

INTRODUCTION

Drought is usually defined in loose terms as a period when insufficient water is available to support the normal activities of a region. Here *normal* is used in the sense of the average over a fairly long period of time. By this type of definition, drought is distinguished from aridity, and it may be expected that both very wet and very dry regions will experience drought. Numerous drought indices have been suggested, but it appears there can be no universal drought indicator--only indicators that will reflect particular aspects of human interest in environmental conditions. Alley (1984) has shown that the well-known Palmer index (Palmer, 1965) must be used with caution, and Cordery and Curtis (1983) have shown that in a given situation, drought severity will be dependent on the precise definition of drought used. There is a need for the development of drought indicators for particular water resources and agricultural activities and, perhaps more importantly, for the education of water users on the wide variety of meanings of the term *drought.*

In order to forecast drought, very careful definition of terms is needed. Drought, therefore, needs to be defined in a number of ways, depending on the interests of the user of the definition (see Wilhite and Glantz, 1985, reprinted in this volume). When the objective is clearly defined, the task of attempting to provide information is much simpler.

MODELING DRYLAND FARMING

A water balance model has been developed for dryland farming situations. The model requires input of rainfall, potential evaporation, and soil water-holding and transmission characteristics. The input variables permit the distribution of input rainfall between storage of soil water, runoff, and evapotranspiration. However, soil-water content and rainfall are the main determinants of runoff and actual evapotranspiration and so, if the soil-water relationships can be determined, it should be possible to estimate the other two. In this study the aim was to use a soil-water budgeting model to estimate real-time soil water movement, and, more particularly, to estimate the resulting changes in soil water storage and the consequential runoff and vegetation development.

The scheme of the water balance model is shown in Fig. 1, and a detailed description of the model is given by Cordery and Graham (1987). However, since this paper focuses on the forecasting of drought, the details of the model will not be discussed here. The model has been based on physical relationships developed by a number of scientists. For example, the energy input and soil layer modeling is broadly based on ideas of Calder, et al. (1983). The energy partitioning between transpiration and soil evaporation is loosely based on work of Tanner and Jury (1976), and the extraction of water from the soil by vegetation comes from Greacen and Hignett (1976, 1984). The development and final production of grain by cereal crops is based on the findings of O'Leary, et al. (1985).

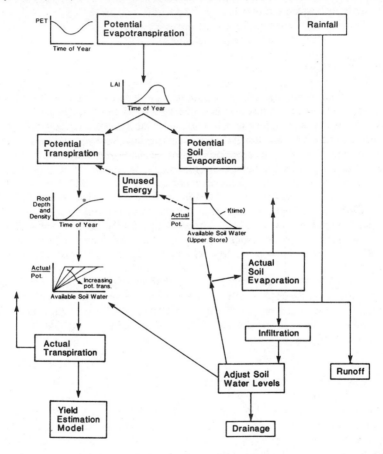

Fig. 1 Schematic of Water Balance (WETBAL) Model.

WATER BALANCE MODEL

A water balance model (WETBAL) has been developed to trace the movement of water in a soil. The model boundaries may be from plot size (encompassing a few square meters) up to river basin size (several thousand square kilometers). The model was developed to reflect the latest thinking on water movement and crop development and incorporates physically based, observed relationships that, on the whole, avoid the need for extensive local calibration. Many of the ideas and relationships involved depend on the work of Greacen and Hignett (1984), Fischer (1979), and O'Leary, et al. (1985). When tested with data for the Gunnedah region in New South Wales, the model gave results such as those shown in Figs. 2 and 3 for a plot of 1 ha and an area of 4,000 km^2, respectively. The results for a large area such as that shown in Fig. 3 must be inferior to those of a small plot since for the large area many variables have been averaged (i.e., date of sowing, daily rainfall depths), and observed yield must also reflect the aggregation of different management practices and causes of loss (such as storms, diseases, and pests) that vary from farm to farm in the region. From these plots it can be seen that the model can provide good estimates of crop production and at the same time provide equally good estimates of soil-water content and runoff depths.

As we have seen, in discussing drought there is always the problem of definition. What do we mean by drought? If drought is defined in terms of any of the model variables, then the model can be used to estimate drought severity, duration, or any other drought characteristic. The literature contains a large number of papers that discuss

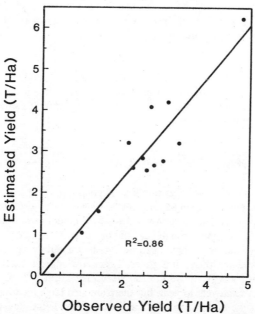

Fig. 2 Grain yield analysis using data from a plot of 1 ha at the Gunnedah Soil Conservation Research Centre, 1973-85.

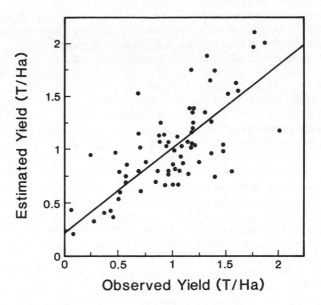

Fig. 3 Grain yield analysis using data from an area of 4,000 km² in the Gunnedah region, 1896-1970.

means of assessing drought severity, particularly of specific (usually notable) or recent droughts. Since the severity of past droughts can be assessed, there is also the possibility of assessing the likelihood of experiencing droughts with particular severity or duration characteristics in the future.

PROBABILISTIC FORECASTING OF DROUGHT

Analysis of observed data permits the examination of the frequency of periods with particular characteristics. Using a long period of data in the water balance model allows the development of frequency curves of any of the model parameters. This activity provides information on the probability of occurrence of particular conditions. However, the same kind of information can be obtained about the future, given the particular state of the variables today. It is generally acknowledged that climatic conditions vary randomly about some fairly well defined seasonal norms. The seasonal average values vary randomly from year to year, but there are also large random variations from day to day. Neither the underlying seasonal average nor day-to-day variations of the climatic variables can be estimated more than a day or two ahead of their occurrence. However, when we consider the overall soil-water balance, the system has a large memory. In most regions the soil water content in the unsaturated zone varies slowly, compared with the climatic factors. This stability (or memory) of the soil-water storage provides the possibility of forecasting, at least probabilistically, the soil-water content some time in the future, even though the major part of the input and output from the system varies randomly from day to day. If soil water can be forecast in this manner, then it should also be possible to forecast other variables that are very much dependent on soil water content, such as runoff volumes and crop yields.

FORECASTING RESULTS

The water balance model has been shown to give good estimates of crop yield (Figs.2 and 3), and so it is possible to forecast the yield, given the soil water status at the time of planting or the soil water status and history since planting from some time during the growing season. To obtain probabilistic estimates of the yield, the model is run for all years of available data (seventy-five years were available for the Gunnedah region), starting at the date of interest using observed or calculated soil water content. In this way a distribution of yield for this current season is obtained, based on all observed data. From this plot it is possible to read off the probabilistic forecasts of yields. For example, from Fig. 4 it can be seen that if only 50 mm of water is available in the upper 2 m of soil on May 15 (in the Southern Hemisphere, planting time is in May; harvest is in November), then there is a 50% chance of harvesting at least 2 tons/ha, an 80% chance of harvesting at least 1.4 tons/ha, and a 20% chance of exceeding 2.8 tons/ha. If at sowing time 190 mm of water were available in the soil profile (approximate field capacity), then the corresponding yields would be 4.1 tons/ha, 2.8 tons/ha, and 4.8 tons/ha, respectively (Fig. 4).

This type of forecast could be invaluable to the farmer who has management choices, such as whether to plant winter wheat now or to wait and plant spring wheat or

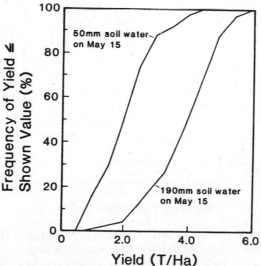

Fig. 4 Wheat yield estimate, Gunnedah region rainfall, 1896-1970 (sine curve estimate of evaporation). Soil water available on May 15—50 mm and 190 mm.

some alternate crops, or whether to leave the land fallow. When drought conditions occur at planting, or the probability of agricultural drought developing is high, this procedure can assist farmers who must make critical management decisions (e.g., evaluate the likelihood that the returns from a crop will exceed costs and by how much).

Similarly, runoff volumes can be forecast, as shown in Fig. 5. If the available soil water can be forecast, then water managers can assess the likely availability of streamflows a number of months into the future. It has been shown (Cordery, 1983) that in very humid areas, streamflow forecasts are impractical because the soil water memory is short. The soil water storage fills frequently; when filling occurs, the memory is lost. However, in subhumid or semiarid regions, where the soil water storage capacity may be more than 30% of the mean annual rainfall, probabilistic forecasts of soil water content could provide significant benefits for water managers. The degree of dependence of future soil water contents on the current soil water level for the Gunnedah region in New South Wales is shown in Fig. 6.

CONCLUSION

Probabilistic forecasts of various aspects of drought are possible using fairly simple water balance and budgeting approaches. It has been shown that volumes of runoff and crop yields can be forecast using a physically realistic model in regions where available soil water storage exceeds about 30% of the mean annual rainfall.

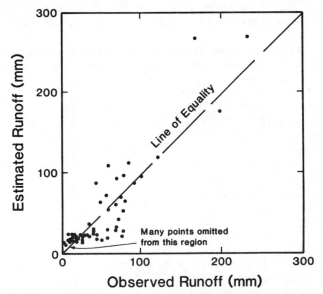

Fig. 5 Comparison of observed annual runoff and annual runoff estimated using water balance model for the Namoi River.

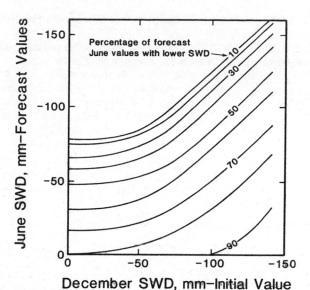

December SWD, mm—Initial Value

Fig. 6 Probability of soil water deficit (SWD) being lower than shown values in six months' time, given current SWD in the Namoi River basin.

REFERENCES

Alley, W. M. 1984. On the treatment of evapotranspiration, soil moisture accounting, and aquifer recharge in monthly water balance models. Water Resour. Res. 20:1137-1194.

Calder, I. R.; R. J. Harding; and P. T. W. Rosier. 1983. An objective assessment of soil moisture deficit models. J. Hydrol. 60:329-355.

Cordery, I. 1983. Forecasting of hydrological drought. Hydrology and Water Resources Symposium, Institute of Engineers, Australia. National Conf. Publ. No. 83/13, pp. 118-123.

Cordery, I.; and B. R. Curtis. 1983. Drought--A problem of definition. Hydrology and Water Resources Symposium, Institute of Engineers, Australia. National Conf. Publ. No. 85/2, pp. 8-9.

Cordery, I.; and A. G. Graham. 1987. Estimating wheat yields using a water budgeting model. Unpublished paper.

Fischer, R. A. 1979. Growth and water limitation to dryland wheat yield in Australia: A physiological framework. J. Aust. Inst. Agric. Sci. 45:83-94.

Greacen, E. L.; and C. T. Hignett. 1976. A water balance model and supply index for wheat in South Australia. CSIRO (Aust.) Div. Soils Tech. Paper 27.

Greacen, E. L.; and C. T. Hignett. 1984. Water balance under wheat modeled with limited soil data. Agr. Water Manage. 8:291-304.

O'Leary, G. J.; D. J. Conner; and D. H. White. 1985. A simulation model of the development, growth and yield of the wheat crop. Agric. Systems 17:1-26.

80

Palmer, W. C. 1965. Meteorological drought. U.S. Weather Bureau, Res. Paper No. 45.

Tanner, C. B.; and W. A. Jury. 1976. Estimating evaporation and transpiration from a row crop during incomplete cover. Agron. J. 68:239-246.

CHAPTER 7

DROUGHT PREDICTION: A HYDROLOGICAL PERSPECTIVE

Vit Klemeš

INTRODUCTION

To predict a drought, a hydrological perspective is not enough. Hydrological processes are among the final steps leading to drought; it is through them that the phenomenon of drought is eventually revealed, usually long after its original causes have been obscured.

In order to predict drought (or to come to a conclusion that this is impossible), we must understand its causes. This means tracing those causes back, indeed very far back, perhaps even to the two penultimate sources of energy powering the climatic engine: the solar processes whose fluctuations, transmitted through solar-terrestrial relations at a variety of energy levels, constitute one set of boundary conditions for the atmospheric processes; and the processes in the earth's interior, which--through geological, geophysical, and oceanographic phenomena--represent the other set.

The synthesis of these two sets of processes, superimposed on the geodetically complicated motions of the earth and modified by extremely complex feedbacks through the biosphere, then produces the irregularly fluctuating climate. This climate is made up of the short-term fluctuations of atmospheric processes that constitute the domain of meteorology. Of these processes, precipitation is the immediate carrier of the "drought signal." For the meteorologist, the drought "buck" stops right here and so it does for all those whose water supply comes directly from precipitation. At the meteorological level, drought is essentially equivalent to a long absence of precipitation.

But there is one more level down the road, the hydrological level. In general, lack of precipitation is not always sufficient to produce drought. Obviously, drought never occurs in the open ocean even if there is no precipitation at all. Similarly, it would be difficult to talk about drought in circumpolar permanently glaciated regions such as those in the Antarctic or Greenland. In order to produce drought, a lack of precipitation over some life-supporting land surface is necessary. However, even this is not sufficient, since precipitation is not necessarily the only direct source of water for every water user: water can also be, and very often is, supplied from storage.

The case of the open ocean is useful to illustrate these basic points. Even in the open ocean a "drought" can arise if we insert there a piece of life-supporting "land surface" in the form, say, of a lifeboat with a shipwrecked sailor. He obviously could have a drought problem, but only after his supply of drinking water has run out. This simplified example highlights the most important fact: even the absence or lack of water as such is not enough to cause a drought--it must pose danger to some form of life. There would be no drought problem in our lifeboat if there were no sailor in it.

This sociobiological aspect is implicit in the very term *drought*; otherwise we would be concerned merely with the lower tail of the statistical distribution of water on the land surface. In the interest of accuracy it should be noted that only the latter problem constitutes the subject matter of hydrology. Strictly speaking, drought is not a hydrological phenomenon; for hydrology, drought is an *effect* of low states of water on some nonhydrologic system, specifically on some life-supporting process that is in some way important to mankind.

To summarize, hydrology takes over from meteorology as the study of water distribution on the land surface after precipitation has reached the ground. In hydrology, precipitation is only an input to be processed. It concentrates on the processes that redistribute this input into various natural storages available on land, on the fluctuations of water in these storages, and on the outflow processes associated with them. In short, the interest of hydrology is focused on processes related to water storage. Hence it has the greatest potential for contributing to the study of drought and to its prediction in those instances where drought results as a consequence of shortages in water supply from natural land-based storage systems.

For the purpose of this discussion, hydrologic storage systems can be divided roughly into three categories:

1. Surface water, representing the water in lakes, depressions, and rivers.
2. Subsurface water in the unsaturated strata, including the soil moisture.
3. Ground water, which is all the water present in the saturated strata.

The differences between these storages are important for two reasons. First, water available from each tends to serve a different purpose and thus its shortage leads to drought symptoms in different areas. Second, their outflow or release processes are dominated by different types of mechanisms, so that the patterns of their fluctuations, and hence the patterns of droughts related to them, are often different.

From this short outline, it should be obvious that hydrology can contribute to the study and prediction of drought mostly by shedding light on the changes that hydrological storages introduce into the patterns of temporal and spatial distribution of water, patterns that have been set by the distribution of precipitation. For the understanding and possible prediction of the precipitation patterns themselves, one must turn to meteorology, climatology, and other disciplines in the hierarchy of processes mentioned earlier.

The Long-Term Perspective

Hydrology can do little to predict droughts far in advance or long periods of drought. But it can contribute significantly to the understanding of why such predictions may be difficult, perhaps even impossible.

Prediction in real time, referred to as *forecasting* in hydrological usage (*prediction* is used only in connection with an unspecified lead time, generally for predictions of statistical frequencies), is possible only if the phenomenon to be forecast exhibits some deterministic pattern. For long-term drought forecasting, the main prerequisite for success is a discovery of trends or periodicities in the climate that could be traced to some underlying deterministic processes in the hierarchy outlined earlier. The two strongest candidates for such processes have been those underlying the formation of sunspots and those triggered by geodetic motions of the earth.

The literature trying to establish a correspondence between these two types of periodicities and the fluctuations in rainfall, river runoff, lake levels, and glaciers is extensive in volume but very modest in conclusive evidence. Most of it relies on statistical correlations between records of the various water-related phenomena and the sunspot numbers or the computed solar energy fluctuations attributable to the geodetic motions. Although these correlations may sometimes seem impressive, there is a conspicuous paucity of documented physical mechanisms that could supply the necessary causal linkages. Without such mechanisms the origin of the apparent cyclic features in hydrological time series must be treated with extreme caution. This is because a hydrological process almost always reflects some kind of storage mechanism and a storage mechanism almost always exhibits what has been called pseudocyclic or quasi-periodic behavior even when it operates on a perfectly random input.

In mathematics the storage feature has been known for a long time. However, in mathematics the counterpart of the physical operation of "storing" is the operation of summation, integration, or cumulation, and the phenomenon of pseudocyclicity has been described in connection with these mathematical operations (Slutzky, 1927; Feller, 1966) rather than with the physical process of storing. Improbable as it sounds, theorists working on storage processes, whether in mathematics, engineering, or hydrology, somehow have failed to make the connection. Moreover, many hydrologists have difficulty appreciating the fact that most hydrological processes actually themselves represent the storage or "cumulative" processes. They tend to take the "cyclic features" in these processes at their face value and engage happily in fitting cyclic features with the most sophisticated mathematical constructs, for which there is little physical justification. These problems were discussed in detail more than a decade ago (Klemeš, 1974) and are still relevant.

Since an understanding of the cyclic behavior of geophysical processes in general, and hydrological processes in particular, is crucial to long-term drought prediction, it may be useful to illustrate the main aspects of the aforementioned issues.

Consider a sequence of random numbers. An example of such a sequence, x_t, t = 1, 2,...,50, appears in the second column Table 1 and its plot is shown in Fig. 1A. The numbers come from a population that is uniformly distributed between one and one hundred (Neville and Kennedy, 1964). Suppose that the variable x represents annual precipitation totals in mm. Because our series is purely random, we know that it is impossible in principle to forecast the time of occurrence of a "drought" or its length. Suppose, however, that our "precipitation" series is a real observed record, so that we do not know whether it is a random series or not. In the search for a pattern that would enable us to forecast droughts, we subject the series $\{x\}$ to various types of manipulations and analyses. One of the most common and simple analyses is to make a plot of the cumulative departures from the mean, $y_t = \sum_{i=1}^{t} (x_i - \bar{x})$, as computed in column 4 of Table 1

and plotted in Fig. 1B. Unlike the original series $\{x\}$, its "residual mass curve" $\{y\}$ (as the type of plot shown in Fig. 1B is also known) strongly suggests the presence of cycles, which may encourage us to extrapolate them, correlate them with cycles in other

Table 1
Fifty Uniformly Distributed Random Numbers x_t ($t = 1,2,.....,50$)
and Their First and Second Order Cumulative Sums of Departures
from Mean (residual mass curves), y_t and z_t

Order Number	Random Number	Diff.	Cumulative Sum	Diff.	Cumulative Sum
t	x_t	$x_t - \bar{x}$	$y_t = \sum_{i=1}^{t} (x_i - \bar{x})$	$y_t - \bar{y}$	$z_t = \sum_{i=1}^{t} (y_i - \bar{y})$
1	98	48	48	28.64	28.64
2	25	-25	23	3.64	32.28
3	37	-13	10	-9.36	22.92
4	55	5	15	-4.36	18.56
5	26	-24	9	-28.36	-9.80
6	1	-49	-58	-77.36	-87.16
7	91	41	-17	-37.36	-123.52
8	82	32	15	-4.36	-127.88
9	81	31	46	26.64	-101.24
10	46	-4	42	22.64	-78.60
11	74	24	66	46.64	-31.96
12	71	21	87	67.64	35.68
13	12	-38	49	29.64	65.32
14	94	44	93	73.64	138.96
15	97	47	140	120.64	259.60
16	24	-26	114	94.64	354.24
17	2	-48	66	46.64	400.88
18	71	21	87	67.64	468.52
19	37	-13	74	54.64	523.16
20	7	-43	31	11.64	534.80
21	3	-47	-16	-35.36	499.44
22	92	42	26	6.64	506.08
23	18	-32	-6	-25.36	480.72
24	66	16	10	-9.36	471.36
25	75	25	35	15.64	487.00
26	2	-48	-13	-32.36	454.63
27	63	13	0	-19.36	435.28
28	21	-29	-29	-48.36	386.92
29	17	-33	-62	-81.36	305.56
30	69	19	-43	-62.36	243.20
31	71	21	-22	-41.36	201.84
32	50	0	-22	-41.36	160.48

33	80	30	8	-11.36	149.12
34	89	39	47	27.64	176.76
35	56	6	53	33.64	210.40
36	38	-12	41	21.64	232.04
37	15	-35	6	-13.36	218.68
38	70	20	26	6.64	225.32
39	11	-39	-13	-32.36	192.96
40	48	-2	-15	-34.36	158.60
41	43	-7	-22	-41.36	117.24
42	40	-10	-32	-51.36	68.88
43	45	-5	-37	-56.36	9.52
44	86	36	-1	-20.36	-10.84
45	98	48	47	27.64	16.80
46	0	-50	-3	-22.36	-5.56
47	83	33	30	10.64	5.08
48	26	-24	6	-13.36	-8.28
49	91	41	47	27.64	19.36
50	3	-47	0	-19.36	0.00
Sum	2,500	0	968	0.00	
Mean	$\bar{\chi} = 50$		$\bar{y} = 19.36$		

series, and so forth. This, of course, all would be in vain if the original series were random (as it actually is), because the cycles in the mass curve {y} are just a typical example of "the summation of random causes as the source of cyclic processes," as is pointed out in the title of Slutzky's 1927 paper, mentioned above. On the other hand, in a true precipitation series, the cycles (or perhaps some of them) could be real. The point is that the pattern itself can in no way tell whether it is spurious or real--this can only be judged by the presence or absence of evident physical mechanisms behind the pattern.

The difficulty of the problem increases as we move from precipitation records to records of hydrological processes, which by themselves already reflect the effect of some hydrologic storage and thus, in their raw form, already represent cumulative processes or include them as their components. Consider, for example, a hydrological series represented by a record of levels in a hypothetical closed lake whose only input is the random "precipitation" series {x} displayed in Fig. 1A and whose only output is evaporation. For simplicity, let's assume that the evaporation is constant and equal to the mean of the precipitation, $\bar{x}$, and that the lake has steep banks so that its area does not appreciably change with the lake level. In such a case, the lake level series would be identical with the precipitation residual mass curve {y} in Fig. 1B. The storage in the lake physically performs the summation of the residuals that was carried out arithmetically in Table 1--it accumulates the differences between the precipitation inputs x_t and evaporation $\bar{x}$ so that we can "leave the computation" to the lake and get the results by taking a record of its levels y_t. Thus, in this case, already the *original* "hydrological

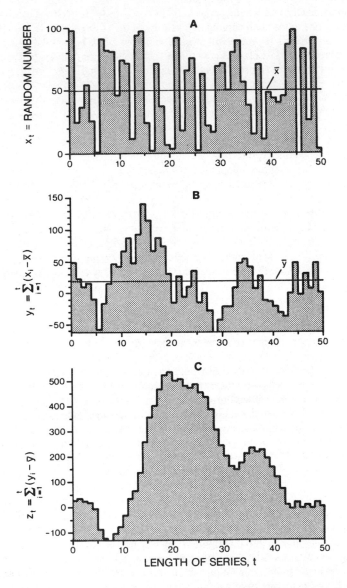

Fig. 1 Series of fifty random numbers x (A), and its first-order (B) and second-order (C) residual mass-curves, y and z, respectively.

record" {y} seems to exhibit a cyclic pattern. We of course would process this "raw" record mathematically and would perhaps again compute its residual mass curve {z}. This has been done in the sixth column of Table 1 and the plot is shown in Fig. 1C. It is apparent that the process {z} has a still more pronounced cyclic pattern than the underlying lake-level record {y}. Yet, we know that no deterministic periodic mechanism is involved here; we observe just pseudocyclic behavior of a "second order" produced by the strengthening of a pseudocyclic pattern of the "first order" by one more integration. Repetition of this operation would lead to further strengthening of the cyclic pattern; indeed, an nth order residual mass curve rapidly converges to a sine wave (Klemeš and Klemeš, 1987).

Thus, in general, hydrological series have a tendency to exhibit more pronounced and smoother cycles than precipitation series. They pose a greater danger for those who suffer from the myopic inclination to search for cycles merely by mathematical processing of time series divorced from an understanding of the underlying physical processes.

The following two quotations illustrate that mathematicians (the good ones) have been aware of these dangers much more acutely than physical scientists and engineers, who (one would assume) should be those with a more deeply ingrained tendency to base their analyses on an understanding of physical causality, as opposed to purely mathematical manipulation. More than thirty years ago, M. S. Bartlet, the eminent English statistician and probabilist, warned that "unless the statistician has a well-defined and realistic model of the actual process he is studying, his analysis is likely to be abortive" (quoted from Klemeš, 1978). More than twenty years ago, William Feller had this to say in regard to the pseudocyclic behavior of cumulative processes: "Most stochastic processes in physics, economics, and education are of this nature and our findings should serve as a warning to those who are prone to discern secular trends in deviations from average norms" (Feller, 1966).

Examples of cumulative sums of deviations from the mean for 100-year-long annual streamflow series of three European rivers are shown in Figs. 2a, 2b, and 2c; for comparison, examples of similar sums for three random series of the same length, drawn from the same gamma-distributed population, are shown in Figs. 2d, 2e, and 2f.

The Short-Term Perspective

Hydrology has a great potential for short-to medium-term forecasting of the so-called hydrological droughts (i.e., low stages in and low releases from hydrological storage reservoirs). Taking the precipitation process as an input, hydrology studies the distribution of precipitation into the different types of storages in a river basin, and interaction among and releases from those storage types. In doing so, hydrology not only can assess the impact of low precipitation on the various hydrologic processes and thus forecast the arrival and severity of a drought, but it can also contribute to a better understanding of the drought phenomenon in general and explain some of the apparent inconsistencies and differences in drought perceptions reflected in various disciplinary views and definitions as recently reported, for example, by Wilhite and Glantz (1985; also reprinted in this volume).

88

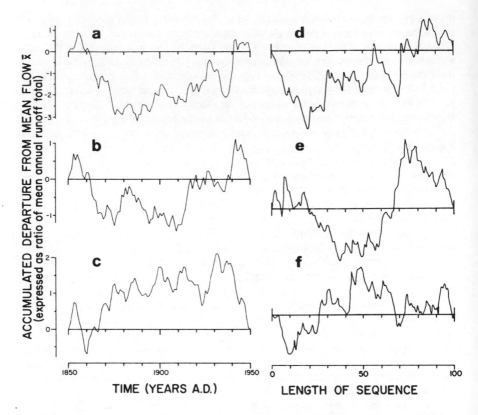

Fig. 2 Residual mass curves of three 100-year series of mean annual flows and of three samples of 100 random numbers: a—Elbe River, Děčín, Czechoslovakia; b—Danube River, Orsova, Romania; c—Gota River, Vanersborg, Sweden (from Klemeš, 1982a); d, e, f—random samples.

The key to unlocking the potential of hydrology is a thorough appreciation of the fact that hydrological processes, being affected by storage mechanisms, are often related much more closely to some integral of the precipitation input process than to this input process itself. The second most important factor is an awareness of the differences between the mechanisms operating on the different types of hydrological storages, which may result in different drought patterns in the respective processes.

To illustrate the first point in general terms, we may first note the difference between a function and its integral for two simple mathematical functions that represent typical idealized prototypes of the precipitation process. One is a sine wave that reflects the basic features of the common seasonality within the annual cycle and is changed into a cosine wave by integration. Thus a physical integrating device with a sine input would produce a cosine output. In other words, the system would introduce a $\pi/2$ phase shift into the input process. Another useful function is the Dirac delta function, defined as an instantaneous impulse of a unit magnitude. On a short time scale, it displays the basic feature of a sudden rainfall burst during a rainless period; on a longer time scale it shows a short period during which precipitation is significantly higher (or lower) than "normal." On integration, the delta function becomes a step function, thus indicating that, for instance, a couple of extremely precipitation-deficient years may introduce a downward jump in the equilibrium level of some hydrological process. In other words, a short "meteorological drought" may trigger a long-lasting period of "hydrological" drought.

The effect of reservoir storage on inflows confirms these generalizations of the features of integration. In hydrology and hydraulics, the transformation of reservoir inflow into outflow by the storage mechanism is usually referred to as storage, or reservoir, "routing" (for a comprehensive review of reservoir routing, see Klemeš, 1982b). Figure 3A shows how a typical "flood wave" might be routed in the course of its passage through a small or large reservoir system such as a cascade of lakes or a ground-water basin; in this case, the time scale would typically be such that the duration of the inflow wave would be between several hours and several days. By inverting the diagram, we have a picture of the reservoir routing effect on a "drought wave" in the input (Fig. 3B). Here a more representative time scale would be such that the duration of the "input drought" would be between several weeks and several months. With the aid of this diagram, some of the observations collected by Wilhite and Glantz (1985; also reprinted in this volume) are easily explained, and some pronouncements that seem contradictory become entirely logical.

Thus it becomes obvious why "meteorological droughts do not necessarily coincide with agricultural droughts" and why "hydrologic droughts are often out of phase with both meteorological and agricultural drought." Meteorological drought roughly coincides with precipitation shortage (i.e., with the "input drought" in Fig. 3B), while agricultural drought may be more closely related to the depletion of soil moisture storage (i.e., with, say, the drought in the output from the "small" reservoir system); and "hydrologic" drought defined on the basis of low streamflows may correspond to the drought in the output from our "large" reservoir system, which could represent the ground water storage supplying the "baseflow component" of streamflow. It is, of course, perfectly in order that all three "droughts" are out of phase with each other since the speed with which an input wave moves through a reservoir depends on the size of reservoir storage and on its release mechanism. Mathematically, the phase shifts can be traced to the aforementioned phase shift of a sine wave under integration. In addition to a phase shift, an input perturbation is attenuated in the course of passage through a storage; it emerges in the output in a smoothed-out form. Mathematically, this effect can be traced to the change of the delta function under integration. This smoothing effect explains the assessment of a recent Brazilian drought as a five-year drought according to policy makers and as only a two-year drought according to meteorologists, and a similar disagreement in 1984 between Australian meteorologists and agriculturists (Wilhite and Glantz, 1985; also reprinted in this volume). Obviously, meteorologists have based their assessment on precipitation corresponding to our "input drought," while the policy makers and agriculturists base their assessment on drought attenuated by storage in some type of hydrological reservoirs (e.g., on a drought related to soil moisture, ground water, or surface water storage).

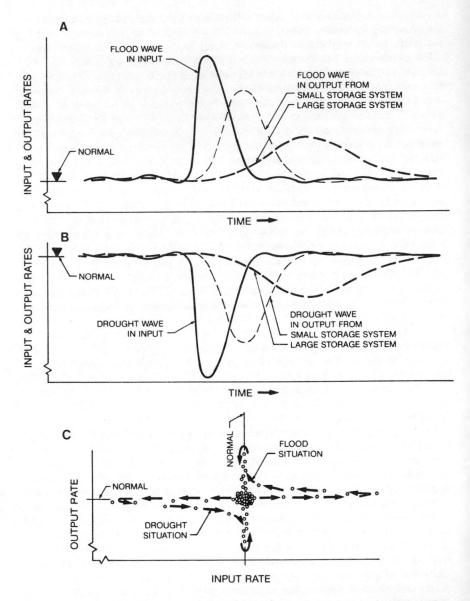

Fig. 3 Schematic representation of routing effect of a storage reservoir: A—"flood wave" routing; B—"drought wave" routing; C—input-output relationship for cases A and B.

A lack of appreciation of the difference between the precipitation process and the hydrological processes caused by a transformation of the former by a storage system has often led, on one hand, to the pursuit of correlations that do not exist and, on the other, to potentially erroneous reconstructions of ancient rainfall and drought patterns based on the assumption that such nonexistent correlations do exist. Examples of the first activity are the repeated attempts to find correlations between, for instance, groundwater levels and precipitation, or soil moisture and precipitation (e.g., Yu and Cruise, 1982). The inevitable findings that such correlations are poor or nonexistent are often presented as profound and unexpected discoveries and attributed to various exotic causes without ever mentioning the obvious reason--that there is no reason to expect a good correlation between a function and its integral (except in some special cases like the exponential function). This can be seen readily even by a cursory examination of the diagrams shown in Figs. 3A and 3B: high or low inputs may occur while the outputs are still more or less normal and the outputs may culminate long after the inputs have returned to normal. The resulting relationship between inputs and outputs then looks like the one shown in Fig. 3C. Not much imagination is needed to see that for a fluctuating input process and the corresponding output from a reservoir with an appreciable storage, the input-output correlation can be very low since the scatter of points on an input-output plot can be extremely high. From this it follows that reconstructions of past precipitation series--based on an assumption of their simple correlation with chronologies of lake deposits, tree rings, and so forth--can be misleading if the dynamics of the water-transfer mechanisms are not considered, since the latter processes may often more closely reflect fluctuations of large storage reservoirs like lakes and ground-water basins than fluctuations of their precipitation inputs.

Having illustrated the overall importance of storage for a proper understanding of the potential of hydrology for drought prediction, let's now return to the second most important aspect mentioned at the beginning of this section--the differences in the mechanisms that control inputs into and releases from the different types of hydrological storages.

Allowing for some simplification, we may say that inputs into and outputs from the surface water storage are dominated by mechanical and thermodynamical forces (gravity and friction controlling surface runoff and infiltration, radiation and heat transfer controlling evaporation); soil moisture movement is controlled by mechanical, thermodynamical, and electrochemical forces (infiltration, percolation, evapotranspiration, chemical bonding of water in the soil, water transport by plants); and ground-water movement is dominated by mechanical forces. Fluctuations of these forces have different rhythms, which may impose different frequencies and patterns on droughts exhibited by the different hydrological processes. It is difficult to speak about a "hydrological" drought in general since individual hydrologic processes have a wide spectrum of behaviors and because these processes may be combined in a wide variety of ways. Thus, the pattern of a streamflow record may be dominated by direct (surface) runoff, glacial melt, ground-water runoff (baseflow), evaporation, and so forth. For example, recently Fairbridge (1984) observed that the Nile River streamflow cannot be properly regarded as a result of one hydrological regime, but must be seen as a composite of two different regimes--the Blue Nile regime, dominated by the Ethiopian monsoons, high slopes, and moderate surface storage; and the White Nile, shaped by the precipitation on the equatorial plateau, the large storages of lakes Victoria, Kyoga, and Albert (Mobutu),

92

and the enormous evaporation in the Sud region. These two regimes dominate the downstream flow in different seasons so that the regimes of spring and fall water shortages are quite different.

Another specific example of the differences in the regimes of different hydrological storages in the same river basin is shown in Fig. 4, reproduced from Klemeš (1983). The solid upper line shows the fluctuations of the total amount of liquid water stored in the basin; the dotted caps represent the accumulation of snow. It would be tempting to take the minima of this solid line as indicators of drought conditions in the basin and use them at least for a statistical prediction of drought frequencies, if not for real-time forecasting. The difficulty is that the line represents the sum of different types of storages whose relative proportions in the sum vary with time. A first step in trying to shed some light on the problem involved separating fluctuations of storage of gravity-controlled water from fluctuations of storage of "tension" water (mostly soil moisture). Although its accuracy is unknown, the result represented by the solid lower line (gravity-controlled storage) and the dashed line (tension storage) well illustrates the importance of such a differentiation for drought prediction. For example, it indicates that periods of soil moisture depletions—which often are the cause of an "agricultural"

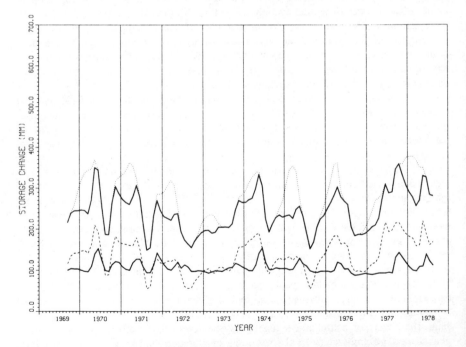

Fig. 4 Time series of storage fluctuations in Rainy Lake basin, Ontario, Canada: solid upper line = all liquid water; dotted segments = snow; solid lower line = gravity-controlled liquid water; dashed line = tension water (from Klemeš, 1983).

drought—tend to be shorter than periods of low ground-water levels, which may be indicative of "hydrological" droughts in terms of water supply shortages (drying up of wells, disappearance of springs, and so forth). Note, for example, that a longer drought is revealed in the solid lower line in 1976-77 than in the solid upper line, where the drought is obscured because of its partial compensation by abundant soil moisture.

To summarize, hydrology has a great potential for tracing the effects of meteorological droughts through the various hydrological subsystems and hence for real-time forecasting and statistical prediction of droughts or water shortages that affect users dependent on different sources of water supply.

CONCLUSIONS

It is beyond the scope of hydrology to offer an exhaustive analysis and complete understanding of the phenomenon of drought. Drought has many causes; hydrological causes are last among these. However, hydrology provides important insights, both into the effectiveness of methodologies used to analyze geophysical records for periodic or cyclic patterns to use in long-term drought forecasting and into the physical processes responsible for the modifications and transformations of the basic "drought signal" supplied by the precipitation record. These latter processes are of paramount importance to the short-; and medium-range forecasting of droughts that affect users dependent on different sources of water supply. In both cases, the value of the contribution of hydrology is directly proportional to the depth of insight into and understanding of the physical mechanisms controlling the various types of hydrological processes; it does not depend much on skill in fitting hydrological records with formal mathematical models aimed merely at preservation of various parameters and patterns of historic records. Unfortunately, present-day hydrology is dominated by the latter tendencies and, although the realization of their sterility is slowly increasing, much effort is needed to change hydrology's course to a direction in which its great potential can bear fruit.

REFERENCES

Fairbridge, R. W. 1984. The Nile floods as a global climatic/solar proxy. pp. 181-190. In N. A. Mornerand and W. Karlen,eds. Climatic Changes on a Yearly to Millennial Basis. D. Reidel, Dordrecht, Holland.

Feller, W. 1966. An Introduction to Probability Theory and Its Applications. 2nd ed., vol. 1. John Wiley and Sons, New York.

Klemeš, V. 1974. The Hurst phenomenon: A puzzle? Water Resour. Res. 10, no. 4 (August):675-688.

Klemeš, V. 1978. Physically based stochastic hydrologic analysis. Adv. Hydroscience 11:285-356.

Klemeš, V. 1982a. Empirical and causal models in hydrology. pp. 95-104. In Scientific Basis of Water-Resource Management. National Academy Press, Washington, DC.

Klemeš, V. 1982b. The essence of mathematical models of reservoir storage. Can. J. Civil Eng. 9, no. 4:624-635.

94

Klemeš, V. 1983. Conceptualization and scale in hydrology. J. Hydrol. 65:1-23.

Klemeš, V.; and I. Klemeš. 1987. Variations on the themes of Slutzky, Hurst and Yule. National Hydrology Research Institute, Environment Canada, Saskatoon, Saskatchewan (submitted for publication).

Neville, A. M.; and J. B. Kennedy. 1964. Basic Statistical Methods for Engineers and Scientists. International Textbook Company, Scranton, PA.

Slutzky, E. 1927. The summation of random causes as the source of cyclic processes. (In Russian). Problems of Economic Conditions 3, no. 1 (reprinted in English in an expanded form, 1937, in Econometrica 5:105-146).

Wilhite, D. A.; and M. H. Glantz. 1985. Understanding the drought phenomenon: The role of definitions. Water International 10:111-120.

Yu, S. L.; and J. F. Cruise. 1982. Time series analysis of soil moisture data. pp. 600-606. In A. H. El-Shaarawi and S. R. Esterby, eds. Time Series Methods in Hydrosciences. Elsevier, Amsterdam.

PART 3

Monitoring and Early Warning

CHAPTER 8
SURFACE WEATHER MONITORING AND THE DEVELOPMENT OF DROUGHT AND OTHER CLIMATE INFORMATION DELIVERY SYSTEMS

Kenneth G. Hubbard

INTRODUCTION

Computers have been used to schedule weather data collection for some time. Technological advances in computer microelectronics and communication systems continue to decrease computation costs and improve the performance of computer equipment. These hardware improvements, which were initially applied to data logging during the late 1970s, have enabled weather data users to obtain more weather data, over wider areas, with less effort and in a more timely fashion than ever before. Some data loggers now offer a programmable interface between the analog signals coming from meteorological sensors and the digital storage media. Although care must be taken to match meteorological sensor requirements to the characteristics of the data logger, data collection technology is becoming increasingly flexible.

For years there has been a data void between the time that hired professionals reported their measurements in real-time and the time that volunteer observers reported their measurements at the end of the reporting period (usually a month). The need for current climate information was noted in a recent publication (NAS, 1982). Current climate information is a natural result of the advances in data logging and collection technologies, whereby the void between data collected for climate records and data collected for describing the current state of the atmosphere is being filled. In the past, data collected at climate stations often were not processed and disseminated for several months. The collection of near-real time climate data has solved that problem.

Many near-real time climate networks are forming because further applications for this type of data are anticipated. The near-real time aspect of these networks makes it possible for scientists to develop decision-making computer aids for use in agricultural operations such as planting, irrigating, harvesting and storing crops, and feeding and marketing cattle.

DEVELOPMENT OF SURFACE WEATHER MONITORING NETWORKS

In the United States, federal agencies have developed surface weather monitoring networks for a multitude of purposes. These include describing the country's climate, providing input to predictive weather models, and determining fire weather danger ratings. Surface weather monitoring and some recent developments are discussed below.

Established Networks

Most surface weather networks require that the observations made at particular sites be transmitted to a center from which the data, or information based on that data, can be widely shared.

Personnel are key to the operation of U.S. surface weather networks. The National Weather Service (NWS) employs hundreds of meteorologists across the country at locations known as first-order stations. Their duties, which primarily involve forecasting, include transmitting the local weather data to other NWS offices. The data become available at scheduled times throughout the country on a distribution system known as AFOS (Automation of Field Observation Systems).

Another federal network involves 11,000 to 12,000 volunteers who make daily observations of temperature and precipitation. The stations operated by these observers are known as second-order weather stations or cooperative stations. The observers measure the daily maximum and minimum temperatures and precipitation using instruments furnished by NWS. They also take other special observations, such as the occurrence of snowfall, lightning, thunder, dust, and so forth. These observations are tabulated on a form that is mailed to a central collection point at the end of each month. There the data are examined for quality (quality control), incorporated in publications, and archived.

Certain benefits and limitations exist in the operation of these first- and second-order surface networks. At locations where a full-time meteorologist makes the measurements, users have the benefit of obtaining the data in near-real time. However, the networks have not received the funding necessary to increase the number of manned stations, so the number of these first-order stations has remained relatively constant. Users obtain near-real time data from this network by subscribing to a satellite weather service or by following public broadcasts of this information. The climatological cooperative network provides data of significant value in describing climate and the magnitude of climatic variations over the entire country. However, the data from this volunteer network is not easily accessible to those with questions about the current weather situation.

Some additional reporting has extended the usefulness of both networks. For example, weekly mailings of data from selected observers in the cooperative network to the NWS offices are sometimes arranged. Another technique adopted at preselected stations is to report, by telephone, data that exceed a predetermined threshold value. The Remote Automatic Meteorological Observing Station (RAMOS) was also developed for obtaining measurements from unstaffed locations. Measurements from RAMOS are transmitted to NWS offices via dedicated phone lines, VHF, or satellite link.

The use of radio waves to transmit precipitation data from mountainous regions is an example of an early attempt to use electronic devices to collect weather information. Telemetry systems were established to collect data from locations a hundred miles distant, provided a radio-signal path was available.

Later communication systems do not require line-of-site paths along the earth's surface for the collection of weather data. The recent meteor burst system (Crook, 1977) takes advantage of frequent but transient meteor dust trails in the upper atmosphere. Interrogation codes are beamed at a meteor trail and reflected to the remote site. Data are then transmitted back in the opposite direction along the same atmospheric path to the collection center.

Satellites have also been used to obtain environmental surface measurements from specific surface sites. Remote Automated Weather Stations (RAWS) were developed by both the Bureau of Land Management (BLM) and the United States Forest Service (USFS) in efforts to measure weather parameters affecting fire fuel conditions on rangelands and forested mountain lands. The RAWS were interrogated via satellite until 1978, when communications were achieved by means of the meteor burst system.

Recent Developments

The new ROSA system of the NWS features the ability to receive measurements from the cooperative network on a daily basis. This project in the north central region features a touch-tone data pad for the observer to key in data from his observation. When the data has been keyed in at the pad, a call is made to the ROSA computer. The observer connects the touch-tone pad to the telephone with a coupler and then pushes a button on the face of the data pad that causes the keyed information to flow immediately through telephone lines to the computer, where it is collected and transmitted to the NWS data dissemination network.

The NWS plans to develop the Automated Surface Observing System (ASOS), using a system that can handle routine observing and record keeping and reduce staff time spent in taking observations. An operational test-bed for the first demonstration phase was formed in 1985 by installing seven demonstration systems in Kansas. Climatic test beds were also installed at Fairbanks (Alaska), Daytona Beach (Florida), San Francisco (California), and Richmond (Virginia). The kinds of observations being considered for ASOS are pressure, wind speed and direction, air and dew point temperature, current weather (rain, freezing rain, and so forth), precipitation accumulation, cloud height, and visibility. These variables have been routinely used in preparing and verifying forecasts and in characterizing aviation weather.

The individual states have been active as well in using the new computer and data-logging technology to collect information on a variety of meteorological variables. In 1980, Nebraska (Hubbard, et al., 1983) and Ohio (Curry, et al., 1981) began planning and installing automated weather stations. Nebraska's Automated Weather Data Network will be discussed in more detail below. In California the NOWCASTING concept was developed (Hauser, 1981) to provide forest and farm managers with improved local weather information for decision making. To this end, automated stations were installed in the Sacramento Valley.

Some of the states that have established automated weather observing stations are listed below:

Arizona	Kansas	Ohio
California	Louisiana	South Dakota
Connecticut	Minnesota	Utah
Illinois	Nebraska	Wisconsin
Indiana	New Mexico	

100

Other states are considering the need for an automated weather data network. Municipalities, public resource managers, and the private sector are also active in collecting weather data from automated stations.

With the establishment of so many new networks, all manner of sampling rates and resulting data formats have been employed. In addition, the installation height of sensors and the scientific units used to represent the measurements have sometimes varied. In response to concern over this lack of uniformity among new networks, the American Association of State Climatologists formed a committee on instrumentation and data standards and passed a resolution with recommendations on the subject. This, together with communication between the various network managers, has helped to reduce the measurement differences between networks.

Nebraska's Automated Weather Data Network

In 1981, the Center for Agricultural Meteorology and Climatology (CAMaC) of the University of Nebraska-Lincoln purchased and installed five automated weather stations in Nebraska to begin continuous collection and reporting of near-real time weather data. Four of these stations were purchased with a grant from the National Climate Program Office (NCPO) and a fifth station was provided by the University to begin the Automated Weather Data Network (AWDN). More stations were subsequently added, and the network now is being extended regionally to support drought monitoring, soil moisture assessment, and other studies. At this time, forty-nine stations are reporting daily by telephone to CAMaC. Each station is able to represent an area fifty miles in diameter. Additional reference to this network can be found in Hubbard, et al. (1983), and Millard (1984).

Collection. Collection of weather data begins at a remote site where a weather station is installed. A complete weather station consists of a Campbell Scientific Model CR21 or CR21x data logger and associated weather instruments mounted on a 9.8 ft. (3 m) tower. A cup anemometer and wind vane are used to measure wind speed and direction, respectively. These are mounted atop the tower. Air temperature, humidity, and solar radiation are measured at 5 ft. (1.5 m). Air temperature is measured with a thermistor and humidity is measured by an electronic hygrometer. The temperature and humidity sensors are mounted in a small instrument shelter. Global radiation is measured with a silicone pyranometer mounted on a horizontal surface at about 2 m. A soil temperature probe consisting of a shielded thermistor is installed at a depth of 4 in. (10 cm) below the soil surface. This depth was chosen because it is representative of seed placement depth at planting time. Each site is also equipped with a tipping bucket rain gauge for measuring precipitation. The tipping mechanism records each 0.04 in. (1 mm) of precipitation received.

A microprocessor with solid-state memory is a part of each weather station. The microprocessor serves as an on-site data manager and is linked to a telephone with a DC-powered modem. The calibration constants for the various weather sensors are entered into memory for use in converting analog sensor signal to digital (in the electronic sense) form during the collection process. Sensors are monitored by the microprocessor once each minute, and hourly averages or totals are calculated. These hourly values are then stored in the memory of the station microprocessor.

Communication

Collection also involves communications between a microcomputer (IBM PC AT), located in the CAMaC offices on the East Campus of the University of Nebraska, and each of the weather stations. Once daily, a communication link is established over the telephone lines. At the station, a modem receives the incoming call and activates a response from the microprocessor where the data are stored. The data and periodic checksums are transmitted in binary and a summation procedure is used to check the binary records received at the microcomputer. This ensures that records received are identical to those transmitted by microprocessors located on-site. All calls take place over conventional phone lines and each weather station site requires only a private telephone line.

Software to automatically accomplish the collection and archiving of weather data was written by CAMaC staff. The computer language used to write the software was Professional Fortran. The telecommunications program was written in Turbo Pascal by Campbell Scientific Inc. of Logan, Utah.

Quality Control. Summarization of the data begins with quality control and flagging procedures that have been implemented on the CAMaC microcomputer. Data are compared to reasonable upper and lower limits for each parameter and any outliers are flagged and checked by the AWDN technician. The diurnal cycle of radiation from the sun is used to double-check the data logger's internal clock. Flags are attached to any data not fitting the diurnal cycle. Intercomparisons of data are routinely made and any bad or missing data are estimated by a distance-weighted interpolation process.

Overview. A general schematic of the linkages present in AWDN is shown in Fig. 1. Near-real time hourly climate data is retrieved from each weather station at about 1 a.m. The collection of weather data for the previous twenty-four-hour period is automated, requiring no human intervention. The telecommunications package developed by CAMaC also permits manual interrogation of the weather stations at any time.

After calling each weather station, the CAMaC computer stores the new measurements in the master data archive. Another program does a preliminary check of the weather data collected to identify suspicious data. Appropriate messages are printed so that the data so identified can be checked by a specialist. The computer then organizes the data for the most recent twenty-four-hour period and prepares it for transmittal to a mainframe computer, where subscribing users can conveniently access weather-related programs.

The mainframe computer in this case operates an agricultural management network, known as AGNET. Many users (Fig. 1) have access to the data generated by the AWDN and stored on AGNET. The weather data stored in the AGNET system can be accessed directly or used indirectly in specific programs (see below) by telephone communication from any terminal.

DEVELOPMENT OF CLIMATE INFORMATION DELIVERY SYSTEMS

Delivery of near-real time climate information to users is as important as the data collection. In general, the worth of the information delivered is inversely related to

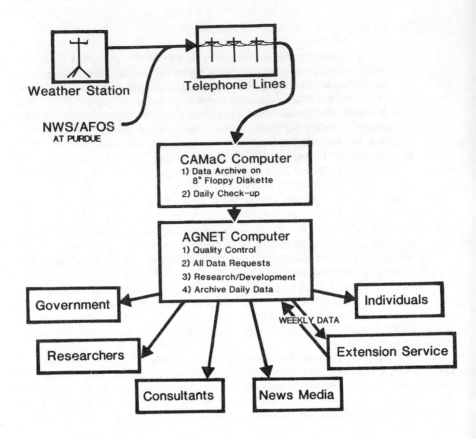

Fig. 1 Schematic of the linkages in the Automated Weather Data Network.

the period of time that elapses between measurement and delivery. For instance, an agricultural producer who must fit an irrigation decision into a busy schedule needs to know how recent weather has affected the need for an irrigation. If an irrigation must be scheduled in the next two days, any delay in receiving pertinent information will leave less time to alter the work schedule, and a delay of two or more days is, of course, not acceptable.

With the advances in computer technology, a number of climate and weather information delivery systems have been developed. The federal government has been responsible for developing several of these systems:

1. Climate Analysis Center developed a climate assessment data base (Finger, et al., 1985) that incorporates forecasts of the National Weather Service for five-day and six- to ten-day periods, outlooks for monthly and seasonal periods, and listings of the Palmer Drought Index into a user's menu.

2. As early as 1977 the Midwest Agricultural Weather Service Center had initiated an information system. This Automated Data Network (ADN) now acquires data from the AFOS (Automation of Field Operations and Service) system of the National Weather Service. This system can deliver local weather conditions, forecasts, agricultural weather, past weather, and severe weather data and bulletins.

3. The National Climatic Data Center initiated a climatic data delivery system in 1983. Newly digitized climate data is made available on this system long before it can be obtained on magnetic tape, giving climate data users an opportunity to update their files with the most recently digitized data.

States have been active in developing delivery systems as well. The AGNET system developed at the University of Nebraska (Thompson, 1981) is an example of a system developed for use in the agricultural management environment. The CLASS system was developed at the Illinois Water Survey to deliver weather data and products in near-real time (Changnon, et al., 1985). The California Irrigation Management and Information Service (CIMIS) was developed at the University of California and NOW-CASTING was developed at Chico State University (Hauser, 1981). It seems logical to assume that these computer information systems will be modified and adapted for use in other states.

Developments That May Affect Information Delivery

Several changes in the area of communications may have impacts on the future of information delivery. The National Science Foundation is supporting the design of University Data (UNIDATA), multilevel systems designed to support (1) access to "global" services, including current and archived weather data and forecasts; (2) local interactive computing; (3) communications between computers; and (4) interactive data collection and management of field observation programs. This communication system (UNIDATA) is aimed at providing linkages and interactive computing capabilities to the atmospheric science community within universities. Such an effort could generally improve the access to climate information at universities and lead to the adoption of a unified climate information delivery system. The system, designed by the University Corporation for Atmospheric Research, will support UNIX, VMS, or MSDOS work stations.

The NWS plans to change their nationwide delivery system by phasing out AFOS and replacing it with the AWIPS-90. The service will also provide a subscription service not now available to users outside of NWS. The NWS collects a considerable amount of the climate and weather data; therefore, easy access to the NWS dissemination system in real time has important consequences for climatologists in the United States.

On a different scale, the use of the microcomputer is increasing dramatically in climatology and meteorology. Both microcomputer links (networks) and dial-up service on microcomputers (e.g., bulletin boards) provide new opportunities to deliver climate information economically and efficiently to end users.

An Integrated Approach

Information delivery requires an integrated approach in order to reach the largest audience. Although terminals, modems, and microcomputers are proliferating, a large proportion of the potential user community still cannot access a computer information system because they lack the essential hardware.

In Nebraska, conventional and new forms of computer information delivery are supported. Personal contact and requests made through the mail are still popular, but the volume of requests handled is dependent on manpower in both cases and the time delay in normal mail service may be unacceptable. Some types of information can be transcribed by voice onto a tape so that anyone who calls can hear a recording of pertinent information. The daily evapotranspiration estimates are placed on a tape recording in many counties in the state.

Another approach has been to provide a group of specialists with a detailed update on the climate and weather situation and ask them in turn to provide a public advisory outlining key considerations that producers should keep in mind. This approach is discussed below.

Nebraska Agricultural Climate Situation Committee. The Cooperative Extension Service established this Committee in the spring of 1981 to provide up-to-date information and advice on current climatic conditions for Nebraska's agricultural industry. The Committee consists of specialists in subject areas covering all important agricultural commodities produced in Nebraska, and a journalist (writer). The specialties of agronomy, soil science, plant pathology, entomology, rangeland science, forestry, animal science, veterinary medicine, climatology, and meteorology are represented.

The Committee meets at 1:30 p.m. each Monday afternoon during the growing season to review near-real time weather and climate data from the previous week. This information includes data from thirty-one AWDN stations and seven AWS first-order stations; ROSA and other AFOS temperature and rainfall reports from sixty cooperative climatological observing stations in Nebraska (assembled with the assistance of the NWS's Omaha Office); and the Weekly Weather and Crop Bulletin and Monthly and Seasonal Outlooks. Climatological analyses and summaries prepared in previous years are also available.

After a thorough review of the current weather-related agricultural problems, advisories are prepared. The journalist composes a press release from notes on the Committee's discussion. The press release is checked by a Committee member and released at about 3:00 p.m. the same day. That Committee member also prepares a tape recording for release to radio stations.

A brief look at the situation in 1981 illustrates the kinds of problems with which the Committee has dealt. The fall of 1980 was dry following a severe heat wave, and soil moisture was depleted in the top 5 ft. (the root zone for most of Nebraska's major crops). The winter of 1980 was extremely dry and warmer than usual. Hence, the spring began with low soil moisture throughout much of the state and with unusually warm soils. Dry surfaces early in the season led some farmers to consider planting earlier than normal. The Committee advised against such action by emphasizing that the probability of a killing frost remained great, despite the unusual warmth. As the spring progressed with little rainfall, the Committee urged that farmers, particularly those on unirrigated land, hold open their options to plant alternative crops, such as sorghum and soybeans, that are generally more drought-resistant than corn.

Another result of the warm, dry spring weather was an unusually early break in winter wheat dormancy. The Committee was fully aware of the potential vulnerability of the wheat to late spring frost because of this early break in dormancy, but it could recommend nothing to reduce the risk. State agencies were, however, alerted to this potentially serious problem. A freeze occurred in early May, when wheat was prematurely in flower, causing an estimated $100 million loss to farmers.

Sorghum appeared to be a good alternative to corn, since the spring continued to be dry. However, wheat fields in southeastern and south central Nebraska were infested with chinch bugs. Sorghum is particularly vulnerable to this pest, and so, the Committee determined, sorghum planted near wheat fields would be particularly susceptible to attack as the chinch bugs migrated out of maturing wheat fields. Thus, where both corn and sorghum appeared risky, the Committee recommended that farmers plant soybeans. The interdisciplinary structure of the Committee was particularly valuable in cases such as this. For example, the entomologist pointed out that land prepared for corn or sorghum might already have been treated with an herbicide antagonistic to all broadleaf plants such as soybeans. Thus, the Committee urged farmers to review herbicide treatment history of their land before deciding to plant soybeans.

Rangeland in northern and western Nebraska was also extremely dry in the spring. Through June, hay harvest was almost negligible. The Committee encouraged ranchers to use Extension Service assistance in locating supplies of hay or finding markets for their excess animals.

Trees in cities showed serious moisture stress by early summer. Homeowners were advised to soak the area around their trees thoroughly to augment the weekly half-inch lawn irrigation otherwise recommended.

This brief summary describes some of the events and agricultural problems that the Agricultural Weather Situation Committee dealt with from March through June. In late June, good rains began, and the 1981 summer crop season was a good one. The Committee continued to function throughout the growing season. During this time, radio and television stations and newspapers throughout the state widely and regularly disseminated the findings of the Committee.

The AGNET Information Delivery System. Information delivery systems are capable of near-real time functions that serve user needs for climate and weather data. In Nebraska, the AGNET system is accessed about 14,000 times per year for different kinds of weather summaries and analyses.

AGNET (Agricultural Management Network) began in 1975 with the installation of computer terminals linking a district office to a central computer at the University of Nebraska. A development grant from the Old West Regional Commission in 1977 funded AGNET's expansion to a five-state region. In 1982, AGNET became a self-funded organization of the University, with subscribers throughout the United States and in other countries. AGNET currently has more than two hundred computer programs to serve its users, including management models dealing with agricultural production, marketing, and finance; electronic mail service; and dissemination of published reports. The six AGNET production programs shown in Table 1 use current weather data from AWDN and NWS sources. One program, CROPSTATUS, has twenty options related to crops and livestock (see Table 2).

Table 1
Weather Programs for AGNET—1984

APPLIED

BEEFGROWER - simulates the performance of beef cattle in the feedlot.

BINDRY - estimates drying time in a natural air grain drying system and the rate at which grain can be loaded in the bin.

CROPSTATUS - provides 20 up-to-date weather summaries related to crops and animals.

IRRIGATE - determines a crop watering schedule, user records rainfall, irrigations and soil moisture and computer projects on irrigation window based on recent weather.

ET - calculates Penman evapotranspiration for selected times and crops by station or for regions of the state.

WEATHER - lists and/or summarizes weather data by stations or in maps of the state.

RESEARCH

GREENHOUSE - simulates the energy and moisture balance within single span greenhouses.

REALSOY - simulates growth and development of soybean plants and estimates final seed yield.

CORNGRO - simulates growth and development of corn and estimates final seed yield.

CUPID - simulates the environment within a crop canopy.

Table 2
Options for CROPSTATUS Program (AGNET)

WEATHER ASSESSMENT

A Precipitation to date
B Precipitation between any 2 dates
C Heating Degree Days
D Cooling Degree Days
E Probability of Precipitation for spring planting
F Probability of Freeze
G Weather Data Listing
H Regional Soil Temperatures
I Regional Climatic Summary
J Regional Historical Climate
K Regional Climate Outlook
L Livestock Stress
M Wind Chill

GROWING SEASON ASSESSMENT

R Growing Degree Days
S Estimated Emergence Date
T Developmental Stage
U Minimum Stage now for Maturity by average freeze date
V Estimated Maturity Date
W Yield Assessment
X Crop Water Use by Region or Location

Drought Assessment and Response System. Another special mechanism for use and dissemination of weather information in Nebraska is the Drought Assessment and Response System (DARS). DARS was initiated in 1985 to deal with drought. The adverse impacts of drought may be widespread geographically and diverse in terms of physical and social damage. Impacts may continue after a drought ends and, in some cases, may not be apparent until after drought conditions have abated.

Some state and federal government programs assist county and local governments and individual citizens in mitigating the impacts of drought. In some cases these programs are incomplete. Inefficiencies due to overlap or poor information lead to a less than satisfactory response. To avoid overlaps and poor decisions it is important to have a systematic organization to identify the types and magnitudes of impacts and determine needs that extend beyond existing programs. DARS was created to fill this need in Nebraska in order to allow a careful and deliberate response to drought rather than a "crisis management" response. Similar plans exist in at least six other states in the United States (see Wilhite, this volume).

The specific objectives of the Nebraska Drought Assessment Response System (DARS) are:

1. To provide timely and systematic data collection, analysis, and dissemination of drought information.
2. To establish criteria for start-up and shut-down of various assessment and response activities by state and federal agencies during drought emergencies.
3. To provide an organizational structure that assures information flow and defines the duties and responsibilities of all agencies.
4. To maintain a current inventory of state and federal agency responsibilities in assessing and responding to drought emergencies.
5. To provide a mechanism for improving methods of assessing drought impacts on agriculture and industry.

The Nebraska Drought Assessment and Response System is built around the System Coordination Group. This group coordinates activities between state and federal agencies and provides information and recommendations to the governor.

The three basic functions of the system are monitoring moisture conditions, assessing impacts of drought, and responding to drought with actions or recommendations. The monitoring function consists of tracking moisture availability in the state's soils, streams, reservoirs, and ground water. Assessment involves gathering and analyzing impact information from a broad range of sources to determine the extent of drought impacts. The response function marshals available resources to alleviate drought-related problems that cannot be met locally and provides a mechanism to identify problems that are not met by existing drought response programs. The Moisture Situation Committee collects and interprets near-real time weather data that serves as the triggering mechanism for the overall system. Although each element of the system is important, the key components are the System Coordination Group and the Moisture Situation Committee.

System Coordination Group. This group is the core of DARS. The primary functions of the group are dissemination of information to the governor, public, and participants in DARS. The group seeks alternative solutions to problems and makes recommendations to the governor.

The group is composed of representatives from the following:

1. Department of Agriculture
2. Civil Defense
3. Department of Health
4. Natural Resources Commission
5. Policy Research Office
6. Agricultural Stabilization and Conservation Service
7. Federal Crop Insurance Corporation
8. Moisture Situation Committee
9. Cooperative Extension Service -University of Nebraska-Lincoln (UNL)

The representative from the Natural Resources Commission acts as chairperson for the group. The chairperson receives reports from the Moisture Situation Committee and is responsible for relaying the information to the governor and the members of the coordination group. The decision to fully activate DARS is made by the governor. The chairman of the coordination group implements the decision by calling the group into session, and the group continues to meet on an ad hoc basis until the drought and resulting impacts have subsided.

During drought situations the group activates the impact assessment process and initiates communications with response agencies. The group is responsible for reviewing and compiling impact assessment reports. They review problems that are not addressed by existing programs and explore alternative solutions to those problems. The group prepares reports containing impact assessments, response efforts, and recommendations for solutions to unaddressed problems.

Moisture Situation Committee. This committee is responsible for monitoring water supply and moisture conditions across the state. The committee is composed of representatives from:

1. Conservation and Survey Division (UNL)
2. Center for Agricultural Meteorology and Climatology (UNL) and the Agricultural Climate Situation Committee
3. National Weather Service
4. Department of Water Resources
5. United States Geological Survey
6. Department of Agronomy (UNL)
7. Soil Conservation Survey

The Conservation and Survey Division is responsible for leadership of this committee and arranges meetings when appropriate. An initial meeting is held each year during the first week of April. Subsequently, the frequency of meetings is based on the severity of conditions.

The Moisture Situation Committee is responsible for making assessments of precipitation, stream flow, reservoir levels, ground-water levels and soil moisture conditions. The committee reports the results of each meeting to the chairman of the System Coordination Group.

Assessment. The function of the assessment element of the system is to collect and analyze drought impact information. The information is provided to the System Coordination Group for summarization, interpretation, and subsequent presentation to the governor and the public. The information is provided to response agencies as an aid in planning a response to drought-related problems. Assessments may be prepared when seeking additional state or federal assistance to respond to needs that cannot be met by existing programs and funds. The impact assessment task forces are water systems and health; agriculture and wildlife; and economics and energy.

CURRENT AND POTENTIAL APPLICATIONS OF CLIMATE INFORMATION

Current Use Patterns

The products available on AGNET are accessed 400-2,000 times per month (Table 3). As would be expected, the products dealing with crops are most often used during summer months, while those dealing with storage of grain and beef production are heavily used in fall, winter, and spring.

The AGNET system served a considerable audience of weather data users—approximately 14,000—in 1985. A survey of AGNET weather data products users

Table 3
Use of AGNET Weather-Based Products, 1985: Number of Accesses

PRODUCT	JAN	FEB	MAR	APR	MAY	JUN	JUL	AUG	SEP	OCT	NOV	DEC	TOTAL
BEEF	640	464	709	608	229	163	205	346	418	452	273	335	4842
BINDRY	49	8	718	554	176	810	12	3	9	182	23	22	2566
CROPSTATUS	38	147	277	317	457	166	392	447	245	196	37	30	2749
ET	167	17	40	33	63	130	465	286	118	15	37	7	1378
IRRIGATE	4	6	16	8	12	38	32	15	2	7	11	1	152
WEATHER	125	95	188	265	294	331	270	219	177	164	46	72	2246
TOTALS	1023	737	1948	1785	1231	1638	1376	1316	969	1016	427	476	13933

(Meyer, 1986) showed that the audience includes people from a wide cross section of commerce: Cooperative Extension (50%), crop and livestock production (20.5%), agribusiness (10.6%), agricultural consulting firms (4.5%), government (5.3%) and other (9.1%—mainly vocational training schools, financial institutes, and radio stations). Other background information showed that spring and summer were, by far, the most active times of the year for the majority of users. Those who used AGNET most frequently in the spring cited information concerning planting decisions and planting delays, crop selection, choice of crop, and effects on calving and feedlot performance as reasons for using the system then. In summer, information on irrigation scheduling, monitoring heat stress and drought conditions, and insect development for timing of pesticide application encouraged some people to use AGNET more frequently. Interest in both fall and winter was considerably less. Respondents used AGNET in the fall for information on harvest and harvest delays, crop drying and storage, fall tillage, and planting of winter wheat. In winter, respondents were concerned primarily with livestock breeding, survival rates, feedlot performance, feed consumption, and ration balancing.

Potential Uses of Climate and Weather Information

More research is needed to understand the relationship between climate and events important to man. Topics of potential research are too broad to fully discuss here, but a few agriculturally related climate products that will be possible in the near future are the following:
1. Crop status indices for more specific characterization of drought and other anomalous weather events.
2. Soil moisture models to estimate the water balance from precipitation and evapotranspiration over regions.
3. Insect progress indicators to characterize the development of insects and to warn of insect outbreaks.
4. Precipitation probability decision aids for use in preventing erosion and determining planting dates and fertilization rates.
5. Outlooks or forecasts of evapotranspiration based on NWS forecasts.

CONCLUSIONS

Pertinent weather data and information distribution, when accomplished in near-real time, will bring about a large user audience. The technology for accomplishing weather data collection, quality control, and archiving on a microcomputer has been demonstrated, and those who are interested in such a near-real time system can employ the AWDN as a model to readily implement a weather monitoring system. However, near-real time weather monitoring alone will not solve the problems of every agricultural region. Based on our experience, a successful system must have the full commitment of its participants. Participants must determine what climatic issues are of highest priority to all groups served by the system and then develop a comprehensive plan to address these issues. Those involved in near-real time weather monitoring systems must also be willing to commit resources (people, money, and equipment) to the project. Organizational structures such as the Agricultural Climate Situation Committee and the Drought Assessment and Response System of Nebraska are necessary to ensure the exchange of information (and benefits of such an exchange) obtained from the system.

REFERENCES

Changnon, S. A.; J. L. Vogel; and W. M. Wendland. 1985. New climate delivery system developed in Illinois. Bull. Am. Meteorol. Soc. 65:704-705.

Crook, A. G. 1977. SNOWTEL: Monitoring climatic factors to predict water supplies. J. Soil Water Conserv. 32:294-295.

Curry, R. D.; J. C. Klink; J. R. Holman; and M. J. Sciarini. 1981. Development of an automated weather station network in Ohio. ASAE Paper No. 81-4502. ASAE, St. Joseph, Michigan.

Finger, F. G.; J. D. Laver; K. H. Bergman; and V. L. Patterson. 1985. The Climate Analysis Center's user information service. Bull. Am. Meteorol. Soc. 66:413-420.

Hauser, R. K. 1981. A McIDAS-based regional weather system in a joint public/private setting. pp. 134-142. In A. Weiss, ed. Computer Techniques and Meteorological Data Applied to Problems of Agriculture and Forestry: A Workshop. American Meteorological Society, Boston.

Hubbard, K. G.; N. J. Rosenberg; and D. Nielsen. 1983. Automated weather data network for agriculture. J. Water Res. Planning Manage. 109:213-222.

Meyer, S. J.; K. G. Hubbard; N. J. Rosenberg; and D. A. Wilhite. 1986. Improving Nebraska's near-real time weather-based products through user interaction. CAMaC Progress Report 86-4. Center for Agricultural Meteorology and Climatology, University of Nebraska-Lincoln.

Millard, P. 1984. The changing direction in weather information. Farming With Pride 4:4-11.

NAS. 1982. Meeting the challenge of climate. National Academy of Sciences. National Academy Press, Washington, D.C.

Thompson, T. L. 1981. Interactive systems for agricultural management. pp. 95-104. In A. Weiss, ed. Computer Techniques and Meteorological Data Applied to Problems of Agriculture and Forestry: A Workshop. American Meteorological Society, Boston.

CHAPTER 9
AGROCLIMATIC MONITORING DURING THE GROWING SEASON IN SEMIARID REGIONS OF AFRICA

M. Konaté and K. Traoré

INTRODUCTION

The severe and persistent drought that affected the Sahelian countries during the 1970s was devastating for human beings as well as for animals. It demonstrated the fragility of the ecosystem and pointed out that the meteorological and hydrometeorological services in those countries affected were poorly prepared to deal with drought-related problems of this magnitude. In 1975, eight African countries created a joint program in agriculture, hydrology, and meteorology in response to these problems. This program, called AGRHYMET, was formed with financial and technical assistance from the international community.

The main objective of the AGRHYMET program was to reinforce the meteorological and hydrological services of member countries in order to improve and coordinate drought-monitoring efforts, and to provide agro-hydro-climatic assistance to agriculture. This, in turn, was intended to support the socioeconomic development of these countries, since their economies are based mainly on a rainfed type of agriculture. After seven years of staff training and resource development by the AGRHYMET program, the Mali Agrometeorological Service was capable of issuing bulletins assessing the impact of climate on food production. These bulletins were useful to technically trained people from government agencies and the representatives of international organizations.

The results of this program were promising. However, a key question was, Could these bulletins be used by Mali's illiterate or poorly educated farmers in their day-to-day operations? The answer was obviously no.

In 1982, Mali established a pilot project in agrometeorology in an attempt to respond to this problem. Agronomic and climatic data were used by a multidisciplinary team to make advisories for a small group of farmers in order to assess how the use of weather information in farming practices affected yield. This program was established in response to the devastating drought. Other factors, such as the availability of scientific information on which advisories could be based and the relatively low level of financial resources required to develop such a program, made the development of the program possible. Because of the drought, food self-sufficiency had already become the first priority in Mali's food strategy. This new program was viewed as one method that would help the government achieve that goal.

The operational stage of the AGRHYMET project began in 1983. The primary goal was to create a data bank of agrometeorological information for use by member nations. Under this project each member country would acquire the capability to monitor agrometeorological conditions during the rainy season and be able to assist decision makers at all levels (e.g., government officials with food planning, farmers with decisions regarding daily operations). Many of the goals of this program were inspired by the initial results of the Malian pilot project.

In this paper, some of the results of the Malian pilot project, including prospects for the future, will be presented. The case study of crop monitoring during the rainy season in Mali as organized by AGRHYMET will also be presented.

PART 1: THE PILOT EXPERIMENT

The site of the pilot experiment is located 60 km southwest of the capital city of Bamako. The area is in the sector of Bancoumana, which is under the jurisdiction of an agricultural extension organization known as Operation Haute Vallee (OHV). This sector has an area of 4,290 km^2. The main food crops, millet and sorghum, are grown on 5,980 ha. The mean annual rainfall varies between 800 mm and 1,000 mm.

Protocol

The primary objective of the AGRHYMET project is to implement an agrometeorological information system to enable farmers to make more efficient decisions in their agricultural activities. The procedure followed to accomplish this objective is summarized below.

1. Basic meteorological parameters (rainfall, temperature, wind, humidity, sunshine) are measured at a reference agrometeorological station. Because of its high spatial variability, rainfall is measured in rain gauges at additional sites installed close to selected fields; soil data (water-holding capacity, runoff coefficient) and plant data (phenological stages, crop coefficients, pests and diseases, weeds) are also collected.
2. Agroclimatological functions (PET, water balance models) are computed.
3. Knowledge of soil-water-crop relationships and agricultural practices adapted to the behavior of plants (tilling, planting date, weeding, application of fertilizer) is used to issue advisories.
4. Directives are disseminated to extension workers in a form understandable to farmers.

Selected Places and Cultivars for the Experiment

Four villages were selected: Bancoumana, Kenieroba, Kongola, and Makandiana (Fig. 1). An improved variety of sorghum (Tiemarifing, 120 days) is grown in Bancoumana and Kenieroba while a local variety of millet (Toutoucoun, 130 days) is grown in Kongola and Makandiana. Both cultivars are widespread in the area. Four

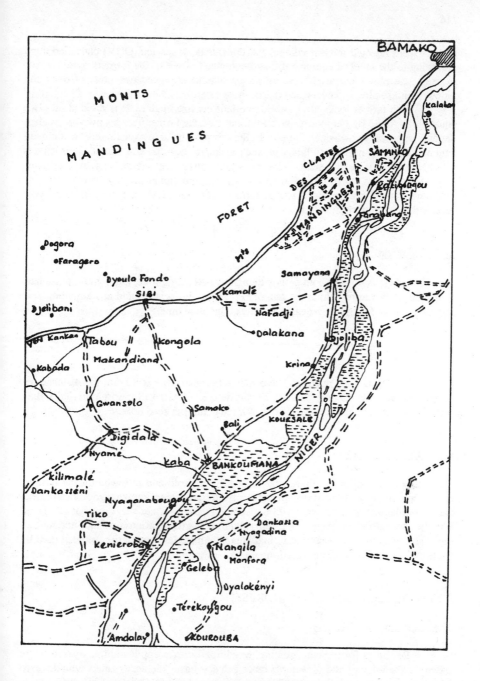

Fig. 1 Agrometeorological pilot zone.

farmers were selected in each village, and the extension service (OHV) classified them according to the level of equipment that they owned. Two of the farmers owned a pair of oxen, one plow, and a multiuse plow; the other two owned two pairs of oxen and plows, multiuse plows, seeders, and one or more carts.

Each farmer looks after a field one-half hectare in size. It is divided into two equal plots, A and B. On plot A, the traditional plot, the farmer uses his own crop calendar and empirical knowledge. On plot B, the test plot, he is to execute only recommendations made by a multidisciplinary team according to climatic conditions. This team is in charge of the experiment. The team comprises agronomists, meteorologists, agrometeorologists, crop protection specialists, and functional literacy specialists. The recommendations are provided to the farmers via the OHV extension officers, who receive the instructions by radio.

Soil Preparation

Tillage is done in both plots with a plow. At tilling time, ammonium phosphate is applied to the entire field at the rate of 100 kg/ha. Urea is applied at stem elongation stage at a rate of 50 kg/ha. Weeding is done at the same time.

Sowing and Thinning

Sowing is done in rows. The distance between rows is 80 cm; the distance between seed holes is 45 cm. Sowing density is 0.80 m x 0.40 for sorghum and millet. Thinning is carried out at the rate of two to three plants per seed hole.

Fixing Crop Calendars

For the traditional plots, crop calendars are fixed and followed by the farmers according to their own criteria. Currently only an *a posteriori* knowledge of these calendars is available; however, more will be learned through farmer surveys. For test plots, activities are carried out according to agrometeorological conditions on fields and following instructions from the multidisciplinary team. An explanation of the methods used by the team is included in the next section.

METHODOLOGY AND PROCEDURES

The Water Balance Principle

Decisions for plowing, sowing, weeding, fertilizer application, and so forth are based on a ten-day period of water balance calculations. The water balance model used here was suggested by Forest (1974) and Forest and Lidon (1984). This model takes into account soil data (available soil water) and crop data (crop coefficients). Climatic input includes daily and decadal rainfall and mean values of decadal potential evapotranspiration (PET).

The model estimates actual evapotranspiration (AET) using Eagleman's function (1971), soil water storage, and crop water requirement satisfaction rate (AET/PET, where PET is the potential evapotranspiration, estimated as suggested by Frere and Popov, 1979). Then, using statistics from the rainfall, the model determines the probability of receiving the rainfall required to meet crop needs during the next ten-day period. Based on this analysis the team then issues recommendations. Water balance calculations are done either with a pocket calculator using an appropriate calculation sheet or with a microcomputer program.

Decision to Plow

The water balance is calculated from the time of the first rainfall. If, at the end of a ten-day period (i), an AET_i/PET_i ratio of 0.2 is obtained and there is at least an 80% probability that the $AET_i + 1/PET_i + 1$ will be 0.2 for the next ten-day period, the team recommends that farmers begin plowing during the next ten days. Franquin (1973) has determined that these soil moisture conditions are favorable to plowing.

Decision to Sow

A study of sowing dates based on a frequency analysis of climatic balance (see, for example, Meteorologie et IER, 1984) shows that, at Bancoumana, sowing on May 20 is successful in one out of two years (probability 0.5). It appears also that after July 5, the soil becomes too moist for sowing in one out of two years (agroclimatic event B1, as defined by Franquin, 1973). Sowing is, therefore, planned for the period between May 20 and July 5.

Using the water balance calculated from the plowing period, if AET = 0.3 PET at the end of a ten-day period between the two dates above and if the probability is at least 80% that it will be so for the next ten-day period, then sowing may take place. This means that when the soil moisture condition is favorable for germination, the decision to sow is made—provided that moisture is likely to be sufficient for sprouting. However, if these conditions occur late and if sowing is delayed further, for whatever reason, a different variety is chosen, if possible.

Throughout the season, the ten-day PET values for the calculations are estimated using Penman's formula from agrometeorological parameters measured at the reference station at Samanko. The 80% probability thresholds used for the plowing and sowing decisions correspond to minimum failure risks of 20% (two out of ten years). Nonetheless, it would have been more effective to couple these forecasts, which are based on statistical rainfall analysis, with dynamic meteorological forecasts covering several days. This is a technical problem that the Directorate of Meteorology is still trying to resolve.

Weeding

The first weeding is carried out after the third leaf appears. The second weeding occurs after stem elongation. Additional weeding takes place as needed according to field observations. Decisions on the need to carry out weeding operations are based on the extent of weed cover and current weather conditions. A two-to three-day forecast would be helpful in trying to schedule weeding operations. For example, weeding may take place one day, but rain on the following day may render the effort useless.

Spreading of Urea

This practice is carried out at stem elongation stage on a day when the soil is considered to be adequately moist. Ideally, this operation should not be done when a long dry spell is forecast, to avoid burning the crops. Again, dependable medium-range forecasts would be useful for the practice.

Crop Protection

The main enemies of the crops in the pilot zone are parasitic plants, diseases, and insects. The main parasitic plant in the area is striga, which farmers uproot, generally before it flowers. This prevents seeds from forming and germinating later in the season.

Various insects and diseases are documented during the season. The main diseases are mildew and smut, for which there is no treatment. The correlations between the appearance of these diseases and various agrometeorological parameters should be studied with a view toward forecasting the disease potential of the area.

DISSEMINATION OF INFORMATION

Time is a precious factor in this experiment since the objective is to advise farmers on the optimal dates for agricultural operations, taking into account meteorological conditions. Thus, information dissemination and interaction among the farmers, extension workers, and multidisciplinary team is of great importance. Figure 2 is a schematic representation of the way information is disseminated in the pilot project. It comprises three main stages:

1. Data collection and transmission. At the end of each ten-day period, two observers collect agrometeorological and crop data in the pilot zone.
2. Data processing and analysis. Pest disease samples, if any, are identified by the Integrated Pest Management (IPM) section of the Agronomic Research Office. Agrometeorological data are processed by the Agromet Division of the Meteorological Service. The multidisciplinary team meets two days after the end of the ten-day period to analyze the processed data and issue recommendations.

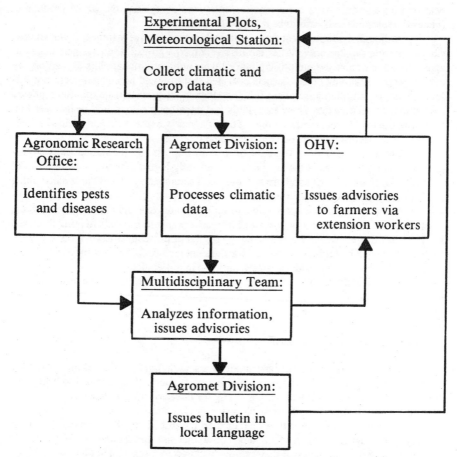

Fig. 2 Schematic representation of the circulation of information in the pilot project.

3. Transmission of directives and issuing of agrometeorological bulletins. The representative of OHV takes the message containing the directives to his headquarters and transmits it by radio to the pilot project zone.

RESULTS

To carry out this experiment, the project management and the so-called pilot farmers agreed on the following arrangements. Project management was to provide farmers with input, but not manpower or farming tools. At harvest, yields were to be estimated from sampled squares called yield squares and seeds were to be selected for the next farming season. After these requirements were completed, the whole production (minus the selected seeds) was to be returned to the farmers.

Although the experiment for this procedure was relatively simple, it was impossible to execute satisfactorily. After the first year of the project, some farmers began to apply the advice from the multidisciplinary team to the traditional plots as well as the control plots. A survey of the farmers revealed that outlined procedures were not followed either because farmers did not fully understand the procedures even after repeated instructions or because they knew that yields and therefore profits would be increased by following the team's recommendations. The first year's experiment had yielded higher production on the test plots than on the traditional plots.

Tables 1 and 2 show the data from both the test and traditional plots over a three-year period. Yields of the test plots are generally higher than yields of the control or traditional plots for both sorghum and millet. The increase in yield has a mean value of 17% for sorghum and 26% for millet.

Since it was not always possible to make farmers execute the experiment in the prescribed manner, the yields in the test plots were compared to yields in other fertilized fields in the village. Tables 1 and 2 show the results of this comparison. Plots that were severely damaged by birds and other animals are not included. The test plots achieved a 41% increase in sorghum yield and a 26% increase in millet yield.

A survey is currently underway to determine the factors that influence the decisions of farmers.

Feedback Effects of the Experiment

Several field visits were carried out to assess the impact of the project. The experiment appeared to have had a positive effect on farmers. They seemed to accept the multidisciplinary team and were willing to pay for the advisories, if necessary. Some indicated that production from the test plots was higher than that from their own family farms, which were two to four times larger than the test plots. The farmers concluded that by using agroclimatic advice, they could increase production while farming a smaller area. Some farmers said they achieved satisfactory results after applying the advice to part of their own farms. As the experiment progressed, more farmers in the area wanted to receive the advisories that were given to the pilot farmers.

PROSPECTS FOR THE FUTURE

The Pilot Project was developed to be carried out in four stages. In the first experimental stage, which is now concluding, researchers collected data and tested agroclimatic methodologies. During the second stage (the assessment stage), the data will be analyzed and methodologies will be selected for future use. The third stage will be an extension stage, during which farmers and extension workers will be involved in data collection and the use of agroclimatic information through training courses and seminars. During the final stage, general assistance will be given to all of the farmlands in the country. Some farmers already have begun taking rainfall measurements.

In the future, the project will be extended over a larger part of the country. The first step will be to include the whole sector of Bancoumana in the project while starting an experimental stage in another sector—Banamba. Banamba has a typical Sahelian climate. Next, the other five sectors of OHV will be covered progressively; the project team then will assess the socioeconomic impact of the experiment in the OHV area. Later, other agricultural extension organizations will be covered.

The basic idea is to work through rural development organizations or agricultural extension organizations, because it is their responsibility to transfer the technologies developed by research services to farmers. The agroclimatic information must be seen as part of the agricultural technological package that is to be transferred to farmers. In addition, the dissemination of information should be improved by establishing a network of radios in the zones to be covered. Farmers would collect rainfall data, and extension workers would make observations on crops.

During a recent seminar it was noticed that older farmers were less receptive to the suggested technology. However, they could be convinced by special radio broadcasts and, if necessary, by demonstrations on plots of their family farms. Also, directives could be disseminated through existing farmer extension groups in the village.

Finally, the methods could be improved by introducing short- and medium-range weather forecasts, operational agrophysiological models, and warnings on pests and disease appearance.

CONCLUSION

The results obtained during the three years of the pilot experiment are quite encouraging. Although it is not easy to quantify the effects of agroclimatic information on the yield potential, the approach used here to issue farming advisories is an effective way to increase crop production.

Farmers who applied the directives to all plots impeded the scientific analysis of the experiment. However, it implies that those farmers have accepted the technology suggested by the project. This is a significant accomplishment, knowing how difficult it is to make farmers in Mali accept new ideas.

Results could have been improved if tools like weather forecasts and agrophysiological models had been available to be used with the methods we have for the advisory-making process. Despite imperfect methodologies and difficulties in implementing the experiment, we do believe that the approach that has been adopted is one of the best ways to provide agriculture in the region with needed operational agroclimatic assistance.

It is hoped that with the improvements mentioned above, operational agroclimatic assistance will help Sahelian farmers cope with the specter of drought-induced famine.

Table 1
Sorghum Yields in the Pilot Fields

	Bancoumana								Kéniéroba							
	1		2		3		4		1		2		3		4	
	T	C	T	C	T	C	T	C	T	C	T	C	T	C	T	C
1983	1635	1485	1675	1617	827	725	1818	1777	1345	863	763	872	405[a]	345[a]	1075	533
1984	1340	1230	1543	1220	1940	1910	1300	1403	1398	920	1050	795	1310	1408	1380	1203
1985	1310	810	1773	1785	1588	1233	1203	1223	1195	320[b]	475[c]	440[c]	960[d]	820[d]	504[e]	483
Mean	1428	1175	1664	1541	1452	1289	1440	1468	1313	892	763	702	892	858	986	740
$100x \dfrac{Y_T - Y_c}{Y_c}$	22		8		13		-2		47		9		4		33	
$100x \dfrac{Y_T - Y_A}{Y_A}$	43		66		45		44		46		1		46		36	

T: Test plot
C: Control plot = Traditional plot
Y_T: Yield in the test plot in kg/ha
Y_c: Yield in the control plot in kg/ha
Y_A: Average yield in the village; Y_A is 1000 kg/ha for Bancoumana and 900 kg/ha for Kéniéroba

(a) Planting occurred very late
(b) The plot was abandoned for one month
(c) Death of young plants for undetermined seasons
(d) Damage due to cattle
(e) Persistence of water puddles in the field

Table 2
Millet Yields in the Pilot Fields

	Kongola								Makandiana							
	1		2		3		4		1		2		3		4	
	T	C	T	C	T	C	T	C	T	C	T	C	T	C	T	C
1983[a]	525	383	755	738	595	483	700	538	803	750	1032	855	585	388	513	410
1984	1050	863	1025	1000	975	908	1028	828	1463	915	1645	733	925	763	995	800
1985	1083	701	1000	780	968	1120	868	785	1300	1278	1325	1046	773[a]	505[a]	903	683
Mean	886	649	927	839	846	837	865	717	1189	981	1334	878	761	552	804	631
$100x \dfrac{Y_T - Y_c}{Y_c}$	37		8		10		21		21		52		38		27	
$100x \dfrac{Y_T - Y_A}{Y_A}$	19		13		8		5		63		75		9		12	

T: Test plot
C: Control plot = Traditional plot
Y_T: Yield in the test plot in kg/ha
Y_c: Yield in the control plot in kg/ha
Y_A: Average yield in the village; YA is 900 kg/ha for Kongola and 850 kg/ha for Makandiana

[a]Damage due to birds (these yields are not taken into account in the comparison with average yield)

PART 2: A CASE STUDY OF AGROMETEOROLOGICAL
AND HYDROLOGICAL MONITORING OF CROPS
DURING THE RAINY SEASON

The AGRHYMET program will participate in early warning systems in member countries by monitoring agroclimatic conditions and making assessments of climate impact on crops and pastures. In Mali, these monitoring activities are organized as follows.

Multidisciplinary Working Group

In Mali, several extension services in the Agriculture Department are working in zones to provide complete coverage of the farmlands. For the crop monitoring system, a multidisciplinary team has been formed; it consists of meteorologists, hydrologists, livestock specialists, and extension services representatives within the Agriculture Department. Each extension service is equipped with radio facilities for communication between rural areas and their headquarters in Bamako, the capital of Mali. The Meteorology Department's agrometeorology division is responsible for coordinating the activities of the team.

Data Requirements

The data collected includes observations of crops, rainfall, river levels, and pastures. Three networks have been set up to collect these data. The network of rain gauges is made up of stations operated partly by the Meteorology Department and partly by the extension services. Since June 1986 a NOAA satellite has been providing information about vegetation conditions for Mali through a vegetation index (see Fig. 3), as suggested by Gray, et al. (1981).

Products

During every ten-day period, data is collected and analyzed by the multidisciplinary working group. The group then prepares a bulletin containing this information, which is disseminated by radio, television, and newspapers. The bulletin assesses the adequacy of rainfall, as a percent of normal or in terms of crop water requirements. It also provides information on river levels and summarizes crop and pasture conditions. An example of the bulletin is given below.

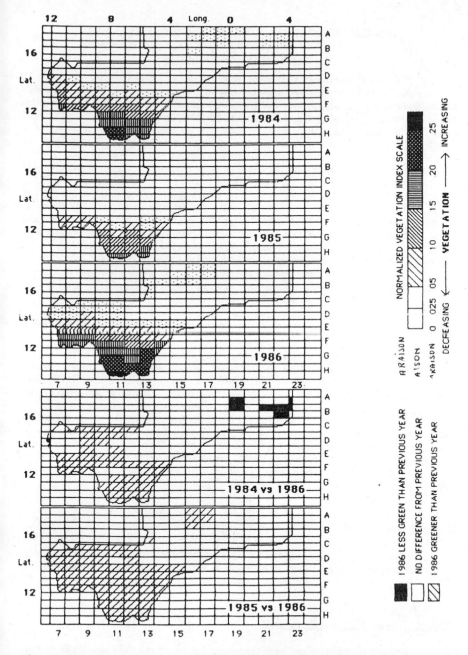

Fig. 3 NOAA satellite normalized vegetation index for Mali, third week of June.

TEN-DAY AGRO-HYDROMETEOROLOGICAL BULLETIN

August 11-20, 1986

The general meteorological situation can be summarized as follows:
During the first three days of the ten-day period, monsoon winds were very weak because of the strengthening of the Saharian high pressure system. This phenomenon has been prevailing since the midpoint of the last ten-day period.

After August 14, stormy weather prevailed because of the development of a trough that resulted in humid conditions in the country. From August 11-13, only light and scattered rains were recorded in the Gao, Koulikoro, and Sikasso regions. From August 14 to the end of the ten-day period, squall lines were frequent, bringing, at times, heavy precipitation. Nevertheless, ten-day rainfall totals have been about 50% below normal in the southern part of Kayes, Koulikoro, Sikasso, and Segou regions, and more than 70% below normal at other locations. Consequently, the cumulative rainfall deficit has increased. In the above- mentioned areas it is less than or equal to 25% below normal and in Mopti and Gao it varies between 30% and 60%. Accumulated rainfall up to August 20 of this year is generally less than that accumulated during the same period in 1985.

Water levels in rivers have risen slightly during the ten- day period, although the rise was less on the Bani River than on the others. Mean ten-day levels are currently below normal; they are also below the levels recorded up to this date in 1984 and 1985.

Biomass and Crop Conditions

The normalized vegetation index from the NOAA satellite suggests that vegetation conditions have increased since the last ten-day period and remain in quite good condition in the southern part of Kayes, Koulikoro, and Segou regions and in the Sikasso region and the southwest Mopti. Although rainfall in these areas was below the normal ten-day amounts, available moisture was enough to meet crop water requirements.

Millet, sorghum, and rice are at the stem elongation stage, maize is at heading stage, and groundnut and cotton are flowering. Crops are generally in good condition, although wilting has been observed at a few locations in the Galo, Fana, and Mopti zones. In northwest Kayes, North Koulikoro, and Segou and in Mopti, Tombouctou, and Gao regions, vegetation coverage still remains low and sometimes in poor condition. Cereals are tillering.

Pasture Conditions

In general, pasture conditions are quite satisfactory in spite of grasshopper infestations in the Mopti area. Water is available in sufficient quantities at cattle watering places.

Prospects for the Next Ten-Day Period

Actual soil moisture and expected precipitation for the next ten-day period are very likely to meet crop water requirements in farmlands located in the southern half of the country—that is, below the latitude of Kayes.

REFERENCES

Eagleman, J. R. 1971. An experimentally derived model for actual evapotranspiration. Agric. Meteorol. 8(4/5):385-394.

Forest, F. 1974. Bilan hydrique efficace et prospective décadaire des besoins en eau des cultures pluviales en zone soudano-sahélienne. Ministère Français de la Coopération.

Forest, F.; and B. Lidon. 1984. Influence of the rainfall pattern in fluctuations in an intensified sorghum crop yield. In ICRISAT. Agrometeorology of Sorghum and Millet in the Semiarid Tropics: Proceedings of the International Symposium. ICRISAT Center, Patancheru, India.

Franquin, P. 1973. Analyse agroclimatique en régions tropicales: Méthode des intersections et periode fréquentielle de végétation. L'Agronomie Tropical 28, no. 6-7.

Frère, M.; and G. F. Popov. 1979. Agrometeorological crop monitoring and forecasting. FAO Plant Production and Protection Paper No. 17. FAO, Rome.

Gray, T. I., Jr.; and D. G. McCrary. 1981. The Environmental Vegetation Index, a tool potentially useful for arid land management. AgRISTARS Report EW-N1-04076, JSC-17132.

Meteorologie et IER. 1984. Contribution à l'étude des dates de semis des princpales cultures pluviales au Mali. Comité National de la Recherche Agronomique.

CHAPTER 10
MONITORING DROUGHT IN AUSTRALIA

Michael J. Coughlan

INTRODUCTION

What is Drought?

A simple answer to the question "What is drought?" is that drought is a protracted lack of adequate water from established sources to meet the needs of users. Although this answer may seem trivial, it embodies the two most important aspects of defining a resource or commodity problem—supply and demand. For the most part, the commonest established source is recent rainfall, although ground water or large surface water storages act as important buffers in many localities when rainfall does not meet expectations or demand.

A further aspect of drought that needs to be clarified is the distinction between aridity and drought. Coughlan and Lee (1978) distinguished them in the following way: *aridity* implies a high probability of rainfall for a given period below an arbitrary but low threshold, while *drought* implies a low probability of rainfall for a given period below an arbitrarily low threshold.

If one accepts these definitions, is it meaningless to talk about drought occurring in those regions of the world where the expectation of useful rainfall is very low—namely, the arid or permanent desert regions? Much of the natural flora and fauna in these regions is very sensitive to water availability, and when rain does fall, their reproductive processes are rapid and prolific. However, the indigenous plants and animals are so well adapted that either complete or at least reproductive dormancy sets in on a return to dry conditions. The period of dormancy may last in some species for many years. In contrast, the reliability of the rainfall is generally far too low in such regions to sustain human activity dependent on supplies from this source.

There are similar factors to consider for those periods during a year when rainfall expectations are very low. Australia, along with many other parts of the world straddling the temperate climatic zones, has large areas with highly seasonal rainfall. On occasions there may be successive years of seasonal rainfall failure in these areas. Whether such multiyear failures should be classed as separate droughts with periods of normal seasonal aridity in between or as one continuous drought is not at all clear. Although this consideration and the others discussed above might seem a trifle pedantic, they are important when one is attempting to assess drought risk, catalogue its incidence, and examine its causes.

In this paper I shall describe how in Australia, the National Climate Centre, a part of the national weather service, monitors drought and operates a national drought watch service. Some attention is given also to the spinoffs from the data base developed to operate this service. These spinoffs enable past droughts to be cataloged, assist in the development of strategies for future droughts, and may provide guidelines for tactical decisions to combat a drought in progress.

Deciles as Drought Indicators

There have been many attempts to develop objective methods of delineating drought-affected regions. Hounam (1970) has tabulated many of these; some are based on simple input parameters such as rainfall or rainfall with mean temperature, while others are based on additional inputs related to water availability or use, such as soil moisture and evapotranspiration. Some of the more complex measures of drought require observations or at least estimations of parameters that are often not routinely observed over wide enough areas to monitor drought effectively. This is certainly the case in relatively sparsely populated Australia. Although a generalized, objective definition of drought and an effective means of delineating its boundaries remain elusive, it is probably fair to say that a prolonged period of significantly below-average rainfall in an area that does not rely entirely on supplies from deep subsurface aquifers or irrigation systems with distant sources remains the best single indicator of drought or potential drought.

The Australian Bureau of Meteorology has for the past twenty years maintained a routine nationwide drought watch system based on a simple index of rainfall deficiency as a primary indicator of water shortage. This terminology was adopted as an acknowledgment that there are more factors to be considered in declaring an area drought stricken than a shortage of rainfall.

Unlike temperature or pressure, rainfall is discontinuous in time and space and its statistical description is rather complex. The most widely recognized measure of central tendency, an essential start for determining any significant shortfall, is the mean (often called the average or normal). In the case of a Gaussian or normal frequency distribution, the mean and the standard deviation as a measure of dispersion are sufficient to describe the distribution completely and to calculate the probability of occurrence of values within a given range. It is common, however, for frequency distributions of rainfall totals not to be normally distributed, particularly in semiarid areas. In such cases one has to resort to using third-order statistics, a transformation of the data, or a different type of theoretical distribution altogether. The normality of a rainfall frequency distribution also tends to decrease with decreasing integration period.

An alternative approach is to use some form of nonparametric method to describe the distribution of rainfall totals. Gibbs and Maher (1967) advocated a system that uses the limits of percentiles, or more specifically the limits of the decile values derived from the cumulative frequency curve. Thus the first decile sets the limit of rainfall for a specified period which has not been exceeded by 10% of the observed totals over previous periods with the same start and end dates. The fifth decile, or median, is the 50% limit; the expectation is that the ninth decile will only be exceeded at a particular location on 10% of all occasions; and so on. Based on a comparison with a comprehensive catalogue of past droughts in Australia prepared by Foley (1957), Gibbs and Maher (1967) decided on the following criteria as a basis for the establishment of the Australian Drought Watch System. Essentially, a *severe deficiency* exists at a location if the rainfall for a period of three or more months does not exceed the fifth-percentile value for that period. A *serious deficiency* exists if the rainfall total lies between the fifth percentile and tenth percentile (first decile). Rainfall is considered to be *average* if it exceeds the third decile and is less than the seventh decile. Figure 1 illustrates the relationship between actual decile values and decile ranges for a normal distribution.

THE AUSTRALIAN DROUGHT WATCH SYSTEM

Lee (1978) has described the System in some detail and only its essential features will be reviewed here. The System relies on the existence of a data set of monthly rainfall totals for about 600 observing stations that record and report their rainfall totals each day. Stations were selected on the basis of optimizing the areal density and the length and quality of the past record. Also included are the records of 107 rainfall district averages, the boundaries of which are shown in Fig. 2. The network of stations for each district is such that it allows a representative total for the district to be calculated as a simple average on a weekly and monthly basis from the daily telegraphic reports. Since the distribution of stations in the larger and more sparsely populated districts is generally poor, the level of activity for which the Drought Watch System is designed is of course commensurately lower. Much of the analysis is computerized but a key work-

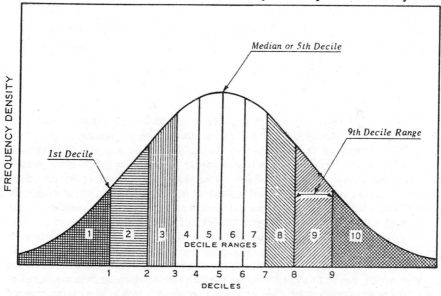

Fig. 1 Deciles and decile ranges for a theoretical normal distribution.

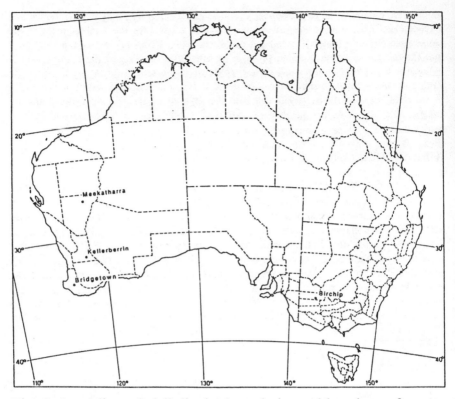

Fig. 2 Australian rainfall district boundaries and locations of towns mentioned in the text.

ing tool is a set of tables of the decile values for one-month to twelve-month totals, starting any month for each station and district derived from the historical record.

The drought watch consists of two phases. The first phase involves an examination around the middle of the month of the district totals to date and an assessment to identify those areas with the potential for serious or severe deficiency by the end of the month. Essentially, this involves looking forward in time in all areas and assessing the amount of rainfall required to meet the specified criteria for rainfall deficiencies. Areas highlighted by this process are flagged for detailed analysis during the second phase after the end of the month using individual station data. Detailed maps delineating affected areas and tables summarizing the rainfall for selected stations during the month are prepared and published. Rainfall deficiency periods, once established over a period of three months, can be delineated over well-defined areas, which are then monitored as the deficiency extends to four, five, or more months. A watch is kept throughout the month on the weekly and, if possible, daily figures to eliminate any marginal areas that receive sufficient cumulative rainfall to exceed the first decile.

A typical drought review map is presented in Fig. 3. It is not uncommon to have several review maps covering more than one overlapping period, since the minimum three-month period of deficiency below the first decile may be triggered in different locations at different times. Further, areas may also move out of deficiency conditions at different times. It becomes a matter of judgment as to the mix of analyses to actually include in the review.

Identifying the triggering point of a rainfall deficiency period for a location is relatively straightforward; defining the break of a drought is less so. Obviously any major weather system producing significant rain may unequivocally eliminate deficiencies. Often, however, the rain may fall sporadically and in varying amounts. The criteria used in the Australian Drought Watch System to signal a break in dry conditions are as follows:

1. Rainfall of the past month already amounts to "average" or better (above the third decile) for the three-month period commencing that month—a heavy rainfall break.

2. Rainfall for the past three months is above average for that period (i.e., above the seventh decile)—a gradual break.

The specification of criteria for drought declarations and drought breaks is no easy task. In Australia, state government usually has this responsibility. Given the

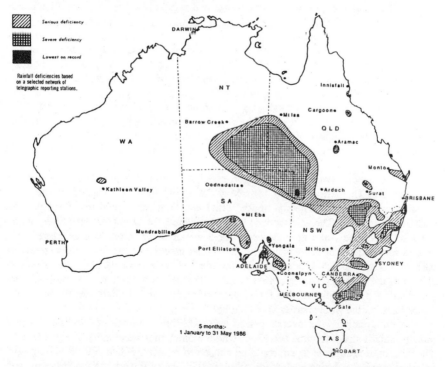

Fig. 3 Typical rainfall deficiency analysis appearing in the Australian Drought Watch Review.

climatic diversity within Australia as a whole, some strong local gradients of rainfall, and a multitude of nonmeteorological factors, there is probably little value in attempting to draw up generalized or uniform criteria (Wilhite, et al., 1985). The criteria adopted as part of the Drought Watch System are not intended to perform this task; they serve only to alert the nation of a potential drought and to monitor the progress of a drought. However, the system is inherently flexible and it would be no major task to operate it with different criteria for a whole range of drought-sensitive activities within an agricultural, hydrological, or general industrial context.

CATALOGING DROUGHTS

Drought by its very nature has an extended lifetime, unlike many of the other natural hazards that beset mankind. A tornado can wreak its havoc in a few minutes, a hurricane in a few hours, and floods over periods from minutes to days. Drought is a slow and insidious process; it may affect only a small area in one year or half a continent in another. In a country the size of Australia, drought may be ending in one part but beginning to take hold in another. Droughts may last for one season or extend over several and, depending on one's definition or perception, may linger on for years.

The cataloging of droughts therefore is a very subjective process unless one is able to quantify the demand side of the drought equation and to measure at least the rainfall, the predominant input on the supply side (Coughlan, 1985). As we have intimated, quantifying the demand side is the more difficult of these tasks. The introduction of new technology, disease, excess rainfall, fluctuating export markets, and even political decisions can also affect the level of outputs from industries that are sensitive to drought. However, using the data base set up for the Drought Watch System, it ought to be possible to develop a method for cataloging past droughts that is based on criteria set with a particular industry in mind. It should be noted that the efficacy of any objective method will be limited by the available data. Adequate Australian rainfall data for this purpose are available for the period since the establishment of the national weather service in 1908.

By way of example, a catalogue of winter/spring droughts has been prepared for Australia. The period chosen, from May through October, corresponds to the major cereal growing season. The six-month period was first subdivided into three periods, each of two months. These subperiods might be related, for example, to the times of germination, dormancy, and growth period for a winter cereal crop such as wheat. The criteria for adequate or inadequate rainfall, termed successes or failures, respectively, in each of the two-month subperiods and for the full six-month period were arbitrarily chosen as the tenth percentiles or first deciles. That is, for May-June, the criterion is the first decile for May-June rainfall for all years of record, and similarly for the other subperiods and for the whole period May-October.

In principle, the overall period could be any number of successive whole months, subdivided into three periods of whole months (not necessarily of equal length). The criteria, it is stressed again, could be chosen to reflect the demands of any drought-sensitive enterprise during each of the subperiods. Further, the criteria might just as easily be a specified amount of rain as a statistically determined limit such as the first decile.

The data set used is the district average rainfall totals referred to previously, the boundaries of which are shown in Fig. 2 (1913 to the present). The data were examined on a district/year basis to determine the number of times that the chosen criteria were not met, using the following principles:

1. If the six-month period registered a failure in any year, the number of two-month subperiod failures was included.

2. If the six-month period registered an overall success (exceeded the first decile), but at least two of the subperiods were failures, the number was included.

The total number of counts meeting either of the two conditions for each district were plotted on a geographical background for all years of record and contoured to give an idea of the intensity and extent of the rainfall deficiencies. Some examples of the maps are given in Fig. 4. The total affected area was also calculated and expressed as a percentage of the continent as a whole. The years in which drought affected more than 25% of the continent are shown in Table 1. It is stressed again that these figures refer to winter/spring droughts only. It is probable that in some years, drought may have taken hold in the preceding months or continued, as in the case of the 1982-83 drought, into the following summer/fall months. Further, the calculations of areal extent were made using whole districts, some of which are quite large. It would be a significantly larger task to redefine the district boundaries or use individual station data to prepare a catalogue or chronology of drought using this or any other objective method based on rainfall statistics.

PROBABILITY OF DROUGHT

Rainfall Reliability

If there is a high expectation of adequate rainfall, then inadequate rainfall is an infrequent situation—just as the occurrence of adequate rainfall is an infrequent situation when there is a high expectation of inadequate rain. This begs the question of what is meant by *adequate*—which is determined largely by the particular enterprise in mind. The notion of rainfall reliability is perhaps best illustrated by examples.

For the sake of argument, let it be assumed that any enterprise will have a satisfactory year if winter rainfall is at least 75% of the median rainfall. In the Meekatharra area, a small town in the arid zone of Western Australia (Fig. 2), the probability, based on past records, of receiving less than 75% of the median rainfall is about 26%. That is, if an enterprise were set up on this basis, one year in four could be expected to be unsatisfactory. The figures for Kellerberrin, a town in the center of the Western Australia wheat belt, are 14%, or one year in seven. Still further south, at Bridgetown (a town in a relatively high winter rainfall zone), the probability of an unsatisfactory year is 12%, or one year in eight. Naturally, the absolute amounts of rainfall are quite different in each area and the respective enterprises will vary accordingly.

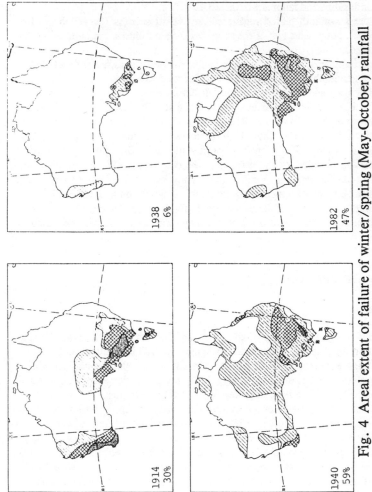

Fig. 4 Areal extent of failure of winter/spring (May-October) rainfall for indicated years. Single hatching denotes failure of season overall, including one two-month period or failure only of two subperiods; double hatching indicates a failure of season and two subperiods; stippling shows a failure of season and all three subperiods (Coughlan, 1985).

1938
6%

1982
47%

1914
30%

1940
59%

**Table 1
Calendar Years in Which the Area of Winter/Spring (May-Oct.)
Droughts in Australia Exceeded 25% of the Continent**

Year	% of Continent Affected
1940	59%
1961	56%
1982	47%
1946	46%
1929	37%
1944	36%
1914	30%
1967	29%
1972	29%

Assessment of Drought Probabilities

Calculations of the above kind can be taken a little further to make more detailed assessments of drought probabilities. The following approach is particularly relevant to areas of high seasonality in rainfall (Coughlan and Lee, 1978). In the Kellerberrin area, approximately 75% of the annual rainfall is registered during the six months from April through September, corresponding again roughly to the major growing season for wheat.

For the sake of convenience, the first decile or 90% exceedance value is again adopted as the basic criterion for success or failure of the growing season. However, simply using this criterion for the entire six-month period is inadequate since it is possible that most of this rain could fall in, say, April and May, with virtually no rain during the remaining four months of the growing season. Although the six-month total would be in excess of the first decile, it is clear that stress within the crop could result from such a skewed temporal distribution of the rainfall. As a refinement, the six months may be divided into three two-month subperiods. Each subperiod may now be examined against a specific threshold.

To objectively assess the threshold for each of the two-month subperiods, the first decile of the six-month period is apportioned by the ratio of the two-month means to the six-month means. For Kellerberrin, the figures are shown in Table 2.

From the decile tables referred to above, for each of the two-month subperiods it is possible to estimate the probability of success or failure to meet the respective threshold. For illustrative purposes, probability curves (Fig. 5) have been drawn up from the decile tables. From these curves, the probabilities of failure in the two-month periods are 0.30, 0.14, and 0.22, respectively, the corresponding probabilities of success being 0.70, 0.86, and 0.78.

The total array of combinations of successes (acceptable or good rainfall) and failures (inadequate or poor rainfall) is shown in Table 3 with the calculated probability for each combination. A notional expected crop response is suggested in the final

Table 2
Statistical Data for Growing Season Rainfall at Kellerberrin

Six-month mean April-Sept.	244 mm
90% exceedance value April-Sept. (90,6)	162 mm
Two-month mean April-May	64 mm
Two-month mean June-July	111 mm
Two-month mean Aug.-Sept.	68 mm
Ratio April-May to April-Sept. (r_1)	.27
Ratio June-July to April-Sept. (r_2)	.45
Ratio Aug-Sept. to April-Sept. (r_3)	.28
April-May threshold r_1 x (90,6)	42 mm
June-July threshold r_2 x (90,6)	74 mm
Aug-Sept. threshold r_3 x (90,6)	45 mm

Table 3
Distribution of Probabilities for the Eight Possible Combinations of Subseasonal Outcomes in Growing Season Rainfall at Kellerberrin

EARLY SEASON	MID-SEASON	FINISH	TOTAL CHANCE	CROP
Good	Good	Good	47%	Good +
Good	Good	Poor	13%	Fair#
Good	Poor	Good	8%	Fair#
Good	Poor	Poor	2%	Poor-
Poor	Good	Good	20%	Fair#
Poor	Good	Poor	6%	Poor-
Poor	Poor	Good	3%	Poor-
Poor	Poor	Poor	1%	Poor-

column. These figures can be further summarized to suggest a 47% chance of a good crop (+), 41% chance of a fair crop (#), and 12% chance of a significant crop failure (-). As a basis of comparison between wheat-growing areas, the calculations done for Keller-berrin have been carried out with similar results for Birchip in northwest Victoria (Fig. 2), both summarized in Table 4.

The analysis can be extended. If, for example, there was a complete failure of rains during the first one or even two months of the growing seasons, an assessment of the probabilities for the distribution of the same basic amount of rainfall can be made. The recalculated probabilities for the same two towns for growing seasons delayed by one and two months are given in Table 5.

The effect of the seasonality of rainfall in the Western Australia wheat belt in comparison to the more evenly distributed rainfall in the Victoria wheat belt is clearly

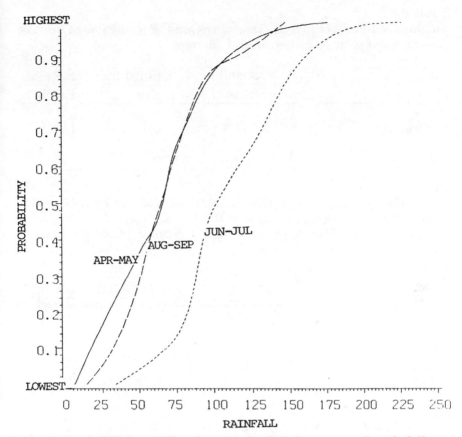

Fig. 5 Probability profiles for accumulated two-month rainfalls as indicated for Kellerberrin, Western Australia. End points of curves are the highest and lowest accumulated rainfall totals recorded for each two-month period.

evident in the higher probabilities of a poor result with an early failure in seasonal rain at Kellerberrin. Since the wettest six months in Birchip start in May, the probability of a good result actually increases there with a one-month delay and is still higher after a two-month delay. Obviously, other indirect factors must be considered in the event of a late start for the seasonal rains, but the concept provides an objective starting point at least for an overall evaluation of a final crop yield.

FORWARD ASSESSMENT OF RAINFALL DEFICIENCIES

Using many of the concepts employed in the Drought Watch System and the other analyses outlined above, Lee (1980) proposed the idea of a forward assessment, up

Table 4
Summarized Probabilities of Obtaining Good, Fair, or Poor Growing Season Rainfall at Kellerberrin and Birchip

Location	Probability of Notional Seasonal Result		
	Good	Fair	Poor-Nil
Kellerberrin	47%	41%	12%
Birchip	47%	40%	13%

Table 5
Summarized Probabilities of Obtaining Good, Fair, or Poor Growing Season Rainfall at Kellerberrin and Birchip, Calculated on the Basis of One and Two Month Failures to the Onset of Growing Season Rains

Location/ Delay	Probability of Delayed Season Results		
	Good	Fair	Poor-Nil
Kellerberrin			
One Month	43%	42%	15%
Two Month	28%	45%	29%
Birchip			
One Month	52%	38%	10%
Two Month	49%	39%	12%

to several months, of the probability of an area being in a rainfall-deficient situation. The criteria for serious deficiencies (the first deciles) are known for periods that extend into the future. Knowing the amounts of rainfall already received and making the assumption that there will be no significant change in the rainfall profile, it is a simple matter of subtraction to arrive at the amount necessary to exceed any specified criteria. Given these amounts and the probability profiles for the appropriate periods, it is therefore only a simple matter to evaluate the probability of exceeding or failing to exceed the criteria. When carried out on a district-by-district or station-by-station basis, analyses mapping the probabilities can be prepared. The technique is currently being evaluated and further refined by the Australian National Climate Centre, and the details of the approach will be presented elsewhere.

It should be stressed that the technique is not a true forecast in the generally accepted meteorological sense but, in addition to an intrinsic value of its own, the technique should provide a benchmark against which more physically based forecasts could be tested. Further, if a seasonal forecast based on the Southern Oscillation/Australian rainfall connection (see, for example, the paper by Nicholls in this volume) were to be made, it would be a straightforward matter to run the statistical assessment on data that have been stratified to include only those years believed to be more appropriate. A confident forecast of below-average seasonal rain based on an expected major swing in the Southern Oscillation, for example, would suggest *a priori* that the statistical forward assessments ought to be calculated only on those data below the mean (or median), or, better still, if sufficient data were available, only on those years when similar swings were observed.

CONCLUSIONS

The Australian Drought Watch System, despite its implicitly simple approach and its reliance on rainfall alone as an indicator of drought, has proved to be an effective tool for alerting the nation to incipient drought conditions and monitoring the course of extant drought. Further, the principles involved have provided several spinoffs, which have enabled past droughts to be objectively cataloged and probabilities of future droughts to be estimated. Like most statistical forecasts based solely on past data, its success lies in the principle that there will be no imminent significant change in the frequency distribution of the data being processed. There will be much to concern us if, as feared by some, this assumption will be proved wrong in the decades to come.

ACKNOWLEDGMENTS

I would like to extend thanks to Mr. Dan Lee, who has been responsible for much of the work in the establishment of the Australian Drought Watch System and who has provided valuable assistance in the preparation of this paper.

REFERENCES

Coughlan, M. J. 1985. Drought in Australia. pp. 129-149. In Natural Disasters in Australia. Proceedings of the Ninth AATS Invitation Symposium, Sydney, Australia. Australian Academy of Technological Sciences, Melbourne.

Coughlan, M. J.; and D. M. Lee. 1978. The assessment of drought risk in Northern Australia. In G. Pickup, ed. Natural Hazards Management in Northern Australia. North Australia Research Unit, Australian National University, Darwin.

Foley, J. C. 1957. Droughts in Australia: A review of records from the earliest years of settlement to 1955. Bulletin No. 43, Commonwealth Bureau of Meteorology, Melbourne.

Gibbs, W. J.; and J. S. Maher. 1967. Rainfall deciles as drought indicators. Bulletin No. 48, Commonwealth Bureau of Meteorology, Melbourne.

Hounam, C. E. 1970. Six lectures delivered at a seminar on drought (Lima, Peru). Working Paper No. 131, Commonwealth Bureau of Meteorology, Melbourne.

144

Lee, D. M. 1978. Australian Drought Watch System. pp. 173-208. In M. T. Hinchey, ed. Proceedings of the Symposium on Drought in Botswana. Botswana Society, Gaborone.

Lee, D. M. 1980. On monitoring rainfall deficiencies in semi-arid desert areas. pp.143-151. In J. Mabbutt and S. M. Berkowiz. The Threatened Dry Lands: Regional and Systematic Studies of Desertification. School of Geography, University of New South Wales, Sydney.

Wilhite, D. A.; M. H. Glantz; and N. J. Rosenberg. 1985. Government response to drought in the United States: Lessons from the mid-1970s. Part 5. Drought response in the United States and Australia: A comparative analysis. CAMaC Progress Report 85-5. Center for Agricultural Meteorology and Climatology, University of Nebraska-Lincoln.

CHAPTER 11
SATELLITE REMOTE SENSING OF DROUGHT CONDITIONS

Compton J. Tucker and Samuel N. Goward

INTRODUCTION

The definitions of drought are varied, but they usually involve a deficiency of precipitation and diminished plant growth and development. Although many definitions of drought exist (Wilhite and Glantz, 1985; reprinted in this volume), we will define *drought* as a period of reduced plant growth, vis-a-vis the historical average, caused by reduced precipitation. Satellite remote sensing can be used to quantify the photosynthetic capacity of the terrestrial surface. The ability to use satellite data to detect drought conditions is based on the spectral manifestation of reduced photosynthetic capacity, which is associated with precipitation shortfalls. By analyzing several years of satellite data that quantify the photosynthetic capacity of plant canopies, we can make comparisons between or among years in terms of the satellite-measured estimates of photosynthetic capacity. Reductions from average conditions provide the means to substantiate the occurrence of drought. Our methodology for identifying and quantifying drought is thus based on the assumption that drought results in a decrease in the photosynthetic capacity of vegetation, and this can be detected and quantified with satellite data. We will provide examples from sub-Saharan Africa to illustrate this over a three-year period.

Green plant canopies are highly absorptive of incident visible region radiation (0.4-0.7 μm) as a consequence of plant pigment absorption, and they are highly reflective of near-infrared radiation (0.7-1.1 μm) as a result of scattering and no absorption (Knipling, 1970; Woolley, 1971). Combinations of visible and near-infrared reflected radiation can be used to estimate the intercepted fraction of photosynthetically active radiation (Asrar, et al., 1984, 1985; Hatfield, et al., 1984; Kumar and Monteith, 1982; Daughtry, et al., 1983; Sellers, 1985; Wiegand and Richardson, 1984). Sellers (1985) has shown how visible and near-infrared radiation are indicators of minimum canopy resistance and photosynthetic capacity but are poor indicators of leaf area index or biomass. Monteith (1977) proposed that net photosynthesis is directly related to the integral of the intercepted photosynthetically active radiation (IPAR). Experimental support for this has been reported by Goward, et al. (1985), and Tucker, et al. (1981 and 1985).

Vegetation IPAR can be estimated from polar-orbiting meteorological satellite data. These data can be processed and combined to form largely cloud-free composite images representing the time series of photosynthetic capacity and minimum canopy resistance while minimizing degrading influences such as atmospheric aerosols and off-nadir scanning effects (Fraser and Kaufman, 1985; Holben and Fraser, 1984; Holben, 1986). IPAR time series can be formed with data from the National Oceanic and Atmospheric Administration's advanced very high resolution radiometer (AVHRR) sensor, since this data source obtains global data daily with the required visible and near-infrared spectral bands. Landsat and SPOT data are not viable sources for IPAR time series data since the repeat frequency of observation is approximately once every sixteen days.

EXPERIMENTAL APPROACH

We have selected sub-Saharan Africa to illustrate our use of NOAA AVHRR data to identify and quantify areas within the semiarid zone which are prone to drought conditions. This area lies roughly between 20° W and 50° E longitude and from 5° N to 20° N latitude. It includes portions of the Sahara Desert as well as the Sahel zone, the Sudan zone, and the Saharo-Sahelian and Sudano-Sahelian transition zones of Africa. The mean annual precipitation varies from 100 mm/yr in the Sahara Desert to approximately 1,000 mm/yr in the southern boundary of the Sudan zone (Le Houreou, 1980; White, 1983). These areas have a monomodal period during which rain (varying in length from 1.5 months in the Saharo-Sahelian zone to 3.5 months in the Sudan zone) may occur. The rainy season begins in the south in June/July and usually continues into October. Within the Sahel zone, August and September are usually the months of peak photosynthetic activity. Consequently, we have chosen to compare the maximum satellite-derived estimate of IPAR from this area for August and September, 1983-85.

Data from the AVHRR sensor on NOAA-7 were used from 1983 to 1984 while similar data from NOAA-9 were used in 1985. AVHRR channel 1 (0.55-0.68 µm) and channel 2 (0.73-1.1 µm) were used to produce a normalized difference vegetation index of (2-1)/(2+1). AVHRR channel 5 (11.5-12.5 µm) was used as a cloud mask where pixels cooler than 12° C were labeled as clouds. Daily data from August and September of 1983-1985 were mapped to a Mercator map projection with a grid cell size of approximately 7 km. After mapping, the data were inspected and registered to a common geographical reference. Data for the two months were combined to yield a seasonal maximum value for each year, since the peak of the Sahelian growing season occurs in August or September (Le Houreou, 1980). The data for each year were compared for this three-year period (Fig. 1).

Figure 1 shows that of the three years, 1984 showed the greatest deficiency of maximum photosynthetic capacity for the Sahel zone and Sudano-Sahelian transition zone. In general, 1985 was better than 1983, an assessment that agrees with precipitation data (Nicholson, 1986). Caution must be exercised when attempting to compare satellite data to, or complement satellite data with, measured or estimated precipitation data, because of variable rain use efficiency. Rain use efficiency, defined as the unit of biomass per area per unit of precipitation per year (kg/ha/mm/yr), has been reported as 0.5 kg/ha/mm/yr for depleted subdesert ecosystems; 3-6 kg/ha/mm/yr for arid and semiarid grazing lands; in excess of 10 kg/ha/mm/yr for well-managed grasslands; and up to about 30 kg/ha/mm/yr for heavily fertilized small plots (Le Houreou, 1984). Not only is the amount, type, and distribution of the precipitation important, but site conditions such

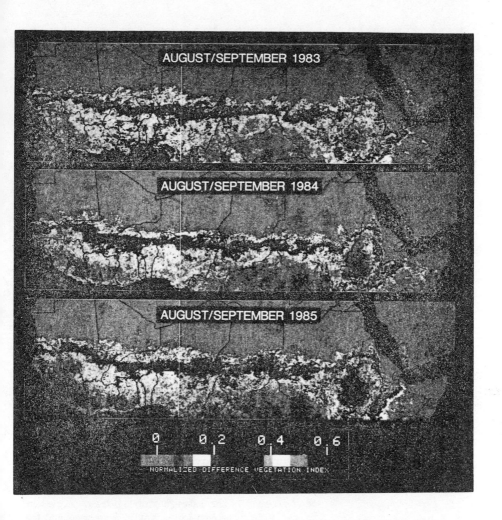

Fig. 1 The normalized difference vegetation index (NDVI) data for sub-Saharan Africa for the months of August-September 1983-85. The maximum NDVI value was selected for each grid cell element from daily 4 km AVHRR data for these two months. We use the NDVI data as an estimate of the intercepted photosynthetically active radiation, which Sellers (1985) has reported as representing the photosynthetic capacity. Sub-Saharan Africa experienced severe drought in 1984; conditions were somewhat better in 1983; and conditions in 1985 were much improved over 1984.

as seed stocks, percolation, runoff characteristics, and vegetation type must also be considered (Le Houreou, 1984). For example, rain use efficiencies from six stations in northern Senegal have been reported to vary from 4.28 in 1981, to 3.31 in 1982, to 2.52 in 1983, to 0.93 in 1984 (Tucker, et al., 1985).

The sub-Saharan Africa maximum normalized difference vegetation index (NDVI) data from August-September of 1983, 1984, and 1985 appear in Fig. 1. These data document the fact that 1985 was the best year and 1984 was the worst year of this three-year period. The gray-tone images in Fig. 1 were produced from a color image; thus the same gray tones can appear more than once (refer to the NDVI scale at the bottom of Fig. 1). The original color-coded representation of Fig. 1 represents an increasing gradient of our satellite index from north to south. Consequently, readers should not confuse the same gray tones from different strata in Fig. 1. For example, the lightest tones appear in two strata separated by the darkest strata. The band of lightest tones *above* the darkest strata represent NDVI values of approximately 0.15-0.17, while the band of lightest tones *below* the darkest tone strata represent NDVI values of approximately 0.41-0.43.

Figure 1 shows that August-September 1983 was significantly better than August-September 1984 in central and eastern Mali and in western Niger. August-September 1985 was significantly better than August-September 1984 throughout Sahelian Africa. The greatest improvements were in eastern Sudan and eastern Chad, followed by northern Senegal, southern Mauritania, and southern Niger. To express the between-year variation in the growing season maximum NDVI from these years of data, we have subtracted 1984 data from first 1983 data and then 1985 data and expressed the difference as a digital image (Fig. 2). A more detailed comparison between 1984 and 1985 for sub-Saharan Africa, including 1 km AVHRR comparisons for Senegal, Mali, Niger, and Sudan, can be found in Tucker, et al. (1986).

Figure 2 provides a description of relative change between years. In terms of primary production, 1984 showed the greatest deficiency of the three years studied. It is our opinion that data such as those we have presented, when available for multiyear periods, will provide the means to identify areas of drought in sub-Saharan Africa within a few days of the end of that year's growing season. Suitable AVHRR data for these purposes exist back to mid-1979 and efforts are now underway at the NASA/Goddard Space Flight Center to process and organize this multiyear, continental-scale data base.

CONCLUSIONS

We have proposed a satellite-based methodology for inferring deficiencies in photosynthetic capacity of terrestrial vegetation at continental and regional scales. To illustrate this, we selected the maximum NDVI value from August-September for three years, using 4 km data. As such, we were only comparing the maximum photosynthetic capacities from three years. Another approach using the same data sources is to compare the time integral of the NDVI data (Tucker, et al., 1985). This provides a comparison between the summed photosynthetic capacities of the growing seasons in question. Recent work in this area supports the hypothesis that time integrals of NDVI data are directly related to primary production (Goward, et al., 1985; Tucker, et al., 1985).

Fig. 2. Difference images formed by subtracting 1984 data from first 1983 (a) and then 1985 (b). The intensity of white tones in these images is proportional to the magnitude of the photosynthetic capacity differences between the years presented in Fig. 1. Note that some areas were markedly different while other areas showed minor or no differences.

150

The data presented in Figs. 1 and 2 are intended to represent an initial indication of the promise of drought monitoring using satellite imagery.

REFERENCES

Asrar, G.; M. Fuchs; E. T. Kanemasu; and J. L. Hatfield. 1984. Estimating absorbed photosynthetic radiation and leaf area index from spectral reflectance in wheat. Agron. J. 76:300-306.

Asrar, G.; E. T. Kanemasu; G. P. Miller; and R. L. Weiser. 1985. Light interception and leaf area index estimates from measurements of grass canopy reflectance. IEEE Trans. Geo. Sci. Remote Sens. (in press).

Daughtry, C. S. T.; K. P. Gallo; and M. E. Bauer. 1983. Spectral estimates of solar radiation intercepted by corn canopies. Agron. J. 75:527-531.

Fraser, R. S.; and Y. J. Kaufman. 1985. The relative importance of aerosol scattering and absorption in remote sensing. IEEE Trans. Geo. Sci. Remote Sens. GE-23:625-633.

Goward, S. N.; C. J. Tucker; and D. G. Dye. 1985. North American vegetation patterns observed with the NOAA-7 advanced very high resolution radiometer. Vegetatio 64:3-14.

Hatfield, J. L.; G. Asrar; and E. T. Kanemasu. 1984. Intercepted photosynthetically active radiation in wheat canopies estimated by spectral reflectance. Remote Sens. Environ. 14:65-76.

Holben, B. N. 1986. Characteristics of maximum value composite images from temporal AVHRR data. Int. J. Remote Sens. (in press).

Holben, B. N.; and R. S. Fraser. 1984. Red and near-infrared sensor response to off-nadir viewing. Int. J. Remote Sens. 5:145-160.

Knipling, E. B. 1970. Physical and physiological basis for the reflectance of visible and near-infrared radiation from vegetation. Remote Sens. Environ. 1:155-159.

Kumar, M.; and J. L. Monteith. 1982. Remote sensing of plant growth. pp. 133-144. In H. Smith, ed. Plants and the Daylight Spectrum. Academic, London.

Le Houreou, H. N. 1980. The rangelands of the Sahel. J. Range Manage. 33:41-46.

Le Houreou, H. N. 1984. Rain use efficiency: A unifying concept in arid-land ecology. J. Arid Environ. 7:1-35.

Monteith, J. L. 1977. Climate and the efficiency of crop production in Britain. Phil. Trans. Royal Soc. B-281:277-294.

Nicholson, S. E. 1986. The spatial coherence of African rainfall anomalies—inter-hemispheric teleconnections. J. Climate Appl. Met. (in press).

Sellers, P. J. 1985. Canopy reflectance, photosynthesis, and transpiration. Int. J. Remote Sens. 6:127-38.

Tucker, C. J.; B. N. Holben; J. E. Elgin; and J. E. McMurtrey. 1981. Remote sensing of total dry-matter accumulation in winter wheat. Remote Sens. Environ. 11:171-189.

Tucker, C. J.; C. L. Vanpraet; M. J. Sharman; and G. Van Ittersum. 1985. Satellite remote sensing of total herbaceous biomass production in the Senegalese Sahel: 1980-1984. Remote Sens. Environ. 17:233-249.

Tucker, C. J.; C. O. Justice; and S. D. Prince. 1986. Monitoring the grasslands of the Sahel: 1984-1985. Int. J. Remote Sens. (in press).

White, F. 1983. The Vegetation of Africa. UNESCO, Paris.

Wiegand, C. L.; and A. J. Richardson. 1984. Leaf area, light interception, and yield estimates from spectral components analysis. Agron. J. 76:543-548.

Wilhite, D. A.; and M. H. Glantz. 1985. Understanding the drought phenomenon: The role of definitions. Water Int. 10:111-120.

Woolley, J. T. 1971. Reflectance and transmittance of light by leaves. Plant Physiol. 47:656-662.

CHAPTER 12
AN OPERATIONAL EARLY WARNING AGRICULTURAL WEATHER SYSTEM

Norton D. Strommen and Raymond P. Motha

INTRODUCTION

Droughts are an important but often-ignored feature of the climate—until they occur. The rise and fall of civilizations have been linked to droughts of varying degrees of intensity or, more properly, a scarcity of food caused by drought. Droughts have existed since the beginning of recorded history, yet the impacts have changed significantly with time and societal structure (Mellor and Gavian, 1987). The nomadic people simply moved to new areas when food supplies became short. However, today most societies have established a permanent home area and have adapted to climate variability by changing customs and applying technology (irrigation, air conditioning, and so forth).

Over the years, national leaders have dealt with climate variability problems related to drought in many different ways. Yet today we cannot find many experts who can agree on a definition that adequately describes when a drought begins and ends, or what appropriate action should be taken. The disagreement is partially related to the many types of drought that can occur—hydrological, agricultural, economic, and so forth. This paper will deal with the application of known weather-plant responses to provide an early alert for potential deviations from normally expected crop development and crop yield potential, and will suggest how these data can be integrated into the nonmeteorologist user community. It is not the intent of this paper to develop an acceptable definition for drought or define the most appropriate actions to be taken.

We would like to begin by briefly describing some of the recent research efforts that have led to the creation of an operational global monitoring capability, the Joint Agricultural Weather Facility (JAWF), located at the U.S. Department of Agriculture (USDA) in Washington, D.C. JAWF's approach to crop assessment is the result of the collection and implementation of ideas assembled from several research efforts undertaken during the past thirty years. The facility is staffed by the National Oceanic and Atmospheric Administration's (NOAA) National Weather Service meteorologists and USDA's agricultural meteorologists. They prepare crop condition assessments and crop yield estimates, using weather data analysis, satellite imagery interpretation, and numerical weather prediction provided by NWS meteorologists and evaluations of current weather and historical climate data by USDA's agricultural meteorologists. Knowledge of year-to-year variability in weather provides a tool that can be used in the assessment of changing crop conditions and estimates of yield variability. The assessment information is used primarily in support of USDA's agricultural economics intelligence work, but it is also extensively used by the agribusiness community. JAWF's biggest single challenge is to convert voluminous amounts of weather data into information that can be easily understood by the department's nonmeteorological user community. Drought occurrences, because of their destructive impacts on crops, have become one of the major focuses of JAWF. However, short-term extreme weather anomalies also play an important role in crop yield fluctuations. These short-term events must be monitored closely to identify their potential impact, which may be as damaging as the longer-term drought occurrences.

Before examining how JAWF accomplishes its crop monitoring and yield assessment work, it is useful to look briefly at selected research programs from which JAWF personnel have been able to extract and modify many useful concepts in support of assessment work.

One of the best-known efforts to systematically attempt to portray drought as a simple index number for domestic use was begun in the early 1960s by W. C. Palmer (1965a). His basic idea was to develop a series of equations that would describe the soil moisture available for plants to use during the course of the growing season. Palmer looked on drought as an accounting problem: "The amount of precipitation required for the near-normal agricultural operation of the established economy of an area during some stated period is dependent on the average climate of the area and on the prevailing meteorological conditions both during and preceding the month or period in question." His initial effort resulted in the Palmer Drought Index (PDI) and later the companion Crop Moisture Index (CMI). These indexes have now been published weekly or monthly during the summer season in the Weekly Weather and Crop Bulletin (WWCB) since the mid-1960s. The WWCB, with some variation, has been published since 1872 and is JAWF's most visible public product for use in the United States and around the world. It has also been used as a model by many nations developing their own reports.

We will discuss some of the major strengths and weaknesses of the PDI and CMI, but time does not permit an exhaustive analysis. Some recent seasonal comparisons made with field soil moisture survey results have shown the Index values to be much better than might initially be expected (personal communication, Robert Shaw, Professor Emeritus, Iowa State University, Ames). The index numbers possess some unique qualities that account for their popularity. First and most important for operational work, they can be derived and updated in a timely and economical manner using the data generated by our current national meteorological observation network. The index numbers also lend themselves to a series of statistical analyses for frequency, intensity, and duration of dry or wet periods. The assumptions used to derive the indexes have been clearly spelled out (Palmer, 1965a). Palmer, during the developmental phase, also made extensive comparisons with available soil moisture totals taken by more traditional methods. A major concern was the assignment of a soil water holding capacity, to be represented by a single value for an entire climatic division. (A climatic division is a region with nearly homogeneous climatic elements; most states have been divided into seven to ten climatic divisions.) We know that soils are highly variable across a climatic division and appropriate caution is urged in using these indexes. Users will find that the PDI changes more slowly than the CMI and is actually a better indicator for hydrological purposes than it is for crop moisture stress conditions. Recognizing this problem in the PDI, Palmer made the modification that produced the CMI, which is responsive to the changes in soil moisture conditions that are reflected by stress placed on the more shallow-rooted crops (Palmer, 1965b).

Developmental work to further improve the PDI and CMI ended in 1973, but the calculations have continued, uninterrupted, to the present. Work has continued on several other approaches to create a soil moisture index that better describes moisture stress placed on crops and/or measures intensity of drought.

The Large Area Crop Inventory Experiment (LACIE), which began in 1974, provided the next opportunity to systematically pull together ideas and research results applicable to crop-climate responses. LACIE's goal was primarily to illustrate the many potential operational uses of remotely sensed data (National Aeronautics and Space Administration, 1978). The pre-LACIE work at Purdue's Laboratory for Applications of Remote Sensing (LARS) and other universities provided a basis for the remote sensing initiative and brought the National Aeronautics and Space Administration (NASA), NOAA, and USDA into an extended cooperative program. However, the application of standard meteorological observations like those by JAWF to monitor and assess changing crop conditions and estimate crop yields as the growing season progressed became a major accomplishment of LACIE. LACIE provided a unique multidiscipline-multiagency setting in which to pursue many interesting ideas on how to evaluate and quantify crop response to various climate-weather parameters. LACIE also resulted in a systematic evaluation of past research on crop-weather relationships and provided a focus for needed future research (National Aeronautics and Space Administration, 1978).

A major obstacle to achieving the proposed goals of the LACIE research was finding adequate historical data sets, both meteorological and agronomic. Thus, a major effort was initially directed to assembling sufficiently high-quality climatic and agronomic data sets for all the major wheat-growing areas of the world. In constructing the data sets for use in model development, it was necessary to place some restriction on the model development research to ensure that the types and quality of input data would be available in real time from the World Weather Watch/Global Telecommunications System (WWW/GTS) of the World Meteorological Organization (WMO). The WWW/GTS provides data only on a synoptic scale. A study was completed to evaluate potential yield model performance bias when operated on estimated input data derived from the synoptic scale WWW/GTS data system versus data estimates derived from a much denser observation network. The denser data network used in the study for comparison was the U. S. Cooperative Observer Network, with one or more stations per county. This provides at least a tenfold increase in data points versus the synoptic scale networks. Yield model estimates derived on data for a twenty-year period from the dense United States cooperative network were compared with results from estimated data using only synoptic reports. Statistically, no differences were found in the yield estimates derived from models driven by input weather estimates made using the different data sets (Sakamoto, et al., 1978).

Tests of various methods to estimate crop growth, soil moisture, and related crop stress were also completed. This work suggested that no one model approach, be it statistical, physiological, or phenological, was clearly superior when used in the wide range of crop yield models being tested. In short, a number of different approaches with varying degrees of complexity provided reasonable and acceptable indications of the soil moisture stress being placed on the plant, crop development rate, and ultimate yield reduction observed over large areas. It must also be pointed out that like the meteorological data, all the agronomic data have a degree of unknown error. However, the agronomic data, yield, phenological information, planting dates, and so forth represent the best and most accurate information available, and thus they are used for developmental purposes and verification of test results. By drawing on the knowledge gained in LACIE and the early phases of the Agricultural and Resources Inventory Survey Through Aerospace Remote Sensing (AgRISTARS) and by making necessary modifications, the operational program at JAWF has evolved over the last six years to its present capabilities. The AgRISTARS project extended the work concepts for yield modeling developed in LACIE for wheat to other crops, including corn, soybeans, cotton, flax, sunflowers, and rice (National Aeronautics and Space Administration, 1980, 1981).

The JAWF facility was established as a world agricultural weather information center in 1978, dedicated to serve the needs of USDA's economic intelligence work. Its primary function is to conduct a daily world agricultural weather watch and assess the impact of anomalous growing-season conditions on crop and livestock production. The National Weather Service's Climate Analysis Center (NWS/CAC) and USDA's National Agricultural Statistics Service (USDA/NASS) cooperate with the USDA's World Agricultural Outlook Board (USDA/WAOB) in operating JAWF. The unit is located at USDA headquarters. JAWF receives near-real time weather data from the global station network as well as products derived from station data and estimated satellite-derived meteorological data, used for outlook and situation work by USDA agencies. Quantified agricultural weather assessments are integrated into USDA's process of systematically updating international crop production estimates at USDA's monthly interagency world crop production meetings and special briefings. JAWF's specific tasks are to:

1. Continuously monitor regional agricultural weather patterns.
2. Synthesize information on crop areas, crop calendars, and cropping patterns.
3. Identify anomalous weather and provide initial qualitative crop impact assessments.
4. Utilize crop-weather relationships to quantify agricultural weather assessments.
5. Interact with agricultural economists and statisticians to integrate quantified yield analyses into the process of commodity production estimates.
6. Provide pertinent, timely information to the secretary of agriculture and USDA staff.
7. Disseminate informative summaries of international crop-weather assessments for release via the Weekly Weather and Crop Bulletin, USDA World Crop Production Report, press releases, and special publications.

The process by which these tasks are accomplished at JAWF is reviewed below.

AGRICULTURAL WEATHER ANALYSIS

Current weather information is obtained primarily from scheduled observation reports of surface conditions received via the Global Telecommunications System (GTS). Daily summaries of global precipitation and temperature from the World Meteorological Center (WMC) Suitland Computer Facility, surface and upper air charts, polar-orbiting GOES Meteosat and GMS satellite images, and automated near real-time meteorological data products are received and processed daily at JAWF for routine monitoring and briefing purposes. Station reports of precipitation and temperature in all agricultural areas are plotted daily for review at the regular briefings.

The emphasis of JAWF's analytical capability is on macroscale (regional) applications of agricultural meteorology; it does not attempt to do microscale (field-size) applications. In regional-scale applications, agronomic and meteorological data are limited and assumptions are required. These two important facts make it imperative that the professional staff ensure that the application does not overextend the informational integrity of the data and that it provides accurate interpretations of the results with due consideration of the underlying constraints. When developing assessments for crop supply and use statistics, an accurate assessment of the direction of crop yield deviations from initial projections several months before the final harvest statistics is often as important as estimating the yield potential during the harvest season. The error in potential yield forecasts should decrease as weather factors accumulate during phenological development. Significant contributions of weather to the yield potential often become apparent by the reproductive stage. Contributions to the yield potential can extend through the harvest season, however. In 1986, persistent and heavy rains during the grain maturation and harvest periods adversely affected both quantity and quality of the wheat crops in Canada and Argentina. Thus, cumulative seasonal effects must be carefully evaluated.

Although surface station data are sparse in some crop areas, agriculturally useful information has been obtained for crop assessment by rigorous monitoring of other upper-level meteorological observations, synoptic reports, and weather satellite imagery. The ancillary information, derived from surface- and upper-level synoptic reports and weather satellite products, is extremely important. Rain-producing convective cells can develop, reach maturity, and dissipate without being detected at station sites, regardless of the density of reporting networks. Synoptic reports provide a general overview of atmospheric conditions that may be conducive to random convective activity. Satellite imagery provides either qualitative or quantitative techniques for identifying cloud coverage as well as the distribution of precipitation over a crop area. Since locally heavy convective activity is a random phenomenon, the impact on regional crop yield potential can only be evaluated by proper monitoring of all available data and information throughout the growing season.

The recent acquisition of a digital weather satellite image system has substantially improved JAWF's capability to monitor global weather systems on a near-real time basis. The system ingests, processes, and stores imagery from GOES, METEOSAT, GMS, and polar-orbiting weather satellites. Images are continuously updated in specified loops that can be magnified, enhanced, or sectorized. This system is used to document weather events and to identify the extent of likely coverage within each crop area. Information is qualitative and is used to provide additional guidance in the weather assessment. Such features as IR temperatures and cloud brightness offer valuable tools in the analysis.

JAWF uses a variety of data products to tailor the global data base to regional agricultural weather assessments. A computer episodic events program monitors the daily global station network for conditions that may develop into yield-related anomalies and identifies stations meeting criteria for specific crop seasons. Episodes of hot and/or dry summer weather, extremely cold winter weather, and temperatures above/below the spring/autumn threshold values for dormancy are flagged. The duration, intensity, and coverage of anomalous weather episodes are factors to be considered for assessment preparation as well as cropping patterns and stages of crop development.

During the summer growing season in both hemispheres, agriculturally important parameters such as vapor pressure deficits (VPD) and potential evapotranspiration (PET) are computed. The vapor pressure deficit is defined as the difference between saturation vapor pressure and the observed vapor pressure at the existing temperature. High vapor pressure deficits (low relative humidities) occur frequently during the summer months, especially in semiarid to arid regions. Numerous agricultural areas are subjected to hot, dry air masses that are generated over large arid regions and advected into the crop area by strong winds. Vapor pressure deficits become very high under these conditions. The terms *sukhovei* in the Soviet Union, *lebeche* in Spain, *sirocco* in southern Europe, and *harmatten* in West Africa are used to describe such atmospheric conditions. This phenomenon also occurs in the U.S. Great Plains, Australia's wheat belt, and South Africa's corn-growing region.

JAWF currently employs two methods to compute PET—the Thornthwaite and modified Penman methods (Palmer, 1965a; Doorenbos and Pruitt, 1977). The Thornthwaite method was developed as a function of monthly mean temperature and day length. This method offers a relatively simple procedure with minimal input, but it is not suited for short time periods. Doorenbos and Pruitt's (Doorenbos and Pruitt, 1977) modified Penman method requires empirical wind and radiation functions as well as vapor pressure deficits. The method provides more satisfactory results over short time periods of the order of days or weeks. The data necessary to compute PET by both methods are available from the global synoptic data base.

The difference between actual precipitation divided by normal precipitation and the actual PET divided by normal PET provides a relative index of moisture available to the crop. Precipitation represents the source of moisture to crops (directly during the growing season and indirectly through storage in irrigation reserves) and PET represents the potential loss of moisture through the soil-plant system. Crop moisture usage depends on specific crop type, growth stage, water availability, and atmospheric conditions. ET is much less than PET during early growth phases, but as more vigorous vegetative growth occurs, crop moisture usage substantially increases. Peak moisture requirements occur during the crucial reproductive and grain development phases. Moisture needs decrease during late filling, and a "dry-down" period helps improve quality content as the crop matures. Differences in moisture usage of specific crops by growth stage are taken into account by crop coefficients (Doorenbos and Pruitt, 1977). Actual soil moisture supplies are the result of the relationship between infiltration and runoff. A regional soil moisture budget model is currently being tested at JAWF to improve the quantification of the soil moisture status at the beginning of the growing season.

A crop calendar, which includes information such as planting, emergence, vegetative, flowering, and mature stages of development, is essential. Early in the season, assumptions may be made about the usual planting period for specific crops. Growing degree days (GDD) are computed to relate heat units accumulated during the growing season with the crop's phenological development. An automated program has the flexibility to be reinitialized when new information is received about the actual planting dates within the crop area. Stress days (temperatures above or below threshold values) are also accumulated during the growing season. Since crop cycles vary by region, relationships between growth stage and GDD have been developed over the past five years according to knowledge of specific crop areas.

A 1981 USDA publication documented cropping zones, crop statistics, and representative climatic profiles for twelve major agricultural regions (U.S. Department of Agriculture, 1981). This document served as a basic reference for more detailed regional analyses. JAWF is working on an updated version that is expected to be published in 1987. Documentation of historical weather events associated with past crop yield fluctuations provides guidance for "expected" yield deviations given similar weather occurrences. For example, soybean yields in the state of Rio Grande do Sul, Brazil, are relatively low when rainfall during either (or both) the spring planting season or summer growing season ranks in the lower 30th percentile. Timing of the rainfall and temperature patterns plays a key role in the final yield outcome. The combination of a cold, wet spring planting season and a dry summer growing season can also lead to a poor yield. These conditions occurred in 1967, 1974, and 1979 in the Canadian spring wheat belt, causing yields to fall substantially below trend projections. Cool, wet springs can delay planting, pushing critical growth phases of the crop cycle into the more vulnerable period of hot, dry summer weather. The occurrence of anomalous weather and its magnitude on crop yields will vary by region.

Various techniques have been developed to model the effects of weather on vegetative growth or the crop yield potential. These include empirical-statistical models, which use regression techniques to relate specific weather variables to crop yields. This approach does not explain cause-and-effect relationships, but it does provide a feasible statistical procedure to evaluate crop yield statistics. JAWF employs the crop-weather analysis models that simulate accumulated crop responses to selected agrometeorological variables as a function of crop phenology. Observed weather data and derived agrometeorological variables are used as input data. Statistical regression techniques are used to evaluate weighting coefficients as crop development progresses from planting to maturity. The analysis models evaluate the effects of weather on crop yields, taking into account the relative importance of weather anomalies according to both crop type and stage of crop development. Computerized estimates of yield departures from the trend provide an objective, first-iteration estimate of the yield potential. These results are compared with historical weather-yield patterns accounting for the progress of the current growing season. The final decision on the monthly estimate of the yield potential is made by the agricultural meteorologist after consideration of all other information provided by meteorologists, economists, and commodity analysts.

The crop-weather analysis approach used by JAWF's agrometeorologists has proved successful for several reasons. The basic reasons are that climatic inputs of the daily global WWW/GTS station database are used, and sufficient data are available from the global synoptic network to compute derived variables such as vapor pressure deficits, potential evapotranspiration, and growing degree days. The daily weather data input allows for adjustments in the "biological" clock of the crop's development progress to aid in monitoring the response of the plants to the observed daily weather events. Detailed information has been compiled on cropping patterns and crop calendars by geographic region in order to model phenological development. Confirmation of the status of crop development is often made by field travel surveys and by the global network of agricultural counselors of USDA's Foreign Agricultural Service. Crop coefficients weight the cumulative effect of weather on the yield potential as crops advance through stages of their development cycle. Model estimates of the crop yield potential are closely scrutinized with respect to cumulative seasonal effects to avoid spurious short-lived fluctuations.

Preplanting crop yield statistics are based on early-season projections, derived from historical trend analyses and current information regarding technological factors such as introduction of new hybrids, fertilizer purchases, and government program changes. Weather data are used to provide indications of planting conditions and subsequent crop establishment. Unusually dry weather may delay planting, as it did during the 1985-86 growing seasons for Brazilian soybeans and South African corn. However, it is generally too early in the growing season to accurately quantify the effects of weather on the crop yield potential because of the random nature of weather events over the remainder of the growing season. For example, unseasonably dry weather delayed wheat planting in both Australia and Argentina during the 1984 growing season. Very late rains extended the planting season well beyond the optimal time, and favorable growing weather yielded near or above average crop yields in both cases. The relative change in monthly yield estimates is small during the early part of the growing season because information is too incomplete to justify large deviations from the early projections. Nonweather information associated with management practices, fertilizer applications, and the introduction of new seed varieties contributed most to any potential change in these early-season estimates. Meteorological input to the yield potential is generally quantified at the national level during the flowering and filling stages of crop development.

Since 1980, JAWF has used this approach to identify weather-related crop losses that occurred in Australia in 1982; in South Africa in 1983 and 1984; in Canada in 1984 and 1985; in the United States in 1980, 1983, and, to a lesser degree, 1984; in Brazil in 1981; and in the Soviet Union and the persistently drought-plagued continent of Africa in several recent years. During the 1985-86 growing season, a prolonged drought caused substantial damage to Brazil's coffee crop and severely stressed soybeans and other summer crops in the major southern growing areas. On the other hand, favorable weather helped produce record or near-record crop yields in the United States in 1981, 1982, and 1985; in Europe in 1984; in Canada in 1983; in Australia in 1983; in Argentina in 1984; and in China in several recent years.

JAWF's yield estimations are integrated into USDA's analytical process for estimation of global area, yield, and production statistics. Non-weather-related production components, including government program changes and fertilizer purchases, are analyzed by other USDA agencies. The data are, in turn, used to evaluate global supply and use estimates. USDA's world crop forecasting process has been implemented so that annual forecasts are updated on a monthly basis. Because these frequent assessments are released to the public, they constitute a major information source for both domestic and foreign agricultural industries and governments. Both qualitative and quantitative assessments of the crop yield potential are provided in international areas for which anomalous growing season weather is identified and selected for review in the monthly meetings. USDA crop analysts evaluate JAWF's objective weather-related analysis and discuss all other interagency analyses before finalizing the monthly crop estimates.

UTILIZATION OF WEATHER ASSESSMENTS

The agricultural weather analysis provides the U.S. agricultural sector with accurate data on potential markets and on supplies of potential competitors. Daily and weekly briefings provide an opportunity for the JAWF staff to interact with USDA commodity analysts and alert them to recent and seasonal agricultural weather conditions. The commodity analysts also provide JAWF with information on crop status and crop condition, based on tours and communications with agricultural counselors assigned to U.S. embassies around the world. Weekly briefings are also given to the secretary of agriculture and his staff to provide them with an overview of global weather conditions that may affect agriculture. A monthly interagency Africa briefing is conducted to provide analysts at USDA and other interested agencies with a detailed account of current weather conditions on the famine-plagued continent.

A significant increase in the demand by commodity analysts and policy-level decision makers for near real-time weather data and assessment information of the type developed by JAWF has occurred recently. In addition to daily briefings of current global agricultural weather, alerts of anomalous conditions affecting agriculture are included in daily highlights summarizing agricultural developments for USDA officials.

SUMMARY

The ultimate goal of JAWF is to provide accurate, concise, and timely information on agricultural weather as it affects global crop production. Agriculture, one of the nation's largest industries, is still an important positive contributor toward reducing the size of the U.S. trade deficit. U.S. farmers have become increasingly dependent on highly variable world markets. Agricultural weather is one factor that affects these markets. Proper use of the global agricultural weather data base, guided by results from experimental field research, may help American agriculturalists maintain the status of a highly efficient, flexible production system capable of meeting national and international food needs.

REFERENCES

Doorenbos, J.; and W. O. Pruitt. 1977. Crop water requirements. FAO Irrigation and Drainage Paper No. 24. Food and Agriculture Organization, Rome.

Mellor, J. W.; and S. Gavian. 1987. Famine: Causes, prevention, and relief. Science 235:539-545.

National Aeronautics and Space Administration. 1978. The LACIE Symposium: Proceedings of Plenary Session. Johnson Space Center, Houston.

National Aeronautics and Space Administration. 1980. AgRISTARS technical program plan. Johnson Space Center, Houston.

National Aeronautics and Space Administration. 1981. AgRISTARS yield model development. Johnson Space Center, Houston.

Palmer, W. C. 1965a. Meteorological drought. Research Paper No. 45. U.S. Department of Commerce, Weather Bureau, Washington, D.C.

Palmer, W. C. 1965b. A Crop Moisture Index, supplement appendix to Research Paper No. 45. U.S. Department of Commerce, Weather Bureau, Washington, D.C.

Sakamoto, C. 1978. Abstract. Thirteenth Session Agricultural Meteorology and Forestry Meetings, Purdue University, Lafayette, Indiana.

U. S. Department of Agriculture. 1981. Major world crop areas and climate profiles. World Agricultural Outlook Board, Washington, D.C.

PART 4

Impact Assessment

CHAPTER 13
CLIMATE IMPACT ASSESSMENT: A REVIEW OF SOME APPROACHES

Martin L. Parry and Timothy R. Carter

INTRODUCTION

The purpose of this paper is to review approaches to and techniques in climate impact assessment, with particular reference to drought impacts. The paper is divided into two parts: Part 1 looks at methodology, outlining definitions, concepts, and approaches to climate impact assessment in general. Part 2 illustrates some techniques that are available for conducting impact analyses, drawing mainly from examples of studies conducted in agriculture.

PART 1: METHODOLOGY

TYPES OF IMPACT

In an assessment of the impact of climatic variation on economies and societies, it is useful to make two broad distinctions: (1) between *approximate* and *proximate* causes and (2) between *contingently necessary* and *contingently sufficient* conditions. *Proximate* causes are those that directly precipitate an impact; *approximate* causes are those that are underlying, indirect, and preconditioning in their effect. Neither proximate nor approximate factors are, on their own, sufficient explanation for an impact. We should thus be wary of assuming meteorological drought, for example, to be the sole "cause" of an economic or social impact when it may, in fact, have served merely to precipitate events that had already been preconditioned by nonclimatic factors such as economic, social, or political developments. In the Sahelian crisis in the mid-1970s, for example, climate may have played just such a triggering role but may not have been the underlying cause of the crisis (Garcia, 1981). This brings us to the second distinction: that between contingently necessary and contingently sufficient conditions (Nagel, 1961). The former are an essential precondition for the effect but are not in themselves sufficient to explain the effect; the latter are not always a necessary precondition, but, when they do occur, they are a sufficient and complete explanation for the effect. To illustrate this condition, we will draw, once again, from the example of the Sahel. Although meteorological drought may have triggered the Sahelian crisis, a broadly similar result could possibly have been triggered by a different short-term event (for example, a political upheaval). An important underlying cause of the crisis was probably the decreasing resilience of Sahelian society to drought as a result of political, social, and economic developments during the 1950s and 1960s (Garcia, 1981). According to this explanation, then, meteorological drought was neither a sufficient nor necessary condition for the effect, merely a proximate factor.

TYPES OF CONCEPTUAL FRAMEWORK

Impact Approach and Interaction Approach

A distinction has been drawn between two broad types of approach in the study of impact from climatic variations: *impact approaches* and *interaction approaches* (Kates, 1985).

The *impact approach* is based on the assumption of direct cause and effect, where a climatic event (for example, a drought) operating on a given "exposure unit" (for example, a human activity) may have "impact" or effect (Fig. 1a). In reality, of course, so many intervening factors operate that it is both misleading and quite impossible to treat these three study elements (drought-activity-impact) in isolation from their environmental and societal milieu, and very few studies (if any) have followed these methods.

An *interaction approach* assumes, first, that the climatic event (drought) is merely one of many processes (both societal and environmental in origin) that may af-

A. Impact approach

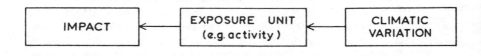

B. Interaction approach

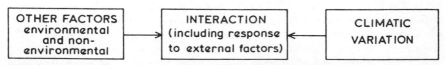

Fig. 1 Schema of simple impact and interaction approaches in climate impact assessment (adapted from Kates, 1985).

fect the exposure unit and, second, that the impact is not separate from the exposure unit (as suggested in Fig. 1a) but is one of the many processes that constitute it (Fig. 1b). Thus, in the Sahel from 1965 to 1972, climate, history, politics, and social change embrace many processes, the convergence of which created, in human terms, a crisis (Garcia, 1981).

Types of Interaction Models

Interaction models have achieved greater degrees of realism by considering the "cascade" of impacts through physical and social systems as *orders of interactions* (Fig. 2). Illustrating this in Fig. 3 are the pathways of drought impacts in the United States. Here the cascade of effects is depicted as it works its way through a hierarchy of scales (from local to global) and through a network of systems (agricultural, economic, social, and political). Additional complexity may be introduced by studying interactions of the same order but between different sectors—for example, between the concurrent effects of drought on agriculture, forestry, water resources, transportation, and so forth.

Interactions between climate variations themselves and other physical systems have only recently gained attention (Fig. 4). Two sets of such interactions can be distinguished:

1. Those in which the effects of the climate variation are transmitted through other physical systems (e.g., by pests and diseases, or by changes in soil structure, soil nutrients, soil erosion, salinization, and so forth).

2. Those in which the effects of the climate variation are themselves affected by other concurrent environmental trends (such as acid deposition and ground-water depletion).

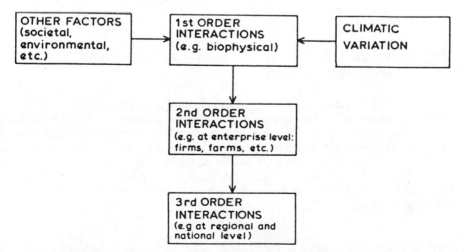

Fig. 2 Schema of interaction approach with ordered interactions within individual sectors (Parry and Carter, 1987).

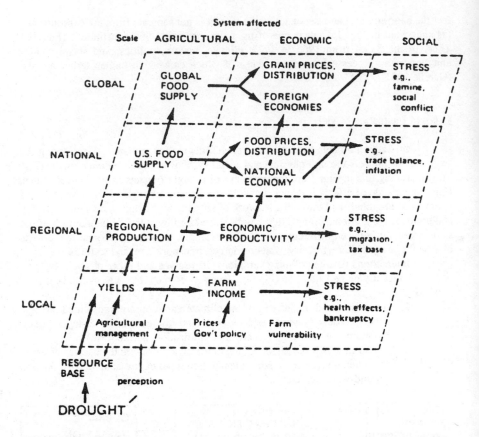

Fig. 3 Hypothetical pathways of drought impacts on society (after Warrick and Bowden, 1981).

Finally, we can allow greater complexity into our conception of interactions between climate and society by considering different types of response. Figure 4 distinguishes between two orders of response: adjustments at the enterprise level (such as at the farm level, where adaptations might include changes of crops, increased irrigation, changes in fertilization); and policy response at the regional, national, and international level. The schema broadly represents the conceptual framework adopted in the IIASA/UNEP project, the results of which will be used to illustrate some of the results discussed (Parry, et al., 1987).

INTEGRATED APPROACHES TO CLIMATE IMPACT ASSESSMENTS

One advantage of distinguishing types of explanation while considering the complexity of interactions is that it discourages acceptance of the operation of causal

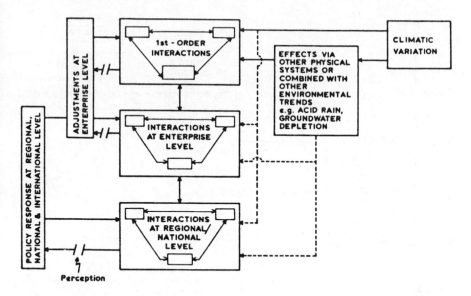

Fig. 4 Schema of the IIASA/UNEP project study method: An interactive approach to climate impact assessment with ordered interactions, interactions at each level, and social and physical feedbacks (Parry and Carter, 1987).

chains, which are conceptually tidy but which massively oversimplify processes of climate impact (see, for example, Fig. 5).

Yet some form of simplification is necessary to make sense of the enormous number and complexity of pathways by which the effects of climatic variations are passed through biophysical, economic, and social systems. One aid to comprehension is a hierarchy of models (Fig. 6), which serves to conceptualize the linkages between the various systems and enables scientists to make an integrated assessment of climate impacts. Such hierarchies of models normally include the following:

1. Models of climatic variation (based on outputs from global climate models or analysis of the instrumental record, or a combination of these).

2. Biophysical models of first-order relationships—that is, relationships between certain climatic variables (e.g., temperature, precipitation, insolation, windspeed) and biophysical supply or demand (e.g., biomass productivity, energy demand). In the field of agriculture, these models would consider the effects of the variables on crop growth, livestock yield, health, and so forth.

3. Economic models of second-order relationships—that is, relationships at the enterprise level (e.g., of farms, firms, agencies, institutions). In the field of agriculture, these models would consider the effects (*inter alia*) of changes in farm-level production on regional and national output and so forth.

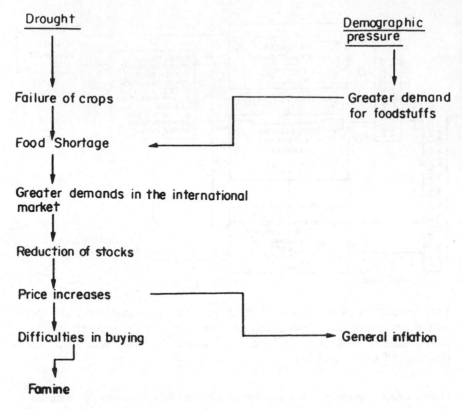

Fig. 5 A "causal chain" purporting to depict the effects of drought in the Sahel in the mid-1970s (from Garcia, 1981). It ignores the distinction between (1) proximate and approximate factors and (2) sufficient and necessary conditions discussed in the text.

    4.   Economic, social, or political models of third-order interactions at the regional, national, or international level.

    This approach yields the following types of integrated assessments: biophysical, enterprise-level, sectoral, and regional (Fig. 6).

TYPES OF ANALYTICAL METHODS

The Direct or "Top-Down" Method

    The scientific method most frequently adopted in climate impact assessment is the *direct method*, in which, for example, the effects of a change in an input variable (such as a change in precipitation) are traced, in a number of steps, along a number of pathways (e.g., precipitation ⇒ crop biomass productivity ⇒ forage level ⇒ carrying

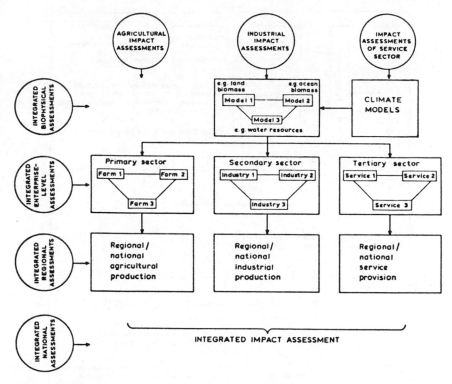

Fig. 6 A hierarchy of models in climate impact assessment (Parry and Carter, 1987).

capacity ⇒ livestock production ⇒ meat and milk supply), as shown in Fig. 7a. The question is thus posed: For a given climate change, what is the impact on (for example) ecosystems, economy, and society? An advantage of this approach is that assessments can be made even if the number of climatic scenarios is restricted (for example, in the case of projected possible future climates), the analysis being conducted on the basis of the character of the climatic changes rather than on their likely impacts.

The Adjoint or "Bottom-Up" Method

An alternative or *adjoint method* (Parry and Carter, 1984) focuses first on the sensitivity of the exposure unit and addresses the following questions:
1. To what aspects of climate is the exposure unit especially sensitive?
2. What changes in these aspects are required to perturb the exposure unit significantly?

Climatic scenarios can then be characterized partly on the basis of these detected sensitivities and partly along lines adopted in the direct approach described above. The steps are illustrated in Fig. 7b. An advantage of this approach is that it can

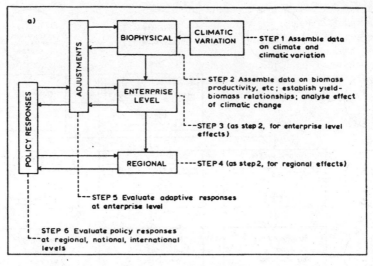

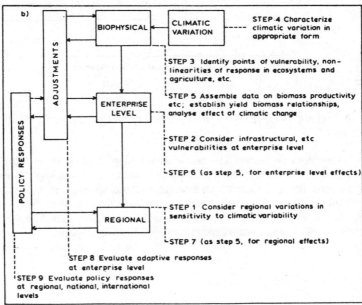

Fig. 7 (a) Direct ("top-down") and (b) adjoint ("bottom-up") methods to climate impact assessment. The adjoint approach was adopted in the IIASA/UNEP project (Parry and Carter, 1987).

help identify sensitivities independently of state-of-the-art climatic scenarios and can allow climatic changes to be expressed in the form that has direct meaning for the exposure unit. In Saskatchewan, for example, recent work has characterized climate impacts on agriculture in terms of the frequency of days of blowing dust, previous sensitivity studies of agriculture having identified such events as critical to the sustainability of cereal production in the region (Williams, et al., 1987).

TYPES OF EXPERIMENTS

For either of the analytical approaches discussed above, two broad types of impact experiment can be conducted (Fig. 8).

Impact Experiments

In these experiments, each set of models in the hierarchy simulates a limited number of feedbacks within its own subsystems. The form of analysis is therefore basically sequential, estimates of effects being based largely on assumed and essentially static sets of biophysical and economic responses.

Adjustment Experiments

By altering some of the assumptions mentioned above, it is possible to evaluate various options available to offset or mitigate the effects. These responses might occur at the enterprise level (for example, a farm-level decision to switch to a different crop) or through a change in government policy (such as a shift in farm subsidies). Experiments for different crops, different amounts of fertilizer, and other actions can enable a new set of impact estimates to be generated which can then be compared with the initial estimates, thus helping in evaluating appropriate policies of response to climatic variations.

In the IIASA/UNEP project, it proved useful to perform these experiments in a sequence, first evaluating impacts on the (unrealistic) assumption that the economic and social systems will undergo no change and then conducting adjustment experiments that incorporate an increasingly complex pattern of assumed responses (Parry, et al., 1987).

SOME INTEGRATING CONCEPTS

In recent years, scientists involved in climate impact assessment have developed a number of integrating themes that allow a common approach to (1) estimating effects of both short- and long-term climatic changes, (2) specifying activities and regions especially sensitive to climate, and (3) considering the options for responding to climatic changes.

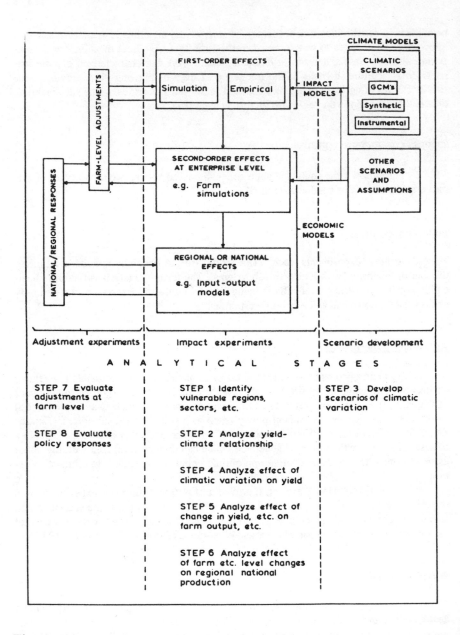

Fig. 8 Conceptual framework and stages of analysis adopted in the IIASA/UNEP project (Parry and Carter, 1987).

Climatic Changes as a Change in Risk

Government interest in climate impacts (e.g., the effects of droughts, floods, cold spells) is largely a short-term concern. Long-term issues, such as the likely future "greenhouse warming," are not always perceived to be of immediate importance. This suggests, therefore, that a useful way to express long-term climatic change for the policy maker is as a change in the frequency of short-term anomalies. For example, estimates indicate that the frequency of drought in Saskatchewan, Canada (defined as a monthly Palmer Drought Index value below -4), would increase from 3% of all months at present to about 9% under a doubled CO_2 climate (see Williams, et al., 1987). One advantage of this type of approach is that the change can be expressed as a change in the risk of impact (Parry, 1985). It would be possible for governments to devise programs that accommodated specified tolerable levels of risk, by adjusting activities as required to match the change of risk. This notion derives in part from the view that economic and social systems adjust to climatic change by responding to changes in the frequencies of unusually disruptive (or beneficial) climatic events, rather than to the long-term change of the average conditions. Moreover, since climate can be regarded as a resource in activities such as agriculture and forestry, adjustments in an activity are likely to be necessary to match changes in the resource levels. Climatic change may thus be interpreted as a change in the range of options that may compete for investment of time, money, and other resources. Finally, the perception of these changed options is often important, because the timing and extent of investment in relation to weather can markedly influence the return on that investment (Parry, 1985).

Delimiting Impact Areas

In order to conduct useful impact analyses, it is important to be specific about the activity or exposure unit being studied and its location. One method of identifying areas that can be affected by climatic variations (such as drought) involves the shift of limits or margins representing boundaries between arbitrarily defined classes. The classifications may include land use, agroecological potential, vegetation, crop yields, and so forth, and the boundaries delimit zones on maps that may be shifted in response to a change in climate, thus defining impact areas. This method has been combined with the "shift-in-risk" idea in a strategy adopted for identifying agricultural areas that are particularly sensitive to climatic variations (Parry and Carter, 1984; see Fig. 9). Other examples include shifts of agroecological zones in Kenya (Akong'a, et al., 1987), precipitation isopleths in the Sahel region (Todorov, 1985), and precipitation effectiveness index in Saskatchewan (Williams, et al., 1987).

Vulnerability at the Margin

Underlying the identification of boundary shifts is the idea that sensitivity to climatic variability may be more readily observed toward the margins of tolerance of an organism or activity, or at the margins of comparative advantage between two competing activities. We can define three types of "marginality" (Fig. 10):

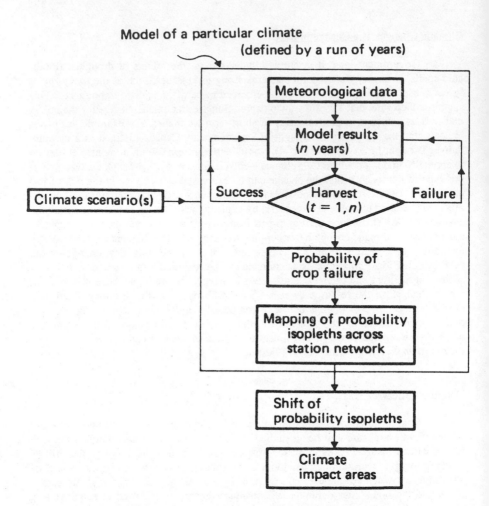

Fig. 9 Steps in the identification of climate impact areas. The weather for a particular year, described by a set of meteorological data, is translated into a measure of annual return on an activity (e.g., harvest failure or success) using an appropriate model. Over a period of years, the frequency (probability) of loss or benefit can be assessed at each of a number of locations and mapped geographically as isopleths. Scenarios of changing climates can then be used as inputs to the model and the probability isopleths can be remapped. The geographical shifts of the isopleths thus delimit areas of specific climate impact (Parry and Carter, 1984).

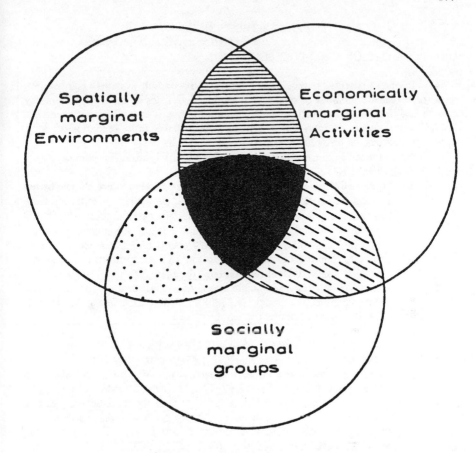

Fig. 10 Types of marginality (Parry and Carter, 1983).

1. *Spatial or geographical marginality*, which describes the edge of a specified region defined economically, biophysically, and so forth (see above).
2. *Economic marginality*, in which returns on an activity barely exceed costs.
3. *Social marginality*, in which an underdeveloped population becomes isolated from its indigenous resource base and is forced into marginal economies that contain fewer adaptive mechanisms for survival (Baird, et al., 1975).

None of these marginal areas or groups is strongly buffered against changes of the environment and, even though they may not coincide, it is reasonable to suggest that each is likely to be particularly sensitive to variations in climate (Parry and Carter, 1983).

PART 2: TECHNIQUES

DEVELOPMENT OF CLIMATIC SCENARIOS

In order to assess the sensitivity of social and economic systems to climate, we need some realistic methods of quantifying the characteristics of both the present-day climate and likely future climatic changes. One technique is to use climatic scenarios. Following the integrated analytical system described above, these scenarios form the upper tier of the model hierarchy in Fig. 6.

Three types of climatic scenario that are particularly useful in climate impact analysis can be identified.

1. *Instrumental scenarios* allow us to specify a plausible future climate by examining the instrumental record for climatic anomalies. We can use these anomalies (which we know have occurred in the past and presumably could occur in the future) as scenarios of future climate, the impacts of which would probably differ from the original events under changed social and economic conditions of a group or an activity. As an illustration, possible anomalies might include an extreme drought year (e.g., 1961 in Saskatchewan or 1982-83 in southeastern Australia), or a dry period of frequent or consecutive drought (e.g., the 1930s in Saskatchewan or the years 1974-75 in parts of central and eastern Kenya.

2. *Synthetic scenarios* comprise climatic data that are generated to simulate an arbitrary climatic change (such as a 10% decrease in rainfall). These are of particular use for testing the sensitivity of impact models.

3. *Scenarios from general circulation models (GCMs)* are a third source of climatic data. GCMs are physically based numerical models of the climate system, one use of which has been to estimate the climatic changes that might be expected given an increase in the concentration of atmospheric carbon dioxide (CO_2) and other radiatively active gases. To date, most experiments have considered the effects of a doubling of CO_2, and the models produce outputs for the whole globe over a network of grid points, showing the simulated change in seasonally averaged climatic variables (e.g., temperature, precipitation rate, and cloud cover) between 1 x CO_2 (present) and 2 x CO_2 (future) equilibrium conditions. Although GCMs have been reasonably successful in reproducing the continental-scale features of present-day (1 x CO_2) temperatures and pressure patterns, other climatic elements, including precipitation, are less well simulated (Gates, 1985). Nevertheless, GCM outputs have been used in a wide range of impact experiments (e.g., see Warrick, et al., 1986; Parry, et al., 1987), the importance of which has been to demonstrate the feasibility of linking climate models and impact models while awaiting more confident GCM predictions in the future.

MODELING FIRST-ORDER IMPACTS

To estimate the impacts of the types of climatic scenarios defined above on a particular biophysical system, we move to the next level of the model hierarchy (Fig. 6), requiring the use of models of biophysical response to climate.

Estimating Biophysical Responses to Climate

Many different types of models can be used to estimate biophysical sensitivity to climate. We will concentrate on agroclimatic models in this paper. Other types that have been used in climate impact experiments include hydrological models (see Gleick, 1986, for a specific example; Beran, 1986, reviews some approaches), forestry models (see Shugart, et al. (1986), for a review of these), and models of energy use and supply (see Jager, 1985).

Within agriculture, a range of agroclimatic models can be used to translate climatic information into a measure of plant productivity or potential. Three main types of models can be identified. The first and simplest method of relating agroclimatic resources to climate is to combine or manipulate meteorological variables into an *agroclimatic index*. Such an index can be particularly useful for identifying areas suited for various crops, since they can incorporate, within a single term, those climatic variables that have most influence on plant growth.

A second type of model is the *empirical-statistical* variety, developed by relating a sample of annual crop yield data to weather data for the same time period and area using statistical techniques such as regression analysis. These models can have a high practical value for large-area yield prediction and usually require only modest quantities of data and computational time. However, the approach does not provide a causal explanation of the relationship between climate and crop yield; it tends to identify only those climatic variables that show a strong statistical association with annual crop yields. Empirical-statistical models are probably most valuable for estimating the impacts of short-term climatic anomalies, the magnitude of which are within the range of conditions under which the model was constructed (i.e., not requiring extrapolation of model relationships). Moreover, assessments using these models are perhaps best conducted in areas where crop yields are highly sensitive to a single climatic variable, such as precipitation in many semiarid regions.

Simulation models are the third type of tool that can be used in assessing plant sensitivity to climate. These are based on an understanding of the relationships between the basic processes of plant and crop growth and environmental factors (such as water supply, temperature, solar radiation, and soil fertility). Despite their general requirements for quite detailed meteorological and physiological data (first for validation and then for applications in impact assessment), simulation models are more firmly based on experimental observation than statistical models, and provide probably the best opportunity to conduct useful climate impact experiments in agriculture (particularly when considering longer-term effects of changes in climate). In the IIASA/UNEP project, simulation models have been used to assess drought impacts on, for example, maize in Kenya (Akong'a, et al., 1987), sorghum in India (Jodha, et al., 1987), barley in Ecuador (Knapp, et al., 1987), and spring wheat in the Saratov region of the USSR (Pitovranov, et al., 1987).

Linking Models of Climate to Models of Biophysical Response

One intention of the hierarchical approach to climate impact assessment is to link models at different levels. In this instance, data from the climatic scenarios are used as inputs to biophysical models. For practical purposes, it is clear that this linkage is a major criterion in selecting the scenarios and impact models. The scenario determines whether the climatic data that are available for impact assessment are suitable for operating a particular impact model, while the impact model's data requirements influence the type of scenario that can be constructed. For example, the temporal and spatial resolution of GCM-derived scenario data is often too coarse for values to be input directly to an impact model. In these circumstances, a synthetic data set may be substituted (for example, by generating daily precipitation values from monthly GCM estimates). If climatic data for a scenario period are missing from the instrumental record and are required as an input to a biophysical model, a sensitivity study of the model may indicate that those data can be approximated by substituting either data from a neighboring meteorological station or long-term averages. For example, in the IIASA/UNEP assessment of maize yield response to climate in Kenya, the simulation model employed was found to be relatively insensitive to interannual variations in all climatic variables except rainfall, so long-term averages of those variables were used along with observed rainfall values (Akong'a, et al., 1987).

Finally, as illustrated in Fig. 9, we can combine the use of biophysical models with the spatial mapping approach to assess areas of impact. For example, using an agroclimatic index of agricultural potential, this approach has been adopted to map shifts in agroclimatic zones for several instrumentally based scenarios of drought in Central and Eastern Kenya (Fig. 11).

INTEGRATING THE ASSESSMENTS OF IMPACT

Up to now we have considered only the upper two levels of the hierarchy of impacts shown in Fig. 6, describing assessments of first-order biophysical responses to scenarios of climate. Recent studies have begun to integrate biophysical effects with their economic and social impacts, both within single sectors (such as agriculture and water resources) and within a regional context.

Sectoral Assessments

Integrated sectoral assessments can be used to trace the impacts of climatic variations through biophysical responses to the enterprise level, and then on to the social and political implications of these. We can illustrate this approach by reference to agriculture in eastern Africa. In the southern rangelands of Ethiopia in the period 1983-84, the effects of reduced rainfall on forage and feed crops (particularly in consecutive years) caused sharp increases in calf mortality (Cossins, 1986). In the past centuries this would probably have led to high death rates among pastoral people but, as Fig. 12 shows for Kenya, this has not been the case in recent decades, with alternative means of making a living sometimes available and famine relief operations a common occurrence. Similar investigations have been reported of the relationships between climate, forage, and meat and milk output elsewhere in Kenya (Akong'a, et al., 1987).

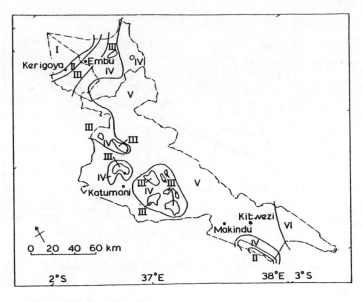

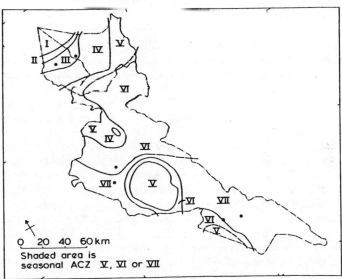

Fig. 11 Agroclimatic zones in Embu, Kirinyaga, and Machakos districts, Kenya, for (a) average (1951-80) climate and (b) the period of March-May rains in 1984 (after Akong'a, et al., 1987).

182

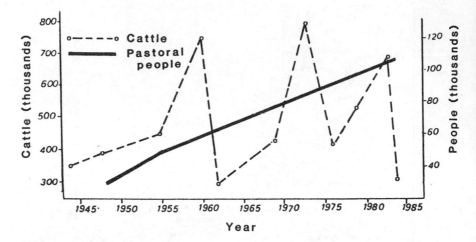

Fig. 12 Changes in cattle and human (pastoral) populations in the Kajiado district of Kenya, 1944-84 (de Leeuw and Bekure, cited in Cossins, 1986).

Regional Assessments

Sectoral studies are, to some extent, conducted as a methodological and disciplinary convenience, because climate impacts are not likely to be restricted to a single sector of a regional economy. Ideally, an integrated regional assessment would consider most or all of the significant interactions both between sectors and between levels of impact. In reality, of course, this is not possible. Yet partly integrated assessments have been successfully implemented. We can illustrate two approaches to assessments of this type, using a single example for each.

1. *Assessments by observation* represent an empirical examination of all available information concerning a climatic event and its biophysical, economic, social, and political impacts. An example is an analysis of the complicity of consecutive drought (1979-80) in northeast Brazil in reducing local food and cash crop production. This, *inter alia*, measurably reduced aggregate regional production and decreased regional participation in the national economy (Magalhães, et al., 1987).

2. *Assessments by simulation* represent attempts to model many of the interactive aspects of a climate impact that are described in the empirical approach. For example, in Saskatchewan, climatic scenarios of altered temperature and precipitation have been used to estimate altered yield levels of spring wheat using a simulation model (Fig. 13). The altered yields were input to farm-level models, converted to production figures, and then aggregated by farm size and soil zone to give provincial production and commodity changes. These were used as inputs to a regional input-output model that considered impacts both on the agricultural and nonagricultural sectors. Finally, changes in output levels for various

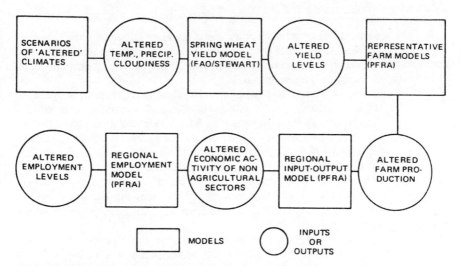

Fig. 13 Hierarchy of models for assessing impacts of climatic change in Saskatchewan (after Williams, et al., 1987).

economic sectors were translated into changes in employment using a third model—an employment model (Williams, et al., 1987).

CONSIDERING ADJUSTMENTS AND ADAPTATIONS

Adjustments to mitigate the effects of climatic variations can be investigated at two levels: the enterprise level and the regional and national policy level (see Fig. 6).

Adjustments at Enterprise Level

Variations of climate frequently prompt a wide range of responses from managers at the enterprise level (e.g., by farmers, irrigation engineers, corporation managers), depending on the perception of the event and its effects. For example, a greater frequency of summer droughts in the Canadian prairies under a 2 x CO_2 climate could encourage farmers to switch from spring wheat to winter wheat or corn (Williams, et al., 1987). Most rural households in drought-prone areas have developed a number of coping strategies for drought, and an extensive literature now exists on these types of adjustment (Jodha and Mascarenhas, 1985). To illustrate, during the 1984 drought in Kenya, in the drier areas about three-quarters of surveyed households reported a shift from their customary staple food to some other food—generally from white maize to yellow (imported) maize (Akong'a, et al., 1987).

184

Policy Responses at Regional and National Levels

In contrast to enterprise-level adjustments are more large-scale and long-term responses by regional and national governments. Here we outline three broad types of policy response: preimpact programs for impact mitigation, post-impact government interventions, and contingency arrangements.

1. *Preimpact government programs* include those policies designed to mitigate possible future effects of climatic variability and change. Programs for drought, in particular, have a long and often checkered history in many countries. These have included Famine Commissions (e.g., those set up by the British Government in India during the nineteenth century); irrigation schemes (e.g., in Saskatchewan following the 1930s droughts); and, more recently, programs for rural development, technological improvement, and economic growth (such as the integrated regional development program of the 1990s for Northeast Brazil, Projeto Nordeste [Magalhães, et al., 1987]).

2. *Post-impact government interventions* include those responses to severe conditions (such as drought) that are initiated because of a combination of the severity of the event and pressure by the public and media. Included within this type of assistance would be relief payments to households in drought-stricken areas such as those in rural Saskatchewan during the 1930s drought years.

3. *Contingency arrangements* describe an array of advance measures that can be employed by government to alleviate the major effects of severe climatic episodes. These range from subsidized insurance policies to low-interest loans. Knowledge of the changes in frequency of such episodes, together with an actuarial assessment of likely damages, can enable government insurance and compensation schemes to be "retuned" to match altered levels of risk stemming from a change of climate (Parry and Carter, 1985).

SUMMARY

In this paper, we have outlined some approaches for analyzing the impacts of climatic variations on society. The connections between a climatic event, its biophysical effects, the economic costs of prevention or compensation, and the social impacts of all of these are imperfectly understood. However, there has been increased interest, and some degree of success, in simulating these connections with a hierarchy of models of varying degrees of complexity. We have illustrated how this approach can be useful for assessing impacts of drought in a range of contrasting regions.

185

REFERENCES

Akong'a, J.; T. E. Downing; N. T. Konijn; D. N. Mungai; H. R. Muturi; and H. L. Potter. 1987. The effects of climatic variations on agriculture in central and eastern Kenya. In M. L. Parry, T. R. Carter, and N. T. Konijn, eds. The Impact of Climatic Variations on Agriculture. Vol. 2. Assessments in Semi-Arid Regions. Reidel, Dordrecht, Holland (in press).

Baird, A.; P. O'Keefe; K. Westgate; and B. Wisner. 1975. Towards an explanation and reduction of disaster proneness. Occasional Paper 11, Disaster Research Unit. University of Bradford, England.

Beran, M. 1986. The Water Resource Impact of Future Climate Change and Variability. International Conference on Health and Environmental Effects of Ozone Modification and Climatic Change. Washington, D.C., June 1986.

Cossins, N. J. 1986. The impact of climate variation on animal production: Commentary on a paper by Dr. J. J. Burgos. Draft paper presented at the Task Force Meeting on Policy Oriented Assessment of Impact of Climatic Variations, International Institute for Applied Systems Analysis, Laxenburg, Austria, June 30-July 2, 1986.

Garcia, R. 1981. Drought and Man: The 1972 Case History. Vol. 1. Nature Pleads Not Guilty. Pergamon, New York.

Gates, W. L. 1985. The use of general circulation models in the analysis of the ecosystem impacts of climatic change. Clim. Change 7(3).267-284.

Gleick, P. H. 1986. Regional Water Resources and Global Climatic Change. International Conference on Health and Environmental Effects of Ozone Modification and Climatic Change, Washington, D.C., June 1986.

Jäger, J. J. 1985. Energy resources. pp. 215-245. In R. W. Kates, J. H. Ausubel, and M. Berberian, eds. Climate Impact Assessment: Studies of the Interaction of Climate and Society (SCOPE 27). Wiley, Chichester, England.

Jodha, N. S.; and A. C. Mascarenhas. 1985. Adjustment in self-provisioning societies. pp. 437-464. In R. W. Kates, J. H. Ausubel, and M. Berberian, eds. Climate Impact Assessment: Studies of the Interaction of Climate and Society (SCOPE 27). Wiley, Chichester, England.

Jodha, N. S.; S. Gadgil; A. K. S. Huda; R. P. Singh; and S. M. Virmani. 1987. The effects of climatic variations on agriculture in central India. In M. L. Parry, T. R. Carter, and N. T. Konijn, eds. The Impact of Climatic Variations on Agriculture. Vol. 2. Assessments in Semi-Arid Regions. Reidel, Dordrecht, Holland (in press).

Kates, R. W. 1985. The interaction of climate and society. pp. 3-36. In R. W. Kates, J. H. Ausubel, and M. Berberian, eds. Climate Impact Assessment: Studies of the Interaction of Climate and Society (SCOPE 27). Wiley, Chichester, England.

Knapp, G.; R. Bravo; L. Canadas; T. Hodges; M. L. Parry; A. M. Planchuelo-Ravelo; A. Ravelo; O. Rovere; and T. Yugcha. 1987. The effects of climatic variations in the central Sierra of Ecuador. In M. L. Parry, T. R. Carter, and N. T. Konijn, eds. The Impact of Climatic Variations on Agriculture. Vol. 2. Assessments in Semi-Arid Regions. Reidel, Dordrecht, Holland (in press).

Magalhães, A. R.; E. R. Rilho; F. L. Garagorry; J. G. Gasques; L. C. B. Molion; M. S. A. Neto; C. A. Nobre; E. R. Porto; and O. E. Reboucas. 1987. The effects of climatic variations on agriculture in Northeast Brazil. In M. L. Parry, T. R. Carter, and N. T. Konijn, eds. The Impact of Climatic Variations on Agriculture. Vol. 2. Assessments in Semi-Arid Regions. Reidel, Dordrecht, Holland (in press).

Nagel, E. 1961. The Structure of Science: Problems in the Logic of Scientific Explanation. Harcourt, Brace and World, New York.

Parry, M. L. 1985. Estimating the sensitivity of natural ecosystems and agriculture to climatic change—Guest editorial. Clim. Change 7:1-3.

Parry, M. L.; and T. R. Carter. 1983. Assessing impacts of climatic change in marginal areas: The search for an appropriate methodology. Working Paper WP-83-77. International Institute for Applied Systems Analysis, Laxenburg, Austria.

Parry, M. L.; and T. R. Carter, eds. 1984. Assessing the impact of climatic change in cold regions. Summary Report SR-84-1. International Institute for Applied Systems Analysis, Laxenburg, Austria.

Parry, M. L.; and T. R. Carter. 1985. The effect of climatic variations on agricultural risk. Clim. Change 7:95-110.

Parry, M. L.; and T. R. Carter. 1987. The assessment of effects of climatic variations on agriculture: Aims, methods and summary of results. In M. L. Parry, T. R. Carter, and N. T. Konijn, eds. The Impact of Climatic Variations on Agriculture. Vol. 1. Assessments in Cool Temperate and Cold Regions, Reidel, Dordrecht, Holland (in press).

Parry, M. L.; T. R. Carter; and N. T. Konijn, eds. 1987. The Impact of Climatic Variations on Agriculture. Vol. 1. Assessments in Cool Temperate and Cold Regions. Vol. 2. Assessments in Semi-Arid Regions. Reidel, Dordrecht, Holland (in press).

Pitovranov, S. E.; A. D. Maximov; O. D. Sirotenko; E. V. Abashina; and V. N. Pavlova. 1987. The effects of climatic variations on agriculture in the Saratov region, USSR. In M. L. Parry, T. R. Carter, and N. T. Konijn, eds. The Impact of Climatic Variations on Agriculture. Vol. 2. Assessments in Semi-Arid Regions. Reidel, Dordrecht, Holland (in press).

Shugart, H. H.; M. Y. Antonovsky; P. G. Jarvis; and A. P. Sandford. 1986. CO_2, climatic change and forest ecosystems: Assessing the response of global forests to the direct effects of increasing CO_2 and climatic change. pp. 475-521. In B. Bolin, B. R. Döös, J. Jäger, and R. A. Warrick, eds. The Greenhouse Effect, Climatic Change and Ecosystems: A Synthesis of the Present Knowledge (SCOPE 29). Wiley, Chichester, England.

Todorov, A. V. 1985. Sahel: The changing rainfall and the "normals" used for its assessment. J. Clim. Applied Meteor. 24:97-107.

Warrick, R., and M. Bowden. 1981. Changing impacts of drought in the Great Plains. In M. Lawson and M. Baker, eds. The Great Plains: Perspectives and Prospects. Center for Great Plains Studies, University of Nebraska, and University of Nebraska Press, Lincoln.

Warrick, R. A.; R. M. Gifford; and M. L. Parry. 1986. CO_2, Climatic Change and Agriculture. Assessing the Response of Food Crops to Increased CO_2. pp.

187

393-473. In B. Bolin, B. R. Döös, J. Jäger, and R. A. Warrick, eds. The Greenhouse Effect, Climatic Change and Ecosystems: A Synthesis of the Present Knowledge (SCOPE 29). Wiley, Chichester, England.

Williams, G. D. V.; R. A. Fautley; K. H. Jones; R. B. Stewart; and E. E. Wheaton. 1987. Estimating impacts of climatic change on agriculture in Saskatchewan, Canada. In M. L. Parry, T. R. Carter, and N. T. Konijn, eds. The Impact of Climatic Variations on Agriculture. Vol. 1. Assessments in Cool Temperate and Cold Regions. Reidel, Dordrecht, Holland (in press).

CHAPTER 14
ASSESSING DROUGHT IMPACTS AND ADJUSTMENTS IN AGRICULTURE AND WATER RESOURCE SYSTEMS

William E. Easterling and William E. Riebsame

INTRODUCTION

Drought impact assessments are conducted for a variety of reasons and by a number of different approaches. The most simple type of impact assessment seeks to answer the question: "What negative impacts did the drought cause; what damages, losses, and hardships were associated with it?" Examples include the impact assessment reports issued by the National Oceanic and Atmospheric Administration's (NOAA) Assessment and Information Services Center (AISC, 1980 and 1982), which evaluate direct impacts (i.e., losses) at the state and national level; and regionally oriented, detailed studies such as Dando, et al. (1981), which assessed economic effects of the 1980 drought in North Dakota. Often, the goal of such studies is to guide the distribution of government drought relief efforts.

A second type of impact assessment focuses on human response and adjustment to drought, taking what has come to be known as the natural hazards approach (see Burton, et al. [1978], for a survey of hazards research). Several such studies are reviewed in Warrick's (1975) benchmark monograph on drought research in the United States and are noted in the Great Plains drought workshop proceedings edited by Rosenberg (1980). Another body of drought impact assessment also centers on human response to drought, as opposed to first-order impacts, from the perspective of government policy or political economy, often via a Marxist analysis (e.g., Watts, 1983) or along more traditional social science lines (Garcia, 1981; Wilhite, 1986). In these studies, emphasis is placed on what people did because of drought, and how economic and political institutions constrained or enhanced the efficacy of their response.

In other drought-related research, impacts have been measured as one step to asking broader questions. For example, Bowden, et al. (1981), studied the impacts of historical droughts on the U.S. Great Plains to test hypotheses about long-term trends in drought vulnerability, and Glantz (1982) assessed the impacts of drought prediction in the Yakima River basin, seeking insight into the usefulness of long-range forecasts. Finally, some studies have attempted to project the impacts of future droughts. For example, Warrick (1984) used a climate-crop model to estimate the yield impacts of a contemporary recurrence of the 1930s drought on the U.S. Great Plains.

The drought impacts literature, as broadly outlined above, illustrates several enduring problems with impact assessment. First, it is easiest to measure first-order impacts (like depressed crop yields or water shortages) than it is to assess second-to-nth order impacts such as economic losses in local and regional economies (e.g., unemployment and other "ripple effects") or social/psychological impacts (stress-related illnesses and so forth). This is partly because data on higher-order impacts are poor or less easily accessible, but it is also related to the difficulty that the careful impact assessor finds in unequivocally linking such impacts to the drought itself. This problem is heightened by the rather fuzzy nature of drought. Although natural hazards researchers may quite credibly link indirect impacts like mortgage default or social pathologies to discreet events like floods or tornadoes, the creeping and pervasive nature of drought makes such linkages less clear. The result of these problems is that drought impact assessments tend to be limited to rather repetitive accountings of first-order impacts, which add little to our understanding of the full social burden of drought, and more comprehensive studies tend to be ideographic and methodologically weak. A second (and related) problem is that impact assessors find it easier to monitor impacts per se than to follow the more critical elements of adjustment. We can more readily cite changes in water costs than follow long-term changes in how a water utility structures its pricing.

The problem of conducting credible and useful drought impact assessments that identify a full range of impacts and adjustments is two-tiered. First, the hypothetical impact sequence or template must be realistic and comprehensive; it should include human adjustment that might attenuate impacts. Second, the researcher must firmly establish the causal link between drought and impact. It is insufficient to rely on logic chains (e.g., "since yields are low, farm income is down, thus farm spending is down, so jobs are being lost in the service sector"); such logical statements should be verified by empirical analysis carefully screened to show the drought signal in key impact variables. In the remainder of this paper, we describe approaches to more credible impact assessment that add to our understanding of how drought and human systems interact. To produce a more realistic impact template, we propose research steps that identify *a priori* drought sensitivities and potential adjustments. We illustrate this approach with analyses of drought impacts on midwestern corn production and western water resources management. To surmount the problem of measuring authentic drought signals in impacts data, we suggest greater reliance on the traditional research designs of longitudinal analysis and "case and control." We specifically propose approaches to case-control analysis at the end of this paper.

Assessing Drought Sensitivities in Agriculture: A Case Study of Midwestern Corn Production

Drought can occur in various degrees of severity and on numerous temporal and spatial scales (Karl, 1983; Karl and Koscielny, 1982). Droughts can develop and end in a matter of weeks or they can persist for years, and no month or season is immune to the onset of drought. Furthermore, droughts can occur at highly localized scales—for example, a few counties—or they can cover supernational regions at any one time. It is this complexity that allows drought to manifest itself in different ways, some of which pose problems for agriculture and some of which do not (Dracup, et al., 1980).

Wilhite and Glantz (1985) identified four major nonmutually exclusive categories of drought: meteorological, agricultural, hydrological, and socioeconomic. They stress that a meteorological drought is not necessarily an agricultural drought, and some of the more common indices of agricultural drought are mentioned, including the Palmer Drought Severity Index (PDSI) and the related Crop Moisture Index. Alley (1984) has severely criticized the PDSI for certain unrealistic assumptions in its calculations. For example, there is no lag between the introduction of moisture as precipitation and its appearance as runoff. From an agricultural standpoint, however, perhaps the greatest problem with this and related indices, as Wilhite and Glantz argue, is that they are usually deployed with too little regard for crop management and phenological drought sensitivities. PDSI values indicating the existence of drought can appear at times during the growing season when moisture requirements of a given crop are low; therefore, as long as moisture is adequate when requirements are high, yields may only be modestly affected, if at all. Yet, there is a tendency to label any drought occurring during the growing season as injurious to crops.

We argue that the initial step in performing an agricultural drought impact assessment is to specify what is meant by the term *agricultural drought*. Thus, there must be an evaluation of the sensitivities of specific crop growth stages to dry conditions and an enumeration of the types of dry conditions (e.g., timing, intensity, persistence, and so forth) that represent drought to a given crop.

In this section, we discuss an approach that is being used to assess drought sensitivities of corn production as part of the Climate Impacts, Perception, and Adjustment Experiment (CLIMPAX) effort. Results of this assessment are used to identify drought-sensitive periods within a crop-growing season.

A Method for Identifying Drought Sensitivities. Much of what is known about agroclimatic sensitivity has been gleaned from formal attempts at weather-crop modeling. Geigel and Sundquist (1984), in their review of these modeling efforts, propose three generations of weather-crop models. The first two generations are a class of models frequently referred to as statistical "black boxes." These tend to be multivariate regressions with a single output, usually expressed as crop yield.

The problem with these approaches, as Katz (1979) points out, is that the weather and technology-independent variables are highly collineated. This makes it difficult, if not impossible, to partition the effects of weather on yields from the effects of technology. Thus, there is little that these models can say about the effect of weather fluctuations on specific phenological processes and management decisions. Moreover, they are of no use in ferreting out potential adjustments farmers may make in response to impacts on yields.

The third generation of models are referred to as deterministic physiological models. These models (e.g., Meyer, et al., 1979) attempt to simulate the effects of weather on individual biophysical processes and management decisions. Model inputs may include daily weather, management, and technology variables, and outputs include impacts on growth stages at any point in the growing season.

Physiological weather-crop models hold the greatest promise for identifying individual agroclimatic sensitivities. These models provide the building blocks of weather-crop development relations, which result in different levels of yield. Unfortunately, these models are not without their problems as well. Most of the models are highly experimental and too poorly developed to be of direct use in a drought sensitivity assessment. Perhaps even more important, the models tend to be parameterized with highly localized empirical relationships that may not be valid at the appropriate spatial scales.

Limitations of the models discussed above notwithstanding, a fairly extensive understanding of agroclimatic relationships has been gained. Many of the relationships have emerged from these extensive modeling efforts along with more basic agronomic research and can be appropriately accepted as "facts." Conversely, many other relationships have not withstood rigorous scientific testing, but their validity is widely accepted nonetheless. Agroclimate experts may not be able to precisely define the causal mechanism for a given crop response to variable weather, yet these experts rely on this relationship as a heuristic "rule of thumb." The problem is that agroclimatic facts and heuristics have yet to be merged into a comprehensive form.

The approach used in CLIMPAX for such a compilation borrows from the field of artificial intelligence and is known as *expert systems*. An expert system is the embodiment within a computer of the detailed reasoning process an expert in a particular field uses in arriving at the solution to a particular problem (see Hayes-Roth, et al. [1983], for a discussion of expert systems).

Figure 1 is a schematic of how an expert system is organized. At the top of the architecture is the "domain problem." This is a reasonably well-defined problem for which a solution is being sought with human expertise. In this research, the central problem is determining what types of climate fluctuations are most likely to produce agricultural impacts and adjustments and for what reasons.

To extract knowledge from a "domain (agroclimatic) expert," a "knowledge engineering" approach is used. Here a scientist, who is familiar with both the domain problem and the way in which expert information will be entered into the knowledge

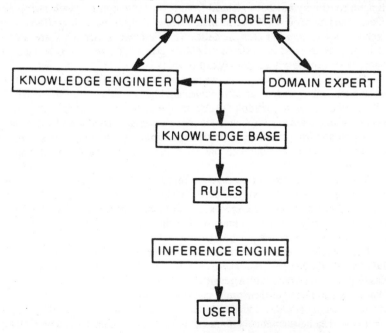

Fig. 1 Typical expert system architecture.

base, has intensive interaction with the domain expert in an effort to precisely capture all of the assumptions, facts, and rules of thumb the expert uses in arriving at a solution. This person is known as the "knowledge engineer." Knowledge engineering involves not only transferring information about crop-climate sensitivity from the expert to the knowledge base but also resolving differences of opinion between experts and demonstrating the knowledge base back to experts for their evaluation as well. Differences of opinion between experts over a certain issue are resolved by reducing the conflicting arguments to their most basic underlying logic and assumptions. If, after this step, conflicts cannot be resolved, a decision on which argument to accept is made by a committee of all of the experts.

The full extent of development of an agriculture-drought sensitivity expert system would additionally include formal specification of a set of rules derived from the knowledge base. These rules would be entered into the actual expert system development software. For purposes here, however, formal completion of the expert system is not necessary. The information to be used to develop sensitivities can be lifted directly from the knowledge base. The only reason to fully develop the computerized version would be to provide a highly structured environment within which the experts might additionally evaluate the knowledge base.

CLIMPAX Knowledge Engineering Approach. The approach used to extract knowledge of corn weather sensitivities is outlined in Fig. 2. Nine experts were recruited for the study, including two agricultural economists, two agricultural meteorologists, three agronomists, a crop consultant, and a climatologist. An initial core of experts from Illinois was used to develop a prototype knowledge base for Illinois corn production that was subsequently extended to corn for all of the Midwest production belt.

Brief Description of Results: The Illinois Case

Obviously, the worst-case drought scenario would call for dry conditions to persist throughout the growing season. The probability of this occurring on a consistent basis, however, is quite low. Thus, the emphasis is placed on identifying periods *within* a given growing season when drought-related weather conditions have the greatest effects on corn production.

Results of the expert system analysis suggested two major periods of drought vulnerability. The first is the corn reproduction (anthesis) and the final grain-fill stage (early to late July in the southern half of Illinois and mid-July to early August in the northern half of Illinois). Moisture and nutrient uptake is high during this period, and insufficient amounts of either are detrimental. This is supported statistically by Huff and Neill (1982).

The second period corresponds with spring planting and emergence. In this period, mild drought can be a positive factor since it facilitates scheduled planting activities and, provided there is sufficient moisture for germination (as there almost always is in Illinois, drought or not), full-season corn varieties have ample opportunity to reach maturity. The drought-related problem during spring planting and emergence actually stems from too much rainfall rather than too little. When this occurs in the emergency phase (May to early June across the whole of the state), the excess moisture discourages vertical penetration of root systems. If rainfall levels remain high during the rest of the

194

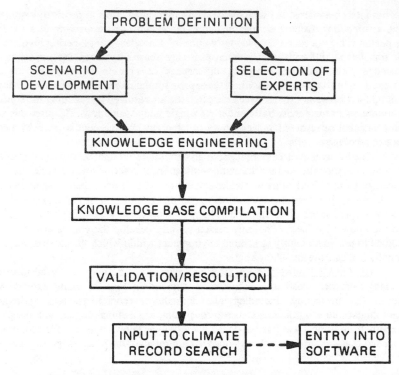

Fig. 2 CLIMPAX expert system approach.

growing season, then problems will be minimal. However, if it becomes dry during the post-emergence part of the growing season after a wet spring, then corn plants are at a higher drought risk than usual since roots cannot reach moisture stored deeper in the soil profile.

The information generated by this approach serves a number of useful purposes. For example, it serves to illustrate the times in the growing season when dry conditions are most likely to produce yield-altering impacts on crops. To this end, expert analysis is being used in Illinois in conjunction with the Palmer Drought Index (Easterling, et al., submitted) to develop an improved method of postaudit agricultural drought detection. Equally important, the expert systems method gives insight into which specific processes and decisions are being affected by dry conditions. This is an important step toward identifying the range of adjustive mechanisms available for coping with drought impacts on agriculture.

ASSESSING DROUGHT SENSITIVITIES, IMPACTS, AND ADJUSTMENT IN WATER RESOURCES

The second section of this chapter (written by William Riebsame) focuses on assessing sensitivities and adjustments to climate impacts on water supply management in the western United States. Based on this work, a drought impact assessment procedure is described that helps the assessor identify a full range of potential managerial adjustments to changes in water availability. Again, the point to be made is that first-order impacts (i.e., streamflow, reservoir storage changes, and changes in water quality) do not tell the whole story of drought impacts because they blend into human adjustments or may be hidden or attenuated by human response. Indeed, it is worth reiterating that the difference between impact and adjustment is semantic, and that a comprehensive impact assessment should include a thorough analysis of resource management changes related to drought rather than simple accounting of shortages or hardships.

Climate Fluctuations and Water Supply Systems

Water supply systems are, in most cases, both drought and flood management systems. Storage reservoirs, transbasin diversions, convergence facilities, and even pricing and allocation protocols are designed to provide a stable and predictable flow of water despite drought and to minimize the physical impacts of floods. Drought and flood management are two sides of the same operational coin, though experience has shown that water resource planners and managers spend more time and effort worrying about drought than floods, especially in the semiarid and arid environments that provide the setting for the world's largest water storage and conveyance systems.

We focus here on systems relying mostly on surface runoff. The typical surface water supply system consists of one or more reservoirs (used for storage, flood control, and hydroelectric generation), some back-up wells, conveyance facilities, treatment plants, and a distribution network. Facilities vary depending on the chief use of the water: agricultural, industrial, or municipal (e.g., household and lawn-watering use). Droughts stress such systems by decreasing the amount of runoff or ground water input to streams feeding the reservoirs or diversions.

Water supply systems are designed to absorb "expected" climate fluctuations and still meet basic demands. Typically, the historical period of hydrological data, or a critical period within the observed record, is used to estimate the physical water supply characteristics that will act as constraints on management, and to which the system should be "adjusted"—that is, designed to absorb impacts without system failure. Public trust and management convention require some level of supply reliability even in the face of stressful climate conditions, though there exist no universally accepted criteria for choosing a level of reliability. A rather wide margin of excess capacity is engineered into most water systems because of both hydrological and social uncertainty. A rich literature exists on water system design addressing the complex problem of managing multiple physical and social variables, constraints, and demands (Maass, et al. [1962], compiled by the Harvard Water Program, is a benchmark work). Climate fluctuation is one of these variables, but it is typically relegated to background status; indeed, climate is generally considered to be stable in hydroclimatological analyses.

Identifying Drought Sensitivity

How a given drought affects the water resources of an area depends on the physical nature of the event *and* the sensitivity of the system affected. Drought impacts are enhanced when water demand closely matches supply and when there is a preexisting imbalance between, for example, the timing of supply and demand (e.g., when supply is low during peak demand, as in most irrigation systems). In these cases, system planners either have sought alternative supplies to supplement what might be called the normal climatically delivered runoff water by developing sources of ground water or imports from other basins, or they have developed large storage capacity that increases the system's ability to absorb supply/demand imbalances by saving excess water for use in dry periods (either intra-annually or interannually).

This buffering capacity is often quite large. At a recent U.S. National Academy of Sciences symposium, the chief of the Los Angeles water supply system argued that the foremost aim of water managers is to avoid shortages by maintaining excess capacity within the confines of economic and social feasibility; water managers are extremely risk- or failure-averse (Georgeson, 1986). At the same symposium, Dziegielewski (1986) noted that the traditional approach to avoiding shortages has been to prepare for a worst-case "design drought" during which the system could still provide a minimum supply. The design drought typically equals either the worst historically observed drought or a statistically synthesized drought unlikely to occur more than once a century. The supply that can be delivered "reliably" by a collection and storage system in the face of drought stress is often called the *safe yield* or *firm yield* and is determined from the relationship of virgin flow (or unmanaged raw water supply) to storage capacity and demand. Although there exists no widely accepted criterion for calculating safe yield, discussions in the literature (e.g., Russell, Arey, and Kates, 1970; Nemec and Schaake, 1982) point to a convergence of *a priori* failure probabilities (i.e., failure to meet demand) on the convenient value of .01. But different social and physical climates make this target more or less difficult to achieve. Russell, Arey, and Kates (1970) found large differences between design and empirical safe-yield values in New England supply systems. In some cases hidden supply cushions (see below) kept systems from failing during the severe mid-1960s drought. Other systems were patently ill-prepared for the period of short supply.

Measures of Drought Sensitivity. Assessing a system's sensitivity is the first critical step in the search for drought impacts and adjustments. A few studies offer some guidance in this process.

The Russell, Arey, and Kates work (1970) is a detailed "inadequacy" study of twenty-two Massachusetts municipal supply systems. They centered on the ratio of use to safe yield. Safe yield was defined by the "design drought" approach. In this case, the 1908-11 dry spell, which had a recurrence interval of roughly thirty years, acted as the design drought. They found that although this ratio, and ancillary data, helped identify particularly sensitive systems, actual drought impacts during the severe 1960s dry spell were counterintuitive to the sensitivity analysis for several systems. Two possible sources of this poor prediction were noted:

    1. In some communities where supplies were adequate, but impacts were severe, it appeared that overcautious management (i.e., large hedging

through conservation in case the drought continued) caused unnecessary shortages.

2. In some apparently inadequate supply systems, there existed a "hidden cushion" of emergency supply not generally made explicit in system descriptions and operating protocols—in essence, managers had added a safety margin to their safety margins.

One reason why such excess buffer might not show up in an initial sensitivity analysis is that it may have been added at another, higher level of decision making (e.g., planners responsible for controlling the number of taps might add a safety margin to the firm capacity claimed by system engineers, "just to be on the safe side"). Such tendencies must be accounted for in sensitivity analysis.

Schwarz (1977) approached drought sensitivity analysis in two ways: selected case studies of large northeastern water systems (e.g., New York and Boston); and simulations of drought-perturbed streamflow, with assessments of its impacts on the Potomac River system. He concludes from the second analysis that the system is relatively insensitive to the worst droughts that might be expected in a thousand-year simulation without significant climate change (i.e., about a 20% flow reduction over fifty-four months), but he also noted:

There are strong indications . . . that major increases in standard deviation are as important as reductions in [mean values of water supply]. There are further indications that sensitivity to changes in   streamflow . . . increase with the degree of development and with a decrease in the level of acceptable risk. In other words, the increase in storage needed to compensate for alternative scenarios and to maintain a specific draft increases with the size of the draft and with a decrease in the acceptable shortage index (p. 118).

That is, systems become more sensitive as they mature, and they may be just as sensitive to climate variability as they are to mean changes in climate.

An Approach to Sensitivity Analysis. Because water systems will be in different stages of development or decay at any given place or time, yielding quite different sensitivities and impacts from similar supply levels, drought impact assessment should include an evaluation of broad drought sensitivities. Such an analysis might begin with two steps: description of the resource system itself and analysis of recent operating records.

To identify points of potential drought sensitivity, water systems should first be examined to produce a resource profile. The resource profile would include basic descriptions of water sources (e.g., snowpack, ground water) and their relative contributions; relationships between supply, storage, and demand (i.e., the system's sensitivity to disruption); the availability of emergency supplies; special factors like in-stream flow requirements, salinity, and other water quality problems; and the basic infrastructural adequacy and flexibility of the system, which illustrates inputs, diversions, storages, transfers, and consumption points.

Physical characteristics of the raw water resource, and the basic relationship between supply and use, determine overall system sensitivity to drought. The chief source of supply determines a system's basic operational sensitivities. For example, snowpack-based systems relying on large surface storage are affected by total amount of snowpack,

the seasonal timing and conditions of its melt and runoff, other inflows (e.g., soil moisture, immediate runoff from rain events), and losses (e.g., evaporation, soil profile
recharge, and vegetative uptake and transpiration). Drought may affect the system via
any of these pathways.

A basic measure of water system sensitivity is the relationship between raw
supply and demand. In humid areas this might be calculated as mean flow of rivers and
extraction or actual use. Mean flow has less relevance in heavily developed, dry climate
systems with large reservoirs. Here the ratio of storage to demand is probably a better
measure of sensitivity, as applied in the cases described below. Systems characterized
by a narrow match between supply (defined in this case as storage capacity) and demand
are more sensitive to drought impacts.

At the simplest level of analysis, one can argue that if the storage-demand
relationship of a water supply system is close to 1:1, then that system will be very sensitive to changes in input, including changes due to drought. Of course, the system is also
sensitive to changes in demand, which are, in most cases, less clearly tied to climate conditions (although water demand might increase during drought, especially if the system
serves irrigated agriculture or large urban demand).

But the concept of system sensitivity is complicated by nonlinear relationships
between system inputs, storage capacities, and operational reliability. Nemec and
Schaake (1982) explored the sensitivities of two derivations of the relationship between
storage and yield: the relationship between the amount of water that can be taken from a
reservoir at a constant level of reliability and the reservoir's storage capacity, and the
change in storage capacity needed to produce a fixed amount of water at a fixed
reliability level. By applying a hydroclimatological simulation model to four stream
basins, with a hypothetical large reservoir in each, they found that the reliability of reservoir yield decreased markedly as total storage neared the average annual runoff (a situation existing in many arid-zone systems). They also found that large increases in reservoir size would be needed to accommodate even small climate changes in basins where
storage closely matched demand. If downstream water needs are accounted for in system operational requirements, then the system does use essentially *all* of the water in its
basin, and the ratio of storage to demand provides a good index of drought sensitivity.
Interpretation of the ratio may be somewhat sensitive to differences in hydroclimatological settings, but it should allow useful comparisons between systems with similar natural
resource profiles.

Identifying Drought Impacts

The chief analytical problem in climate and society research, the rubric under
which we would classify drought impact assessment (see Kates, et al., 1985), is
demonstrating that any impact or response is causally associated with climate fluctuation
rather than with the many other physical and social elements (such as water resource
management) that affect complex human behavior. The resource profile and *a priori* sensitivity analysis can provide a reasonably clear indication of impact potential in a given
water system, while carefully conducted empirical analysis of water system operations
should allow the unambiguous identification of drought impacts and related adjustments.

To overcome the signal-to-noise ratio problem in climate impact assessment, empirical impact studies should more frequently employ traditional research designs such as longitudinal analysis and "case and control." It has been shown that recent droughts and other climate anomalies in the United States exhibit varied spatial and temporal patterns that should allow the researcher to compare cases with and without a given anomaly (often in nearby areas) or follow the development of impacts over time for a given system (see, for example, Karl and Riebsame, 1984). Wherever possible, similar water systems not experiencing drought conditions should be compared in order to measure the true drought signal in the affected system. Actual impact assessment methods applied within these approaches cannot easily be prescribed in advance, but we can identify potentially fruitful approaches. The basic data to be searched for impacts signals associated with a defined drought period are system supply, yield, use, and storage tabulations maintained for most public water systems. When matched with historical narratives of system operation, improvements and additions, and ancillary activities (like power production), these data can be used to describe the system's overall drought sensitivity (see the case studies below). Changes in system yield, inflows to treatment plants, and use may all reflect drought impacts. Time series of storage changes (perhaps analyzed to find any biases toward anomalous periods of increased or decreased precipitation), changes in operational schedules, and price structures may all reflect impacts. The assessor might look for patterns in variables like storage change during, before, and after identified drought episodes or compared between case and control systems. By linking impacts to an a priori sensitivity analysis, some indications of the predictability of impacts should emerge.

Identifying Drought Adjustments

Drought stress and/or system failure should lead to adjustment. As hypothesized in Fig. 3, adjustments might take place because of either a change in climate that increases drought magnitude and/or frequency (Fig. 3a) or changes in the operating limits of the system, often driven by increasing demand (Fig. 3b). Adjustments in water supply management can be divided into routine and extraordinary or emergency actions (e.g., drawing down reservoirs to absorb seasonal runoff versus actually cutting off deliveries). Reservoir systems routinely absorb small variations in climate inputs, but conditions occasionally require actions beyond routine—sometimes even the reassessment of design criteria if managers find themselves often taking actions that in the past were considered extraordinary or emergency measures. There also exist large policy and financial differences between short-term and long-term adjustments (e.g., cutting back supplies to some users versus expanding storage capacity) or between temporary and permanent adjustment, as illustrated in Fig. 3. System redesign, or long-term changes in operating procedures, are paths by which management activities are permanently adjusted to drought. One can imagine an ensemble of adjustments evolving over time to make a system less vulnerable to drought impacts. This is illustrated for agriculture in the U.S. Great Plains in Fig. 4 (from Warrick, 1975).

Changes in either supply or demand will alter the system capacity needed to maintain a constant safe yield, and managers/planners should, theoretically, monitor such changes and attempt to adjust system characteristics accordingly. In reality, adjust-

200

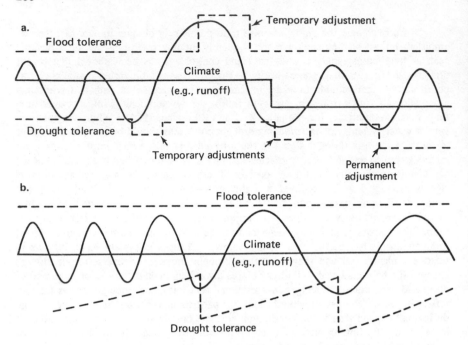

Fig. 3 Hypothetical drought adjustment patterns (a) under a fluctuating climate and (b) with system change (e.g., growing demand) interacting with climate variability.

ments (especially in water resource systems) do not occur uniformly as systems age, but are effected in a steplike manner determined by the long planning time of control facilities. Climate fluctuations such as droughts (as opposed, say, to volumetric or temporal changes in demand) pose especially difficult adjustment problems for several reasons. First, droughts develop slowly and their early indicators are subtle and difficult to detect, and even more difficult to extrapolate into the near future. Second, as demonstrated by Nemec and Schaake (1982), storage capacity is nonlinearly related to reliability of meeting demand, especially in dry climates. Large increments in storage may be needed to accommodate even relatively minor droughts while maintaining the same level of reliability. Recognizing this, arid zone water planners have traditionally maintained rather large storage buffers. For example, the system of reservoirs on the Colorado River in the southwestern United States stores several years of the river's mean annual flow, an extraordinarily high storage-to-flow ratio that most systems cannot afford.

Some indication of adjustment is available from system operation records. Changes in storage reflect decisions to fill or lower reservoirs in response chiefly to changing raw water supply. Annual operational narratives can help the assessor isolate

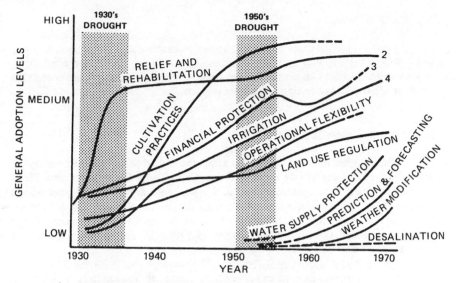

1. Very rough approximation of relative levels of adoption.
2. Institutional arrangements for R&R--not payments.
3. Shape of curve generalized from number of acres insured and amounts of loans in the United States (dip in 1950's reflects lower adoption of insurance at that time).
4. Based on total irrigated acres in the United States.

Fig. 4 Generalized historical trends of drought adjustment.

storage changes that were due to new construction, repair and maintenance activities, or environmental quality activities (like fisheries maintenance) rather than drought.

One approach to identifying adjustments and their possible influences on actual impacts would be to create a "management profile" that lays out both routine and extraordinary activities (e.g., reservoir operations like fill, drawdown, and spilling) plus short-term and long-term options for adjusting system performance to meet new criteria. The management profile might be cast into a seasonal calendar of operations, identifying particular times and activities that are sensitive to climate-related changes in supply or demand. Adjustments to drought should show up as aberrations in system operation (e.g., earlier-or later-than-normal reservoir drawdown). The lesson from Russell, Arey, and Kates's analysis, however, is that it is important to identify a full range of adjustment, perhaps even adjustments that most managers cannot articulate in interviews or that would not be explicit in operational documents. Here the type of flexible case study conducted by Schwarz, or interview techniques that go beyond front-line managers to others who have had some input to system planning, would be appropriate.

TWO CASE STUDIES

Two longitudinal cases of drought impact assessment are now presented. They roughly follow the stepwise approach of assessing sensitivity impact and adjustment. The Denver case focuses on sensitivity and impact, and the California case centers on the role of adjustment in affecting subsequent impacts.

Drought and the Denver Water Supply

The last great enduring drought to affect the United States occurred during the mid- and late-1970s. Parts of the upper Midwest, Great Plains, Rocky Mountains, Sierra Nevada, and Pacific Northwest were hard hit. Drying began as early as 1974, reached its worst in 1977, and rather quickly ended, with above-normal precipitation in many drought areas during late 1978. The Denver water system was one of many western urban systems affected by the drought. Its previous drought experience was a two-year dry spell in 1962-63.

Resource and Management Profiles. The resource profile for the Denver system shows that it derives most of its supply from snowpack in three large basins straddling the continental divide. Water is collected by a complex of transmontane tunnels, diversion/intakes, and streams that empty into several large reservoirs. Treatment for domestic consumption is accomplished on-line before delivery of the raw water into the municipal distribution system. Reservoirs are brought to peak storage during the May-June runoff, and low storage usually occurs around September, at the end of the peak demand season. Immediate runoff from convective summer rains, or early autumnal frontal precipitation, is stored or sent through the system as immediate supply if needed. Excess supply, senior rights water, and minimum stream maintenance flows are passed through the urban area and down the South Platte River.

Denver's water managers operate within the typical restrictions of a municipal and industrial supply system. They attempt to guarantee firm supply by maintaining large storage capacity to absorb impacts from the region's occasional multiyear dry spells. The system's historical development (Milliken, 1985) reflects these constraints and demands. During the post-war years of rapid growth, planners kept system capacity ahead of demand by acquiring more water rights (often through interbasin transfers) and building larger conveyance and storage facilities (Fig. 5a). After about 1965 a set of constraints—nearly complete appropriate of regional supplies, environmental concerns, financial problems (most of the users were not metered, paying a flat rate that fell far short of the water's real costs), and decreasing federal support for water development—hindered further physical expansion, and managers began to concentrate more on controlling use. Nevertheless, as discussed below, the Denver Water Board has decided that further physical expansion (especially of storage) is the preferred means of reliably meeting demand in the future (U.S. Army Corps of Engineers, 1987).

Drought Sensitivity. Low snowpack, lack of summer convective precipitation, and warm summer temperatures in the distribution area (leading to increased demand, especially for lawn watering) constitute the system's worst drought stress scenario, according to managers. Their chief means of adjusting to depressed supplies is to utilize stored water. Although there is no universally accepted "industry standard" for storage-

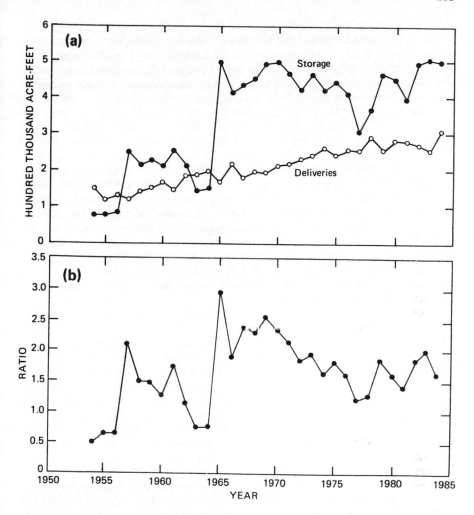

Fig. 5 (a) Annual storage and deliveries for Denver. (b) Ratio of storage to use for Denver.

to-use ratios, Denver's water managers feel that their current (1975-84 average) ratio of about 1.5 (see Fig. 5b) is too low, especially given steady growth in demand. In the past thirty years the system has swung from a low storage/use ratio of 1.2 (1954-63) to a high of 2.05 during 1965-74—the first decade after a major new reservoir was filled. Since then, this two-year storage buffer has been eroded to the current 1.5 years of demand. Thus, the system was at a stage of relatively high drought sensitivity during both of the two recent drought periods, 1962-63 and 1974-77. Yet, there were some differences in the impacts and adjustments associated with these dry spells.

Drought Impacts and Adjustments. The low runoff years in 1962-63 and 1974-77 caused net storage decreases (Fig.5a). In both periods, approximately one-third of the stored supply was used, and only a switch to abnormally wet years at the end of each drought allowed managers to reestablish nearly full capacity in short order. Indeed, 1965 was one of the wettest runoff years on record, allowing not only the refilling of storage depleted during the 1962-63 drought, but also rapid filling of the new Dillon reservoir. Recovery from drawdown during the mid-1970s was somewhat slower, but exceptionally high snowpack seasons beginning in 1979 have brought the system back to capacity. Thus, the system's record may not fully illustrate its drought vulnerability. A dry spell not ended by exceptionally wet conditions could create a longer-lasting deficit.

During the 1962-64 drought, managers did not implement mandatory residential or commercial water conservation because they felt sure that the new reservoir at Dillon, and associated transmontane diversions (allowing Denver to tap previously unused water rights on the west slope), would quickly improve the system's safe yield. They felt confident in drawing one of the system's main reservoirs—Antero—completely dry and using half of the total storage in several other reservoirs, depleting existing storage by 69,755 acre feet, or almost 30% of the capacity then available. This strategy worked. Not only were they able to draw on previously unused sources via Dillon, but exceptionally heavy snowpack in 1965 allowed them to fill the new reservoir extraordinarily quickly (i.e., in less than two calendar years).

The situation was somewhat different during the mid-1970s drought. The system had been operating with an average storage-to-use ratio of 2.1 for the ten-year period before the 1974-77 dry period, but the ratio declined to 1.5 during the dry spell itself. During 1977, managers, uncertain of the ultimate length and severity of the drought, instituted mandatory use restrictions that apparently reduced demand by 5% to 7%, compared to what it would have been without restrictions. The restrictions also reduced peak demand. They used legal restrictions on water use to keep the necessary drawdown to roughly 20% of the now much-enlarged storage capacity because no new supplies were in the offing. The restrictions were made voluntary after the system was brought back to full storage capacity during the above-normal precipitation years following 1978.

One interesting effect of the mid-1970s use restrictions is that they seem to have evolved, even in their voluntary form, into a "permanent" drought adjustment. A recent analysis by the Denver Water Department (Martin, 1986) showed that use still reflects the restrictions several years after they were lifted.

The 1970s experience and the convergence of supply and demand obvious in Fig. 5a have added momentum to managers' perception that additional storage is necessary. System planners now feel quite vulnerable to drought and are pushing for a new 1.1-million-acre-foot reservoir called Two Forks, which would triple the system's storage capacity (U. S. Army Corps of Engineers, 1987). Although we suspect that it could be demonstrated that the perceived need for more storage capacity increased during dry spells, managers pointedly argue that the planned new reservoir has been discussed occasionally during most of this century! Until this reservoir is constructed, or demand falls drastically, the ratio of supply to use will be close to one, and the system will be susceptible to severe restrictions in future multiyear droughts.

Drought Impacts and Adjustments in the California State Water Project

The 1976-78 drought in the western United States was even more severe in northern California. Two exceptionally low streamflow years (1977 and 1978) depleted reservoirs, leading to mandatory use restrictions above those allowed in user contracts. The chief water system of interest in the area is the California State Water Project, which services three types of water: agricultural, industrial, and municipal.

Resource and Management Profiles. The State Water Project (SWP) derives most of its supply from rainfall and, to a lesser extent, snowpack (delayed) runoff in the Sacramento and San Joaquin River basins. Of the current firm yield of roughly 2.4 million acre feet of water, about 75% is used in northern and central areas, while the remaining 25% is contracted (but not always actually delivered) to southern California for use by the Metropolitan District Commission (i.e., domestic water for Los Angeles). The system's actual yield record is shown in Fig. 6, which also illustrates a key source of system flexibility: the difference between firm or "entitlement" water and "surplus" water. Simply speaking, entitlement water is contracted for delivery under all but the most severe supply constraints. The risk criteria for entitlement water has been set at a 1% chance of deficiency in any given year. Surplus water is declared in most years, and sold at a discount, sometimes merely for the cost of delivery. This supply structure allows the system to maintain a reliable core yield but still make beneficial use of the full amount of water available in the average year (in almost all cases, firm yield will be substantially less than average yield-the difference depending, of course, on the reliability criterion applied to firm water supply).

The SWP began deliveries in the early 1960s and rapidly contracted most of its available firm supply. Rapid commitment of supply made the system more susceptible to drought impacts as it erased the buffer of uncontracted water. This buffer has been maintained at a remarkably large value, as illustrated in Fig. 7a. However, the system

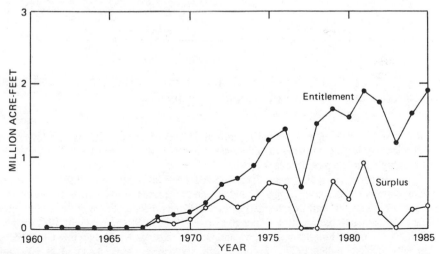

Fig. 6 California State Water Project entitlement and surplus water deliveries.

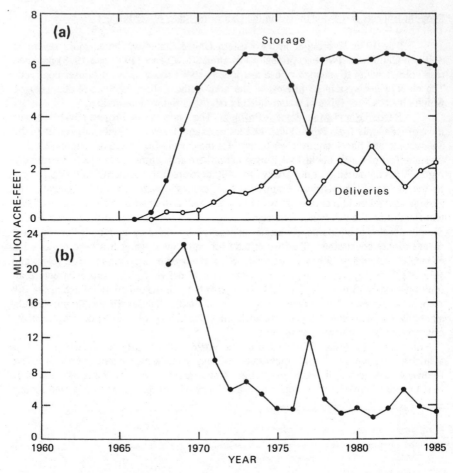

Fig. 7 State Water Project (a) maximum annual storage and total deliveries and (b) ratio of storage to deliveries.

has evolved from a huge buffer during the early years of contract-letting to a lower but still relatively large (compared to other water systems in the western United States) ratio of roughly 4.0 in the past decade (Fig. 7b).

Impacts and Adjustment. The first-order impacts of the recent low-flow years were depressed deliveries (Figs. 6 and 7) and increased unit costs. Physical and economic losses, as well as managerial response, have been detailed in several reports (e.g., California Department of Water Resources, 1978). Streamflows in 1977 ranged from 7% to 56% of long-term averages, and Oroville storage was drawn down to 25% of capacity by September 1977. Enforced use deficiencies were declared at 10% for municipal and industrial users and 60% for agricultural users. Total deliveries declined from 2.0 million acre feet in 1976 to .90 million acre feet in 1977. Deficiencies were eased greatly by the Metropolitan Water District's (MWD) decision to pump its allocation from the Colorado River rather than draw its share of SWP water (almost 25% of SWP's total firm supply). Agricultural losses (lost production and damaged crops) were estimated at $510 million in 1976 and $567 million in 1977. Hydroelectric production, which typically accounts for 20% of the state's electricity, declined by half in 1976 and two-thirds in 1977. Thus, experience shows that the project's service area does, indeed, exhibit large socioeconomic vulnerability to decreased water supply.

Short-term response centered on conservation, ground-water use, and very conservative management of Oroville storage. One of the surprising lessons learned from the dry spell was that use reductions were apparently more easily, and less painfully, instituted by municipal and industrial users than by agricultural users. This is counter to most drought reduction strategies, which target irrigation for initial supply reduction during shortages. These adjustments and above-normal precipitation allowed the system to rebound quickly in 1978; indeed, substantial surplus supply was again declared in 1979.

Perhaps the more interesting impact of the drought was that it, in concert with the SWP's growing drought sensitivity (i.e., demand approaching supply), set in motion a major evaluation of how project water is allocated. The case also illustrates the importance of assessing drought adjustments as well as impacts. In late 1977, during the worst of the drought, users raised concerns that the system was actually not as reliable their contracts implied. Deficiencies allocated to some firm contracts in 1977 suggested that the 1928-34 "design drought" target for firm yield was not sufficient for the system as it had evolved in the 1970s. In response, SWP managers initiated a new "rule curve" (the rules by which water is distributed to users during dry years) that set extremely conservative delivery/deficiency and carry-over (e.g., storage at the end of the year) requirements. It would provide, at something approaching 99% reliability, firm supplies even in the face of several years like 1977. The effect of this more deficiency-averse management is to make defined firm supplies much smaller than average supply. In the case of the new rule curve, redefined firm supplies were less than the ultimate target deliveries stipulated by the SWP's enabling legislation and long-term plan. To provide reliable supplies even in a multiyear drought, the new reliability target required large carry-over during a drought, at the expense of current-year deliveries (see California Department of Water Resources, 1985).

Sufficient precipitation following the mid-1970s drought delayed a climate test of the new protocol for almost a decade. By 1985, following this spell of drought-free years and in light of rapidly growing demand, SWP managers and users were questioning whether this ultrasafe approach was appropriate. The large excess capacity necessary to provide the target yield even during several years like 1977 began to look wasteful. The 1983 update of the state's water plan (California Department of Water Resources, 1983) suggested:

> Uncertainty regarding the capability of increasing developed supplies over the next several decades may justify and in fact may require taking greater risks in delivering water to customers . . . Some water projects [could] take greater risks by delivering a higher annual supply, leaving less carryover storage in case of drought. This would allow growing needs to be met in normal years . . . exist-

ing facilities may be operating in a more conservative manner than is necessary (p. 255).

This set the stage for a reevaluation of drought operating procedures aimed at assuming greater risks to provide a larger annual supply—that is, to meet growing demands without actually increasing raw supply substantially.

Planners have begun working on a new rule curve, a process that received greater impetus when the short, sharp drought in early 1985, combined with the existing conservative protocol, caused projected shortages in current-year deliveries in order to meet carry-over requirements (California Department of Water Resources, 1985). Some users and managers felt that the conservative protocol caused an "overreaction" to this short drought, and they were frustrated by the requirement to save water in case future years were dry.

The new rule curve would require less carry-over and is, essentially, an easing of the definition of firm volumes. It also reflects, as shown in simulations using two proposed new versions of the operating protocol (Fig. 8), an easing of management aversion to potential storage depletion. The rationale, argued by the SWP user consortium, is that since the future is always uncertain, they would prefer larger supplies and would accept the risk of depleted supplies in multiyear droughts. As shown in Fig. 8, the two proposed alternative protocols, when applied to the 1985 dry spell, would allow rapid drawdown to meet current user needs and with less carry-over in the design-drought sequence of 1929-34 weather conditions. A replay of 1929-34 conditions allows some storage recovery in hypothetical years 1987 and 1989, but in 1988 the procedures lead to total storage depletion (Fig. 8a) and to declining deliveries (Fig. 8b).

This proposed change in drought adjustment can be seen as a realignment of SWP policies to user perceptions of what constitutes "safe" water management. It will function best in relatively short drought sequences (e.g., the single-season dry spells experienced in 1981 and 1985) and will bring about system "failure" in a prolonged drought like 1929-34 and even perhaps in a repeat of the shorter mid-1970s drought. But it can also be seen essentially as a change in the definition of what constitutes system failure. Failure will no longer be defined as inability to deliver restricted water supplies in the second, third....nth year of a multiyear drought, but will be seen as any restriction in deliveries during the first year of a drought. The implications of such a realignment of drought management philosophy are profound. The change represents a shift of drought risk from managers to contractors to (ultimately) the consumers of water contractor products.

Discussion

Changes in water system drought sensitivity, differences in response to different periods of drought, and changes in underlying water allocation protocols all complicate the process of assessing the impact of drought on water supply. The Denver and California cases illustrate the complexity of assessing the full implication of drought impacts even within the system under study. We have not, however, begun to explore the propagation of impacts beyond the immediate system managers and users.

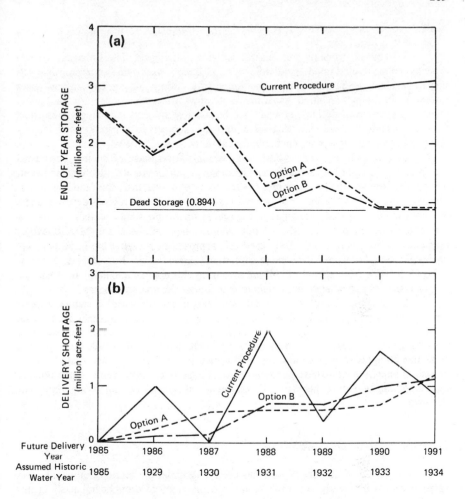

Fig. 8 Hypothetical operating protocols.

The cases show that besides immediate effects on raw water availability, price, use restrictions, and quality, a water system's drought experience affects medium- and long-range planning; the setting of risk levels; and (presumably) user and manager perceptions of risk, vulnerability, and the range of potential and/or desirable drought responses. If we are to answer the critical question of just how vulnerable our water resource systems are to drought impacts, then we must conduct more comprehensive impact assessments of multiple systems, applying criteria and study methods that allow us to draw some generalized conclusions from different systems. Because many water systems, especially those in the western United States, face growing demand and (as always) an uncertain climatic future, it is critical that we now seek a more comprehensive knowledge of system sensitivity and the best means to change that sensitivity.

APPLYING CASE-CONTROL TO DROUGHT IMPACT ASSESSMENT

Natural experiments are a useful tool for isolating credible linkages between drought and associated impacts and adjustments. They also provide an appropriate setting for evaluating the sensitivities mentioned in the foregoing agriculture and water resources examples. Natural experiments borrow from the concept of traditional laboratory experiment designs, in which the behavior of subjects receiving a prescribed treatment is compared with the behavior of untreated subjects in a strictly controlled setting (e.g., agronomic test plots, epidemiological studies).

In a natural experiment design, in which the response of society and broad ecosystems to drought is examined, strict laboratory controls are not possible. However, it is possible to view the behavior of these more complex systems within the contexts of "before," "during," and "after" approaches to drought. Moreover, regions experiencing a drought can be compared with adjacent regions of similar physical and social traits that did not experience a drought. Metropolitan Meteorological Experiment (METROMEX) researchers (Changnon, et al., 1981) used this approach in studying the impacts of urbanization in St. Louis on downwind precipitation characteristics. Researchers in the ongoing CLIMPAX (Kates, et al., 1984) are also using this approach to study the response of biophysical and societal systems to multiyear climate fluctuation epochs.

The combination of temporal and spatial controls advocated in natural experiments provides an opportunity to add scientific precision to the identification of causal linkages derived from the logic chain mentioned in the introduction. Furthermore, climatological analyses (see, for example, Karl and Koscielny, 1980) have demonstrated numerous droughts of various temporal and spatial scales that might serve as the focus of natural experiments. These numerous natural experiment opportunities can provide the compelling evidence necessary to establish linkages along the drought impacts template.

SUMMARY AND CONCLUSIONS

A substantial amount of work has been done under the rubric of climate impact assessment that is directly applicable to the specific study of drought impacts. In this paper, we have outlined some of the approaches taken and some of the enduring problems of these approaches in making credible linkages between drought, its assorted impacts, and adjustments to these impacts. Finally, we have reviewed examples of an ongoing research project focusing on U.S. agriculture and water resources in which drought sensitivities are identified and, in the water resources case, potential adjustments are enumerated. These are currently being evaluated within the context of a series of natural experiments employing case-control to establish more drought-impact linkages than was possible in previous analyses.

In conclusion, we stress the importance of developing more rigorous empirical methods such as natural experiments for tracing the full range of primary and secondary impacts of drought. It is through an accumulation of hindsight analyses of recent droughts using these approaches that compelling evidence can be found to prove the existence of such impacts. In our estimation, it is lessons from our recent past dealing with drought that will give the most insight into impacts of current and near-future drought.

211

As Whitehead noted (quoted by Hare in Kates, et al., 1985), "It is how the past perishes that the future becomes."

REFERENCES

Alley, W. M. 1984. The Palmer Drought Severity Index: Limitations and Assumptions. J. Clim. Applied Meteorol. 23:1100-1109.

Assessment and Information Services Center (AISC). 1980. U.S. Social and Economic Effects of the Great 1980 Heat Wave and Drought. National Oceanic and Atmospheric Administration, Washington, D.C.

Assessment and Information Services Center (AISC). 1982. U.S. Economic and Social Impacts of the Record 1976-77 Winter Freeze and Drought. National Oceanic and Atmospheric Administration, Washington, D.C.

Burton, I.; R. W. Kates; and G. F. White. 1978. The Environment as Hazard. Oxford University Press, Oxford.

Bowden, M. J.; R. W. Kates; P. A. Kay; W. E. Riebsame; R. A. Warrick; D. L. Johnson; H. A. Gould; and D. Weiner. 1981. The effect of climate fluctuations on human populations: Two hypotheses. pp. 479-513. In T. M. L. Wigley, M. J. Ingram, and G. Farmer, eds. Climate and History. Cambridge University Press, Cambridge.

California Department of Water Resources. 1978. The 1976-77 California Drought: A Review. California Department of Water Resources, Sacramento.

California Department of Water Resources. 1983. The California Water Plan. California Department of Water Resources, Sacramento.

California Department of Water Resources. 1985. Review of the State Water Project Rule Curve (draft). Division of Operations and Maintenance, Sacramento.

Changnon, S. A., Jr., ed. 1981. Metromex: A review and summary. Meteorological Monograph 18 (October). American Meteorological Society, Boston.

Dando, W. A.; R. D. Mower; and D. C. Munski. 1981. The North Dakota 1980 Drought: Economic Effects. Department of Geography, University of North Dakota, Grand Forks.

Dracup, J. A.; K. S. Lee; and E. G. Paulson, Jr. 1980. On the definition of droughts. Water Resour. Res. 16 (2):297-302.

Dziegielewski, B. 1986. Drought management options. pp. 65-77. In Water Science and Technology Board. Drought Management and Its Impact on Public Water Systems. National Academy of Sciences, Washington, D.C.

Easterling, W. E.; S. A. Isard; P. Warren; P. Guinan; and M. Shafer. 1987. Improving the detection of agricultural drought: A case study of Illinois corn production. Agricultural and Forest Meteorology (submitted).

Garcia, R. B. 1981. Drought and Man: The 1972 Case Study. Pergamon Press, Oxford, England.

Geigel, J. M.; and W. B. Sundquist. 1984. A review and evaluation of weather-crop yield models. Department of Agricultural and Applied Economics Staff Paper Series, University of Minnesota, St. Paul.

212

Georgeson, D. L. 1986. What are acceptable risks for public systems? pp. 49-64. In Water Science and Technology Board. Drought Management and Its Impact on Public Water Systems. National Academy of Sciences, Washington, D.C.

Glantz, M. H. 1982. Consequences and responsibilities in drought forecasting: The case of Yakima, 1977. Water Resour. Res. 18:3-13.

Hayes-Roth, F.; D. Waterman; and D. Lenat. 1983. Building Expert Systems. Addison-Wesley, London.

Huff, F. A.; and J. C. Neill. 1982. Effects of natural climatic fluctuations on the temporal and variation in crop yields. J. Clim. Applied Meteorol. 21(4):540-550.

Karl, T. R. 1983. Some spatial characteristics of drought duration in the United States. J. Clim. Applied Meteorol. 22(8):1356-1366.

Karl, T. R.; and A. J. Koscielny. 1982. Drought in the United States: 1895-1981. J. Clim. 2:313-329.

Karl, T. R.; and W. E. Riebsame. 1984. Identification of 10-to 20-year temperature and precipitation fluctuations in the contiguous United States. J. Clim. Applied Meteorol. 23:950-966.

Kates, R. W.; S. A. Changnon, Jr.; T. R. Karl; W. E. Riebsame; and W. E. Easterling. 1984. The Climate Impacts, Perception, and Adjustment Experiment (CLIMPAX): A proposal for Collaborative Research. CENTED, Clark University, Worcester, Massachusetts.

Kates, R. W.; J. Ausubel; and M. Berberian, eds. 1985. Climate Impact Assessment: Studies of the Interaction of Climate and Society. John Wiley and Sons, New York.

Katz, R. W. 1979. Sensitivity analysis of statistical crop-weather models. Agric. Meteorol. 20:291-300.

Maass, A. 1962. Design of Water Resource Systems. Harvard University Press, Cambridge, Massachusetts.

Martin, M. 1985. Preliminary analysis of 1985 water use. Unpublished memorandum, Denver Water Department, Denver.

Meyer, G. E.; R. B. Curry; J. G. Streeter; and H. J. Mederski. 1979. SOYMOD/OARDC—A dynamic simulator of soybean growth, development, and seed yield: Theory, structure, and validation. OARDC Research Bull. 1113. Wooster, Ohio.

Milliken, J. G. 1985. Water management issues in the Denver, Colorado, urban area. Unpublished paper. World Resources Institute, Washington, D.C.

Nemec, J.; and J. Schaake. 1982. Sensitivity of water resource systems to climate variation. J. Hydrol. Sci. 27:327-343.

Rosenberg, N.J., ed. 1980. Drought in the Great Plains: Research on Impacts and Strategies. Water Resources Publications, Littleton, Colorado.

Russell, C. S.; D. G. Arey; and R. W. Kates. 1970. Drought and Water Supply. Johns Hopkins Press, Baltimore.

Schwarz, H. E. 1977. Climatic change and water supply: How sensitive is the northeast? pp. 111-120. In Panel on Weather and Climate. Climate, Climatic Change and Water Supply. National Academy of Sciences, Washington, D.C.

U.S. Army Corps of Engineers. 1987. The Metropolitan Denver Water Supply. Draft Environmental Impact Statement, Vol. 1. Omaha, Nebraska.

Warrick, R. A. 1975. Drought hazard in the United States: A research assessment. Monograph No. 4, Natural Hazards Research and Applications Information Center, University of Colorado, Boulder.

Warrick, R. A. 1984. The possible impacts on wheat production of a recurrence of the 1930s drought in the U.S. Great Plains. Clim. Change 6:5-26.

Watts, M. 1983. On the poverty of theory: Natural hazards research in context. pp. 231-262. In K. Hewitt, ed. Interpretations of Calamity. Allen and Unwin, Boston.

Wilhite, D. A.; N. J. Rosenberg; and M. H. Glantz. 1986. Improving federal response to drought. J. Clim. Applied Meteorol. 25:332-342.

Wilhite, D. A.; and M. H. Glantz. 1985. Understanding the drought phenomenon: The role of definitions. Water Int. 10:111-120.

CHAPTER 15
CLIMATE IMPACT ASSESSMENT IN CENTRAL AND EASTERN KENYA: NOTES ON METHODOLOGY

Thomas E. Downing

INTRODUCTION

The long rains, normally occurring between March and May in central and eastern Kenya, failed in 1984, triggering one of the worst droughts in fifty years (Macodras, et al., 1986). The drought had begun in 1983 in most of Eastern Province in Kenya, and spread in 1984 to include the central highlands and much of the pastoral areas of the country. The drought was both extensive, covering most of the country, and intensive, with very little rainfall until the abnormally heavy short rains began in October 1984. Early in 1984 the National Environment Secretariat began to formulate a project to document drought vulnerability in selected areas of Kenya and to assess the range of practicable and effective responses available to smallholders. (The National Environment Secretariat [NES] is a unit of the Ministry of Environment and Natural Resources, charged with coordinating national policy regarding environment.) The resulting activity, called the Climatic Variability and Social Impacts Project, was a direct extension of the Secretariat's district environmental assessment program.

In mid-1984, NES was approached by the International Institute for Applied Systems Analysis (IIASA) to collaborate on the preparation of the Kenya Case Study for an edited volume, Climatic Variability and Agricultural Production in the Semi-Arid Region (Parry, et al., 1987). Gradually contributors to the Kenya Case Study were identified and enlisted, and funding was obtained from the Ford Foundation. This paper describes the methodology employed in preparing the Kenya Case Study (Akong'a, et al., 1987), including a summary of the principal conclusions about the effect of climatic variability on smallholders in central and eastern Kenya. References to the individual papers of the Kenya Case Study are provided in each relevant section. All the data and results presented here are from the case study.

The study area comprised three districts (see Fig. 1)—Kirinyaga in Central Province, and Embu and Machakos in Eastern Province (Downing, et al., 1986). The three districts were chosen because they span a range of environments from the upper slopes of Mt. Kenya (a national park) and the highland tea and coffee zones around Kerugoya and Embu towns; through the maize-sunflower zone typical of middle Kirinyaga and Embu districts and the hills of Machakos district; to the drier cotton, marginal cotton, and livestock-millet zones at lower altitudes (Fig. 2). Rainfall and evaporation, and hence the agroclimatic zones, are closely correlated with altitude. Five rainfall stations were used in the case study to represent the typical environments in the area:

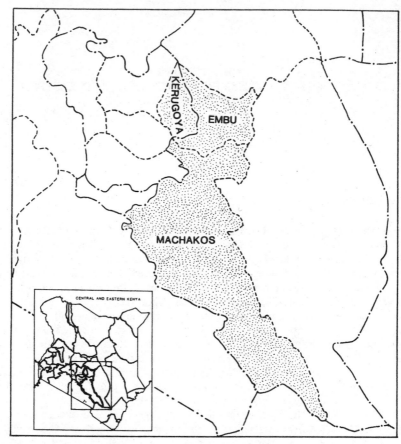

Fig. 1 Location of study area.

STATION	ZONE	DESCRIPTION
Kerugoya	I/II	tea-coffee zone
Embu	III	maize-sunflower-cotton zone
Machakos & Katumani	IV	marginal cotton zone
Makindu	V	livestock-millit zone

Other stations were used to provide spatial detail or to supplement the data available at the above reference stations.

The tea-coffee zone is densely settled. Average households own less than 3 ha, of which 1 ha might be for forage and grazing. The typical household owns less than 4 livestock units (400 kg equivalent), usually grade cows. Tea and coffee provide fairly reliable cash incomes, while maize and beans are grown for both food and cash. A similar land use pattern prevails in the maize-sunflower-cotton zone, with the notable ab-

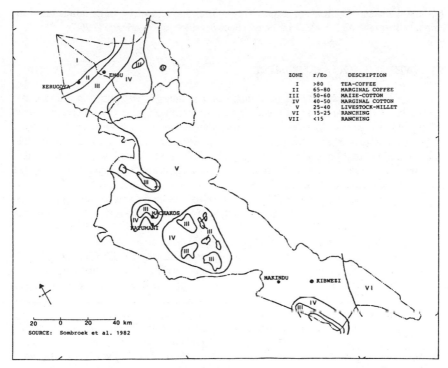

ZONE	r/Eo	DESCRIPTION
I	>80	TEA-COFFEE
II	65-80	MARGINAL COFFEE
III	50-60	MAIZE-COTTON
IV	40-50	MARGINAL COTTON
V	25-40	LIVESTOCK-MILLET
VI	15-25	RANCHING
VII	<15	RANCHING

SOURCE: Sombroek et al. 1982

Fig. 2 Agroclimatic zones of Kirinyaga, Embu, and Machakos.

sence of tea and coffee as cash crops. The average farm is about 3 ha, with 2.5 livestock units (400 kg equivalent).

The lower two zones have more land available for agriculture and grazing. Average farms in the marginal cotton zone are about 10 ha, with eight livestock units (300 kg local, Zebu cattle equivalent). Drought-resistant maize can be grown in good years, but the area is more suited to sorghum and millet. Holdings in the livestock-millet zone average more than 15 ha, with a stocking rate of 3-4 ha per 300 kg equivalent animal on off-farm grazing land. There are few reliable grain crops in this zone, although some sorghums and millets give acceptable yields. Drought-resistant crops such as pigeon peas are common.

In general, development has followed the altitudinal pattern, largely as a result of the general productivity of the farming systems, including income earned from coffee and tea, which are not matched with productive cash crops in the lower zones. The road network, number of markets, health centers and schools, and general nutritional and educational status are greatest in the coffee and tea zones and lowest in the lower zones.

Population densities throughout the study area are high, given the available land resources. In the tea and coffee zones, densities average more than 400 people per km^2, with annual growth rates of about 4.5%. In the maize-cotton zone, densities are lower (about 250 per km^2) and the annual growth rate is just over 2%, indicating a high rate of outmigration. The two lower zones have high growth rates (5.4 and 3.8%, respectively), but low densities (112 and 45, respectively). They have received large numbers of immigrants from the higher zones in the two decades since independence (1963).

CLIMATE IMPACT ASSESSMENT

Climate and society are best understood as interrelated entities in a transactive system in which each component modifies and is modified by every other component. Although this conceptual model is intellectually appealing, it is extremely difficult to use in practical studies of specific localities. A simpler model of climate/society relationships underlies the Kenya Case Study (Fig. 3). This linear model, with feedback from long-term processes, is a modification of the model presented in Kates (1985, p. 32). The principal elements of the model are:

1. Characterization of the climatology of the study area, focusing on the incidence and nature of drought, trends in rainfall, and trends in climatic variability.
2. Sensitivity of agricultural production to climatic parameters.
3. Impact of variability in agricultural production on smallholder economics.
4. The range and effectiveness of responses available to smallholders.
5. Underlying processes that may affect the long-term vulnerability to climatic variability.

The methodology employed in the Kenya Case Study incorporated three objectives. First, the entire drought hazard chain (as presented in Fig. 3) was assessed in the scope of one project. Second, the analysis and presentation were designed to be interpretable by nonspecialists—that is, the staff of government bodies who are called on to advise the policy makers. Third, a consistent set of climatic scenarios was used in each paper to characterize climatic variability and describe its effects on agricultural production and smallholders. The scenarios, defined according to the cumulative probability of exceeding the seasonal rainfall, are defined in Table 1. In addition, the project used the experience of the 1984 drought both as a natural experiment of a severe drought and as a source of anecdotes to illustrate general conclusions of the study.

Background on the project environment is important to an understanding the evolution of the project. The authors of the Kenya Case Study were two lecturers at the University of Nairobi (Akong'a and Mungai), a scientist formerly at IIASA who took a position at the Centre for World Food Studies in Wageningen midway through the project (Konijn), two staff of the National Environment Secretariat (Muturi and Downing), and a scientist at the Kenya Agricultural Research Institute (Potter). Downing was the coordinating editor of the study, on secondment from Clark University. The funding from the Ford Foundation was for a large project, in six districts, for which the Kenya Case Study served as a pilot. The funds were adequate, but precluded paying consultancy fees for additional technical staff, and the authors contributed to the volume as part of, and in competition with, their normal duties. The authors used nine different computers (personal computers and mainframes) in various institutions in Kenya and Europe. Although Nairobi is a center of communications and technology in Africa, communication between the authors (transferring data and reviewing draft papers) was hampered by distance, computer incompatibility, and conflicting work schedules. Even within Nairobi it is difficult to convene enough meetings for the authors to attend and

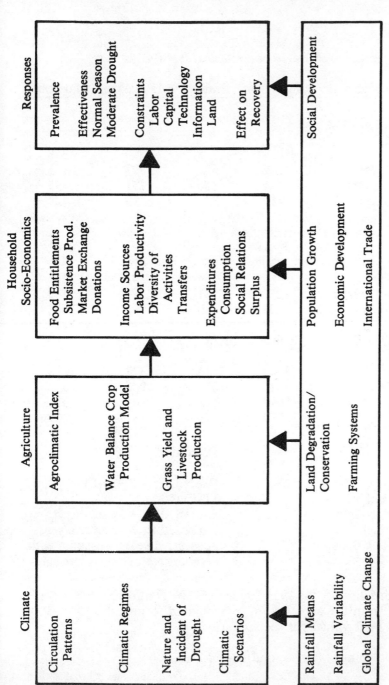

Fig. 3 Overview of climate impact assessment.

Climate	Agriculture	Household Socio-Economics	Responses
Circulation Patterns	Agroclimatic Index	Food Entitlements Subsistence Prod. Market Exchange Donations	Prevalence
Climatic Regimes	Water Balance Crop Production Model	Income Sources Labor Productivity Diversity of Activities Transfers	Effectiveness Normal Season Moderate Drought
Nature and Incident of Drought	Grass Yield and Livestock Production	Expenditures Consumption Social Relations Surplus	Constraints Labor Capital Technology Information Land
Climatic Scenarios			Effect on Recovery

Trends in Vulnerability

Rainfall Means	Land Degradation/ Conservation	Population Growth	Social Development
Rainfall Variability	Farming Systems	Economic Development	
Global Climate Change		International Trade	

Table 1
Climatic Scenarios at Reference Stations (rainfall in mm)

Season/Scenario	Kerugoya	Embu	Machakos	Makindu
March-May (Long) Rains				
Good year	1029	775	590	328
Average year	702	527	397	175
Moderate drought	481	350	211	95
Severe drought	450	231	133	24
October-December (Short) Rains				
Good year	730	657	671	603
Average year	461	354	344	261
Moderate drought	227	201	240	149
Severe drought	203	138	198	103
October-December (Agricultural Year)				
Good year	2043	1516	1377	1016
Average year	1525	1055	905	552
Moderate drought	1097	718	645	331
Severe drought	937	676	581	209

Scenario	Definition
Good year	Exceeded in 10% of the years
Average year	Median
Moderate drought	Exceeded in 90% of the years
Severe drought	Exceeded in 98% of the years
Back-to-back drought	Successive years (seasons) with moderate or severe drought

Note: Rainfall is for the 1951-80 period. The cumulative probabilities are taken from the actual data, interpolated to give the 10%, 50%, 90%, and 98% values for the scenarios.

Source: Downing, Mungai, and Muturi, 1986.

review their progress. In particular, major problems were encountered in transferring the data and programs for Konijn's crop production model, which requires a large amount of data and is written in an assembly language. The result is some inconsistency in the data used and the amount of transfer between one analysis and the next in the hazard chain.

Several kinds of data sets were available, including detailed maps (e.g., soils), aggregated maps (population), point-specific measurements (rainfall), sample surveys (household economics, yields), and case studies (farming systems). A geographic information system could have integrated these data and produced powerful analyses with overlays and composite maps. Because such a system was not available within the scope of the project's funds and technical expertise, much of the analyses were done using simple computer programs or by hand, and the integration between modes of analysis relied on the representative stations mentioned above, rather than coverage for the entire study area.

The next four sections review the methods used and major results of the study in each section of the drought hazard chain and presents a synthesis of the case study findings. The final section makes a few suggestions for climate impact assessment in developing countries.

DROUGHT CLIMATOLOGY

Understanding the climatology of drought is a prerequisite to elaborating the potential impact of climatic variability in Kenya (Downing, et al., 1987). The primary climatic element of economic importance is rainfall. Evaporation is less variable and can be fairly well predicted from altitude, distance from the sea, and number of rain days (a surrogate for cloud cover). Other parameters such as wind, humidity, and radiation are essential inputs to the crop production model. The dominant controls on rainfall in Kenya, in probable order of importance, are the movement and strength of the Intertropical Convergence Zone, altitude, and aspect. Negative rainfall anomalies (drought) cause the most severe and widespread suffering. However, above-average rainfall is also important in understanding the pattern of agriculture in the drier areas. It is the expectation of sufficient rainfall in even a few seasons out of ten that encourages farmers to plant maize in areas traditionally considered suitable only for sorghum and millet. Drought is a recurrent feature of the climatic record. Both drought and above-average rainfall tend to occur in spatially uniform patterns throughout the three districts, indicating a regional climatic mechanism. There are no strong trends in either the average rainfall or its variability, and the established rainfall cycles are not of sufficient strength to allow accurate prediction of drought.

Several seasons were selected to depict the seasonal rainfall patterns. Rainfall in October-December 1976 (Fig. 4a) was mixed, with the slopes of Mt. Kenya and the highlands of Machakos receiving average rainfall, while the lower zones experienced moderate drought. The following season, the March-May (1977) rains (Fig. 5a) were exceptionally good, with almost the entire area receiving above-normal rainfall. Similarly, almost the entire study area received less than 70% of normal rainfall in the 1984 March-May rains (Fig. 6a).

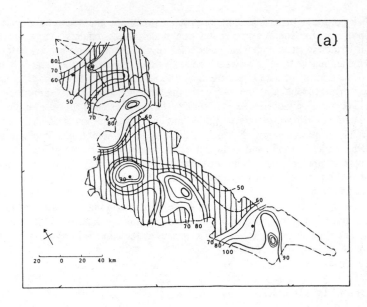

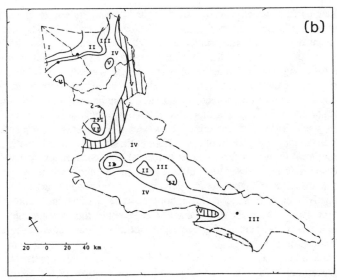

Fig. 4 (a) Rainfall as a percentage of normal in October-December 1976. (b) Agroclimatic zones in October-December 1976.

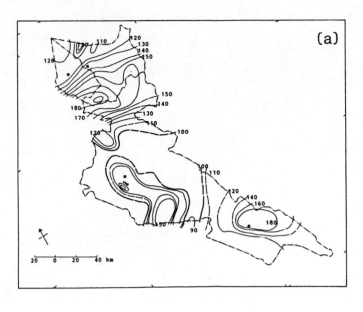

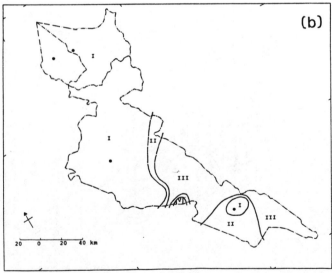

Fig. 5 (a) Rainfall as a percentage of normal in March-May 1977. (b) Agroclimatic zones in March-May 1977.

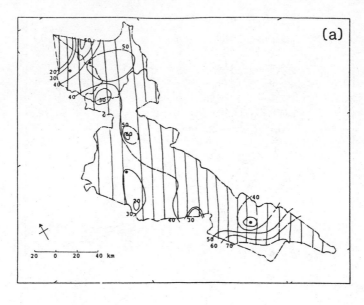

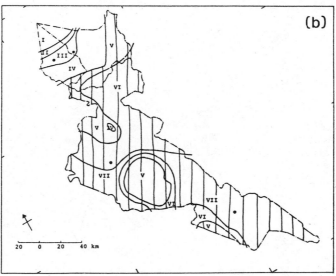

Fig. 6 (a) Rainfall as a percentage of normal in March-May 1984. (b) Agroclimatic zones in March-May 1984.

AGROCLIMATOLOGY

Agroclimatic Index

The Kenya Soil Survey developed an index to delimit agroclimatic zones in Kenya suitable for various crops (Sombroek, et al., 1982). The index is the ratio of annual average rainfall (r) to annual potential evaporation (Eo) (Table 2). The index has been widely used in Kenya as a basis for determining crop suitability and in district plans. It is a simple index, but by incorporating evaporation, it provides a more useful typology of climatic patterns than maps based on rainfall alone.

Agroclimatic zones were computed for seasonal rainfall in the three districts, using average seasonal evaporation based on the monthly proportions of annual evaporation in each zone (Mungai and Muturi, 1987). Thus, using average evaporation, the resulting agroclimatic zones indicate the variability of effective rainfall (although soil water-holding capacities are not included). The seasonal agroclimatic zones indicate wetter conditions than the annual zones, since the six driest months with the highest evaporation are not included. This necessitates provision of an eighth category, 0, for seasons with r/Eo 1. Figure 7 depicts the fluctuations of the seasonal agroclimatic zones for 1951 to 1980 for the four reference stations. The two stations in the upper zones, Kerugoya and Embu, average 0 (March-May rains) and I (October-December rains). Kerugoya rarely experiences drought in either season, while the October-December rains at Embu are less reliable than the March-May rains. The seasonal pattern is different to the south of the study area, with the October-December rains being more reliable than the March-May rains at Makindu.

The agroclimatic zones (0 through VII) were mapped for the same seasons for which rainfall departures from normal were mapped above. The zonation in the October-December 1976 rains (Fig. 4b) was similar to the average conditions. More than 39% of the area was in zone III or a wetter zone (suitable for maize production), and none of the study area was semiarid (zone VI) or arid (zone VII). In the following season, March-May 1977 (Figure 5b), only a very small area (less than 1%) would have been too dry to produce maize. Indeed, some of the wetter areas experienced problems with waterlogging and seed loss. The 1984 drought is evident in Fig. 6b. Only the upper slopes of Mt. Kenya were suitable for maize production, while most of the study area (64%) was arid or semiarid.

Using average figures for maize yields in each agroclimatic zone reported in the Ministry of Agriculture's Farm Management Handbooks (Jaetzold and Schmidt, 1983), potential maize yields under rainfall conditions can be estimated on an annual basis. Few actual measurements of maize yields are available in Kenya; and they have not been sufficient to correlate to the seasonal agroclimatic zones, or to calibrate the crop production model described below. The estimates of maize production in Jaetzold and Schmidt may be termed the best available expert estimates. They can be used to illustrate the fluctuations in production from year to year, but should not be interpreted as estimates of actual production in any given year. Data for the four scenarios and four reference stations are presented in Table 3. Even in good years, Makindu produces little maize. Kerugoya and Embu have high yields in good and average years, and even in severe drought years, Kerugoya produces some maize. Embu and Machakos produce little

Table 2
Agroclimatic Index and Crop Suitability Zones

Zone	I	II	III	IV	V	VI	VII
Description	Tea/Coffee	Marginal Coffee	Maize/Cotton	Marginal Cotton	Livestock/Millet	— Ranching —	
r/Eo Ratio	>80	65-80	50-65	40-50	25-40	15-25	<15
Climatic Designation	Humid	Subhumid	Semi-humid	Semihumid/Semiarid	Semiarid	Arid	Very arid
Ave. No. Growing Days/Year	365	290-365	235-290	180-235	110-180	75-110	<75
Potential Annual Plant Biomass Kg DM/Ha	>30,000	20,000-30,000	12,000-20,000	7,000-12,000	3,000-7,000	1,000-3,000	<1,000

Major Limitations:
1: [———soil fertility———] husbandry [———rainfall———]
2: [———husbandry———] rainfall husbandry
3: [———drainage———]rainfall [———soil fertility———]

Source: Sombroek, et al., 1982

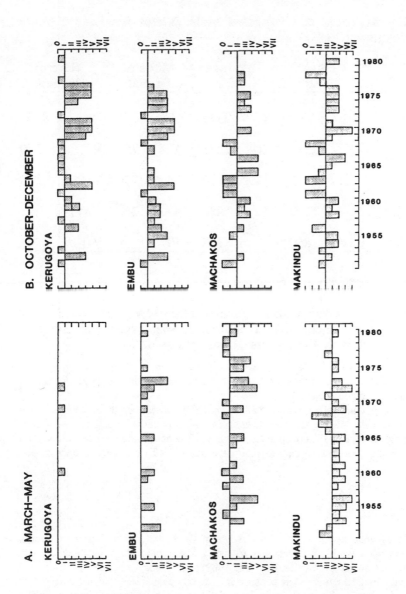

Fig. 7 Seasonal agroclimatic zones at four reference stations.

Table 3
Agroclimatic Zones and Expected Maize Yields for Four Climatic Scenarios (in kg/ha/yr)

Station	Good Year		Average Year		Moderate Drought		Severe Drought	
Kerugoya	0	>2375[a]	I	2375	III	1275	IV	850
Embu	I	2375	III	1275	V	250	V	<250
Machakos	I	2375	IV	850	V	250	V	<250
Katumani	II/	1000	IV	850	V	250	V/VI	0
Makindu	IV	850	V	250	VI	0	VII	0

[a]Subject to flooding and temperatures

Source: Average crop yields for farmers at the low technology level as cited in Jaetzold and Schmidt, 1983, except for Zone V, which is the best guess of case study authors.

maize in moderate or worse drought, but have the largest fluctuations in production between drought and good years.

A map of annual agroclimatic zones could be transformed to indicate estimated potential maize yields. The next step, to estimate total production, would require spatially disaggregated data on the area planted in maize. The case study did not include these two steps because of lack of data to verify the maize yields and lack of data on area planted.

Crop Production

A dynamic crop production model, originally created to model grain production in the developed world, was adapted to assess the relationships between climatic parameters and maize production (Konijn, 1987). The model operated on a one-day time period, but used ten-day data because it is readily available. The first stage of the model used radiation and temperature data to determine the potential biomass production. For one station in Machakos, these results, using actual measurements, were compared to the results when averaged data were used. The correlation was significant (r .90), and averaged climatic (not including rainfall) data were used where actual measurements were not available. The second stage incorporated a water balance equation of soil moisture, rainfall, and evapotranspiration for the crop phenology determined in the previous stage. The resulting water-limited biomass production is then partitioned between the leaf, stem, root, and grain, with the latter being the water-limited potential yield. The water-limited potential yield is the maximum expected with optimum management, soils, and nutrients.

A test of the model results against measured yields on farmers' fields in central Machakos revealed a reasonable correlation, although the model results were much higher than the observed yields. The third stage of the model limits yields based on the available technology and nutrients. This part of the model was not used in the Kenya Case Study. Instead, the water-limited potential yields were multiplied by 0.15 to approximate actual yields, given the low level of technology in the study area. The reduction to 15% of maximum potential yield is in accordance with the results of Njeru (1983) and Bakhtri, et al. (1984).

The model's estimated yields were compared to estimates of maize yields derived from the agroclimatic index. A clear relationship was demonstrated, and the simple agroclimatic index might be a useful method of predicting yields over large areas with little data or processing required.

Yields were estimated for two scenarios (good year and moderate year) at the four reference stations (Fig. 8). The results follow the general pattern noted in the above section. Maize yields at Kerugoya in the March-May rains are similar in both scenarios; the area can hardly be considered drought-prone. In contrast, at Makindu, yields are negligible in the drought year. The yields at Embu and Machakos in both seasons and at Kerugoya in the October-December rains are two to three times greater in the good year than in the drought year.

The model could be used more extensively to present a spatial picture of agricultural drought by including more stations in the analysis. Also, it can capture dynamic changes within the growing season. It could be used to estimate the effectiveness of altering cropping practices in response to an early estimate of the total seasonal rainfall. Preliminary results indicate that the optimum planting time is at the onset of the rains; a delay of ten days could result in a 20% reduction in yield (see also Dowker, 1964; and Goldson, 1963). The model has not been validated with sufficient independent data on yields, agronomic practices, and actual crop phenology. Therefore the results are best interpreted as estimates of the variability of yields, rather than predictions of actual yields and production in the study area.

Livestock Production

The five climatic scenarios were used to estimate the effect of climatic variability on livestock production—milk output in Kerugoya, Embu, and Katumani (used instead of Machakos because it is more representative of the livestock situation in the marginal cotton zone) and meat production in the Makindu area (Potter, 1987). The results are presented in Table 4, based on the livestock holdings and land resources described earlier as being typical for each zone.

The estimates of milk output are the results of research station and on-farm trials with forage and natural grass production, livestock requirements, and milk output. At Kerugoya and Embu, output exceeds 2 kg/day in average and good seasons. There

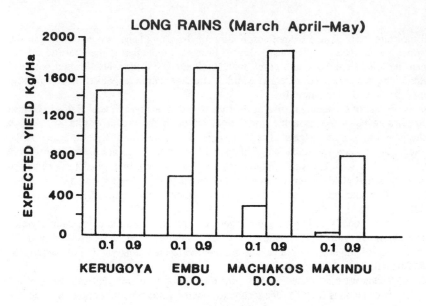

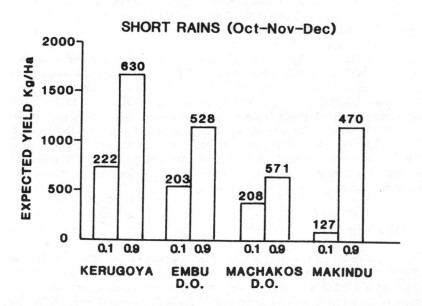

Fig. 8 Crop production model results for maize. 0.1 is the moderate drought scenario; 0.9 is the good year scenario. Numbers at the top of the short rains graph are seasonal rainfall in mm.

Table 4
Livestock Production for Four Scenarios of Climatic Variability

Station	Good Year	Average Year	Moderate Drought	Severe Drought
Kerugoya				
Daily forage Kg DM	52	36	30	25[a]
% of potential intake	95	65	55	45
Milk output Kg/Da	8-10	2-4	0-2	0
Embu				
Daily forage Kg DM	44	27	14	7[b]
% of potential intake	125	78	39	20
Milk output Kg/Da	8-10	3-5	0	0
Katumani				
Daily forage Kg DM	25	6	3	2[d]
% of potential intake	40	11	4	3
Milk output Kg/Da	0-1[c]	0[c]	0	0
Makindu				
Growth periods[e]	12	9	6	5
LWG — Kg/Head/Yr[f]	190	155	118	107
LWG — Kg/Ha/Yr	48	39	27	27

Note: Data are presented for the livestock situations described in the introduction. Daily forage is for the farm holding; % of potential intake and milk output are based on the average livestock units.

[a] Napier grass fodder would survive, but would be sufficient for maintenance only.

[b] Napier grass would not survive. In absence of off-farm grazing or commercial fodder, stock deaths will be high.

[c] Actual milk output related to crop residues and off-farm grazing rather than on-farm grazing or fodder production.

[d] High stock mortality due to poor state of off-farm grazing.

[e] Growth Periods are the number of ten-day periods with more than 20mm rainfall.

[f] LWG is live weight gain.

Source: Potter, 1986.

will be little milk output in moderate and severe droughts, with considerable stock deaths expected in Embu in severe and back-to-back droughts. At Katumani and Makindu, successful livestock production depends on access to off-farm resources, including purchased feeds. At Katumani, stock mortality rates of 70-80% may be expected in a prolonged drought because there will be no crop residues and little off-farm grazing after the first season.

In the lower zones of the study area, livestock are kept for meat production. Live weight gain over the year is related to the length of time for which suitable grazing areas are available. The number of ten-day periods with rainfall in excess of 20 mm is a better predictor of the state of the grasslands than is the total seasonal or annual rainfall. Livestock production can be highly profitable in average and good years, and herds can be maintained during moderate droughts. The outcome of prolonged drought will depend on the access to reserved grazing areas. A high number of stock deaths will be common because the grasslands will produce little additional growth and the variety of grass species available for consumption by animals is limited, thus restricting their diets.

SMALLHOLDER VULNERABILITY AND RESPONSE TO DROUGHT

Climatic variability, particularly drought, has an impact on small landholders in Kenya largely through changes in food entitlements—the access to food produced on one's own holding, purchased in local or distant markets, or donated by friends, relatives, or agencies (Sen, 1981; Akong'a and Downing, 1987). The three categories of food entitlements were also used to group coping strategies according to characteristics of the household economy—its sources of income and patterns of expenditure—and were evaluated for their prevalence, effectiveness in normal seasons and in moderate and severe droughts, impact of recovery from drought, and constraints to their adoption. The result is a descriptive framework for analyzing household drought vulnerability and responses. A rigorous, quantitative model would require more data on household incomes, expenditures, and preferences than were available. However, the available data were sufficient to document the major trends in drought vulnerability and responses. The framework may serve as a guide in the analysis of survey data previously collected or in the design of future surveys of household food security.

The term *vulnerability* describes the fundamental nature of the household and its environment, roughly equivalent to the term *adaptation* (as defined in the natural hazards literature—Burton, et al., 1979; and Wisner, 1977). *Responses,* also termed *adjustments,* are short-term activities triggered by the current state of the environment. The division between *vulnerability* and *responses* is artificial, largely depending on the observer's point of view. In the typology developed in the case study, the two terms were incorporated into one framework under the heading of coping strategies.

Vulnerability to the impact of drought in central and eastern Kenya is primarily determined by nonclimatic factors. Data on nutritional status indicate that the chief causes of malnutrition are low incomes, lack of inputs (including land), and involvement in cash cropping in some areas (Government of Kenya, 1983). Small landholders in the study area are well integrated into the cash economy, often selling maize to pay for school fees, then buying it back for food later in the year. Those with access to off-farm income are best able to cope with the demands for cash in normal years and with food shortages in drought years. The differential impact of climatic variability on households depends on the particular social and economic circumstances of the household.

In much of the study area, rural households have become less flexible in the range of coping strategies available in response to drought. Because population densities have increased and land holdings have been consolidated and adjudicated, fewer agricultural practices can be adopted to reduce vulnerability to drought or to lessen drought's impact. Grazing land is scarce and few farmers have fields in distant locations. The household unit is relatively stable in central and eastern Kenya. During the 1984 drought, few of the households (less than 25%) reported that any family member had left the area for more than a month. Most of the reasons given for moving were not related to the drought. Very few entire households left their homes during the drought. Kin networks appear to be less extensive and less able to support needy families in times of drought, compared to several decades ago.

Except for tea and coffee, household farm production is oriented toward subsistence needs, with low levels of purchased inputs and little use of hired labor. In contrast, household reproduction requires considerable amounts of cash for school fees, transportation, medical care, supplementary foods, housing improvements, and contributions to self-help projects (Harambee). This integration of rural households into the cash economy has resulted in a shift toward monetary drought-coping strategies. During normal years, cash is required for many things and is used to purchase basic and ancillary foods. On average, more than 30% of the households' maize consumption is purchased (Central Bureau of Statistics, 1982). The most effective coping strategies are those that provide off-farm income. In the various zones of the study area, some 10-30% of the households have a nuclear family member permanently employed.

The rural markets function reasonably well throughout the study area. Households have come to rely on purchased foods in normal years, and more so during drought. In 1984 there was not a widespread failure of effective demand. The drought was known as Ni Kwa Ngweta—"I could die with cash"—because people had money, but there was little food in the markets, and it was expensive (one to seven times the usual price, depending on the commodity).

The agricultural frontier has been extended into the drier zones in the two decades since independence, with a corresponding shift toward maize production instead of sorghum and millet. The result has been an increase in the cropping system's sensitivity to drought, and a shift in household adaptations to wetter years. Given the mix of available on-farm labor, changes in food preferences, and reliability of off-farm incomes, it appears that many smallholders should no longer be considered risk-averse farmers adapted to skewed (low and unreliable) rainfall regimes. Rather, they are opportunists, taking advantage of crops which do well in better years and buying food in poor years.

SYNTHESIS AND MAJOR CONCLUSIONS

The impact of climatic variability, defined by a consistent set of climatic scenarios applied to the same representative stations and typical households, is summarized in Tables 5 through 8 (Potter, et al., 1987). The results are presented for an entire year to facilitate a consistent comparison between zones and allow use of the

Table 5
Climate Impact Assessment for the Tea-Coffee Zone

| Scenario | Climatology | | | Agroclimatology | | Smallholder Economics |
	Typical Rainfall mm	% of Normal	ACZ	Production Forage DM Kg/Ha	Maize Kg/Ha	
Good year	2040	134	I	19,000	2400	Good to very good yield from food and cash crops. Off-farm and cash crop income available for investment, education, and household purchases. Adequate feed for grade cows.
Average year	1525	100	II	13,000	1900	Good crop yields for food and cash crops. Income available for investment, education, and household purchases. Grade cows require use of off-farm feed and crop residues to supplement on-farm forage.

Moderate drought	1100	72	III	11,000	1300	Fair crop yields. Proceeds from previous cash crops main source of farm income. Grade cows severely affected by feed shortage. Little milk output and calf losses result.
Severe drought	940	62	IV/V	9,000	250	Poor crop yields but total crop failure unlikely. Proceeds from previous year's cash crop vital. Grade cows severely affected as even off-farm grazing and crop residues in limited supply. Very little milk produced, calf deaths approach 100%.
Back-to-back drought	1300 & 940	—	—	—	—	Poor crop yields in both years. Little cash crop income in second year so credit and off-farm income required to purchase farm needs, food, and subsequent reinvestment. Stock deaths expected as feeds are unavailable in second year.

Note: Based on data for Kerugoya.
Source: Potter, et al., 1986.

Table 6
Climate Impact Assessment for the Maize-Cotton Zone

Scenario	Climatology			Agroclimatology		Smallholder Economics
	Typical Rainfall mm	% of Normal	ACZ	Production Forage DM Kg/Ha	Maize Kg/Ha	
Good year	1520	144	II	16,000	2000	Good to very good yield from food and cash crops. Off-farm and cash crop income available for farm requirements. Adequate feed for grade cows.
Average year	1055	100	III	10,000	1200	Fair to good crop yields. Forage for grade cows will require supplementation from off-farm or crop residue sources.
Moderate drought	720	68	IV	5,000	350	Cash and food crop harvests poor. Previous year's cash proceeds and off-farm income important for farm purchases. Survival of Napier grass marginal; feed supply sub-maintenance with possible stock deaths.

Severe drought	675	64	V	2,500	250	Very little crop or forage growth. Proceeds from previous year's cash crop needed for food and other purchases. Napier grass will die out; stock losses may reach 70-80% in absence of other feeds from off-farm resources.
Back-to-back drought	750 & 675	—	—	—	—	Little or no crop yield or forage growth in first year, followed by similar second year, resulting in no cash crop income and no food available on farm. Credit and off-farm income vital for provision of food and reinvestment in forage, livestock, and seeds after drought.

Note: Based on data for Embu.
Source: Potter, et al., 1986.

Table 7
Climate Impact Assessment for the Marginal Cotton Zone.

Scenario	Climatology		ACZ	Agroclimatology Production		Smallholder Economics
	Typical Rainfall mm	% of Normal		Forage DM Kg/Ha	Maize Kg/Ha	
Good year	1150	169	II/III	6,000	1000	Food crops give fair to good yield with some surplus. Very limited cash cropping. Milk output from crossbreeds depends on off-farm resources and crop residues; on-farm resources adequate for little more than maintenance.
Average year	680	100	IV	1,600	850	Poor crop yields, insufficient even for subsistence. Milk output extremely low; depending on off-farm feed resources as crop residues are very limited. Reliance on stock sales and off-farm income for food purchases.

Moderate drought	450	66	V	600	250	Crops yield little. Stock deaths high because of lack of feed resources both on and off-farm. Without off-farm income, famine relief needed.
Severe drought	440	65	V/VI	500	0	Crop failure. Stock deaths may reach 70-80%. Extensive famine relief required.
Back-to-back drought	450 & 480	—	—	—	—	Situation in year 1 same as for severe drought, but in year 2 stock sales will not be practicable as stock left will be very limited. Extensive famine relief will be required, followed by credit or grants for restocking and planting after the drought.

Notes: Based on data for Katumani, which is more representative of the livestock situation than Machakos, a wetter station in the same zone.
Source: Potter, et al., 1986.

Table 8
Climate Impact Assessment for the Livestock-Millet Zone

| Scenario | Climatology | | ACZ | Agroclimatology Production | | Smallholder Economics |
	Typical Rainfall mm	% of Normal		Forage DM Kg/Ha	Maize Kg/Ha	
Good year	750	150	IV	25	250	Maize crop minimal; more drought resistant crops such as sorghum yield better. Livestock produce little milk; main income from sale of meat. Maximum meat production from natural grazing.
Average year	500	100	V	20	200	Crop situation same as in good year. Reasonable meat production offers some cash income.

| Moderate drought | 350 | 70 | VI | 15 | 0 | Almost complete crop failure. Forage quality only good for short period; meat production limited by lack of grazing of adequate nutritive value. Without off-farm income, stock sales required, but market saturation gives low returns for stock in poor condition. Famine relief probably required. |
| Back-to-back drought | 300 & 250 | — | — | — | — | First year same as for severe drought scenario. Second-year effects depend on previous range condition, but stock deaths widespread. Famine relief required, followed by assistance in restocking and seed purchases after drought. |

Note: Based on data for Makindu.

Source: Potter, et al., 1986.

average annual yield data. The synthesis of the results of the case study is illustrative. As noted above, without a powerful computerized geographic information system, data could only be processed for a few representative stations. The links between productivity (yields), production, and economic impacts are complex and variable. Lacking sufficient data to discuss the entire range of household situations, the case study authors used common socioeconomic characteristics in each zone to illustrate the pattern and trends in the impact of climatic variability. The maize yield data are at least sufficient to illustrate the order of magnitude of climate impacts between zones and scenarios. The impact assessment is a simplification of reality, including only the impact of a short-term climatic event on a static socioeconomic environment. Longer-term feedbacks and other variables, such as insect pest outbreaks, are ignored.

The climatology columns indicate a typical annual rainfall and its percentage of the mean. The definition of moderate drought used in this study (rainfall that is exceeded in 90% of the years) corresponds quite closely to the more common definition of moderate drought (rainfall less than 70% of the median). Under agroclimatology, the annual agroclimatic zone (ACZ), forage or meat production, and maize production are given. The estimates of potential maize yields are based on the ACZ for the scenario year. The results of the crop production model are not included since they are seasonal rather than annual estimates of yields. The expected consequences of each scenario on smallholders are described in the last column.

The good and average years will be very productive in the tea-coffee and maize-cotton zones, enabling farmers to store excess food and invest profits. In the marginal cotton zone, a good year results in adequate production, while in average years households will have to rely on drought-resistant crops and off-farm resources. Even a good year in the livestock-millet zone will not produce high maize yields, although livestock will be productive. Only severe and prolonged droughts will have serious consequences in the tea-coffee zone, while a moderate drought in the maize-cotton, marginal cotton, and livestock-millet zones can have serious impacts in the absence of off-farm resources.

The implications of the Kenya Case Study for policy fall into three general categories: agricultural development, marketing and pricing, and food security. Agricultural technology and management practices among the majority of smallholders have stagnated in the last decade or so. Since most of the land suitable for agriculture is now under cultivation, the pressing need is for research stations and extension services to promote ways and means of increasing yields. In many areas, particularly in the drier zones, labor during the critical periods is a major constraint. The most promising approach appears to be "response farming." This involves tailoring farm practices to a prediction of the total seasonal rainfall based on the starting date of the rains and the rainfall in the first few weeks of the season.

Many crops could be more profitable for the smallholder if the marketing systems were improved. Maize, wheat, milk, meat, cotton, sorghum, beans, horticultural crops, coffee and tea-important crops in the study area—are controlled by government or marketing boards. In most cases, there is considerable room for improvement in the pricing structure, provision of credit, access to markets, and timeliness of payments. The shift in smallholders' economics, from maintaining large on-farm stores and being self-sufficient in food production to reliance on local markets for a large portion of their food requirements even in normal seasons, means that the government, as the principal

243

marketing agent, must ensure that the local markets are well supplied throughout the course of a drought. There must be sufficient food available in the market to keep prices at a reasonable level.

The present government policy is to maintain a strategic food reserve of six months of the national requirements of maize and beans, the principal food crops (Government of Kenya, 1981). In 1984, the strategic reserve was barely adequate to meet national needs before commercially imported maize arrived.

CLIMATIC IMPACT ASSESSMENT IN DEVELOPING COUNTRIES

The Kenya Case Study illustrates several problems in conducting integrated climate impact assessments. The problems are likely common to all such assessments, although several issues are of particular interest to professionals in developing countries. There is an inescapable tension between methodologies that are ideal, judged by academic qualities, and those that promise to yield demonstrable, practicable results.

The case study was probably the first attempt in Kenya to conduct an integrated climate impact assessment involving scholars from different institutions and specific models of agricultural production. The results are clearly useful. The process could be improved by involving more participants and reviewers within Kenya in a program with higher visibility, and by developing a process whereby policy makers are able to evaluate the short-and long-term effects of climatic variability and climate change. It is most important that future assessments be carried out within the country itself, in close collaboration with appropriate research and development institutions. The professional staff and computing facilities are available or can be developed. Application of the results requires broad review and synthesis at many levels within the research program and among policy makers.

The assessment could be considerably expanded—to other districts, by using more detailed data bases, and by developing more rigorous models. Such a project would require a significant commitment of funding, for at least two years. In particular, computer programmers and data entry personnel would be required. Professional staff must work full-time on the project, and provisions must be made for appropriate training of all project participants. Short courses and workshops are insufficient to provide competent participants in technical disciplines, and may actually impede the progress of the project.

One practical outcome of an attempt to integrate the results of different models and analyses is that gaps in current knowledge are identified. Data collection and research can then be focused on aspects that promise the highest yields. The Kenya Case Study has noted the lack of consistent, complete data on agricultural yields, which is urgently required to verify predictive models. One important lesson learned in the 1984 drought was that a useful nutrition monitoring system is necessary. A pilot growth-monitoring system has since been implemented.

Many agencies are working in fields related to climate impact assessment. In spite of the importance of drought, the lack of clear analyses of vulnerability to drought, and the paucity of relevant data, there is little coordination between related projects. Climatic variability must be included as an essential aspect of resource assessments and agricultural development planning. The entire chain of impacts and responses to

244

climatic variability must be included in assessment and planning efforts in order to identify the linkages that are most amenable to policy intervention.

REFERENCES

Akong'a, J.; and T. E. Downing. 1987. Smallholder Vulnerability and Response to Drought. In M. Parry, T. Carter, and N.Konijn, eds. The Impacts of Climatic Variations on Agriculture, Volume II: Assessments in Semi-Arid Regions. Reidel, Dordrecht, Holland (in press).

Akong'a, J.; T. E. Downing; N. Konijn; D. Mungai; H. Muturi; and H. Potter. 1987. Climatic Variability and Agricultural Production in Central and Eastern Kenya: The Kenya Case Study. In M. Parry, T. Carter, and N. Konijn, eds. The Impacts of Climatic Variations on Agriculture, Volume II: Assessments in Semi-Arid Regions. Reidel, Dordrecht, Holland (in press).

Bakhtri, M. N.; S. Gavotti; and J. K. Kimemia. 1984. On-farm research at Katumani: Pre-extension trials experience (with special reference to semi-arid areas of Eastern Province of Kenya). E. Afr. Agric. For. J. 44:437-443.

Burton, I.; R. W. Kates; and G. F. White. 1978. The Environment as Hazard. Oxford University Press, New York.

Central Bureau of Statistics. 1982. Seasonal Variation in Food Crops: Evidence from IRS4. Ministry of Economic Planning and Development, Nairobi.

Dowker, B. D. 1964. A note on the reduction in yield of Taboran maize by late planting. E. Afr. Agric. For. J. 21:33-34.

Downing, T. E.; J. Akong'a; D. N. Mungai; H. Muturi; and H. Potter. 1986. Introduction to the Kenya Case Study. In M. Parry, T. Carter, and N. Konijn, eds. The Impacts of Climatic Variations on Agriculture, Volume II: Assessments in Semi-Arid Regions. Reidel, Dordrecht, Holland (in press).

Downing, T. E.; D. N. Mungai; and H. R. Muturi. 1987. Drought climatology and development of climatic scenarios. In M. Parry, T. Carter, and N. Konijn, eds. The Impacts of Climatic Variations on Agriculture, Volume II: Assessments in Semi-Arid Regions. Reidel, Dordrecht, Holland (in press).

Goldson, J. R. 1963. The effect of time of planting on maize yield. E. Afr. Agric. For. J. 20:160-163.

Government of Kenya. 1981. Sessional Paper No. 4 of 1981 on National Food Policy. Government Printers, Nairobi.

Government of Kenya. 1983. National Five Year Development Plan for 1984-88. Ministry of Finance and Planning, Nairobi.

Jaetzold, R.; and H. Schmidt. 1983. Farm Management Handbook of Kenya: Natural Conditions and Farm Management Information. Ministry of Agriculture, Nairobi.

Kates, R. W. 1985. The Interaction of Climate and Society. pp. 3-36. In R. W. Kates, J. H. Ausubel, and M. Berberian, eds. Climate Impact Assessment. SCOPE 27. John Wiley, New York.

Konijn, N. T. 1987. The effects of climatic variability on maize yields. In M. Parry, T. Carter, and N. Konijn, eds. The Impacts of Climatic Variations on Agricul-

245

ture, Volume II: Assessments in Semi-Arid Regions. Reidel, Dordrecht, Holland (in press).

Macodras, M. W.; J. Mwikya; and P. M. Nthusi. 1986. Synoptic Features Associated with the Failure of the Long Rains in Kenya. Meteorological Department, Nairobi.

Mungai, D. N.; and H. R. Muturi. 1987. The effects of climatic variability on agroclimatic zones and agricultural production. In M. Parry, T. Carter, and N. Konijn, eds. The Impacts of Climatic Variations on Agriculture, Volume II: Assessments in Semi-Arid Regions. Reidel, Dordrecht, Holland (in press).

Njeru, N. 1983. Some Physiological Properties of Different Maize Varieties at N.A.R.S. Kitale. In J. C. Mohucs and W. H. Tahir, eds. More Food from Better Technology. Food and Agriculture Organization, Rome.

Parry, M. L.; T. Carter; and N. T. Konijn, eds. 1987. The Impacts of Climatic Variations on Agriculture, Volume II: Assessments in Semi-Arid Regions. Reidel, Dordrecht, Holland (in press).

Potter, II. L. 1987. The effects of climatic variability on livestock production. In M. Parry, T. Carter, and N. Konijn, eds. The Impacts of Climatic Variations on Agriculture, Volume II: Assessments in Semi-Arid Regions. Reidel, Dordrecht, Holland (in press).

Potter, H. L.; J. Akong'a; T. E. Downing; D. N. Mungai; and H. R. Muturi. 1987. Implications for Policy. In M. Parry, T Carter, and N, Konijn,eds. The Impacts of Climatic Variations on Agriculture, Volume II: Assessments in Semi-Arid Regions. Reidel, Dordrecht, Holland (in press).

Sen, A. K. 1981. Poverty and Famine. Oxford University Press, Oxford.

Sombroek, W. G.; H. M. H. Braun; and B. J. A. Van der Pauw. 1982. Exploratory Soil Map and Agroclimatic Zone Map of Kenya. Kenya Soil Survey, Nairobi.

Wisner, B. G. 1977. The Human Ecology of Drought in Eastern Kenya. Ph.D. Dissertation. Clark University, Worcester, Massachusetts.

CHAPTER 16
INTERNATIONAL DROUGHT EARLY WARNING PROGRAM OF NOAA/NESDIS/AISC

Clarence M. Sakamoto and Louis T. Steyaert

INTRODUCTION

Since 1979, the Assessment and Information Services Center (AISC) of the National Oceanic and Atmospheric Administration/National Environmental Satellite, Data and Information Service (NOAA/NESDIS) has been providing drought early warning alerts and climate impact assessments to national and international agencies that require such information for disaster preparedness and agricultural assessment. A related activity has been the transfer of AISC technical assistance to developing nations that are implementing their own early warning crop monitoring systems.

The work of AISC has led to an operational system that is cost effective and simple to implement. The system's products, which are both qualitative and quantitative in content, are continually being evaluated. Additional tools to complement the existing system are also being investigated.

This paper describes the drought early warning program of AISC, including procedures and tools used, technical assistance, problems encountered with transferring the system to developing nations, and potential benefits. Suggestions for improving the assessments and information flow are outlined.

PROGRAM OVERVIEW

In 1979, NOAA/NESDIS/AISC began developing its international climate impact assessment technology with support from the U.S. Agency for International Development (AID), Office of U.S. Foreign Disaster Assistance (OFDA). The program was developed cooperatively by AISC and the University of Missouri-Columbia's Atmospheric Science Department. In 1985, the cooperative activities of NOAA and the University of Missouri were formalized with the creation of the Cooperative Institute for Applied Meteorology (CIAM).

The purpose of the early warning program is to provide U.S. government agencies (e.g., AID, Department of State, U.S. Department of Agriculture, Central Intelligence Agency), U.S. missions abroad (American embassies and U.S. AID missions), and United Nations agencies (e.g., FAO, WMO, UNDP, ESCAP) with brief, qualitative cables assessing the potential impact of weather variability on food crops. More than eighty countries throughout the tropics have been included (Fig. 1). The objective of

Fig. 1 The climate impact assessment technology program scope of NOAA/NESDIS/AISC.

these cables is to increase the lead time available for agencies and governments to implement plans for food security. Studies of the program have shown that these assessments, issued one month before harvest, can provide useful and reliable information three to six months before socioeconomic impacts become evident. The qualitative assessment reports are based primarily on rainfall data and provide agencies with information on potential drought and its impact on crops.

In addition to routine cable reports, special assessment bulletins have been issued to provide food security analysts with greater detail, based on information from additional sources (e.g., meteorological, satellite, and ancillary data). Since 1982, more than thirty of these special assessment reports have been provided to AID and its country missions for countries in Africa, Asia, Latin America, and the Southwest Pacific Basin. These data sources are provided to the field offices so that analysts can better understand the products and make local adjustments as in-country data become available. Based on recent advances in the use of meteorological satellite data for agricultural assessment, these special assessments were made quantitative during 1985 for the African Sahel and Horn countries.

An operational assessment capability requires a multidisciplinary staff that can work not only with each other, but also with counterparts from other agencies and countries as well. The assessment capability also requires rapid-response communication facilities to ensure that information reaches the end user as rapidly as possible. Weather-associated products by their nature are highly perishable—that is, their value decreases very rapidly with time. Furthermore, when potential drought impact can affect lives and economic costs, the cables must be timely. Therefore, AISC relies on NOAA and AID communication systems as well as on commercial telex or cable facilities. Materials that cannot be transmitted electronically are sent by express mail. This service, however, can be very expensive and is sometimes unreliable.

Because many different types of data are used to prepare assessments, a coordinated plan involving several subsystems, including historical data bases, has been developed so that operational products can be prepared and delivered in a timely manner (see Fig. 2). The AISC assessment process and assessment tools, developed over several years, are referred to as the NOAA Drought Early Warning System.

DROUGHT EARLY WARNING SUBSYSTEMS

The NOAA Drought Early Warning System is based on three subsystems: agroclimatic indices, satellite assessment models, and crop yield forecast models. As indicated in Fig. 2, several different assessment tools are derived from data bases under each subsystem. These assessment tools include NOAA Metsat products (vegetation index maps, vegetation index time-series, and color- coded images), agroclimatic indices, and various statistical crop yield forecast models. The tools are analyzed in the context of the Geographic Information System (Fig. 3), which involves overlaying, integrating, and evaluating various data sources that are cross-checked with each other for consistency and convergence of information. Various resource maps (e.g., land use) and ancillary data are used to develop quantitative special assessment reports (Steyaert, 1985).

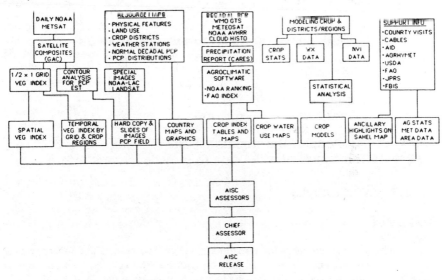

Fig. 2 Task flow chart for the 1986 Sahel/Horn Special Assessment System, illustrating the use of different types of data and assessment tools for operational assessment by AISC.

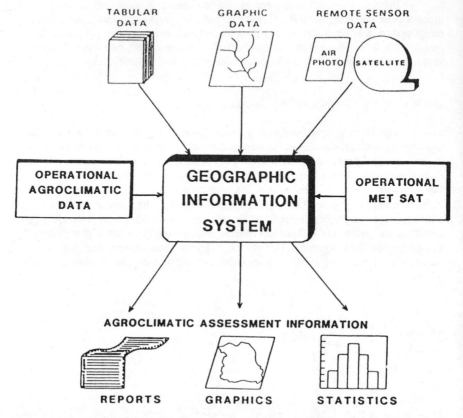

Fig. 3 The Geographic Information System concept uses different data sources and integrates the data to provide relevant information.

AGROCLIMATIC INDICES

Rainfall Data

The major requirement for agroclimatic indices is a reliable and timely rainfall data base. Rainfall reports are received daily through the WMO Global Telecommunications System (GTS). These data are supplemented with less timely, but usually more reliable, reports from such sources as USAID missions, the Regional AGRHYMET Center in Niamey, Niger, or other telegraphic or mail sources. Published data are frequently obtained through trainee contacts in developing countries; these usually arrive later than desired, but still provide useful information. AISC places considerable emphasis on quality control of historical and real-time rainfall data.

In addition to being plotted spatially for regional analysis, rainfall data are also used as input for agroclimatic indices that are based on either monthly or ten-day time periods, e.g., water budgeting or weighted crop water use analyzed with respect to historical records. Ranking historical indexes represents one useful approach to estimating the probable occurrence of weather conditions affecting crops. For example, Fig. 4 shows the ranking of a simple agroclimate index for Haiti. In this case, index values below the thirtieth percentile are often associated with moderate to severe drought, while index values below the twentieth percentile are associated with drought-induced food shortages. The appropriate threshold for assessing potential impacts is determined by an analysis of the historical index data in conjunction with the use of an episodic (or ancillary) data base. An episodic data base is simply a record of the historic impacts of crop damage due to droughts, floods, and other anomalous weather events. With this data base, the agroclimate index ranks are calibrated to establish the critical threshold. Better results have occurred when the rankings are prepared for critical growth periods in the crop cycle. Although this approach is very qualitative, it does provide a useful relative

AGROCLIMATIC INDEX FOR AUTUMN MAIZE
NORTHERN HAITI (1947-1977)

NOAA/NESDIS/AISC

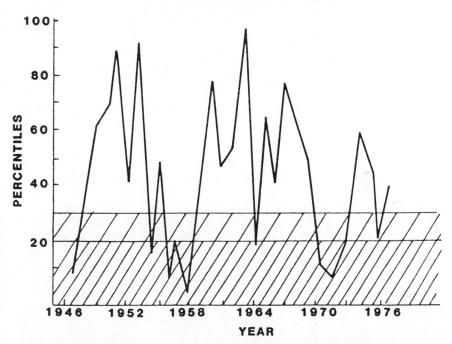

Fig. 4 Ranking of an agroclimatic index (in this case, autumn weighted rainfall). The shaded areas have been calibrated with historical episodic data. Moderate to severe droughts were associated with values below the thirtieth percentile.

measure of the impact; for example, an observer might note, "This drought is the worst in 15 years when production was 'x' metric tons in 1970." Procedures for ranking different agroclimate indexes are discussed further by Sakamoto, et al. (1984).

Ten-day rainfall data are used as input to calculate the soil moisture budgets and crop indexes based on procedures referred to as the "FAO Index" (Frere and Popov, 1979). Concepts such as potential evapotranspiration, crop water requirements, and available water are applied in this index. The FAO index was developed primarily for use in the Sahel, although illustrations of its use in Asia have also been reported by the authors. Use of this index with independent data has shown it to be insensitive to high moisture levels, but it appears to be sensitive to extreme drought conditions. The use of this index for quantitative application has led to mixed results. Work is underway to modify the algorithms to determine whether adjustments can lead to greater sensitivity for a larger range of soil moisture levels.

Ancillary Data

Ancillary data provide information that can be used to supplement the information content of the weather impact assessment. For example, locust infestation is weather-related and can directly affect crop yield. Favorable soil moisture is associated with higher crop yields; however, high moisture can also lead to locust problems. Therefore, locust infestation can mean lower than anticipated yield from favorable soil moisture alone. Floods, civil strife, bird infestation, and plant diseases can be useful as ancillary data if the degree of damage (or impact) to food crops is described. As mentioned previously, these data are important for calibrating agroclimatic indices where reliable concomitant crop yield data are not available. An example of an ancillary data base for Sri Lanka is shown in Table 1; in this case, all of the data were secured from FAO reports (Frere and Popov, 1979).

SATELLITE ASSESSMENT MODELS

AISC uses data from the European Space Agency's Geostationary Meteorological Satellite (METEOSAT) and the NOAA Polar Orbiting Satellite. METEOSAT imagery of Africa is secured from facsimile charts that are used to estimate rainfall amount according to cloud types and coverage (through time) based on the process of cloud indexing. This approach estimates regional rainfall amount. For sparse or nonreporting areas, these estimates represent the only source of rainfall data. The METEOSAT-derived rainfall analysis is also compared with the mean outgoing longwave radiation map, published weekly by the Climatic Analysis Center of NOAA, National Weather Service. Low levels of outgoing radiation are generally associated with rainfall occurrences (Fig. 5). METEOSAT is also used to identify large-scale patterns such as the Intertropical Discontinuity (ITD) or the Intertropical Convergence Zone (ITCZ).

The NOAA satellite provides daily data from the Advanced Very High Resolution Radiometer (AVHRR), which has a spatial resolution of 1.1 km. The signals from the satellite can be received directly by local field stations as the satellite passes in the vicinity. Two types of data can also be recorded for later transmission to receiving sta-

Table 1
Sample Ancillary Data Base for Sri Lanka

MONTH	COMMENTS
March	Total rain for the period 1 September 1978 - 11 February 1979 was seriously deficient in the Western and Uva Provinces. Cyclone damage late last year and prolonged drought in some areas is likely to reduce 1979 Maha production.
April	The 1978/1979 Maha (Main) rice crop is harvested. The rainfall deficiency previously reported did not seriously affect yields, but due to insufficient rains, land preparation for Yala crop was delayed in some areas. The 1979 Yala crop was reduced by drought.
	Good yielding 1978/1979 Maha rice was harvested. A larger area had been planted.
	There was deficient rainfall from September 1978 to April 1 in the West and Uva Provinces and there was widespread damage due to brown plant hoppers. Yala rice crop land preparation was delayed in some areas due to insufficient rains. Aid is being given to cyclone victims. Also aid is being given for the rehabilitaton of agricultural production in the flood-affected areas.
June	Rains are seriously deficient in most provinces.
July	Deficient and erratic southwest monsoon rains have affected Yala, which accounts for 30% of the total rice production.
Sept.	Late arrival of the southwest monsoon and poor rains have seriously affected the Yala Paddy crop. The country is still dry.
Dec.	Good rains from November to mid-December helped sowings of Maha rice, which is harvested in February and March.

Source: Frere and Popov, 1979.

MEAN OUTGOING LONGWAVE RADIATION (DAY+NITE)/2

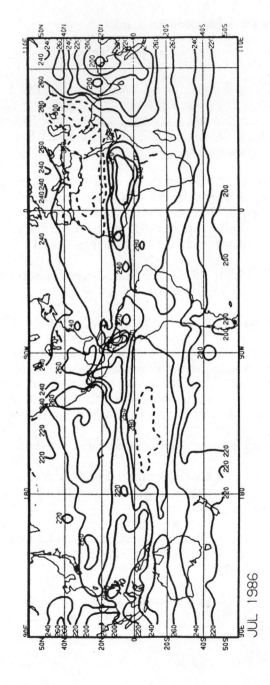

JUL 1986

Fig. 5 The radiation chart developed by Climatic Analysis Center/NOAA is used by AISC to compare large-scale rainfall patterns and the relative position of the ITCZ.

tions operated by NOAA/NESDIS. Selected 1 km data can be recorded and are termed *LAC* (for "Local Area Coverage"). The complete set of 1 km data observed continuously by the satellite are also sampled internally to obtain 4 km resolution data, termed *GAC* (for "Global Area Coverage"). NESDIS subsequently samples the GAC data to produce a 16 km resolution product called "SUPERVEGE." The use of LAC, GAC, or SUPER-VEGE must be tempered with the objectives, cost, hardware requirements, and timetable imposed for the operational system in mind. Generally, it is less expensive to obtain SUPERVEGE versus LAC or GAC, but information content may be compromised simply because of the sampling scheme. Studies are underway at AISC to determine the thresholds associated with the information content of LAC, GAC, and SUPERVEGE.

For agricultural assessment, AISC uses three of the five radiation channels from the polar orbiting satellite: channel 1 (visible, 0.55-0.68 μm), channel 2 (near infrared, .725-1.10 μm) and channel 4 (thermal infrared, 10.5-11.5 m)μ. To remove cloud contamination, AISC digitally composites daily data over intervals of seven to thirty days by selecting the greenest pixel. The composited data are then used to produce vegetation/biomass indexes and color images as part of the NOAA satellite assessment models subsystem.

Vegetation/Biomass Index

The normalized vegetation/biomass index (NVI) is defined as:

$$NVI = \frac{Channel\ 2 - Channel\ 1}{Channel\ 2 + Channel\ 1}$$

Studies by van Dyk (1986) have shown that changes in look angle, atmospheric moisture content, and pollutants can produce highly variable NVIs when calculated from daily data. Much of this variability (or noise), however, can be removed by compositing cloud-free pixels and spatially averaging NVIs over assessment regions. Specifically, pixels within a specified threshold in a composited assessment polygon (e.g., 1/2° latitude by 1° longitude) are averaged each week and assembled to provide an NVI time series. In the present compositing algorithm, pixels with channels 1 and 2 values of 150 or greater are treated as clouds and not included in the NVI averaging. Consideration is also being given to using channel 4 in the process for selecting a threshold to exclude clouds in averaging the values for the "greenest pixels" before spatial averaging. The variability in the time series based on regionally averaged composited data is also high, but not as great as with the daily data. Again, this variability is due to several factors, including satellite look angle and atmospheric contamination. To reduce this variability, the weekly time series are further smoothed (Fig. 6) by using a selected smoothing algorithm (van Dyk, et al., 1986; Velleman and Hoaglin, 1981). As shown in Fig. 6, it is evident that the smoothing process depicts discernable NVI time series differences for three years (1983-85) in southeastern Senegal and western Mali. The spatially averaged and temporally smoothed NVI data are also mapped for year-to-year comparative analyses at key times during the crop growing season.

256

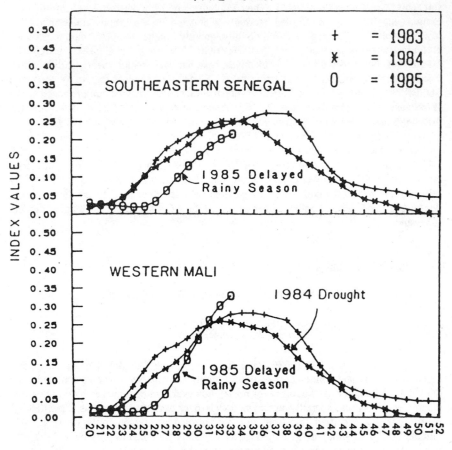

Fig. 6 The smoothed normalized vegetation index for southeastern Senegal and western Mali in 1983, 1984, and 1985. Note the reduced vegetation for 1984 and the delayed 1985 rainy season.

NOAA Satellite Images

There are many useful color coordinate systems available for developing satellite imagery. Each has its own advantages and disadvantages for display and analyses. AISC uses the Ambroziak Color Coordinate System (ACCS) (Ambroziak, 1984, 1986). The ACCS shows the health of the vegetation using natural colors as perceived by the human mind—green for vegetation, red-brown for bare ground. The mind processes the color information for qualitative analysis of patterns. Therefore, it is an analytical tool.

Different hues (red-orange-yellow-green-cyan-blue) separate vegetation and water from soil and clouds using the visible (channel 1) and near infrared (channel 2) portions of the electromagnetic radiation reflected signals. Saturation (red-pink-white) is used to identify clouds with the thermal infrared band (channel 4)—cloud tops are colder than the ground surface and they become white when the saturation of the colors is reduced for pixels with low temperatures. Clouds are cold and bright; sand is light colored, warm, and bright. Sand therefore has a red hue. Another dimension in the ACCS is the scene brightness or intensity. This is the distance from the origin as shown in the coordinate system of Fig. 7. Sharp boundaries on the image, shown as large changes in hue, indicate sharp changes in surface vegetation such as forest and stressed crops. The interpretation of the colors is defined in Table 2.

It is important to recognize that the satellite imagery must be used in conjunction with the observed NVI values. Low NVI values may be related to cloud cover, which can be visually observed from the composited imagery, thereby qualifying the interpretation of the greenness index or NVI in terms of the health of the vegetation.

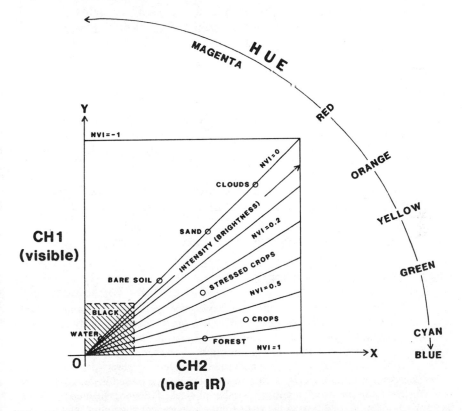

Fig. 7 The Ambroziak Color Coordinate System (ACCS), showing hue and intensity as a function of channels 1 and 2.

Table 2
Interpretation of Hue and Intensity in the ACCS Display

	INTENSITY	
HUE[a]	DARK ——— Increasing Brightness ——— BRIGHT	
Red	Wet or dark soil[b]	Sand or low clouds
Yellow	Emerging or sparse plant cover over wet or dark soil[b]	Emerging or sparse plant cover over sand or under scattered clouds
Green	Very healthy plants combined with standing water or forest	Healthy fields crops or similar plants
Cyan (greenish-blue)	Dense forest	Dense forest, maize or rice cover
Magenta (purplish-red)	Clear shallow or slightly turbid water	Highly turbid, very shallow, or partially cloud covered water

[a]Colors without hue include black (clear deep water or dark shadow) and white (clouds, snow, or colder high terrain)

[b]Dark reds, oranges, and yellow are shades of brown

CROP YIELD FORECAST MODELS

AISC uses two kinds of crop yield models for operational assessment. One uses satellite NVI data and the other uses rainfall in a simple regression analysis. Figure 8 shows a sample NVI yield model for millet in the Sahel countries. The best interpretation of these NVI models is achieved when information on crop calendar, critical growth stages of crops, and climate of the area are used collectively. Figure 6 depicts the type of NVI curves that are calculated for crop-reporting regions and used in development of models. In the current model, a selected number of weeks following greenup (noted by an upswing of the curve) is used as the value for the independent variable.

A more complex situation is illustrated by the model developed for parts of Ethiopia, where a bimodal rainfall distribution is observed. The bimodal rainfall distribution is associated with the movement of the Intertropical Convergence Zone (ITCZ) as it

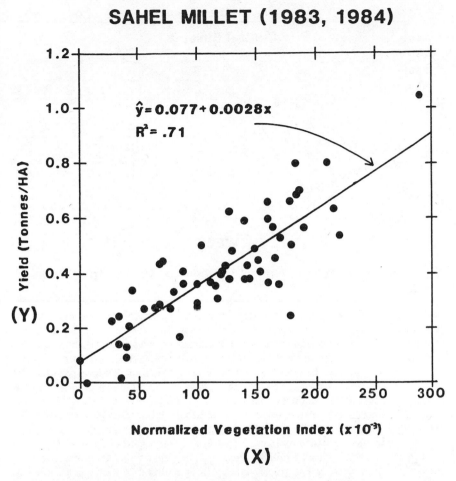

Fig. 8 Sahel millet yield model as a function of normalized vegetation index.

shifts north and south during the year. This bimodal rainfall distribution is also reflected in the vegetation index time series (Fig. 9). Ethiopia's major crop, teff, is usually planted in June-July, with the critical heading period in September-October. To develop the NVI/crop yield model, the critical growth period must be known so that the proper NVI value can be selected from the NVI time series. For teff, the period eight to ten weeks after emergence is the critical heading and flowering period. For the NVI/teff yield model, the NVI value at nine weeks following emergence was selected. However, overall greenup, as indicated by increasing NVI, may not always coincide with emergence (e.g., teff). Therefore, it is important to know when a specific crop is sown. In some years, replanting is necessary; therefore, feedback from in-country users as well as

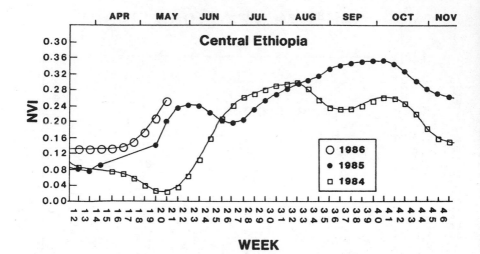

Fig. 9 NVI time series in Central Ethiopia for 1984-86 from weeks 12 through 46.

verification from other field reports (e.g., FAO, AID mission) may be essential for proper utilization of these simple models. NVI values also have different ranges for different geographic areas as well as for different climatic regimes. Careful analysis of the time series is essential to determine the NVI value for quantitative estimation.

AISC also uses the classical statistical rainfall/yield modeling approach. The limitations and benefits of this type of model have been previously discussed (Katz, 1979; Sakamoto, 1981). Although much criticism can be leveled at the use of monthly data, valid information on the response of the crop during critical periods can be revealed by these models. The variables are selected with the agronomic importance of the variable in relation to the known crop phenology. The outputs of the models are best used in conjunction with all available data, including spatial and temporal maps and graphs. As is commonly known, the quality of agricultural data obtained from host country governments varies considerably and should be used cautiously. The guide to this issue is whether the agronomic response in the model is consistent with the weather observations and other known cultural practices.

Beginning thirty days before harvesting, AISC prepares quantitative crop yield forecasts. These forecasts are based on the combined interpretation of the recently developed NVI/yield models, the classic rainfall/crop yield statistical models, and a crop-condition analysis based on the products of the Agroclimate Index and Satellite Assessment Models Subsystems. Because the quality of agricultural statistics for most Sahel countries is suspect, AISC references yield projections to a consensus baseline average yield. Crop yield forecasts are sent by cable to USAID missions for their use and distribution. The forecasts provided by AISC represent only one component of a famine early warning program that also considers human population, nutrition, and socioeconomic factors.

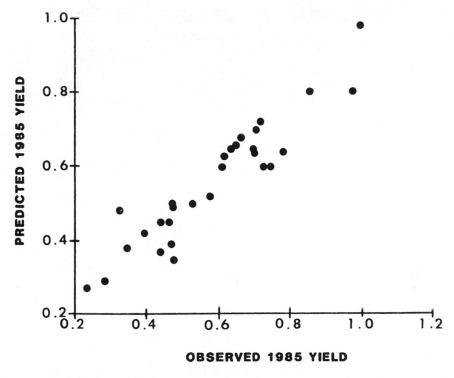

OBSERVED 1985 YIELD

Fig. 10 Predicted versus observed millet yields (Mt/Ha) in the Sahel for 1985.

Preliminary verification of AISC millet yield forecasts for the 1985 season in the Sahel is shown in Fig. 10. Verification results for the sorghum forecasts are also shown for three countries (Fig. 11). The verification procedure suggests results are reasonable; additional verification is being done for 1986.

TECHNICAL ASSISTANCE PROGRAM

The NOAA/NESDIS/AISC Early Warning Program also includes provisions for assisting countries in the development of their own operational assessment capability. Since 1981, AISC has assisted more than thirty countries within Latin American, Caribbean, African, and Asian regions (Fig. 12). The exchange of information during technology transfer helps not only the recipient country, but also the AISC assessment process. The reciprocal benefits can easily be seen when one considers the constant need for data, current land use resource maps, crop data, crop calendar information, ground truth information for satellite data verification, and operational rainfall reports not readily available through the GTS system.

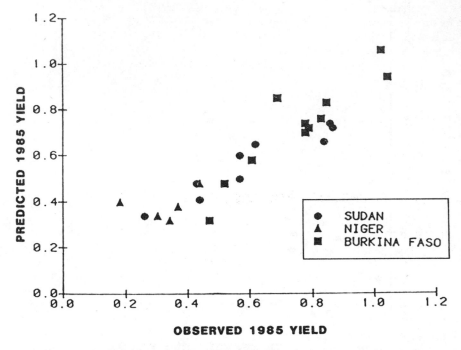

Fig. 11 Predicted versus observed sorghum yields (Mt/Ha) in Sudan, Niger, and Burkina Faso for 1985.

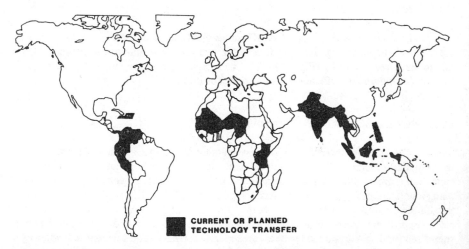

Fig. 12 Technology transfer program scope of NOAA/NESDIS/-AISC for the drought early warning assessment system.

Over the past several years, AISC has formulated a deliberate "process model" for transferring assessment technology to developing countries. This process is multidisciplinary and interagency in scope. It includes several phases:

1. Professional training courses for technicians.
2. Preparation of trainee reports that include methods and implementation plans.
3. Workshops for midlevel managers to brief them on the methods and to gain their support.
4. Seminars for policy makers to inform the top-level managers of the program and benefits and to gain their support and involvement in the development of a national plan.
5. Preparation of quasi-operational assessments by host countries as directed by the policy makers and midlevel managers.
6. AISC/University of Missouri in-country technical assistance to monitor progress and introduce new techniques.
7. Follow-up seminars by midlevel managers and policy makers to report on progress, problems, national plans, and future directions.

Follow-up assistance is provided as necessary to conduct training and monitor progress.

Implementation of an operational program requires considerable coordination within a country. Some of the problems encountered in these countries are the same kinds of problems that exist in the United States, such as determining who has responsibility for agricultural assessment and other components of the plan. Therefore, much time is spent developing an "atmosphere" and establishing the framework under which disciplines from different agencies can work together. Usually the agrometeorologist (or agronomist) is assigned to the agricultural ministry while the meteorologist is in a separate ministry; coordination is required. The agricultural economist or statistician is also brought into the program to form a multidisciplinary team. This interagency team plus the office responsible for drought/disaster management and food security are asked to participate in the development of a country plan. Government support for agrometeorology programs may often be deferred in favor of high-visibility infrastructure development.

Another major problem faced by the countries is the high turnover of professionals. Although most of the participants are highly qualified, some participants may be selected for political reasons and not primarily for their technical qualifications. Because the more qualified persons rapidly move into management positions, training must be a continuing effort. This often means that the program does not progress as rapidly as desired. Technicians do not have policy-making authority; consequently, it is important to keep top-level management informed of the benefits from the program. In some cases, government reorganization involving midlevel and ministerial level personnel has also slowed progress; when new managers begin, they must be briefed to gain their support for continuing the program.

AISC has found it advantageous to work with international agencies or through centers located within the region of interest to promote the transfer of assessment technology. In Asia, for example, AISC has worked with the United Nations' Economic and Social Commission for Asia and the Pacific (ESCAP), which has agricultural and remote sensing programs. In the case of the Sahelian countries, AISC has been working with the Regional AGRHYMET Center located in Niamey, Niger, which represents the focal point through which AISC methodology can be transferred. Their familiarity with local customs and the political infrastructure has been a key asset. The first three steps in the technology transfer process model have been completed for the Sahel, and all steps have been completed for nine Asian countries.

The production of a periodic assessment bulletin by each country represents a major goal of the program. In Latin America, agroclimatic assessment bulletins are being prepared in Peru, Ecuador, Jamaica, Costa Rica, and Belize. The program in Asia, which began in 1981, involved nine countries from south and southeast Asia (Indonesia, Malaysia, Philippines, Thailand, Bangladesh, India, Nepal, Pakistan, and Sri Lanka). Eight of these nine countries have implemented an operational climate impact assessment program, beginning with the distribution of periodic assessment bulletins for various users. In two of the nine countries (Thailand and Malaysia), additional training has been completed to incorporate NOAA/AVHRR data in their operational assessment (Tung and Pilus, 1985; Martchaipoom, et al., 1985). In Africa, participants from the Sahelian countries received an intensive six-week training program during April 1986 and have now begun to use satellite NVI data in their assessment for 1986 under the AGRHYMET Project.

The training aspect of the AISC technology transfer program is intensive and considered unique. It involves various levels of management in developing countries. It is multidisciplinary and multiagency, and it involves established institutional agencies located in the region. Three types of training are provided: U.S.-based six- to eight-week courses, regional courses, and "on-the-job" training associated with in-country visits conducted jointly by AISC and CIAM. Hands-on experience is also provided in the use of the microcomputers. The participants are requested to bring necessary data with them; these are used during the training course to produce models, resource manuals, probability tables, agroclimatic indices, and so forth. The United States-based course requires that a training report be completed by each participant. These reports serve as useful references for the country and for AISC. Reports have been completed in English, French, and Spanish. The course for the Sahelian countries in April-May 1986 in the United States (Columbia, Missouri; and Washington, D.C.) was taught simultaneously in French and English. Lesson plans, including exercises, have been incorporated into the training program. Allowances are made for weekly critiques, so course adjustments are possible to serve the needs of the participants. Since 1981, AISC/CIAM has trained nearly a hundred participants from thirty countries.

ASSESSMENT PRODUCTS

End users determine the type of products and format of the assessment. AISC users include planners and managers within the Agency for International Development in Washington, D.C., and in the field. The assessments are shared with international agencies and other U.S. government agencies as well as with the host country governments through the USAID missions. For illustration purposes, the 1986 Special Assessment for the Sahel/Horn of Africa is described. It includes three types of assessments: (1) the Executive Summary, (2) the Regional and Country Analysis, and (3) the Cable Update.

Executive Summary

The Executive Summary highlights major impacts within the region. This bulletin is intended for mid- and top-level managers who are primarily interested in the major weather problems as related to future food needs. They need a concise assessment of the situation. Alert areas are noted on the front cover with a narrative explanation of impacts included within. The total number of pages does not exceed five. Graphics that can be quickly and easily analyzed are desirable. A major component in this summary is a regional map of two to three countries with problem areas highlighted (Fig. 13). This map is based on high resolution analyses of satellite data and imagery.

Regional and Country Analysis

A more detailed publication with additional data is also published. These data are provided so that local analysts can verify or amplify the assessment. Additional graphics include time series of NVI data (Fig. 14), comparative NVI analysis (Fig. 15), and decadal and monthly rainfall (including normals and ranking of observed data). The position of the ITD is also provided. Hard-copy color imagery is included to provide a synoptic view of the situation. A written impact assessment summarizes the graphics and tables.

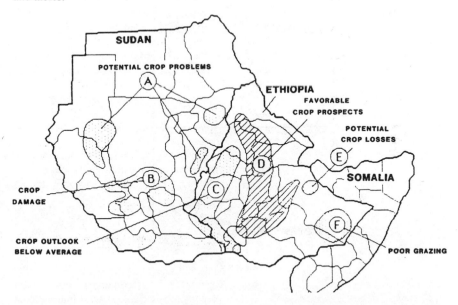

Fig. 13 Weather impact highlights of Sudan, Ethiopia, and Somalia at the end of July 1986. A more detailed written assessment (not shown) for each area is noted below the map.

□ : 1984
● : 1985
O : 1986

SENEGAL

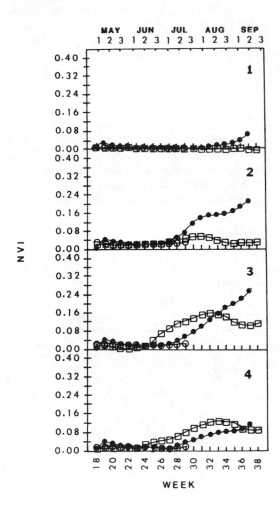

Fig. 14 NVI time series for four sites in Senegal for 1984-86, as illustrated in the 1986 special regional country assessment for the Sahel.

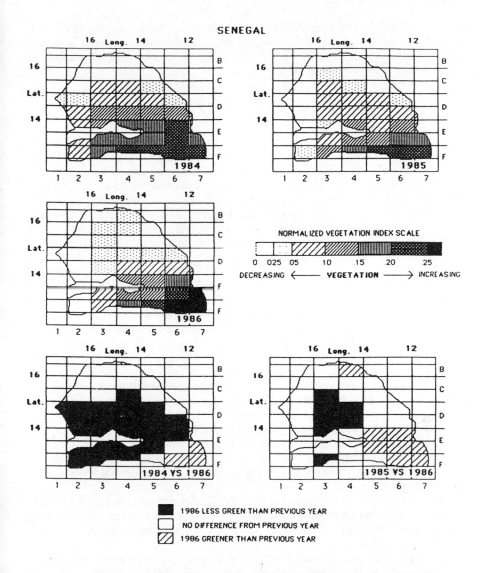

Fig. 15 A sample assessment product showing comparative NVI during the third week of July in Senegal, with 1984, 1985, and 1986 data.

Cables

Cables are used to update the monthly assessment bulletins and are issued every ten days. These are concise so that timely reports can be provided to the user with minimum delay. At this time, cables are also the only way that quantitative estimates of crop yield are issued by AISC to the field.

BENEFITS OF THE PROGRAM

The benefits derived from mitigating drought impact through improved early warning alerts can vary. The economic savings from reduced costs of food imports through advanced purchases before commodity prices increase can easily reach millions of dollars. Prepositioning of food relief stocks, reduced transportation costs of goods, and reduced costs of other logistical considerations such as warehouse storage and mode of transportation can lead to huge savings by relief agencies. For some countries, economic disaster can lead to civil strife and, consequently, additional costs for restoring order. One country in Asia, for example, required an additional 250,000 metric tons of maize. The world market price of maize increased $20 per ton between the time the local crop was damaged by drought and the time the grain was needed. This represented a potential savings of $5 million if action had been taken at the time of the local impact assessment (Steyaert, 1984). In another case, involving Malaysia, the rice production in 1984 was 10% higher than anticipated because of favorable weather conditions. This was not known until the end of the crop season, when sufficient storage facilities were not available. Consequently, 10% of the crop was lost to rot, insects, and rodents. If the impact of the favorable weather had been assessed, the savings could have been in the millions of dollars, according to Malaysian government sources.

Early warning information from a crop yield assessment program can strengthen food security, enhance price stability programs at the national level, and provide the food ministry with information on international trade markets that affect foreign exchange. The assessment can also be viewed as an independent source of information to complement reports from probability and nonprobability agricultural surveys. These surveys are usually the most accurate way to obtain crop production estimates, but for many countries, established procedures are still under development, nonexistent, or not very timely.

History has revealed that drought-induced economic problems can lead to civil strife. Problems are compounded if drought goes undetected until impacts are evident; therefore, an early warning system is essential to help mitigate the problems resulting from food shortages.

The costs to implement a drought early warning program include (1) human resources, (2) data, (3) computer hardware and software, and (4) development of assessment methodology. Processing of the satellite data can be time-consuming, but it can be completed economically. To process daily GAC data for a ten-day composite for the entire Sahel, for example, requires about seven hours on the VAX 730 (this time can be reduced considerably with larger computers) to provide a composited disk data set for analysis on a personal computer.

POTENTIAL IMPROVEMENTS

The AISC Drought Early Warning System can be improved in several ways to upgrade the quality, timeliness, and quantification of the assessments. These include (1) techniques development, (2) computer hardware, (3) communications, and (4) expansion of technical assistance.

Techniques Development

Satellite technology has provided the opportunity for developing new assessment tools to quantify the impact of weather variability. Current NVI/crop models must be further verified by isolating specific crop areas and obtaining additional ground-truth data. Crop data provided by national governments are often gross estimates; therefore, satellite data need to be compared with reliable data gathered from the field. Other ways to use the NVI data for crop response must be investigated. These include the use of more than one period over the season, rather than the current practice of using a single week.

The use of remote sensing data to estimate pastureland biomass and its potential animal carrying capacity is another area of interest. Nomadic populations in many Sahelian countries rely on the pastures which are rainfed in association with the movement and strength of the Intertropical Convergence Zone (ITCZ). In 1986, many African nations were affected by an epidemic locust situation. This led to destruction of large fields and consequently caused a need for replanting. Can remote sensing be used to assess the damage? Can areas of favorable hatching be detected sufficiently early? What type of products will be helpful to alert countries to the control of this potential hazard?

Another tool that can complement existing models for crop yield forecasting is the simulation crop model. This type of model requires daily data inputs and needs to be tested for use in the Sahel. A test of the CERES-Maize model was completed for the United States in 1985 and showed positive utility for large-area crop assessment (Hodges, et al., 1986; Botner, et al., 1986). A model for sorghum (or other major crops), if available, could be tested to develop various "what if" scenarios and could be of great use in the Sahel.

The use of sea surface temperature and its association with rainfall in the Sahelian countries is another potential tool that could complement existing subsystems. Sea surface temperatures are also very important in estimating coastal fishery populations during the season.

Rainfall estimation in data-sparse areas is a major problem. A system of providing estimates of rainfall from satellite-derived parameters would enhance the accuracy of the assessments. The most significant improvement, however, should come from developing a rapid, automated (yet quality-controlled) way of displaying several data sources quickly and simultaneously. Data sources include meteorological, satellite, agrophysical (including soils, topography, rivers, and lakes) and other supplemental data (for example, population and transportation). With such a system, analysts are able to spend more time analyzing. This concept is, of course, the Geographic Information System (GIS).

Computer Hardware Requirements

It is becoming increasingly evident that many nations rely on the use of microcomputers. Therefore, the AISC approach in developing the assessment subsystems has been to view the PC as a key hardware element in assessment. Easily maintained software can be developed and updated with the use of microcomputers. A data base (historical and current) is essential to the process of a drought early warning system. The data base includes meteorological satellite and other types of data. Therefore, a data base management system is essential. Many countries are not able to process the voluminous data adequately.

Timely and reliable communication is an essential factor for improving the early warning program. Relying on regular mail service is unsatisfactory. Express mail systems may be faster but not totally adequate, particularly in remote countries. In addition, it is very costly. Telex systems are rapid, but visual aids, graphs, and other material cannot be sent through the system.

Technical Assistance

The goal of providing technical assistance could be intensified to a level at which the countries are using their own resources to provide the assessment information. In-country training must expand. The long-range objective of providing highly qualified personnel to train others within their own country should be pursued. Individual countries providing the training may have their own training infrastructures. Although it may seem difficult, pooling international resources to conduct training courses is a cost-efficient way to proceed. Decision makers, including top-level management, must be continually briefed and kept informed of the program. A great deal of coordination is required.

SUMMARY

The Drought Early Warning program of the Assessment and Information Services Center is an operational program that includes assessment modeling, assessment reporting, and development of technical assistance in less-developed countries. It involves several subsystems, including new satellite assessment models that are supplemented by conventional ground-observed meteorological data. Additional refinements and investigation into the reliability of these assessment tools are in order.

The system relies on the Global Telecommunications System for its meteorological data and the Polar Orbiter for its daily satellite coverage. The system considers large areas. As interest in smaller areas develops, the AVHRR data can be supplemented with higher-resolution satellite data to enhance the accuracy of the program. However, the cost of processing the higher-reduction data must be kept in mind.

Technical assistance to developing countries is an important part of the AISC program. The goal is to assist developing countries in implementing their own early warning crop monitoring system. AISC has demonstrated that with little cost, an effective early warning program using new satellite technology can upgrade the quality of agricultural impact assessment for developing countries. However, new assessment tools must not only be continually developed and verified, but capability must also exist to rapidly transmit early warning information to the user.

ACKNOWLEDGMENTS

Appreciation is expressed to our colleagues in Columbia, Missouri, who helped in developing the contents of this paper. We would like to thank the staff of the Cooperative Institute for Applied Meteorology (CIAM), including Dr. Albert van Dyk, whose methodology for satellite yield models established a breakthrough in this technology; Tyeece Little, who processed numerous drafts of the paper; and Kyle McReynolds, for drafting services. Our NOAA/NESDIS/AISC staff, including Dr. Gary Johnson, remote sensing scientist, and Ms. Rita Terry, writer and editor, contributed with discussions on the content of the paper.

REFERENCES

Ambroziak, R. A. 1984. A new method for incorporating meteorological satellite data into global crop monitoring. Eighteenth International Symposium on Remote Sensing of the Environment: Paris, France. October 1-5.

Ambroziak, R. A. 1986. Real time crop assessment using color theory and satellite data. Ph.D. dissertation, University of Delaware.

Botner, D.; C. Sakamoto; T. Hodges; and S. LeDuc. 1986. CERES-Maize Growth Model: 2. Results in the U.S. Cornbelt. Conference on the Human Consequences of 1985's Climate, Asheville, N.C., August 6-7. Sponsored by the American Meteorological Society.

Frere, M.; and G. F. Popov. 1979. Agrometeorological crop monitoring and forecasting: Plant production and protection. Paper 17, Food and Agriculture Organization of the United Nations, Rome.

Hodges, T.; D. Botner; C. Sakamoto; and J. Hayes-Haug. 1986. CERES-Maize Growth Model: 1. Adaptation to the U.S. Cornbelt. Conference on the Human Consequences of 1985's Climate, Asheville, N.C., August 6-7. Sponsored by the American Meteorological Society, Boston.

Katz, R. 1979. Sensitivity analysis of statistical crop-weather models. Agric. Meteorol. 29:291-300.

Martchaipoom, S.; S. Karnchanasutham; and S. Wongparn. 1985. Application of NOAA satellite data for crop assessment in Thailand: A training report. NOAA/NESDIS/Assessment and Information Services Center, Columbia, Missouri.

Sakamoto, C. 1981. Climate-crop regression yield model: An appraisal. In A. Berg, ed. Application of Remote Sensing to Agricultural Production Forecasting. A. A. Balkama, Rotterdam.

Sakamoto, C.; R. Achutuni; and L. Steyaert. 1984. User's Guide: Development of Agroclimate/Crop Condition Index Assessment Models. NOAA/NES-

DIS/AISC in cooperation with Atmospheric Science Department, University of Missouri, Columbia.

Steyaert, L. T. 1984. Climatic impact assessment technology: Disaster early warning and technical assistance in the developing world. U.S. Department of Commerce, NOAA/NESDIS/AISC, Washington, D.C.

Steyaert, L. T. 1985. A geographic information systems analysis for quantitative crop forecasting in semi-arid regions of Africa: Technical planning document. NOAA/NESDIS/AISC, Columbia, Missouri.

Tung, N. P.; and Z. B. Pilus. 1985. Application of NOAA satellite data for crop assessment in Malaysia: A training report. NOAA/NESDIS/Assessment and Information Services Center, Columbia, Missouri.

van Dyk, A. 1986. A crop condition and crop yield estimation method based on NOAA-AVHRR satellite data. Ph.D. dissertation, University of Missouri-Columbia.

van Dyk, A.; S. L. Callis; C. M. Sakamoto; and W. L. Decker. 1986. Smoothing vegetation index profiles: An alternative method of reducing radiometric disturbances in NOAA/AVHRR data (approved for publication).

Velleman, P.; and D. C. Hoaglin. 1981. Applications, Basics and Computing of Exploratory Data Analyses. Duxbury Press, Boston.

CHAPTER 17
FOOD SHORTAGES ASSESSMENT AND PREDICTION: METHODS OF THE EARLY WARNING SYSTEM OF ETHIOPIA

Teferi Bekele

INTRODUCTION

In response to the major disaster of the 1973 drought, which claimed about 200,000 human lives, the Ethiopian government established the Relief and Rehabilitation Commission (RRC), with the primary objectives of providing relief assistance to victims of manmade and natural disasters and coordinating and supervising the implementation of relief and rehabilitation activities undertaken in Ethiopia. Officials realized that the RRC could act more effectively if they were knowledgeable about areas and numbers of people likely to be affected by drought and if they maintained food reserves from the country's major food aid donors to cover all eventualities. In order to fulfill the former objective, the Early Warning System was established in 1976 for the purpose of informing all its possible users, including government and donors, of impending food shortages as early as possible. As one of the major users of the outputs of the program, RRC is responsible for coordinating the system.

The following paper will briefly describe the food shortages assessment and prediction methods of the system.

BACKGROUND INFORMATION ON THE SYSTEM

Formation of the System

The drought in the northern parts of the country, which was first publicized by the media in 1973, underlined the need to concentrate and strengthen the government's capacity to produce information quickly in order to respond to acute food shortages. At the end of 1974, the Inter-Ministerial Technical Working Group (ITWG) was convened under the auspices of the RRC to advise the Commission on the technical aspects of a system that would help monitor food and nutrition. The ITWG recommended that a permanent system be established to continuously collect information related to food and nutrition, a system that would be based on the activities of government agencies with mandated responsibilities for various aspects of agriculture and food. Accordingly the following agencies, in collaboration with the RRC, were recommended to implement the program: Central Statistical Office, National Meteorological Service Agency, Ministry of Agriculture, Ministry of Education, and Ethiopian Nutrition Institute. The actual technical direction of the activities of the program was to be the responsibility of a project implementation group, now called the Project Coordinating Committee (PCC). The PCC consists of professionals from the participating government agencies, each responsible for implementing a sector of the program.

The program was officially launched in January 1977. Most of the arrangements of the system are still in operation; the only change has been the inclusion of the Ministry of State Farms Development and the Agricultural Marketing Corporation as members of the PCC.

Objectives of the System

In broader terms, the objectives of the system can be stated as follows:
1. The early warning of impending food shortages.
2. The identification of both deficit and surplus-producing areas for market stabilization.
3. The management of regional food shortages.
4. The management of national food security.
5. The management of food commodity marketing.
6. The planning of sectoral and intersectoral regional development with regard to food supply.

In order to attain these objectives, a set of strategies has been carefully developed. The strategies include the following:
1. The establishment of a regular system of crop monitoring.
2. The establishment of a system of monitoring pastoral conditions and animal production in rangeland areas.
3. The establishment of a system of monitoring prices and supplies.
4. The strengthening and extending of meteorological reporting, with particular application to agricultural conditions.
5. The establishment of a system for efficient data processing and intersectoral analysis.
6. The establishment of a system to relay analyzed data, in a clear and understandable form, to all agencies responsible for action.
7. The development of models to define the relationships between the various aspects that determine food availability.

Organizational Structure

General. The program, coordinated by the RRC, is a collaborative activity of different government agencies. Required information is collected and channeled through the existing infrastructure of relevant government agencies, which use the information to achieve their own institutional objectives and goals; thus the system avoids duplication of efforts. By locating the Early Warning System within the RRC, both prediction and response mechanisms were established within the same institutional framework, thus making efficient and timely responses possible.

The number of member agencies participating in the program has now reached eight; their responsibilities and areas of participation are as follows:

1. The Relief and Rehabilitation Commission coordinates the implementation of the overall program through its Early Warning and Planning Department (EWPD). The RRC receives the required information and data from member agencies on a regular basis, analyzes and interprets the data, and provides the results of the analyses in the form of periodic reports. The department has two divisions directly linked to the program: one deals with the early warning aspect (monitoring the food situation and making predictions), and the other is responsible for making detailed assessments (based on predictions from the other division) of the possible magnitude and impact of disaster and for disaster preparedness and planning. The head of the Early Warning and Planning Department of the Commission is the chairman of the Project Coordinating Committee.

2. The Central Statistical Office, in addition to providing technical guidance, collects crop performance information from 537 districts and market situations at selected sites and forwards this information to the Early Warning and Planning Department at monthly intervals. It also conducts regular training and supervision of the field staff, in collaboration with the EWPD.

3. The National Meteorological Services Agency collects and analyzes meteorological data from selected stations and provides the data to the EWPD at regular intervals.

4. The Ministry of Agriculture is responsible for collecting rangeland information and providing manpower support to collect and analyze crop data.

5. The Ethiopian Nutrition Institute conducts nutritional surveys in some randomly selected areas of the country. In particular, the Institute collects and provides, every three months, nutritional status information on children under five years of age and assists in the analysis of the data.

6. The Ministry of State Farms joined the program recently as a member agency and is responsible for providing the Early Warning and Planning Department with state farms production data and market situation figures for the areas in which it operates.

7. The Agricultural Marketing Corporation joined the program recently as a member agency with the responsibility of providing the EWPD with product prices and other related information for the areas in which it operates.

8. The Ministry of Education is responsible for providing manpower (students and teachers) in rural areas to collect and report data on rainfall and market situations.

Central Coordinating Office. A central support and coordinating office for the program has been set up under the administrative and technical control of the Early Warning and Planning Department of the RRC. The office has two sections, the Marketing and Rangeland Statistics Section and the Crop Statistics Section, which have the following major functions:

1. Collaborate with the technical staff of the participating agencies to ensure technical integration of the program, evaluation of data quality, and technical modifications.

2. Collect and process data from the field and member agencies.
3. Undertake statistical analysis required to test the validity of trends and values of collected data, for data quality control, and for the statistical interpretation of the data output.
4. Produce and disseminate monthly, quarterly, and seasonal reports to all concerned government and international organizations.

Field Structure. The structural network of the program reaches down to the field level: reporting agents from the participating agencies are posted throughout the country and are responsible for collecting data relevant to the system. This network provides a resource for the participating agencies as well as the Early Warning and Planning Department to use for their own purposes.

SYSTEM METHODOLOGY

Food Supply Systems (FSS) in Ethiopia

The central governing concept of the program is to monitor the links between factors that determine food production, distribution, and consumption in a unified matrix. This chain of events—which begins with the determinants of food production and eventually leads to the access people have to good quality food of sufficient quantity—is seen as a single entity. The chain of events is described as a food supply system. For each "food supply system" chain, a matrix of indicators has been selected. The regular measurement of these indicators will provide a continuous assessment of the performance of the food supply system as a whole, and of each of the components individually, so that the cause for a change in food availability for a particular population group can be identified at once. The analysis of changes observed in the indicators standing for each link in this chain provides predictive as well as up-to-date information on food availability.

Details of the major food supply systems in Ethiopia are given below.

1. Subsistence Crop Dependent Food Supply System.
  • About 75% of the total population of the country depends primarily on its own production, which is mainly grain, for its food supply. Production over the food and seed requirement is sold.
  • Production is dependent to a large extent on good climatic conditions, absence of pests and diseases, and adequate human and animal labor input.
  • Most of the food consumed is grown rather than bought, so the importance of the market to the croppers is limited. However, in times of crop failure, the croppers buy grain by selling their livestock. In general, purchasing power in subsistence economies is low and disappears rapidly if crops fail.
  • Because Ethiopian crop production is almost totally dependent on rainfed agriculture, the subsistence crop dependent food supply system is vulnerable to food shortages caused by climatic variations, which occur frequently.
  • Whenever farmers in this food supply system believe the season is going to be bad (crop failure due to hail, floods, pests, diseases, or lack of rain),

their first reaction is to withhold whatever marketable grain they may have, which results in price increases and supply shortages in the markets. However, when the production shortfall is significant, the reserve grain does not last long, and they depend on the market for the sale of their livestock and remaining assets. This resource also is soon exhausted.

- This food supply system has a better potential for recovery than the livestock-dependent FSS.

2. The Livestock-Dependent Food Supply System (Pastoralists).

- This food supply system, which includes about 10% of the population of the country, operates in the lowland areas, where people depend on animals for food through milk, meat, and blood products. Animal products are supplemented by grain crops in good years.
- The size of the herd and its productivity are dependent on pasture and water, which are in turn dependent on adequate rain. Thus rainfall is the major determinant of animal production.
- The market plays an important role in the pastoralists' food supply, since animals are regularly exchanged for grain in local markets. Thus their food supply is directly or indirectly dependent on animals.
- The ratio of animal price to grain price has an important bearing on the pastoralists' food supply, because grain prices are determined by supply and animal prices are determined by the size, age, and condition of the animal. A poor year in the cropping areas coinciding with a drought in the pastoralist areas means high grain prices and, because the animals' condition is poor, a greater supply of animals to the market, with lower prices than usual.
- Pastoralists have developed a number of strategies in the event of a dry year, such as the use of dry season grazing areas. Mobility and labor sharing are an important part of the strategy within the clan. Thus instead of the steadily increasing food shortage pattern observed in cropping areas, the pastoralists' food shortage is hidden until the clan's resources are totally exhausted. Large numbers of drought-stricken people then suddenly appear in urban areas.
- Pastoralists may better withstand shortages, but once animal reserves are depleted, recovery may take many years.

3. The Market-Dependent Food Supply System.

- The market-dependent population, which is about 15% of the country's population, includes the urban and cash crop producing rural population. It has a cash income with purchasing power and is fed from the market by a number of production sources—state farms, food processing plants, surplus-producing rural populations, and so forth.
- Market prices and supply are the major factors that determine the food availability for this group of the population. The stability of supply and price depends not only on stability of production but also on smooth transit through the transportation, warehousing, and retailing system.

Sampling Strategy

In order to achieve a satisfactory evaluation of national food supply system performance for a country like Ethiopia, with its complex agroclimatic zones, a wide sample is required. Because aggregated information is not helpful in identifying food deficit and surplus areas, the sample is designed so as to provide reliable disaggregated information. When aggregation becomes necessary, the highest is the wereda level. The general approach is as follows:

1. In order to obtain national coverage, information of a qualitative nature is obtained from all areas of the country. Data on crop performance, condition of livestock, pasture, and water and market supplies are mainly qualitative.

2. Major markets from Regional, Awraja, and major Wereda capitals are selected as samples. With the increase in the Early Warning System's capability, attempts are being made to include all wereda markets as well as the major lower-level rural markets in the sample.

3. About thirty to forty meteorological stations (mostly those located near airports and research stations and where good communication facilities exist) are used as a sample and therefore are not necessarily representative of the country.

4. When household-level surveys (such as pastoral area and disaster area assessments) are made, proper scientific sampling methods are applied. Peasant Associations are the primary sampling units and households within the selected Peasant Associations are secondary sampling units. When nutritional status assessments are made, subsamples are taken from the selected households.

Data Collection

Data Acquisition. All data have been obtained by a ground-based reporting network. However, the Early Warning System is now trying to augment this network with remote sensing techniques in collaboration with other international organizations, particularly the International Livestock Centre for Africa (ILCA).

Frequency of Collection. The crop and market information is collected monthly; pastoral information, quarterly; and rainfall information, daily.

Data Transit. All data, except for meteorological information, are sent from the headquarters of the responsible member agencies to the central coordinating office at the RRC for processing. The meteorological information is aggregated to ten-day and monthly periods, analyzed in the agency concerned, and sent in the form of a report to the coordinating office one week after the end of the ten-day or monthly period.

All other data must arrive at the headquarters of the agencies three weeks after they have been collected. The coordinating office collects the field questionnaires from the agencies at set intervals, usually twice a week.

Data Processing

Since most of the information collected is qualitative, a manual data processing system is being used. However, an electronic data processing system will be used when the capability exists for a continuous flow of quantitative or multisectoral data from the field.

Reporting

The output of the program is issued regularly in the form of the following reports.

1. Ten-day, monthly, and seasonal agrometeorological reports are issued by the National Meteorological Service Agency.
2. Monthly Early Warning System reports compare normal and actual crop activities, inadequacy of rain for agricultural activities, any disruption in agricultural activity and its effect on expected production, performance of crops, and grain price trends.
3. Quarterly Early Warning System reports examine, in greater detail, the factors included in the monthly reports. Most of the information is displayed in the form of maps and graphs for easy visual interpretation.
4. Synoptic reports are issued at the end of every production period, updating the quarterly reports and providing a final picture of the food situation.
5. Disaster Area Assessment reports are issued after the surveys and reports listed above are conducted.

ASSESSMENT AND PREDICTION OF FOOD SHORTAGES IN FOOD SUPPLY SYSTEMS

In order to measure changes in the food supply system, a number of early warning indicators are identified for each system. For the systems to be effective, we must first determine (1) the relevance of the indicator to the food supply; (2) the effectiveness of the indicator to predict change; and (3) the likelihood of the indicator to provide sufficient lead time between the identification of the problem and the occurrence of the disaster. Timeliness also plays a crucial role in the usefulness of early warning indicators.

Crop-Dependent Food Supply System

Early warning indicators are mainly related to crop production and market situation. Limited indicators on consumption and nutrition situations are also considered. Crop assessments are made at district levels by altitude zones (for high, middle, and low altitudes). For each altitude zone, five major food crops are identified and their performance is monitored over a period of time. The conditions of the identified food crops, timeliness of general agricultural activities, cause and degree of damage to crops, and so forth are carefully assessed in qualitative terms at monthly intervals. The expected production of the five major crops in the district that is under consideration is then estimated in qualitative terms—whether the production is good, satisfactory, poor, or very poor, and how it compares with production from the previous year; and whether there is a surplus and how much of a surplus—enough for food and seed, enough for food only, enough for seed only, or complete destruction (no production).

The five crops are then ranked and aggregated to give a food forecast. A weighted average of the expected production of the five major food crops in an area is taken to identify whether that area is expecting adequate production or not. If the aggregated forecast indicates enough production only for seed (which is related to the rainfall condition, disruption of crop activities, and crop damages), the area is identified and immediately reported as a possible disaster area. If the aggregated forecast indicates surplus, the area is rated as a surplus area; if production is expected to provide enough for food and seed, the area is rated as sufficient. When the production forecast indicates that the crop will provide enough for food only, the area is rated as "below requirement."

Along with the crop assessment, a market assessment is made. This involves the collection of market information during the major market day in the middle of a month for the major cereals, pulses, and oil seeds. Price and supply of major crops are the major indicators of the food prospect. Normally when peasants anticipate a poor harvest, they withhold whatever marketable grain they have, and this leads to price increases and supply shortages. If crop failure is indicated, its effect on the food supply is evaluated. The assessment at this stage includes checking the availability of stock carried forward from the previous harvest and livestock that could be sold to purchase food from a local market. If the people do not have either stock from the previous harvest or enough livestock for sale, and if crop failure is imminent and the aggregate forecast shows serious food shortage, information is collected on numbers of people likely to be affected, numbers likely to face food shortages, alternatives for alleviating the shortages, and the length of time that assistance is likely to be required.

In areas where food shortages are serious and likely to affect a large number of people for a longer period of time, the Disaster Area Assessment Team of the Early Warning and Planning Department conducts a thorough assessment of the area. Teams make detailed household-level assessments of the amount produced, amount in storage, livestock holding, price situation (for grain and livestock), nutritional status of children under the age of five, and health condition of the population. The teams also recommend short-term and long-term measures. Other disaster indicators—such as migration, human and livestock deaths, and appearance of capital goods in the markets—are also checked.

Livestock-Dependent Food Supply System (Pastoralist)

Field teams from the RRC are deployed on a quarterly basis in each district inhabited by pastoralists. They assess antecedent rainfall conditions, which in turn determine pasture and water availability. The teams also assess water and livestock condition and adequacy of pasture in the whole district and in selected households. The household-level assessment includes determining the herding size of the household. The normal migration pattern of the population is then compared with the actual pattern to see if there are displacements from the traditional routes.

A detailed market assessment is also made to ensure compatibility between live-stock prices and grain prices and to detect abnormalities in the number and type of animals brought for sale. Once the condition of the animals deteriorates and the market situation is disturbed by declining animal prices, increased flow of animals in poor condition, and rising grain prices, then a serious food shortage is forecast. The district is declared a potential disaster area and the number of pastoralists likely to be affected is determined for relief and rehabilitation measures.

Market-Dependent Food Supply System

This population is assumed to have a cash income and can acquire supplies wherever surplus is available. It is therefore of less concern to the Early Warning System. However, information on price and supply and production prospects, particularly in areas expecting surplus production, is provided to the government marketing agency to help it in its operation.

USE OF OUTPUT BY DECISION-MAKING BODIES

The Relief and Rehabilitation Commission is one of the major users of the Early Warning System: RRC estimates its relief requirements and also plans and executes its relief operations based on the information obtained through the system. The RRC has already started the Food Security Reserve Project, which stockpiles emergency food in strategic locations around the country. The Early Warning System provides the information necessary to release grain from the stock and call forward replacement supplies.

The major user of information on surplus areas of the system is the Agricultural Marketing Corporation (AMC), which is a member of the Project Coordinating Committee. The AMC uses the information to extend its capacity to buy from surplus-producing areas and sell stock to stabilize supply in market-dependent communities. Ethiopian embassies abroad also receive copies of the Early Warning System reports, which they use, along with other information, to make the international community aware of the food situation in the country.

MAJOR PROBLEMS OF THE SYSTEM

Since its establishment, and despite several constraints, the Early Warning System has played a valuable role in monitoring the food situation in the country. Constraints have included shortage of funds, lack of transport facilities, and lack of field personnel and trained manpower. The system's capacity to carry out quick surveys and monitor ongoing disaster situations is also limited, as is its access to quick and reliable information through other techniques such as remote sensing. The qualitative nature of the information used has constrained effective determination and understanding of the magnitude of the food shortages in the country.

CONCLUSIONS

The Early Warning System continues to be vital to the Relief and Rehabilitation Commission as a planning tool for guiding internal aid allocations and requests for international aid. Every effort is being made to strengthen and improve the capacity of the system in the following four general areas so as to increase both the types of information provided and the number of user agencies, and to strengthen the system's links with the response and intervention system:

1. The direct technical improvement of the Early Warning System and its component parts and the strengthening of the system's ability to undertake research and mapping exercises when necessary.
2. Increased cooperation between and within government agencies participating in the system, and between the system and international organizations and nongovernment organizations.
3. The improvement of the collection and dissemination of early warning and other general information.
4. The improvement of specific intervention mechanisms in response to early warning and other general information.

REFERENCES

Ali, A. 1986. Prediction of Food Shortages and the Response System of the RRC. Department of Aid Coordination and International Relations, Addis Ababa.
Relief and Rehabilitation Commission. 1985. Early Warning and Planning Services. The Early Warning System—Ethiopia. Description of Its Major Activities and Technical Basis. RRC, Addis Ababa, Ethiopia.
Relief and Rehabilitation Commission. 1980. Food and Nutrition Surveillance Program, Project Document. RRC, Addis Ababa, Ethiopia.
Relief and Rehabilitation Commission and UNICEF. 1984. Joint RRC-UNICEF Workshop on Technical and Institutional Improvements in the Early Warning System, Nazareth, August 15-18, 1984. RRC, Addis Ababa.
Relief and Rehabilitation Commission and UNICEF. 1984. Review of the Early Warning System of the Relief and Rehabilitation Commission. RRC, Addis Ababa.

CHAPTER 18
WOULD BETTER INFORMATION FROM AN EARLY WARNING
SYSTEM IMPROVE AFRICAN FOOD SECURITY?

John McIntire

INTRODUCTION

The famines of 1984 and 1985 have again brought the world's attention to ways of reducing Africa's vulnerability to catastrophic food shortages. The long-term solution is of course to increase food production, or to increase the capacity to import food using export earnings. Short-term solutions involve food aid, in kind or in cash. These solutions are only partly independent, because many food-aid programs intend to contribute to food production in the longer run. This paper will concentrate on the short-term issue, which involves severe food shortages, the food security programs to prevent shortages, and the role of information in such programs.

I make the obvious assumption that food aid, stored locally or imported, will be a necessary part of any food security program. Food aid is subject to many criticisms. One is that aid has disincentive effects on local food production. A second is that supplies of food aid are plentiful when world grain prices are low and the purchasing power of needy countries is therefore high; but supplies are scarce when world prices are high and purchasing power is therefore low. This countercyclical behavior of food-aid quantities and world grain prices means that aid is least available when it is most necessary. A third criticism is that aid is subject to administrative delays in donor countries and to handling delays in recipient countries. A fourth is that aid is used for political purposes by recipient countries, and does not reach the needy. A fifth is that because aid grain is often rice or wheat, recipients accustomed to consuming other grains or root crops become dependent on aid grain. This dependency encourages imports of such grains, to the ultimate detriment of traditional staples. Finally, because of uncertainty about the terms of food aid that is not stored nationally, it is said that food aid held abroad imposes the costs of uncertainty on recipients.

Each of the criticisms involves elements necessary for efficient food aid: production, prices, consumption, transport, conditionality. If information about these elements were more widely available or better used, then it might be possible to reduce disincentive effects, administrative and handling delays, political misadministration, and dependence on aid grains—all but the latter to the obvious benefit of the recipients.

Two kinds of information important for famine relief issues are staple production and the climatic conditions of production. Such information is notoriously unreliable in Africa, being of low quality, high variability, and late arrival. Poor production data can lead to serious misestimates of the amount, timing, and distribution of necessary aid. If data arrive late, then aid might arrive too late to prevent famine. Poor climatic data, especially thin coverage of remote areas, can lead to underestimates of impending dangers. Poor data can also lead to overestimates of the quantities of aid required, and perhaps aggravate disincentive effects.

One technique proposed for reducing the error in African food production and climatic data involves the use of remote-sensing data to predict food production directly or indirectly. Because such data are available rapidly, cover a wide area, and are objective, it has been argued that they can provide early warning of drought (Brumby and Cossins, 1985). The United Nations Food and Agriculture Organization (FAO) has used drought early-warning systems in the Sahel countries of West Africa, so the idea is not new. What is new is the use of digitized satellite imagery to estimate biomass production. Such techniques offer, in principle, an accurate crop forecast several months before other techniques. The apparent attractiveness of the technique must be analyzed carefully, however. Using it in a food security system might give a false sense of security about the areas and groups at risk and is justified only if certain conditions hold. Information is a complement, not a substitute, to insurance. Several questions arise: Can the same information be had more cheaply? Is the information provided necessary and/or sufficient? Is a lack of accurate, timely production information really a cause of famine?

This paper examines the conditions in which famines have occurred and tries to indicate if investments in information, like early-warning systems, can contribute to food security in sub-Saharan Africa. The following section reviews some of the sad history of recent African famines: whether famines are unique to the post-independence era, which groups suffered, and why. The third section studies the role of information in those disasters, examining the types of information gathered and how they were used. The fourth section answers the question, Was lack of information on production conditions, leading to a slow relief response, a major cause of the famines?

Are the famines in the last fifteen years unique and do famines appear to be becoming more frequent or more severe?

These famines are well studied in two excellent books (Mesfin, 1984; Sen, 1981), which are used here as sources. *Famine* is defined as an acute shortage of food, for whatever reason, resulting in serious malnutrition, in disease consequent to the malnutrition, and in deaths from starvation or from diseases related to the malnutrition. The discussion here is not of chronic malnutrition.

The books by Mesfin and Sen note recurrent famines in Ethiopia; Mesfin's book, in particular, reviews many famines from the mid-1950s to the mid-1970s. The work of Bonte (1975) on Mauritania reported many famines. Watts' (1983) book on northern Nigeria found famines in the nineteenth century. The evidence referred to does not suggest that droughts causing severe food shortages are unique to Africa after independence; nor does any other evidence of which I am aware.

The historical record of the severity of previous famines is incomplete. Even well-studied catastrophes, such as the Bengal famine of 1943, are the subject of much conjecture about their real magnitudes. My opinion—and it is only that—is that African famines are probably less severe and less frequent since World War II than in the nineteenth century. I say this because there have been improvements in (1) income, allowing greater accumulation of wealth to draw on in times of need; (2) transportation, allowing better shipment of relief; and (3) health, allowing reduction of mortality in the years after the original crisis. There has also been population growth in Africa, which would have been difficult to sustain if there had been frequent and major famines.

Were there regularities in the recent famines?

Agroclimates and susceptible climates have shown regularities, but not in periods between famines. The susceptible climates are those where rainfed agriculture dominates. The West African famine of 1972-74 and the Sudanese famine of 1984-85 were in the semiarid tropics (SAT) [1], while the worst of the Ethiopian famines, as reported by Mesfin, were in the lower highlands of that country. In none of those regions is irrigation important. Extensive harvest failures occurred in the semiarid tropics of Botswana, but did not lead to famine (Campbell, 1978; Holm and Morgan, 1985). Famines in Uganda and Mozambique occurred in war areas and were only partly related to climatic conditions.

Although the humid and subhumid tropics have been subject to rainfall shortages, their populations have been much less affected by them. In recent years in Nigeria, the government has organized relief to the afflicted areas (Wetherell, Holt, and Richards, 1978) to lessen the impact of drought. The subhumid and humid tropics may also be less susceptible to droughts that cause complete crop failures because their absolute rainfall is higher and because of the prevalence of drought-security crops, like cassava.

It seems fair to conclude that droughts, leading to severe food shortages, are most common in the semiarid tropics, where rainfed cereal cultivation is widely practiced. The semiarid tropics have a high relative variability of rainfall (Cocheme and Franquin, 1967); low income, including low import capacity; poor transportation; and poor communication. The Sahel, Ethiopia, and Botswana all have population pressure on high-quality land; while population density, particularly in the Sahel, is low in aggregate, it is much higher on the best lands.

Which groups have been most affected?

Of all the West African groups, the herders have been most affected by droughts. During droughts, animals die or are sold in extremis, grain prices rise rapidly while animal prices fall, and the herders' purchasing power collapses. Because herders do not have food reserves and because their animal capital dies, they suffer what Sen calls an *entitlement failure*. (By this he means a lack of income or wealth to convert into consumption.) Their crisis is that they have no income to buy food, not that their food production is low. Sen argues in fact that herders may suffer this fate even if grain production is relatively good, although in the years in question it was bad.

Nutritional studies in the Sahel in July and August of 1973 (Kloth, 1974) and the province of Harerghe in Ethiopia (RRC, 1974) in 1974-75 show the fate of the herders. The Sahel studies of children in refugee camps in Niger, Mauritania, Mali, and Burkina Faso (then Upper Volta) found many more children of nomads in the camps.

Of the children examined, greater numbers of nomads' children were moderately or severely malnourished. There is oral evidence, reviewed by Brun (1975), that many nomad adults died before they could reach the camps.

The Center for Disease Control (CDC) did a second round of Sahel nutrition studies in June and July 1974. These studies did not confirm a higher proportion of malnourished nomadic children than sedentary children; small differences were found between sedentary and nomad groups, but they were not statistically significant. The 1974 study casts some doubt on the argument that herders suffering entitlement failure were most severely affected by the drought. The circumstances of the study—especially the strong possibility that many herders were already in camps and the reported fact that some of the people surveyed in their villages were already receiving food aid—makes the results difficult to interpret.

The Ethiopian groups included cultivators and noncultivators. In the 1973-74 famine around Harerghe, herders were affected for some of the same reasons as the West African herders. In the 1973-74 famine in Wello, nonagricultural populations and landless laborers were affected for the same reasons—lack of income—while some marginal tenants of small plots and even minor landholders suffered as well. In fact, Sen (1981) argues that grain production in Wello was only just below average and certainly not catastrophically low. [2]

Mesfin (1984) analyzed Ethiopian famines from the 1950s to the 1970s. He concluded that districts reporting famine conditions were those where subsistence farming dominated. More affluent farming districts had fewer famines. Those people affected in the 1984-85 Ethiopian famine, centered in Wello and Tigray, were cultivators. Recalling that Sen's analysis of the 1973-74 famine concentrated on the origins of the cultivators in relief camps, it would be useful to know more about these people, but this is not now possible. The cause of their distress was low production over (at least) two seasons.

From this brief review, we can conclude that the groups most vulnerable are those that depend indirectly on agriculture—that is, herders who do not farm and agricultural laborers—and poorer cultivators who cannot accumulate reserves. If Mesfin's evidence is general, cultivators suffer when they are subsistence producers whose crops (apparently) have failed for more than one year. Where crops fail for only one year, cultivators can keep adequate reserves. One should be cautious about generalizing from Mesfin's evidence for the rest of Africa. Ethiopian peasants under the imperial regime were subject to many taxes, which were paid partly by reducing consumption and partly by reducing savings that might have been held as grain reserves. West African peasants were probably less oppressed and might therefore have been better able to accumulate reserves. Because landless and urban classes are much less numerous in Africa than in Asia, they have not suffered from famines as much their counterparts in Bangladesh and Bengal have, again as recounted by Sen (1981). [3]

If it is indeed nonfarming groups that are most vulnerable, and if they are vulnerable even in years with reasonable production, then this suggests that information on production can be seriously misleading. Information on prices of livestock products, staples, and incomes would be required to predict distress of nonfarming groups.

What was the response to indications of famine in the affected countries?

Posing the question in terms of response to famine is a weak test. Famines occur some time after droughts or exceptional price increases [4], so that a better test would be response to indications of drought or market disruptions. However, even by the weaker test, there have been significant delays from the times at which indications of serious distress were available and the times at which governments acted. Such delays have occurred for political or bureaucratic reasons, not for lack of information.

Mesfin's (1984) book recounts the pathetic (and successful) attempt of Haile Selassie's government to ignore the famine of 1973-74, just as it had ignored similar catastrophes in the past. Relief was organized largely by the revolutionary government after it consolidated power in September 1974. Mesfin argues that there were reliable accounts of the disaster for at least eighteen months before the revolutionary government came to power. It is well known that the political disruptions of 1974 were related to the distress of the famine areas; this again suggests that information was available, which the government ignored. Mesfin also tells the almost unbelievable history of the Tigray famine of 1958, in which much the same pattern of events occurred.

The leaders of the military coup in April 1974 in Niger justified their actions by pointing to the civilian government's inability to resolve the food problem and by making allegations that government officials had profited from it. Relief organization had started in 1973, but this was more than a year after the first indications of a disaster in the summer of 1972 (Brown, 1975). This again suggests that information was available to authorities, who chose to ignore it. A similar, perhaps even more blatant, disregard for information occurred in Chad and contributed to the overthrow of the government in 1975 (Ormieres, 1975). [5]

Although one can say that the agrometeorological networks in the Sahel and Ethiopia were poorly developed and therefore could not have been expected to provide reliable information rapidly, there had been indications of low rainfall for some time. For example, Kelly wrote that "empirical evidence show[ed] that the northward penetration of the monsoon rains in West Africa had been curtailed since the late 1960s" (Kelly, 1975). Such evidence, even if it was from a small number of stations, was available well before the famine.

Sen's (1981) book has several accounts of famines that were ignored by authorities in Africa and elsewhere. In every case, some information was available—weather reports, crop estimates by extension agents, reports of unusual movements of people seeking aid. Brun (1975) cites large and unusual movements of people into small Mauritanian cities in early 1973, to give just one example. Campbell (1978), writing of Botswana, noted that "although all the signs were present . . . the drought of the 1960s took people by surprise."

Do drought cycles exist?

Although effort has been devoted to discovering cycles in African rainfall, the evidence is controversial. In terms of food security in Africa, cycles are not really an important issue. First, if there are regular cycles, then it is still necessary to organize relief administration. If the experience of African famines tells us anything, it is that relief administration has not been well organized except *after* a disaster. Second, if there are no cycles, then it is still necessary to organize relief. With or without cycles, there is still great variability in rainfall, crop output, and incomes in these countries, and that variability must be dealt with. Third, even if cycles could be clearly estimated, the confidence intervals for their lengths would still be greater than the period in which a drought is likely to lead to famine. Recall that herders, especially in West Africa, have often been the most afflicted by famines and that they can be afflicted by drought lasting as little as one year if it is severe enough. In sum, the statistical evidence about cycles is weak, while that about variability is strong, so we might as well accept the conclusion of Glantz and Katz: "For all practical purposes, including planning for the impact of future droughts, we might as well view drought as an 'aperiodic' phenomenon" (Glantz and Katz, 1983).

What information is gathered?

Evidence indicating famine can be direct (people are starving or are behaving in a manner consistent with food shortages) or indirect (the season looks bad because rainfall is low or because crops are suffering).

African governments rely on rainfall and crop estimates made by local officials. Food supply is assessed by synthesizing information on climate, crop growth, crop prices, and informed appraisals. Mesfin (1984) recounts the evidence provided by officials in Ethiopia, who reported whether or not a famine situation existed in their districts; this is probably still a typical procedure in Ethiopia, the difference being that the Relief and Rehabilitation Commission (RRC) exists as a central authority to receive and act on such reports.

In the Sahel, rainfall reporting systems vary in coverage and timeliness. I do not know what the situation was before the 1980s, but now precipitation data from remote areas can be sent to central authorities within two weeks. Authorities can also have crop and animal price data of thinner coverage, probably with a longer delay, but the collection network is less dense. I do not know if there are any formal methods of direct reporting in these countries. In Botswana, a more formal information gathering process is part of an official system to warn of drought as well as to provide relief.

Two important criticisms can be made about rainfall data (apart from the fact that they might be slow to arrive). The first is that rainfall data are only indirect measures of crop growth. Since crop growth depends on rainfall distribution as well as amount, reports of amounts only are inadequate. Second, rainfall stations are too dispersed to provide general information, even if that information is a good crop estimator.

The first criticism is accurate. It can be resolved by using cumulative distributions, whether of the total amounts or the total deficits, in a given period. Using cumulative distributions might then aggravate the timeliness problem. The second criticism is also accurate and the obvious solution is to have more stations. One advantage of a remote sensing system is that it is perhaps cheaper than a greater density of rainfall stations.

What food security systems have been proposed?

Four principal systems have been proposed or are being used. They are similar on one fundamental point—each requires resources from outside the affected area, either from the domestic budget or from aid. The merits and demerits of each are described briefly here.

The first system centers on public grain reserves. Two assumptions justify public reserves. The first is that privately held reserves in poor countries are too small to cover large shortfalls in food production. The second assumption holds that if famine threatens because of an entitlement failure, then releases from private reserves, whatever their sizes, would not be free and therefore would not help the needy. The merits of public systems are that you can't eat money: reserves are in kind, are held in deficit areas, and can be released immediately. The demerits are that reserves are expensive (even if the grain to fill the reserves is donated), subject to physical or economic deterioration, subject to political misuse, and do not necessarily reach the needy. [6]

A second system is food import insurance (Konandreas, Huddleston, and Ramangkura, 1978). This is an insurance policy against shortfalls in domestic food production or increases in the food import bill; countries' cash drawings on the policy would be used to buy imports. Its merits are that it is less expensive than holding physical reserves and (maybe) less subject to political manipulation. Its demerits are that you can't eat money: an insurance scheme might be slow, might be needed in years of high world prices (thus reducing its purchasing power), and grain bought with it might not reach the needy.

A third system is a countercyclical trade policy. Governments tax exports in surplus years to stabilize domestic prices and producers' incomes; they subsidize imports in bad years to stabilize domestic consumption and consumers' welfare. Such a policy could be implemented with a stabilization fund and any profits from the fund could be used for drought relief. Even if there were no pecuniary profits to the fund, there would still be benefits in terms of reduced price instability. The merits and demerits of this system are the same as those of the food insurance scheme, with the added demerits that it requires a great deal of information on domestic prices that is not likely to be available, and it is especially susceptible to corruption.

A fourth system is public works. The government keeps a list of labor-intensive projects in areas that are likely to be affected. When necessary, those projects are implemented by hiring needy persons who are paid in kind or in cash. This has been done in Botswana (Holm and Morgan, 1985) and in India. Its merits are that it yields productive investment, responds to entitlement failures by providing income, and allows a more normal life among the affected population. Its demerits are that it is subject to political manipulation, especially in defining the criteria and sites for relief.

I once committed myself too enthusiastically to a market-oriented system, mixing trade policies, grain reserves, and import food insurance (McIntire, 1981). Such a mix has failed—or at least there is no evidence that it has worked in the poorest countries of Africa—because of administrative delays, lack of transport capacity, and lack of information necessary to make a trade policy or an insurance system work. There is still no reason in principle that such a mixed system would not work, but the fact that it has not worked is strong enough evidence that something else is necessary.

I now argue that the three components of a successful food security system for the poorest countries in sub-Saharan Africa are:

1. Public grain reserves equal to roughly 5% of expected annual consumption.
2. A commitment from the historical food aid donors to supply another 10% as grain on demand.
3. A commitment from the historical food aid donors to provide whatever is necessary beyond that 15% from a food insurance scheme to be used exclusively for public works in affected areas on terms to be agreed on well in advance.

The first component provides immediate relief without compromising the use of other resources, such as aid or commercial imports. The second provides for extreme dangers, in particular those occurring among farming populations holding their own grain reserves. The third allows for the political interests of both receiving and giving nations, by giving each some leverage in the choice of projects and in other terms of the scheme. In particular, if terms were made for relief works programs in advance, then several administrative problems could be solved, at least partly: the most susceptible regions, the political demands of competing regions, donor concerns about project choice, and recipient concerns that they are being taken for granted. The three components could provide for a reasonable measure of consumption security while establishing some basis for resistance to future catastrophes. According to Holm and Morgan (1985), this is more or less what the government of Botswana has done successfully.

What would be the role of information in such schemes?

The role of information would be (at most) secondary, really affecting only the food insurance and relief works components. The grain reserves would still have to be managed with little external interference. It might be possible to direct governments' attention to danger areas with early warning information, but it is unrealistic to think that highly quantitative information (about rain, production, or prices) will serve as a trigger for the release of public grain reserves in poor countries. Because drought risk areas can be predicted reasonably well, grain reserves could be located in the areas of greatest need. [7]

The role of information would be largely historical in the food insurance component. And, because this is the second defense, early warning would be less vital. The information needed for calculating insurance premiums includes world prices and domestic transport costs, which are available without an early warning system. What economists like to call "moral hazard"—that is, negligence induced by the availability of insurance, in this case defined as excessive drawings on the insurance fund—might be encouraged by a food insurance scheme. However, this could be alleviated by putting a cap on cumulative drawings in each period, by reviewing drawings, and by using that review to set the limit in the following period.

Information would be important to the relief component, but timeliness is not vital. What is vital is historical information on droughts and technical information on relevant public works investments. Data and analyses would be necessary to identify famine-prone areas and relief projects there. "Data and analyses" refers not only to the meteorological and production type, but also to the historical and economic type presented by Mesfin and Watts.

CONCLUSIONS

In thinking about the food crisis in Africa, and in insisting on the role of information, it seems that observers have fallen into a fairly simple fallacy. The fallacy is the following: famines are produced by crop failure in one season; crop failure in one season is (necessarily) sudden; therefore, if such failures could be predicted then it would be possible to prevent famines, by timely expedition of emergency relief.

The evidence I have tried to assemble establishes another line of reasoning: famines largely affect people who grow few or no crops (such as pastoralists) and who constitute relatively small parts of the population. Famines can occur even when there is only a small production shortfall—this is the most important lesson of Sen's book. Although food shortages and chronic malnutrition are the lot of many, these shortages are not famines and have to be remedied by other measures. Famines do not occur with any identifiable period, but they do occur in known areas. If famines do endanger large populations in such areas, then the rainfall deficits that produced them probably occurred for more than one year.

Under this reasoning, the role of better information about production and production conditions is small—not absent, but small—and the role of sophisticated forecasts is also small. The needed information is analysis of the historical data. Such analysis would be used to:

1. Identify sites for the grain reserves necessary as a first line of defense.
2. Identify administrative deficiencies in the reporting of famine situations from the field.
3. Calculate necessary transport facilities and buy or build them.
4. Estimate the availability of foreign exchange so as to make intelligent use of commercial imports.
5. Use estimates of availability of foreign exchange to make intelligent use of food insurance schemes.
6. Plan public works in afflicted areas, to be funded partly by relief grain (food-for-work programs).

It is clear that a sophisticated early warning system has some value, especially a dramatic one. (I do not mean to sneer at the latter, by the way.) The practical difficulties of using it are not insurmountable. However, promoting it as a tool that can do very much to improve African food security rests on the false assumption that information is what is lacking. What is lacking is (1) good use of the available information; (2) reasonable appraisal of who is at risk; and (3) plans and means to respond to droughts and the famines that sometimes ensue from them. Better information will have some effect, but only if it leads to better preparation.

292

NOTES

1. The semiarid tropics (SAT) are those regions of the tropics receiving between 400 mm and 1100 mm of rain per year in a single season. In Africa, they include the Sahel, the northern band of the West African coastal countries, and much of the lowlands of Eastern Africa.

2. This ignores the possibility that the cumulative deficit over several years may have been quite large, even if the production deficit in the crisis year may have been small. In addition, Sen's analysis is based on district data; farm surveys show that the within-district variation is large in Ethiopia and the Sahel. These facts do not invalidate Sen's thesis, but they increase the information burden of relief authorities.

3. None of the above should be taken to mean that urban classes in Africa were not affected by the price increases. They did suffer income losses and malnutrition must have increased, but there was much less starvation. It should also not be taken to mean that there is no long-term malnutrition in Africa; extensive research shows that there is.

4. The second part of the sentence is weaker than the first, because there are highly vulnerable populations in which catastrophes can occur rapidly. Ravaillon (1986) showed significant rice market failures in Bangladesh for short periods from 1972 through 1975. In spite of the brevity of these periods, severe famine occurred in 1974; the famine was partly related to the market's failure to move rice from surplus to deficit areas.

5. Ormieres reports declarations by Chadian officials that relief would be withheld from regions supporting an insurrection.

6. The academic literature also insists on the possible displacement of private storage by public storage. This concern is valid in developed countries, with well-functioning grain markets and active speculation, but it is not a problem in developing countries. Others have suggested that a further demerit is the absence of an insurer; that is, who would be willing to bear these risks?

7. Admittedly, such reserves would have to be filled at the outset with concessional imports, and the demerits noted above would still apply.

REFERENCES

Bonte, P. 1975. Pasteurs et nomades—l'exemple de la Mauritanie. pp. 62-86. In J. Copans, ed. Secheresses et famines du sahel: II. Paysans et nomades. Francois Maspero, Paris.

Brown, D. S. 1975. Drought perceptions and responses of the international donor community. pp. 1-13. In J. L. Newman, ed. Drought, Famine and Population Movements in Africa. Foreign and Comparative Studies/Eastern Africa XVII. Maxwell School, Syracuse University, Syracuse, New York.

Brumby, P. J.; and N. J. Cossins. 1985. NOAA-7 Satellite imagery: A better early warning system for the Sahel. ILCA Newsletter 4(January):2-3.

Brun, T. 1975. Manifestations nutritionelles et medicales de la famine. pp. 75-108. In J. Copans, ed. Secheresses et famines du Sahel: I. Ecologie, Denutrition, Assistance. Francois Maspero, Paris.

Campbell, A. C. 1978. The 1960s drought in Botswana. pp. 98-109. In M. T. Hinchey, ed. Proceedings of the Symposium on Drought in Botswana. Botswana Society, Gaborone.

Cocheme, J.; and P. A. Franquin. 1967. Study of the agroclimatology of the semiarid area south of the Sahara in West Africa. Technical report prepared for the FAO/UNESCO/WHO Interagency Project on Agroclimatology. FAO, Rome.

Copans, J., ed. 1975. Secheresses et famines du Sahel. 2 vols. Francois Maspero, Paris.

Glantz, M. H.; and R. W. Katz. 1983. African drought and its impacts: Revived interest in a recurrent phenomenon. United Nations Environment Program, Nairobi.

Hinchey, M. T., ed. 1978. Proceedings of the Symposium on Drought in Botswana. Botswana Society, Gaborone.

Holm, J. D.; and R. G. Morgan. 1985. Coping with drought in Botswana: An African success. J. Modern Afr. Studies 23 (September):463-482.

Kelly, T. J. 1975. Climate and the West African drought. pp. 14-31. In J. L. Newman, ed. Drought, famine and population movements in Africa. Foreign and Comparative Studies/Eastern Africa XVII. Maxwell School, Syracuse University, Syracuse, New York.

Kloth, T. I. 1974. Sahel nutrition survey: 1974. Center for Disease Control, Atlanta.

Konandreas, P.; B. Huddleston; and V. Ramangkura. 1978. Food security: An insurance approach. IFPRI Research Report No. 4, Washington, D.C.

McIntire, J. 1981. Food security in the Sahel: Variable import levy, grain reserves, and foreign exchange assistance. IFPRI Research Report No. 26, Washington, D.C.

Mesfin, W. M. 1984. Rural vulnerability to famine in Ethiopia: 1958-1977. Vikas, New Delhi.

Newman, J. L., ed. 1975. Drought, famine and population movements in Africa. Foreign and Comparative Studies/Eastern Africa XVII. Maxwell School, Syracuse University, Syracuse, New York.

Ormieres, J. L. 1975. Les consequences politiques de la famine. pp. 131-145. In J. Copans, ed. Secheresses et famines du Sahel: I. Ecologie, Denutrition, Assistance. Francois Maspero, Paris.

Ravaillon, M. 1986. Testing market integration. Am. J. Agric. Econ. 68(1):102-109.

Relief and Rehabilitation Commission (RRC). 1974. Harerghe under drought: A survey of the effects of drought upon human nutrition in Harerghe province. RRC, Addis Ababa.

Sen, A. 1981. Poverty and Famines: An Essay on Entitlement and Deprivation. Clarendon Press, Oxford, England.

Watts, M. 1983. Silent Violence. University of California Press, Berkeley, California.

Wetherell, H. I.; J. Holt; and P. Richards. 1978. Drought in the Sahel: A broader interpretation, with regard to West Africa and Ethiopia. pp. 131-141. In M. T. Hinchey, ed. Proceedings of the Symposium on Drought in Botswana. Botswana Society, Gaborone.

PART 5

Special Papers

CHAPTER 19
DROUGHT AND ECONOMIC DEVELOPMENT IN SUB-SAHARAN
AFRICA

Michael H. Glantz

INTRODUCTION

The purpose of this chapter is to remind those concerned with economic development issues how drought can, and often does, affect the process of development in sub-Saharan Africa. This reminder might seem unnecessary because of what now seems to be a widespread awareness of the devastating impacts of drought in developing countries. Yet, many troublesome signs constantly reappear, suggesting that such a reminder is clearly warranted.

A review of how the West African Sahel, plagued by drought in 1968-73, and Ethiopia, affected by drought in 1972-74, were treated by scholars, policy makers, governmental and nongovernmental development agencies, and of course the media, once those droughts and their impacts had seemingly ended, raises concern about how drought is viewed over the long run. While a drought is in progress, it is on everyone's mind. Once it ends, however, the interest in, as well as the perceived importance of, drought rapidly disappears.

The latest surge in awareness of African droughts and their societal impacts seems to be a direct result of recent news accounts of deaths and suffering of humans and livestock and of the stark photographs of a degraded African environment. This was clearly the case in the early 1980s for Ethiopia (e.g., BBC film on the subject was aired in October 1984), as it was in the early 1970s both for the West African Sahel (e.g., Morentz, 1980) and for Ethiopia (e.g., Shepherd, 1975). These accounts dramatize some of the more visible impacts of climate variability (e.g., drought) on society and on the environment in sub-Saharan Africa's arid and semiarid areas.

The drought-ridden seventeen-year period in the West African Sahel that began in 1968 (actually, after the 1967 harvest) prompted the publication of scores of books and hundreds, if not thousands, of articles on various physical aspects of drought and its impacts on various economic and social activities. The focus of these publications encompasses various levels of social organization, from herder and farmer to households and tribal groups, to the state, to the international community. A similar situation arose forty years ago as a response to drought in the U.S. Great Plains; Tannehill (1947) noted that "each time there is a serious drought millions of words are written on crop failures, misuse of the land, overpopulation, rainfall record" (p. 18).[1]

Yet, even with all these words during the past few years, many concerned with the study of drought have been left with an uneasy feeling that drought is still generally viewed as either an "idiosyncratic" occurrence, a transient event, or a temporary climatic aberration. Evidence shows that such views are misleading and that in some areas, meteorological drought is a recurring but aperiodic phenomenon; it is a part of climate and not apart from it. As such, drought is closely related to the problem of achieving sustained agricultural production in sub-Saharan Africa. It should no longer be ignored in development planning.

AFRICAN CLIMATE SINCE INDEPENDENCE

Post-independence African leaders have had to cope with innumerable problems of nation-building in a world rent by political, economic, and ideological cleavages. At the same time, several of those leaders have been forced to cope with the environmental and societal impacts of one of their worst and most prolonged drought episodes in recent times.

Peter Lamb has developed a regional rainfall index for an area somewhat broader than the West African Sahel (Lamb, 1982, 1983; Kerr, 1985). The rainfall record used by Lamb encompasses the years 1941-84. As Fig. 1 shows, rainfall in this area declined drastically within a relatively short time. By coincidence, this decline followed political independence of the countries whose rainfall stations are included in the index.

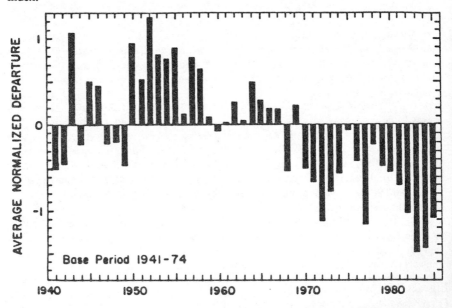

Fig. 1 Rainfall index for twenty sub-Saharan stations in West Africa west of the 10 °E between 11 °N-19 °N developed by Lamb (1985).

Changes in rainfall amounts at the local level are also quite graphic, as shown in the following figure for Gao, Mali. Figure 2 shows rainfall box plots in terms of the annual rainfall quartile ranges, medians, and highs and lows. It also compares the rainfall record before independence, after independence, and for the total time series. When one combines the post-independence years with the rest of the time series, the recent decline in rainfall is overshadowed by the longer (of the two) time series segments. Clearly, rainfall at this particular location has been considerably lower since independence than in the preindependence period. However, this does not mean that the current downward trend in annual rainfall will continue, just as the above-average rainfall years of the 1950s and early 1960s (see Fig. 1) did not mean that the wet conditions prevailing at that time would continue.

Although many sub-Saharan African countries, like Mali, have been plagued by drought-related constraints on domestic food production during a large part of their post-independence period, there is no simple correlation between meteorological drought and declines in agricultural production. However, as the box plots for Gao and Lamb's regional rainfall index do suggest, drought conditions in the post-independence period

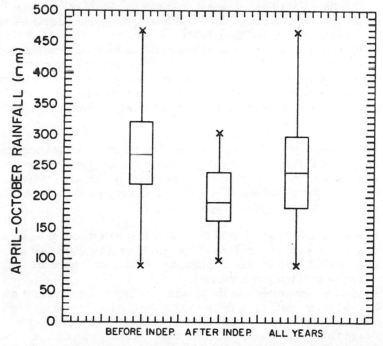

Fig. 2 Box plots of preindependence (1920-60), post-independence (1961-84), and combined (1920-84) wet season rainfall at Gao, Mali. These plots give the minimum (indicated by an x), lower quartile (the bottom of the box), and maximum (indicated by an x) of the probability distribution.

should receive more attention than they have in the past; they should be included as one of the several main factors contributing to declining per capita agricultural production in many African countries. Drought should also be seen not only for its direct societal and environmental impacts but for the varying degrees to which it exacerbates other related problems in Africa, such as balance of payments, debt repayment, food imports, and urbanization.

To better understand how climate, drought, and development issues should be considered in the future, it is useful to look at how they have been considered in the past.

CLIMATE AND DEVELOPMENT: A REVIEW OF THE LITERATURE

Until the most recent Sahelian and Ethiopian droughts, climate has been presented in the scientific and popular literature primarily as a boundary condition—that is, as a fixed and relatively unchanging precondition affecting society's development. Scientists and policy makers who perceive climate as a set of boundary conditions suggest that there is little, if anything, one might do to alter the climate or its impacts in a large-scale way, except for technological fixes such as those suggested during the past century for various parts of Africa (Glantz, 1977).

Many discussions that assess the effects of climate on human activities begin with comments on a book by Ellsworth Huntington, Climate and Civilization (1915), in which he hypothesized about the effects of climate on levels of development of different cultures. He concluded that there was an ideal temperature and degree of "storminess" that made possible the development of industrialized societies. Brooks (1926) noted that, according to Huntington,

> [A] certain type of climate, now found mainly in Britain, France and neighbouring parts of Europe, and in the eastern United States, is favourable to a high level of civilization. This climate is characterized by a moderate temperature, and by the passage of frequent barometric depressions, which give a sufficient rainfall and changeable stimulating weather (p. 292).

Huntington viewed inhabitants in the northern temperate regions as industrious and energetic, as a result of climatic factors (especially temperature), while those in the tropical areas were subjected to enervating climatic conditions that sapped them of the desire and energy to undertake productive work.

Huntington's views represent the thinking of a group of geographical determinists who tend to reduce the ills of the developing world (as well as the successes of the industrialized world) to climatic differences between these two regions. [2] Several books followed Huntington's Climate and Civilization, including such titles as Climate through the Ages (Brooks, 1926), Climate and the Energy of Nations (Markham, 1944), and World Power and Shifting Climates (Mills, 1963). Although some authors later adopted and modified some of the stances taken by Huntington, many challenged them as being at best ethnocentric and at worst racist. Still others felt that he had overplayed the importance to society and culture of natural climatic factors.

After World War II, attention to the relationship between developing countries and climate shifted from an explanation of why the levels of development of the tropical countries were so different from those in the temperate regions to discussions of how to develop tropical countries, given their climatic boundary conditions. [3] Paul Streeten (1976) observed that after World War II, a new optimism had emerged, suggesting that development could be brought about by simply supplying some missing economic elements:

> It is part of the stages-of-growth mythology that all countries tread inexorably the same path to eventual "take-off" and self-sustained economic growth; that the speed of this march is determined by savings ratios, investment ratios, and capital-output ratios; and the role of rich countries is to supply missing components, like foreign exchange or skills (p. xi).

According to Streeten, "the neglect of the role of climate fitted well into the new optimism" (p. xi).

In the early 1950s the U.S. Council on Foreign Relations established the Study Group on Climate and Economic Development in the Tropics. Their concern for convening such a study group was raised by the following observation: "By any rational definition of 'underdeveloped country' most of them lie entirely or partially in the tropics. Is climate the common factor that keeps them underdeveloped?" (Lee, 1957, p. vii). The study group's report discussed climate in terms of its effects on soil fertility, human and livestock health, plants, storage and handling of crops, and so forth. Nowhere in the report, however, was either climate variability or drought mentioned.

In 1969 Bernard Oury, an economist with the World Bank, lamented the lack of interest that economists, in their consideration of the development process, show in the effects of weather and climate on societies. He noted, "From the earliest times, the weather and climate have influenced, if not controlled, the progress of civilization. Yet, in spite of its obvious importance and often dramatic impact, professional economists generally take little interest in the weather as a prime factor in economic development" (p. 24). This article appears to be one of the first from the World Bank to consider weather and development.

In the 1970s another World Bank economist, A. M. Kamarck, discussed climate and economic development in the tropics (Kamarck, 1976). Kamarck, unlike the geographic determinists writing earlier this century, did not reduce all ills of countries in the midst of economic development to climatic factors. He noted that

> None of this is to claim that climate has a mechanical one-to-one relation to economic development, nor that climate with its effects is the only ruling constraint on economic development, nor that if the effects of climate were removed as a constraint in today's poor countries development would be unbounded. Rather, in today's poor countries climatic factors have hampered economic development through their impact on agriculture. . . . These effects need to be better understood (p. 11). [4]

Although Kamarck commented on the neglect of climate factors by earlier students of economic development, he provided little additional information about how drought or, more generally, climate variability might affect development. Yet, the importance of considering the impacts of drought, as an element of climate, on the development process should not be underestimated.

Biswas (1984), like Kamarck, presented a cursory review of the works of economists who made references to climate and development, such as Myrdal (1968), Galbraith (1951), Lewis (1955), and Tosi (1975). Biswas raised an interesting and important issue: "One can, however, ask if development economists have failed miserably to consider climate as an important factor for development planning, why have not the climatologists ensured that such a neglect is not allowed to continue" (p. 7). He then suggested, "Much though the climatologists know about climate, they have not ventured out of their own discipline: they have tended to remain isolated within their own field. . . . Accordingly one is indeed hard pressed to name more than a handful of climatologists who are even active in the fringe areas of development" (p. 7). Further, he suggested that it was no surprise that at the World Climate Conference convened by the World Meteorological Organization, "not a single paper analyzing the relations between climate and overall development" was presented (WMO, 1979, p. 7).

One such recent attempt at a "new" approach to understanding the relationship of climatic characteristics and development was the seminar convened in 1978 by the Institute of Development Studies at the University of Sussex, in which seasonality and its relationship to various aspects of rural poverty were addressed (Chambers, et al., 1981). Underscoring the relevance to development of seasonality (as a characteristic of climate), Chambers, et al., succinctly stated the case, as follows:

> Most of the very poor people in the world live in tropical areas with marked wet and dry seasons. Especially for the poorer people, women and children, the wet season before the harvest is usually the most critical time of year. At that time adverse factors often overlap and interact: food is short and food prices high; physical energy is needed for agricultural work; sickness is prevalent, especially malaria, diarrhea and skin infections; child care, family hygiene, and cooking are neglected by women overburdened with work; and late pregnancy is common, with births peaking near harvest. This is a time of year marked by loss of body weight, low birth weights, high neonatal mortality, malnutrition, and indebtedness. It is the hungry season and the sick season. It is the time of year when poor people are at their poorest and most vulnerable to becoming poorer (p. xv).

Thus, a more effective way to assess the impacts of climate on the development process is to move away from considerations of climate as a boundary condition and to focus on seasonality and other characteristics of climate, such as variability, changes in climate regimes, and droughts and their impacts on the environment and on human activities. To do so means that we can move on to a new phase in the consideration of climatic factors by integrating them into the long list of factors that constrain the development process.

303

CLIMATE VARIABILITY AND DEVELOPMENT

Understanding Drought

There are several major difficulties in dealing with drought. One is that it is a creeping phenomenon. Its onset as well as its end are often difficult to identify, because they lack a sharp distinction from nondrought dry spells. Tannehill (1947), for example, suggested, "The first rainless day in a spell of fine weather contributes as much to the drought as the last day, but no one knows precisely how serious it will be until the last dry day has gone and the rains have come again" (p. 2).

Another difficulty is that drought is generally viewed as a transient phenomenon. As a result, it is usually not taken seriously, once the rains have returned. Yet, drought is a major disruptive force with which policy makers must reckon. The return time for droughts in various parts of sub-Saharan Africa is on the order of decades, while the length of tenure in office for policy makers is most often on the order of years. How does one get these decision makers to keep in mind events that recur on a decadal scale when structuring development policies for their countries?

Yet another problem relates to identifying the impacts of drought on human activities. Impacts of drought are pervasive; although there are some obvious effects (e.g., withering crops, dry watering points, reduced forage for livestock), we often are less aware of second- and third-order effects (e.g., price increases, increased food imports, surges in rural-to-urban migration rates). Therefore, many of the impacts that might be attributable to drought are difficult to identify.

The view of drought as an idiosyncratic event that does not need to be taken seriously once it has passed is subtly reinforced by the fact that in many instances drought is not the sole factor responsible for a variety of social dislocations. [5] Yet, drought can, and often does, exacerbate existing sociopolitical, economic, or cultural factors that vary from one country to another and from one point in time to the next.

As another example of how drought exacerbates existing societal conditions, a U.S. Department of Agriculture situation report (USDA, 1984) for sub-Saharan Africa noted that "the continuing economic crisis in the region was worsened by the drought"; that "drought in addition to aged plantation trees and disease reduced the output of cocoa in Cameroon"; that "drought and continued weak finances among farmers adversely affected crop yields by reducing the need for, and use of, fertilizers"; that "the combination of guerrilla disruption and drought has had a disastrous impact on food production [in Mozambique]" (p. 17); and that "during the last year the drought and import restrictions caused severe distortions in the corn price" (p. 9). Along similar lines, Lester Brown (1985) argued, "Three forces are acting in concert to put Africa on the skids in terms of food supplies (population growth, widespread soil erosion and government neglect of agriculture) . . . Only now has this situation been brought into sharp focus by severe drought" (p. 71). And finally, with respect to famines, many authors have explained why droughts need not result in famine and famines do not necessarily have their origins in drought (Bush, 1985; Torry, 1984; Watts, 1983; Sen, 1981).

Thus, although drought may not be solely or even directly responsible for many of the societal disruptions that occur during drought episodes, its combination with other factors specific to a country at a given time can make a bad situation worse and can be devastating to the development process.

Another difficulty in dealing with drought is that drought means different things to different people, depending on their specific interest in, or need for, rainfall. Here, only meteorological, agricultural, and hydrological droughts are discussed (for a more detailed discussion on drought, see, for example, Wilhite and Glantz, 1985, reprinted in this volume; Palmer, 1965; Tannehill, 1947).

Meteorological drought can be defined, for example, as a 25% reduction of the long-term average rainfall in a given region. There are scores of variations of this definition. A meteorological drought is sometimes difficult to identify with any degree of reliability, in part because of the nature of the phenomenon and in part because meteorological and climatological information in many African countries has only been available for relatively short time periods or is of relatively poor quality. [6]

It is not always the case, however, that rainfall information by itself is of immediate, direct, or prime use to policy makers and agricultural planners. Agricultural drought occurs when there is not enough moisture available at the right time for the growth and development of crops. As a result, yields and/or absolute production declines. Many people now realize that the timing of precipitation throughout the growing season is as important as the absolute amount of seasonal or monthly precipitation. What appears to have been adequate seasonal rainfall (in terms of amounts) may have been poorly distributed throughout the season (see, for example, Palutikof, et al., 1982). Crops have varying moisture needs throughout their growth and development cycles, and thus the timing of rainfall is crucial in rainfed agricultural regions in determining whether there will be a good harvest or a poor one. Dennett, et al. (1985), have recently shown that there has been a change in the seasonal distribution of Sahelian rains, primarily a reduction in August rainfall. Such a change is detrimental to agricultural development plans but can only be detected (as a trend) in retrospect. Also, different crops require different amounts of moisture. Thus, many argue, drought must be defined in terms of the water requirements of specific crops.

Hydrologic drought has been defined as one in which streamflow falls below some predetermined level (Dracup, et al., 1980). Most often, that level is defined in terms of a reduction in streamflow that interrupts the successful undertaking of human activities, such as irrigated farming. In the West African context, an added dimension to the impact of such a drought would be the inability to cultivate land along the edge of a river or a body of water (i.e., flood recession farming), during periods of extremely low flow.

When discussions of drought take place, there is often confusion between meteorological and agricultural droughts. There have been a growing number of references to the "seventeen-year drought situation" in sub-Saharan Africa (Kerr, 1985; Nicholson, 1983; Winstanley, 1985). Lamb's index, shown earlier, suggests that meteorological drought has occurred in the West African Sahel for this length of time. Winstanley (1985) suggests that, based on *his* interpretation of yet-unpublished data, "the current 17-year drought in sub-Saharan Africa has a 1 in 125,000 probability of occurrence." Aside from the issue of whether the actual meteorological situation can accurately be called a seventeen-year drought or whether such a probability statement can be justified, the agricultural production situation does not necessarily reflect the same adverse conditions for these seventeen years. In 1974, for example, observers were convinced that the Sahelian drought had "broken." Meteorological drought (or at least its devastating impacts) was absent in 1975 and, to some observers, in 1976 as well. Nicholson (1983) noted, "Rainfall in 1974 and 1975 was still 15-20% below normal . . . but compared to the previous years [1968-73], conditions had dramatically improved and drought was generally presumed to have ended. The apparent return of 'normal' economic and human conditions supported this assumption" (p. 1646).

On a local scale, the spatial variability of rainfall was (as usual) quite large. Campbell (1977) noted that, for example, "Tahoua (Niger) had below average precipitation in 1969, 1971, and 1972 and above average precipitation in 1968 and 1970. A few hundred kilometers away, however, at Ingall (Niger), a run of dry years began in 1968" (p. 178).

More recently, the 1984 USDA situation report for sub-Saharan Africa referred to increases in agricultural production in the early 1980s, despite meteorological drought. It mentioned, for example, that in 1983 "only marginal areas of Mali were affected by drought, so national cereal production increased slightly" (p. 2). More generally, the 1984 situation report noted, "The drought of 1983 followed two years of average to above-average harvests, which contribute to the economic gains made by most of these [Sahelian] countries during 1982 and 1983" (p. 2).

A similar situation occurred in southern Africa, as noted by Bratton (1986), who, commenting on the resourcefulness of peasant farmers in Zimbabwe during their worst drought this century, wrote the following:

> How, in the face of drought, can we account for the fact that peasant farmers grew and sold more maize in the first five years of independence? What factors were at work to counteract the failure of the rains? We recognize that surplus production emanated principally from the areas of highest potential where drought was least severe. Nonetheless, expansion of food crop output is most unusual under drought conditions.

Thus, although there have been interannual and intraseasonal reductions in regional rainfall, such reductions did not necessarily translate into reduced agricultural production for each drought year in various locations.

PERCEPTIONS ABOUT DROUGHT AND DEVELOPMENT

It is not necessary to search long and hard for reasons why one might feel uneasy about how drought in sub-Saharan Africa is perceived, as it relates to development prospects. All too often the pervasive impacts of drought as a recurrent phenomenon receive too little sustained attention. For example, a recent issue of Time Magazine (Time, 1984), devoted to Africa, identified (on its cover) Africa's woes as coups, corruption, and conflict. Only a few sentences in that issue mentioned drought. Yet, the issue appeared in mid-January 1984, a time when tens of thousands of Ethiopians, among other Africans, were dying from drought-related food shortages.

Recurrent drought has also been ignored by development planners. A vice-president of the World Bank commented:

> Despite all our achievements, I think it is fair to say we have failed in Africa along with everybody else . . . We have not fully understood the problems. We

have not always designed our projects to fit the agroclimatic conditions of Africa, and the social, cultural, and political framework of the African countries (Walsh, 1984, p. 22).

Bradford Morse (1986) also called attention to this problem when he commented, "I quite agree with those who assert that national decision makers and development practitioners have paid too little attention to drought in the past."

Perhaps one of the most alarming examples (to this author) of how drought is perceived by those who have an influence on development planning in the Third World is a 1981 report (prepared by the U.S. Department of Agriculture [USDA, 1981] for the U.S. Agency for International Development) discussing factors that affect the food balance situation in sub-Saharan Africa. Figure 3 depicts the way in which those who prepared this particular report viewed the role of weather (and, therefore, drought) in food production, an activity in which a large majority of the population of sub-Saharan Africa engages.

This figure suggests that the most important and direct impact of weather is on crop yields. Yet, weather (especially drought) also affects to varying degrees several other factors shown on the schematic, such as migration, labor supply (urban and rural), acreage planted, on-farm grain storage, home consumption, food imports, export crop acreage (in some instances), and land quality. Although the importance of the direct and indirect impacts of drought on the food balance situation will vary greatly from one location to another and from one time to another, and although drought is but one factor among many others that require consideration, its importance must not be underestimated. Some of the factors that have not been well represented in the chart or in the supporting text of the USDA report are briefly discussed in the following paragraphs. As these are not mutually exclusive factors, the discussions within the following sections overlap.

Land Quality

In the years before the outbreak of the Sahelian drought in the late 1960s, when rainfall in the region was more abundant, wetter prevailing conditions masked the adverse effects of inappropriate land use practices on land quality. Wetter conditions also prompted governments and farmers to encroach on and cultivate parts of the seemingly seldom-used rangelands. In addition to depriving the pastoralists of their sorely needed dry- as well as wet-season pastures, this action increased the vulnerability of farmers, since these former rangelands were in the long run unable to sustain agriculture, as a direct result of an inevitable return to drier conditions in that semiarid or arid region.

With the onset of the multiyear drought in the late 1960s, many of the impacts of inappropriate land use practices became visible. The slow process of environmental degradation became accelerated by prevailing drought conditions. Drought not only exposes and accelerates existing land quality problems, it can also initiate new ones. The cultivation of lands subject to a high degree of rainfall variability makes the land extremely susceptible to wind erosion (and desertification) during prolonged drought episodes, as the bare soils lack the density of the vegetative cover necessary to minimize the effects of aeolian processes. *Desertification* has become a catchall term for environ-

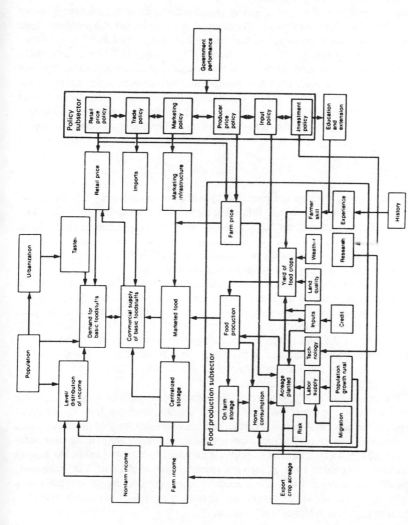

Fig. 3 Interaction among food balance factors, sub-Saharan Africa (USDA).

mental degradation in arid and semiarid lands. It can result from natural or human causes, or a combination of the two. The term now encompasses soil erosion due to wind and water, soil compaction due to trampling, firewood gathering, reduced fallow time, salinization and waterlogging, and so forth.

As the fertility of the land and crop yields decline, farmers (and their governments) search for new land to cultivate. Assuming that the best rainfed agricultural land is already in production, farmers are forced to cultivate lands considered increasingly marginal from the standpoint of soil quality, terrain slope, and rainfall (see Glantz, et al., 1986). Thus, newly cultivated lands are high-risk areas in the long run for rainfed agricultural activities: high risk from the standpoint of soil fertility and reduced fallow time and from the standpoint of their proneness to the adverse effects of prolonged droughts. The relationship among drought, environmental deterioration, and agricultural stagnation is too often ignored in the formulation of agricultural development strategies.

Acreage Planted

In most years, farmers are prepared to make several attempts at planting. If rain does not fall within a certain time following the sowing of seed, the seeds die or germinate and then die. Each time the farmers reseed, they draw down their grain reserves. Successive planting failures reduce the reserves and seed becomes scarce. The farmer must then decide whether to plant the remaining seed or use it for consumption. Eventually, there is nothing left for planting and little for consumption.

The farmer is then obliged to borrow, offering his labor or perhaps a portion of a future harvest as payment for the loan. In the event of a prolonged drought, the farmer may drift to the urban centers in search of work or the entire family may abandon their land in search of emergency food supplies at famine relief centers. Those who remain to farm the land in case the rains return are operating under conditions in which there will be fewer and weaker family members to till the land and in which most, if not all, of the necessary draft animals may have perished (McCann, 1986). Clearly, drought conditions affect the amount of planted acreage.

The amount of acreage planted to food crops is also affected by land quality. The poorer the land, the lower the yields and, therefore, the more land that must be brought into production to maintain a certain required absolute level of production. To maintain the same level of production, there is considerable pressure to bring even more land into production, forcing farmers to cultivate climatically marginal lands. As a result of the movement into these areas, human activities become vulnerable to an increase in the probability that a drought will affect their activities, not because the climate of the newly cultivated area will have changed but because people will have undertaken activities more appropriate to higher rainfall areas.

Export Crop Acreage

One activity generally considered to be insulated from the impacts of drought is the production of agricultural commodities for export. Governments usually give these commodities favored treatment, allowing them to be grown in the relatively better watered and most favored agricultural areas. They receive costly but necessary inputs such as better seed varieties, technology, water resources (including irrigation and well-drilling technology), fertilizer, and so forth. They earn foreign exchange and, as a result, are perceived to be essential for long-term development. They are considered so important that the export of cash crops continued or increased during the droughts and famines in the Sahel and Ethiopia in the early 1970s and 1980s (e.g., Lofchie, 1975; Shepherd, 1975; Hancock, 1985), while the production of food crops sharply declined. Much criticism has been leveled against this practice, especially in the midst of famine.

In many instances the record shows that foreign exchange earned from agricultural exports does not necessarily feed back into the development process and, more particularly, into agricultural development. It is often diverted to support other non-development-oriented government programs, such as the military, or it is used to subsidize the food demands of urban populations by importing nontraditional food supplies for their consumption.

Some studies do suggest, however, that prolonged drought can affect cash-crop production. de Wilde (1984), for example, notes that "widespread, repeated droughts may reverse, for some time, a trend toward the growing of cash crops, particularly if no effective steps have been taken to provide food relief, even if the prices of cash crops appear attractive" (p. 8). Campbell (1977), too, has noted that

> As food production decreases so the amount available at the market declines more rapidly due to the increasing proportion of the harvest used for consumption at the farm. In the event of a prolonged drought the amount of food available at the market would decline and its price rise and farmers might attempt to sow food crops . . . in place of cash crops, or increase their consumption of edible cash crops (p. 130).

Thus, even cash crops grown in relatively fertile and better watered areas might not be immune from the indirect effects of prolonged droughts.

Migration, Labor Supply, and Urbanization

As climate variability (or, more specifically, drought) is a common feature of arid and semiarid parts of sub-Saharan Africa, so too is migration. Migration has been resorted to as a mechanism for survival for centuries (e.g., Baier, 1980) by regional inhabitants, herders and farmers alike, on a seasonal basis (e.g., Rempel, 1981, pp. 210-14) as well as during prolonged drought episodes (e.g., Caldwell, 1975).

Baier (1980) noted, for example, that during the 1910-14 drought in this region, "migration to the south was an age-old reaction to climatic downturn" (p. 139). Migration tactics and strategies depend to a great extent on the duration and intensity of meteorological drought and on the degree of its impacts on food production processes.

With the advent of a major drought, men often leave their villages in search of income-producing labor. Campbell (1977) noted about the 1968-73 Sahelian drought:

> A large proportion of the strategies for dealing with drought . . . involve the movement of people away from their homes in search of means for minimizing

the possibility of famine arising as a consequence of drought. For example, once the Hausa realized that a food shortage was imminent, greater numbers of men began to move in search of employment, and later, as the problems became more severe, whole families abandoned their homes and moved to other areas in search of sustenance (p. 177).

This robs the rural areas of some of their labor supply, placing the total burden of agricultural activities on the shoulders of the women, children, and elderly. Drought, therefore, accelerates a process already underway, even in normal rainfall years, when some segments of the population migrate from rural to urban areas seeking wage labor to repay money borrowed for seed and, perhaps, food supplies required in order to get through the "seasonal hunger" that precedes annual harvests (e.g., Watts, 1983).

In addition, as people and households migrate from their villages in search of food, an increasing burden falls on those agricultural areas less directly (or less harshly) affected by drought conditions. With respect to the recent situation in Ethiopia, its Relief and Rehabilitation Commission (RRC) noted:

> In recent years, particularly since 1980, prolonged rain failures (mostly drought but also inappropriate and untimely precipitation) have caused widespread crop and pasture failures. Over the same period, cultivators and pastoralists . . . have been forced to migrate in masses in search of relief and resettlement (RRC, 1984, p. 7).

Urban centers in sub-Saharan Africa are relatively small, compared to cities in Asia and Latin America. Yet, their growth rates have been quite high, even in the absence of droughts. A recent report on Africa (U.S. Office of Technology Assessment, 1984) noted: "The rate of urban growth, at 5 to 7 percent per year (2.7% growth rate results in a doubling of population in about 10 years), is the highest in the world . . . Immigrants to African cities often come from impoverished rural areas and their movements add to the destabilizing effects of rapid urbanization" (p. 19). During extended drought, existing migration from rural to urban areas becomes accelerated (Campbell, 1977, p. 180; Caldwell, 1975, pp. 23-31). Many who go to the cities in either their own or neighboring countries do not return to the rural areas. As urban populations expand in pulses during drought episodes, the rural areas become increasingly stressed.

> There is at present in Ethiopia a catastrophic displacement of population which is putting enormous pressure on agriculturally favoured areas of the country . . . the burden of feeding the affected population is being undertaken by local people (some of who may themselves be drought affected) and by the RRC (RRC, 194, p. 7).

In sum, many have written about the rural-urban conflict over scarce resources within developing countries and have criticized the bias of national governments toward the urban populations at the expense of those in the rural areas (Lipton, 1977). Drought episodes serve not only to highlight such disparities but also to exacerbate them.

Food Imports

During extended droughts, food imports, as either aid or trade, are required to sustain the nutritional needs of urban and rural populations. Even when food imports are primarily geared to the needs of the urban populations, drought also comes into play because, during such periods, there are influxes of migrants into urban areas in search of food or employment. Increased rates of urbanization not only deprive the rural areas of agricultural producers, as noted earlier, but increase the need for imported food for the expanding urban populations.

Because urban areas are the centers of power for the ruling elites, they are supplied with inexpensive, often subsidized, food either drawn from the rural areas or imported from abroad. The artificially low prices for agricultural products act as a disincentive to produce greater quantities of food; they also discriminate against the rural population.

Food imports for urban populations are usually easily prepared convenience foods such as wheat and rice, purchased with scarce foreign exchange. These inexpensive, subsidized food imports also alter the tastes and, subsequently, the food preferences of the urban population, away from the traditional crops grown in the countryside, such as millet, sorghum, and cassava. As noted earlier, the urban population is constantly expanding as a result of the influx of migrants from rural areas. As the urban population swells and people develop a preference for, and dependence on, wheat and rice, the situation takes on the appearance of a vicious circle. In response to this particular situation, some governments have resorted to import substitution by growing wheat and rice in their own country. However, to do so is not without cost and sacrifice in many cases, since it requires the displacement of traditional crops from certain cultivated areas, as well as costly inputs of fertilizers and irrigation equipment.

Rural Poverty

Rural poverty exists in sub-Saharan Africa, even in years of rainfall favorable for agriculture and livestock raising. In the villages there are both rich and poor farmers. Frequently, the poorer farmers borrow from those more well-to-do, repaying them with labor or with a share of the crop they produced. During times of drought stress, the disparities between the rich and the poor increase, as the former are in a position to pay low prices for livestock as well as exact high interest for grain they lend. More often than not the relatively richer peasants are in a position of having grains in reserve that they can sell in the marketplace when grain prices rise sharply, as they do during drought periods. Some of the poorer peasant farmers might eventually sell their land for food and become part of a migrant labor force of landless peasants (see, for example, Colvin, et al., 1981; Chambers, et al., 1981).

CONCLUSIONS

These examples identify some ways that drought affects components of the food balance system and, hence, the development process. They are by no means exhaustive. Clearly, many publications now exist that discuss how drought has affected a local community, the environment, water resources, livestock, a sector of an economy, international trade, foreign assistance, and so forth. These publications constitute a large body of case-specific information, not only for sub-Saharan Africa but for other developing and developed countries as well. Yet, the literature related to economic development has focused little attention on drought (a recurring, aperiodic phenomenon) as a constraint to economic development.

To gain a proper understanding of why societies that are partially or wholly in the arid and semiarid tropics and subtropics have had great difficulty in developing their economies, one must consider, along with other relevant factors, the implications of recurrent prolonged meteorological, agricultural, and hydrologic drought. Paraphrasing the adage that war is too important to be left to the generals, I would assert that drought considerations are too important to be left only to the meteorologists.

This paper does not claim that all constraints on development in African societies are the result of droughts (or, more broadly, climate variability). It does claim, however, that drought must be integrated into the already lengthy list of natural and societal influences that can adversely affect the economic development in sub-Saharan Africa.

NOTES

1. Drought is not a problem for developing countries alone. Coping with recurrent drought episodes has also been a formidable task for leaders of industrialized countries, as was the case, for example, in the 1930s and 1950s in the U.S. Great Plains and in the mid-1950s in Soviet Central Asia (Brezhnev, 1978). There is considerable speculation among scientists today about whether and how society in the United States could cope with a return of a 1930s-like U.S. drought in, say, the 1990s (e.g., Bernard, 1980; Warrick, 1984; Bowden, et al., 1981).

2. In fact, the belief that the climate of the tropics is a primary factor in underdevelopment and the climate of the temperate regions is a factor in industrialization persists today, not only among "northerners" but among some "southerners" as well. For example, Bandyopadhyaya (1983) wrote:

In India and other tropical countries I have noted farmers, industrial labourers, and in fact all kinds of manual and office workers working in slow rhythm with long and frequent rest pauses. But in the temperate zone I have noticed the same classes of people working in quick rhythm with great vigour and energy, and with very few rest pauses. I have known from personal experience and the experience of other tropical peoples in the temperate zone that this spectacular difference in working energy and efficiency could not be due entirely or even mainly to different levels of nutrition. I had no doubt at all in my mind that the principal interpretation lay in the differences in temperature and humidity between the two climatic zones (p. vi).

3. Streeten (1976) referred to these boundary conditions as initial conditions. By initial conditions he meant those conditions that the migrants (in the North American

case, the immigrants) discovered upon arrival; for the developing countries he apparently referred to the existing conditions with which they had to cope at the time of independence. He noted the reluctance of writers "to admit the vast differences in initial conditions with which today's poor countries are faced compared with the pre-industrial phase of the more advanced countries"(p. 9).

4. Although Kamarck (1976) referred only in passing to the adverse impacts of the Sahelian drought of the early 1970s, he was one of the first to draw attention to drought as having an adverse effect on the development process. In reference to drought in Northeast Brazil, he noted, "Although these droughts [in Brazil] are a major obstacle—perhaps the biggest one to economic development—development approaches heretofore have tended to invest mainly in fixed capital of various kinds rather than in necessary research to find out how best to handle the droughts" (p. 20).

5. Torry's (1984) reference to a distinction between underlying (ultimate) and catalytic (proximate) causes of famine are of direct relevance to discussions of drought and its societal impacts. Torry noted:

Proximate causes are situational and originate shortly prior to or during an emergency. Ultimate causes can be construed as predisposing conditions transforming proximate causes into famine distresses....In fact proximate causes (e.g., drought) can land a household in the clutches of famine with or without the involvement of ultimate causes (p. 8).

However, while a specific drought may be considered a proximate cause of famine, droughts as recurrent phenomena can be considered an underlying cause.

6. In the past, most African countries have put a relatively low value on their meteorological services. Such services were considered of value mostly for aviation, not only during colonial times but during post-colonial periods as well. Recently, there has been a growing interest in, and support for, many of the national and regional (e.g., AGRHYMET in Niamey, Niger) meteorological services in sub-Saharan Africa. Some of these services have become more active in assisting decision makers by identifying how meteorological information might improve the value of their decisions. Meteorological services are increasingly being called on to provide input for decision-making processes regarding agricultural development and for early famine warning systems.

REFERENCES

Baier, S. 1980. An Economic History of Central Niger. Oxford University Press, Oxford, England.

Bandyopadhyaya, J. 1983. Climate and World Order: An Inquiry into the Natural Cause of Underdevelopment. South Asian, New Delhi.

Bernard, H. W., Jr. 1980. The Greenhouse Effect. Ballinger Publishing, Cambridge, England.

Biswas, A. K. 1984. Climate and development. In A. K. Biswas, ed. Climate and Development. Natural Resources and the Environment Series, Vol. 13. Tycooly International Publishing, Dublin.

314

Bowden, M. J.; R. W. Kates; P. A. Kay; W. E. Riebsame; R. A. Warrick; D. L. Johnson; H. A. Gould; and D. Weiner. 1981. The effect of climate fluctuations on human populations: Two hypotheses. pp. 479-513. In T. M. L. Wigley, M. J. Ingram, and G. Farmer, eds. Climate and History: Studies in Past Climates and Their Impact on Man. Cambridge University Press, Cambridge, England.

Bratton, M. 1986. Drought, food and the social organization of small farmers in Zimbabwe. Chap. 10. In M. H. Glantz, ed. Drought and Hunger in Africa: Denying Famine a Future. Cambridge University Press, Cambridge, England.

Brezhnev, L. 1978. The Virgin Lands. Progress Publishers, Moscow.

Brooks, C. E. P. 1926. Climate through the Ages. 2nd rev. ed., 1970. Dover Publications, New York.

Brown, L. 1985. "Human element" not drought causes famine. U.S. News and World Report (February 25), pp. 71-72.

Bush, R. 1985. Drought and Famines. Review of African Political Economy 33:59-64.

Caldwell, J. The Sahelian drought and its demographic implications. American Council on Education, Overseas Liaison Committee Paper No. 8, Washington, D.C.

Campbell, D. J. 1977. Strategies for coping with drought in the Sahel: A study of recent population movements in the department of Maradi, Niger. Ph.D. dissertation, Clark University, Worcester, Massachusetts.

Chambers, R.; R. Longhurst; and A. Pacey, eds. 1981. Seasonal Dimensions to Rural Poverty. Allenheld, Osmun and Co., Totowa, New Jersey.

Colvin, L. G.; C. Ba; B. Barry; J. Faye; A. Hamer; M. Soumah; and F. Sow, eds. 1981. The Uprooted of the Western Sahel: Migrants' Quest for Cash in the Senegambia. Praeger, New York.

Dennett, M. D.; J. Elston; and J. A. Rodgers. 1985. A reappraisal of rainfall trends in the Sahel. J. Clim. 5:353-361.

de Wilde, J. C. 1984. Agriculture, Marketing, and Pricing in Sub-Saharan Africa. University of California African Studies Center and African Studies Association, Los Angeles.

Dracup, J. A.; K. S. Lee; and E. G. Paulson, Jr. 1980. On the definition of droughts. Water Resour. Res. 16(2):297-302.

Galbraith, J. K. 1951. Conditions for economic change in underdeveloped countries. Am. J. Farm Econ. 33:693.

Glantz, M. H.; R. W. Katz; A. R. Magalhaes; and L. Ogallo. 1986. Drought follows the plow [draft]. National Center for Atmospheric Research, Boulder, Colorado.

Glantz, M. H. 1977. Climate and weather modification in and around arid lands in Africa. pp. 307-331. In M. H. Glantz, ed. Desertification: Environmental Degradation in and around Arid Lands. Westview Press, Boulder, Colorado.

Hancock, G. 1985. Ethiopia: The Challenge of Hunger. Victor Gollancz, London.

Huntington, E. 1915. Civilization and Climate. Reprinted 1971. The Shoe String Press, Hamden, Connecticut.

Kamarck, A. M. 1976. The Tropics and Economic Development: A Provocative Inquiry into the Poverty of Nations. The Johns Hopkins University Press, Baltimore, for the World Bank.

Kerr, R. A. 1985. Fifteen years of African drought. Science 227:1453-1454.

Lamb, P. 1982. Persistence of Subsaharan drought. Nature 299:46-48.

Lamb, P. 1983. Subsaharan rainfall update for 1982: Continued drought. J. Clim. 3:419-422.

Lee, D. H. K. 1957. Climate and Economic Development in the Tropics. Harper and Brothers, New York.

Lewis, W. A. 1955. Theory of Economic Growth. Allen and Unwin, London.

Lipton, M. 1977. Why Poor People Stay Poor: Urban Bias in World Development. Temple Smith, London.

Lofchie, M. F. 1975. Political and economic origins of African hunger. J. Modern African Studies 13(4):551-567.

Markham, S. F. 1944. Climate and the Energy of Nations. Oxford University Press, London.

McCann, J. 1986. The social impact of drought in Ethiopia. Chap. 11. In M. H. Glantz, ed. Drought and Hunger in Africa: Denying Famine a Future. Cambridge University Press, Cambridge, England.

Mills, C. A. 1963. World Power Amid Shifting Climate. The Christopher Publishing House, Boston.

Morentz, J. W. 1980. Communications in the Sahel drought: Comparing the mass media with other channels of international communication. In Disasters and the Mass Media, Proceedings of the Committee on Disasters and the Mass Media Workshop, February 1979. National Academy of Sciences, Washington, D.C.

Morse, B. 1986. Africa beyond the famine: New hope. Keynote address. In M. H. Glantz, ed. Drought and Hunger in Africa: Denying Famine a Future. Cambridge University Press, Cambridge, England.

Myrdal, G. 1968. Asian Drama: An Inquiry into the Poverty of Nations. Vol. 3:2121-2138. New York: Pantheon.

Nicholson, S. E. 1983. Sub-Saharan rainfall in the years 1976-80: Evidence of continued drought. Mon. Weather Rev. 111:1646-1654.

Oury, B. 1969. Weather and economic development. Finance and Development 6:24-29.

Palmer, W. C. (1965). Meteorological drought. Research Paper No. 45. U.S. Department of Commerce, Weather Bureau, Washington, D.C.

Palutikof, J. P.; G. Farmer; and T. M. L. Wigley. 1982. Strategies for the amelioration of agricultural drought in Africa. In Proceedings of the Technical Conference on Climate: Africa, 25-30 January 1982. WMO Secretariat, Geneva.

Relief and Rehabilitation Commission (RRC). 1984. Project Proposal for the Strengthening of the Food and Nutrition Surveillance Programme. RRC, Addis Ababa.

Rempel, H. 1981. Seasonal outmigration and rural poverty. pp. 210-214. In R. Chambers, R. Longhurst, and A. Pacey, eds. Seasonal Dimensions to Rural Poverty. Allenheld, Osmun and Co., Totowa, New Jersey.

Sen, A. 1981. Poverty and Famines: An Essay on Entitlement and Deprivation. Clarendon Press, Oxford, England.

Shepherd, J. 1975. The Politics of Starvation. Carnegie Endowment for International Peace, Washington, D.C.

316

Streeten, P. 1976. Foreword. pp. ix-xii. In A. M. Kamarck. The Tropics and Economic Development: A Provocative Inquiry into the Poverty of Nations. Johns Hopkins University Press, Baltimore, for The World Bank.

Tannehill, I. R. 1947. Drought: Its Causes and Effects. Princeton University Press, Princeton, New Jersey.

Time. 1984. Africa's woes: Coups, conflict, corruption. Vol. 123, No. 3, January 16.

Torry, W. I. 1984. Social science research on famine: A critical evaluation. Human Ecology 12(3):227-252.

Tosi, J. 1975. Some relationships of climate to economic development in the tropics. In The Use of Ecological Guidelines for Development in the American Tropics, New Series No. 31. International Union for Conservation of Nature, Morges, Switzerland.

U.S. Department of Agriculture. 1981. Food Problems and Prospects in Sub-Saharan Africa. Government Printing Office, Washington, D.C.

U.S. Department of Agriculture. 1984. Sub-Saharan Africa: Outlook and Situation Report. Economic Research Service, USDA, Washington, D.C.

U.S. Office of Technology Assessment. 1984. Africa Tomorrow: Issues in Technology, Agriculture, and U.S. Foreign Aid. Office of Technology Assessment, Washington, D.C.

Walsh, J. 1984. Hunger in West Africa: A crisis in development. Technology Review 87(6):22-23.

Warrick, R. A. 1984. The possible impacts on wheat production of a recurrence of the 1930s drought in the U.S. Great Plains. Clim. Change 6(1):5-26.

Watts, M. 1983. Silent Violence: Food, Famine and Peasantry in Northern Nigeria. University of California Press, Berkeley.

Wilhite, D. A.; and M. H. Glantz. 1985. Understanding the drought phenomenon: The role of definitions. Water Int. 10:111-120.

Winstanley, D. 1985. Africa in drought: A change of climate? Weatherwise 38:75-81.

World Meteorological Organization. 1979. Proceedings of the World Climate Conference, 12-23 February. WMO, Geneva.

CHAPTER 20
DROUGHT AND CLIMATE CHANGE: FOR BETTER OR WORSE?

Norman J. Rosenberg

INTRODUCTION

It seems natural enough that when severe and persistent drought occurs in a region, we wonder whether it evidences some sort of climatic change. However, the instrumental record and surrogate evidence indicate quite clearly that drought is a recurrent phenomenon, and one need not invoke climatic change as the cause. Even the drought that has most effectively captured world attention in recent decades—that in sub-Saharan Africa, beginning in the late 1960s and continuing to some extent until now—is not entirely unprecedented. Figure 1 from Lamb's (1982, 1983) analyses of rainfall records for Africa, showing an unusually long run of dry years in the Sahel preceded by wetter than (current) average conditions from 1950 until the onset of the recent drought, is suggestive of a significant climatic change. Yet Nicholson (1983), in searching noninstrumental records from the nineteenth century in Africa, was able to identify one drought period between 1820 and 1840 at least as long and severe as that of the period 1968-84.

There is evidence, based on tree-ring analyses, pollen analysis, anthropology, chronicles, folklore, newspaper accounts, and instrumental observations, that drought is indeed a recurrent feature of the North American climate. Elsewhere, I have assembled evidence of drought incidence from Mexico, the United States, and Canada that supports this assertion (Rosenberg, 1983).

A strong case can be made that, virtually everywhere, drought is within the normal range of climatic conditions. But drought can, indeed, be a manifestation of a persistent climate change as well. Some examples: Bryson and Murray (1977) speculate that the decline of the Indus Valley civilization that once thrived in what is now the Rajasthan or Thar Desert of India and Pakistan was due to a changed climate and failure in monsoon rains. Some six thousand years ago, during the "climatic-optimum," North Africa had a wetter climate than it has today (Sarnthein, 1978). The Hopi and Zuni civilizations of the American Southwest may have developed in a more humid, benign climate than exists in that region today. Nonetheless, most of the droughts of which we have record appear to fall within the "noise" of normal climatic variation. However, we cannot rule out the possibility that any drought may signal a one-directional climatic change.

We must consider, as well, the possibility that man's activities are, somehow, exacerbating normally occurring dry spells. Bryson (1973) suggested that increasing at-

318

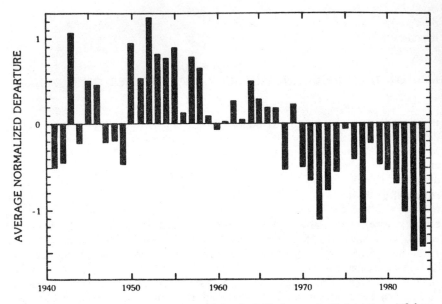

Fig. 1 Departures from normal rainfall in sub-Saharan Africa, 1941-85 (Lamb, 1982, 1983; updates shown in Glantz, 1986).

mospheric turbidity (due in large part to man) and greenhouse warming (due to carbon dioxide)—both of which are probably attributable to man—might be implicated as causes of the Sahelian droughts. Both effects, in Bryson's view, tend to cause the zone of subtropical high pressure (anticyclones) to move equatorward—thereby suppressing monsoonal rains in the northerly portions of the regions normally watered by these rains.

Evidence now available shows that the earth's atmosphere is not, in fact, becoming more turbid. There have been no long-term changes in the amount of small particles suspended in the air sampled over Mauna Loa, an observatory on the island of Hawaii that, because of its location in the mid-Pacific and its altitude (approximately 3,350 m or 11,000 ft.), represents the condition of the mixed or "average" global atmosphere. [1] Additionally, the effect of a significant greenhouse warming would likely be to decrease the equator-to-pole temperature gradient, which is not consistent with a southward movement of the subtropical anticyclone.

Another mechanism was proposed by Charney (1975) and elucidated by Charney, et al. (1975). It was suggested that overuse of land "feeds back" to intensify drought conditions. According to this theory, an increase in land albedo (reflectivity for solar radiation) such as occurs when land is denuded of vegetation leads to a decrease in net incoming radiation and an increase in the radiative cooling of the air. [2] This would cause the air to sink to maintain thermal equilibrium by adiabatic compression. Cumulus convection and its associated rainfall would be suppressed. Lower rainfall further reduces plant cover, raises albedo, and amplifies the effect.

Researchers have considered the Charney hypothesis (e.g., Chervin, 1980) but, as one would expect, verification of this effect is extremely difficult, and unequivocal evidence of its reality is not yet available. Nicholson (1985) makes the argument that the very persistence of the Sub-Saharan drought is a sort of confirmation of the Charney hypothesis.

MECHANISMS OF CLIMATE CHANGE

Climate changes are induced by a number of natural phenomena over which man has no control; but man's interventions are beginning to play a significant role in inducing change—perhaps in amplifying or suppressing natural change, as well.

The climate of the earth is determined by the rates at which the spinning land and ocean surfaces of the planet and its atmospheric envelope absorb, redistribute, and dispose of solar radiation. This rate is determined by the rate at which the sun emits radiation, by the angle at which the sun's rays strike the surfaces on earth, and by the transparency of the atmosphere to solar radiation and the counter radiation from the earth's surface to space.

Radiation and Energy Exchange

The rate at which the sun emits radiation fluctuates on a monthly basis by as much as 0.3% (e.g., Eddy, 1982). Because of the gravitational effects of other bodies in space, the shape of the earth's orbit around the sun and the longitude in orbit when earth is closest to the sun (the precession) vary in cycles of about 90,000 and 21,000 years, respectively. The tilt of the earth on its axis, now about 23.5°, varies between 21.8° and 24.4° in the course of a cycle of about 41,000 years. As a result of these cyclic fluctuations and the daily and seasonal cycles with which we are more familiar, the flux density (intensity per unit area per unit time) of solar radiation received at any particular latitude and place is also subject to considerable variability.

The amount of solar radiation received at the top of the atmosphere—about 1367 W m^{-2}—is depleted as it penetrates the atmosphere to the surface of the planet. The atmosphere reflects and absorbs a considerable amount of the solar radiation. The radiation that penetrates to the surface is reflected or absorbed. The absorbed energy is eventually reradiated to space.

The flux density of radiation emitted by the sun and by the earth differ greatly in quantity since the rate of emission depends on the fourth power of the temperature - 6,000° K in the case of the sun and 300° K as a general average for the earth's surface. Additionally, as shown in Fig. 2a, the spectra of the radiation emitted by sun and earth also differ greatly. The solar spectrum ranges from the ultraviolet to the near infrared (about 0.15 to 4.0 μm), with about half of the total radiation in the visible waveband (0.4 to 0.7 μm). Terrestrial radiation occurs in the infrared (about 3.0 to 80 μm), with the bulk emitted in the 8-14 μm waveband. Thus, the solar and terrestrial spectra virtually do not overlap.

Both the quality and the quantity of the solar radiation stream are affected by the constituents of the atmosphere. These constituents are listed in Table 1, and the absorption spectra of certain of these gases are shown in Fig. 2b. Water vapor (H_2O), carbon dioxide (CO_2), nitrous oxide (N_2O), and methane (CH_4) are all essentially transparent

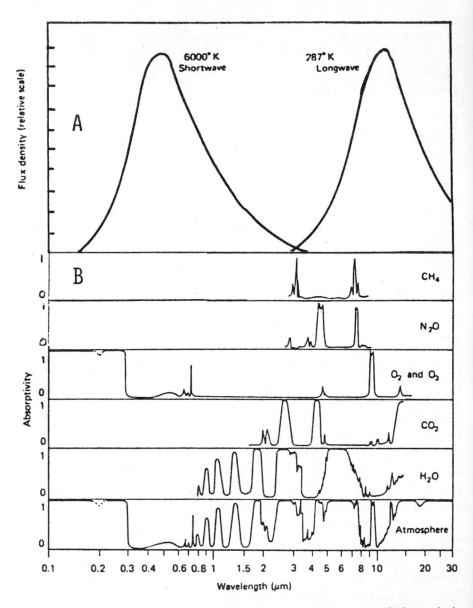

Fig. 2 (a) Spectra of solar and terrestrial radiation scaled to their maximum flux densities; (b) absorption spectra for important constituent gases of the atmosphere. Note the log-scale of the common abscissa (adapted from Reifsnyder and Lull, 1965; and Fleagle and Businger, 1963).

Table 1
Constituents of Clean, Dry Air

Constituent	Volume %
Nitrogen	78.08
[a]Oxygen	20.95
Argon	0.93
Carbon dioxide	0.035
Neon	1.8×10^{-3}
Helium	5.24×10^{-4}
Krypton	1×10^{-4}
Hydrogen	5×10^{-5}
Xenon	8.0×10^{-6}
Radon	6.0×10^{-18}
Ozone	Variable; about 1.0×10^{-6}

Plus

[b]Methane, CH_4	1.6×10^{-4}
[b]Nitrous Oxide, N_2O	3.0×10^{-5}
[b]Freon 11, CCl_3F	2.3×10^{-8}
[b]Freon 12, CCl_2F_2	4.0×10^{-8}
[b]Carbon Tetrachloride, CCl_4	1.3×10^{-8}
[c]Water vapor	0-3% +
[c]Dusts, pollens	Highly Variable

[a]Concern has been expressed that oxygen might decrease in concentration as a result of industrial pollution of the atmosphere or as a result of a reduction in the quantity of photosynthesizing vegetation following changes in land use. Observations show, however, that the concentration remains stable at 20.946% (Machta and Hughes, 1970; Machta, 1985 personal communication).

[b]Estimated average values at the end of 1985.

[c]Vary substantially in space and/or time.

Source: Based on List, p. 389, and other cited sources.

to incoming solar radiation but are strong absorbers in the infrared. They behave somewhat like glass in a greenhouse, which lets in the sunlight but traps outgoing thermal radiation. The greenhouse analogy is imperfect since the gain in heat within a greenhouse is due largely to the suppression of convective transport; nonetheless, the terms *greenhouse effect* and *greenhouse gas* have become commonplace. The term *radiatively active trace gas* more correctly describes the behavior of the gases mentioned above.

Water vapor is the most important of the infrared absorbing gases, but carbon dioxide has strong absorption peaks at about 4 and 15 μm where water vapor is less absorptive. As a result of man's activities the concentration of carbon dioxide has increased in the global atmosphere by at least 25% since 1750 (280 ppm then, compared to 345 ppm today). The increase in CO_2 concentration continues at this time and is expected to double the preindustrial concentration by sometime in the first half of the coming century. Additionally, the concentrations of other radiatively active trace gases, nitrous oxide, methane, carbon tetrachloride, and the chlorofluorocarbons (CCL_2F_2 and CCl_3F, known commercially as Freon 11 and 12) are also increasing at an even more rapid rate than CO_2. N_2O and CH_4 may be increasing as a result of man's activities, but natural sources and sinks for these gases are known. The Freons and CCl_4 are industrial products and can only be the result of man's activities. The radiatively active trace gases CH_4, N_2O, CCl_4, and Freons 11 and 12 can, together, generate as strong a greenhouse effect as that caused by CO_2.

The "greenhouse effect" is a cause for concern. Increasing atmospheric absorption of infrared radiation must lead to a warming of the lower layers of the atmosphere. The capacity of the atmosphere to hold water vapor is an exponentially increasing function of temperature. A warmer atmosphere (all other factors remaining unchanged) leads to greater rates of evaporation. Hence, the CO_2-induced greenhouse effect can "feed back" positively by increasing the quantities of water vapor in the atmosphere, unless increased cloudiness compensates for this effect.

Much has been written on the difficulty of identifying the "greenhouse" signal in the noise of natural climatic variation (e.g., Hayashi, 1982). Despite the difficulty, a recent paper by Jones, et al. (1986), based on near-surface temperature data over land and oceans of both hemispheres during the past 130 years provides evidence for a general warming during this century and a rapid warming since the mid-1970s.

The Impact of Land Use Change

Man can (and has) influenced the radiation balance of large tracts of earth. His influence is exerted through changes in land use that alter reflectivity and surface temperatures. The extent to which these conversions may alter local climate can be illustrated with a few examples. Consider the conversion to grassland of a hectare of land in the middle of a forest. Reflectivity of the surface will increase from, say, 18% to 24%, effecting a reduction in the net radiation. Trees that are deep-rooted can usually continue to extract water after shallow-rooted grass has exhausted its supply. Transpiration is the primary mechanism that allows leaves to remain cool even as they absorb the short-and long-wave radiation that impinges on them. Thus the mean temperature of the forest at noon might be 25° C, compared to 35° C for grass under the same weather conditions. This difference in leaf temperature would account for an increase in outgoing long-wave radiation of about 14%, further reducing the net radiation (or available energy) over the grass.

Under these circumstances, net radiation at midday would be reduced by about 5%, from 720 W m^{-2} in the forest to 690 W m^{-2} in the grassed area. But, the net radiation or available energy is not necessarily partitioned in the same ways in grassland and forest. After the grass has exhausted the water from its shallow root zone, its transpiration rate is sharply reduced. The surface becomes warmer than the air above and transfers heat to it. The air above the grass becomes warmer, its ability to hold water vapor (an exponential function of the air temperature) increases, and relative humidity falls. The warm dry air over the grass can be carried by the wind into the adjacent forest. There, if soil water is still available to the tree roots, it may supplement the energy from the sun and increase the rate of evapotranspiration above that prevailing in the rest of the forest.

The example given above describes the effects of land conversion at a "microscale." The same principles apply when large areas of land undergo alterations in use. When rainfed agricultural lands are irrigated, when forests are removed, when rangelands are overgrazed and denuded, even when portions of large lakes or seas undergo color changes because of algal blooms, their radiation and energy balances are altered with consequent effects on the local climate and the climate of adjacent lands (or waters) downwind. All changes in land use, large and small, have an impact on the global energy balance and the global climate.

Other Potential Causes of Change

To this point, we have dealt with three of the most important mechanisms of climate change. These are changes in the supply of solar energy, changes in the transmissivity of the atmosphere for both incoming and outgoing radiation, and changes in land use that alter the radiation balance. Schneider and Londer (1984) list other possible causes. These include: (1) the release of heat (thermal pollution) that warms the lower atmosphere directly; (2) the upward transport of chlorofluoromethanes and nitrous oxide into the stratosphere, where photochemical reaction of their dissociation products probably reduces stratospheric ozone with a consequent increase in ultraviolet irradiation of the surface and its inhabitants; and (3) the release of trace gases (e.g., nitrogen oxides, carbon monoxide, or methane) that increase ozone concentration in the troposphere (lower 15 km atmosphere, approximately) by photochemical reactions. Tropospheric ozone causes a large atmospheric heating that enhances both solar and greenhouse heating of the lower atmosphere.

Schneider and Londer also list large-scale nuclear war as a potential cause of climatic change. Such an event could lead to very large injections of soot and dust into the troposphere and stratosphere, causing transient cooling that might last for weeks to months (the so-called nuclear winter phenomenon).

PREDICTING CLIMATIC CHANGE

Simple one-dimensional models of the atmosphere indicate that the lower layers will warm and the upper layers will cool as a result of the greenhouse effect. To understand how this phenomenon will alter global climate requires the use of more complicated models and analyses. Three approaches are described below.

Mathematical Models

Virtually all components of the climate system, including land, ocean, atmosphere, and cryosphere (snow and land and sea ice) can be described mathematically. The equations can be solved either separately or in concert to study limited interactions or fluctuations of the entire system.

There are many types of climate models, ranging in complexity from the one-dimensional, in which some change in the atmosphere (e.g., an increase in dust or smoke) alters the vertical distribution of temperature, to the general circulation model (GCM), which deals with changes in the three-dimensional atmosphere over a fourth dimension—time.

Meehl (1984) points out that the general circulation models are presently the most complex and expensive in terms of computer time, but they are also the most realistic in the way they explicitly simulate many elements of the climate system. Despite their sophistication, these models are not without problems.

The "state-of-the-art" in general circulation models has recently been assessed by MacCracken and Luther (1985):

Atmospheric general circulation models are capable of simulating almost all of the observed large-scale features of the climate, and they reproduce the general character of day-to-day variations as well as seasonal changes of the circulation winter to summer. However, these models do not yet adequately represent the observed regional features that are needed for making detailed climate projections and assessments of ecological, agricultural and societal impacts.

Nonetheless, GCMs are the best tools for predicting in the near future the direction and degree of climate change, and a review of their findings with respect to the "greenhouse effect" is worthwhile. MacCracken and Luther (1985) reviewed results of the most recent "experiments" involving GCMs, in which the increasing atmospheric concentration of CO_2 is allowed to perturb the current atmosphere. Although CO_2 is increasing slowly in the atmosphere (as are the other radiatively active trace gases), it is easier for the GCMs to calculate what might happen if a large stepwise change in CO_2 concentration were to occur.

When the models proceed without consideration of feedback processes (changing cloudiness, oceanic capture, or release of heat), the GCMs are in close agreement, predicting a change in global average surface temperature due to a doubling of CO_2 concentration in the range of 1.2° C to 1.3° C. However, the models that include feedback processes differ considerably in their predictions—1.5° C to 4.5° C for a CO_2 doubling.

MacCracken and Luther's summary of GCM experiments indicates that the models predict a greenhouse warming of the global average surface air temperature of about 3.5° C to 4.2° C and an increase in the global average precipitation rate of about 7% to 11%. The models agreed closely with respect to global average surface temperature, but much less closely in their projections of the regional patterns of such changes.

Figures 3, 4, and 5 from Schlesinger and Mitchell (1985) illustrate the projections made by three GCMs of changes in climate (temperature, precipitation, and soil moisture, respectively) to follow a doubling of the global atmospheric CO_2 concentration. The figures have been redrawn for simplicity and show only Africa and North America in June, July, and August.

Differences between the models of the Geophysical Fluid Dynamics Laboratory (GFDL), Goddard Institute of Space Studies (GISS), and National Center for Atmospheric Research (NCAR) are shown in Figs. 3-5. Predictions of temperature increases in the middle of North America range from 2° C to 8° C, depending on model. Projections for precipitation in this region during June, July, and August range from -1 to +1 mm/day. In western Africa precipitation changes range from +2 to -1 mm/day. Perhaps most critical is the soil water difference that results from changes in precipitation and evaporation. GFDL predicts as much as 3 cm soil water deficit for the summer season in North America. GISS predicts no change there while NCAR predicts from zero to -1 cm reduction in soil water. In western Africa the predictions differ widely as well.

Another interesting comparison assembled by Schlesinger and Mitchell (1985) is shown in Figs. 6 and 7. Figure 6 compares the GFDL, GISS, and NCAR latitude-time

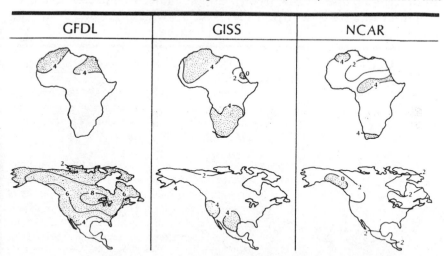

Fig. 3 The distribution of surface air temperature change (°C) for a doubling of atmospheric carbon dioxide concentration for June, July, and August, simulated by the global climatic models of GFDL (left), GISS (center), and NCAR (right). Stipple indicates temperature increases greater than 4 °C (redrawn from Fig. 4.39 of Schlesinger and Mitchell, 1985).

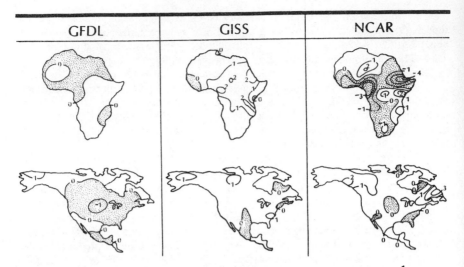

GFDL	GISS	NCAR

Fig. 4   The distribution of precipitation rate change (mm d^{-1}) for a doubling of atmospheric carbon dioxide concentration for June, July, and August, simulated by the global climatic models of GFDL (left), GISS (center), and NCAR (right). Stipple indicates a decrease in precipitation rate (redrawn from Fig. 4.42 of Schlesinger and Mitchell, 1985).

GFDL	GISS	NCAR

Fig. 5   The distribution of soil water change (cm) for a doubling of atmospheric carbon dioxide concentration for June, July, and August, simulated by the global climatic models of GFDL (left), GISS (center), and NCAR (right). Stipple indicates a decrease in soil water (redrawn from Fig. 4.45 of Schlesinger and Mitchell, 1985).

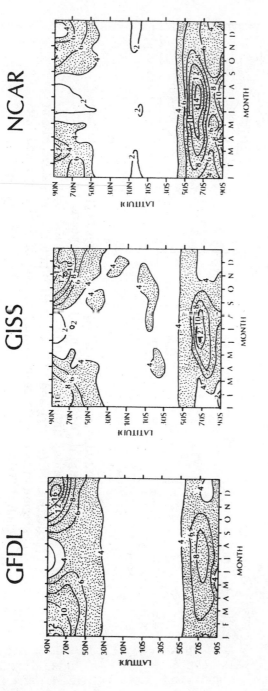

Fig. 6 Latitude-time cross section of the zonal mean surface air temperature change (°C) for a doubling of the atmospheric carbon dioxide concentration, simulated with the global climatic models of GFDL (left), GISS (center), and NCAR (right). Stipple indicates temperature increases greater than 4 °C (redrawn from Fig. 4.40 of Schlesinger and Mitchell, 1985).

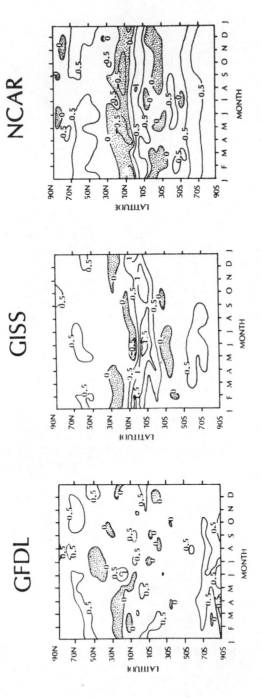

Fig. 7 Latitude-time cross section of the zonal mean precipitation rate change (mm d^{-1}) for a doubling of the atmospheric carbon dioxide concentration, simulated with the global climatic models of GFDL (left), GISS (center), and NCAR (right). Stipple indicates a decrease in precipitation rate (redrawn from Fig. 4.43 of Schlesinger and Mitchell, 1985).

cross sections of zonal mean surface air temperature change for a doubling of atmospheric CO_2 concentration. GFDL predicts that the region between latitudes 30° N and 50° N will be at least 4° C warmer throughout the year. GISS also predicts that the same zone will be that much warmer, but not from late spring through much of the fall. NCAR indicates that the 30-50° N latitude belt will not be 4° C warmer at any time.

Similarly, Fig. 7 displays the latitude-time cross section of the zonal mean precipitation rate in mm d^{-1} for a doubling of the atmospheric CO_2 concentration. For the latitude belt 30-50° N, GFDL predicts a period of summer dryness. The other two models predict no change or a slight increase in precipitation.

Figure 8 displays latitude-time cross sections of zonal mean soil water change in cm for a doubling of the atmospheric CO_2 content. This simulation applies only to the ice-free lands. Throughout most of the year all three models simulate a band of decreased soil moisture near 20° N and a band of increased soil moisture near 10° S. All three models show a moistening of the soil within the belt 30-60° N from October to April. GFDL predicts a drying everywhere from April to September. GISS predicts late summer drying south of 50° N and NCAR predicts a moistening north of 30° N throughout the year.

Obviously, then, the "state-of-the-art" in global climatic modeling is not yet good enough to provide agreement as to what will happen in a doubled-CO_2 world. Certainly the detail needed for regional planning purposes is lacking. The models are, in my opinion, good enough at this point to alert us to the probability of significant change in the temperature regime, in the spatial and temporal distribution of precipitation, and in the seasonal availability of soil moisture. They are also sufficiently good to alert us to the possibility that CO_2-induced climatic change might lead to more frequent, more severe, or more protracted droughts. However, careful examination of Figs. 3-8 raises the possibility that droughts might actually be moderated by forthcoming climatic change. The issue is complex and much more information must be brought to bear before we begin calling possibilities by the more commanding term *probability*.

The results of three GCM projections of temperature, precipitation, and soil moisture in a doubled CO_2 atmosphere were discussed above. The most severe predictions stem from the GFDL model, and a very recent "experiment" with that model (Manabe and Wetherald, 1986) produced particularly ominous conclusions with respect to summer dryness in the midlatitudes. In this scenario, soil moisture is reduced in summer over extensive regions of the middle and high latitudes, including the North American Great Plains, western Europe, northern Canada, and Siberia. With what could be interpreted as a greater than 90% statistical certainty, Manabe and Wetherald predict as much as a 3 cm decrease in mid-continental soil moisture in North America in summer (June, July, August) due to doubling of atmospheric CO_2. This corresponds to as much as a 50% decrease in available soil moisture. [3]

These findings must be treated with caution for a number of reasons. First, in their parameterizations, Manabe and Wetherald assume a single globally uniform soil of 1 m depth that can hold 15 cm of liquid water when wetted to field capacity. Second, the rate of evaporation from this soil is treated as a function of the water content of the soil and potential evaporation. Third, potential evaporation is treated as approximately equal to the total radiative energy absorbed by continental surfaces, notwithstanding the fact that the regional redistribution of energy by the transport of sensible heat (advection) has a great impact on the distribution of evaporation rates.

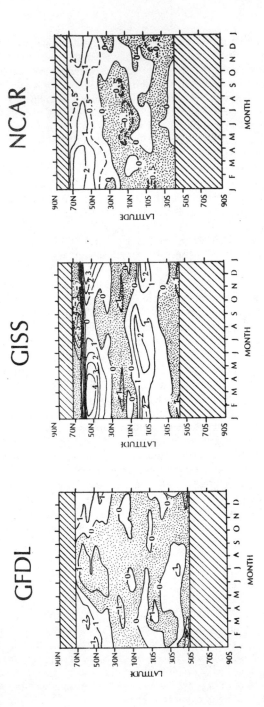

Fig. 8 Latitude-time cross section of zonal mean soil water content change (cm) over ice-free land for a doubling of the atmospheric carbon dioxide concentration, simulated with the global climatic models of GFDL (left), GISS (center), and NCAR (right). Stipple indicates a decrease in soil water; hatching indicates latitudes where there is no ice-free land (redrawn from Fig. 4.46 of Schlesinger and Mitchell, 1985).

This latter point is illustrated by data on evapotranspiration from Mead, Nebraska (41° 09' N; 96° 30' W; 354 m above m.s.l.). At that location, precision weighing lysimeters (Rosenberg and Brown, 1970) have been used to measure water use in a wide range of crops subjected to various conditions of water supply and to other imposed treatments. Evapotranspiration rates at Mead and Cozad, Nebraska, from alfalfa crops well supplied with water—essentially under conditions of potential evapotranspiration—are shown in Fig. 9. [4] Since net radiation on clear days in this environment provides enough energy for the evaporation of about 5.0-7.0 mm/day, it is evident that a secondary source of energy is available to drive the evaporation process. That energy source has been shown by Rosenberg (1969), Rosenberg and Verma (1978), and Brakke, et al. (1978), to be the advection of sensible heat, primarily from regions to the south and southwest. Other reports are available on the role of sensible heat advection in the Great Plains region (e.g., Hanks, et al., 1971; Wright and Jensen, 1971). Brakke, et al. (1978), have shown that the quantities of sensible heat attributable to regional advection are closely related to windiness. Frequently, regional advection is responsible for 50% of the total evapotranspiration.

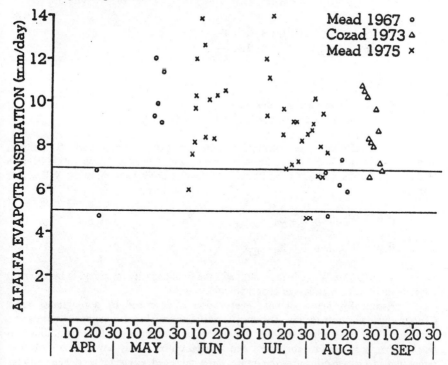

Fig. 9 Daily total of evapotranspiration (ET) by alfalfa well supplied with water. The band indicates the range of daily ET that can be attributed to net radiation. The excess is attributable to sensible heat advection (from Rosenberg, 1982).

In an earlier paper (Rosenberg, 1982), I analyze the GFDL approach to calculating evaporation from land surfaces. This is an aerodynamic approach first used by Manabe (1969) and again by Manabe and Wetherald (1980). It is still being used by GFDL (R. T. Wetherald, personal communication, August 20, 1986). Potential evaporation, E_0, is given by:

$$E_0 = \rho(h) \cdot CD(h) \cdot |V(h)| \cdot [r_{ws} - r(h)] \tag{1}$$

where:

$\rho(h)$ is density of air at height h,
$V(h)$ is velocity of the wind at height h,
r_{ws} is the saturation mixing ratio of water vapor at the surface, a function of surface temperature T_*,
$r(h)$ is the mixing ratio of water vapor at height h,
and
$CD(h)$ is the drag coefficient at height h given by:

$$CD(h) = \frac{k_0^2}{\ln\left(\dfrac{h}{z_0}\right)} \tag{2}$$

where:

k_0 is von Karman's constant,
z_0 is the roughness parameter, assumed to be 0.1 m.

Since conditions for potential evaporation (Eo) do not prevail at all times, Manabe (1969) used Budyko's (1956) approach to determine actual evaporation (E) as a function of available soil water. In Budyko's scheme a critical soil moisture, WK, exists such that:

$$\text{if } W \geq W_K, \text{ then } E = E_0 \tag{3}$$

$$\text{if } W < W_K, \text{ then } E = E_0 \frac{W}{W_k} \tag{4}$$

$W_K = 0.75 \times W_{F_c}$ where Fc indicates the field capacity (assumed to be 15 cm in a 1 m depth of soil, regardless of geographical location).

Essentially, then, potential evaporation is described by a roughness term, CD(h), which accounts for the efficiency of turbulent mixing, a wind speed term and a term describing the gradient in water vapor concentration between the evaporating surface and height h. Surface roughness and turbulent mixing may not necessarily be different in the CO_2-rich climate of the future, but wind speed will be reduced, generally because of the reduction in equator-to-pole temperature gradient from which a weakening of the Hadley cell circulation must follow. Additionally, the poleward displacement of the circumpolar vortex and the storm tracks associated with it also argue for a reduced windiness in the midlatitudes.

In a world of diminished equator-to-pole temperature gradient, wind speed should, overall, be decreased. The Manabe-Wetherald paper of 1980 is not explicit with respect to surface winds. Assuming no other changes in the right-hand terms of Eq. (1), a reduction in windiness can only act to reduce the potential evaporation. Further, the simple aerodynamic model used in Eq. (1) should be sensitive to thermal stratification, which is likely to be affected by a CO_2-induced climatic change. Transpiration is also influenced by stomatal regulation. Plants in a warmer climate may close stomates; in a more humid environment they may open more.

The temperature-humidity relationships in a CO_2-changed climate are complex. According to Eq. (1) we should, for example, expect an increase in temperature to increase E_0 through its influence on the gradient in saturation mixing ratios of water vapor [r_{ws} -r(h)]. However, a warmer atmosphere does not, in itself, alter the mixing ratio (essentially the specific humidity) of air over an affected region. While Manabe and Wetherald (1980) predict an increased mixing ratio regardless of latitude, it is possible, of course, that the air over certain zones would be less humid because of reduced precipitation and because mixing ratio increases less rapidly than surface temperature. A warmer surface, on the other hand, leads unequivocally to an increase in the saturation mixing ratio of water vapor at the surface. Increased evaporation may lower surface temperatures, assuming water is available. But decreased precipitation and greater evaporative demand may dry the surface, raising temperatures and increasing r_{ws}.

The foregoing discussion is intended to show that the simple algorithm employed by GFDL cannot do justice to the complexities of "real-world" evapotranspiration estimation. Further, the discussion of evaporation and transpiration given above assumes no change in plant behavior due to the enrichment of the atmosphere with CO_2. But there is evidence from many studies that transpiration is affected by CO_2 concentrations, and this factor must be considered as well.

GCMs are used to predict changes in mean climatic conditions. But changes in variability of climate may prove to be at least as important in practical terms. We need to know, for example, whether the numbers of days with maximum temperature above certain critical thresholds will increase or decrease, whether runs of hot, cold, wet, or dry days (or any combination; e.g., hot/dry) will increase in frequency or persistence. Mearns, et al. (1984), are among the few climatologists attempting to deal with this issue.

Analogy with the Climatic Optimum

We see, then, that problems associated with the use of GCMs in predicting climate change are many. Other approaches are being used by climatologists to project regional conditions in a world warmed by the greenhouse effect. One approach relies on proxy climatic data from the distant past or paleoclimatic analogues. These analogues are developed from tree-ring records, pollen layering in sediments, isotype ratios in wood or sediments, and a number of other techniques. One such analogue that has received considerable attention is shown in Fig. 10, from Kellogg and Schware (1981), in which a regional distribution of climatic conditions has been reconstructed for the period known as the "climatic optimum" (sometimes called the "Altithermal") about

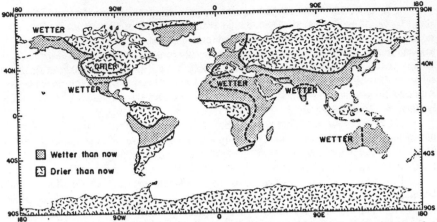

Fig. 10 Scenario of possible soil moisture patterns on a warmer earth. Based on paleoclimatic reconstruction, comparisons of recent warm and cold years in the northern hemisphere, and a climate model experiment (from Kellogg and Schware, 1981, p. 49).

6000 to 9000 years BP. Continental interiors are believed to have been drier during this period, when temperatures were perhaps 2° C higher than today.

Peter Lamb (1986) is critical of this approach. He points out that global mean surface temperature for the period of the climatic optimum cannot be reliably established. Additionally, dating of paleoclimatic phenomena is not certain. Perhaps more importantly, the seasonal and spatial distribution of incoming solar radiation then differed radically from the regime today. Likely, atmospheric circulation patterns were also very different from today because the ice sheet did not finally disappear in North America until around 6000 BP.

<u>Analogy with Climates of the Warm Years (The Instrumental Record)</u>

Another approach used to predict the climatic conditions that may prevail in the CO_2-rich world of the future is based on the actual instrumental record. Sets of warm and cold years are selected from the modern climatic record. Differences between specific regions in surface pressure, temperature, and precipitation patterns are determined. Notable among studies that have used this approach are Wigley, et al. (1980), and Lough, et al. (1983). Lamb (1986) has reviewed the various specific approaches to formulating scenarios of greenhouse-warmed climate. He points out a number of disadvantages. Among them:

1. The selection of warm and cold years or periods of years has been based on Northern Hemisphere land data—not on the globe as a whole.
2. The temperature differences identified in the instrumental record are small compared to those expected to result from future greenhouse warming.
3. A CO_2-doubling is likely to produce significant changes in the oceanic and cryospheric boundary conditions.

4. The regional details of such warm year-cold year comparisons depend strongly on the time period(s) used.

5. The response of the climate system to a steady increase in CO_2 (as is likely to occur in the future) and to a step-function CO_2 change may be quite different.

In a forthcoming paper, Wigley, et al. (1986), use the period of warming in the early twentieth century as the analogue of a warmer world. Their results for North America indicate higher and less variable temperatures throughout the year, but especially south of 50° N in summer. Midcontinent summer rainfall is reduced.

Lamb (1986) points out that, despite their many difficulties, the GCM, climate-optimum, and instrumental approaches to predicting climate in the CO_2-enriched world of the future are not totally inconsistent in their predictions.

BIOLOGICAL EFFECTS OF CO_2 ENRICHMENT

Background

To this point our attention has been fixed on the effects of CO_2 (and other radiatively active trace gases) on climatic processes and climatic change. Of these gases, carbon dioxide has the most clearly established influence on plant growth, development and water use. Tropospheric ozone is deleterious to plant growth, but this gas is not so uniformly distributed as CO_2 and is, in fact, a product of photochemical reactions with atmospheric pollutants. The other gases—N_2O, CH_4, and so forth—are still in such low concentration that, despite their relatively rapid increase, important biological impacts have yet to be associated with them.

The green plants upon which we depend for food, feed, and fiber and for ground cover to protect the soil are classified into three major groups on the basis of their photosynthetic mechanisms. C_4 plants utilize the C-4 dicarboxylic acid chemical pathway for photosynthesis. C_4 species are generally the tropical grasses, such as corn, sorghum, millet, and sugar cane, but other grasses and forbs are included. C_3 species utilize a photosynthetic pathway involving a three-carbon intermediate product. The C_3 group includes the small grains (e.g., wheat, barley) and legumes (e.g., alfalfa, soybean) and many other species. A third, but relatively minor, group of plants accomplish photosynthesis through crassulacean acid metabolism (CAM). These plants maintain stomates open at night, during which time they fix CO_2 in the form of organic acids. During daytime, the stored CO_2 is reduced photosynthetically. Pineapple is one of the few cultivated CAM plants.

The potential effect of increased global CO_2 will be different for C_3 and C_4 species. All plants consume, by respiration, some portion of the photosynthate they produce. Respiration proceeds in both C_3 and C_4 species by an essentially identical biochemical pathway throughout the day and night. However, the C_3 plants have an additional respiratory mechanism that is controlled by light and the availability of oxygen. The respiratory mechanism common to C_3 and C_4 plants is called *dark respiration* since it occurs regardless of light. The additional respiratory mechanism of C_3 plants is called *photorespiration* and occurs only during daytime.

Characteristics of C_3 and C_4 plants are given in Table 2 (from Goudriaan and Ajtay, 1979). At the light compensation point (that level of irradiance at which

Table 2
Some Characteristics of C_3 and C_4 Plants

	C_3	C_4
CO_2 assimilation rate in high light	2-4 g CO_2 m^2 h^{-1}	4-7 g CO_2 m^2 h^{-1}
Temperature optimum	20-25 °C	30-35 °C
CO_2 compensation point in high light	50 ppm	10 ppm
Photorespiration	present	not present

photosynthesis and respiration are in balance), the internal CO_2 concentration is considerably greater in the leaves of C_3 plants, due to the rapid release of CO_2 in photorespiration. The CO_2 compensation point (leaf internal CO_2 concentration at high irradiance) is considerably greater in the C_3 than in the C_4 plants.

C$_4$ plants have a greater photosynthetic potential under their optimum conditions, which involve strong solar irradiance and high temperatures. C_3 plants, given their optima of lower irradiance and temperature, produce photosynthate at about half the rate of C_4 plants.

In order to better understand the mechanisms of photosynthesis and evapotranspiration as they may be affected by increasing CO_2 concentration in the atmosphere, we may use Ohm's law as a starting point:

$$I = \frac{V}{R}$$

where I is electrical current flow, V is voltage, and R is resistance to current flow. Transpiration is the flux of water vaporized within the leaf into the atmosphere. The transpiration process (T) may be treated as an analog of the flow of electric current:

$$T = (C) \ \frac{e_1 - e_a}{r_a + r_s} \tag{6}$$

where e_a is vapor pressure of the air in contact with the leaf, e1 is the vapor pressure within the leaf's substomatal cavities, and (C) represents a group of physical constants. Thus, the driving force or voltage for transpiration is the difference or gradient in vapor pressure from leaf to air. Vapor leaving the leaf must pass through the stomates. Stomates exert a resistance (r_s) to the passage of vapor which depends on their degree of openness. The air itself exerts a resistance (r_a) to further passage of the vapor molecules. If the air is still, vapor can move only by molecular diffusion—a very slow process compared to the turbulent diffusion that occurs when the air is in motion; with increasing wind speed the aerial resistance is reduced.

Similarly, photosynthesis (P) can be approximated by the flux of carbon dioxide from the air above (F_c), which is given as a functional analogue of Ohm's Law:

$$P = F_c = (C') \frac{[CO_2]_a - [CO_2]_g}{r_a' + r_s' + r_m'} \qquad (7)$$

Here the driving force is the CO_2 concentration gradient between air, $[CO_2]_a$, and the leaf internal CO_2 concentration $[CO_2]_g$ (g for grana—the subcellular organelle where the photosynthetic reaction takes place). Since its concentration is greater in the atmosphere than it is within the leaf during daylight, CO_2 diffuses from the air into the plant leaf. This diffusion is resisted by air itself (r_a') and a further resistance is exerted by the stomata (r_s'). The primes are used to indicate that the constants and resistances to diffusion of H_2O and CO_2 are numerically different because of physical differences between these molecules.

In the case of photosynthesis, an additional resistance affects the pathway since the CO_2 molecule must diffuse to the grana against certain physical and chemical barriers. This combined resistance is termed the *mesophyll resistance* (r_m'). The resistances to water vapor and CO_2 flux under normal conditions are about 10-30; 20-500; 400-1000 s m-1 for r_a', r_s', and r_m', respectively.

Effects of CO2 Enrichment on Photosynthesis

When air is enriched in CO_2, the gradient or "driving force" in the numerator of Eq. 7 is increased. This is true for all species, but the effect is greater on C_3 plants because $[CO_2]_g$ is greater in plants having photorespiration and the gradient is normally smaller than in C_4 species. Additionally, in the case of C_3 species, increased ambient CO_2 acts to suppress photorespiration since that process proceeds at a rate that depends on competition between oxygen molecules and CO_2 molecules for enzymatic sites (Cholett, 1977; Ehleringer and Bjorkman, 1977). This phenomenon is illustrated in Fig. 11 (from Lemon, 1983).

The response of typical C_3 species to increasing $[CO_2]$ is illustrated schematically in Fig. 12. C_3 plants saturate at between 30% and 40% full sunlight. C_4 plants are still unsaturated at full sunlight and their rate of CO_2 fixation is not diminished. When the air is enriched from 300 ppm CO_2 (the current global mean concentration is about 345 ppm) to 600 ppm, C_3 plants are no longer light-saturated, even at full sunlight, and they photosynthesize like C_4 plants.

338

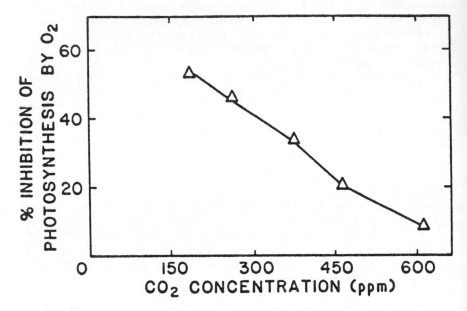

Fig. 11 Inhibition of photosynthesis in potato leaves by 21% (air) at increasing CO_2 levels (from Lemon, 1983, Chap. 2).

Effects of CO_2 Enrichment on Transpiration

Stomata open when exposed to light. However, they tend to close (the stomatal resistance is increased) with increasing concentration of CO_2 in the atmosphere. Stomatal opening is also affected by other environmental factors—temperature, relative humidity of the ambient air, and the availability of soil moisture. Normally, those factors that induce moisture stress result in stomatal closure that may be partial or complete in the event of very severe moisture shortage or extreme atmospheric evaporative demand. These factors all interact to determine the state of the leaf resistance (integration of the stomatal resistances on both sides of the leaf).

The influence of CO_2 on stomatal closure is more consequential in the process of transpiration than it is in photosynthesis. Reference to Eq. (6) will show that, except in almost windless conditions, r_s is the primary determinant of the resistance to vapor transport from plant to atmosphere. Any significant increase in r_s should then lead to a reduction in transpiration rate.

Experimental evidence supports this hypothesis. Figure 13 (from Akita and Moss, 1972) illustrates the relative decrease in transpiration rate for three C_3 and three C_4 species that occurs with increasing CO_2. The transpiration of these plants was observed in a leaf chamber in the dark and under strong illumination. Clearly, stomates of the C_4 species respond more sharply, and this response holds true in the range of CO_2 concentrations currently found in the field air and anticipated in the foreseeable future. In Fig. 13 it is seen that, in the light, the response of the C_3 species to realistic ambient

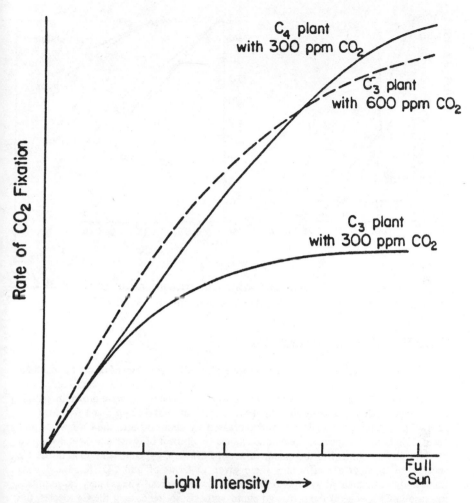

Fig. 12 Influence of light intensity on C_3 and C_4 photosynthesis rate. The effect of a doubling of CO_2 concentration on the photosynthesis rate of the C_3 plant is also shown (from Lemon, 1983, Chap. 3).

CO_2 concentration is very slight. The response is considerably greater in the dark. Since most transpiration occurs during the daytime, however, the response in darkness is probably of minor importance.

340

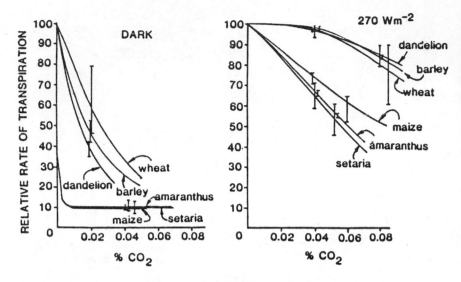

Fig. 13 Effect of CO_2 concentration on transpiration of C_3 and C_4 species in light and darkness (after Akita and Moss, 1972).

<u>Effects of CO_2 Enrichment on Water Use Efficiency</u>

Thus, as we have seen from the foregoing, CO_2 enrichment of the atmosphere affects both photosynthesis and transpiration. Table 3 illustrates the overall effects of CO_2 enrichment on two C_3 species and one C_4 species. The plants were grown in a number of experiments with controlled light and temperature at 330 ppm and 640 (or 660) ppm of CO_2. Photosynthetic rate was increased by about 50% in the C_3 species and about 25% in the C_4 species. Leaf conductance (reciprocal of resistance) was decreased by the CO_2 enrichment to the extent of about 22% in C_3 species and 33% in the C_4 species. The water use efficiency (here given in terms of mol CO_2 fixed/mol H_2O transpired) was increased by 86% to 95% in the three species. The primary cause of this increase in C_3 species is the enhanced photosynthesis; in the case of the C_4 species, the primary cause is the reduced transpiration.

THE BIOLOGICAL INTERACTIONS WITH DROUGHT

The foregoing sections have dealt with observation of the direct effects of CO_2 enrichment of the atmosphere on photosynthesis, transpiration,and water use efficiency, based primarily on growth chamber research. How might these responses manifest themselves in real-world crop production in the semiarid and arid zones of the world that are prone to drought? How might unmanaged ecosystems respond? We must, for simplicity, consider drought to be an exacerbation of the moisture stress that frequently affects the regions of our primary concern.

Table 3

Response of Leaf Photosynthesis, Leaf Conductance, and Photosynthetic Water Use Efficiency to Growth under Increased CO_2 Concentrations

	CO_2 Concentration ppm	Photosynthesis $\mu mol\ m^{-2}\ s^{-1}$	Ratio	Leaf Conductance $mmol\ m^{-2}\ s^{-1}$	Ratio	Water Use Efficiency $\mu mol\ CO_2$/ $mmol\ H_2O$	Ratio
Nerium oleander (C_3)	660	35.9	1.48	200	.77	2.7	1.95
	330	24.2		261		1.4	
Gossypium Hirsutum (C_3)	640	51.1	1.50	390	.79	6.4	1.87
	330	34.2		495		3.4	
Zea mays (C_4)	640	65.3	1.23	260	.67	12.5	1.86
	330	53.0		390		6.7	

Source: From Chapter 4 in Lemon, 1983—see original for details of the experiments.

In a recent review article, Kimball (1985) summarizes known and likely responses of plants to stimulation by carbon dioxide enrichment. He does this in order to predict the trends in adaptation of plants that are likely to occur as we move into a CO_2-richer world. The responses are:

1. Leaf and canopy photosynthesis rates will increase with increases in CO_2 concentration to at least 1000 ppm.
2. Plants will be bigger, with differences in size response among species.
3. C_3 species will respond more strongly than C_4 species.
4. Leaf area, weight per unit area, leaf thickness, stem height, branching, and seed and fruit number and size will likely increase.
5. Root-to-shoot ratios will increase.
6. Agricultural yields will likely increase with a doubling of current CO_2 concentration by an average of 32%.
7. Partial closure of leaf stomata, induced by CO_2 enrichment, will lead to decreases in leaf transpiration rates and increases in daytime leaf temperature. C_4 species respond more strongly than C_3 species in this regard.
8. Growth stimulation due to CO_2 enrichment appears relatively constant with light intensity and temperature.
9. The partial stomatal closure with increasing CO_2 concentration may compensate somewhat for water stress, and salinity stress and damage due to pollutants may be reduced.
10. When nutrients are limiting, the relative response to CO_2 enrichment may be reduced. This may be compensated partly by increased root volume and depth and possible stimulation of mycorrhizal fungi, which make phosphorus and water more available to the plant. Nitrogen fixation by legumes is stimulated by increased CO_2 concentration.

Since drought is the subject of our concern here, and since expected climate changes may increase the frequency, severity, and duration of drought, further exploration of the possible interactions of CO_2 enrichment and climate change on plant-water relations is needed.

In growth chamber studies, doubling of CO_2 concentration yielded, on the average, a 34% reduction in transpiration (Kimball, 1985). In the field, however, leaf area will likely be increased and the demand for water thereby will be increased. Root systems will be larger and able to extract more water from the soil. Reductions in evaporation make more thermal energy available, which by interrow advection of sensible heat can increase soil evaporation, thereby reducing the potential for water savings.

Stomatal closure and leaf area-increase work in opposite directions in controlling transpiration. Photosynthesis is relatively unaffected by CO_2 enrichment in C_4 plants, but their stomates are relatively responsive. Therefore, these plants are most likely to show a significant decrease in consumptive use of water.

Another important consideration identified by Kimball (1985) is the relative improvement in plant internal water condition in plants grown in a CO_2-enriched atmosphere. Through the mechanism of stomatal closure, plants in the enriched atmosphere maintain a higher water potential for longer periods than do plants grown in normal CO_2 concentrations. Thus, under drought stress, the enriched plants are able to maintain turgor and photosynthesize more actively. The effects of CO_2 enrichment under drought stress and under well-watered conditions for a range of C_3 plants were summarized by

Kimball (1985). He found that doubling [CO_2] resulted in growth or yield increases of 43% and 76% in well-watered and drought-stressed conditions, respectively. Drought-stressed CO_2-enriched plants grew (or yielded) an average of 91% as well as well-watered unenriched plants. This suggests that CO_2 enrichment of the atmosphere may compensate to some degree for the increasing aridity that is predicted to result from climatic changes in regions of the world that are now prone to drought.

SUMMARY AND CONCLUSIONS

Climate changes because of natural events that alter the amount of solar energy reaching our planet, the transparency of the atmosphere to this radiation, and its seasonal and geographic distribution at the earth's surface. Deserts have been created and have been reclaimed as the result of long-term climatic changes. The frequency and severity of the droughts in any specified region have also been affected by long-term climatic change.

We recognize the inevitability and immutability of the natural processes described above. But in recent years we have come to recognize that man's activities also have an impact on the atmospheric processes that control climate. By altering the surface in vast regions we change their radiation and energy balances. By emitting large amounts of radiatively active trace gases and suspensoids into the atmosphere we change its transparency to incoming short-wave solar radiation and, even more, to outgoing long-wave terrestrial radiation.

The processes involved in climatic change are very complex, and the prediction of changes that may follow natural and man-made perturbations in the atmospheric system require the use of extremely sophisticated analytical methods. Global climatic models are one such tool. GCMs have been used extensively in recent years to predict the geographic distribution of changes in surface temperature, precipitation, and soil water availability expected to follow from the "greenhouse effect" caused by a significant increase in the atmospheric carbon dioxide concentration above its preindustrial level. There has already been a 25% increase in CO_2 concentration, and a doubling could occur by the mid-twenty-first century. The rapid increase in the atmospheric concentration of other radiatively active trace gases (methane, nitrous oxides, chlorofluorocarbons, and others) could hasten and/or intensify the "greenhouse effect."

The GCMs predict profound changes in the distribution of surface temperature and precipitation. Although the available models disagree about specific regions, it is clear that the climate of the earth, as a whole, will warm and that precipitation as a whole will increase, as will evaporation. The GFDL model projections, in particular, indicate that the midlatitudes of the Northern Hemisphere ($\sim 37°$ to $50°$ N) will experience a significant shortfall in soil water availability, especially in summer. Since this is the latitudinal zone in which much of the world's grain is produced and since portions of this belt are already "droughty," this prediction is ominous. That other GCMs do not agree in specific detail with the GFDL model is not necessarily cause for reassurance. Perhaps all that can be said with certainty at this time is that some of the drought-prone regions of the world will be negatively affected by impending climate change and other regions may benefit. The state-of-the-art is inadequate to do more than alert us to the *probability* of change and the *possibility* that it could be quite serious in certain regions of the world.

Our knowledge of the direct response of plants to carbon dioxide enrichment of the atmosphere is more secure. Photosynthesis rate will increase in all the higher plants, but most in the C_3 species; transpiration will be reduced in all higher plants, but most in the C_4 species. Because of stomatal closure induced by CO_2, the C_4 species, important in the subhumid and semiarid zones, might be able to avoid or minimize the impact of increased aridity. Plants grown in CO_2-enriched air also reduce the impact of water stress on photosynthetic rate and yield by maintaining a better internal water balance (greater turgor). Deeper rooting habit, increased soil organic matter content with its consequent increase in soil water holding capacity, and other responses stimulated by CO_2 enrichment of the air may also tend to alleviate the moisture stress that would follow from the reduced precipitation and increased evaporation rate in regions so affected by climatic change.

Assessing that which is known and that which is yet unknown about the mechanisms of climatic change, the regional specificity of the changes to expect from the "greenhouse effect," and the direct effects of carbon dioxide enrichment on plant growth and water use leaves us uncertain as to whether the drought-prone areas of the world will be better off or worse. But we are now aware that climatic change is highly probable and that the changes may be profound in many places. The drought-prone regions may have less resilience and their resources may already be severely strained; hence, they are among the regions that require attention most urgently.

In my view, it is essential that governments and international agencies give considerable support to study of the potential impacts of a wide range of possible climatic changes on the natural resource base and on the societal and economic implications of such changes. Decisions will, of necessity, be required and it is our task, as scientists and administrators, to reduce the degree of uncertainty facing decision makers as much and as quickly as possible.

ACKNOWLEDGMENTS

I am indebted to Mrs. Sharon Kelly, Miss Sheila Smith, and Miss Deborah Wood for stenographic, graphic arts, and bibliographic work required in preparation of this manuscript. I am also indebted to colleagues at the Center for Agricultural Meteorology and Climatology, University of Nebraska-Lincoln, and Resources for the Future, Washington, D.C., for the insights they have shared with me on many of the issues dealt with in this paper.

NOTES

1. B. G. Mendoca, Geophysical Monitoring for Climate Change Division, NOAA. Unpublished data on atmospheric transmission of solar radiation at Mauna Loa Observatory, 1958-85.

2. The albedo of green vegetation fully covering the ground is in the range of 18-24%. Bare light-colored sandy soil may have an albedo of 40-50%.

3. In a recent (Aug. 20, 1986) telephone conversation with R. T. Wetherald, I learned that the control case (1xCO2) predicts that mean seasonal (J, J, A) soil moisture content is equal to 6 cm in the total root zone 1 m deep. The Manabe-Wetherald model does not consider the geographic distribution of real soil types and moisture-holding capacities.

4. The measurements at Cozad were made by means of the Bowen Ratio-Energy Balance method.

REFERENCES

Akita, S.; and D. N. Moss. 1972. Differential stomatal response between C3 and C4 species to atmospheric CO2 concentration and light. Crop Sci. 12:789.
Brakke, T. W.; S. B. Verma; and N. J. Rosenberg. 1978. Local and regional components of sensible heat advection. J. Appl. Meteorol. 17:955-963.
Bryson, R. A. 1973. Drought in Sahelia: Who or what is to blame? Ecologist 3:366-371.
Bryson, R. A.; and T. Murray. 1977. Climate of Hunger. University of Wisconsin Press, Madison.
Budyko, M. I. 1956. Heat Balance of the Earth's Surface. Gidrometeoizdat, Leningrad.
Charney, J. G. 1975. Dynamics of deserts and drought in the Sahel. Quart. J. Roy. Meteorol. Soc. 101:193-202.
Charney, J. G.; P. H. Stone; and W. J. Quirk. 1975. Drought in the Sahara: A biogeophysical feedback mechanism. Science 187:434-435.
Chervin, R. M. 1980. On the simulation of climate and climate change with general circulation models. J. Atmos. Sci. 37:1903-1913.
Chollett, R. 1977. The biochemistry of photorespiration. Trends Biochem. Sci. 2:155-159.
Eddy, J. A. 1982. Changes in the solar constant and climatic effects. Nature 300:689-693.
Ehleringer, J. R.; and O. Bjorkman. 1977. Quantum yields for CO2 uptake in C3 and C4 plants. Plant Physiol. 59:86-90.
Fleagle, R. G.; and J. A. Businger. 1963. An Introduction to Atmospheric Physics. Academic Press, New York.
Glantz, M. H. 1986. Drought, famine and the seasons in sub-Saharan Africa. Manuscript prepared for the WMO/UNEP/WHO Symposium on Climate and Human Health, Leningrad, September 22-26, 1986.
Goudriaan, J.; and G. L. Ajtay. 1979. The possible effects of increased CO2 on photosynthesis. pp. 237-249. In B. Bolin, E. T. Degans, S. Kempe, and P. Ketner, eds. The Global Carbon Cycle (SCOPE 13). Wiley, New York.
Hanks, R. J.; L. H. Allen, Jr.; and H. R. Gardner. 1971. Advection and evapotranspiration of wide-row sorghum in the central Great Plains. Agron. J. 63:520-527.
Hayashi, Y. 1982. Confidence intervals of a climatic signal. J. Atmos. Sci. 39:1895-1905.
Jones, P. D.; T. M. L. Wigley; and P. B. Wright. 1986. Global temperature variations between 1861 and 1984. Nature 322:430-434.

346

Kellogg, W. W.; and R. Schware. 1981. Climate Change and Society: Consequences of Increasing Atmospheric Carbon Dioxide. Westview Press, Boulder, Colorado.

Kimball, B. A. 1985. Adaptation of vegetation and management practices to a higher carbon dioxide world. Chap. 9. In B. R. Strain and J. D. Cure, eds. Direct Effects of Increasing Carbon Dioxide on Vegetation. DOE/ER-0238. U.S. Dept. of Energy, Carbon Dioxide Research Division, Washington, D.C.

Lamb, P. J. 1982. Persistence of sub-Saharan drought. Nature 299:46-48.

Lamb, P. J. 1983. Sub-Saharan rainfall update for 1982: Continued drought. J. Clim. 3:419-422.

Lamb, P. J. 1986. A state-of-the-art review of the development of climatic scenarios. Paper presented at the Task Force Meeting on Policy-Oriented Assessment of Impact of Climatic Variations, IIASA, Laxenburg, Austria, June 30-July 2, 1986.

Lemon, E. R., ed. 1983. CO_2 and Plants: The Response of Plants to Rising Levels of Atmospheric Carbon Dioxide. AAAS Selected Symposium 84. Westview Press, Boulder, Colorado.

List, R. J., ed. 1966. Smithsonian Meteorological Tables. 6th rev. ed., Smithsonian Misc. Collections, Vol. 114. Smithsonian Institution, Washington, D.C.

Lough, J. M.; T. M. L. Wigley; and J. P. Palutikof. 1983. Climate and climate impact scenarios for Europe in a warmer world. J. Clim. Applied Meteorol. 22:1673-1684.

MacCracken, M. C.; and F. M. Luther, eds. 1985. Projecting the Climatic Effects of Increasing Carbon Dioxide. DOE/ER-0237. U.S. Dept. of Energy, Carbon Dioxide Research Division, Washington, D.C.

Manabe, S.; and R. T. Wetherald. 1986. Reduction in summer soil wetness induced by an increase in atmospheric carbon dioxide. Science 232:626-628.

Manabe, S. 1969. Climate and the ocean circulation: I. The atmospheric circulation and the hydrology of the earth's surface. Mon. Weather Rev. 97:739-774.

Manabe, S.; and R. T. Wetherald. 1980. On the distribution of climate change resulting from an increase in CO_2 content of the atmosphere. J. Atmos. Sci. 37:99-118.

Mearns, L. O.; R. W. Katz; and S. H. Schneider. 1984. Extreme high-temperature events: Changes in the probabilities with changes in mean temperature. J. Clim. Applied Meteorol. 23:1601-1613.

Meehl, G. A. 1984. Modeling the earth's climate. Clim. Change 6:259-286.

Nicholson, S. E. 1983. Sub-Saharan rainfall in the years 1976-80: Evidence of continued drought. Mon. Weather Rev. 111:1646-1654.

Nicholson, S. E. 1985. Notes: Sub-Saharan rainfall 1981-84. J. Clim. Applied Meteorol. 24:1388-1391.

Reifsnyder, W. E.; and H. W. Lull. 1965. Radiant Energy in Relation to Forests. Tech. Bull. No. 1344. USDA, Forest Service, Washington, D.C.

Rosenberg, N. J. 1969. Seasonal patterns in evapotranspiration by irrigated alfalfa in the central Great Plains. Agron. J. 61:879-886.

Rosenberg, N. J.; and K. W. Brown. 1970. Improvements in the van Bavel-Myers automatic weighing lysimeter. Water Resour. Res. 6:1227-1229.

347

Rosenberg, N. J.; and S. B. Verma. 1978. Extreme evapotranspiration by irrigated alfalfa: A consequence of the 1976 midwestern drought. J. Appl. Meteorol. 17:934-941.
Rosenberg, N. J. 1982. The increasing CO_2 concentration in the atmosphere and its implication on agricultural productivity. II. Effects through CO_2-induced climatic change. Clim. Change 4:239-254.
Rosenberg, N. J. 1983. When the rains don't come: Droughts in North America. Feature article in Science and the Future, Yearbook of the Encyclopedia Brittanica, pp. 108-129.
Sarnthein, M. 1978. Sand deserts during glacial maximum and climatic optimum. Nature 272:43-46.
Schlesinger, M. E.; and J. F. B. Mitchell. 1985. Model projections of the equilibrium climatic response to increased carbon dioxide. Chap. 4. In M. C. MacCracken and F. M. Luther, eds. Projecting the Climatic Effects of Increasing Carbon Dioxide. DOE/ER-0237. U.S. Dept. of Energy, Carbon Dioxide Research Division, Washington, D.C.
Schneider, S.; and R. Londer. 1984. The Coevolution of Climate and Life. Sierra Club Books, San Francisco, California.
Wigley, T. M. L.; P. D. Jones; and P. M. Kelley. 1980. Scenario for a warm, high CO_2 world. Nature 283:17-21.
Wigley, T. M. L.; P. D. Jones; and P. M. Kelley. 1986. Empirical studies: Warm world scenarios and the detection of a CO_2-induced climatic change. In B. Bolin, B. R. Doos, J. Jager, and R. A. Warrick, eds. An Assessment of the Role of Carbon Dioxide and Other Radiatively Active Constituents in Climatic Variations and Associated Impacts. Scientific Committee on Problems of Environment (SCOPE) (forthcoming).
Wright, J. L.; and M. E. Jensen. 1971. Peak water requirements of crops in southern Idaho. J. Irrig. Drain. Div. (ASCE) 98:193-201.

PART 6

Adaptation and Adjustment

CHAPTER 21
ADAPTATION AND ADJUSTMENTS
IN DROUGHT-PRONE AREAS: RESEARCH DIRECTIONS

Steven T. Sonka

INTRODUCTION

Drought and its societal effects are of obvious importance. One doesn't need graduate-level training to discern the human suffering that occurs because of prolonged droughts. The economic and social consequences are severe and are vividly transmitted to us by means of modern communications.

The role of social science research should be to assist societies in developing improved mechanisms to deal with drought (Doulding, 1985; Chen, 1983). As I will stress later, however, actions to deal with drought must not be separated from the broader issue of the interaction of climate and society. The discussion that follows attempts to raise a number of concerns about the more traditional means of evaluating drought's effect on society. Doing this is not an attempt to quarrel with the worth or need for such approaches. Rather, this paper's goal is to suggest the possibility of expanding research efforts to serve society.

The remainder of the paper is divided into four segments. The first briefly reviews a portion of the extensive literature on drought and climate impact analysis. The purpose of that review is not to summarize the effectiveness of adaptations actually used. Instead a number of common themes from those analyses that suggest a need for advancing research thrusts are identified. The second section considers the drought problem from a decision-making perspective. Implications of this approach for understanding societal responses to drought are suggested. The decision-making framework is used as an underpinning for the paper's third section, which refers to implementation of that framework in a research approach. The potential for integrated quantitative models as a means to evaluate climate/human interactions is evaluated. The final section is a short summary of major points.

BACKGROUND

In reviewing the considerable body of research findings relating to the effects of drought on society, I was impressed with the richness and diversity of work that has been accomplished. Even if limited to the narrower aspects of adjustments and adaptations to drought, there still is an impressive body of literature on which to build. It is not my intent, however, to comprehensively summarize the findings of that work. To do so would strain available time resources as well as my intellectual capabilities. Instead I have attempted to highlight a limited number of important points.

Maunder and Ausubel (1985) found that the economic sectors considered most often in previous work were those related to agriculture and water resources. Most of these works show a historic orientation, typically analyzing the impacts of a previous major drought on society. Speaking in a general sense, the literature seems to have three common themes:

1. Individual persons and societies do adapt in significant ways to the potential for drought.
2. Human actions, often taken at times other than when a drought is occurring, may critically affect a society's vulnerability to drought.
3. Individual persons and societies often act in ways implying that they are surprised by the occurrence of drought, even in locations where severe droughts are part of modern history.

A few brief examples will illustrate these themes.

Numerous studies have documented that both private and public decision makers take actions suggesting their concern about the possible occurrence of drought. For example, in self-provisioning agricultural societies, farmers pursue activities such as diversification of enterprises and production strategies; maintenance of flexible patterns of resource use, including consumption; adaptations of the environment, often through supplemental irrigation; and development of networks for rural cooperation (Jodha and Mascarenhas, 1985).

Warrick and his colleagues offer similar results for developed agricultures in the American Great Plains region (Warrick, 1980; Warrick and Riebsame, 1983). Their hypothesis of a lessening effect of the adverse consequences of drought over time implies that adaptations occur. This work indicates that even when the direct physical impact of drought (for example, on crop yields) cannot be shown to be diminished, the adverse impacts on the local area can be reduced by spreading the negative effects over a broader segment of the population.

Numerous investigations have documented that drought is not solely a physical phenomenon. Heathcote (1973) notes it may be useful to define drought in agricultural and hydrological terms as well as in meteorological terms. The importance of the economic and social system is stressed in emphatic terms by Garcia (1981, p. 219): "Climatic events per se are not the root cause, in our times, of great disasters, famines, increased misery." Although they note that climate's role is important, Garcia and many others have found that a society's vulnerability to drought is as much a function of human and social actions as it is of climate events (Garcia, 1981; Warrick and Riebsame, 1983; Heathcote, 1985).

The final common theme is that individual citizens and societies often tend to act as if they are surprised when droughts occur (Hill, 1973; Heathcote, 1973). The public's treatment of drought as an unexpected event can reasonably be attributed to the desire to attract relief. It is interesting that such relief, particularly for the agricultural sector, is generally forthcoming—even when the agriculturalist has not taken actions, such as holding excess stocks of feed or purchasing crop insurance, to reduce the adverse effects of drought. At times, human actions taken to reduce vulnerability actually exacerbate the problem. For example, actions to restrict nomadic movement in the Sahel appear to have made those societies more vulnerable to drought (Garcia, 1981). Planting of more drought-susceptible crops indicates that sometimes decision makers take actions suggesting that drought is not expected.

Viewed as a group, these three general themes present somewhat of a paradox. On the one hand, the presence of adaptations and the knowledge that human actions can make societies more vulnerable to drought suggests an awareness of climate/societal interactions. Conversely, the idea that drought is unexpected, whether suggested by pronouncements or by actions, indicates a lack of perception of and sensitivity to the potential for drought. Undoubtedly the truth lies somewhere in between those contradictory viewpoints. In the following discussion, a different perspective for analysis of human/drought interactions is suggested. Viewed from this perspective, the previously mentioned paradox might not exist.

A DECISION PERSPECTIVE

As I have noted above, a substantial amount of important scholarly research has addressed the issue of man's adaptation to drought. In general, these projects have employed the extreme events approach (as described by Heathcote, 1985). These works have been essential in defining the responses that individual citizens and societies have employed in reacting to adverse weather phenomena.

The remainder of this discussion will adopt a perspective that is markedly different, however, from the methodologies previously employed. Rather than focusing on analysis of past extreme events, the perspective to be employed centers on decisions and the decision-making process. Before beginning this discussion, I would like to reiterate that advancing this perspective is not meant to suggest that prior or future extreme event historic analyses are not important. In fact, as will be noted subsequently, these efforts are essential to the effective conduct of research using the decision perspective being proposed (de Vries, 1985).

Decision and Production Processes

Kenneth Boulding (1985, p. 10) has stated, "A decision essentially involves a choice among different images of the future that we conceive to be within our power to achieve." Weather events affect those images. Generally our power is not to forestall the weather event. Rather our choices revolve around responding to the potential that drought may occur or reacting to the presence of drought. From the economist's view, the charge is to "optimally" adjust to our climatic endowment, including its characteristics of variability and change (Lovell and Smith, 1985).

A Simplified Example

To illuminate the issues associated with drought and decision making, a simplistic example will be discussed. Initially we will consider an example for crop production in a commercial agricultural setting. Then this example will be expanded to consider implications for a subsistence agricultural situation and for the public decision maker.

Figure 1 presents a schematic of the decision and production process as it might occur in selection of operating inputs for an annual crop such as cotton, wheat, or corn. The processes are illustrated in a manner that is quite dissimilar to that typically used to indicate societal adaptations to drought (Kates, 1985; Warrick and Riebsame, 1983).

The topmost section of Fig. 1 relates to the planning process. In this section, expectations play a major role. (In Fig. 1, factors enclosed by ovals are uncertain expectations; those noted by rectangles are factors known at the time the decision is made; and those noted by trapezia occur during or are results of the production process.) Expectations of future weather events, which include some realization that drought could occur, are one source of uncertainty to the producer. Although a source of variability, this approach allows us to also consider climate as a natural resource (Riebsame, 1985). An important factor in many agricultural situations, climate expectations are but one of the many economic, social, and physical factors that the decision maker somehow weighs in making a production choice.

The potential for drought affects production decisions through the expected profit oval in Fig. 1. It is likely, however, that the three factors shown as affecting the production decision are not independent but in reality are interrelated. For example, a producer in a very secure financial position may have a different attitude toward drought than does a producer in a marginally secure position. Although it is likely that these interrelationships exist, we know very little about their empirical effect. For example, we might expect the poorly financed producer to adopt strategies that are more conservative than those of the well-financed producer. In reality the more marginal producer may have to assume that drought cannot occur—because if it does the firm will not survive no matter what actions the producer pursues. Given that framework, the producer in the weaker financial position may adopt practices that appear to be relatively risky.

The second section of Fig. 1 relates to actual events. Notice that the actual events occur after the planning process and production decision are completed. This, of course, is just another way of saying that uncertainty is a major characteristic of decision making.

To this point we have considered the production process at the important level of the individual decision maker. But there are many producers, and financial outcomes cannot be determined until the totality of production is weighed against the total demand for the commodity. Therefore the third section of Fig. 1 is labeled *market effects*. Here demand and supply conditions interact to determine market prices. In today's highly interdependent world, market effects are volatile and affected by events literally on the other side of the world from individual producers.

These market effects can mitigate or exacerbate the effects of the drought. For example, the drought of 1983 in the central United States was offset by relatively high market prices and government programs. For producers in the southern United States in 1986, however, drought has been coupled with relatively low output prices. Financial effects in this latter case are particularly devastating.

The final section of Fig. 1 emphasizes the continuous nature of decision and production processes. The current year's results are very important in conditioning the following year's processes. These interrelations have many dimensions, including the following.

1. Physical factors such as soil moisture and ground-water availability.
2. The financial constraints within which the individual firm operates.

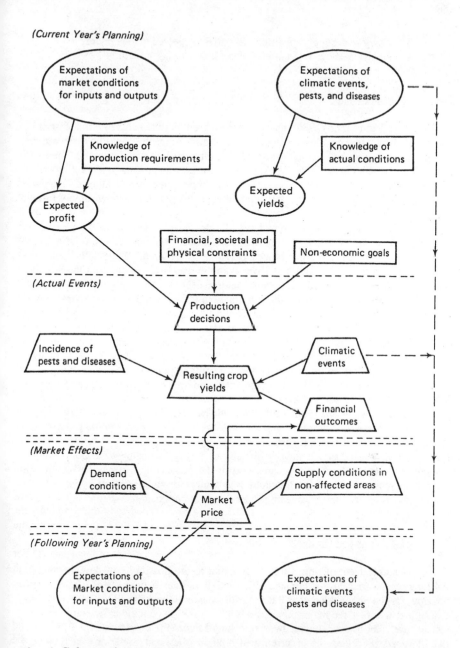

(Current Year's Planning)

Expectations of
market conditions
for inputs and outputs

Expectations of
climatic events,
pests, and diseases

Knowledge of
production requirements

Knowledge of
actual conditions

Expected
profit

Expected
yields

Financial, societal and
physical constraints

Non-economic goals

(Actual Events)

Production
decisions

Incidence of
pests and diseases

Climatic
events

Resulting crop
yields

Financial
outcomes

(Market Effects)

Demand
conditions

Supply conditions in
non-affected areas

Market
price

(Following Year's Planning)

Expectations of
Market conditions
for inputs and outputs

Expectations of
climatic events
pests and diseases

Fig. 1 Schematic of climate's impact on an economic activity viewed
from a decision-making perspective.

3. Carry-over supply conditions that affect expected market prices.
4. Decision-maker expectations of possible climatic conditions.

The Crucial Role of Time

Lovell and Smith (1985) assert that three prominent features of climate must be incorporated into frameworks relating to its economic impacts. Two of these are the stochastic nature and the potential for broad geographical impacts of climate. These are depicted in the schematic outlined in Fig. 1. The third aspect is the temporal nature of climate's effects. The annual component of this temporal nature was alluded to above. However, the sequential nature of decision making is a key component worthy of further discussion.

A significant simplification of Fig. 1 was the presentation of the production decision as a single decision. In reality, production is seldom the result of a single decision. Instead a series of interrelated decisions is required. Table 1 illustrates the structure of decision making for a specific example that is consistent with the previous framework, that of corn production in the midwestern United States. Within Table 1, these operational production decisions are linked to the time periods when those choices need to be made.

For midwestern corn production, it is well known that drought conditions during the summer period can devastate yields. Dramatic examples have been experienced in 1974, 1980, and 1983. But notice that essentially no decisions occur during this period. (The fertilization decision noted must take place very early in June, at the start of the summer period.) This depiction again underscores the importance of expectations in operational decision making.

The decisions shown in Table 1 are interrelated, in that choices made early in the production process affect the flexibility of decision making later in the process. For example, the decision to plant corn often results in fall application of fertilizer in this region. Once that occurs, it is very difficult to justify switching to a more drought-tolerant crop such as oats or soybeans, even if the producer's expectations of drought were to increase. The option of switching to a more drought-resistant variety of corn remains, however, and might have important financial implications.

Types of Decisions and Droughts

Another facet of time's role in adapting to the possibility of drought refers to the long-term variability of climate. Figure 2 illustrates a time series of streamflow amounts for the Senegal River at Bakel for this century (Faure and Gac, 1981). Within that figure, we see three major time periods when drought conditions severely restricted streamflow. These data suggest two interesting factors for consideration. First notice that the years preceding the occurrence of drought often had ample or excess rainfall. This has important implications for decision makers' expectations about future weather events. Notice that persons born either in the 1915-20 or 1945-50 periods would not have experienced severe droughts until they were well into their twenties. These persons had expectations that may not have included severe prolonged droughts. Their decisions may well have reflected that restricted experience base.

As we learn more about how managers manage and make decisions, the hectic and overloaded nature of decision making is becoming more apparent (Van de Ven, 1985). Managing the manager's attention is being recognized as an increasingly critical factor. With respect to drought and its temporal variability, is it likely that a producer who has just seen a run of good rainfall years will expect a drought this year?

A second implication of the uncertainty associated with drought is the recognition that the possibility of drought has an economic effect, even in years of adequate or excessive moisture. This pervasive effect of the possibility of drought does not seem to have received adequate recognition. Often analyses have focused on the suffering and losses that result when drought occurs. In those instances, human practices that have worsened the effects of the drought are typically identified. Examples such as restricting nomadic movement in the Sahel or crop production in arid regions quickly come to mind. Analyses that concentrate only on the extreme event tend to document the adverse

Table 1
Production Choices and Time Period When Climate Forecast Information Could Potentially Be Useful for Corn Production, Central Illinois

Production choices	Decision Time Periods				
	Fall/ Winter (Sept.- Mar.)	Early Spring (Apr.1- May 15)	Late Spring (May 16- Jun.10)	Summer (Jun.11- Sept.30)	Fall (Sept.- Nov.)
Choice of crop	X	X	X		
Fertilization (timing and amount)	X	X	X	X	
Tillage (timing and amount)	X	X	X		
Planting date		X	X		
Variety selection	X	X	X		
Plant population		X	X		
Time of harvest					X

Source: Sonka, et al., 1986.

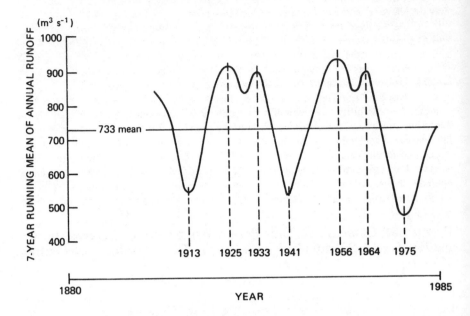

Fig. 2 Mean annual modulus of River Senegal runoff (7-year running mean) measured at Bakel (from Faure and Gac, 1981).

effects of those actions during the drought but discount to zero the benefits of those actions in nondrought years. Where irreversible physical effects are the variable of interest, this may be appropriate. For economic analyses, however, this approach is not satisfactory.

Results of a recently completed analysis for corn production in the midwestern portion of the United States will illustrate this point (Mjelde, 1985). Using a decision analysis framework, this effort estimated outcomes for a hypothetical corn producer over the fourteen-year period from 1970 through 1983. As one part of the analysis, the producer was assumed to make decisions as if the producer believed that drought conditions were going to occur every year. This was compared to an alternative assumption of normal weather conditions. Over the fourteen-year period, the pessimistic producer would have averaged about $6 per acre less in net returns than did someone assuming normal conditions.

Of course in a drought year the pessimistic producer would have done significantly better than the more optimistic producer. Someone evaluating the results of the extreme event of 1983 might have discovered that producers who assumed average conditions had taken actions that made them more vulnerable to drought. The "cost" of being right in 1983, however, was reduced returns over the entire period.

Let me stress that I am not suggesting that actions which are more vulnerable to drought are necessarily preferable. The costs that occur during the drought may significantly overwhelm the benefits in other periods. It is not appropriate, however, to use only evaluation methods that consider a portion of the range of possible climate events.

Some Implications of the Decision-Making Perspective

The preceding discussion suggests several implications for scholars concerned with either the physical or societal impacts of drought. A few will be mentioned here, but this certainly is not an exhaustive list.

Expectations. As we consider means to improve our decision responses to drought, the key role of improving decision makers' expectations is highlighted. Several alternatives come to mind. The first of these is the development of skillful climate forecasts with sufficient lead time to be useful to producers. The scientific problems associated with seasonal climate forecasting are certainly significant. One of the key issues is to determine levels of accuracy that would be useful to decision makers. Forecasts that may not meet statistical tests of significance may be desired by producers who have to make decisions no matter what the standard error of the estimate is.

Forecasts do not form the only basis for decision makers' expectations, however. Knowing the true statistical chances for drought may have value, even for producers who have considerable experience in a specific location. For that matter, we know very little about how individual producers develop their prior expectations with respect to the probability of occurrence of particular weather events and what information they use in that process. There is considerable evidence that individual producers perform poorly in experiments in which probabilistic information is of importance and, probably as importantly, they consistently have overconfident views of their capabilities (Kahneman and Tversky, 1982).

As documented in Fig. 1, the relevant expectations include economic as well as physical factors. Knowledge of physical conditions in competitive producing areas, the size of actual or potential carry-over stocks, and factors affecting demand are examples of factors for which the producer may want to develop expectations. The factors noted are important because they indicate the vulnerability of the entire market system to production shortfalls from events such as drought.

Interrelation of drought and decision-maker constraints. In a preceding section, the potential for complex interactions between the producer's financial position and adjustments or responses to drought were suggested. Decision makers typically face more than financial constraints. Physical factors may be constraints that the decision maker needs to consider. For example, the planting of windbreaks and other agronomic practices were adopted as responses to the Dust Bowl conditions of the 1930s (Worster, 1979). These constraints affect the production system every year because of the possibility that drought conditions may develop.

Constraints such as windbreaks are relatively permanent in nature. During or after a period of dry conditions, however, drought can temporarily alter the physical environment with which the decision maker works. Annual conditions, such as soil moisture before planting, could materially alter the choices the producer will make.

Lessening the negative effects of drought. A better understanding of the effects of drought on decision making and society is, of course, desirable. A more compelling goal is to develop mechanisms that will reduce the negative consequences of drought, when it occurs. Three types of mechanisms come to mind: (1) new technologies that are less susceptible to adverse weather, (2) societal policies, and (3) new management practices. The decision-making framework is quite helpful in identifying how such mechanisms could assist society.

Focus on climate/human system interaction. The framework shown in Fig. 1 concentrates on drought's impact on a particular aspect of society. This framework explicitly identifies the complexity of the interrelations of human systems and the range of climate events possible. In this agricultural setting the decision maker is continually responding to the effects of previous, current, and future weather events. Drought obviously is of major importance and occupies part of the manager's attention with respect to climatic events. It is not, however, the only event possible or under consideration by the manager. Understanding the decision maker's perspective relative to drought, therefore, requires a broader perspective than is possible if we only evaluate climate/human system interactions when droughts have occurred.

An interesting extension of this broader focus is the impact of society's reactions to drought, as well as the drought itself, on the decision maker. The human suffering associated with prolonged drought can be extensive. In addition, those effects are often vivid and can be described visually. Given the availability of modern television communications, news media find that the effects of drought are easily transmitted to their audiences.

Publics have responded to these vivid and visual reports of suffering. A natural reaction in such situations is to attempt to reduce that suffering. In this decade the sequence just described has occurred in the African Sahel drought and in the 1986 drought in the southeastern United States. In the first case, worldwide actions were implemented to deliver relief aid. In the second, feedstuffs have been delivered to maintain cattle herds.

Such humanitarian actions undoubtedly reduced the immediate suffering of those afflicted. The decision-maker framework, however, allows us to identify an additional effect of such actions. In Fig. 1, expectations are shown to be central to the decision-making process. Our expectations, or what Boulding (1985) referred to as images of the future, are also affected by those humanitarian actions. An implication of these altered expectations is that it is now plausible for the individual decision maker to choose to maintain a smaller internal reserve of food, feedstuffs, or cash. This comment is not meant to imply that humanitarian relief actions should not occur. Instead, the decision-making perspective does alert us to the natural human reaction to expect such actions to occur if similar conditions reappear in the future.

Expanding the Analysis

The previous discussion considered a commercial agricultural situation. This situation is, of course, not representative of much of the world's agriculture. In subsistence agricultures, at least two additional factors must be considered: a typically more diverse pattern of production and the need to explicitly include consumption within the decision framework (Jodha and Mascarenhas, 1985; Spitz, 1980). Fortunately it is possible to expand the decision framework to consider subsistence agriculture.

In the commercial agricultural setting, financial reserves play a major role in mitigating the potential effects of drought. In subsistence agricultures, financial reserves are not available and physical reserves must be used. These reserves are in the form of both livestock and crop inventories. The rate at which the reserves are depleted is an important consideration for decision makers. The cost of depleting reserves too rapidly is severe. In addition to serving as food reserves, grain inventories also are often the seed stock for future crops. However, there are also costs associated with maintaining reserves that are too large.

Of course, all important decisions are not made by private decision makers. Public sector managers have critical choices to make that can affect society's adaptability to drought. The decision-making framework previously considered can be altered to accommodate this setting as well. Many of the decision features are relevant for both private and public sector managers. The role of expectations and uncertainty exists in both cases. Each manager has numerous institutional and physical constraints. A major distinction between the two is likely to be the means by which good or bad decisions are graded. The private decision maker measures outcomes in terms of changes in income or revenues. Less direct measures influence the public sector manager. Although the actions of the public sector manager can have major influences on society's adaptability to drought, the personal income of the manager may not be directly affected. Often political processes are involved. In such circumstances, the attributes of a good decision may have different characteristics than those of a private-sector decision.

THOUGHTS FOR THE RESEARCH COMMUNITY

The following remarks will extend the implications just noted. First, a brief review of an integrated modeling approach to decision analysis will be provided. Then implications of using such an approach will be discussed. The use of models is suggested as an extension of the body of work related to drought's impacts. It is not suggested as a complete substitute for more traditional forms of analysis.

Integrated Models for Assessing Drought's Impact

The decision framework of Fig. 1 represents a useful conceptual underpinning for application of quantitative models to the analysis of drought's impacts on society. As we think of the problem setting depicted in Fig. 1, it is apparent that several dimensions are identified (Warrick and Riebsame, 1983). One of the dimensions is the types of processes identified. These range from microphysical processes to macroeconomic linkages. The relevant geographic scale similarly varies from a subunit of the farm to the larger economic region and, by implication, to the world. Although necessary, the conceptual framework needs to be made operational if further gains in understanding are to be realized. I would propose that we need to develop linked quantitative models of the several processes involved to achieve that operational state. Figure 3 lists the three

362

Physical _____ Physiological, plant
processes   growth simulations

Firm _____ Stochastic, adaptive
decisions   decision models

Market _____ Economic models of
forces   supply and demand

Fig. 3 Types of integrated models needed to conduct an economic analysis of drought and society.

types of models and associated processes that could be used to begin to attack this problem for the agricultural example.

Plant-growth models for the relevant crops would be the first component of the three tiers of models needed. Assuming a regional study area, results of these physical models would be required for several locations within the area. These locations should include central as well as marginal areas. Inclusion of marginal regions would allow identification of the important shifts among enterprises in such areas (Parry, 1985). Data, modeling, and resource constraints will determine the number of locations that could be addressed in each specific research effort.

Physical models in themselves cannot completely capture the time and variability influences of drought. The effect of the decision maker, including the whole array of constraints, expectations, and attitudes, must be included. Dynamic modeling techniques, considering the sequential nature of decision making, are required (Katz, et. al., 1982; Winkler, et. al., 1983). These firm-level models could be used to evaluate new technologies, alternative management practices, and societal policies. An important point is that an integrative modeling approach can be used to perform *ex ante* evaluations of these mechanisms. Several research teams have successfully developed linked bioeconomic models relating to agricultural situations (Ahmed, et al., 1976; Boggess, 1984). Included among these are efforts relating to climate and society (Sonka, et al., 1986; Mjelde, et al., 1986).

Effects of drought and potential adaptations to drought are not limited to the individual firm, however. Linkages to regional market economies will markedly effect the desirability of alternative mechanisms. Therefore the modeling system must include a market-level analytical capability. Such a macromodel could exist at different ranges of aggregation, from regional to national or international levels. At whatever level, this model should incorporate effects of exogenous forces outside the study area, such as population changes and production in other regions. Efforts to link microprocess and regional models have not been successful in general. Liverman (1983) notes the poor performance of large-scale, global models in responding to climate fluctuations. Possibly this results because of the lack of microlevel and firm-level processes in those models.

Perceived Advantages

Calling for improved quantitative models can be a simplistic and naive response to a problem. Hopefully that is not true in this case. In the following paragraphs, a number of reasons for this proposal are advanced.

Responding to decision makers' needs. Chen (1983) has noted that social science research should address the question of "so what." The "so what" related to drought is discovering and evaluating mechanisms to reduce the adverse consequences of drought. Casting those efforts in the context of public and private decision makers should allow researchers to have a positive impact on that actual decision process.

An extremely important feature of an integrated modeling approach is that it can take a forward-looking as well as historic view. Identification of past mistakes is useful, but the decision maker by necessity often focuses on current and future events. The decision maker needs information that incorporates the entire range of climate events, rather than results that are optimal only if drought occurs (Lamb, et. al., 1985).

A major research unknown deserving further attention relates to the decision maker and the process by which the individual interweaves the potential for drought and other climate events into the decision-making process. De Vries (1985) asserts that an important research focus should be the process of decision making in a probabilistic framework. Given advances in both computational power and techniques of behavioral research, it is increasingly possible to delineate the climate-related information needs of individual producers (Fischoff and Furby, 1983).

Numerous researchers (e.g., Ausubel and Biswas, 1980; Garcia, 1981; Warrick, 1980) have proposed drought-related research agendas with the goal of improving societal well-being. Several common threads are interwoven in those agendas. Included among these are analysis of the direct effects of drought on specific sectors of society, vulnerability of alternative social structures, and assessment of the distribution of impacts. If we are to address such issues for the entire range of climate events, quantitative tools are more likely to be useful for separating the independent effects of climate.

Interdisciplinary analyses. Review of any set of climate-impact-related articles is likely to uncover the assertion that an interdisciplinary research approach is required before we can effectively evaluate climate impacts. Yet interdisciplinary efforts are notorious for being difficult and frustrating. In reviewing alternative methodologies, Swanson (1979) notes that modeling approaches are most likely to achieve effective integration of effort. This occurs because the needs of the model are specific and concrete. Therefore efforts to satisfy those needs tend to overcome the disciplinary biases of the various researchers. In essence, the model can become a neutral integrator of the expertise from several disciplines.

Need for coefficients. Nix (1985) suggests four major problems in the modeling of agroclimatic relationships. These are lack of basic understanding of underlying processes, inadequacies in climate data, unavailability of consistent data sets across different settings, and a heritage of descriptive and static analyses. Because integrated models as suggested here would be heavy demanders of coefficients, it may seem strange to list the need for coefficients as a perceived advantage.

On the positive side, modeling approaches make coefficient needs more explicit and clear-cut. In so doing, they tend to force researchers to focus their efforts on achieving more specific goals. The results often are advances in understanding of the underlying physical processes.

Coefficients are not the only factor required in order to develop complex models. Fortunately, computational advances are increasing our research capabilities and at the same time lowering costs. Conceptual modeling challenges abound in an effort to link models of different processes and geographic levels. A particular challenge would be to satisfactorily integrate individual firm-model results with a macromodeling capability.

Training and education. The potential exists to use models as well as research tools in training and educational settings. Such direct applications could be used to expand the images of decision makers with respect to climate (Lave and Epple, 1985) and in so doing improve the actual decision-making process. As noted previously, decisions made in years of normal or excessive rainfall often have major effects on the drought vulnerability of society. Conversion of research models to educational tools may help decision makers see a fuller range of outcomes from their decisions. A further benefit of the research community participating in such efforts could be the greater understanding gained by researchers of the cognitive processes actually used by individual citizens (Fischoff and Furby, 1983).

Integration of climate impact-related work. Analysis of climate's impact on the individual and society is typically categorized by topical areas such as drought, flooding, weather modification, forecasting, information provision, climate change, and climate impacts. Clearly, however, these issues do not represent independent phenomena. Yet it is often difficult to discern underlying common features from descriptive, historical analyses. If a linked modeling approach could be successfully implemented in a decision analytic framework, the potential exists to analyze behavior and climate impacts across the wider spectrum of potential climate events. These efforts, in conjunction with carefully conducted analyses of extreme events, would allow us to proceed more rapidly in understanding the broader implications of man's interaction with climate.

CONCLUDING REMARKS

The goal of this paper is to extend our thinking about research approaches focused on adaptation and adjustment to drought. Considerable excellent work has been completed by historically investigating extreme drought events. The approach proposed in this paper is suggested as a means to further the contributions of social and physical scientists in assessing alternative responses to drought.

A decision-making perspective is advanced as a framework for analysis of drought. This framework is illustrated for an agricultural situation, although the approach is applicable in a wide range of situations. Implementation of this approach can be achieved through the use of quantitative models. The concept of linking models of physical and economic processes over different levels of aggregation is proposed.

Implementing the concepts advanced will require considerable effort and ingenuity in specific situations. The payoff from successful efforts, however, can be substantial. Included as potential advantages are the following factors:

1. Improved societal responses to drought depend on actions of decision makers; therefore, the viewpoint of decision making is a natural perspective to generate useful investigations.

2. The decision-making perspective allows evaluation of mechanisms to reduce societal drought vulnerability over the entire range of possible weather events.

3. The uncertainty associated with climate variability can be identified explicitly.

4. The interaction of climate and nonclimate factors (such as economics, individual behavior, and physical constraints) in affecting drought-related decision making can be assessed.

5. The interdisciplinary, problem-oriented nature of drought can be effectively accommodated using quantitative models in a decision analytic framework.

REFERENCES

Ahmed, J.; C. H. M. van Bard ; and E. A. Hiler. 1976. Optimization of crop irrigation strategy under a stochastic weather regime: A simulation strategy. Water Resour. Res. 12:1241-1247.

Ausubel, J.; and A. K. Biswas. 1980. Introduction and overview. pp. 1-12. In J. Ausubel and A. K. Biswas, eds. Climatic Constraints and Human Activities. Pergamon Press, New York.

Boggess, W. A. 1984. Discussion: Use of bioeconomic simulations in production economics. South. J. Agric. Econ. 16:87-89.

Boulding, K. E. Human Betterment. 1985. Sage Publications, Beverly Hills.

Chen, R. S. 1983. Research in climate change and society. pp. 1-2. In R. S. Chen, E. Boulding, and S. H. Schneider, eds. Social Science Research and Climate Change. D. Reidel Publishing Company, Boston.

de Vries, Jan. 1985. Analysis of historical climate-society interaction. pp. 273-294. In R. W. Kates, J. H. Ausubel, and M. Berberian, eds. Climate Impact Assessment. John Wiley and Sons, New York.

Faure, H.; and J. Y. Gac. 1981. Will the Sahelian drought end in 1985? Nature 291:475-478.

Fischhoff, B.; and L. Furby. 1983. Psychological dimensions of climatic change. pp. 180-207. In R. S. Chen, E. Boulding, and S. H. Schneider, eds. Social Science Research and Climate Change. D. Reidel Publishing Company, Boston.

Garcia, R. V. 1981. Drought and Man: The 1972 Case History. Vol. 1. Pergamon Press, New York.

Heathcote, R. L. 1973. Drought perception. pp. 17-40. In J. V. Lovett, ed. Drought. Angus and Robertson, Sydney, Australia.

Heathcote, R. L. 1985. Extreme event analysis. pp. 369-402. In R. W. Kates, J. H. Ausubel, and M. Berberian, eds. Climate Impact Assessment. John Wiley and Sons, New York.

Hill, M. K. 1973. Farm management for drought mitigation. pp. 195-219. In J. V. Lovett, ed. Drought. Angus and Robertson, Sydney, Australia.

Jodha, N. S.; and A. C. Mascarenhas. 1985. Adjustment in self-provisioning societies. pp. 437-468. In R. W. Kates, J. H. Ausubel, and M. Berberian, eds. Climate Impact Assessment. John Wiley and Sons, New York.

Kahneman, D.; and A. Tversky. 1982. The psychology of preferences. Sci. Am. 246:160-174.

Kates, R. W. 1985. The interaction of climate and society. pp. 3-36. In R. W. Kates, J. H. Ausubel, and M. Berberian, eds. Climate Impact Assessment. John Wiley and Sons, New York.

Katz, R. W.; A. H. Murphy; and R. L. Winkler. 1982. Assessing the value of frost forecasts to orchardists: A dynamic decision making approach. J. Appl. Meteorol. 21:518-531.

Lamb, P. J.; S. T. Sonka; and S. A. Changnon, Jr. 1985. Use of climate information by the U.S. agribusiness. National Oceanic and Atmospheric Administration Technical Report NCPO 001. Washington, D.C.

Lave, L. B.; and D. Epple. 1985. Scenario analysis. pp. 511-528. In R. W. Kates, J. H. Ausubel, and M. Berberian, eds. Climate Impact Assessment. John Wiley and Sons, New York.

Liverman, D. M. 1983. The use of a simulation model in assessing the impacts of climate on the world food system. Ph.D. dissertation, University of California, Los Angeles.

Lovell, C.; A. Knox; and V. K. Smith. 1985. Microeconomic analysis. pp. 293-322. In R. W. Kates, J. H. Ausubel, and M. Berberian, eds. Climate Impact Assessment. John Wiley and Sons, New York.

Maunder, W. J.; and J. H. Ausubel. 1985. Identifying climate sensitivity. pp. 85-104. In R. W. Kates, J. H. Ausubel, and M. Berberian, eds. Climate Impact Assessment. John Wiley and Sons, New York.

Mjelde, J. W. 1985. Dynamic programming model of the corn production decision process with stochastic climate forecasts. Ph.D. dissertation, University of Illinois at Urbana-Champaign.

Mjelde, J. W.; S. T. Sonka; B. L. Dixon; and P. J. Lamb. 1986. Integration of dynamic programming and simulation models to value lead time of information forecasting schemes. Department of Agricultural Economics Staff Paper DIR 86-1 SP-4, Texas A & M University, College Station.

Nix, H. A. 1985. Agriculture. pp. 105-130. In R. W. Kates, J. H. Ausubel, and M. Berberian, eds. Climate Impact Assessment. John Wiley and Sons, New York.

Parry, M. L. 1985. The impact of climatic variations on agricultural margins. pp. 351-368. In R. W. Kates, J. H. Ausubel, and M. Berberian, eds. Climate Impact Assessment. John Wiley and Sons, New York.

Riebsame, W. E. 1985. Research in climate-society interaction. pp. 69-84. In R. W. Kates, J. H. Ausubel, and M. Berberian, eds. Climate Impact Assessment. John Wiley and Sons, New York.

Sonka, S. T.; P. J. Lamb; S. E. Hollinger; and J. W. Mjelde. 1986. The economic use of weather and climate information: Concepts and an agricultural example. J. Clim. 6:447-457.

Spitz, P. 1980. Drought and self-provisioning. pp. 125-147. In J. Ausubel and A. K. Biswas, eds. Climatic Constraints and Human Activities. Pergamon Press, New York.

Swanson, E. R. 1979. Working with other disciplines. Am. J. Agric. Econ. 61:849.

Van de Ven, A. H. 1985. Central problems in the management of innovation. Strategic Management Research Center Paper #21, University of Minnesota, St. Paul.

Warrick, R. A. 1980. Drought in the Great Plains: A case study of research on climate and society in the USA. pp. 93-123. In J. Ausubel and A. K. Biswas, eds. Climatic Constraints and Human Activities. Pergamon Press, New York.

Warrick, R. A.; and W. E. Riebsame. 1983. Societal response to CO_2-induced climate change: Opportunities for research. pp. 20-61. In R. S. Chen, E. Boulding, and S. H. Schneider, eds. Social Science Research and Climate Change. D. Reidel Publishing Company, Boston.

Winkler, R. L.; A. H. Murphy; and R. W. Katz. 1983. The value of climatic information: A decision-analytic approach. J. Clim. 3:187.

Worster, D. 1979. Dust Bowl. Oxford University Press, New York.

CHAPTER 22
ADAPTATION AND ADJUSTMENTS IN DROUGHT-PRONE AREAS: AN OVERVIEW—SOUTH AUSTRALIAN STUDY

R. J. French

INTRODUCTION

Australia is a country of about 7.7 million km^2, situated between latitudes 10° and 43° S. It has a population of almost 16 million people. The Australian environment ranges from the tropics to deserts to a Mediterranean type of climate in the southern areas. The major part of Australia consists of arid rangelands in the center of the continent. These occupy 74% of the area and have only 3% of the country's population. Most of the agricultural production comes from within 150 km of the coastline, and agriculture contributes about 45% of the country's export earnings.

Australia is frequently affected by droughts. The early explorers recorded such events, and later poets incorporated the impact of droughts on the communities into the folklore.

> The crops are done, the chorus ran
> Its keeping dry no doubt.
> We'll all be rooned [ruined], said Hanrahan
> Before the year is out
> "John O'Brien"

The effects of droughts were worse when they coincided with economic depressions. Although in most years there is a drought somewhere, it is not often that more than 40% of Australia is affected by drought at the same time.

In general, technology and farming practices have reduced the impact of drought, and many farmers are learning to cope much better. Wheat yields and livestock numbers do not decline as much now in drought years as they did thirty to forty years ago. The loss in rural production in a drought year is only a small percentage of the domestic product. That loss has changed little from the 2-3% recorded nearly twenty years ago (McIntyre, 1973). Nevertheless, in some states or regions the effects of drought can be particularly devastating from time to time and drought relief policies must be implemented. In the past there has been little planning, and drought management has largely been a reaction to a crisis. Nowadays there is a greater coordination between the federal and state governments on drought policies, a feature commented on favorably by Wilhite, et al. (1985). Drought is one of the declared natural disasters, and policies are being developed under the guidance of the National Drought Consultative

Committee. In the past eight years, about A$940 million has been provided for drought relief in Australia by the combined governments from a total national disasters outlay of A$1.7 billion. In South Australia, drought payments have been A$96 million, from a total disaster outlay figure of A$129 million.

In general, droughts in Australia mean low crop yields, little feed for livestock, shortage of water on some farms, land degradation, and no money for farmers and associated agribusiness. There is no shortage of food for the people, since this can be brought in, and these days the big cities are not greatly affected by a shortage of water. In fact, most city people enjoy the warmer winter weather of a drought year.

Although droughts have been a feature of the country since settlement, they still tend to be regarded as an unfortunate event and not as a permanent part of the Australian climate (Heathcote, 1969). "It had better not be a drought this year; I can't afford it" is not an uncommon sentiment.

DROUGHT IN SOUTH AUSTRALIA

Australia is made up of seven states; one of these is South Australia, in the south central part of the continent. South Australia occupies about 13% of the continent. About 83% of the area is arid rangelands with less than 250 mm of annual rainfall; this area has 800 landholders. Some 14% of the land, with rainfall between 250 mm and 500 mm, is used for mixed cereal-livestock farming and has 12,000 landholders. Another 3% has rainfall of more than 500 mm and is used for pastures and livestock by its 5,000 landholders. South Australia is often called the driest state in the driest continent, and one of its features is that as the rainfall gets lower, the variability increases. Droughts in South Australia do not always coincide with droughts in the other states.

Following settlement in 1836, land development rushed northward to the margins of the arid lands on the catch phrase, "Rain follows the plow." A severe drought in 1865 led to an investigation by the surveyor general, Goyder, who defined a line beyond which farming was considered too risky. This line still has some relevance today. Subsequent droughts led to three southward retractions of the areas sown to wheat. Abandoned wheat farms were repurchased by a government scheme and the land was returned to arid rangelands grazing.

The effect of a recent drought on the South Australian economy can be gauged from the value of the agricultural production listed in Table 1. Here the values are compared for three successive years, with a drought in the middle year.

The rainfall in the drought year was only 57% of that in the previous average year. The value of the total agricultural production was 83% of the previous year, but the value of the cereal production was only 58%. Wheat yields were only 42% of the previous year, while sheep numbers were 92%. There were only small reductions in the value of the fruit production, mainly because much of it is under irrigation.

The year following the drought was marked by a big increase in the returns from cropping, due to a high yield and an increase in the area of cropping: a common practice of farmers in South Australia is to crop their way out of the drought.

The effects of drought in the different parts of the state are more variable and are shown in Table 2. In general, the numbers of sheep were maintained over this one-year drought, but this has not always been the case. Wheat yields vary in the districts

Table 1
Value of Agricultural Production in South Australia

	1981 Average Year	1982 Drought Year	1983 Good Year
Average annual Rainfall[a] (mm)	382	218	407
	(in millions of dollars)		
Crop - wheat	265	121	466
barley	174	98	273
other	97	91	132
	536	310	871
Fruit - grapes	72	58	73
citrus	36	34	38
vegetables	75	62	92
other	42	41	44
	225	195	247
Livestock - slaughtering	331	336	275
products	338	352	390
	669	688	665
Total Value	1430	1193	1783
Wheat sown (m.ha)	1.43	1.40	1.56
yield (t.ha)	1.19	0.50	1.82
Sheep numbers (million)	16.71	15.45	16.37

[a] = values derived from averaging rainfalls in different regions

Table 2
Examples of Yields of Wheat and Livestock Numbers in Different Areas

		1981	1982	1983
Arid rangelands -	rainfall (mm)	237	112	167
	sheep (M)[a]	1.6	1.4	1.5
Central Livestock Districts				
Murraylands -	rainfall (mm)	350	169	438
	wheat (t.ha^{-1})	0.97	0.25	1.39
	sheep (M)	2.2	2.0	2.2
Eyre -	rainfall (mm)	360	222	403
	wheat (t.ha^{-1})	0.98	0.42	1.57
	sheep (M)	2.5	2.4	2.5
Central -	rainfall (mm)	412	261	473
	wheat (t.ha^{-1})	1.61	1.45	2.44
	sheep (M)	5.6	5.2	5.3
High rainfall				
South East -	rainfall (mm)	630	365	660
	wheat (t.ha^{-1})	1.77	0.90	2.23
	sheep (M)	4.7	4.6	4.8

[a]M = million

from 26% to 90% of the yield of the previous year. These variations in the effect of drought on different farming industries in different districts serves to highlight the difficulty of defining a drought and implementing drought relief policies.

Thus there can be an agricultural drought when there is insufficient rain to grow crops and pastures in their normal growing season; there can be a hydrological drought when there is insufficient rain to cause runoff in the catchments of reservoirs; or there can be a meteorological drought (e.g., no rain) over a summer period which has little effect on crops and pastures but may seriously affect vines and fruit trees in the same district. It is for these reasons and because of the variation in rainfall over short distances that whenever a drought declaration is made in South Australia, the whole of the state is included.

APPROACH TO DROUGHT MANAGEMENT

Drought management has many different aspects. These include research into understanding the causes of drought, prediction and statistical probability, survival, lack of feed, land degradation, and shortage of finance. Another essential part of the equation is the farmer, and the effects of drought on the landscape, for better or worse, depend on his skills and resources.

This case study deals with the effects of an agricultural drought on mixed cereal-livestock farms of 500-1,500 ha in areas of 250-500 mm annual rainfall. In the past, farmers have survived droughts by rugged stoicism, but today many more variables are involved. The farmer is concerned not only with variable rainfall but also with variable costs on and off the farm, and variable prices and interest rates. He is involved in the management of uncertainty, for the effects of drought are no longer overcome with a rainfall of 50 mm. This paper deals with the interaction between scientists and farmers in the technical and social responses to drought.

UNDERSTANDING THE CLIMATE AND WEATHER PATTERNS IN SOUTH AUSTRALIA

Drought Frequency

Droughts are a normal part of the climate of South Australia, and it is important to have a record of their frequency. The rainfall patterns over the years can be classified according to the decile system (Gibbs and Maher, 1967). In this system, the probability of an amount of rain in any month, group of months, or year is evaluated from past records. In Table 3, the rainfall for the decile rankings are shown for the town of Kimba, in the cereal district. Thus a yearly rainfall of 391 mm is rated as decile 7; that is, in seven years out of ten, the rainfall will be equal to or less than this amount. A seasonal drought is said to occur when the rainfall is in decile 1 for three or more consecutive months. A drought year occurs when the rainfall for the year is in decile 1 and occasionally in decile 2. In Fig. 1, the distribution of annual rainfall for Georgetown is shown, with drought years identified by rainfall less than decile 2.

Patterns of Yearly Rainfall

Although it is generally not possible to predict the onset or frequency of drought, there is some evidence to suggest that patterns of rainfall do occur. One means of identifying such patterns is to calculate the residual mass and the cumulative sum of the deviations of the monthly rainfall from the long-term monthly mean (Russell, 1981). These calculations can identify groups of years with positive and negative accumulations of rainfall. Thus in Fig. 2 the December values of the cumulative sum of the rainfall deviations from the monthly mean are shown for each year since 1874. Gains and decreases can be seen over various groups of years. For the years 1903-26, the average annual rainfall was 510 mm; for the years 1927-45, it was 407 mm. For 1946-56, the

Table 3
Decile Values of Rainfall for Kimba for Each Month of the Year and for Combinations of Months During the April to October Growing Season

Kimba

Rainfall Deciles (millimeters)
Calculated for 1920 - 1985

Months

	J	F	M	A	M	J	J	A	S	O	N	D	Year
Highest on record	141	163	77	104	113	130	128	95	138	117	135	97	582
Decile 9	35	59	44	51	73	73	70	72	71	73	49	38	518
8	28	38	29	43	59	58	55	60	55	53	39	30	426
7	21	26	21	35	48	48	49	55	45	35	29	21	391
6	12	20	16	24	37	39	42	46	38	28	23	17	365
5	9	13	9	19	28	34	37	42	32	22	19	14	338
4	6	9	6	14	25	27	34	39	27	19	14	10	302
3	2	2	3	10	17	21	29	33	19	13	11	7	289
2	1	1	1	4	12	18	22	21	14	8	6	4	251
1	0	0	0	2	6	10	19	16	7	6	1	1	209
Lowest on record	0	0	0	0	3	1	9	6	4	0	0	0	176
Average	16	22	16	24	36	38	41	43	36	31	23	18	345

Combinations of Groups of Months

	Apr -Oct	May -Oct	Apr -May	Jun -Oct	A-M -J	July -Oct	A-M -J-J	Aug -Oct	AMJ JA	Sep -Oct	AMJ JAS	Oct	Apr -Oct
Highest on record	104	451	163	362	228	279	344	220	383	164	443	117	495
Decile 9	51	340	114	266	173	227	218	171	263	129	331	73	364
8	43		92		141		192		236		286		317
7	35		78		122		157		210		249		281
6	24		64		106		141		186		233		266
5	19	222	50	188	83	138	129	107	177	58	207	22	250
4	14		41		74		112		158		189		223
3	10		31		63		102		148		172		204
2	4		28		53		86		124		153		186
1	2	135	17	121	36	94	71	57	99	21	120	6	145
Lowest on record	0	87	4	80	12	38	41	28	65	11	77	0	87
Average	24	225	60	189	98	150	139	109	182	67	219	31	250

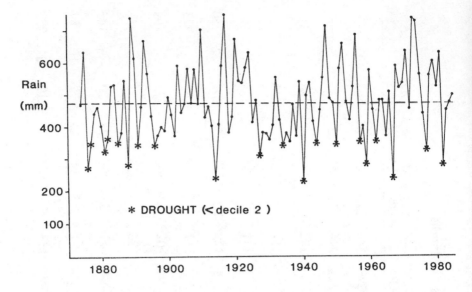

Fig. 1 The annual rainfall for Georgetown in the cereal districts of north central South Australia, showing the fluctuations about the long-term average and the frequency of drought years.

average was 536 mm; the years 1957-67 show an average of 407 mm; and the years 1968-81 have an average of 559 mm. The trends can be related to water supply, yield of wheat, and stock numbers in these periods.

Use of Deciles in Predicting the Nature of the Growing Season

Drought has been described as a "creeping phenomenon," and thus the development of any growing season is always somewhat uncertain. The decile approach enables us to progressively update the probability of rain during the growing season. Thus in the lower half of Table 3, the actual rainfall for April can be added separately to three probabilities of rainfall—namely, deciles 9, 5, and 1 for the remaining months (May-October) of the growing season—and the totals can be compared with the April to October values. This gives a first set of estimates of rainfall in the growing season.

At the end of May, the combined rainfall for April and May is added to the rainfall deciles 9, 5, and 1 for the months June through October. This process is repeated at the end of each month, using the actual rainfall for that month and the probabilities of rainfall for the remaining months of the growing season. In Fig. 3, the three updated rainfall probabilities for Kimba are plotted at the end of each month, and they indicate a clear trend of what the outcome of the seasonal rainfall will be.

This updated rainfall data can also be used in growth models to predict crop and pasture yields and to assist in decisions such as whether to buy new machinery or to sell livestock. In Fig. 4, the trend in the estimate of wheat yield, calculated from a simple

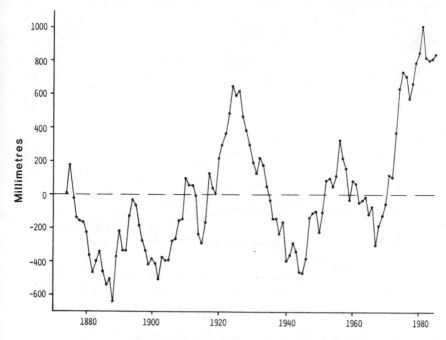

Fig. 2 The cumulative sum of the deviations of the monthly rainfall from the long-term mean for each month for Georgetown. The point for each year is the December value.

growth model that uses the rainfall data together with day-degrees of temperature, crop phenology, and evaporation during the growing season, identifies the approximate harvested yield.

IMPROVING THE WATER USE EFFICIENCY

In recent years an increasing emphasis has been given to research and extension programs that aim to make crops and pastures more productive per unit of water use. Some of the research programs we are carrying out in this area are:

1. Defining the potential yield. Field measurements of water use by wheat crops, taken over many years, have led to the formulation of a potential yield model (Fig. 5). The research showed that, on average, 110 mm (4 in.) of rainfall is lost by direct evaporation from the soil and the plant, but the remaining water supply can produce 20 kg/ha grain per mm, equal to 2 1/2 gas per acre per inch (French and Schultz, 1984a, 1984b). Currently, however, the average district yield is only about half this potential for the water supply.
    The factors that gave increased yields and those that decreased yields are illustrated in the figure. Potential yield would rarely be reached through re-

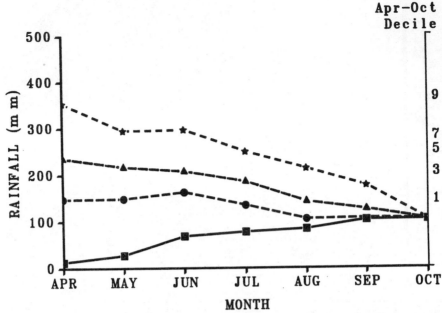

Fig. 3 A method for predicting the trend in rainfall during the growing season (April-October) at Kimba, South Australia. The actual rainfall to the end of each month is added separately to the rainfall for deciles 9, 5, and 1 for the remaining months of the growing season.

■ actual rain,   ★ actual rain + decile 9,   ▲ actual rain + decile 5,   ● actual rain + decile 1 for remaining months.

search on a single factor; the important need therefore is to conduct multifactor research and develop a technological package for farmers to adopt. Key issues in this package are healthy plant roots free from root diseases and weeds, early time of sowing, adequate nutrition (particularly nitrogen), minimum tillage, chemical fallow, and stubble mulching. The reduced tillage programs keep the soil covered longer, do not damage the soil structure, and enable a higher production per unit of water supply. The same principles should be applied to other crops and pastures if the most efficient production per unit of water supply is to be obtained.

2. The use of Landsat imagery and infrared photographs to detect changes in vegetation. Research in Landsat imagery is aimed at detecting changes in soil water and vegetation over large areas of land. Landsat can probably play a key role in the management of extensive grazing areas. However, low-level infrared photography of individual fields is now being used by farmers in cereals districts to detect variability in crop and pasture yields on their farms. These photos indicate where improved practices are necessary to overcome this variability and therefore give higher production.

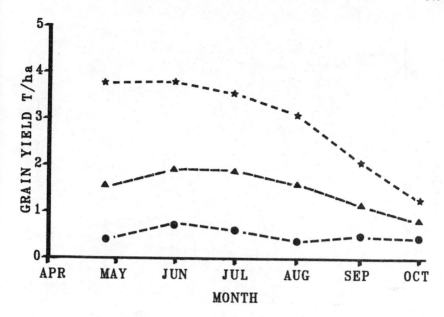

Fig. 4 The estimate of wheat yield, using a simple growth model and the updated rainfall estimates outlined in Fig. 3.

★ based on decile 9 rainfall, ▲ based on decile 5 rainfall, ● based on decile 1 rainfall.

3.   Contour farming. Water use efficiency can be improved by building contour banks (terraces) on land with slopes between 2% and 10% slope to prevent runoff. About 12,000 ha per year are treated in this way in South Australia. Most banking is now carried out in group conservation catchment schemes, each scheme involving twelve to fifteen farmers in projects that are supported financially under the National Soil Conservation Programme.

BUILDING RESERVES TO BUFFER THE EFFECTS OF DROUGHT

In Australia, there is no shortage of food for the population in a drought. Even if an area is severely affected, food can be transported in from other districts. The main crises in a drought are shortage of feed and water for livestock, degradation of land, and shortage of money for the landholders.

380

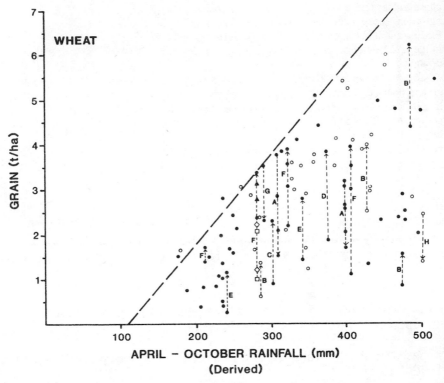

Fig. 5 The relation between grain yield of wheat and the estimate of water use. The black dots are results from experiments, the open circles from farmers' fields. Yield increases were obtained from the application of nitrogen (points linked by a B line), phosphorus (C line), copper (D line), control of eelworms (E line), and multifactors (F line). Yield decreased because of delayed time of sowing (A line), weeds (G line), and waterlogging (H line) (from French and Schultz, 1984b).

Fodder Supplies for Livestock

The three main agricultural divisions of South Australia—the arid rangeland, the crop-livestock farming area, and the high rainfall pasture zone—are linked by a reasonably good network of highways and railways. This enables feed to be transported to the livestock; livestock may also be transported to more favorable areas for agistment or to market.

In the arid rangelands where sheep are grazed at the rate of 13-18 per km[2] and there is no cropping, successful graziers either relocate livestock to the remaining dams with a water supply or bring in water. They do not mate their livestock, but may purchase fodder (preferably with the help of a fodder subsidy), sell off the older sheep, or agist their sheep on properties elsewhere. The latter is usually cheaper than maintenance feeding and it helps to prevent serious overgrazing of their property. In general, research in the arid lands has not given the landholders many new practical options to survive a drought.

In the crop-livestock farming areas where crop yields in a drought year are greatly reduced, farmers concentrate on livestock management, particularly on adjusting livestock numbers. Immediate objectives are to sell off surplus livestock; highest returns are obtained if the farmer has some predictive data about the way the season is developing, so that he can sell before the prices fall. The second objective is to try to retain the breeding flock, and a practice that is becoming more acceptable calls for farmers to store grain in small silos on the farm and feed this to their livestock, held in small paddocks or in feedlots.

Although some hay has to be conserved to balance the diet, farmers are now showing a preference for storing grain. Examples of the practices adopted by farmers are:

1. Storing one bushel of barley per head of sheep at harvest in December. If the following growing season (from April onward) is favorable, the grain can still be sold to the barley board at the end of winter.
2. Storing three bushels of oats per head for stud sheep.
3. Storing grain legumes, particularly lupins and vetch.
4. Transporting the screenings from wheat and barley harvesting to a factory where they are mixed with protein material and made into pellets.

In general, little conserved fodder is given to livestock until after the stubbles of the crops have been grazed. From then on the method of feeding varies. Some farmers feed hay and grain to the stock in the stubble paddock. However, because sheep graze paddocks unevenly, bare patches develop and erosion may occur. Other farmers spread a mixture of grain, such as lupins and barley, by means of a fertilizer spreader into the areas of the fields that still have good cover, and let the livestock look for it. A few restrict their sheep to parts of the field by means of mobile electric suspension fences that are solar powered. Several kilometers of these fences can be erected in a few hours.

A more recent development is for farmers to hold and feed sheep in small paddocks or feedlots. In the last major drought in South Australia, eighty farmers in one district on Eyre Peninsula alone hand-fed more than 50,000 sheep in small paddocks for up to eighteen weeks.

A number of steps are necessary to ensure the success of lot feeding (Ashton and Hannay, 1984). Ewes must be vaccinated against enterotoxaemia and drenched for worms. An ideal feed is 70% grain and 28% hay (e.g., 2 kg barley and 1 kg hay per head per week) together with 1% ground limestone and 1% salt. The hay should be fed before the grain and the feed should be provided daily for the first two to three weeks, then provided twice a week.

It is preferable to restrict the stocking to about 500 sheep in each feedlot of 3-6 ha and to remove those sheep that do poorly in a feedlot, as well as ewes that are not in lamb (determined by using the latest ultrasound technique). Deaths are not often in excess of 2% of the flock, and the cost of feeding varies from A$0.6 to A$1.2 per head per week.

In drought feeding, the nutrient most required is metabolizable energy (ME), which is influenced by the fiber content of the feed and the cost per unit of energy. Thus 1 kg of oats has an ME of 12, compared with 1 kg straw with an ME of 6. However, the energy can come from stored cereal or legume grain, baled pasture hay, or baled straw treated with urea and molasses. The relative costs of feed are determined by the cost per kg of feed divided by the ME per kg.

In Table 4, metabolizable energy and protein content of different fodders and wheat are compared. These comparisons enable calculations to be made of the materials available and their cost, and thereby help determine the best ration for the livestock. Information such as this forms the basis for a drought feeding calculator that indicates what mixtures of grain, hay, straw, molasses, and so forth can provide about 35 kg ME and 8-12% protein for a sheep for a week. Similar principles apply to the feeding of cattle, except that cattle need a higher percentage of hay in their feed.

Table 4
Energy and Protein Contents of Various Fodders Compared with Wheat

	No. of Kg to Give Metabolizable Energy Equivalent to 1 kg Wheat = 12.6 MJ	No. of Kg to Give Protein Content in 1 kg Wheat = 11.7%
Grain - wheat	1.00	1.00
- barley	1.02	1.08
- oats	1.21	1.19
- lupins	1.06	0.43
Molasses	1.33	3.70
Hay - oaten	1.43	1.44
- grass	1.38	1.00
- clover	1.40	0.87
- lucerne	1.43	0.57
Silage	4.34	15.20
Cereal straw	2.33	4.33

Calculations based on 90% dry matter for grain and hay, 70% dry matter for molasses, and 30% for silage.

Based on data of Cochrane, et al. (1983).

Improving the Water Supply for Livestock

Although many farmers in South Australia are connected to a government water pipeline, the need for additional water supplies in drought years on farms is common. Farmers often set aside an area of land above a dam as a source of runoff, and, in general, about 12% of the rainfall runs off into the dams. However, improved runoff occurs when the catchment is designed and graded into bays separated by undisturbed headlands. Up to 35% of the rain runs off into the dam. These "roaded" catchments have proved effective in increasing water supply in both agricultural and arid pastoral areas (personal communication from S. D. Moore).

Emergency Tillage

During a drought, the land often becomes bare and subject to erosion by wind and water. One emergency operation involves plowing this bare ground with single furrows up to 25 cm deep and 3-10 m apart, depending on soil type. The aim is to produce large clods to resist erosion.

Shortage of Money for Landholders

Farmers need to be innovative and develop approaches that enable them to survive financially during a drought and retain their assets. Some of the "practices" being used by enterprising farmers are:

1. Alternative sources of production that are less influenced by rainfall. Among the enterprises now operating on farms are intensive pig or poultry units, limited irrigation of special products such as freshly cut flowers, and tourist accommodation units. It is obvious that only a few of each of these enterprises are possible in any one district, but they do present options for enterprising farmers.
2. Purchasing land away from their normal farming environment. Included here are practices such as buying a part share in an irrigation block that adjoins dryland country or the purchase of a small block with irrigation in high rainfall areas. About half the leases in our arid rangelands have an interest in land elsewhere.
3. Off-farm investments. Again, this approach is mainly used by the innovators. It includes part-time employment in a nearby town for the husband or wife, investment in a block of flats in the cities, or investments in shares and government bonds. A number of farmers have sufficient investments off-farm to provide funds for the seed, fertilizer, and fuel for sowing the next year's crop.

GOVERNMENT DROUGHT RELIEF MEASURES

In the past, governments have tended to react to the financial distress of landholders in a drought with hastily prepared assistance schemes. Governments prefer to be seen as coping with a calamity rather than developing long-term plans. However, many of these schemes have tended to distort the realities of drought; subsidies have more often gone to the imprudent farmers or have been given for specific practices such as seed or fertilizer rather than for total farm management.

Yet there is a general feeling that farmers need some help through a drought in order to protect the basic resources of land, soil, and livestock. Many farmers do not have funds of their own to do this in a drought year, as Table 5 illustrates. The table compares the cash operating surplus of funds (i.e., the money a farmer has to live on and use for income tax payments, loan repayments, and replacement of equipment). However, because of a skewed distribution, 60% of the farmers are below the average and therefore have few funds to be innovative or to change their established practices.

In Australia, national disasters are handled by arrangements established between the federal and state governments. Drought is included in this general area, and drought policy is set by the National Drought Consultative Committee. Funds are provided under separate acts for drought relief and for general adjustments to farming properties. With drought, each state government has to first provide an initial financial threshold for drought relief (in South Australia, this has risen from A$3 million in 1978-79 to A$7 million in 1986) and then the remaining costs are shared in a ratio of 1:3 between the states and the federal government.

The funding policies vary between states, but in South Australia, drought funding is associated with general funds for rural assistance. The main aim is to help a farmer stay viable by allowing him to use money in a way that suits his farming system rather than to allocate funds for specific inputs such as fertilizer, seed, and so forth.

Features of our drought relief funding are:

1. Declaration of drought. Drought declaration procedures vary between states. In some states, declarations are made on the basis of specific Pastoral Districts, and drought is declared when half the crops are failing or half the livestock is threatened. But in South Australia, drought is declared

Table 5
Surplus Funds on Farms in a Drought Year (1982-83) and in the Following Good Year (1983-84)

	1982-83 $	1983-84 $
Top 25% farmers	27,270	72,160
Average farmers	20,150	60,550
Bottom 25% farmers	390	22,900

on a statewide basis, following the recommendation of an advisory committee.

2. Eligibility for drought relief. The criteria have changed over the years. Eligible farmers are those who earn 50% of their income from primary production and have the capacity to remain viable over the next five years. A farmer is required to provide data on his cropping and livestock programs, costs, yields, returns, and expenditures for the last three years, and a list of debts verified by a bank manager.

3. Method of funding. The main form of drought relief funding is the carry-on loan, which provides a successful applicant with up to $50,000 at a concessional rate of interest of 8% per annum for up to ten years, subject to regular review.

   In the 1977-78 drought, 227 of the 1,445 applicants for carry-on loans were rejected either because they could not show viability or because they still had sufficient cash or credit on hand. In the 1982 drought, about 2,000 of the state's 18,000 commercial farmers sought drought relief, and 1,600 were granted funding. Currently, 600 of these farmers have repaid their loans following the introduction of an interest incentive scheme for early repayment. In addition, because of the economic difficulty, another 2,000 farmers (equal to 60% of applicants) have been granted funding from the Rural Assistance Branch.

4. Specific subsidies for the transport of fodder, water, and livestock to and from agistment. In general, the provision of these subsidies varies with the decision of the government at the time. They have ranged from a 50% subsidy for the purchase of fodder to a 75% subsidy of the transport cost. Some claim that these subsidies distort the reality of the drought, allowing livestock to be retained on the property and degrading the land. Others claim that the cost of feeding sheep from subsidized fodder is no more than the cash return from the wool, and it preserves the national flock. The scheme has a high administrative cost because it involves large numbers of small subsidies. In 1982-83, only 6% of the total drought relief was allocated to transport subsidies.

   In some droughts, a livestock slaughter subsidy has been provided to dispose of stock that cannot be sent to markets or agisted on other areas. The subsidy was given because of a potential public health risk and an increased erosion hazard. The amount was $10 a head for cattle and $1 a head to the local government authority to help dispose of carcasses.

5. Household support. When a farmer has been refused a carry-on loan because of his nonviability, assistance can be given to the household for one to three years at the level of the community unemployment benefits.

6. Drought bonds and income equilisation deposits. These have been introduced at times by government and then withdrawn. The aim was to encourage farmers to invest in the bonds with surplus funds earned in the good years.

   Drought bonds were not widely used because they were restricted to grazing industries and only paid low rates of interest. They were replaced in 1976 by Income Equilisation Deposits, in which the deposits made by farmers were deductible from income tax in the year of deposit, but were taxed when withdrawn. This approach was accepted by many farmers, for in the 1982-83 drought, some 475 farmers withdrew an average of $8,500 in the first six months, while 1,200 still possessed deposits averaging $13,300. However, changes to the tax averaging system increased the risk of farmers having to pay more tax. Farmers now prefer to invest directly in the money market, although attempts are being made to restore the deposits on more equitable terms.

7. Specific funds to local government authorities. In some districts, particularly those with sandy soils that drift readily in drought years, funds have been provided to the authorities to clear away the drift and keep the district roads open.

In general, it is recognized that the carry-on loans are the best form of drought relief. They cause less distortion about the reality of drought and provide money to keep farmers viable. This in turn supports agribusiness, helps to preserve the viability of the local town, and reduces the size of the rural social problem. However, there is a tendency for some farmers to regard these loans as a permanent form of assistance, for there is a high recurrence of applicants with each drought.

It is now recognized that an additional service that could be provided to farmers affected by drought is a personal counseling service to help them choose a new direction and to help them retain their dignity.

Not all the effects of drought are negative, however. People who derive benefits from drought are city housewives with cheaper meat, transport firms involved in shifting fodder and livestock, and tourist organizations. Often there is also a lower incidence of pests and diseases.

FUTURE DROUGHT ASSISTANCE

Two things are certain: the climatic pattern will continue to produce droughts, and the government will provide some sort of assistance in the next drought in spite of the rhetoric from economists that such funds distort the allocation of resources between the rural sector and the rest of the economy. It is probable that the criteria for eligibility will vary, for members of drought planning conferences have difficulty in making firm policy recommendations. However, the overall aim should be to lessen the impact of a drought on the people, particularly farm families, and on the livestock and land resources. To this end, our Department of Agriculture has formed the Rural Assistance Branch, which has the dual role of approving loans to farmers to help them maintain viability and allocating specific funds as drought relief measures. The aim is to assist farmers, through research and extension, in developing strategies and new resources so that they can handle the next drought. The strategies should include a study of the variability of the weather patterns, the need for funds for resowing after the drought, the need to maintain breeding herds and land resources, and the need to provide a reasonable living standard.

Key features in such a strategy are:

1. Education programs for landholders. Farmers have a much greater need for educational courses today than previously. Farming is no longer a way

of life; it is a technical and economic business. Courses are needed to help farmers understand weather patterns, farming technology and soil management systems, finance, and alternative investments off the farm. These educational programs should be supported by local boards, such as Land Management Boards, in which farmers with interests in soil conservation, land tenure, finance, and welfare are represented.

2. Predictions and growth modeling. One of the big deficiencies in agricultural research is the inability both to predict the probability of rainfall during the growing season and to estimate yield and economic returns of different crops. This is an area of modeling that should be developed, for on-farm weather boxes, which can be tied in with home computers, are now available.

Although simple models for determining crop yields, pasture production, and livestock numbers now exist, greater cooperation is needed between research officers, meteorologists, economists, and extension officers to develop and adopt models that can use the farm weather data during the growing season and progressively estimate the likely yield and economic return.

Farmers need to be able to compare this year's rainfall with that of other years, and to be able to ask "what if" questions of their computer to determine what crop will give the best economic return this year, or whether they should sell livestock or invest off the farm. Farmers also need to be able to estimate how productive their farming is in relation to potential yield models for the water supply.

3. Encourage practices that cut and store fodder and grain for livestock. Excess fodder is only available in some years, so storage capacity should be built to carry up to two years in reserves for the livestock.

4. Investment off farms. Farmers' returns are influenced not only by rainfall but also by costs and prices, which are influenced by the total world market. Farming is therefore an investment in a multifactor, fluctuating environment. It is increasingly necessary to invest funds off the farm to insulate the farmer from adverse rural economic cycles. The investments should rotate between properties and equities during periods of inflation and bonds and debentures during times of deflation.

5. Continuation of carry-on loans from government sources. This approach is now regarded as the most realistic way of helping farmers and country towns through droughts. It is important, however, that the conditions for such loans be clearly stated and known in advance of a drought. It is also argued that the interest rate should be the same as commercial interest rates.

6. Provision of a social welfare component. Social welfare services should be provided to give more equitable support to farmers and others in country towns affected by the drought. People should be given a chance to look for other opportunities without losing their dignity.

7. Prizes for innovative farming practices. In all drought relief programs, the funding tends to go to the farmers in trouble—there are no rewards for the prudent, efficient farmers who have knowledge and innovations to help them through a drought. The possibility of awarding annual prizes in a dis-

trict to the farmer who develops an efficient practical method for reducing the effects of drought should be considered.

8. Support programs should be developed to assist farmers in replanting trees and improving the aesthetics of the environment.

Overall, the policies, guidelines, and arguments for and against drought relief funding have changed little over the last twenty years. In general, the policies are based on a crisis management response. But drought must be seen as a normal part of the climate. Continuing programs need to be developed in all years to encourage the farmer to adopt practices that enable him to build resources to withstand the effects of drought and other weather hazards, such as floods and winds. Financial assistance will probably be available to farmers in future droughts, and it should be allocated, at commercial rates of interest, to farmers who are likely to remain viable.

Droughts generally have affected the farming community in the past, but there is increasing evidence that water supplies to cities and industries will be affected in future droughts, and this in turn could influence the amount of funds available for farmers.

ACKNOWLEDGMENTS

The author wishes to thank Mr. B. Handscombe and Mr. T. Newberry of the Department of Agriculture for their comments on this paper, and acknowledges the contributions from numerous farmers in South Australia.

REFERENCES

Ashton, B. L.; and J. N. Hannay. 1984. Lot feeding of sheep through the 1982 drought. Technical Report No. 67. Department of Agriculture South Australia.

Cochrane, M.; B. Bartsch; and J. Valentine. 1983. Feed composition tables, Fact Sheet 29/83, Department of Agriculture, Adelaide.

French, R. J.; and J. E. Schultz. 1984a. Water use efficiency of wheat in a Mediterranean type environment. I. The relation between yields, water use and climate. Aust. J. Agric. Res. 35:743-64.

French, R. J.; and J. E. Schultz. 1984b. Water use efficiency of wheat in a Mediterranean type environment. II. Some limitations to efficiency. Aust. J. Agric. Res. 35:765-75.

Gibbs, W. J.; and J. V. Maher. 1967. Rainfall declines as drought indicators. Commonwealth Bureau of Meteorology Bulletin No. 48, Melbourne.

Heathcote, R. L. 1969. Drought in Australia: A problem of perception. Geogr. Rev. 59(2):175-194.

McIntyre, A. J. 1973. Effects of drought in the economy. pp. 181-192. In J. V. Lovett, ed. The Environmental, Economic and Social Significance of Drought. Angus and Robertson, Sydney.

Russell, J. S. 1981. Geographic variation in seasonal rainfall in Australia—An analysis of the 80 year period 1895-1974. J. Aust. Inst. Agric. Sci. 47:59-66.

Wilhite, D. A.; N. J. Rosenberg; and M. H. Glantz. 1985. Government response to drought in the United States: Lessons from the mid-1970s. Part 5. Drought response in the United States and Australia: A comparative analysis. CAMaC Progress Report 85-5. Center for Agricultural Meteorology and Climatology, University of Nebraska-Lincoln.

CHAPTER 23
TECHNOLOGICAL AND SOCIOPOLITICAL ADAPTATION AND
ADJUSTMENT TO DROUGHT: THE INDIAN EXPERIENCE

J. Venkateswarlu

INTRODUCTION

Drought indicates dryness or lack of rainfall or water. The National Commission on Agriculture (1976) classifies droughts as meteorological, hydrological, or agricultural. In a meteorological drought, a significant (more than 25%) decrease in normal precipitation occurs over an area. When this drought is prolonged, it becomes a hydrological drought, with marked depletion of surface water and subsequent drying of reservoirs, lakes, streams, and rivers; cessation of spring flows; and decreases in groundwater levels. Agricultural drought is said to occur when soil moisture and rainfall are inadequate for healthy crop growth during the growing season, leading to extreme crop stress and wilt. This results in reduced productivity or even total loss of crops.

Of the three types of drought, agricultural drought has the greatest consequences for drylands. In India, agricultural drought can occur anywhere, depending on the distribution of the rainfall. For instance, in 1972, rainfall was deficient in twenty-one out of thirty-five subdivisions; seventeen subdivisions experienced deficient rainfall in 1979.

Based on long-term rainfall data, the Indian Meteorological Department found higher variability with lower rainfall and considered more than 30% departure from normal as an index of drought. Sarkar (1979) identified the areas that are more subject to drought (Fig. 1). The World Bank (1974) reported that 60 million ha in about seventy-two districts were drought-prone, affecting more than 70 million people.

EFFECT OF DROUGHT

Effect on Food Grain Production

The overall effect of drought is a reduction in the productivity of dryland crops. Nageswara Rao and Manikiam (1985) noted that weather, primarily rainfall, is responsible for 50% of the variation in yield of crops. In fact, over the last two decades in India (with the advent of high-yielding varieties of crops), drought has led to a total reduction in the production of food grains (Fig. 2). The production increased from 95 million tons in 1967-68 to 152 million tons in 1983-84, with significant troughs during 1972 (97 million tons) and 1979 (110 million tons). In other words, although Indian

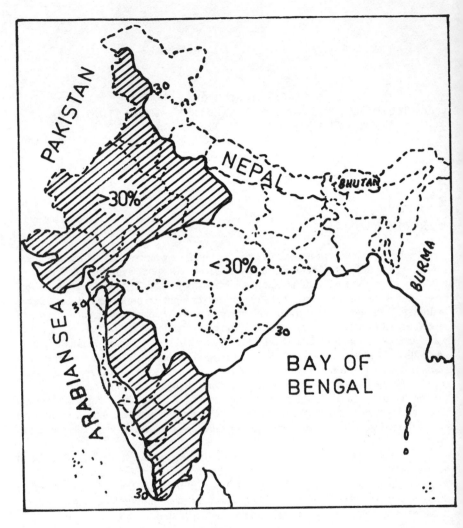

Fig. 1 Drought-prone areas in India (from Sarkar, 1979).

agriculture has been making progress, it has not been possible to keep the trend going during the drought years.

A closer examination of the respective crops is more revealing. Figures 3-6 indicate the production trends of individual commodities. In the case of rice, the yield fluctuations are more severe (Fig. 3). This is understandable since 60% of the rice in India is rainfed and is grown, in many places, in hostile environments. The same is true of coarse grains (Fig. 4) and food legumes (Fig. 5), both of which are mostly (up to 95%) grown in dryland areas. But wheat production (Fig. 6) was more stable because 65% of that crop is irrigated in India. On the whole, the compound growth rate in food production was 2.14%, while that of the population was 2.25% for the period 1967-86.

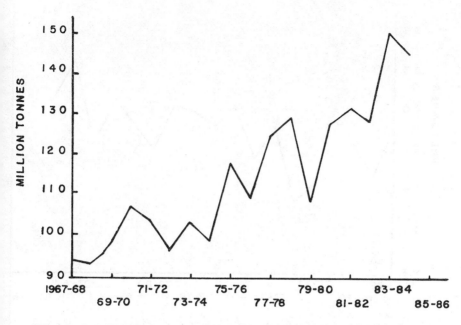

Fig. 2 Food-grain production (D E & S, Government of India).

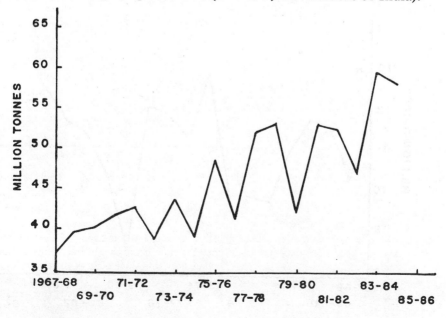

Fig. 3 Rice production (D E & S, Government of India).

394

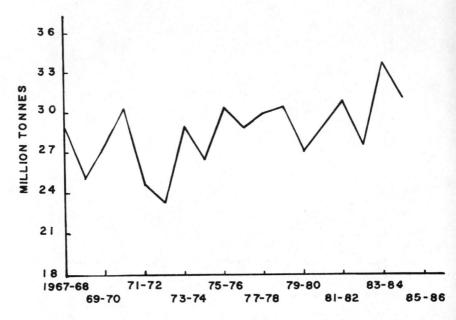

Fig. 4 Coarse cereals production (D E & S, Government of India).

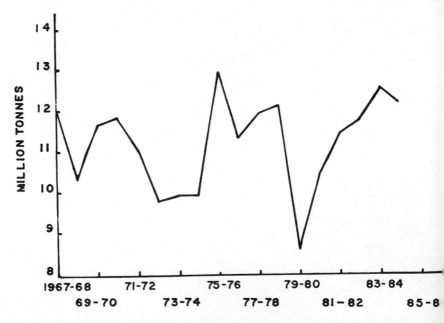

Fig. 5 Pulses production (D E & S, Government of India).

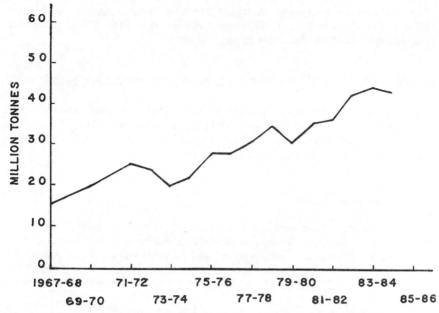

Fig. 6 Wheat production (D E & S, Government of India).

Effect on Fodder Production

Fodder is another important consideration. During drought, fodder as well as food grain would be scarce. It is well known that animals supply 50% of the draft requirement in Indian agriculture. Animals are an integral part of Indian agriculture, and their fodder demands must be attended to more carefully than before.

Effect at Farm Level

To cope with drought, farmers have adopted some of the following strategies:
1. Reduce consumption.
2. Postpone social arrangements such as marriages.
3. Migrate to better areas with livestock, or sell stock.
4. Take consumption loans.
5. Sell assets like gold ornaments as a last resort.

Some develop their own systems of food grain and fodder storage to tide them over during poor rainfall years.

Farmers also adapt to risk through the diversification of crops and cropping systems. Jodha and Mascarenhas (1985) and Walker and Jodha (1986) found that diversification of crops within an area as small as a village enhanced yield stability in some ecological settings. Although Walker and Jodha (1986) did not believe that intercropping led to yield stability, Singh and Walker (1984) and Randhawa and Venkateswarlu (1986) stated that it was a perfect hedge against complete crop failure, even though one of the components in the system was frequently not harvested or was harvested for low yields. In fact, Rao and Wiley (1980) found variability reduced to 39% with intercropping as compared to 49% when growing sorghum alone.

GOVERNMENTAL INTERVENTION TO MITIGATE DROUGHT EFFECTS

Droughts are not uncommon to India. In the nineteenth century and early twentieth century, drought caused acute food shortages, starvation, and deaths. For instance, 1 million people died in famines in 1800-1825; 0.4 million died in 1825-50; 5 million died in 1850-75; and 15 million died in 1875-1900 (Das, 1981).

Early Drought Relief Efforts

The Indian government made several efforts to mitigate the impacts of these droughts. From 1860 to 1878, the government remitted land revenue, extended irrigation facilities, streamlined communications, and provided employment through relief works. These measures were further updated by the famine commissions of 1898, 1901, and 1944. However, no permanent gains resulted from these endeavors.

Relief Efforts during the Last Two Decades

During the last two decades, attempts have been made to improve disaster management. Model relief manuals were made available for guidance. Governmental and nongovernmental agencies worked together to alleviate many of the drought-stricken people by initiating the following.
1. Ground-water exploitation.
2. Construction of rural godowns (storage facilities).
3. Health and nutrition programs.
4. Minor irrigation works.
5. Soil conservation programs.
6. Afforestation programs.
7. Communications improvements.

Later the government included programs for livestock development and assistance to small and marginal farmers as well as landless labor. But even though US$150 million was spent on such programs, no significant improvements occurred in these areas. Subsidy was overemphasized. Unfortunately, these programs were assessed on the basis of the amount of money spent rather than on the results, which probably explains the lack of impact of these programs.

More Recent Efforts

More recently, efforts to fight drought have included on-farm water harvesting and conservation, alternate crop planning, and compensatory programs. For this purpose, the government developed:

1. Crop weather watch groups at the national and state levels.
2. Food security through buffer stocks.
3. Priority in the most seriously affected areas through "Food for Work"/National Rural Employment Project and other programs.
4. High priority in food production in the most favorable areas as compensatory programs.
5. Optimum input use.
6. Rural godowns to avoid crash sales.
7. Crop insurance schemes.

The performance of some of these programs is discussed in the following paragraphs.

Crop Weather Watch Groups. These groups are formed by drawing personnel from extension and research groups at the national and state levels. They review the progress of the monsoon and suggest appropriate action in areas affected by drought and floods. They develop contingency crop plans by comparing crop/variety performance for different dates of sowing in different agroclimatic situations. In situations of moisture stress, they suggest proper weeding and soil mulching. Other compensatory measures are also considered, such as thinning plant stands under stress, increasing plant population for delayed sown crops, and applying nutrients for crops that received some precipitation after a period of stress. The government has stored seed of alternate crops and varieties in seed banks for use in tests to determine the performance of those crops. In a normal year, the losses incurred by holding such buffer seed, if any, are to be written off by the government.

Food Security. Because of technological advancements, it has become possible to have adequate buffer stocks of food grain. The buffer stock was 22.48 million tons in July 1984 and 28.65 million tons in July 1985. Such huge buffer stocks are useful for drought mitigation and prevention of deaths due to starvation. Still, some argue that the country's food supplies are only meeting the market demand for food and not the food requirement of all the people—particularly the rural poor, who spend more than 75% of their income on food. Of this, 80% is spent on cereals alone. Even in normal years these people cannot purchase food with ease. The task of buying food would be much more difficult in drought or flood years. These considerations emphasize that food production at the rural level (and perhaps even the farm level) should receive more attention.

Compensatory Programs. When a drought persists for a longer period, the monsoon crop may be affected. Then, compensatory programs have to be developed. One such strategy pays attention to the post-rainy season crops. Venkateswarlu and Singh (1979) reviewed the 1979 drought in India and found that the onset of the monsoon was delayed seven to ten days, with long breaks in the monsoon rains from the second fortnight of August on. In some areas, early withdrawal of the monsoon rains was also observed. The problem was accentuated by temperatures 5-6° C above normal, leading to more dry surface soil. Over the entire country, seventeen out of thirty-six sub-divisions were affected by drought. Suggested compensatory programs included:

1. A concerted drive to improve productivity in the better rainfall areas.
2. Arrangements for deep seeding or opening dry surface soil to place seed in the moist zone for post-rainy season crops in deep soils of high rainfall regions.
3. Suggestions for choosing efficient crops for areas during the post-rainy season.

All of these suggestions were to be further strengthened by the timely supply of resource inputs (e.g., fertilizer).

Crop Insurance. Agricultural production is a risky enterprise, more so under rainfed conditions. To insulate the system of dryland farming against failure, the government extended crop insurance to dryland crops, on a trial basis, for some areas. The farmers pay a small premium and are assured of 75-90% of the average yield through the insurance program. If the crop fails, the farmer is paid a certain amount (indemnity). The farmers also get crop loans at 7.5% interest through the state/district cooperatives. The state government is a cosponsor, underwriting 25% of the losses, if they occur. The scheme gives preference to small and marginal farmers, who are also given a 50% subsidy to cover the cost of the premium. Dendekar (1985) reviewed the progress of this scheme for the 1979-83 period. The ratio of total claims versus premiums paid was 1.1, meaning a loss for the government. This does not include staff and other incidental expenses. Hazell, et al. (1986), presented case studies on crop insurance in the United States, Japan, Mexico, Brazil, and Costa Rica. Their conclusions, which were corroborated by Walker, et al. (personal communication, 1986), were not encouraging. They considered it preferable to raise agricultural productivity through the direct utilization of funds and by focusing on reducing crop yield variability instead of unnecessary expenditures on the administration of the crop insurance scheme.

TECHNOLOGICAL EFFORTS

The drought-prone areas of India are characterized by intense rainfall interspersed with drought and short rainy seasons. The soils are shallow, low in organic matter, and poor in natural productivity. They are, at times, low in infiltration capacity. They suffer from severe runoff and soil erosion. The farms are small and fragmented. The farmers have few resources; humans and draft animals provide the labor. So the technological advances of the West are not transferable to India without adaptation (Randhawa and Venkateswarlu, 1979).

Research

Certain concepts and related research results that may be useful in moderating the effect of moisture stress due to drought are discussed below.

Breeding for Drought Tolerance. This is not an easy task. Field techniques are laborious and time consuming, and any laboratory technique can only provide an approximation. Perhaps a more realistic goal would be to achieve high yield potential, taking into consideration the area's rainfall regime.

The high yield potential of the improved varieties of crops could be useful in combatting drought, which is mostly a nonspecific stress. Krishnamoorthy, et al. (1971), found that high yield potential sorghums performed well even during periods of drought.

With an analysis of long-term rainfall records, and by knowing soil characteristics, it is possible to ascertain the growing season for a given region. Cultivars can then be selected for a given ecological system. For example, in the post-rainy season Vertisols of Deccan, the local variety of sorghum, a 150-day hybrid, could not yield more than 200 kg/ha. On the other hand, CSH 1 (a 100-day hybrid) yielded up to 800 kg/ha with the same level of management. This is because the hybrid was not affected by the moisture stress resulting from late December cracks in these Vertisols. Krishnamoorthy, et al. (1975), used this drought escape mechanism together with rainfall data to suggest suitable varieties of upland rice for eastern Uttar Pradesh.

Physiological Approaches. Asana, et al. (1986), give an excellent review of different crops in this area of research. For upland rice, they showed that shorter-duration varieties (e.g., 100 days) can escape drought. Their findings were based (in part) on considerations of seedling vigor, moderate tillering ability, and moderate ability to recover after drought. Venkateswarlu (1984) found that adequate water at flowering time was necessary to obtain good rice yields. The yields obtained were 0-3,150 kg/ha, with 15-600 mm rainfall received during the one-month anthesis period. In post-rainy season sorghum, good traits are timely flowering (to escape atmospheric and soil drought) and better root penetration.

In tillering cereals like pearl millet, the rapid rate of recovery after water stress should prove useful for drought tolerance. Mahalakshmi and Bidinger (1985, 1986) found that water deficit during panicle development in pearl millet might affect the main shoot, but this could be compensated for by the tillers, which act as an important adaptive mechanism. Crop duration in relation to prevalent weather conditions is important for short duration pulses (Asana, et al., 1986).

Stability in Production with Improved Management. Improved practices give stability to the production of dryland crops, especially when the crops are chosen to fit the environment. These high-yielding varieties and hybrids have deeper and denser root systems and, with fertilizer, use soil moisture more efficiently (Singh, et al., 1975). In the process they encompass a greater volume of soil and so are better able to withstand mild stress. Some data (Table 1) show that the coefficient of variation for yield is less with increased rainfall. Improved management also reduces variability. Thus improved crop production practices insulate dryland crops against mild stress.

Aberration in rainfall. The variability of rainfall increases as the amount decreases. So drought-prone areas are subject to larger aberrations. Broadly speaking, these aberrations include delayed onset of monsoon; "breaks" in the rains during the monsoon; early cessation of rainfall; and extended rainfall. The research undertaken by the All India Coordinated Research Project for Dryland Agriculture over the last fifteen years on some of these aspects provided useful results.

Delayed Onset of Monsoon. The timing of the sowing of crops is dependent on rainfall in the drylands. When rains are delayed or the farmer is delayed in sowing, alternative varieties are needed. However, this seed may not be available to farmers. In this case the government should provide seed through seed banks, as pointed out earlier. If

Table 1
Yield Variability of Crops in Different Agroclimatic Regions

Center	Soil Type	Average Rainfall (mm)	Crop	Average Yield (kg/ha)	S D	C V(%)	Remarks
Varanasi	Entisols	1080	Rice (Improved)	2250	400	14.6	Monsoon crop
Hoshiarpur	Inceptisols	1000	Wheat (Improved)	3150	1010	32.0	Post-monsoon crop
			Wheat (Traditional)	1870	550	29.4	Post-monsoon crop
Hyderabad	Alfisols	760	Sorghum (Improved)	3550	1420	39.0	Monsoon crop
			Sorghum (Traditional)	1920	750	39.3	Monsoon crop
Bellary	Vertisols	508	Sorghum (Improved)	1890	860	46.0	Post-monsoon crop
			Sorghum (Traditional)	770	480	62.0	Post-monsoon crop
Jodhpur	Aridisols	380	Mung bean (Improved)	930	650	65.1	Monsoon crop

Source: Annual reports of the respective centers, All India Coordinated Research Project for Dryland Agriculture, Hyderabad.

the delays are longer, crops may need to be changed, and governmental support again will be necessary. Venkateswarlu (1983) has provided the needed information on alternate crop strategies for different agroclimatic regions of India.

"Breaks" in the Rains and Mid-Season Corrections. During the monsoon period, these "breaks" in rain may extend from days to weeks. Depending on the time and extent of moisture stress, decisions may need to be made about the crop.

If the crop sown is only a week or ten days old and the moisture stress is extended, it would be preferable to resow the crop. On the other hand, when such a stress occurs after six to eight weeks of growth, other methods such as ratooning and thinning should be practiced. A ratooned drought-affected sorghum crop that subsequently received rain yielded 800 kg/ha, compared to 200 kg/ha for drought-affected sorghum without ratooning. Similarly, in the case of pearl millet, the yield of a ratoon was 2,510 kg/ha, compared to 1,600 kg/ha without ratooning (Venkateswarlu, 1983). But ratooning is a high-management system, and success depends on the general vigor of the drought-affected crops.

Thinning of plant population by removing every third row was found to mitigate stress in post-rainy season sorghum in the Vertisols of 500 mm rainfall in India (Table 2). The effects were significant in below-normal years.

Researchers have found that if the break in the monsoon is very brief, soil mulching is effective in extending the period of water storage in the root profile in the post-rainy season areas. Organic mulches have very little place in crop production during the rainy season. However, in post-rainy season crops, they were found to be useful. In Sholapur (an area with Vertisols), organic mulch at 4 t/ha gave 1,640 kg/ha as against 980 kg/ha with control. Similarly, in a loamy sand of Gujarat, local tobacco yield was 1,840 kg/ha with 4 t/ha of pearl millet mulch material, compared to 1,330 kg/ha with control (Randhawa and Venkateswarlu, 1979). However, in India the byproducts of crops have many uses, such as fodder, fuel, and manure. So the use of organic mulches may not be possible even in the post-rainy season areas.

Dilute nutrient solutions on drought-affected crops gave mixed results. In one test, boron was found to increase the yield of drought-affected pearl millet (Ramamurthy and Das, 1977), but in another trial they found that even water spray gave a significantly increased yield of wheat over the control system.

Early Cessation of Rains. Not much can be done when the rains recede early. If high-yielding varieties of crops are used, they may escape drought, since they generally require a shorter season. If not, irrigation must be provided.

Extended Rains. In the case of long-duration or perennial crops like pigeon pea and castor beans, extended rains would be useful. Additional nitrogen might be needed for nonlegumes like castor beans to fully exploit the extended rains. A cereal might be ratooned for grain or fodder, depending on the rain. Otherwise, a short pulse of the vigna group can be sown.

Crop Life Saving. Rains are the only source of water for dryland crops. Infiltration of rain can be improved through better soil management. Several land configurations have been identified for various locations in India (Table 3). These configurations have uniform, on-farm rainwater recharge in the root profile. They reduce the movement of soil from plot to plot and provide extended time for rainwater to infiltrate the soil and reach the root profile. All these configurations allow a 15-25% increase in crop yields (Venkateswarlu, 1986).

Table 2
Effect of Thinning on Yield of Post-Rainy Season Sorghum in Vertisols of Deccan (Bellary)

Thinning System	Grain Yield (kg/ha)			
	1974-75 (sub-normal)	1975-76 (above normal)	1977-78 (sub-normal)	1978-79 (above normal)
Original population (90,000 plants/ha)	1550	2420	540	2490
Every third row removed (60,000 plants/ha)	2110	2020	920	2330

Source: Venkateswarlu, 1983.

Table 3
Efficient Land Configurations for Various Agroclimatic Situations

Area	Rainfall	System of Land Configuration
Alfisols (semiarid)	Medium	Sowing across the slope and ridging the land between the crop rows with the subsequent interculturing operations
Alfisols (semiarid)	Medium	Graded border strips of 130 x 11 m with 0.1% grade
Alfisols (semiarid) (shallow)	Low intervals	Dead furrows at 2.4 to 3.6 m
Vertisols (semiarid)	High	Broad bed and furrow with a bed of 100 cm and 50 cm of shallow furrow which has a depth of 15 cm
Vertisols (semiarid)	Low	Contour farming
Aridisols (semiarid)	Low	Interplot water harvesting of cropped to uncropped land (1:1 ratio), the slope of uncropped area being on both sides
Aridisols (semiarid)	Low	Interrow water harvesting with a treatment of ridges with runoff-inducing substances like tank silt or polythene

Source: Venkateswarlu, 1986.

More recently, serious attempts have been made to develop areas on the basis of watersheds. This approach is based on the holistic development of an area and includes soil and water conservation programs coupled with good crop husbandry. It aims at involving the farmer as a partner in the endeavor and attempts to increase income and rural employment through increased crop productivity.

After establishing several of the soil and water conservation measures on a watershed basis, researchers observed that ground-water recharge was improved (Table 4). Use of such water conjunctively with rain has a very high payoff—200 kg/cm for

Table 4
Ground Water Recharge with Soil Conservation Measures

| Location | Treated Area | | Area in ha | Ground Water Recharge Wells (No.) | | | |
	System			Initial	After Treatment	Initial	After Treatment
G. R. Halli (Alisols-Karnataka)	Graded bunds; gully-plugging; check dams; diversion drains		314	27	30	22.4	33.4
Naranka (Vertisols-Gujarat)	Percolation tanks (95); Nala plugging and check dams		2603	81	121	270.0	370.0
Indore (Vertisols-Madhya Pradesh)	Diversion drain: gully-control with gabion, chute, and loose boulder structures		2203	120	287	160.0	571.0

Source: Randhawa and Venkateswarlu, 1986.

cereals and 100 kg/ha/cm for oilseeds and food legumes (Randhawa and Venkateswarlu, 1986).

FODDER BANKS

Finding adequate fodder during a drought is also a serious problem. However, optimized crop production systems would provide a large part of the needed fodder. For example, intercropping sorghum with pigeon pea provides food, fodder, and fuel. The food is from the grains of both the crops. Fodder comes from the stalks of the sorghum and fuel comes from the sticks of the pigeon pea. Fodder and fuel can be provided on a permanent basis if alley cropping is practiced. Alley cropping is an extension of the intercropping system. In this system, woody perennials are deliberately grown with arable crops seeking mutually beneficial interactions. For instance, *Leucaena leucocephala* can be grown as hedges at set intervals, and arable crops can be grown in the alleys. In the first two years, the hedge rows may not have any effect on arable crops. In the subsequent years, however, the arable crops would experience a decline in yield, which would continue as aridity increased. In fact, alley cropping may not lead to increased biomass, as compared to intercropping in bad years (Table 5). In good years, intercropping gave significantly higher biomass production than alley cropping, and this could be the result of mutual shading in the latter system. The main advantage of alley cropping is the permanency of the hedge rows. The geometry, choice of the woody perennial, and system of their management need to be fully resolved before implementing alley cropping on farmers' fields.

Concurrently, marginal lands could be brought under improved pastures, when 5-10 tons of forage can be harvested compared to 1-2 tons from native pastures. *Cenchrus ciliaris* 1 kg/ha with *Stylosanthes hamata* 4 kg/ha seed broadcast with 50 kg P_2O_5/ha (through single superphosphate) provides 4-6 tons of improved forage in Alfisols and Vertisols. Combining trees with improved pastures provides forage in lean periods. Some trees that can be usefully included besides *leucaena* are *Acacia albida*, *Acacia senegal*, *Prosopis cineraria*, and *Sesbania grandiflora*.

SUMMARY

Drought occurs every year in some part of India, but more often in lower rainfall regions. Researchers have identified 60 million ha in the country as drought-prone.

Earlier efforts to moderate drought effects included remission of land revenue, extension of irrigation facilities, rural employment through relief works (such as soil conservation and construction of roads), livestock improvement, and afforestation. More recently, on-farm activities (such as alternate crop strategies, compensatory programs, and crop insurance) were included.

Over the last fifteen years, researchers have concentrated on methods of increasing crop production under dryland conditions in order to mitigate drought effects at farm level. Simple and easily implemented practices were developed for obtaining at least a 100% increase in yields. This improved crop husbandry insulates crops against mild stress and helps increase yield stability. To meet weather aberrations, researchers

Table 5
Biomass Production in Intercropping and Alley Cropping in SAT Alfisols

System	Yield (kg/ha)	
	Below Normal Year	Normal Year
Sorghum + pigeonpea		
Grain	1726 + 389	3612 + 768
Straw/sticks	2236 + 1107	8027 + 2842
Leucaena leucocephala + sorghum		
Grain	787 (1963)	1366 (2003)
Sorghum straw/*Leucaena*	1914 + 2537 (4057)	3771 + 1181 (5522)

Note: Figures in parenthesis are for sole crop of sorghum

Source: Annual reports of All India Coordinated Research Project for Dry land Agriculture 1979-85.

developed alternate crop strategies, mid-season correction, and crop life saving techniques. A system for augmenting fodders was also suggested.

The holistic development of watershed areas is now being attempted, with the purpose of providing these areas with systems of drought-proofing or drought management, as well as generating income and rural employment.

ACKNOWLEDGMENTS

I wish to thank Dr. N. S. Randhawa, director general, Indian Council of Agricultural Research, and secretary, DARE, Government of India, for providing me constant encouragement and guidance while preparing this manuscript.

REFERENCES

Asana, R. D.; V. Balasubramanian; and V. Mahalaskshmi. 1986. Physiological investigations on the rainfed crops of India: An over-view. Indian National Science Academy, New Delhi (in press).

Das, P. K. 1981. A historical perspective—Droughts and famines in India. pp. 3-12. In R. P. Pearce, ed. Tropical Droughts: Meteorological Aspects and Implications for Agriculture. World Meteorological Organization, Geneva.

Dendekar, V. M. 1985. Crop insurance in India: A review, 1976-77 to 1984-85. Econ. Politic. Weekly 20, A-46-A.59.

Hazell, P.; C. Pomareda; and A. Valdes. 1986. Crop Insurance for Agricultural Development—Issues and Experience. Johns Hopkins University Press, Baltimore.

Jodha, N. S.; and A. C. Mascarenhas. 1985. Adjustment in self-provisioning societies. In R. W. Kates, J. H. Ausubel, and M. Berberian, eds. Climate Impact Assessment. John Wiley, New York.

Krishnamoorthy, C.; S. Freyman; and E. D. Spratt. 1975. Concept of non-specific stress. Symposium on Crop Plant Responses to Environmental Stresses. VPKAS, Almorah, India.

Krishnamoorthy, C.; S. V. S. Shastry; and W. M. Freyman. 1971. Breeding rice for tolerance to drought and salinity. Oryzae 8(2) Suppl. 47-54.

Mahalakshmi, V.; and F. R. Bidinger. 1985. Flowing response of pearl millet to water stress during panicle development. Ann. Appl. Biol. 106:571-578.

Mahalakshmi, V.; and F. R. Bidinger. 1986. Water deficit during panicle development in pearl millet: Yield compensation by tillers. J. Agric. Sci. Camb. 106:113-119.

Nageswara Rao, P. P.; and B. Manikiam. 1985. Satellite remote sensing for better disaster forecast and management for agricultural purposes. Tech. Rep. TR-56-85, NNRMS, Bangalore, India.

National Commission on Agriculture. 1976. Report on Climate and Agriculture. Part IV, pp. 1-124. Government of India, New Delhi.

Ramamurthy, B.; and S. K. Das. 1977. Improving pearl millet production in areas of acute moisture stress. Proceedings of Millet Workshop, Bhubaneswar, India.

Randhawa, N. S.; and J. Venkateswarlu. 1979. Indian experience in the semi-arid tropics: Prospect and retrospect. Proceedings of the International Symposium on Development and Transfer of Technology for Rainfed Agriculture and SAT Farmers. ICRISAT, Patancheru, India.

Randhawa, N. S.; and J. Venkateswarlu. 1986. Farming systems research—Indian experience. IARCS Workshop on Farming Systems Research. ICRISAT, Patancheru, India.

Rao, M. R.; and R. W. Wiley. 1980. Evaluation of yield stability in intercropping. Studies on sorghum/pigeonpea. Exp. Agric. 16:105-116.

Sarkar, R. P. 1979. Droughts in India, their predictability. pp. 33-40. In Proceedings of the International Symposium on Hydrological Aspects of Droughts, IIT, New Delhi.

408

Singh, R.; Y. Singh; S. S. Prihar; and P. Singh. 1975. Effect of N fertilization on yield and water use efficiency of dryland winter wheat as affected by stored water and rainfall. Agron. J. 67:593-603.

Singh, R. P.; and T. S. Walker. 1984. Crop failure in the semi-arid tropics of peninsular India: Implications for technological policy. Indian J. Agric. Econ. 39:29-39.

Venkateswarlu, J. 1983. Contingent crop production strategy in rainfed areas under different weather conditions. Project Bulletin No. 5. All India Coordinated Research Project for Dryland Agriculture, Hyderabad, India.

Venkateswarlu, J. 1984. Drought problems in rice production. pp. 69-76. In A. Deepak and K. R. Rao, eds. Application of Remote Sensing for Rice Production. A. Deepak Publishing, Hampton, Virginia.

Venkateswarlu, J. 1986. Efficient resource management systems for drylands: Fifteen years of dryland agricultural research. Souvenir, CRIDA, Hyderabad.

Venkateswarlu, J.; and S. N. Singh. 1979. Contingency plans for rainfed *rabi* crop. Indian Farming 29, no. 7 (October):17-20.

Walker, T. S.; and N. S. Jodha. 1986. How small farm households adapt to risk. pp. 17-34. In P. Hazell, C. Pomareda, and A. Valdes, eds. Crop Insurance for Agricultural Development Issues and Experience. Johns Hopkins University Press, Baltimore.

World Bank. 1974. An appraisal of drought prone areas project, India. Rep (IBRD) No. 533-1-ln. World Bank, New York.

CHAPTER 24
PERCEPTIONS OF DROUGHT IN THE OGALLALA AQUIFER REGION OF THE WESTERN U.S. GREAT PLAINS

Jonathan G. Taylor, Thomas R. Stewart, and Mary W. Downton

INTRODUCTION

This paper examines farmers' perceptions of drought in the Ogallala Aquifer region of the western U.S. Great Plains. The Ogallala Aquifer extends from the southern edge of South Dakota deep into the Panhandle of Texas, and underlies most of the region labeled as the 1930s "Dust Bowl" (see Heathcote, 1980; Worster, 1979). Major droughts have been documented for the region roughly in alternate decades from the 1890s through the 1950s (Warrick and Bowden, 1981), and can be expected to occur again.

The social, biological, and economic impacts of future droughts on regional agriculture will depend in large measure on how farmers of the region prepare for and respond to drought. The farmers' actions, in turn, are influenced by how they recognize and interpret drought. Appropriate adjustments and adaptations can lessen negative impacts whereas inappropriate actions can increase them. Therefore, understanding drought impact requires an understanding of human perception and behavior.

Perception of climate in the Great Plains region has been studied by Bowden (1976), Kollmorgen and Kollmorgen (1973), and Lawson (1974). Heathcote investigated perception of desertification on the Great Plains (1980) and perception of drought in Australia (1969, 1974), and Warrick (1975) includes commentary on perceptions in his assessment of drought hazard research in the United States. Most closely aligned to the present study was the work done by Saarinen (1966), Perceptions of the Drought Hazard on the Great Plains.

This paper presents the perceptions of drought held by farmers in the Ogallala Aquifer region of the western U.S. Great Plains, based on interviews of farmers during the spring of 1985. It follows, by twenty years, the work done by Thomas F. Saarinen; it replicates many of his survey questions and shares two of his study counties. Perception of drought was a central concern of both Saarinen and the present study, and in this aspect we now have comparative data from the mid-1960s and 1980s.

METHOD

During the spring of 1985, we interviewed ninety-nine farmers from six counties overlying the Ogallala Aquifer: Yuma and Phillips counties in northeastern Colorado; Frontier and Finney counties from southwestern Nebraska and Kansas, respectively; and Texas and Swisher counties in the panhandles of Oklahoma and Texas, respectively. Aquifer condition can greatly affect a farmer's ability to respond to drought. In the northernmost county (Frontier County, Nebraska), farmers had experienced little aquifer depletion at the time of the study, but in the southern counties, especially in Swisher County, Texas, and Finney County, Kansas, aquifer depletion was seriously affecting farming operations (Gutentag, et al., 1984).

Farmers were interviewed in their homes about their farming operations and local climate. They were asked for their opinions regarding irrigation versus dryland farming and different economic approaches to farming [1], and they also were questioned in detail about drought. They were asked to define drought, recall droughts that they had experienced, and discuss the effects of past droughts. Then they were asked about their expectations for future droughts, including whether another drought like that of the "Dirty Thirties" could come again, and what the effects of such a drought would be now; whether drought years follow one another; whether droughts are becoming more or less frequent; what frequency of drought they anticipate in their areas; and whether they had found effective ways of overcoming drought losses.

Results of this survey, as well as meteorological data for the substate regions where the surveying was conducted, are the foundation for the discussion that follows.

RESULTS

Experience of Drought

Farmers' drought experience was compared with the Palmer Drought Severity Index (Palmer, 1965) in each of the counties surveyed during the time each farmer was farming in the area. The Palmer Index, or PDSI, is based on water balance, and classifies weather conditions for each month as departures from "climatically normal conditions for the month and location" (see Table 1). Although the PDSI has been criticized (Alley, 1984; Karl, 1985; Oladipo, 1985), it remains in widespread use. The PDSI was used in this study for two reasons: interviewing was conducted in some of Palmer's original test areas; and Saarinen (1966) used the PDSI for comparison with farmers' recollections of drought. This allowed direct comparison of the 1965 and 1985 results.

Figure 1 is a comparison of the years of drought recalled by farmers (solid line) and the meteorological pattern of drought that has occurred in the Ogallala Aquifer region (dashed line) since 1930. [2] As indicated in Fig. 1, the Ogallala region experienced severe drought lasting almost a decade during the Dust Bowl of the 1930s and lasting five years during the 1950s. These classic drought episodes were clearly remembered by the farmers interviewed. The fairly serious drought years of 1963-64, which were recalled by more than 50% of Saarinen's sample, were almost entirely forgotten by our respondents in 1985. Drought periods since the 1960s have been fairly mild and brief. From about 1960 to the present there appears to be little meaningful relationship between recorded drought and years recalled as personal drought experience.

In general, farmers tended to recall drought either as the prolonged, extreme events that occurred in the region in the 1930s and 1950s or as short-term events in recent years (the 1980s). People remember the most recent droughts by year, the more distant severe droughts by decade.

Table 1
Palmer Drought Severity Index

Value	Classification
= >4.00	Extremely Wet
3.00 to 3.99	Very Wet
2.00 to 2.99	Moderately Wet
1.00 to 1.99	Slightly Wet
0.50 to 0.99	Incipient Wet
0.49 to -0.49	Near Normal
-0.50 to -0.99	Incipient Drought
-1.00 to -1.99	Mild Drought
-2.00 to -2.99	Moderate Drought
-3.00 to -3.99	Severe Drought
< = -4.00	Extreme Drought

Time is an important component in farmers' memory of drought, as would be expected. The percent of farmers who identified any year in which they were farming as a drought year is negatively correlated with how long ago it occurred. [3] Note that the solid line in Fig. 1 (the number of farmers who recalled drought that year) trails off from right to left between 1985 and 1960: as the length of time increases, the number of farmers identifying a year as a drought year decreases.

This pattern of recalling the most severe and the most recent droughts can be explained by analogy. It is similar to standing on the plains, looking up toward nearby mountains. One can see the closest foothills in detail, the tallest mountain peaks somewhat less precisely. The intermediate ranges are hidden from view. This description of memory pattern seems intuitively logical; it fits with our own experience. It also fits with the results reported by Kirby (1974) of farmers' perceptions in the Oaxaca Valley of Mexico. These farmers' rainfall memory included the most recent wet year, then progressively wetter years beyond. In addition, the previous year's moisture was recalled regardless of the relative wetness. Kirby felt that the latest, wettest year blocked memory of earlier years. This was supported by her finding that farmers interviewed immediately after a particularly wet year were unable to recall any previous wet years.

The analysis of farmers' drought memories indicates that memories of all but the most prolonged and severe drought events fade rapidly. To examine the relationship between farmers' drought memories and meteorological measures of their experience, multiple regression analysis was used to control for the effect of fading memory. For the dependent variable in the regressions, a "drought rating by farmers" (DRF) was computed for each year in each location. The DRF for a location is the proportion of respondents farming there at the time who identified each year as a drought year. For the period 1960-84, DRF was significantly correlated with the reciprocal of how many years past (YP) the identified drought year occurred (1/YP, where YP is the number of years

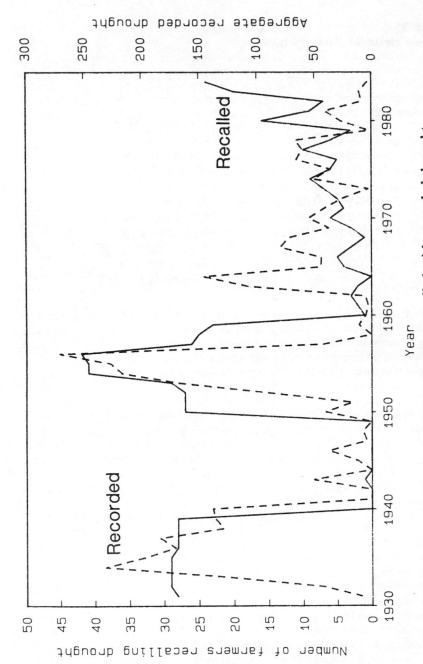

Fig. 1 Comparison of drought years recalled with recorded drought in the Ogallala Aquifer region.

between 1985 and the year of drought occurrence). Thirty-two percent of the variance in DRF was explained by fading memory alone.

Because of the vagueness in farmers' identification of drought in earlier years, stepwise multiple regression analyses were run just on the years 1974-84. For these years, 1/YP still explained 30% of the variance in DRF, and regressions on March-August monthly rainfall and temperature revealed July temperature as the only other significant predictor. Surprisingly, rainfall did not emerge as a significant predictor.

Regressions using monthly March-August PDSI values as predictors showed July and June values as significant, together explaining 20% of the variance in DRF in addition to that explained by 1/YP. [4] The percent of variance explained by the PDSI was equal to that explained by July temperature. Since the PDSI measures differences from normal regional and temporal conditions, it was probably doing somewhat better than July temperatures in explaining farmers' recollection of drought.

Of course, the older farmers have experienced (and therefore recall) more droughts than have younger farmers. Farmers over fifty averaged 2 or more droughts recalled; for farmers under fifty, the number recalled was 1.5. Quite logically, the proportion of farmers who mentioned the classic droughts of the 1950s and 1930s increases with age: 100% of those sixty or older, 78% of those in their fifties, and 55% of those in their forties. None of the farmers under forty recalled these classic droughts.

The proportions of farmers who mentioned drought years in the 1980s is shown in Table 2. Fairly consistently, farmers under forty recall drought in the 1980s; farmers over fifty recall the classic droughts of the 1950s and 1930s.

Younger farmers reported less damage from past droughts. Of the farmers under forty, 33% reported no serious impact on their own farming operations from the last drought of their experience, as compared with 21% of the farmers forty and older.

Table 2
Age and Experience of Farmers Compared with Recalled and Expected Droughts

	Years of Farm Experience (median)	Number of Farmers	Number of Farmers Identifying Drought in Period: 1980-84	Number of Farmers Identifying Drought in Period: 1982-84	Expected Drought Years (median)
Under 40	9.5	16	13 (81%)	11 (69%)	22.5
49-49	24	33	14 (42%)	7 (21%)	11
40-59	33	23	8 (35%)	7 (30%)	15
60 & over	45	27	7 (26%)	6 (22%)	15
Overall	28	99	42 (42%)	31 (31%)	13

414

However, the majority of the latest droughts being reported by these youngest farmers occurred in the early 1980s, which, as noted above, was not a period of very serious drought.

Meteorological conditions during the period of a farmer's experience have a profound effect on his beliefs about which moisture levels are normal and which are abnormally dry. Figure 1 shows that people who began farming in the Ogallala Aquifer region after 1964 would have a very limited experience in relation to the potential severity of drought there.

Figure 2 illustrates how experience can influence a farmer's concept of normal wetness and the range of wetness to dryness. The three lines indicate, for April through August in southwestern Kansas, the most extreme wetness (top line), the median wetness to dryness (center solid line), and the most extreme dryness (bottom line) experienced, depending on when a person had arrived there. For example, one of the farmers in our survey who began farming in Finney County, Kansas, in 1965 would have experienced, between 1965 and 1985, a median PDSI value almost exactly equal to the thirty-year

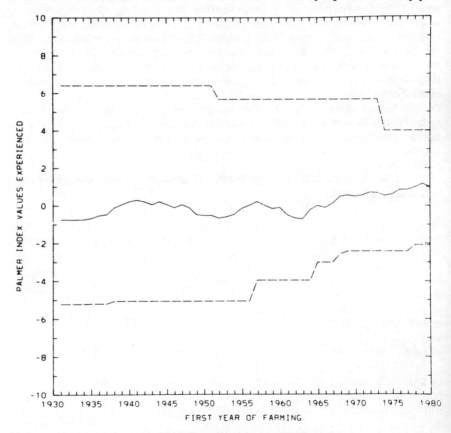

Fig. 2 Breadth of "wetness-to-dryness" experience in southwest Kansas, depending on first year of farming.

average; drought to a PDSI value of -3, the threshold of severe drought; and extreme wetness up to +5.67. He would lack experience of the severe or extreme droughts that occurred before 1964. The "step function" shifts in PDSI experience, illustrated in Fig. 2, show that a person could farm for quite a few years in an area (twenty in the example above) and still have a very limited direct experience of the region's drought potential. Similar patterns of experience were found for the other four study areas.

Drought Definition

The first mention of the term *drought* in the 1985 interviews occurred when farmers were asked for their definitions: "What do you think of as a drought?" This was immediately preceded by a series of questions concerning weather and climate, so a tendency to answer in meteorological terms was expected.

Drought was defined in terms of deficient rainfall, lack of moisture, or a "dry spell" by eighty-nine of the farmers; twelve mentioned high temperature or winds in addition to dryness. The remaining farmers defined drought in terms of low crop yields or crop failure. Several included both low crop yields and dryness in their definition, and two farmers specifically mentioned economic impacts in addition to dryness or low crop yield. Opinions differed on how long a dry spell must be to constitute a drought. Of the sixty-six farmers who mentioned a time span, 68% specified a single season or a period under eight months, and 32% specified one year or longer. Of those who defined drought as a dry season, many specified summer or the growing season; a few specified spring. Many farmers pointed out that seasonal variations in precipitation and temperature are much more important in farming than are annual averages. A wet-winter/dry-summer year, with average annual precipitation, could constitute a functional drought year for summer crops.

The severity and duration aspects of drought definition were found to be linked. Of the farmers in Kansas, Oklahoma, and Texas who used the word *drought* for the mildly dry conditions of 1982-84, only one had defined drought as lasting as much as a year. In contrast, the farmers who did not consider 1982-84 to be drought years were almost evenly split between short duration (one season, less than eight months) and long duration (a year or more) definitions. [5]

A farmer's experience depends on both his location and the number of years he has been farming. It was expected that these, in turn, would influence his definition of drought. There was some tendency for the farmers under forty to use a shorter time-span definition: 75% of the farmers under forty defined drought as lasting seven months or less, compared to only 50% of the farmers aged forty and over, but this difference was not statistically significant. Thus, the expected duration of a drought was not significantly related to either location or years of experience for these farmers.

The level of severity required for a dry spell to be called a drought, as indicated by the farmer's willingness to label a year between 1982 and 1984 a drought year, was related to the farmer's experience. In Texas, Oklahoma, and Kansas, the PDSI indicated some periods of mildly below-normal moisture in 1982-84. In these three states, we can distinguish between a group of twenty-nine farmers who identified drought in this three-year period and another group of thirty-one farmers who did not mention an occurrence of drought in the same time period. Examination of the crops and livestock grown by the two groups revealed no apparent differences. Instead, the two groups differed significantly [6] in their definitions of drought duration and in their years of farming experience. Definition of drought duration explained 19% of the variance; years of farming experience explained an additional 10%. Those who identified drought in 1982-84 were much more likely to use a short-term definition of drought. More experienced farmers were less likely to identify these years of mild moisture deficiency as drought years.

Expectations of Drought

The farmers' expectations of future droughts were related to their definitions of drought and to their farming locations. Farmers were asked to estimate drought frequency: "If you were to live here one hundred years, how many drought years would you expect to have?" Responses ranged from one to ninety years per hundred, but fifty-five of the ninety-nine farmers interviewed expected a number in the range of ten to twenty years. The median number of expected drought years per hundred was thirteen.

The farmers who used a shorter duration or a drought definition of lesser intensity or severity expected droughts to occur significantly more often. Table 3 shows that farmers using a short-term drought definition (under eight months) expect a median of twenty drought years in one hundred, while farmers using all other drought definitions expect a median of only ten to twelve drought years in one hundred. [7] These results in-

Table 3
Definitions of Drought Compared with Recalled and Expected Droughts

Drought Definition: Duration of Deficient Ppt.	Number of Farmers	Number Identifying 1980s Drought	Expected Drought Yrs/100 (median)	Years Farming Experience (median)
Under 8 Months	45	28 (62%)	20	27
One Year	12	3 (25%)	10	28
Two Years	9	0 (0%)	11.5	34
Not Specified	17	6 (35%)	12	32
Rainfall not Mentioned	16	5 (31%)	10	28.5

dicate consistency in a farmer's use of the word *drought,* since inclusion of milder dry spells expands the number of events to which the word will be applied.

Farmers in the southerly locations expected more frequent droughts than did farmers in the northern locations. The significant north-south split was between Nebraska and Colorado in the north, whose farmers expected a median of ten and eleven drought years, respectively, and Kansas, Oklahoma, and Texas in the south, where farmers expected a median of nineteen, fifteen, and eighteen drought years, respectively. [8] From the present data we cannot determine whether differences in recent experience or differences in area temperatures contributed more to these north/south differences in farmers' estimates of drought frequency.

Whether farmers felt drought had become more or less frequent is significantly related to farming experience at a 95% confidence level. Farmers who had experienced the 1950s or even the 1930s droughts were more likely to feel that drought had become less frequent in recent years. [9]

The farmers interviewed were also asked whether another drought as severe as that of the "Dirty Thirties" would occur again and, if it did, whether the effects be as bad. A majority of the farmers (55%) believed that such a drought would *probably* recur, and a fourth felt it *definitely* would recur. Most (71%) of the farmers felt that a recurrence of such a drought was at least possible. An even larger percentage (80%) of the farmers interviewed, including all but one of the farmers under forty, felt that the effects of another Dust Bowl drought would not be as severe as they were in the 1930s. This was attributed primarily to changes in agricultural technology that have occurred since 1940, including irrigation.

The expected impact of drought was also examined. Farmers were asked, "Have you found effective ways to overcome drought losses?" The responses were significantly related to both age and experience, at a 95% confidence level. [10] Most (84%) of the farmers under age sixty felt they had found ways to overcome drought losses, while only 52% of those sixty and over felt that way. Combining this response with the tendency of more experienced farmers to use a more severe definition of drought, we conclude that the oldest group of farmers, the only ones who were farming in both the 1930s and the 1950s, tended to see drought as something more severe and more difficult to overcome than the dry spells experienced in recent years.

CONCLUSIONS

Comparisons Between 1965 and 1985

Results of the 1985 survey substantiate and expand on Saarinen's description of how drought is recalled. Saarinen identified a distinctive pattern of drought recollection among Great Plains farmers. Farmers remembered the most recent drought, the most severe droughts, and to some extent the "drought of primacy" (i.e., the first drought they experienced as farmers). The 1985 Ogallala region survey found that farmers tended to recall recent, moderately dry years as drought years; beyond that immediate time horizon, they recalled only extreme drought events. Nearly a third mentioned a drought that occurred within their first two years of farming, their "drought of primacy."

However, three-fourths of these latter also fall within the 1930s and 1950s classic severe drought periods for the region.

Saarinen noted that even the most recent "incipient drought" was recalled, in Adams County, Nebraska, by more than 50% of the farmers interviewed. This memory, however, was inversely correlated to farming experience; old timers did not mention the incipient drought of 1963-64, but newcomers did. A refinement of this pattern of drought memory that Saarinen demonstrated is suggested by the results of the 1985 survey. Not only are the most recent droughts recalled, but the most recent *years* are recalled as drought years even if they showed only short, mild dry periods. But the most recent years are not recalled as drought years by everyone. Less experienced farmers remembered the most recent dry periods of seasons as droughts; experienced farmers remembered their most severe droughts—the "classics."

It is important to note that Saarinen's survey immediately followed a two-year period of rather severe drought (1963-64). Using the aggregated PDSI drought scale shown in Fig. 1, drought severity/duration for 1963-1964 totaled 254 for the Ogallala region included in the 1985 survey. The total drought severity/duration in this same region for the two years preceding the 1985 survey was fourteen. Saarinen conducted his survey in Nebraska, Kansas, Colorado, and Oklahoma; Finney County, Kansas, and Frontier County, Nebraska, were included in both surveys, so the survey areas are reasonably analogous.

Despite the very different conditions preceding the two surveys, there is a great deal of similarity in the results. However, the 1985 results differ in *magnitude* from the 1965 results, especially in terms of the most recent years recalled as drought years. Saarinen reported that drought episodes recalled by "at least half of the farmers who were there at the time" included the most recent drought (1962-64 or 1963-64), plus the classic drought episodes of the 1950s and the 1930s Dust Bowl. In the 1985 Ogallala survey, none of the most recent drought years were recalled by half of the farmers present. But the classic drought episodes, as in Saarinen's survey, were recalled by more of the farmers surveyed than were actually farming there during the 1930s or 1950s. Thus the 1985 survey results differ in amplitude from those of 1965, but the pattern is essentially the same.

Perception of Drought

Farmers in the hotter, southerly areas of the Ogallala region expected more droughts than those in the cooler areas, indicating that they see their location as more drought-prone. Under meteorological definitions like the PDSI, the term *drought-prone* has little meaning since each location is compared only to its own normal conditions. Many farmers appear to use a definition of drought that focuses on the discrepancy between local moisture supply and crop water demand, an interrelationship that is not captured by the PDSI.

Wilhite and Glantz (1985; reprinted in this volume) have pointed out a similar division over drought definitions between academic disciplines. Meteorological definitions of drought, like the Palmer Index, generally focus on deviations from long-term mean moisture conditions for an area, while agricultural definitions of drought are more likely to focus on plant water demand. As a result, "meteorological droughts do not necessarily coincide with periods of agricultural drought."

Experience seems to pervade the model of drought perception offered here. Limited experience will yield a limited perspective on weather variability. A number of drought perception characteristics separate our sample into farmers with an extended drought horizon and farmers with a limited drought horizon.

Farmers who have an extended drought horizon tend to be older. They have experienced more droughts and thus recall more droughts, and their experience has included extreme drought. Older farmers are more likely than younger farmers to define drought as harsh and long. With greater severity and duration in their definition, they tend to expect fewer such droughts to occur, but droughts that will certainly be felt. They also note a recent reprieve; they feel that drought frequency has decreased in the past few years. Although these more seasoned farmers feel that changes in farming technology will greatly change the nature of future drought impacts, they don't feel that drought has been overcome. They have experienced the deprivation that has resulted from extreme, prolonged drought.

By contrast, young farmers, with a more limited drought horizon, have not seen as many droughts and so, of course, do not recall so many. Because of the pattern of drought history in the region, this experience has not included drought of truly classic proportions. They have only rather limited drought episodes to recall, and thus they tend to define drought as shorter and less severe, and they expect to see more of these milder droughts. More of the farmers in this group feel that they have found effective ways to overcome drought losses.

This relationship between experience and drought perception is of critical importance. Younger farmers, lacking experience of really extreme drought, feel they have drought pretty well in hand, that innovative farming practices will pull them through. The older farmers who have experienced deprivation resulting from extreme drought, although they feel that changes in farming technology will greatly change the nature of future drought impacts, don't feel that drought has been overcome. "Stubble will keep the soil from blowing, but you can only go for so long without rain and still have stubble to leave." "When you can't afford to pump water, irrigation won't be able to protect you from drought, will it?"

As we have suggested, the Ogallala Aquifer is experiencing very different conditions in different areas. To the south, especially in the Texas Panhandle, farmers are running out of irrigation water. Unfavorable economic conditions are constraining irrigation throughout the region and rates of new irrigation development over the Ogallala Aquifer have greatly declined (see Taylor, Downton, and Stewart, in press). Thus, a demonstrated adaptation that modifies the effects of drought, irrigation from the Ogallala Aquifer, is faltering. Heathcote (1980) notes, in his study of desertification on the Great Plains, "Even if the swings of the seasons are not greater than those previously experienced, the impact of drought is likely to increase because of the recent expansion of irrigated farming, which has already produced significant reduction of local water tables and fears for their ultimate exhaustion." When extreme, prolonged drought does come again to the Ogallala Aquifer region, as history suggests it will, today's young farmers, especially those who are running short on irrigation water supplies, may be in for a very harsh awakening.

420

NOTES

1. More details, and results from other lines of questioning, can be found in Taylor, Downton, and Stewart (in press).

2. Monthly PDSI values were aggregated for comparison with farmers' recollections of "drought years." PDSI values of -1.0 or below (Palmer's "drought threshhold") were added to give a rough index that includes both drought severity and duration. Separate PDSI plots of values for each of the five study areas revealed very similar patterns. Therefore, the values were added across the five regions, and the results are plotted in Fig. 1.

3. The Pearson product-moment correlation coefficient was -0.65 for the period 1960-84.

4. The regression coefficient for June was smaller than the coefficient for July and of opposite sign, so its effect was to *remove* some of the cumulative moisture information contained in the July Palmer Index value.

5. This difference between groups was statistically significant at a 99% confidence level, using a chi-squared test.

6. Based on a stepwise discriminant analysis.

7. This difference in drought expectation is statistically significant at a 95% confidence level based on nonparametric analysis of variance using the Kruskal-Wallis test.

8. The north-south difference is statistically significant at a 99% confidence level using a Wilcoxon test.

9. Based on a nonparametric analysis of variance using the Kruskal-Wallis test.

10. The comparison with age used the chi-squared test; the comparison with experience used the Wilcoxon test.

REFERENCES

Alley, W. M. 1984. The Palmer Drought Severity Index: Limitations and assumptions. J. Clim. Applied Meteorol. 23:1100-1109.

Bowden, M. J. 1976. The Great American Desert in the American mind: The historiography of a geographical notion. pp. 119-147. In D. Lowenthal and M. J. Bowden, eds. Geographies of the Mind: Essays in Historical Geography in Honor of John Kirkland Wright. Oxford University Press, New York.

Gutentag, E. D.; F. L. Heimes; N. C. Krothe; R. R. Luckey; and J. B. Weeks. 1984. Geohydrology of the High Plains Aquifer in parts of Colorado, Kansas, Nebraska, New Mexico, Oklahoma, South Dakota, Texas, and Wyoming. U.S. Geological Survey Prof. Paper 1400-B. U.S. Government Printing Office, Washington, D.C.

Heathcote, R. L. 1980. Perception of desertification on the Southern Great Plains: A preliminary enquiry. pp. 34-59. In R. L. Heathcote, ed. Perception of Desertification. United Nations University, Tokyo.

Heathcote, R. L. 1974. Drought in South Australia. pp. 128-136. In G. F. White, ed. Natural Hazards: Local, National, Global. Oxford University Press, New York.

Heathcote, R. L. 1969. Drought in Australia: A Problem of Perception. Geographical Review 59:175-194.

Karl, T. R. 1985. The sensitivity of the Palmer Drought Severity Index and Palmer's Z-index to their calibration coefficients including potential evapotranspiration. J. Clim. Applied Meteorol. 25:77-86.

Kirby, A. V. 1974. Individual and community response to rainfall variability in Oaxaca, Mexico. pp. 119-128. In G. F. White, ed. Natural Hazards: Local, National, Global. Oxford University Press, New York.

Kollmorgen, W.; and J. Kollmorgen. 1973. Landscape Meteorology in the Plains Area. Annals Assoc. Am. Geog. 63(4):424-441.

Lawson, M. P. 1974. The Climate of the Great American Desert. University of Nebraska Studies, New Series No. 46. University of Nebraska-Lincoln.

Oladipo, E. O. 1985. A comparative performance analysis of three meteorological drought indices. J. Climatol. 5:655-664.

Palmer, W. C. 1965. Meteorological drought. U.S. Department of Commerce, Weather Bureau Research Paper 45.

Saarinen, T. F. 1966. Perception of the Drought Hazard on the Great Plains. Department of Geography Research Paper No. 106, University of Chicago.

Taylor, J. G.; M. W. Downton; and T. R. Stewart. 1987. Adapting to environmental change: Perceptions and farming practices in the Ogallala Aquifer region. In Proceedings: Arid Lands, Today and Tomorrow. An International Arid Lands Research and Development Conference (in press).

Warrick, R. A. 1975. Drought Hazard in the U.S.: A Research Assessment. Institute of Behavioral Studies, University of Colorado, Boulder.

Warrick, R. A.; and M. J. Bowden. 1981. The changing impacts of drought in the Great Plains. pp. 111-137. In M. P. Lawson and M. E. Baker, eds. The Great Plains: Perspectives and Prospects. University of Nebraska Press, Lincoln.

Wilhite, D. A.; and M. H. Glantz. 1985. Understanding the drought phenomenon: The role of definitions. Water Int. 10:111-120.

Worster, D. 1979. Dust Bowl: The Southern Plains in the 1930s. Oxford University Press, New York.

PART 7

Planning and Response by Government

CHAPTER 25
THE ROLE OF GOVERNMENT IN PLANNING FOR DROUGHT:
WHERE DO WE GO FROM HERE?

Donald A. Wilhite

INTRODUCTION

During the twentieth century, governments have typically responded to drought by providing emergency, short-term, and long-term assistance to distressed areas. Emergency and short-term assistance programs are often reactive, a kind of "band-aid" approach to more serious land and water management problems (Rosenberg, 1980; Hamer, 1985; Wilhite, et al., 1986). Actions of this type have long been criticized as inefficient and ineffective by the scientific community and government officials, as well as by recipients of relief. Long-term assistance programs are far fewer in number, but they are proactive. They attempt to lessen a region's vulnerability to drought through improved management and planning.

The vulnerability of developed and developing societies to drought has been reemphasized as a result of recent drought occurrences in Africa, Australia, Brazil, China, and the United States. These droughts have demonstrated the need for additional planning to help mitigate the possible worst effects of future droughts. The need for national drought planning exists in all drought-prone regions, as noted in the recent memorandum from the World Meteorological Organization (1986). Case studies of recent drought episodes, impacts, and governmental response in Botswana, northeast Brazil, and India are included in this section of the proceedings.

The purpose of this paper is to briefly review and evaluate the policies adopted by governments in response to recent episodes of severe drought. The mid-1970s droughts in the United States and Canada and the more recent droughts of the early 1980s in Australia and South Africa will be used as examples of prior drought mitigation efforts. Furthermore, recommendations will be made on how governments can improve drought mitigation efforts. The concept of drought policy and planning will be discussed in this context.

GOVERNMENTAL RESPONSE TO DROUGHT: U.S. AND CANADA

Droughts of the Mid-1970s

United States. Several episodes of widespread, severe drought have occurred in the United States during the past decade. The droughts of the mid-1970s, 1980, 1983,

1985, and 1986 are most noteworthy. Each of these recent droughts produced significant impacts and major economic losses. However, the mid-1970s droughts were the last episodes to result in massive response efforts by the federal government. This response effort culminated in 1977 after two or more consecutive years of drought in large sections of the Far West, northern Great Plains, and upper Midwest states.

The years 1974, 1976, and 1977 stand out as those in which the greatest economic losses occurred. Impacts were most critical in the agricultural sector, but the municipal, industrial, and recreational sectors were also affected. In 1974, the timing of the precipitation deficiency and heat wave resulted in reduced yields of corn and other grains, particularly in the central and southern plains states.

Weather conditions improved considerably during 1975, but drought returned in 1976 to many western states (Wagner, 1976). By May, the drought-affected area included all of California. By July, two pockets of extreme drought had developed. The first was in California and adjacent states. The second drought area extended from north central Nebraska through eastern South Dakota, southeastern North Dakota, and southern Minnesota to Wisconsin.

It became apparent by January 1977 that, because of below-normal snowpack in the Far West, irrigation water would be short the following summer. For example, precipitation deficits for the period October-February ranged from 125 mm to 510 mm in the Pacific Northwest (Dickson, 1977a). By April, moisture conditions improved in parts of South Dakota and the central plains while the drought intensified in Wisconsin and Minnesota (USDA, 1977). Drought conditions in the upper Midwest and West deteriorated further during April and May, and the total area affected expanded significantly. By the end of May, moderate to extreme drought affected the northern half of the eastern United States and most of the West as well.

Moisture shortages and high temperature conditions were moderating by August, but the spatial extent of drought had changed only slightly (Fig. 1). The situation had improved slowly by September, first in the Far West, central plains, and central Midwest, then in the northern plains. From December 1977 through March 1978, weather conditions improved considerably in the far western states. Precipitation was normal or above normal during the entire period, which considerably improved the water supply outlook for irrigation during the summer of 1978.

Canada. The drought that affected the Canadian prairie provinces of Alberta, Manitoba, and Saskatchewan during the 1976-77 period was largely an extension of a widespread drought that was occurring simultaneously in the United States. The drought began during the winter months of 1976-77. Precipitation during the period of September 1976 to April 1977 was 50% of normal in the southern portion of Saskatchewan and Manitoba and a small portion of Alberta. By April the region's moisture conditions were characterized by below-normal snowpack, low soil moisture reserves, and reduced streamflow and ground-water reserves. By the end of May, heavy precipitation throughout the region had alleviated the impending threat of widespread drought.

Drought Policy and Assistance Measures During the Mid-1970s

United States. Although many programs are now available to alleviate economic and physical hardship caused by natural disasters, only a few of these

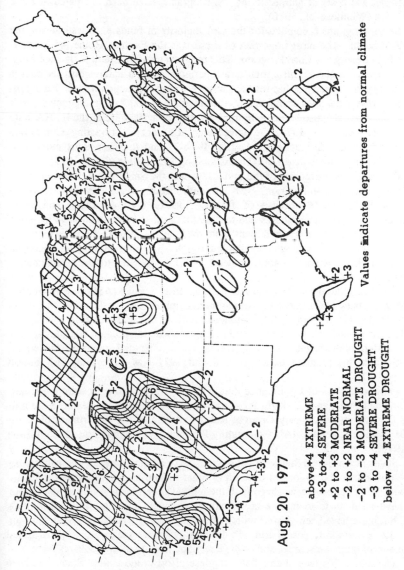

Aug. 20, 1977

above+4 EXTREME
+3 to+4 SEVERE
+2 to +3 MODERATE
-2 to +2 NEAR NORMAL
-2 to -3 MODERATE DROUGHT
-3 to -4 SEVERE DROUGHT
below -4 EXTREME DROUGHT

Values indicate departures from normal climate

Fig. 1 Palmer Drought Severity Index values for the United States, August 20, 1977.

programs are designed specifically to cope with drought. The total funds allocated during 1974-77 to lessen the effects of the drought through various loan and grant programs, plus the costs of administering the programs, have been estimated at more than $8 billion (Wilhite, et al., 1986).

Seven programs accounted for the vast majority of funds disbursed during the mid-1970s drought. The most important of these was the Farmers Home Administration's (FmHA) Emergency Loan Program. This program provides credit assistance to established farmers, ranchers, and agricultural operators when a natural disaster causes physical damage to property or has resulted in severe crop production losses. Emergency loans are made in counties designated by the president as major or emergency disaster areas. Designations can also be made by the secretary of agriculture or the FmHA state director. After April 25, 1977, the Interagency Drought Coordinating Committee (IDCC) also triggered designations. During 1976-77 and the first eight months of FY1978, FmHA made more than 92,000 loans totaling $3.23billion (GAO, 1979).

A second major program of the mid-1970s was the Small Business Administration's (SBA) Disaster Loan Program. SBA was authorized to make loans as determined necessary and appropriate because of floods, riots or civil disorders, and other catastrophes. Crop production losses due to drought or other events were first included in SBA's program in June 1977, and loans were made available to farmers beginning in July 1977. Two types of loans were available through SBA: physical disaster loans and economic injury loans. Congress appropriated $1.4 billion for SBA to meet the demands of farmers (GAO, 1979).

The Agricultural Stabilization and Conservation Service (ASCS), a subagency of the United States Department of Agriculture, administered the Disaster Payments Program. Under this program, a farmer whose production was reduced by natural disaster to less than two-thirds of his historical average production became eligible for payment of one-third of the target price level (ASCS, 1976). The total amount disbursed nationally through this program between 1974 and 1977 was more than $1.8 billion (ASCS, 1974-77).

Other programs of significance during the mid-1970s drought were the Emergency Fund and Emergency Drought Programs of the Department of Interior, $130 million; the Community Emergency Drought Relief Program of the Department of Commerce, $175 million; and FmHA's Community Program Loans and Grants, $225 million (GAO, 1979).

States in the United States do not have fiscal or administrative responsibility for relief measures under conditions of drought or other natural disasters. Since the 1930s, this responsibility has been centralized with the federal government (Wilhite, 1983). Attempts have been made to initiate cost-sharing measures, such as during the 1950s drought, but these have been viewed with disfavor by state government (Wilhite, et al., 1984). State opposition to cost-sharing on drought assistance measures has been based on arguments of limited resources and/or the interstate inequity of available resources.

The mid-1970s federal and state response effort in the United States has been documented and evaluated elsewhere (GAO, 1979; Wilhite, et al., 1984). The latter study demonstrated that governments in the United States often respond to drought through crisis management rather than by risk management. This was true not only in the mid-1970s but also in previous episodes of widespread and severe drought. In crisis management the time to act is perceived by decision makers to be short. Reaction to crisis often results in the implementation of hastily prepared assessment and response procedures that may lead to ineffective, poorly coordinated, and untimely response. The studies cited above suggest that if planning were initiated between periods of drought, the opportunity would exist to develop an organized response that might more effectively address issues and impacts specific to drought. Also, the limited resources available to government to mitigate the effects of drought might be allocated in a more beneficial manner.

Both of the studies cited above recommend the formulation of a national plan as a means of improving federal drought assessment and response activities. The components of a drought plan will be discussed later in this paper. Wilhite, et al. (1984), also recommend greater involvement by state government in drought planning to complement and facilitate the federal effort. To date, no formal action on these recommendations has taken place at the federal level. State planning efforts, largely in response to the mid-1970s and subsequent droughts, have been completed in Colorado, South Dakota, New York (Wilhite and Wood, 1985), and (most recently) Nebraska and South Carolina.

Canada. In response to the threat of significant impacts in the prairie provinces from the short-term drought of 1976-77, both the provincial and federal governments responded with emergency financial and technical aid programs. Assistance was made available for drilling farm and municipal wells, transporting livestock and feed, and constructing stock ponds.

Liverman (1980) evaluated governmental response to this short-term drought. She concluded that the organizational structure set up to deal with emergencies such as drought was ignored during the 1976-77 period. Instead, a hierarchy of new committees was established within the government. Another coordination problem occurred because the jurisdictional units administered by various governmental agencies had different boundaries. This resulted in poor coordination between agencies at various levels of government.

There was also considerable disagreement between key decision makers over what constitutes a drought. This led to disagreement and indecision over the need for action. Also, reliance on precipitation statistics to determine the severity of impacts resulted in poor assessments of probable impact. The lack of good information and the overpublicizing of the event by the media led to overreaction by government. In the final analysis the drought was of moderate severity and produced few negative impacts. Liverman (1980) concluded that in most cases drought assistance was not justified.

Droughts of the Early 1980s

Australia. The 1982-83 drought was confined primarily to eastern Australia (Fig. 2), but portions of this area had been experiencing less severe droughts for a number of years. South Australia and New South Wales, for example, had experienced drought in each year since 1976 and 1979, respectively (Reynolds, et al., 1983). Clearly, the droughts preceding 1982-83 increased the vulnerability of agricultural producers to added effects of severe drought.

The "official" drought in New South Wales began in May 1979, when eight of the fifty-eight Pastoral Protection Districts were drought declared. By January of 1980,

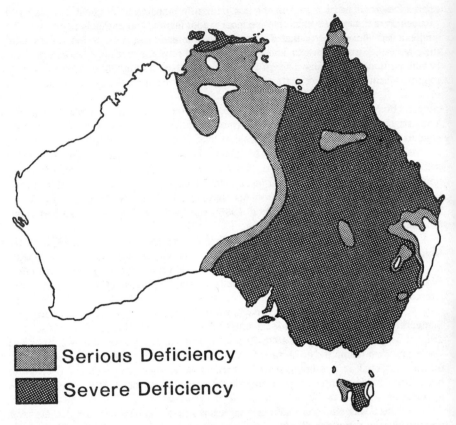

Serious Deficiency

Severe Deficiency

Fig. 2 Major drought-affected areas in Australia, 1983. The spatial extent of the drought was basically the same during 1982.

the rainfall situation had deteriorated still further and twenty-three districts were declared. Drought persisted but was of variable spatial extent and severity until August 1982, when a further rapid deterioration occurred. Between September 1982 and April 1983, more than fifty districts were drought declared. As a consequence of the drought, sheep numbers declined from a peak of about 73 million in the 1970s to about 43 million in 1983. Cattle numbers declined from a peak of 9 million in 1976 to about 4 million in 1983. The 1982-83 wheat crop was reduced from the normal 7 million to 1.5 million metric tons, for a loss of approximately A$825 million (New South Wales Department of Agriculture, 1983). The magnitude of the agricultural impacts in the other eastern states was similar to that in New South Wales. Over the entire country, farm debt increased by about 7%; in Victoria, the debt increased by almost 15%.

South Africa. Droughts are a normal feature of the climate of South Africa. In 1980 and the early months of 1981 the South African drought was mostly confined to the extreme southwest and northern parts of the country. During 1981 the drought area spread eastward and southward. By early 1982 Palmer Drought Severity Index (PDSI) values were in the -2.0 (moderate drought) to -3.0 (severe drought) range for the central regions and -4.0 or less (extreme drought) in the extreme west and north. By mid-1983 the area of extreme drought had expanded significantly in spatial coverage; all but a small portion of the Transvaal was affected by at least moderate drought (Department of Agricultural Technical Services, 1980-83).

The drought resulted in severe hardships for farmers and also had a catastrophic impact on the nation's economy. South Africa, normally a major exporter of grains and other agricultural products, suddenly became an importer. Usually the world's third leading exporter of corn, South African imports in 1983 were expected to be about 2 million tons. Also, exports to neighboring states and to those in East and West Africa were significantly reduced as a direct result of the drought. This drought has not been confined to South Africa, but rather has affected a large portion of southern Africa. The impacts of and associated governmental responses to this drought in Botswana are the focus of a paper in these proceedings by T. C. Moremi.

Drought Policy and Assistance Measures of the Early 1980s

Australia. The Australian constitution does not delegate specific powers covering natural disaster relief to the federal government. These powers belong primarily to the states, which, as a result, have taken a more active role in drought response than state governments in the United States and elsewhere.

Before 1971, natural disaster relief and restoration was provided at a state's request by joint federal/state financing on a 1:1 cost-sharing basis. No limit was set on the level of funding that could be provided by the federal government. In 1971 the Natural Disaster Relief Arrangements (NDRA) were established, whereby states were expected to meet a certain base level or threshold of expenditures for disaster relief from their own resources (Department of Primary Industry, 1984). Disasters provided for in this arrangement are droughts, cyclones, storms, floods, and bushfires. These expenditure thresholds were set according to 1969-70 state budget receipts and, therefore, varied between states. The base levels were raised in 1978 and 1984 (National Drought Consultative Committee, 1984; Keating, 1984). Under the NDRA arrangements, the federal government agreed to provide full reimbursement of eligible expenditures after the thresholds for state expenditures on natural disasters were reached. The NDRA formalized, for the first time, joint federal-state natural disaster relief arrangements.

At the time of the establishment of NDRA, a special set of core measures (i.e., federal government-approved drought assistance measures) had evolved in each state on the basis of thirty years of government involvement in disaster relief. These measures were particularly relevant to the needs of each state because they had been designed by state government in response to its own disaster-related experiences.

Tables 1 and 2 provide data on state and federal expenditures for drought aid from 1970-71 to 1983-84 under the NDRA. The magnitude of state expenditures is significant, especially when compared to the limited financial responsibility of states in the United States. The total for all states was just over A$570 million. Of this total, approximately A$180 million was expended during 1982-83 and A$120 million was spent during 1983-84. Federal expenditures to the states for drought aid under the NDRA ar-

Table 1
Expenditures in Australian States Under Natural Disaster Relief Arrangements, By Type of Disaster, 1970-71 to 1983-84 (A$ Thousands) (National Drought Consultative Committee, 1984)

	New South Wales	Victoria	Queensland	South Australia	Western Australia	Tasmania	Northern Territory	TOTAL
				DROUGHT				
1970-71	3,239	—	15,623	—	—	596	—	19,458
1971-72	458	—	3,143	—	—	—	—	3,601
1972-73	—	—	—	—	—	—	—	
1973-74	987	—	—	—	—	—	—	987
1974-75	160	—	—	—	—	—	—	160
1975-76	—	—	—	—	—	—	—	
1976-77	1,120	1,626	—	—	3,023	—	—	5,769
1977-78	2,620	1,228	2,785	13,580	17,999	—	—	38,212
1978-79	3,013	1,422	5,165	9,257	8,070	—	—	26,927
1979-80	—	—	2,208	2,225	12,560	—	—	16,993
1980-81	66,810	—	22,768	—	20,142	—	—	109,720
1981-82	31,018	—	9,608	—	5,081	295	—	46,002
1982-83	53,645	34,796	51,982	27,380	12,653	1,282	—	181,738
1983-84 (estimate)	21,500	8,100	63,300	4,600	22,100	1,900	—	121,500
Total	184,570	47,172	176,582	57,042	101,628	4,073	—	571,067

Table 2
Commonwealth of Australia Payments Under Natural Disaster Relief Arrangements, Estimated by Type of Disaster, 1970-71 To 1983-84 (A$ Thousands) (National Drought Consultative Committee, 1984)

	New South Wales	Victoria	Queens-land	South Australia	Western Australia	Tasmania	Northern Territory	TOTAL
				DROUGHT				
1970-71	450	—	13,632	—	—	16	—	14,098
1971-72	—	—	1,502	—	—	—	—	1,502
1972-73	—	—	46	—	—	—	—	46
1973-74	38	—	—	—	—	—	—	38
1974-75	114	—	—	—	—	—	—	114
1975-76	—	—	—	—	—	—	—	—
1976-77	779	716	—	—	2,134	—	—	3,629
1977-78	1,458	399	3,091	12,350	15,269	—	—	32,567
1978-79	743	173	2,942	5,430	6,036	—	—	15,324
1979-80	—	-229	1,224	-270	6,922	—	—	7,647
1980-81	42,447	—	14,780	-737	13,523	—	—	70,013
1981-82	14,554	—	5,162	—	2,239	267	—	22,222
1982-83	32,557	22,695	37,297	18,368	7,731	—	—	118,648
1983-84 (estimate)	11,800	4,600	45,300	4,300	15,300	600	—	81,900
Total	104,940	28,354	124,976	39,441	69,154	883	—	367,748

rangements (Table 2) were just under A$370 million, or about A$200 million less than the total state expenditures. The largest share of the assistance was provided to Queensland and New South Wales.

In addition to the cost-sharing measures described above, two federal drought assistance schemes were available during the 1982-83 drought. These were the Drought Relief Fodder Subsidy Scheme and the Drought Relief Interest Subsidy Scheme (National Drought Consultative Committee, 1984). The Fodder Subsidy Scheme provided a payment to drought-declared primary producers to help defray the cost of fodder for sheep and cattle. The administrative costs of this program were covered by the states. The amount of the subsidy was based on 50% of the price of feed wheat and the nutritive value of the fodder relative to wheat; Commonwealth expenditures under this program were about A$104 million during 1982-83 and A$18 million through February 1984.

The Drought Relief Interest Subsidy Scheme provided payments to eligible primary producers to cover all interest payments exceeding 12% per year. To be eligible, producers had to have been drought declared and could not have available financial assets in excess of 12% of the total farm debt. Expenditures for the program, not including administrative costs, were about A$3 million in 1982-83 and A$23 million through February 1984.

The Livestock and Grain Producers Association (LGPA) of New South Wales has strongly commended the state and federal governments of Australia for their drought assistance measures. LGPA based its conclusions on the achievement of what it considers to be the first priority of drought aid in Australia—the preservation of the national sheep and cattle herd. Through the preservation of these resources, farm and nonfarm income was able to recover more quickly than after previous episodes of severe drought. LGPA estimated that, had government not intervened in 1982-83, some 15 to 20 million sheep would have been slaughtered. As a result, post-drought recovery would have been delayed, at a cost to the national economy of A$500 million over a five-year period (Anonymous, 1983). However, the Working Group for the Standing Committee of the Australian Agricultural Council (1983) concluded, "With the exception of concessional finance and information, existing policy measures, including those introduced during the current (1982-83) drought, do not perform well in achieving the objectives of drought policy which it considered important. In summary, the nearly $300 million of expenditures was not cost effective."

These contrasting views of the cost effectiveness of recent drought measures in Australia reflect the recent controversy over state and federal involvement in drought aid. Several other studies have been completed (National Farm Federation, 1983; South Australian Department of Agriculture, 1983; Stott, 1983), each providing recommendations for future drought policy. The three Australian Academies of Science (1984) are also working together to try to resolve this issue. At stake is the role that government will play in attempting to alleviate or mitigate the hardship caused by drought and, possibly, other natural disasters as well.

The National Drought Consultative Committee (NDCC) was appointed by the Minister for Primary Industry in 1984 to review Australian drought policy. In a recent report (Ministry for Primary Industry, 1985) NDCC recommends two objectives for a national drought policy: (1) to encourage the efficient allocation of national and regional farm resources; and (2) to minimize the economic hardship caused by drought. In addition, the report identifies several specific national objectives and recommends drought policy measures it considers to be the most effective. The committee also addressed issues concerning the administration, eligibility, and purpose of drought programs, as well as drought declaration and revocation procedures.

South Africa. Until recently, actions taken by the South African government in response to droughts typically have been poorly coordinated and assistance programs have been largely ineffective (personal communication from C. R. Baard, 1985). According to C. R. Baard, chief director of Regulatory Services of the Department of Agricultural Economics and Marketing in Pretoria, South Africa, the government has had difficulty assessing drought impact and making subsequent declarations, as have governments of most of the world's drought-prone regions. And, no routine comprehensive evaluation of government drought policy and response efforts has been completed.

For many decades, drought assistance programs in South Africa have concentrated largely on providing relief to the livestock industry, with little attention to crop farming, either dryland or irrigated. A similar situation has existed in Australia. The rationale behind this emphasis on the livestock industry in South Africa has been that 85% of all agricultural land in the country remains under native pastures, most of which lie in the dry zones of the western and northwestern part of the country. The incidence of drought (i.e., less than 70% of normal precipitation) in these drier zones is about one year in three. Only 15% of South Africa receives precipitation in excess of 500 mm per year.

The drought that began in 1978 has affected, to varying degrees, 75% of the country. Farmers in the crop regions of the Transvaal, Orange Free State, and Natal were hardest hit, as crops were destroyed in four consecutive years. Farmers in these states were unable to obtain credit from local cooperatives or commercial banks. Therefore, the government introduced new drought relief measures, such as debt consolidation loans through the Land Bank and Agricultural Credit Board. During the 1984-85 fiscal year the government spent approximately R447 million in support of these various drought relief programs (personal communication from C. R. Baard, 1985).

As a result of the extended drought period and the ineffectiveness of government drought programs, the South African government recently undertook a substantial reevaluation of their drought policy. The Phase Drought Relief Scheme, in effect since 1946, is now being gradually eliminated. This review of drought policy and programs has resulted in a clearer concept of what the objectives of drought relief policy should be. Assistance programs, the instruments of that policy, are being revised accordingly. The primary objective of the new drought relief strategy for the livestock regions of South Africa is to introduce measures that will ensure optimum utilization of the agricultural resources while avoiding detrimental effects on pasture lands.

DROUGHT POLICY COMPARISONS

A comparative analysis of drought policy in the United States and Australia during recent severe drought episodes has been completed and appears elsewhere (Wilhite, 1986). The results of this study will be presented here as examples of two approaches followed by governments to assess and respond to drought.

For purposes of comparison, the principal features of drought policy are grouped into three categories: organization, response, and evaluation (Table 3). *Or-*

Table 3
Comparison of Drought Policy Features: United States and Australia Status as of 1984

Features	United States	Australia
ORGANIZATION:		
National drought plan	None	Study in progress
State drought plans	In selected states	Through NDRA agreements
National drought early warning system	Joint USDA/NOAA Weather Facility	Bureau of Meteorology
Agricultural impact assessment techniques	Available, but generally unreliable	None available
Responsibility for drought declaration	Federal	State
Geographic unit of designation	County	Unit varies between states
Declaration procedures	Standard for all states, varies by program/agency	Varies between states; standard within states

RESPONSE:

State fiscal responsibility for assistance measures	Negligible, if any	Defined by NDRA agreements up to base amounts, varies by state
State administrative responsibility for assistance measures	No responsibility for federal measures	Defined by NDRA agreements and by federal measures
Eligibility requirements and provisions of drought assistance measures	Standard within programs for all designated counties	Varies by state for NDRA core measures, standard for federal programs
National crop insurance program	All-risk federal program	Rainfall insurance feasibility study in progress

EVALUATION:

Post-drought documentation and evaluation of procedures and measures	No routine evaluation by government	Routine evaluation by federal and state governments

ganizational features are planning activities that provide timely and reliable assessments, such as a drought early warning system; and procedures for a coordinated and efficient response, such as drought declaration and revocation. These characteristics would be the foundation of a national drought plan. Only a few states in the United States have drought plans (Wilhite and Wood, 1985). State drought plans exist only in a loose form in Australia under the NDRA agreements.

Response features refer to assistance measures and associated administrative procedures that are in place to assist individual citizens or businesses experiencing economic and physical hardship because of drought. Numerous assistance measures are available in the United States but few are intended specifically for drought. Relief arrangements in Australia are, for the most part, included under the NDRA agreements. An all-risk crop insurance program has been evolving in the United States since 1939 (Federal Crop Insurance Corporation, 1980). The Australian Bureau of Agricultural Economics has studied the feasibility of a rainfall insurance scheme and recommends the adoption of such a scheme under new drought policy guidelines. Hail and flood insurance is provided by commercial insurance companies in some areas.

Evaluation of organizational procedures and drought assistance measures in the post-drought recovery period is the third category of drought policy features. Governments in Australia have been more conscientious in their evaluation of recent drought response efforts. In the United States, government does not routinely evaluate the performance of response-related procedures or drought assistance measures. The General Accounting Office (1979) made an evaluation of the 1976-77 drought response activities at the request of the chairman of the Subcommittee on Environment, Energy, and Natural Resources, the late Congressman Leo J. Ryan. Wilhite, et al. (1984), evaluated governmental response to the mid-1970s drought under sponsorship of the National Science Foundation. These were the first systematic evaluations of federal drought response efforts in the United States.

THE OBJECTIVES OF DROUGHT POLICY

The underlying question is this: Should government be involved in providing assistance to those economic sectors or persons that experience hardship in times of drought? Because of the frequency, severity, and spatial extent of drought, governments in the United States, Canada, Australia, South Africa, and elsewhere have elected to provide assistance, and through a wide range of measures. These drought assistance measures are the instruments of a *de facto* policy that has evolved over the past fifty years. The decision on whether to provide aid has been based more often on political than economic reasoning. Thus, government involvement in drought relief seems to be a political reality, and one that should be dealt with in a more effective and efficient manner.

Previous discussion has concentrated on government response to recent episodes of widespread, severe drought in the United States, Canada, Australia, and South Africa. These drought relief attempts have been shown to be largely ineffective, poorly coordinated, and untimely. In these examples, governments have reacted to, rather than prepared for, recurrent and inevitable episodes of drought.

For purposes of contingency planning, the objectives of any government drought policy must be stated explicitly. Without clearly stated drought policy objectives, contingency planning will lack direction and purpose. Also, the effectiveness of drought assessment and response actions will be difficult to evaluate. In response to recent experiences, Australia and South Africa have begun stating drought policy objectives and formulating institutional plans and programs to carry out these objectives.

I propose three objectives for a national drought policy. First, assistance measures should not discourage agricultural producers, municipalities, and other groups from the adoption of appropriate and efficient management practices that help to alleviate the effects of drought. Second, assistance should be provided in an equitable, consistent, and predictable manner to all without regard to economic circumstances, industry, or geographic region. Third, the importance of protecting the natural and agricultural resource base must be recognized. Although these objectives may not be achievable in all cases, they do represent a model against which recent drought policies and measures, the instruments of that policy, can be evaluated. Drought policy objectives are also the foundation of any planning effort by federal and state governments.

DROUGHT PLANNING: WHAT IS IT?

Drought planning can be defined as actions taken by government, industry, individual citizens, and others in advance of drought for the purpose of mitigating some of the impacts associated with its occurrence. For purposes of this paper, drought planning should include, but is not limited to, the following activities:

1. A monitoring/early warning system to provide decision makers at all levels with information about the onset, continuation, and termination of drought conditions and their severity.
2. Operational assessment programs to determine, reliably, the likely impact of the drought event.
3. An institutional structure for coordinating governmental actions, including information flow within and between levels of government, and drought declaration and revocation criteria and procedures.
4. Appropriate drought assistance programs with predetermined eligibility and implementation criteria.
5. Financial resources to maintain operational programs and to initiate research required to support drought assessment and response activities.
6. Educational programs designed to promote the adoption of appropriate drought mitigation strategies among the various economic sectors most affected by drought.

DROUGHT POLICY/PLANNING RECOMMENDATIONS

For government in the United States to significantly improve its drought assessment and response capability, progress must be made in four key areas. The experiences of Australia, South Africa, and Canada have been similar to those of the United States, suggesting that the following recommendations will be applicable in these countries as well.

1. Reliable and timely informational products. Reliable and timely informational products (advisories, reports, management recommendations) and information dissemination plans must be developed. For example, few can question the significance of more reliable and timely information about appropriate drought management strategies. Campbell (1973) has argued that Australian farmers have not exploited the available management strategies to their fullest. It would appear that this conclusion applies equally well to most farmers in drought-prone areas. Government or the private sector should provide information to producers, not only about the relative costs and benefits of alternative management strategies, but also about the probability of droughts of various duration and intensity. Such information could reduce drought impact as well as the need for government assistance. Government must also inform potential recipients more effectively about the availability and provisions of drought assistance measures.

2. Improved impact assessment techniques. Impact assessment techniques must be improved. In the case of agriculture, usually the first economic sector to experience the hardships of drought, new tools must be developed to provide decision makers in government and business with the types of information necessary to identify the onset and termination of drought and to better understand the severity of drought and its likely impact. These tools would be used by government to identify periods of abnormal risk and to trigger various assistance measures.

3. Centralized designation and revocation procedures. Designation procedures in the United States, for example, must be centralized under a single agency or committee with complete authority to determine eligibility for all assistance programs. Criteria must be determined in advance of drought, well publicized when drought occurs, and applied consistently to all affected states, counties, and localities. Revocation procedures must be similarly defined.

Procedures for drought designation and revocation must be specific to each country, reflecting differences in the system of government, the relative importance of the various economic sectors, water supply and management characteristics, cultural differences, and so forth. In Australia, for example, the declaration of drought areas is a state responsibility, and procedures differ considerably between states. It may not be feasible to standardize procedures between the states because of the large precipitation gradients that exist over much of the country. In contrast, drought declaration decisions in the United States are a federal responsibility, considered at a state's request. Declaration procedures vary between agencies and, at times, between programs and within agencies. Drought policies with respect to revocation of declarations must be better defined and take into account the lingering effects of drought.

4. Adoption of a proactive approach to drought assistance program development. Assistance measures must be developed in advance of drought—that is, a proactive approach should be taken to avoid the delays in program for-

mulation and congressional approval such as occurred in the United States during the mid-1970s. Programs should be administered by a single agency through the mechanism of an interagency committee in which federal agencies with responsibility in drought assessment and response are represented. Representatives of the affected states and/or regions should be included in the membership of this committee. Assistance measures must address the specific problems associated with drought.

Another question deserving considerable attention in the discussion of national drought policy is the degree of fiscal and administrative responsibility that states should have in support of assistance measures. The Australian approach of cost-sharing these programs has been quite successful and may be applicable in the United States and elsewhere. Such an approach would allow states to have greater fiscal and administrative control over assistance measures. These measures could also be tailored to reflect the unique water supply problems and specific drought-related impacts of each state.

More attention should be directed to the development of assistance measures that encourage producers to incorporate appropriate levels of risk management in individual farm plans. Recipients of drought aid would benefit from knowing, in advance, what types of assistance will, and will not, be provided. Generally, Australians prefer assistance in the form of loans because recipients retain the flexibility to use the money in a way that best suits their farming situation; that is, farm management decisions remain with the farmer. Loans also have an important secondary effect: farmers can continue to spend at relatively normal levels and the economy of neighboring communities is not disturbed substantially. Equity requires that loans be made available to all. The Australian government has concluded that feed reserves and freight subsidies for water and feed can discourage the adoption of appropriate risk management techniques. These measures promote soil degradation by keeping livestock on the land during periods when the vegetation is severely stressed.

SUMMARY AND CONCLUSIONS

The purpose of this paper is to evaluate and compare current drought policy and government responses to recent droughts and to offer recommendations for policy change. The experiences of the United States, Canada, Australia, and South Africa were used as examples. Four critical needs were identified: (1) reliable and timely informational products and dissemination plans that provide producers with better information about drought, alternative management strategies, and assistance measures available; (2) improved impact assessment techniques, especially in the agricultural sector, for use by government to identify periods of abnormal risk and to trigger assistance measures; (3) administratively centralized drought declaration procedures that are well publicized and consistently applied; and (4) equitable, consistent, and predictable standby assistance measures that encourage producers to develop and maintain appropriate levels of risk management. These measures must not discriminate against good farm managers. Most of these recommendations will be applicable to drought policy and planning needs in developed and developing countries alike.

Governments in the United States have responded to drought by crisis management rather than risk management. This approach has been grossly ineffective. Several recent studies have addressed the issue of drought policy, or lack of it, in the United States and have concluded that we should now move toward drought planning with the aim of improving its efficiency. The development of a national drought plan is proposed as an effective way of implementing these recommendations in the United States. In Australia, two national drought committees have considered the benefits of a national drought policy that would be the basis for a plan. A national drought policy, although only recently formulated, has now been adopted. Similar progress has been made in South Africa. Actions of this type have been called for in all drought-prone nations by the World Meteorological Organization (1986).

In the United States a national drought plan could encourage and perhaps provide incentive to states to take a more active role in planning for drought. In fact, drought planning should be coordinated between the states and federal government. In the past, most states have played a passive role, relying almost exclusively on the federal government to come to the assistance of residents of the drought-affected area. Although the federal government has accepted this role, improving government response to drought requires a cooperative effort. States must develop their own organizational plan for collecting, analyzing, and disseminating information on drought conditions. Cost-sharing of drought assistance measures should be pursued as a means of involving state government in drought assistance. The level of state involvement in drought planning in other countries must be determined on a case-by-case basis.

REFERENCES

ASCS. 1974-77. Annual Reports: Feed Grain, Wheat and Cotton Program, Disaster Provision. U.S. Department of Agriculture, Washington, D.C.
ASCS. 1976. Annual Report, Nebraska. U.S. Department of Agriculture, Lincoln, Nebraska.
Anonymous. 1983. LGPA submits priorities for government assistance in future drought situations. Livestock and Grain Producer 6:1-3.
Australian Academies of Science. 1984. National strategy for drought—Background and objectives. Notes for joint study of Australian Academies of Science. Prepared by Garth Paltridge, CSIRO, Aspendale, Victoria, Australia.
Australian Agricultural Council. 1983. An evaluation of existing drought policies given the current drought experience. Report by Standing Committee on Agriculture Working Group, Canberra, Australia.
Campbell, K. O. 1973. The future role of agriculture in the Australian economy. In J. V. Lovett, ed. The Environmental, Economic and Social Significance of Drought. Angus and Robertson, Sydney, Australia.
Department of Agricultural Technical Services. 1980-83. Maps of the Palmer Drought Severity Index for South Africa. Published monthly. Pretoria, South Africa.
Department of Primary Industry. 1984. Review of the Natural Disaster Relief Arrangements. Prepared for the National Drought Consultative Committee, Canberra, Australia.
Dickson, R. R. 1977. Weather and circulation of February 1977. Mon. Weather Rev. 105:684-689.

Federal Crop Insurance Corporation. 1980. An Inside Look at All-Risk Crop Insurance. Washington, D.C.

General Accounting Office. 1979. Federal Response to the 1976-77 Drought: What Should Be Done Next? Report to the Comptroller General. Washington, D.C.

Hamer, W. I. 1985. A Review of the 1982-83 Drought. Victoria Department of Agriculture, Technical Report Series No. 104, Melbourne.

Keating, P. J. 1984. Payments to or for the states, the Northern Territory and local government authorities, 1984-85. Treasurer of the Commonwealth of Australia, 1984-85. Budget Paper No. 7. Canberra, Australia.

Liverman, D. 1980. Coordination of response to drought in the Canadian Prairies. Proceedings, Association of the American Geographers Annual Meeting. Association of American Geographers, Washington, D.C.

Ministry for Primary Industry. 1985. Report by the National Drought Consultative Committee on Drought Policy, Canberra, Australia.

National Drought Consultative Committee. 1984. Drought assistance—Financial arrangements. Notes from meeting, March 28, 1984, Canberra, Australia.

National Farmers' Federation. 1983. Drought policy. National Farmers' Federation, Canberra, Australia.

New South Wales Department of Agriculture. 1983. Drought policies. Prepared by the New South Wales Department of Agriculture, Sydney, Australia.

Reynolds, R. G.; W. D. Watson; and D. J. Collins. 1983. Water resources aspects of drought in Australia. Water 2000: Consultants Report No. 13. Australian Government Publishing Service, Canberra, Australia.

Rosenberg, N. J., ed. 1980. Drought in the Great Plains: Research on Impacts and Strategies. Water Resources Publications, Littleton, Colorado.

South Australian Department of Agriculture. 1983. Rural adjustment: Interim report on drought relief measures. Submission to Industries Assistance Commission Inquiry. South Australian Treasury Department, Adelaide, Australia.

Stott, K. J. 1983. An economic assessment of assistance measures for the 1982-83 drought and for future droughts. Internal Report Series. Department of Agriculture, Victoria, Australia.

United States Department of Agriculture. 1977. Weekly Weather and Crop Bulletin (April 5). Published jointly with the Department of Commerce, Washington, D.C.

Wagner, A. J. 1976. Weather and circulation of January 1976. Mon. Weather Rev. 104:491-498.

Wilhite, D. A. 1983. Government response to drought in the United States: With particular reference to the Great Plains. J. Clim. Applied Meteorol. 22:40-50.

Wilhite, D. A.; N. J. Rosenberg; and M. H. Glantz. 1984. Government Response to Drought in the United States: Lessons From the Mid-1970s. Parts 1-4. Final Report to the Climate Dynamics Program, National Science Foundation. Progress Report 84-1 to 84-4. Center for Agricultural Meteorology and Climatology, University of Nebraska-Lincoln.

Wilhite, D. A.; and D. A. Wood. 1985. Planning for drought: The role of state government. Water Resour. Bull. 21:31-38.

Wilhite, D. A.; N. J. Rosenberg; and M. H. Glantz. 1986. Improving federal response to drought. J. Clim. Applied Meteorol. 25:332-342.

444

Wilhite, D. A. 1986. Drought policy in the U.S. and Australia: A comparative analysis. Water Resour. Bull. 22:425-438.

World Meteorological Organization. 1986. Model Drought Response Plan, Annex 1 to Permanent Representatives of Members of WMO from G. O. P. Obasi, Secretary-General.

CHAPTER 26
DROUGHT PLANNING AND RESPONSE:
BOTSWANA EXPERIENCE

Tswelopele C. Moremi

INTRODUCTION

Botswana is a landlocked country that straddles the Tropic of Capricorn in the center of the southern African Plateau. The country's total land area is 582,000 km^2, about the size of France or Kenya. Botswana shares borders with Zimbabwe, the Republic of South Africa, Namibia (including the Caprivi Strip), and Zambia.

The country is vast and relatively flat, with occasional rocky hills rising from the land. It is divided into three main geographical areas. In the northwest, the Okavango River drains inland from Angola to form an extensive swamp—the Okavango Delta. This unique water source covers 10,000 km^2 and is rich in wildlife and vegetation. In the east, the Limpopo River Valley gradually descends from 900 m in the south to 500 m at its confluence with the Shashe River.

The eastern part of the country has a less harsh climate and more fertile soils in comparison to the rest of the country. Arable land is scarce. It is estimated that less than 5% of Botswana's land area is cultivable, and much of this land is in the east. It is in this part of the country that most of Botswana's population lives. The remaining two-thirds of the country is covered with the thick layer of Kalahari Sand. This sand layer is up to 120 m thick. The Kalahari supports a vegetation of scrub and grasses, but surface water is almost completely absent.

CLIMATE

The geographical position of Botswana in the center of the southern African land mass and the country's latitude (most of Botswana lies north of the Tropic of Capricorn) make for a semiarid continental climate. The average annual rainfall is only 475 mm, and this is erratic (especially in the south) and unevenly distributed. Rainfall distribution ranges from less than 250 mm in the south to more than 650 mm in the northeast. More than 90% of this rain falls in the summer months (from November to April), but in a highly unpredictable manner. Vegetation patterns are closely related to climate and soil type.

Almost all the rainfall occurs during the summer months (from October to April); the period from May to September is generally dry. Most rainfall occurs as localized showers and thunderstorms, and its incidence is highly variable both in time and space.

The prevailing climate conditions are such that apart from the Okavango System, surface water is scarce. Most rivers are ephemeral; the country has few perennial springs, and surface water held in pans or dams evaporates rapidly. Some underground aquifers are recharged by heavy rain, but in the Kalahari most rain is trapped in the top few meters of sand and then lost through evaporation and transpiration. Because of the absence or unreliability of surface water in most parts of the country, boreholes are an important source of water supplies. The low, erratic, and unevenly distributed rainfall makes drought a regular occurrence.

POPULATION CHARACTERISTICS

Botswana's population is small relative to the size of the country. It is growing very rapidly as a result of a high birthrate and declining mortality rate. The country's population is estimated at 1.3 million and is growing at a rate of about 3.4% per annum, making it one of the highest growth rates in Africa. As a result of this high birthrate and the low mortality rate among the population, Botswana has a high proportion of children and young people.

SOCIAL AND ECONOMIC SITUATION AT INDEPENDENCE

Botswana's independence in September 1966 came at the end of a series of severe drought years which had lasted for more than five years. The drought resulted in the loss of about 400,000 cattle and left about one-fifth of the population depending on drought relief food rations. It severely affected the already fragile food and agricultural situation in the country and seriously impaired the rural economy. Planning for social and economic development had to be done on a very meager budget, which had to be substantially supplemented by the United Kingdom. Like persons in many other African countries, more than 95% of Botswana's population lived in the rural areas at the time of independence. Presently, about 84% of the population lives in rural areas. Because the majority of the people depended mainly on agriculture, the country needed to reduce the vulnerability of the population—especially children and pregnant and lactating women—to drought and unreliable food production.

At independence, therefore, Botswana was one of the poorest and least developed countries in the world, with a per capita income of about 60 pula (P60) per annum (then equivalent to about US$80). The economy at the time was supported by migrant labor and some beef exports. The human resource base, in terms of skills, was made up largely of migrant laborers and livestock producers as well as those involved in arable agriculture. Skilled manpower was almost nonexistent in areas that required management and technical skills, and in industry. It became even more urgent for the government to develop a sound infrastructure for social and economic planning in order to ensure effective and efficient utilization of scarce resources.

In light of the country's situation, policy making in the immediate post-independence period was concerned with establishing the economic viability of Botswana, achieving fiscal self-sufficiency, and initiating a small number of relatively large-scale and capital-intensive mining projects (the Selibe-Phikwe Cooper Mine and Letlhakane and Orapa diamond mines). Of great importance on the economic front, Botswana gained preferential access to the beef market of the European community through the First Lome Convention.

Once the economy had been established on a firm basis in the early 1970s, the government developed a broad-based rural development strategy. The core of this strategy, which has remained the centerpiece of successive National Development plans, was to secure the rapid and large returns from the mining sector and other export industries and reinvest these in overall development, with special emphasis on rural development.

DEVELOPMENT OF BOTSWANA'S DROUGHT RELIEF PROGRAMME

In addition to shifting the focus of policy making to broad-based development, the government also needed to recognize drought as a recurring phenomenon that affects, in particular, the poorest sections of Botswana's population.

The most important consideration in developing a policy for drought planning was the acquisition of knowledge and information on the nature of drought as well as the resources required to respond to drought. As a result, in 1976 a consultant was commissioned to investigate the problem of drought, with special reference to the livestock sector. The concern over the effects of drought on the livestock sector is a result of the importance of the beef industry in Botswana's economy, at least during the immediate post-independence period. The consultant's report emphasized the need to develop a human relief program as part of government contingency planning for drought. As a result, in 1977, the Inter-Ministerial Working Group was formed under the chairmanship of the Rural Development Unit of the Ministry of Finance and Development Planning. This Working Group, among others, was to give active consideration to developing a national policy on drought. In 1978, the Botswana Society organized a symposium on drought, which focused on the effects of drought on humans. The results of the symposium provided more information to the government on drought policy planning. An example of the government's increasing concern with drought was the decision in 1978 to develop the Nutritional Surveillance Programme, which would help to determine the effects of drought on certain vulnerable sections of the population.

In 1979-80, the country was once more drought-stricken. The most notable outcome of this drought was not so much the drought mitigation achievements of the government but rather its desire to document and evaluate the 1979-80 Drought Relief Programme. Consequently, in 1980, the government commissioned two consultants to evaluate the 1979-80 Drought Relief Programme and make appropriate recommendations for the future. This evaluation provided an important input to drought policy development. A major recommendation was to strengthen the institutional framework for dealing with drought.

DROUGHT RELIEF PLANNING AND MONITORING

The evaluation of the 1979-80 Drought Relief Programme reinforced the system of drought monitoring, relief coordination, and implementation. At the national level, relief programs are coordinated by the Inter-Ministerial Drought Committee. This Committee is assisted by the Early Warning Technical Sub-Committee in monitoring drought. The Inter-Ministerial Drought Committee meets, on average, every two months. The meetings for this Committee are preceded by meetings of the Subcommittee of the Early Warning Technical Committee, which reports to the Inter-Ministerial Drought Committee. At the local level, district drought committees assume a role similar to that of the Inter-Ministerial Drought Committee.

The Food Resources Department was also created in 1982. The Department's responsibilities include obtaining and distributing food supplies during drought and non-drought years to primary schools, health facilities, children, and other vulnerable groups. The Department also coordinates the labor-based relief program, which provides supplementary income to the able-bodied members of the rural communities. The Food Resources Department represents an important part of the country's attempts to create an adequate drought (and emergency) response capacity as well as to undertake post-drought recovery measures.

The strengthening of the institutional framework as outlined above has created an additional capacity for both anticipating and monitoring the effects of drought. The government of Botswana therefore has been able to reduce the adverse effects of the current drought, which is considered to be the worst five-year drought in recorded history.

CURRENT DROUGHT RELIEF PROGRAMME

As already illustrated, Botswana's Drought Relief Programme has evolved over a period of years and was, in particular, a result of the critical evaluation of the 1979-80 Drought Relief Programme.

The current Drought Relief Programme has the following main objectives:

1. Supplementation of food supplies as a preventive measure to reduce the incidence of, or forestall increases in, malnutrition among those groups considered at high risk. These include the non-able-bodied vulnerable groups (preschool children, pregnant and lactating women, tuberculosis patients, and temporary or permanent destitutes), primary school age children, and those living in remote locations.
2. Supplementation of rural incomes in order to compensate in part for agricultural production lost because of drought.
3. Treatment of malnourished children.
4. Securing water supplies for human consumption.
5. Alleviation of drought effects on livestock.
6. Provision of assistance to crop farmers to increase their ability to regain productivity in the seasons following harvest failure.

In line with these objectives, the Drought Relief Programme has the following components.

Human Relief. This portion of the relief program contains four elements—supplementary food distribution for vulnerable groups on a monthly basis through health facilities; an expanded primary-school feeding program; direct (on-site) feeding for malnourished persons at health facilities in order to effect rapid weight gains; and a special logistical relief effort to bring food supplies to remote areas without shops or social services.

Labor-Based Relief Project. People are employed at a daily wage on village improvement schemes selected by their village development committees in the agricultural slack season. This provides large numbers of rural people with temporary income-earning opportunities. Socially useful or productive structures are created in the process (dams, airstrips, accommodations, storage facilities, access roads, and so forth).

Water Relief. Special funds are made available to district council water units to increase their capacity to make repairs to existing water systems and to transport water to settlements whose normal supplies have been affected. A certain number of new water systems are also constructed in hard-hit areas on an emergency basis if required. A facility is available for farmer groups wishing to improve their water sources for livestock watering or small-scale irrigation.

Agricultural Relief. In an effort to alleviate the constraints imposed by the drought on farming recovery, seed packages are made available to all farmers free of charge; stock feed is sold at highly subsidized prices; cash grants are given to farmers to clear and prepare arable land; and draft power is heavily subsidized for households.

The following are some of the results of the implementation of the programs during 1985-86.

Supplementary feeding reached 384,000 persons in vulnerable groups of the rural population in 1985-86 and also provided food to 18,000 remote-area dwellers. The number of beneficiaries within the vulnerable groups was reduced slightly from the previous year because fewer categories of recipients are eligible in recovery zones. The rations provide one-third of the daily caloric requirements for one person. Almost all districts reported efficient food distribution. They were assisted by the operation of eight new depots and the placement of four new regional officers and four U.N.V. regional advisors in Botswana. In addition, 222,000 primary school children received supplementary food to take home during school vacations. Approximately 53,000 metric tons of foodstuffs were used in the supplementary feeding program in 1985-86.

The labor-based relief program is a cash-for-work program in which participants receive a wage for participating in a village project. However, demand is much greater than the number of jobs available, so participants share the jobs. The program is suspended for several weeks during the planting season, which reduces the total available wages possible for each household. A recent survey found the wage per annum to be P35 to P250 per household in different areas, partly depending on variation in demand by region.

CONTINGENCY PLANNING

The government's concern with the performance of arable agriculture in Botswana, which is characterized by extreme variations (due to erratic rainfall) in both yields per hectare and hectares planted, necessitated that they request additional donor assistance to establish a strategic grain reserve. The government had developed a strategic grain reserve against unexpected food shortages and other emergencies. Unfortunately, because of the need to draw on the reserve during the current drought cycle, the target level (of grain) has not been achieved. In light of the present unstable economic situation, growth in population, and the need to ensure food security, it has been decided to expand the reserve to hold at least a six-month supply of grain. The reserve is therefore an important part of the government's emergency response plans, as has been evidenced by the use of the reserve during the current drought. In addition, as already indicated, it has become a very important part of the government's contingency planning efforts. The expanded project calls for additional food-aid assistance to increase the reserve to the required level.

The concern over inadequate food production as a result of internal crop failure, the persistently inadequate nutritional status of certain groups of Botswana's population, and the need for national food security led to a government decision in 1983 to develop a national food strategy for Botswana as part of National Development Plan VI. The main objective of the National Food Strategy, which was adopted by Parliament in December 1985, is to reduce dependence on foreign sources of basic foodstuffs both at the national level and at the household level. More specifically, the National Food Strategy aims to achieve broad-based recovery in arable production after the current drought cycle, national self-sufficiency in the staple crops of maize and sorghum (both food and seed), and at least a minimum acceptable diet for all Botswana, thus progressively eliminating malnutrition. The National Food Strategy is also aimed at building up the capacity to deal with drought and other related emergencies at the national level.

The National Food Strategy should be seen against the government's long-standing commitment to promote rural development and productive employment opportunities in the rural areas. The objectives of the National Food Strategy have been reflected in the project that the various concerned ministries have developed for National Development Plan VI.

SUMMARY

Because of poor, erratic, and unreliable rainfall and generally poor soils, Botswana is highly vulnerable to drought. In the immediate post-independence period, the government's policy-making efforts were devoted to creating a viable economic base for sustained development. Once the economy had started to "take off," other issues such as drought became crucial items on the policy-making agenda. The evaluation of the 1979-80 Drought Relief Programme enabled the government to strengthen the institutional framework for dealing with drought in Botswana.

Botswana is currently experiencing the worst five-year drought in its recorded history. However, because of the government's past experience in handling drought and the strengthening of the institutional arrangements, the government has so far successfully organized an extensive relief program.

In recognition of recurring drought, the government has cooperated with the World Food Programme since 1977 in developing a strategic grain reserve; this has become a very important part of Botswana's overall contingency planning effort. The government also has developed a long-term national food strategy as a framework for the development of arable agriculture.

REFERENCES

Gooch, T.; and J. MacDonald. 1981. Evaluation of 1979-80 Drought Relief Programme. Gaborone, Botswana.
Hinchey, M. T., ed. 1979. Botswana Drought Symposium. Botswana Society, Gaborone, Botswana.
Ministry of Finance and Development. 1985. Botswana National Development VI: 1985-91. Reports on National Food Strategy. Government of Botswana Printer, Gaborone.
National Assembly. 1985. Government White Paper No. 2; National Food Strategy. Gaborone, Botswana.
World Bank. 1986. Public expenditure and development in Botswana. World Bank Document, June 3. Report Number 6031-BT. World Bank, New York.

CHAPTER 27
DROUGHT MANAGEMENT IN INDIA:
STEPS TOWARD ELIMINATING FAMINES

Suresh K. Sinha, K. Kailasanathan, and A. K. Vasistha

INTRODUCTION

There was a time when India was identified as having a potential for famine, but fortunately this description is no longer accurate. In 1943, four years before India gained independence, the most serious famine of this century claimed 3 million lives in Bengal. There was no drought; the failure of the administrative system led to this avoidable famine (Bhatia, 1967; Chattopadhyay, 1981). Two consecutive droughts in 1965 and 1966 created food shortages in Bihar which led to famine conditions. Administrators learned valuable lessons from the 1965 and 1966 droughts. Subsequently, these experiences were applied to droughts of far greater magnitude that occurred in 1972, 1979, and 1982. No famine resulted. During the last two of these droughts (1979 and 1982), no food grains were imported, giving officials a feeling of accomplishment. How has this been achieved? Can the Indian experience be emulated by other countries? These are important questions. This paper describes some of the worst droughts in India and their impact on agriculture. The policy decisions of the government which may have played an important role in eliminating famines are also presented.

RAINFALL OVER INDIA

Most of the rainfall in India occurs as a result of the southwest monsoon and is concentrated between June and September. Despite extensive meteorological studies, including the renowned Monax experiment, causes for aberrant monsoons remain elusive (Das, 1984). "Normal" monsoon rainfall is an average over a variable time period ranging from 30 to 100 years, depending on the availability of data. On the basis of total rainfall and the average distribution, the easiest and simplest prediction is that no year will have a "normal" monsoon (Sinha, 1986). Nonetheless, averages do provide some basis for the classification and assessment of productivity potential. The broad areal distribution of rainfall is given in Table 1. The duration of the rainfall varies from 30 days to 180 days in different parts of the country (Fig. 1). Northern India receives some of its rain during the winter while some rainfall in the coastal regions is received from October to December. This large variation in the distribution of precipitation in the country creates an array of agroclimatic conditions in combination with different soil types and

Table 1
Areal Distribution of Rainfall in India

Mean annual rainfall (cm)	Geographical area (%)
0- 75	30
75-125	42
125-200	20
Above 200	8

atmospheric temperatures. However, rainfall remains the primary factor in determining agricultural production.

DEFINING DROUGHT AND ITS MAGNITUDE

There are many definitions of drought (Hounam, et. al, 1975; Krishnan, 1979; see also the paper by Wilhite and Glantz, 1985, reprinted in this volume). When drought is defined in relation to precipitation or agriculture, the limits of the definition, though arbitrary, are important to scientists, administrators, planners, and policy makers. However, definitions may hold little value for farmers.

The India Meteorology Department uses two measures—the first describes rainfall conditions while the second represents drought severity. Rainfall conditions are defined as follows:

Excess	+ 20% or more of the average of 70-100 years
Normal	+ 19% to -19% of the average of 70-100 years
Deficient	- 20% to -59% of the average of 70-100 years
Scanty	- 60% or less of the average of 70-100 years

The precipitation is expressed on a weekly and monthly basis. *Drought* is described as moderate or severe if the seasonal rainfall (southwest monsoon) deficiency is 26-50% or more than 50% of the normal, respectively. The criteria used by the India Meteorology Department is the most generally accepted measure of drought, principally because of its simplicity. Other measures of drought have been proposed. Subrahmanyam (1964), for example, defined drought intensities using standard deviation of the aridity index, while Krishnan and Thanvi (1971) used the aridity index of the *Kharif* (monsoon season) cropping season to describe drought intensity. A *drought-prone area* is defined as one in which the probability of a drought year is greater than 20%. A *chronic drought-prone area* is one in which the probability of a drought year is greater than 40%. A *drought year* occurs when less than 75% of the "normal" rainfall is received.

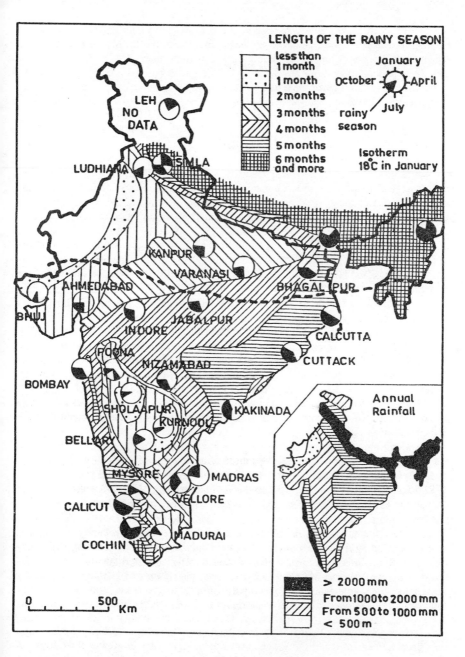

Fig. 1 Length of the rainy season.

The rainfall criterion described above is useful for a continuous monitoring of the monsoon season. The sum of the season's rainfall becomes the basis for describing a region under moderate or severe drought. When more than 50% of the area in the country is under moderate or severe drought, the country is described as severely affected by drought; and when the affected area is 26-50% of the country, it is described as an incidence of moderate drought.

ANALYSIS OF THE VARIOUS DROUGHTS

The spatial characteristics, intensity, and frequency of a drought in a given meteorological subdivision are important from the point of view of the agriculture and economy of the country. The incidence and intensity of some of the worst droughts in India are shown in Fig. 2, along with some "normal" monsoon years. The 1918 drought was the worst in this century; the droughts of 1965, 1966, 1972, 1979, and 1982 were quite serious.

The country is divided into thirty-one meteorological subdivisions (in recent years Andaman and Nicobar Islands, Laksha Dweep, Hills of West U.P. and Nagaland, Manipur, Mizoram, and Tripura have been added to reorganize the country into thirty-five subdivisions). In 1918, drought affected twenty-three subdivisions, of which fifteen had moderate drought and eight had severe drought. Drought covered 73% of the total area of post-independent India. In subsequent droughts, ten to sixteen subdivisions (covering 37-54% of the country's total area) were affected. It must, however, be emphasized that the same subdivisions were not always affected by drought during the above-mentioned drought years. The subdivisions that experienced drought more often were East U.P., Punjab, Himachal Pradesh, Jammu and Kashmir, Rajasthan, East M.P. and West M.P., Vidharbha, Bihar Plain, and Bihar Plateau. The probability of occurrence of a drought in a five-year period in different regions is given in Table 2. The drought-prone areas are shown in Fig. 3.

Drought conditions become a great menace if the drought occurs consecutively for more than one year in the same region. Severe drought occurred in West Rajasthan in 1904 and 1905. The same region experienced moderate droughts in 1980, 1981, and 1982. Punjab and Haryana experienced moderate droughts in 1980, 1981, and 1982. Punjab and Haryana experienced moderate droughts of two consecutive years on two occasions or more. Similarly, moderate droughts occurred in 1965 and 1966 in East Uttar Pradesh, Rajasthan, East Madhya Pradesh, and West Madhya Pradesh. Such consecutive years of drought have a more serious effect than a severe drought of only one year, and agricultural industries are the most seriously affected. Fortunately India has not faced this situation except in some small areas of the country. Indian droughts almost never affect the whole country. Various parts of the country always receive excess rainfall even during the poorest monsoon season (Anonymous, 1979).

Fig. 2 Incidence and intensity of droughts in India.

Table 2
Probability of Occurrence of Drought in Drought-Prone Meteorological Subdivisons

Meteorological Subdivisions	Frequency of Deficient Rainfall (75% of normal or less)
Assam, Northeast Region	Very rare, once in 15 years
West Bengal, West Madhya Pradesh, Konkan, Coastal Andhra Pradesh, Maharashtra, Kerala, Bihar, Orissa	Once in five years
South Interior Karnataka, Eastern Uttar Pradesh, Vidarbha, Gujarat, Eastern Rajasthan, Western Uttar Pradesh	Once in four years
Tamil Nadu, Kashmir	Once in three years
Rayalaseema, Telangana, Western Rajasthan	Twice in five years

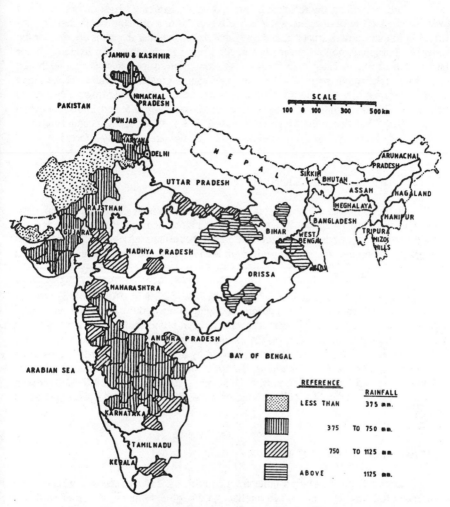

Fig. 3 Drought-prone area in India.

IMPACT OF DROUGHTS

Physical aspects

Droughts mean less rainfall. They have an immediate effect on the recharge of soil moisture and they result in reductions of streamflow and reservoir levels. Temperatures are usually above normal and humidity is reduced. By the middle of September (when the monsoon normally withdraws) in 1979, the reservoir level in major reservoirs in north India such as Gobindsagar (Bhakra), Pong (Beas), Ramaganga, Gandhisagar, and others was down 3-11 m. This influenced both power generation and irrigation.

Drought affects the recharge of ground water, reducing irrigation potential and even the availability of drinking water in wells. In 1986, a drinking water shortage occurred in Maharashtra, Karnataka, and Rajasthan because either the wells dried up or the water level dropped too low. In regions dependent on ground water for irrigation, poor farmers are affected because their wells are shallow. Rich farmers have deeper wells and can afford higher pumping costs. Thus drought causes greater disparities. Since many canal irrigation projects are diversions from rivers, a decrease in river flow further limits irrigation. The availability of water, therefore, is not only affected in the monsoon season (*Kharif*) but also in the winter crop season (*Rabi*). When drought occurs consecutively for two years, hydropower generation and irrigation are adversely affected.

AGRICULTURAL PRODUCTION

India continues to have a predominantly agricultural economy. Even now, despite heavy industrialization, 50% of the gross national income is derived from agriculture. Therefore, any adverse environmental factor that effects agriculture also influences the national economy. The effects of drought are felt at the individual level as well as at the national level.

The major droughts of 1918, 1965, 1966, 1972, 1979, and 1982 caused losses in food grain production ranging from 3.7% in 1982-83 to 32.3% in 1918 (Table 3). An important aspect of production is that despite drought, an upward trend in grain production has been maintained and the import of food has been eliminated. There are peaks and valleys in grain production (Fig. 4); for example, a peak of 131.4 million tons of food grains was reached in 1978-79. It was followed by a severe drought in 1979, lowering production by 17% to 109 million tons. In 1980-81 and 1981-82 food grain production reached 129.5 and 133.3 million tons, respectively. The drought of 1982-83, however, caused a reduction of only 5 million tons, or 3.7% over the peak production period of 1981-82.

SOCIAL AND ECONOMIC IMPACT

Droughts have occurred quite frequently in the Indian subcontinent and have often been followed by famines. References to droughts, famines, and relief work are found in some of the earliest writings (see Nehru, 1947). There were twenty-one famines, eight of which occurred between 1770 and 1880. A commission was subsequently set up to inquire into the problems of the 1860-61 famine of Orissa and Bengal, with Colonel Baird Smith as its chairman. His statement of 1860-61 is relevant even today: "Indian famines are rather famines of work than of food; for, when work can be had and paid for, food is always forthcoming."

Thus the genesis of famines in India in the past did not lie in food shortage, but in the shortage of purchasing power. There was not enough money and prices of food articles rose sharply (Bhatia, 1967). The beginning of famines and creation of landless labor is shown in Fig. 5. Failure of the monsoon caused reduced food production, leading to borrowing from moneylenders who charged very high interest rates. Having become indebted, the farmers eventually lost their land. This can be seen by an enormous

Table 3
Extent and Impact of Drought in Important Drought Years

Drought year	% of the Country Affected	% Reduction in Food Grain Production Over the Previous Peak Year	Total Food Grain Production (in million metric tons)	Import of Food Grains (in million metric tons)
1918-19	73	32.3		
1965-66	54	18.8	72.4	10.6
1972-73	43	7.7	97.0	3.6
1979-80	41	17.0	109.0	0
1982-83	37	3.7	128.4	0

Net import between 1966-67 and 1976-77 was approximately 47.7 million tons.

increase in land transactions during and immediately following drought periods (Spitz, 1981). Even those farmers who had a good harvest became indebted because they could not afford to build up assets or save money. This was a vicious circle, which no doubt was initiated by a bad monsoon and which ultimately resulted in famines.

Some nineteenth-century officials took an interest in resolving the problem. Colonel Baird Smith recommended extension of the irrigation system, improvement of communication, and remission of land tax in 1860-61. The Famine Inquiry Commission under General R. Stratchey (1878) said, "The paramount duty of the State was to offer protection to the people of India from the effects of uncertainty of the seasons."

Other commissions were set up in 1897-98 and 1901; these ultimately led to the development of the Famine Code. But although several commissions recommended measures to improve production and assistance, the government did not pay any attention to the food supply and regulation of trade and prices of food grains during famines.

FAMINE CODES

On the basis of the report of the first Famine Commission (appointed in 1878), the Famine Codes were promulgated from 1883 on and were adopted by several provincial governments. The main concerns of these codes were:

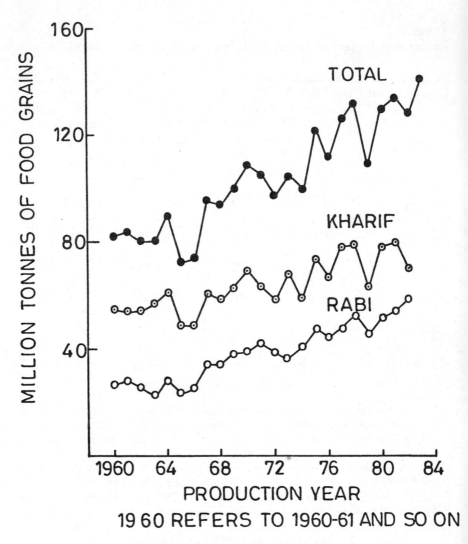

Fig. 4 Food-grain production in India since 1960.

1. Opening of relief works in famine areas.
2. Prescribing the scales and systems of wages for labor employed on relief works.
3. Providing for the treatment of destitutes, women, children, and ill and elderly victims.
4. Grant of *taccavi* loans to the farmers for resuming agricultural activities at the end of the famine.
5. Remission and suspension of payment of land revenue demand.

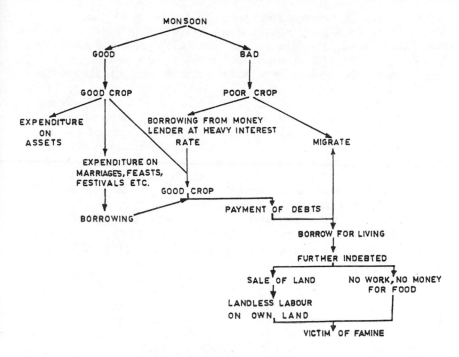

Fig. 5 Path to famine.

6. Supply of grain and fodder for the cattle.

Many of the features of the Famine Codes were good, but they could not be implemented because of the definition of the drought. The drought was defined by the *Annawari* system, which expressed the loss of crop. An area was called drought-affected if production was 37% of the normal. When production went below 25%, the area was declared a famine area and the Famine Code came into operation. Thus any relief work had to start only after the crop had been damaged. This was too late to salvage agricultural crops. Unfortunately, the same Famine Codes were used in post-independent India when the droughts of 1965 and 1966 occurred.

POST-INDEPENDENCE EXPERIENCE

In post-independent India, the country accepted the policy of democracy, socialism, free press, and welfare state. Therefore, the government was bound to respond with much greater concern and assistance to people affected by natural calamities. The free press highlights the problems of the people, which keeps the leadership alert about the needs of the disaster-affected region. But the government did not respond effectively in 1966 and 1967 when famine conditions occurred in Bihar. The exact number of deaths is not known but unofficial sources estimated 273 and 2,344 deaths in 1966 and 1967, respectively. Grain production fell (Fig. 4) and was approximately 50% of normal in Bihar during the droughts of 1965 and 1966. The wholesale price of food grains increased sharply by 1967 (Table 4). In Bihar and West Bengal the wholesale price of rice increased from Rs.93.7 to Rs.180.8 per 100 kg and Rs.68.1 to Rs.156.5 per 100 kg, respectively. During the same period there was only a marginal increase in the wholesale price of rice in Andhra Pradesh, Madhya Pradesh, and Tamilnadu.

Two factors other than reduced production contributed to such an abnormal rise in price in West Bengal and Bihar. First, the government did not permit any interstate movement of food grains. Second, there was no adequate arrangement for the distribution of food grains to the people. In the absence of enough earnings to buy food at elevated prices, the poorer sections of the society suffered the most. Corruption became rampant under such conditions. Only nongovernment agencies, such as that organized by Jayaprakash Narayan, could save thousands of lives through public kitchens.

A study by Jodha (1975) noted the effects of drought on the daily per capita consumption of food grains in Rajasthan. In October 1963, about 71% of the people received 601-750 g of food grains per day; 21.2% received 451-600 g; and 7.7% received 300-450 g. But by April 1964, only 5.8% of the people received 601-750 g of food grains daily; 69.2% received 300-450 g.

It is impossible to describe adequately the effects of the 1965 and 1966 droughts without mentioning the call given by Prime Minister Lal Bahadur Shastri. Because of the political strings attached to the import of food grains under the PL 480 scheme, he asked the people to forego one meal a week on Monday evening. No food was cooked in his own house, and no restaurant served any cereal preparation on Monday evenings. Food grain imports in 1966 reached 10.7 million tons in an attempt to meet the deficit caused by drought. This led to a change in policies in the agricultural

Table 4
Average Wholesale Price[a] of Rice in Moderately Droughted and "Normal" States, 1965-67 and 1978-80

	Year					
State	1965	1966	1967	1978	1979	1980
West Bengal	68.1	81.3	156.5	176.5	208.0	221.7
Bihar	93.7	133.2	180.8	168.6	190.6	220.4
Andhra Pradesh	65.6	67.8	73.0	162.8	163.1	190.4
Madhya Pradesh	60.9	67.8	71.7	195.0	210.3	234.6
Tamil Nadu	63.1	65.1	68.1	153.7	168.0	192.5

[a]Price in Rupees per 100 Kg.

sector, and food grain self-sufficiency became the top priority in the country. Among other changes, in 1970, the Dryland Agriculture Research Project was established with the assistance of the government of Canada.

FROM FAMINE CODE TO DROUGHT CODE AND GOOD WEATHER CODE

A roving seminar, "Crop Life Saving Research," was organized by the Indian Council for Agricultural Research in 1975 to discuss the approaches to increase production in drought-prone areas. A major effort in this seminar was to emphasize a change from Famine Code to Drought Code and Good Weather Code.

The Drought Code outlines for each agroecological region a list of anticipatory measures and alternative cropping strategies that should be adopted when there is evidence of drought. The kind of programs and information include the following:

1. Early-season anticipation of conditions of scarcity.
2. Maximizing production and alternating cropping patterns when necessary in irrigated areas.
3. Mid-season corrections in crop planning in unirrigated areas.
4. Introduction of life-saving techniques in the drought-affected areas.
5. Building up of appropriate seed and fertilizer buffers to implement the drought cropping strategy.

The Good Weather Code outlines the scientific, administrative, and planning steps necessary to take full advantage of a good monsoon season to increase production of food grains. Thus a shift in thinking occurred, from curative measures to preventive measures against adverse effects of drought.

THE 1979 DROUGHT

The experience of the 1979 drought can be considered a major step in drought management for India. The monsoon in 1977 and 1978 had been good, but one could not necessarily expect a continuation of these conditions in 1979. M. S. Swaminathan, secretary of the Department of Agriculture, wrote to state governments urging them to keep themselves prepared to face a poor monsoon. At regular weekly and biweekly intervals, monsoon development was monitored. However, it started late and was erratic, causing prolonged dry spells in August. The states affected included Andhra Pradesh, Bihar, Haryana, Punjab, Uttar Pradesh, West Bengal, Madhya Pradesh, Orissa, Karnataka, Maharashtra, and Rajasthan. The rainfall deficiency ranged from 12% and 16% in Orissa and West Bengal, respectively, to 55% in Madhya Pradesh. The major food-grain-producing states—Uttar Pradesh, Haryana, and Punjab—recorded deficiencies in rainfall between 21% and 41%.

The Ministry of Agriculture set up a watch group consisting of representatives from the Department of Agriculture, India Meteorology Department, Indian Council of Agricultural Research, Ministry of Information and Broadcasting, and others. A two-pronged strategy was adopted which focused on curative and preventive measures. A meeting of the chief ministers of drought-affected states was convened in September.

This meeting was addressed by the prime minister. Watch groups were established in all state capitals and district headquarters. They were to provide weekly reports of rainfall, agricultural operations, employment, and other activities or occurrences affected by drought.

Curative Approach

The prime minister announced a twelve-point program that provided for the following:

1. Full-time relief officers.
2. Monitoring.
3. Availability of food grains.
4. Fair-price shops.
5. Checks on antisocial elements.
6. Food for work.
7. Afforestation.
8. Food for nutrition program.
9. Contingency plan.
10. Public health measures.
11. Rigs for boring drinking water wells.
12. Cattle camps and relief camps.

The twelve-point program was created to avert what is referred to as *Trikal* (*Akal, Jalkal,* and *Tinkal*), which means that food, water, and fodder are not available. Although drought affected 240 districts and 220 million people, the severity was not widely felt because of the buffer stocks of food grains. This is substantiated by the fact that the increase in prices of food grains was much less than that of the period 1965-67 (Table 4). The central government allocated 19.6 million tons of food grains to the states, incurring an expenditure of Rs.1,569.5 million. As many as 6.2 million people were given employment under employment-generating schemes, including the Food For Work Program (Jaiswal and Kolte, 1981). Relief measures on such a large scale were never before undertaken. As a result of these measures, no starvation deaths were reported. If the country had had to import food grains to meet the shortage of 22 million tons, the cost would have been US$4.6 billion at the prevailing international market price (Jain and Sinha, 1981). Importation of food at this level would have been impossible for the country.

Although all aspects of the prime minister's twelve-point program were important, the Food for Work Program deserves special mention and will be briefly described in a subsequent section.

Preventive Measures

Since the failure of the monsoon affected the *Kharif* (monsoon season crop), it was necessary to attempt higher production in *Rabi* (winter season crop), which has always been more productive (Anonymous, 1903; Sinha, et. al, 1985). Arrangements were made for the supply of seeds, fertilizers, diesel fuel, and electricity to farmers

(Anonymous, 1979). This was to be monitored by all chief ministers in their states and reported to India's Ministry of Agriculture and the prime minister's secretariat at weekly intervals. The policy of increasing production in *Rabi* has been successful, as can be seen from Fig. 4. This has provided a buffering capacity against fluctuations in food grain production, which are mostly due to wheat production. Of course, it has created problems of disparity among different regions and also shortages in production of oil-seeds and pulses.

Food For Work Program

The program had the following objectives:
1. To generate additional gainful employment for a large number of un-employed and underemployed persons (both men and women) in the rural areas, which will improve their incomes and, consequently, their nutritional levels.
2. To create durable community assets and strengthen the rural infrastructure, which will result in higher production and better standards of living in the rural areas.
3. To use surplus food grains for development of human resources.

An evaluation of this program in ten states, covering twenty districts and eighty villages involving 793 households, showed that the program helped with the following: construction and repair of village roads and streets; minor irrigation works; construction of community works; drainage programs; and soil conservation and forestry and other works. Up to November 1979, this program released 1.36 million tons of food grains and generated 286.4 million man-days of work, with the greatest number of days in West Bengal (Anonymous, 1980).

PRESENT APPROACH

It is recognized that the country has to be prepared to face the challenge of an aberrant monsoon in the future. At present, approximately 28% of the cultivable land is irrigated; the upper limit is 50% of the country. Therefore, the problems of drought-prone areas have to be tackled on a long-term basis to minimize the adverse effects of drought. Such a program should include the following:
1. An early forecast of the monsoon to enable farmers to be prepared for a good, normal, or bad season.
2. Improved communication systems.
3. Availability of resources such as credit, fertilizers, pesticides, and power for increasing production.
4. Proper assistance to farmers in the years when the monsoon fails.
5. Adequate prices for produce in good years.
6. Building reasonable buffer stocks of food grains, which should be located strategically so as to be made available in the shortest possible time.
7. An improved transportation system.

Above all, the welfare state must realize its responsibility toward its people, as mentioned in Arthashastra (Economics) by Chankya in 32 B.C.: "Famine relief was a special care of the State, and half the stores in all the State Warehouses were always kept in reserve for times of scarcity and famines." In modern times we might say that it is the duty of the government of the day to ensure the welfare of the people during periods of natural calamities. Fortunately, the successive governments in post-independent India have been conscious of this responsibility. The free press has played an important role in keeping both government and citizens informed about droughts, floods, and cyclone-damaged areas, as well as problems of those who have been affected.

Two major programs announced by the government of India in the VIIth Five-Year Plan need to be mentioned. The first, the Technology Mission on Agro-met Service, has the following specific objectives:

1. Improve weather predictions on various time scales.
2. Prepare climatological information related to specific agricultural requirements, including control of pests and diseases.
3. Provide a fast and responsive communication channel for collection and dissemination of data, information, charts, and bulletins.
4. Provide advice on agricultural operations on contingencycrop practices and dryland farming.

The Mission has three components, dealing with meteorological forecasts and information, appropriate communication systems, and agricultural input management. The Mission will have a joint advisory committee with representatives from different ministries. The cost of the Mission would be approximately one billion rupees during the VIIth Five-Year Plan period.

The government of India and state governments introduced the second program, crop insurance schemes, to ensure some returns to the farmers even in bad years. Initially the crops of paddy, wheat, millets, oilseeds, and pulses would be covered. This type of scheme has some difficult operational problems, but a beginning has been made.

CONCLUSIONS

It appears that India has to some extent succeeded in eliminating food scarcity and hence famines in different parts of the country. The famine path as depicted in Fig. 5 has been broken by starting the Food for Work Program for farmers and stopping the practice of borrowing from moneylenders. Credit is available from nationalized banks and other government agencies.

Being a large country, India has the advantage of never having experienced drought over the entire country. Increase in irrigation potential, both through surface and ground water, has helped to enhance *Rabi* production. Thus, the loss in production in one region can be compensated by excess production from other regions. Small countries may not be able to emulate the example of India. Therefore, it may be useful for several small countries to organize a joint program to combat drought.

The availability of power and the extensive infrastructure of railways, road transport, and satellite communication together provide additional advantages. However, several problem areas still remain. Among these problems, some of the following should be mentioned:

1. The security of the food system at the national level does not mean food security at an individual level. Despite a buffer stock of 30 million tons of food grains, some people do not have adequate food supplies. The need is, therefore, to ensure food security to all the people under all conditions.
2. Development of water harvesting and watershed management would help ensure the prosperity of individual farmers. This requires community action, which is difficult in a democratic society.
3. Past experience shows that only in 1978 and 1918 has drought-year production dropped below 10% of the peak production. Therefore, maintaining a buffer stock of 12.5-15% of the peak production should be adequate. It would also help if crop production could be diversified, oilseed imports reduced, and the deficiency of pulses eliminated.

REFERENCES

Anonymous. 1903. Report of the Indian Irrigation Commission. Office of the Superintendent of Government Printing, Calcutta.
Anonymous. 1979. Stabilizing crop production under conditions of drought and unfavourable conditions. Conference of State Chief Ministers, September 27, 1979. Ministry of Agriculture and Irrigation, Government of India, New Delhi.
Anonymous. 1980. Evaluation of Food for Work Program. Final Report. Program Evaluation Organization Planning Commission, Government of India, New Delhi.
Bhatia, B. M. 1967. Famines in India. Asia Publishing House, New Delhi.
Chattopadhyay, B. 1981. Notes towards understanding of the Bengal Famine of 1943. CRESSIDA 1:112-153.
Das, P. K. 1984. Monsoons. Indian National Science Academy, New Delhi.
Hounam, C. E.; J. J. Burgos; M. S. Kalik; W. C. Palmer; and J. Rodda. 1975. Drought and Agriculture. Report of the CAgM Working Group on the Assessment of Drought. Technical Note No. 138. World Meteorological Organization, Geneva.
Jain, H. K.; and S. K. Sinha. 1981. Droughts and the new agricultural technology. WMO Symposium on Meteorological Aspects of Tropical Droughts. World Meteorological Organization, Geneva.
Jaiswal, N. K.; and N. V. Kolte. 1981. Development of Drought Prone Areas. National Institute of Rural Development, Hyderabad.
Jodha, N. S. 1975. Famine and famine policies: Some empirical evidence. Economic and Political Weekly, Oct. 11, 1975.
Krishnan, A. 1979. Definitions of droughts and factors relevant to specifications of agricultural and hydrological droughts. pp. 67-102. In Hydrological Aspects of Droughts. International Symposium, Dec. 3-7, 1979. Indian National Committee for IHP.CSIR, New Delhi.
Krishnan, A.; and K. P. Thanvi. 1971. Occurrence of droughts in Rajasthan during 1941-1960. Proceedings of All India Seminar on Dryland Farming, New Delhi.

Nehru, Jawahar Lal. 1947. The Discovery of India. Asia Publishing House, New Delhi.

Sinha, S. K. 1987. The 1982-83 Drought in India: Magnitude and Impact. pp. 37-42. In M. Glantz, ed. The Societal Impacts Associated with the 1982-83 Worldwide Climate Anomalies. National Center for Atmospheric Research, Boulder, Colorado.

Sinha, S. K.; Aggarwal, P. K., and R. Khanna-Chopra. 1985. Irrigation in India: A physiological and phenological approach to water management in grain crops. Advances in Irrigation 3:130-213.

Spitz, P. 1981. Drought and Self Provisioning. CRESSIDA 1(2):18-35.

Subrahmanyam, V. P. 1964. Climatic water balance of the Indian arid zone. pp. 405-411. Proceedings of the Symposium on Problems of Indian Arid Zone, Jodhpur.

Wilhite, D. A.; and M. H. Glantz. 1985. Understanding the drought phenomenon: The role of definitions. Water Int. 10:111-120.

CHAPTER 28
DROUGHT IN NORTHEAST BRAZIL: IMPACT AND
GOVERNMENT RESPONSE

Dirceu M. Pessoa

DROUGHT IN A REGIONAL CONTEXT

Periodic droughts occur in the vast semiarid hinterland (see Fig. 1) of the northeastern region of Brazil. The hinterland is referred to by the government as the Drought Polygon. It is located between two humid zones: the Green-Coastal Zone on the east and the pre-Amazon region on the west. Table 1 lists statistical information about the semiarid zone and the entire Northeast.

The semiarid zone is the largest and most densely populated region in the Northeast, with an area of 850 km^2 and a population of 19.2 million inhabitants (1980 census). Its population constitutes 54% of the population of the Northeast and includes a rural population of 11 million inhabitants (or 62% of the rural population of the whole region). The rural economy of the whole zone is characterized by cattle breeding and nonirrigated agriculture. The semiarid zone produces 72% of the cattle raised in the Northeast. Most farmers use native green forage, which grows during the rainy season, and crop residues for feed. The more modern farmers cultivate irrigated greenfodder. Historically, the principal motive for settling the land was cattle breeding. Because it has been the dominant activity of proprietors of large and medium-size farms and because of the value of the herds, cattle breeding has always occupied a privileged position. Agriculture's principal objectives have been to ensure a food supply for the workers and to produce feed (crop residues) and financial support (through cotton production) for cattle raising.

Drought in this region is not only caused by low precipitation (the average annual rainfall is approximately 600-800 mm) but also by the high rate of evapotranspiration—approximately 1,800 mm per year, which causes systematic annual deficits in the balance of evapotranspiration minus precipitation. Another characteristic is the seasonal concentration of precipitation: two-thirds of the annual precipitation occurs in one three-month period. The climate is also characterized by a six- to seven-month dry season, with almost no rainfall. A final natural characteristic of the region is the crystalline base of most of the soil, which has a low capacity to absorb water. The region has a relatively high population density of 23 inhabitants/km^2 (1980 census).

As in other drought-prone regions, drought does not occur in a uniform pattern over Brazil's vast northeastern semiarid zone. Studies on the frequency of its occurrence have identified its epicenter in the northern area (Fig. 1), including parts of the states of Rio Grande do Norte, Paraíba, Pernambuco, Piauí, and (especially) Ceará (Carvalho,

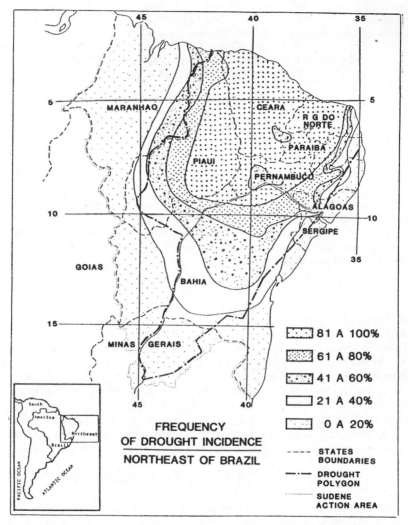

Fig. 1 Frequency of drought in Northeast Brazil (SUDENE, 1981a).

1973; SUDENE, 1981a). This area coincides with the area of the cattle-cotton system known as the northern backlands (*Sertão Norte*) (Melo, 1978; Silva, 1982).

Records of drought occurrence date back to the beginning of the colonial period, more than four hundred years ago. In his famous "Epistolary Narration of a Jesuit Voyage and Mission," Father Fernão Cardim recorded the 1583 drought that crossed the frontiers of the semiarid region and reached the humid belt of the eastern Northeast.

Table 1
The Semiarid Zone within Northeast Brazil

	Great NE Zones			Total	
	Green Littoral	Semiarid	West Frontier	NE	Brazil
Area (in 1,000 km²)	95.6	850.2	700.9	1,646.7	8,511.9
Resident population (in millions)					
Total	10.3	19.2	6.3	35.9	119.1
Rural	2.7	11.0	4.1	17.9	38.6
Urban	7.6	8.2	2.2	18.0	80.5
Density 1980 (inhab/km²)					
Total	107.4	22.6	9.0	21.8	14.0
Rural	28.2	13.0	5.8	10.8	4.5
Growth 1970-80 (%/year)					
Total	2.7	1.6	3.6	2.1	2.5
Rural	0.4	0.1	1.7	0.4	-0.6
Urban	3.7	4.2	8.6	4.1	4.4
Urbanization rates (in %)					
1970	67.1	32.9	27.1	41.2	55.9
1980	73.8	42.7	34.9	50.2	67.6
GNP *per capita* 1980 (in US$)	——	——	——	808.0	1,885.0
Bovine herd					
Total 1980 (in millions of cattle)	1.7	16.9	4.9	23.5	118.1
Density 1980 (head/km²)	17.8	19.9	7.0	14.3	13.9
Growth 1970-80 (%/year)	4.7	4.0	5.4	4.3	4.2

Source: IBGE for areas, population, and herd; FGV for GNP Brazil, SUDENE-CPR for GNP Northeast

The year of 83 had such a great drought and sterility in the provinces (something rare and unaccustomed, because it was a land of continuous rain), that the [mills powered by] water wheels did not grind much of the time. Many sugar cane and cassava plantations dried up, and there was great hunger, principally in the backlands of Pernambuco, where the whites, caught by hunger, were aided by four or five thousand Indians. Nevertheless, when the hunger passed, those who could returned to the backlands, except those who remained in the homes of the whites or in their own or against their will (Cardim, 1925, p. 331).

Since Cardim's account, which contains the first reference to drought in the region, others have recorded a succession of droughts (Alves, 1953; Carvalho, 1973, SUDENE, 1981a). Nevertheless, the great 1977-79 drought first caused great national concern because of the increasing dimension of its principal impacts: unemployment (associated with the interruption of agricultural activity); impoverishment of a considerable part of the population; increasing influx of rural inhabitants into urban centers; and intensification of migration to other regions.

GOVERNMENT RESPONSE

The government's response to drought includes long-range policies and emergency policies that result in short-term programs during drought years.

Long-Range Policies

These policies reflect the regional perception of drought. Government policies and programs take four approaches (Hirschman, 1965; Pessoa and Cavalcanti, 1973; Guimarães, 1982; Fundação João Pinheiro, 1983).

The Naturalistic Approach. This approach is based on an understanding of natural phenomena and a desire to discover the ecological, especially the climatological, conditions that are the cause of the region's economic and social vulnerability. Euclides da Cunha best expressed this desire: "The tormenting of man, there, is a reflection of a greater torture, wider, including the general economy of life. It is born from the secular martyrdom of the land" (Cunha, 1981, p. 44). It is a torment that wrings all the cruelty from the spectacle of the drought, extending through the entire region, "the same scene, desolate: agonizing vegetation, sick and shapeless, exhausted from the painful spasm...the *silva horrida* of Martius, revealing its breast, the light of tropical nature, a desert vacuum" (Cunha, 1981, p. 34).

To this desolate state there is a rapid reversal in the cycle of the "general economy of life," with the sudden advent of the rains:

Abruptly in minutes, the firmament is buffeted with rapid lightning, successive, deeply cutting the black form of the tempest. The loud thunder reverberates harshly. The downpour of rain falls, heavy, in intervals, over the ground, soon uniting into a watery deluge . . . And returning from his trip, the traveler, amazed, no longer sees a desert. Over the ground, that the amaryllis blankets, triumphantly resurge the tropical flora. It is a change of glorification . . . And the backlands are a paradise (Cunha, pp. 35-36).

The desire to understand this intriguing natural reality increases when one realizes "how many remote factors can influence a subject that interests us both for its superior scientific concern and for its more intimate meaning involving the destiny of a great part of our country" (Cunha, p. 28).

During the great drought of 1877-79, which coincided with the end of the Empire, these concerns about drought were transcribed into practical terms for the first time, in the form of a series of studies, discussions, and publications related to the northeastern droughts. By the end of 1877, the "memorable sessions" and discussions among scientists and engineers of the Polytechnic Institute of Rio de Janeiro (Instituto Politécnico do Rio de Janeiro) had been followed by the creation of the Imperial Inquiry Comission

(Comissão Imperial de Inquérito), which was responsible for studying ways to avoid similar disasters in the future.

Federal institutionalization of public policies for the region resulted in the creation of the Department of Works to Overcome Drought (Inspectoria de Obras Contra as Secas—IOCS) in 1909. The department was later transformed into the Federal Department of Works to Overcome Drought (Inspectoria Federal de Obras Contra as Secas—IFOCS), and in 1954 it became the National Department of Works to Overcome Drought (Departamento Nacional de Obras Contra as Secas—DNOCS). One of the department's first concerns was the collection of basic information about the region, including technical-scientific studies, maps, and the installation of climatological and hydrological observation stations. Hirschman (1965) emphasized that the studies of the first ten years, which initiated permanent interest in discovering the natural characteristics of the region, were particularly important.

In the 1960s, this interest in the region's natural characteristics was responsible for the creation of the Superintendency of Northeast Development (SUDENE) and the Department of Natural Resources, which was responsible for the considerable development and systematization of previous accomplishments, especially maps showing soil and mineral resources (SUDENE, 1980b). Hydroclimatological research developments under SUDENE and the Department of Natural Resources have included a network of more than two thousand stations; hydrogeological research, for which SUDENE had ample foreign technical and financial support; meteorological research (seventy-five stations in the Northeast, integrating the world's network); and integrated studies of potential natural resources and the social and economic conditions in the hydrographic basins of the Jaguaribe, São Francisco, Apodi, Acaraú, Paraguaçu, Parnaíba, Itapecuru, and Mearim rivers (SUDENE, 1980b, pp. 65-77).

The Engineering Approach. Notwithstanding the scientific questions of the naturalists, the most immediate and intuitive way drought is perceived is through its most evident manifestation: a shortage of water for human and animal consumption and agriculture. The solution is elementary: store water in normal years for later use. The possibility of underground reservoirs is remote because of the predominantly crystalline geological formation, so the drought must be fought mainly through the storage of surface water, with the identification of appropriate sites for the construction of dams.

Since the construction of the first 128 million m^3 capacity Quixada Dam, begun in 1884, DNOCS has constructed 1,121 dams (as of December 31, 1983), with a capacity surpassing 15 billion m^3 of water (IBGE, 1984). If these were added to all other dams constructed by public and private groups, the total number of dams would be in the thousands. During the last great drought, 8,604 dams and reservoirs were constructed under the government emergency plan (SUDENE, 1984). The dams are justified not only because of the occurrence of periodic drought or interannual precipitation irregularities, but also by a need to ensure that rural producers will have a dependable water supply during the dry season of normal years.

Human and animal consumption represents an insignificant amount of water when compared with the water requirements for irrigation. The decision to allocate water involves an element of uncertainty because the use of water for irrigation in the normal dry season can mean a lack of water—empty reservoirs—if there should be a drought the following year. If stored water is held back for a possible drought year, evapotranspiration losses are high and must be added to production losses that result from the decision not to use the water for irrigation.

But this explanation does not fully explain why the area under irrigation is so small in spite of the profusion of dam construction: only 260,000 hectares were irrigated in 1980, and only 180,000 hectares were privately developed (SUDENE, 1986). The risk of completely emptying a reservoir is not the only reason, because many reservoirs are sufficiently large to withstand a year of drought. Besides, drought defined as a deficiency in the soil moisture necessary for crop production (Wilhite and Glantz, 1985) is due more to the rainfall distribution than to the volume of the rainfall itself. Even in years of drought, concentrated rainfall can be sufficient to fill a reservoir. It is also possible to construct combination reservoir-wells, from which the reservoir water could be used for irrigation while the well water could be reserved for human and animal consumption in a dry year.

The reason irrigation is not widely used is related to the pattern of landownership. According to official real estate records, three-quarters of the land in the northern backlands, the epicenter of the northeastern drought, is divided among fewer than a fifth of the landholdings in the form of large properties (see Table 2). Because they own more land, large landowners are better able to construct dams and reservoirs on their property. Because they often are absentee landowners interested in extensive cattle breeding, their main concern is directed more toward storing water for animal consumption rather than irrigated agriculture.

The Ecological Adjustment Approach. After the 1958 drought, government response to drought took a new approach: exploring how common agricultural practices

Table 2
Sertao Norte: **Land Distribution and Rural Real Estate**

Categories	Real Estate Number	%	Total Area 1000 ha	%	Average Area
Small Property	209,940	81.6	4,679.2	26.1	22
Rural Enterprise	2,350	0.9	773.4	4.3	329
Latifundium per exploration	45,011	17.5	12,387.1	69.3	275
Latifundium per dimension	2	0.0	16.8	0.3	8,400
Total	257,311	100.0	17,856.5	100.0	69

Source: INCRA - Cadastrais, 1972

were adapted to the environment. Of the three most common practices (subsistence agriculture, cotton cultivation, and cattle raising), subsistence agriculture, especially corn culture, was particularly vulnerable to drought. Annual crops with a short growing season require a minimum period of rainfall; without this minimum, they must be replanted during the next rainfall period or else continue to grow under precarious conditions with a serious reduction in production.

Mocó cotton, which is a perennial xerophyte, grows deep roots, which partially compensates for the lack of topsoil moisture. Production may be less in a drought year than in a normal year, but the plant survives, and the production of the normal year can compensate for that of the drought year.

Cattle raising is the least vulnerable activity because it has greater possibilities for compensating for the effects of drought. It is easier to transport water for cattle than to irrigate crops. It is also possible to transport food for cattle. It is possible if necessary to move the herd itself, in accordance with current practices of some large cattle owners.

These observations led the Working Group for a Developed Northeast (Groupo de Trabalho para o Desenvolvido Nordeste—GTDN), coordinated by economist Celso Furtado, to recommend the development of more stable production systems resistant to rainfall irregularities: "The reorganization of the economy of the semiarid zone of the Northeast requires specialization in xerophile culture and cattle raising and in reducing subsistence agriculture" (GTDN, 1967, p. 82). This new ecological adjustment attempt has resulted in increased livestock raising (especially cattle breeding), which has been associated with more intensive management practices: pasture improvement, division of pastures with fences, genetic improvement of the herds, and disease prevention.

However, the increase in cattle breeding, as opposed to an increase in farming (Melo, 1980), has had some negative effects: unemployment, proletarianization, reduction of agricultural produce, and increased price of agricultural products. According to GTDN strategy, these effects would be counteracted by two complementary plans—the diversification of the sugar cane monoculture in the Green Coastal humid zone and the expansion of the agricultural frontier in the pre-Amazon humid zone—designed to increase the food supply and absorb the surplus population resulting from the reorganization of the semiarid zone economy. These steps were intended to solve the drought problem by increasing the food supply and lowering urban salaries to encourage industrialization, which was a basic component in the economic development strategy recommended for the Northeast. SUDENE was created to direct this development process.

In reality, except for the industrialization process, none of the steps were effectively implemented: the diversification of the sugar cane monoculture was blocked by the resistance of large landowners and by the ultimate organization of the National Program for Alcohol (Programa Nacional do Alcool—PROALCOOL), and the opening of an agricultural frontier was halted by the illegal occupancy of the land and the appropriation of great tracts of land for speculation or extensive cattle raising.

The Social Differentiation Approach. The GTDN report called attention to the existing relationship between production and the common practices of ranchers and laborers:

> The income generated by cattle raising is appropriated almost totally by the rancher: the income generated by the mocó cotton culture is divided into equal

parts between the landowner and the worker. For the rural laborer the share of cotton is less important than the subsistence agriculture . . . the most important activity from the laborers' point of view is the subsistence agriculture and from the ranchers' point of view the cattle raising (GTDN, 1967, p. 63).

After the 1970 drought, the focus changed from the sporadic occurrence of drought to the chronic poverty that drought exacerbates (Pessoa and Cavalcante, 1973; Pessoa, 1983). The degree of vulnerability of those affected by drought is determined by level of income: the higher the income, the greater the capacity to compensate for drought-year losses with income from normal years. Vulnerability is also determined by a person's position in the existing production relationship. The large landowner is naturally better able to resist drought: if he thinks that drought will occur, he simply stops paying his sharecroppers and hiring salaried workers. This results in the automatic reduction of those workers to refugee status. Between those two extremes—landowners' relative immunity to drought and sharecroppers' and laborers' indigence—the small direct producers try to survive by using their small savings, getting loans, selling part of their small assets, and registering as refugees for the emergency programs improvised by the government.

This approach to understanding drought—an approach that centers on the concentration of drought effects on the homogeneous social class that is deprived of access to the land and is stigmatized by rural poverty—was responsible for the creation of special programs intended to fight rural poverty through integrated rural development projects. Examples of such projects include the POLONORDESTE and, more recently, the Northeast Project (Projeto Nordeste), which is being developed with the support of the World Bank. The greatest difference of this new focus is that it specifies target groups (such as small rural producers) instead of relying on government intervention through regional channels, which always strengthens the structures responsible for generating rural poverty and its consequent vulnerability to droughts.

Emergency Actions

In spite of all the efforts and accomplishments in terms of understanding the natural causes of drought, improving basic service facilities (particularly water supplies), and modernizing cattle raising practices, and in spite of all the speeches and technical-bureaucratic apparatus favoring the small producer in the scope of the special projects, the landless classes and the small producers were even more vulnerable during the last drought. And the dimensions of government emergency operations were without precedent in regional history. Referring to government intervention as an "emergency" conveys the idea of urgency that has led to the abuse and corruption known as the "drought industry." But the recurrent character of the challenges of drought also emphasizes the elements that Hirschman (1965) identified as responsible for the plan of the organizational structure that directs drought emergency planning and implementation.

Organizational Structure. The government drought emergency planning effort, which goes back to the creation of SUDENE, was established through the following legislation:

1. Law 3,692 of December 1959, which created the Superintendency of Northeast Development (Superintendencia do Desenvolvimento do Nordeste—SUDENE).
2. Law 4,329 of June 27, 1963, which created the Emergency and Supply Fund of the Northeast (Fundo de Emergência e Abastecimento do Nordeste—FEANE).
3. Decree 47,890 of March 9, 1965, which established the guidelines for the emergency plan of SUDENE.

Later, Decree 67,347 of October 5, 1970, consolidated laws that established policies and guidelines for the permanent defense against public calamities. The decree created the "Special Group for Matters of Public Calamities" (Grupo Especial para Assuntos de Calamidade Pública—GEACAP). According to the current system, the general coordination of the emergency operation is SUDENE's responsibility through its superintendent or his representative. To meet this responsibility, SUDENE has created the office of Civil Defense Coordinator (Coordenadoria de Defesa Civil—CORDED), in charge of the mobilization and coordination of necessary support for preparing and implementing emergency operations.

At the federal level, the job of preparing and implementing emergency operations is the responsibility of the Ministry of the Interior (MINTER), through its special secretary for civil defense. Collaborating federal agencies are DNOCS, Company for the Development of the San Francisco Valley (Companhia de Desenvolvimento do Vale de São Francisco—CODEVASF), the Brazilian Food Company (Companhia Brasileira de Alimentos—COBAL), the National Roads Department (Departamento Nacional de Estradas de Rodagem), and the Armed Forces (army, navy, and air force). At the state level, various government departments and the Committees for Civil Defense are mobilized. On the county level, local governments are prominent; and, if one exists, the County Committee for Civil Defense (Comissões Municipais de Defesa Civil—COMDEC) works with representatives of local government and local leaders. In September 1984, approximately 42%, or 600, of the region's counties had COMDECS (SUDENE, 1984).

The first duty of the Task Force coordinated by SUDENE is the preparation of the Civil Defense Plan. The agencies involved are invited to present emergency response proposals to SUDENE, which SUDENE then consolidates, following guidelines of MINTER, previous plans, and suggestions received from other institutions. The most recent version of this process is the Civil Defense Plan for 1985 (SUDENE, 1984). It is divided into three chapters: the first, General Considerations, defines the objectives and organizational basis of the planning process; the second deals specifically with drought problems; and the third is dedicated to floods and other phenomena.

The 1985 plan's proposed objective "is to update a group of measures, work projects, and services of Civil Defense, destined to limit or prevent the risks to which the population is subject and losses of resources and material assets, and assisting the people by giving aid and rehabilitating the affected area" (SUDENE, 1984). The chapter relative to droughts begins with a synopsis of the last great drought and a listing of the facilities already constructed (or in progress) in response to the drought.

The plan provides for triggering a drought emergency program from information from the Hydrometeorological Division of SUDENE, which controls a network of 1,716 rainfall measuring stations. Of these, 46 are strategically located and send daily reports by radio; 485 send information every ten days by telegraph. The others send monthly reports. More specifically, the plan calls for the National Meteorological Institute (INEMET) to issue reports through its 3rd Meteorological District, with jurisdiction from Piauí to Bahia. The reports include:

1. A daily climate bulletin, which contains an analysis of the synoptical chart and other meteorological data such as maximum and minimum daily temperatures, total daily rainfall, relative humidity, and a weather forecast for the next twenty-four hours, including probable cloud cover, wind direction and speed, and visibility.
2. Special meteorological notices, issued when adverse meteorological conditions (rainstorms or intense rain, dry periods, strong winds, heat waves, and so forth) are identified, with the possibility of exchanging this information with other areas of the country.
3. Meteorological alerts issued during the quarters of January/March, April/June, July/September, and October/December, with climatological information referring to the seasons of the year.

Once a calamitous situation due to drought is detected, a state of emergency is declared in the affected localities by the state government; SUDENE then conducts an impact assessment *in loco* as a prerequisite to requesting MINTER to recognize the state of emergency. If MINTER recognizes SUDENE's request, special credit is liberated to provide emergency assistance to the affected localities.

Basically, data for the *in loco* impact assessment include soil characteristics, water deficit, rural demographic density, and need for public works. The plan states that the "differences in the situations in each state are considered and the needs of each microregion are respected" (SUDENE, 1984, p. 34). The plan stipulates that for each situation, SUDENE will invite representatives of the states and executive agencies in order to detail the proposed objectives and sign agreements for the immediate implementation of top-priority actions, taking into consideration the following:

1. Critical areas of the special programs should be intensified and adjusted to emphasize the expansion of rural credit, improvement of water supply, and eventually the distribution of food.
2. Public works projects should exclusively employ rural refugees paid a monthly salary established by the federal government.

The plan provides a detailed list of regulations relating to public works (destination, size, location, control, and so forth); water supply by tank trucks (restrictions and conditions for subcontracting private vehicles); and employment offered to needy laborers (priorities and hiring conditions). Participating institutions must send SUDENE monthly follow-up reports of their activities, the amount of available manpower, status of the services, expenditures and projected needs, and other relevant information (SUDENE, 1984).

The action lines that could be developed according to the plan are very comprehensive: public works (with an emphasis on the water infrastructure); food production (near dams, rivers, and in microclimatic areas); water supply (usually by tank trucks); basic food supply (strategic low-priced staples); food distribution (in case of social tension); forestation and reforestation; dissemination of drought-resistant greenfodder; supplying seeds; supporting small irrigation operations; human resources programs (literacy programs); distributing construction materials and tools; and mining services.

The chapter on droughts ends with a listing and consolidation of available services and works, identified with the help of the states, executive agencies, and other institutions involved with the problem. The plan was devised to ensure work to up to three million small agricultural producers through the construction of public facilities. A 500 billion cruzeiro cost was predicted, corresponding to the amount spent by the government in the last year of drought (Table 3.) At the prices of the time, December 1984, this amount corresponds to approximately US$160 million, or 60% of the federal expenditures in the first year of the last great drought (1979). The expenditures for other programs were not stated in the plan.

The 1979-83 Drought. The emergency operation caused by the 1979-83 drought followed the general procedures of the established organizational structure: an initial emergency plan (SUDENE, 1979) was activated and reactivated throughout the period (SUDENE, 1979, 1980a, 1981b, 1982). This plan consisted mainly of public works projects to provide employment for the refugees.

The 1979-83 drought was unusual because of the great number of counties and the extensive portion of the population affected. In the two great droughts of 1958 and 1970, the number of refugees was half a million workers; in this last great drought, the number rose to three million, corresponding to half the population working in agriculture, according to the 1980 census (Table 3). It should be pointed out that the increase in the number of workers hired in emergency operation "work fronts" was accompanied by the reduction of their real wages, which dropped from 90% to 30% of the regional minimum wage. This is even more dramatic if one considers the policy of wage compression of the military government in power since 1964. The minimum wage in the five years of drought represents, in terms of real value, approximately two-thirds of the 1960 minimum wage. In this same period—the 1960s and 1970s—the Brazilian and Northeast Brazilian economy showed an outstanding GNP growth of 7% per year. Therefore, the growth in the number of refugees absorbed in the "work fronts" and paid at such reduced wages reflected the whole process of relative and absolute impoverishment to which the population had been subjected in the previous decades.

The increase in workers and reduction in wages was doubtlessly associated with the recession that characterized the Brazilian economy in the early 1980s, when the country's GNP rates, which had been very high in the last two decades, dropped suddenly to -1.6% in 1981, 0.9% in 1982, and -3.2% in 1983, with obvious effects on employment and income. Converted at the exchange rates of the period, monthly wages paid to the workers of the "work fronts" (Table 3) correspond to US$67 and US$63 dollars in May and November 1979, respectively; approximately US$50 from May 1980 to May 1983; and US$33 and US$17 in May and November 1983, respectively.

The levels of poverty suggested by this situation are consistent with the findings of the Joaquim Nabuco 1979 field research (Cavalcanti and Pessoa, 1983) concerning the refugees' situation in the 1978 normal year. Data were as follows:

PRINCIPAL STATUS	PERCENTAGE
Agriculturalists owning property	20.1
Agriculturalists not owning property	75.1
Other	4.8
Total	100.0

Table 3
Progression of the Drought in the Northeast, 1979-83

	1979 Apr79-Feb80	1980 May80-May81	1981 Jun81-May82	1982 Jun82-May83	1983 June83-May84
Counties affected:					
Number	513.0	988.0	1,100.0	898.0	1,328.0
Index (base:1979 = 100)	100.0	192.6	214.4	175.0	258.9
Percentage of total region	36.2	69.7	77.6	63.4	93.7
Area affected:					
Area (100 km^2)	538.7	1,400.0	1,442.0	1,391.0	1,590.0
Index (base:1979 = 100)	100.0	259.9	267.7	258.2	295.2
Population assisted in each emergency:					
Maximum number (in thousands of workers)	459.6	719.9	1,168.7	746.8	3,009.0
Index (base:1979 = 100)	100.0	156.6	254.3	162.5	654.7
Monthly salary in an emergency:					
Current cruzeiros: May	1,591.4	2,480.2	4,071.7	7,700.0	15,300.0
November	1,962.2	2,996.1	5,730.0	11,225.0	15,300.0
% of Minimum Salary: May	88.5	72.2	57.1	54.0	50.0
November	83.0	62.5	56.2	54.1	30.4

Resources Distributed (in billions current Cz):

Works and Services	6.4	24.9	72.2	56.5	550.0
Credits	2.3	12.6	5.1	—	—
Total	8.7	37.5	77.3	56.5	
Water Supply:					
Number of tank trucks	625.0	1,261.0	2,061.0	2,845.0	5,462.0
Index (base 1979 = 100)	100.0	201.8	329.8	455.2	873.9
Volume of water affected (10^6 m^3)	2.0	4.1	7.3	13.1	29.9
Index (base:1979 = 100)	100.0	205.0	365.0	655.0	1,495.0

Source: SUDENE/CORDEC

Note that of the 20% of farmers owning property, 60% own areas of up to 20 hectares and 92% own areas of up to 100 hectares. These data reflect a social structure responsible for the fact that one homogeneous social group, the landless, is more vulnerable to drought than any other.

Financial expenditures of the federal government in this emergency operation were estimated by SUDENE/CORDEC at 730 billion current cruzeiros as of 1983 (General Price Index, Internal Availability), or approximately US$2.3 billion at the corresponding annual rate. According to the way SUDENE grouped the expenditures (see Table 3), the operation consisted basically of the execution of work projects and services, with a small fraction of the amount allocated to a line of special credit (2.7% at current prices or 15.2% in constant cruzeiros as of 1983—General Price Index, Internal Availability).

Let us observe closely how the government responded in each of the drought years. In 1979 it introduced a new program to resolve the problems associated with the "work fronts": long distances between work places and workers' homes, low quality and productivity standards, poor facilities, bad food, poor sanitation, high maintenance costs, and so forth. The innovations consisted of the replacement of the traditional "work fronts" with a "working within the property" system, which included constructing and repairing watering places, wells, cisterns, and irrigation channels; clearing areas; constructing fences; and repairing houses.

For properties up to 20 hectares, the federal government financed up to five workers, including the owner's family. For properties from 20 to 100 hectares, the government permitted hiring up to ten workers and provided 80% of the financing, with the landowner contributing the remaining 20% through his family's labor. For properties of more than 100 hectares, the limit on the number of workers was not established. Properties of 100 to 500 hectares were allowed expenditures for 70% of the labor, with the remaining 30% to be financed through special credit lines with an interest rate of 2% per year and a twenty-year payment term that included a six-year payment holiday before payment began. For properties of more than 500 hectares, the same conditions prevailed but expenses were divided on a 50-50 basis. From April 1979 to February 1980, approximately sixty properties benefitted from this program. Government expenditures rose to 8.7 billion cruzeiros in 1979, which corresponded to approximately US$270 million at 1979 exchange rates.

Notwithstanding the practical advantages of the new system for the program operators, dissatisfaction arose because the system favored the private interests of the landowners receiving the benefits. The 1980 plan maintained the "working within the property" system as its main strategy, but it introduced variations and began incorporating public and community work projects through DNOCS, the First Engineering Sector of the Army, CODEVASF, and some other state institutions. The modifications introduced in the system included alteration of the size criteria, financing limits, and numbers of workers to be hired by the largest properties. Credit conditions were also modified: interest rates were increased to 7% per year and payment terms were reduced to twelve years, including a four-year payment holiday. This plan benefitted 244,000 properties from May 1980 to May 1981. Expenditures increased to 37.5 billion historical cruzeiros, corresponding to approximately US$600 million dollars (November 1980 exchange rate).

In 1981 the "working within the property system" was discontinued. From June 1981 to May 1982, the number of workers employed surpassed 1 million, and all resources were allocated for the execution of community and public works. This action, which coincided with efforts to establish COMDEC and ensure its participation in the plan's implementation, doubtlessly had an impact on the November 1982 elections for state, federal, and local officials, elections that resulted in a very important victory for the governing party in the Northeast.

Government expenditures rose to 77.3 billion historical cruzeiros, corresponding to US$640 million dollars in terms of the November 1981 exchange rates. The special credit for landowners was restricted to 6.6% of this amount and was eliminated in the following year. Nevertheless, there are records of transfers of funds (although amounts were not revealed) from emergency programs to the PROHIDRO program, a subsidized credit program for the implementation of hydraulic work in rural properties (SUDENE, 1984, p. 17).

The strategy implemented in 1981 was maintained the following years (SUDENE, 1984, p. 24). From June 1982 to May 1983, expenditures rose to 56.2 billion historical cruzeiros, which corresponds to a little more than US$600 million (at the exchange rate as of November 1983).

In addition to the "work fronts" (created to provide employment and income to the drought victims) and credit lines (which were granted to the landowners), the government initiated a program using tank trucks to provide water. Private trucks were rented to transport water tanks (purchased by the government) to needy communities. Among the drought indicators listed in Table 3, this shows a continuous growth. This information not only reveals the accumulated effects of continued drought on the water supply; it also reflects the special interests created by the rental of private trucks paid for by the government in a time of economic recession.

Other failures pointed out in several documents issued by the Federation of Rural Workers (Federação de Trabalhadores Rurais) in the states of the Northeast and by the National Conference of the Bishops of Brazil (Conferencia Nacional dos Bispos do Brasil—CNBB) were included in an unpublished report (Avaliação do Plano de Defesa Civil do Nordeste—Programa de Emergencia, 1979-1983—IPLAN/IPEA/SEPLAN-PR, Brasília; 1983), from which I have listed some excerpts:

1. Information on program criteria, proposed measures, and decision making was not shared with the workers.
2. Rural workers did not participate, through their representative organization, in the formulation, execution, and control of the program.
3. Landowners included "ghost workers" (nonexistent workers) in their reports to government officials in order to receive more money.
4. Persons who were not part of the rural working class were often enrolled in the program for political reasons, to the detriment of the target group.
5. The program did not allow the enrollment of women, single men, retired people, and minors, which caused increases in the number of civil marriages among minors and falsified statements to gain access to work.
6. Some workers were not provided with tools, forcing them to use their own.
7. Work hours were not consistent: in some places, people worked ten hours per day for three days a week; in others, men worked five to seven hours per day, Monday through Friday, or only two or three days a week.

8. The quality of the work—especially the dams, which were constructed of sand instead of cement or stone—caused discontent among the enlisted people.

9. Late payments were not timed with either the sale of food by the Brazilian Food Company (COBAL) in the urban areas or the days of the street markets, and the workers consequently were exploited by merchants because they were obliged to buy food on credit.

FINAL NOTES AND CONCLUSIONS

The analysis of government involvement with the Northeast drought reveals a rich history of learning through the painful process of understanding, conceptualizing, and intervening over a period of time; of the creation of organizational structures for the planning and implementation of emergency programs; and of vivid experience in the operation of the programs themselves.

Notwithstanding all of the accomplishments, the problems caused by the drought in the Northeast remain challenging because they are related to the social structure.

Overshadowed by the size of the affected area is the problem of the deep separation of the principal decision makers from those afflicted by drought. The main decision makers are the large property owners who have most of the land and water and control access to credit and other support services. The principal victims are the small landless producers, sharecroppers, salaried workers, and, on a smaller scale, small landowners. The last drought repeated the scenario of the previous ones: the big landowners laid off their sharecroppers and salaried workers, who also suffered from the lack of jobs in the cities (due to recession) and the closing of the frontiers (due to large-scale speculative land appropriation).

How has the government responded? By enlisting the refugees, paying them a meager salary, and returning them for free to the large landowners, who had been granted special credit that they would never be expected to repay. This background will permit us to better evaluate the government's performance in terms of the four key areas established by Wilhite, et al. (1985)—adequate information, impact assessment, designation procedure, and organizational structure.

The information system activated by the government had very restricted objectives. Very little was done in terms of long-term planning to reduce the impact of the drought and the consequent need for government assistance. In fact, the main decision makers knew very well that the price would be paid by the government, which functions as a regulation/preservation device. But those involved in the program failed to make clear the nature of the criteria and measures for emergency action.

The impact assessment was done on the basis of hydrometeorological data and information gathered from the counties and states, complemented by *in loco* observations. Because much of the information was quite general and because of the interests involved, political pressures led to frequent diagnoses and decisions that did not reflect the real situation. Designation procedures to determine the eligibility of counties for the assistance programs was centralized and based on well-defined criteria. However, the effectiveness of this procedure is questionable because of the problems with impact assessment. In terms of organizational structure, the plan is administered by a single agency, SUDENE, and an interagency committee.

In addition to the achievements made in drought planning, the government needs to define more accurately the objectives of the policy to assure greater equity and more incentives to adopt adequate practices to overcome the old "drought industry" that unfortunately is still active in the Northeast. One of the principle obstacles is the regional agrarian structure, which is responsible for the fact that in the new Projeto Nordeste, born in the surges of the last drought and destined to incorporate the old special programs, the landowners have been given fundamental consideration.

If the New Republic is able to fulfill its promises of agrarian reform—an accomplishment that will basically depend on the political support the group can gather—the government should ensure not only access to the land but also the sensible integration of the various approaches to strengthen the small landless producers and the small landowners. Water supply studies, technological support, and services should be directed to meet the needs of this vulnerable section of the population.

ACKNOWLEDGMENTS

The author wishes to thank the Northeast Civil Defense regional coordinator, Dr. José Magalhães Sobrinho, for his assistance in collecting basic information about the 1979-1983 Northeast drought emergency program. Special thanks are also extended to Norma Liza Gerjoy for her assistance with translating my original Portuguese text into English, Inalda Silvestre for helping with the library research and classification, and Iêda Pires for typing the manuscript and helping with the preparation of the illustrations that appear in this paper.

The editors would like to thank Elizabeth and Erasmo da Silva for their help in translating and editing the manuscript.

REFERENCES

Alves, J. 1953. História das secas. Instituto do Ceará, Fortaleza, Brazil.

Cardim, F. 1925. Tratados da terra e gente do Brasil. Livraria J. Leite, Rio de Janeiro.

Carvalho, O. 1973. Plano integrado para o combate preventivo aos efeitos das secas no Nordeste. MINTER, Brasília.

Cavalcanti, C.; and D. Pessoa, eds. 1983. A seca nordestina de 79-80. Fundação Joaquim Nabuco, Recife, Brazil.

Cunha, E. 1981. Os sertões: Campanha de canudos. 3rd ed. F. Alves, Rio de Janeiro.

Fundação João Pinheiro. 1984. Um reexame da questão nordestina. Belo Horizonte, Brazil.

Grupo de Trabalho para o Desenvolvimento do Nordeste. 1967. Uma política de desenvolvimento econômico para o Nordeste. 2nd ed. SUDENE, Recife, Brazil.

Guimarães, L. 1982. Formas recentes de atuação do Estado no Nordeste: In Anais do Seminário Internacional sobre Disparidade Regional. Forum Nordeste/ SUDENE, Recife, Brazil.

Hirschman, A. O. 1965. Brazil's North-East. In A. O. Hirschman. Journeys toward Progress. Doubleday, New York.

IBGE. 1984. Anuário Estatístico do Brasil. IBGE, Rio de Janeiro.

Melo, M. L. 1978. Regiões agrárias do Nordeste. SUDENE, Recife, Brazil.

Melo, M. L. 1980. Os Agrestes—Estudo dos espaços nordestinos do sistema gado-policultura de uso de recursos. SUDENE, Recife, Brazil.

Pessoa, D.; and C. Cavalcanti. 1973. Caráter e efeitos da seca nordestina de 1970. SUDENE/SIRAC. Recife, Brazil.

Pessoa, D. 1983. Estratificação social e vulnerabilidade à seca. B. Sobre População Emprego e Renda no Nordeste 2, no. 1 (January/April):125-138.

Silva, M.; and D. A. Lima. 1982. Sertão-Norte: Área do sistema gado-algodão. SUDENE, Recife, Brazil.

Smoll, H. L. 1914. Geologia e suprimento d'água subterrânea no Piauí e parte do Ceará. IOCS, Rio de Janeiro.

SUDENE. 1978. Plano de emergência contra as calamidades públicas para 1979. Recife, Brazil.

SUDENE. 1979. Plano anual de Defesa Civil—1980, versão preliminar. SUDENE/GEACAP/CORDEC, Recife, Brazil.

SUDENE. 1980a. Calamidades públicas: Plano de emergência para 1981, versão preliminar. SUDENE/CORDEC-NE, Recife, Brazil.

SUDENE. 1980b. SUDENE vinte anos. Recife, Brazil.

SUDENE. 1981a. As secas do Nordeste. DRN, Recife, Brazil.

SUDENE. 1981b. Calamidades públicas no Nordeste: Plano de defesa civil para 1982, versão preliminar. Recife, Brazil.

SUDENE. 1982. Plano de defesa civil para 1983, região Nordeste. SUDENE/COR-DEC-NE, Recife, Brazil.

SUDENE. 1984. Plano de defesa civil para 1985, região Nordeste. SUDENE/COR-DEC-NE, Recife, Brazil.

SUDENE. 1986. Programa de Irrigação do Nordeste-PROINE, 1986/1990. Recife, Brazil.

Wilhite, D. A.; and M. H. Glantz. 1985. Understanding the drought phenomenon: The role of definitions. Water Int. 10:111-120.

Wilhite, D. A.; N. J. Rosenberg; and M. H. Glantz. 1985. Government response to drought in the United States: Lessons from the mid-1970s. Part 5. Drought response in the United States and Australia: A comparative analysis. CAMaC Progress Report 85-5. Center for Agricultural Meteorology and Climatology, University of Nebraska-Lincoln.

CHAPTER 29
INTERACTION BETWEEN SCIENTIST AND LAYMAN
IN THE PERCEPTION AND ASSESSMENT OF DROUGHT: SOUTH AFRICA

Roland E. Schulze

INTRODUCTION

The layman is often thoroughly confused when trying to perceive objectively the complex drought phenomenon with its attendant social and economic implications. Southern Africa is only now recovering from a major subcontinental drought that extended into the mid-1980s. Frequently called a "two-hundred year event," this drought has taken its toll agriculturally, economically, socially, and environmentally, costing billions of dollars of taxpayers' money (both internally and through foreign aid in largely ad hoc, reactive crisis responses). For the scientist involved in drought studies, the 1980s drought has provided both satisfaction (at seeing real-world decisions made based on scientific research) as well as frustration (at the misrepresentation and misinterpretation of scientific concepts and the lack of pre- and post-drought response to an environmental crisis that is likely to recur.

This paper summarizes selected research approaches and experiences in the interaction between scientist and layman in the perception of this recent drought in southern Africa, with emphasis on agricultural impacts.

TERMINOLOGY

Scientist

In the context of this paper, the scientist is assumed to possess systematized knowledge (based on sound scientific principles) to assess the drought phenomenon and its impacts objectively in order to help resolve practical problems using scientific know-how. Let us assume further that the scientist is usually not a decision maker per se, but rather someone who provides scientific information and options to the water resources decision maker both proactively, in examining alternative scenarios before drought sets in, and reactively, in responding to the decision maker's dilemma once an existing drought crisis requires scientifically sound ad hoc answers. We will also assume that the scientist has an educational function.

Layman

A layman is one who is not an expert in a particular branch of knowledge. The layman, when viewed from the scientist's purist perspective, includes the following.
1. The politician, who makes (sometimes profound) public pronouncements on topics of a scientific nature.
2. The technocrat, frequently a scientist-turned-administrator, who often has to convert scientific information into feasible management options.
3. The media, which influences perceptions considerably.
4. The population at large, which has to respond to the drought.

Perception

Perception of a phenomenon like drought can be genuine (by direct experience of and response to the consequences of drought) or induced (for example, by the media engendering a feeling of sympathetic suffering at a heightened experience level). It is well known that perception of the drought hazard varies according to personality differences and in time (as population increases and intensified agriculture make heavier demands on a finite amount of water). The order in which groups of people in southern Africa probably would perceive drought is given below.
1. The subsistence agriculturalists and pastoralists of the Third World, who have no buffers of technological know-how, adaptive mechanisms, loan facilities, other means of income or savings.
2. The inexperienced (first-generation) but more technologically advanced dryland farmers, operating in humid or subhumid areas.
3. The experienced (already conservation-conscious) farmers, operating in humid or subhumid areas.
4. The arid zone farmers, who have adapted in approach and response by displaying resourcefulness to frequent and often severe dry spells.
5. The low-income urban dwellers, whose meager budgets cannot absorb drought-induced food price hikes.
6. The middle- to upper-income urbanites, to whom the drought frequently implies inconvenience and nuisance rather than genuine suffering.

PREDROUGHT INTERACTION THROUGH FARMER EDUCATION

Premises on Which Drought Education Should be Based

In agriculture, predrought research can result in major savings in drought aid. In scientists' interaction with farmers and the extension service, we should take note of certain premises set out by French (1983):
1. The onset of a drought cannot be forecast.
2. Drought should be viewed by the farmer not as an abnormal event, but as a recurring (if irregularly so) environmental feature.

3. Drought management is essentially part of the general management of soil, plants, and animals.
4. Amelioration of drought effects is achieved only if government and farmer work together openly and honestly.
5. A fundamental ecological principle during drought is to use available water efficiently and effectively.

In addition to French's premises, the following should be noted.

1. The farmer should know, in quantitative and comparative terms, what intrinsic drought risks prevail in the long run at his location in order to anticipate and/or take buffering precautionary measures.
2. A strong case can be made for applying differential drought aid, giving earlier or relatively more assistance to the farmer who has implemented sound soil and water conservation practices or has taken other protective measures.
3. Procedures adopted in quantifying drought aid should be known in advance in general terms (considering a region's agricultural significance and intrinsic drought risk) and also in specific terms (regarding the potential of the individual farm or land and the current level of farm management).

Proactive Measures Example: Fodder Production Planning and Banking

The most common cause of income losses in livestock farming in Natal, South Africa, is inadequate quantity of feed supplies. A solution to this problem is fodder production planning as a basis for building up a fodder "bank" to be used in times of drought. The range species *Eragrostis curvula* is used widely as a fodder, and R. I. Jones (personal communication, 1982) has derived a formula for estimating *E. curvula* yield, Y,

$$Y(kg/ha/yr) = 31.9N + \frac{N^2}{57.9} + 3939\ln (\text{Annual Precipitation, mm}) - 22450 \qquad (1)$$

in which
$$N = kg \text{ nitrogen applied/ha/hr.}$$

On the basis (personal communication from R. I. Jones, 1982) that the *minimum* fodder bank accumulation (MFBA) from a year of excess precipitation (and thus excess yield) should be an accumulated amount large enough to provide additional fodder to cater for the "average dry" year (i.e., with precipitation one standard deviation below the mean, occurring statistically about one year in six [Schulze, 1982]), the MFBA is the difference in yield between an average year, with precipitation = MAP, and an "average dry" year, with precipitation = DRY. As a percentage of a farm's total average fodder production,

$$MFBA(\%) = \frac{Y(MAP) - Y(DRY)}{Y(MAP)} \; 100 = \frac{393900 \ln (MAP/DRY)}{31.9N - \frac{N}{57.9}^2 + 3939 \ln MAP - 22450}$$

Using mapping procedures detailed in Schulze (1982), Fig. 1 illustrates the considerable regional differences in Natal in MFBA, ranging from % to 50%, assuming native *E. curvula* range (i.e., N = 0 kg/ha). Because it is senseless to expect a fodder bank to be built up indefinitely, R. I. Jones (personal communication, 1982) suggests restricting the size of the fodder bank to a level that could supply forage for the worst drought expected once in twenty years, thereby introducing the concept of the so-called ideal fodder bank size. By substituting the annual rainfall exceeded with a 95% probability as the value for "DRY" in the above equation and mapping the results, the ideal fodder bank map (Fig. 2) indicates those areas of Natal where less than 40% and more than 70% of the mean annual *E. curvula* production of a livestock farm should be "banked" as a buffer against severe drought. These examples are among several given in Schulze (1982) which illustrate what topics should be researched and promoted, and what changes should be effected in the scientist's interaction with the farmer/extension service to ensure proactive management under drought conditions.

OBJECTIVE ASSESSMENT OF DROUGHT SEVERITY

It remains inevitable that comparisons of current and historical droughts are made with respect to their severity and areal extent. Comparisons, based often on unfounded and personal experience, can be highly distorted. Extensive climatic data bases, data networks, and computers have enabled the scientist only recently to undertake more or less "objective" assessment of drought severity as a guide to the disbursement of drought management aid. Two techniques used during the 1980s drought in southern Africa are illustrated below.

Agricultural Drought Severity at a Point Using the ACRU Model

Agricultural drought occurs when soil moisture stress causes crop yield reductions. Crop yield (dry matter production) may be related directly to accumulated actual evapotranspiration—i.e., the interplay of daily effective rainfall, soil moisture status, atmospheric demand, crop growth/phenological stage, root development, and timing/severity of plant stress.

The ACRU model (Schulze, 1986) is a physical-conceptual agrohydrological simulator using readily available climatic data. It was created particularly for use in developing countries, and it has input options at different levels of sophistication and multiple output (options including runoff components, reservoir yield, and irrigation water supply and demand as well as crop yield estimates). Being a multi-soil-layer moisture budgeting model with emphasis on estimating actual evapotranspiration and plant stress day by day, ACRU could be particularly useful as a crop yield estimator.

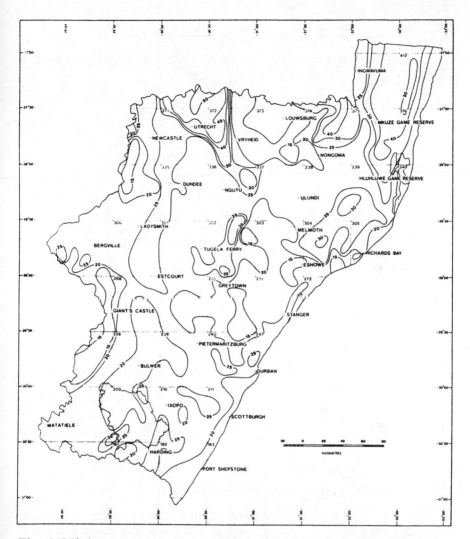

Fig. 1 Minimum percentage fodder bank accumulation in Natal (Schulze, 1982).

The ACRU model (with maize and sugarcane submodels) was applied to fifty-one years of daily climatic data for Sevenoaks (29° 12'S; 30° 35'E) in Natal on different local soils on a farm. The resultant crop yield simulations (with genetic/technological levels assumed at mid-1980s levels) plotted in Fig. 3 illustrate the following.

1. At a given local economic break-even threshold of 3.8 tons/ha, the extended late 1970s-early 1980s drought was indeed severe.
2. The shorter drought of the mid-1940s gave an even lower individual annual estimation of maize yield.

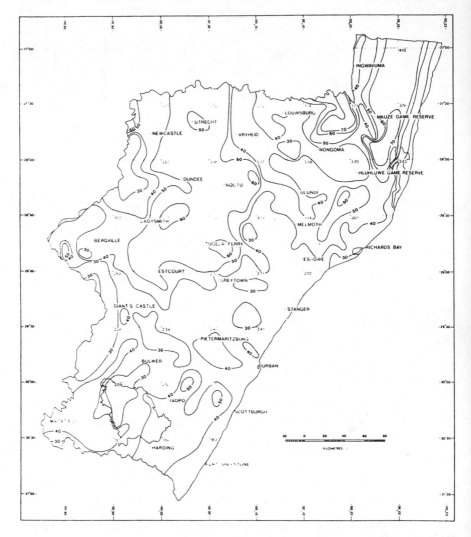

Fig. 2 "Ideal" fodder bank size in Natal, as a percentage of mean annual fodder production (Schulze, 1982).

3. The moisture buffer provided by deeper soils resulted in increased yields by nearly 1 ton/ha on average.

4. Irrigation, with an economic threshold yield of 5.5 tons/ha, would provide excellent insurance against crop failure at this location.

The alternative crop to maize at Sevenoaks is sugarcane. By applying actual 1985 producer prices of maize and sugarcane to crop yield simulations at Sevenoaks, Table 1 shows that during severe drought, lower losses would have been incurred with

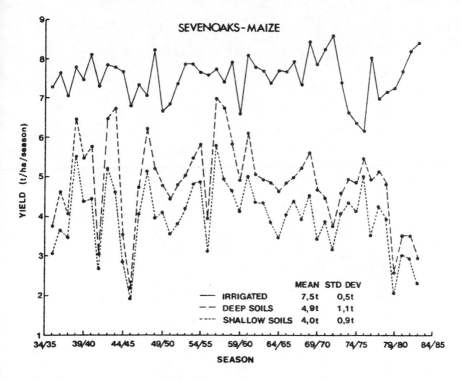

Fig. 3 Maize yield simulations under different conditions at Seven-oaks, Natal (Schulze, 1986).

sugarcane than with maize. These results illustrate the application of a simulation model in assessing severity and economic impact of agricultural drought at a specific location under different crops.

Assessment of Spatial Extent of Drought

Publicized as a two-hundred-year event, the drought of the 1980s in Southern Africa was perceived as being more severe than droughts of the early 1930s, mid-1940s, and late 1960s, probably largely through extensive television coverage. This publicity also led to widespread acceptance of the idea that the drought was fairly uniformly severe throughout much of the subcontinent.

A study by Dent, et. al (1986), has attempted to assess "objectively" the severity and spatial extent of the drought of the early 1980s for the summer rainfall region of southern Africa. Using data from 2,408 rainfall stations with long duration records up to March 1984, summer rainfall totals were calculated, then cumulated over one, two, three, and four consecutive years. The totals were then used as the basis for a drought severity index. According to this index, very severe droughts (category 1) occur when

Table 1
Simulation of Drought Effects on Economic Returns from Maize and Sugarcane at Sevenoaks

Crop	Condition	Percentage Years Economic Threshold Not Reached	Profit/ha Year of Median Production	Profit/ha Worst Year in 5	Profit/ha Worst Year in 20
Maize	Deep Soil	19	R 231[a]	R 27	R-231
	Shallow Soil	35	63	-147	-336
	Irrigated	0	462	315[2]	189[b]
Sugarcane	Deep Soil	8	257	66	-163
	Shallow Soil	38	75	- 86	-255

[a]US$ = R2.25
[b]Not related to drought

Source: Schulze, 1986.

an area receives less than 10% of the mean summer precipitation above the driest summer precipitation for the period on record; moderately severe (category 2) droughts occur when 11-35% of the mean is received; and mild (category 3) droughts occur when more than 35% of the mean is received (Dent, et al., 1986). The rainfall totals are also mapped, using polynomial spline interpolation routines, for major drought sequences from 1930 on.

Figure 4, depicting three-year drought sequences, compares the 1930s drought with the 1980s drought, illustrating that spatially the categories of drought delimited by the procedures detailed in Dent, et al. (1986), present a patchy rather than regionally uniform picture. The most severe droughts (category 1) have been concentrated in different parts of southern Africa during major drought periods (e.g., in central areas in the drought of 1930-31 and 1932-33 and along the eastern seaboard in the drought of 1980-81 and 1982-83). During major drought periods, large areas may be experiencing relatively "mild" (category 3) droughts only; and areas of "mild" and "very severe" drought may be in very close proximity to one another.

Although the indices used above are not ideal, such spatial analyses help us better understand the issues associated with the temporal and spatial comparisons of drought severity. Furthermore, at each location, intracomparisons (rather than intercomparisons) of climate records are made, thereby incorporating the local rainfall climate into the method—an important consideration when drought is conceived as an agent determining the long-term ecological interactions that are unique to any specific location.

HELPING PREVENT CONFUSION CREATED BY MEDIA AND POLITICIANS

Modern media, selling news most effectively when it is the "worst," "most severe," "biggest," or "smallest," may blur and distort our perception of drought. Newspaper articles on drought during 1983 contain information, humor, hard sell, soft sell, threat, and criticism. Television gives us instant coverage of the suffering caused by drought, not only in our own regions, but throughout the world. It is small wonder the layman may become confused by impressions gained from the media. In such times the scientist must also be an educator, writing at a level that people other than scholars may understand and clarifying unqualified or misinterpretable statements made frequently in public.

Explaining Drought Terminology

It is imperative that in our communications with media, laymen, or politicians we make it quite clear that:
1. One has to distinguish between agricultural, hydrological, and meteorological drought.
2. Different types of drought do not necessarily coexist at a location or region at a given time.
3. No one can forecast the onset of drought, and we only know about a drought once we are already in it.

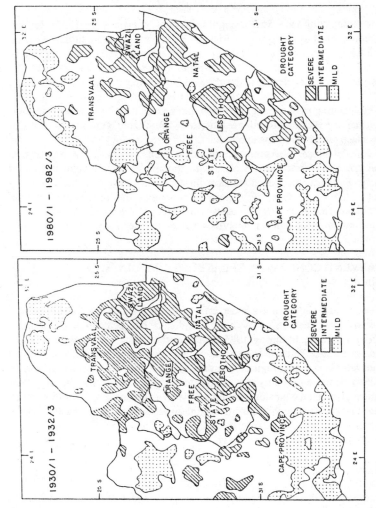

Fig. 4 Spatial depiction of drought severity categories for accumulated three-year summer rainfall totals in the early 1930s and
1980s (after Dent, et al, 1986).

4. Drought is a relative phenomenon, to be understood regionally and locally in terms of supply and demand and in terms of long-term balances in nature.
5. Drought, a temporarily abnormal condition, must not be confused with aridity, a more or less permanently dry climatic condition.
6. Droughts should be assessed by objective means with regard to their severity, duration, time of occurrence within the annual cycle, and areal extent.

Problems with the Concept of Drought Recurrence Intervals

During the drought of early 1980s in southern Africa, the media initially called it the "drought of a lifetime"; within months it was commonly known as the two-hundred-year drought and later even the five-hundred-year drought.

The concept of the recurrence interval, useful as it may be, is fraught with danger of misinterpretation and misuse. Scientists, in advising decision makers (who in turn advise politicians, who tell the media), must ensure they are not misunderstood, by stressing that:

1. The calculated recurrence interval gives an average return period, based on the sample available for analysis, and an event of equal or greater magnitude may in fact occur within years or, alternatively, not for centuries (i.e., that this predictive tool is not a forecasting tool in that we cannot say when the extreme event is going to be equaled or exceeded).
2. In working with probabilities, we cannot meaningfully extrapolate beyond the length of observed records that may not be temporally representative and are usually much shorter than highly publicized two-hundred-year droughts.
3. The confidence with which we can give our answer is usually enveloped in a wide range of what statistically is the true answer (e.g., the computed answer from a 68-year rainfall record at Cedara, Natal, indicated that by 1983 the area was in the grips of a 143-year drought; within 95% confidence limits it could have been anything from a 40- to 250-year drought).

When it is with utmost difficulty that we get fellow scientists to use the concept of the return period with the care it deserves, it is with some consternation that we turn this concept loose for the layman and politician!

Experiences with the Concept of So-Called Drought Cycles

Whether or not oscillations of climate exist is not at issue here; rather, we are concerned with the response of laymen to so-called drought cycles and the role of the scientist in dispelling misinterpretation of possible oscillations.

In South Africa, Tyson and Dyer wrote a series of papers in the late 1970s in which a 70- to 100-year time series of regional annual rainfall data was smoothed and filtered, producing persistent "quasi-periodic fluctuations" of annual rainfall (Fig. 5) with a major oscillation of 17-23 years (e.g., Dyer and Tyson, 1977). On the basis of their

500

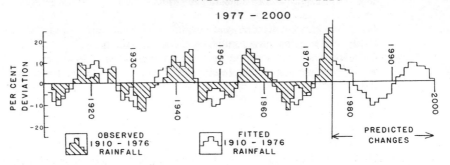

ESTIMATED WET AND DRY SPELLS

1977 – 2000

Fig. 5 Possible future extended wet and dry spells over the summer rainfall region of southern Africa (after Tyson and Dyer, 1978).

results they forecast the likelihood of droughts in southern Africa in the 1980s (Fig. 5; for example, see Tyson and Dyer, 1978). Their work received publicity through the media, particularly when a series of dry years occurred at the beginning of the 1980s.

Tyson and Dyer as well as other authors were cautious in their scientific writing, avoiding the "cycle" concept and stressing instead phrases like "tendencies for wet and dry years to cluster," or "organized variations." They also emphasized that no forecasts shorter than five-year general trends could be made, let alone predictions of annual rainfall for a single year, because major annual perturbations within general trends occurred. The notion of southern Africa being in a drought "cycle" nevertheless caught on to the extent that it became known as the Tyson-Dyer Syndrome. The maize industry expressed concern in the early 1980s, and certain farmers would not even plant maize, because Tyson and Dyer had forecast a drought and there would therefore be no hope of achieving any yield anyway until the drought "cycle" had passed.

The above experiences exemplify the caution that has to be exercised in conveying scientific concepts related to drought to the media and laymen, and the repercussions that well-intentioned dissemination of research findings can have.

CONCLUSIONS: ON THE POST-DROUGHT ROLE OF THE SCIENTIST

It is a common experience for a large proportion of the population that soon after a drought has passed, little remains of the cumulative experience, except the accumulated debt of (mostly) farmers. Disquietingly soon, "business as before" is the order of the day. It is in this post-drought stage that those responsible for scientific review and reassessment should collaborate closely with governmental or paragovernmental institutions. Many examples of scientific research possibilities are cited in Yevjevich, et al. (1983), and will not be repeated here. Regarding agricultural/meteorological drought, a few other examples suffice:

1. Setting up improved, coordinated climatic data bases and networks in terms also of drought assessment and aid.

2. Examining environmental deterioration, both permanent and temporary (e.g., the replacement of palatable plant species by less useful ones; range rehabilitation rates).
3. Inventorying, computerizing, and updating future potential drought aid to farmers, farm by farm, according to assessments of each farmer's water and soil conservation and grazing management practices. This information would be conveyed to the farmer before the next drought for future drought-aid funding or tax incentive.
4. Reassessing the effectiveness of drought indices (including improving drought severity models in terms of crop yield estimations under moisture stress) and the effectiveness of soil, water, and grazing conservation management on soil water status.
5. Prompting funding agencies to fund research before the onset of droughts, because sound drought research is measured in hundreds of thousands of dollars, but drought aid is measured in billions of dollars.
6. Concentrating even more research and interaction into the complex socio-politico-environmental Third World, with its unique problems in respect to drought.

ACKNOWLEDGMENTS

My attendance at the International Symposium on Drought was made possible by grants from the Utah Water Research Laboratory and the South African Council for Scientific and Industrial Research.

REFERENCES

Dent, M. C.; R. E. Schulze; H. M. M. Wills; and S. D. Lynch. 1986. Spatial and temporal analysis of the recent drought in the summer rainfall region of Southern Africa. Water S. A. (in press).

Dyer, T. G. J.; and P. D. Tyson. 1977. Estimating above and below normal rainfall periods over South Africa, 1972-2000. J. Appl. Meteorol. 16:145-147.

French, R. J. 1983. Managing environmental aspects of agricultural droughts: Australian experience. pp. 170-187. In V. Yevjevich, L. da Cunha, and E. Vlachos, eds. Coping with Droughts. Water Resources Publications, Littleton, Colorado.

Schulze, R. E. 1982. Agrohydrology and climatology of Natal. Water Research Commission, Pretoria.

Schulze, R. E. 1986. The ACRU model for agrohydrological decision-making: Structure, options and application. Proceedings of the 2nd South African National Hydrology Symposium. Department of Agricultural Engineering, University of Natal, Pietermaritzburg. ACRU Report 22:345-362.

Tyson, P. D.; and T. G. J. Dyer. 1978. The predicted above-normal rainfall of the seventies and the likelihood of droughts in the eighties in South Africa. S. Afr. J. Sci. 74:372-377.

Yevjevich, V.; L. da Cunha; and E. Vlachos. 1983. Coping with Droughts. Water Resources Publications, Littleton, Colorado.

PART 8

The Role of Donor Organizations in Responding to Drought and Famine

CHAPTER 30
DROUGHT AND AGRICULTURAL DEVELOPMENT

H. E. Dregne

INTRODUCTION

Drought is a recurring phenomenon in the drylands, its impact on human populations depending on the severity and longevity of the event. For the most part, a one-year agricultural drought presents only a moderate problem to the local inhabitants. Two consecutive years of crop failure make the problem a serious one. Three or more consecutive years of drought have a severe or disastrous effect on cultivators and pastoralists and affect a host of other segments of society. Whether or not famine accompanies a drought is a function of numerous other factors, the most important of which is the economic status of the affected population. Poverty begets famine (Mellor and Gavian, 1987).

In dry regions, temporal and spatial variability of rainfall is high. Even when large regions within a country are experiencing severe drought, it is not unusual to find that some places have normal or near-normal rainfall (Warrick, 1984). Rainfall variability is greater in the drier climatic zones and smaller in the wetter zones. Interannual variability tends to be greater in summer rainfall zones (such as the Sahel) than in the winter rainfall zones (such as North Africa). A consequence of high rainfall variability is the high risk that cultivators and pastoralists face in the dry regions.

My discussion will deal with the role of international organizations in coping with famine and drought effects on agricultural production systems. Emphasis will be on developing countries in the dry regions. The international development organizations used as examples are the World Bank and the U.S. Agency for International Development (AID).

AGRICULTURAL ADJUSTMENTS TO ARIDITY

Agriculturists have devised various means of coping with dryness and variability. Fallowing land for water conservation or nutrient restoration is an age-old practice of proven value in modern and traditional agriculture. Deep seeding and wide spacing of plants increases the chances of soil moisture being available for seedling establishment and growth. Both small-scale and large-scale water harvesting (the concentration of water from a large area onto a small area where it can be used by a crop) have been practiced for millennia. Terracing to reduce runoff is of similar antiquity. Nomadism and transhumance are direct responses to climatic variability. Cultivators in dry regions make frequent decisions about crops to plant. If rains come early, long-season cultivars are planted to take advantage of their greater yield-producing potential. If rains are late or if dry periods kill crops planted early, short-season cultivars of the same crop or a different crop are planted. Management decisions of this type are a normal response to temporal variability in rainfall, whether or not the season turns out to be drought-affected.

Survival of agriculturists in drylands demands storage of profits accumulated in good years to compensate for losses in poor years. The biblical admonition to save up food during the seven fat years to provide for the seven lean years is as relevant in arid regions today as it was in ancient Egypt. Storage can and does take a variety of shapes, from saving money to storing grain to investing in additional livestock or land. Obviously, if the adverse impact of poor years is to be minimized, advantage must be taken of the yield potential in the good years. A logical conclusion of this line of reasoning is that research and technology transfer should be concentrated on achieving maximum economic returns in average or above-average rainfall years. A corollary would be to concentrate research and extension on agricultural production in the more favorable climatic zones, but this tactic will not work if movement of food from one part of a country to another is restricted.

In the United States, farmers and ranchers have been exposed to the vagaries of arid region climates for more than a hundred years. Much success and many costly failures have accompanied the expansion of agriculture from the humid east to the land area west of the ninety-eighth meridian, an area that constitutes 60% of the forty-eight contiguous states. Progress in reaching a reasonably satisfactory accommodation of people to the arid environment has been the result of technological advances. Constant experimenting with new ideas has characterized United States agriculture. Much of that experimentation is done by enterprising farmers and ranchers working with research, extension, and industry personnel.

Science and technology applied to United States dryland agriculture has led to a number of significant developments. The key to success has been an emphasis on understanding basic soil-plant-climate relations and adapting that knowledge to field conditions. Among the notable contributions to sustained crop production are the development of sweep tillage, minimum tillage, efficient summer fallow system, weed and insect control, mulching, chisel plowing, conservation bench-terracing, wind erosion control, improved cultivars, and effective use of fertilizers (Dregne and Willis, 1983). Range management has been brought to the level of a science for the first time. Rotation and deferred grazing management has halted and reversed the land degradation of the late nineteenth and early twentieth centuries. Range plant introductions, reseeding, brush control with machines and herbicides, soil pitting, and judicious use of fertilizers have all contributed to a greater stabilization of rangeland productivity.

TECHNOLOGY TRANSFER

Coping with aridity and climatic variability is a matter of crop selection, moisture conservation, erosion control, and maintenance of soil fertility. The principles are the same everywhere; only the actual management practices differ. Techniques in use in mechanized, advanced-technology societies seldom can be transferred to new environments without adaptation. Nevertheless, the idea behind the technique may well be adaptable to different circumstances. Child, et al., (1984), expressed this point well in a description of the value of several grazing management systems. They noted that the main problem in transferring those systems was their rigid application to new environments. Even the best system needs local adaptation.

The use of sandfighters to control wind erosion in Texas and Niger provides an example of how technology transfer can function. The sandfighter is a device consisting of small paddles or fingers attached to an axle that may be as much as 10 m long. As the axle rotates when pulled by a tractor, it kicks up soil clods that resist wind erosion. On West Texas sandy loam soils, the sandfighter works well when pulled rapidly across fields. It is much less effective when pulled slowly. A Texas A&M University team involved in the TropSoils Collaborative Research Support Project (financed by the Agency for International Development) proposed testing the sandfighter in Niger. Since tractors are scarce in Niger, oxen and donkeys were used to pull the sandfighter, even though it was feared that the machine would not be effective when pulled at the pace of animals. It turned out to be highly successful because the physical properties of Niger's sandy soils were different from those of West Texas sandy soils. If the sandfighter had been tested only with a tractor, it would have had limited utility.

How ideas are generated and technologies are adapted is also illustrated by the history of furrow diking. This technique for capturing and holding water on the land consists of constructing dams at intervals in furrows. It was first developed in the 1920s or 1930s in the western Great Plains. It was then called *basin listing*. The technique worked excellently, but damming furrows meant that tractors bounced across the field and cultivation was impossible. Its use was short-lived. In Nigeria, scientists at the International Institute of Tropical Agriculture (IITA) seized the basin listing concept when they were searching for ways to conserve water in northern Nigeria. They used hand labor to construct the dams and they called the practice *tied ridging*. It is now a commonly used practice.

In the 1970s, the U.S. Department of Agriculture and Texas A&M University engineers, searching for better ways to conserve water and aware of the effectiveness of tied ridges, decided to adapt the practice to West Texas conditions. They came up with a tractor attachment that constructed and removed dikes in the furrows. Furrow diking is now used widely in the southern Great Plains. The principle of tied ridging and furrow diking is the same; only the method of construction differs.

Agricultural technologies are, for the most part, location specific. This means that there must be local testing and adapting of introduced technologies. There must be experimentation and change, followed by more experimentation and change until the technology is found to be either suitable or unsuitable. But experimentation and adaptation call for trained people, working in cooperation with local cultivators and pastoralists. Trained people are in short supply in the developing countries, and research stations and universities are handicapped by poor facilities. Beautiful buildings are not enough.

INTERNATIONAL DEVELOPMENT AGENCIES

International aid agencies have their own special interests in supporting agricultural development (Table 1). The World Bank provides money for large-scale projects, principally in the areas of agricultural and rural development; major irrigation project construction; and livestock production, marketing, and veterinary services. Most of the rurally oriented projects involve construction (roads, irrigation and drainage systems, power systems, water supplies, and buildings) and management (extension services, watershed development, irrigation projects, health services). Short-term training in management and operation of Bank-supported projects is a component of nearly all projects.

For the ten-year period from 1970 to 1980, World Bank financial commitments to agricultural projects in arid regions of developing countries amounted to approximately $1.7 billion (UNEP, 1982). Of that amount, 51% went to agricultural and rural development, 33% to irrigation, 10% to livestock, 4% to drought rehabilitation (Sahel countries), and 2% to forestry. Agricultural and rural development and livestock projects usually are intended to strengthen the infrastructure of the agricultural economy, not to provide direct technical assistance. Technical assistance is provided for irrigation projects. By country, 51% of Bank funds went to Africa, 22% to Mexico, 17% to Asia, and 10% to South America.

During that same ten-year period, the Agency for International Development (AID) spent nearly $700 million on agricultural projects in the drylands. Most of the money (76%) went to projects in Africa. Asian projects received 16% of the funds and Latin American projects received 8%. The projects included strengthening of rural infrastructure (roads, water supplies, and so forth), crop research and extension, watershed management, irrigation management, and institution building. Training of nationals at

Table 1
Orientation of Agricultural Development Projects Supported by Three Organizations, 1970-1980

Type of Project	Development Organization			
	World Bank	AID	FAO	Total
	— Number of Projects —			
Livestock improvement	28	12	7	47
Range improvement	14	9	1	24
Dryland crop production	12	21	8	41
Erosion control	10	6	5	21
Irrigation development	19	11	8	38
Institution building	37	39	11	87

Source: Dregne, 1984

the university level has always been an important part of AID operations, along with short-term training. Most training is done in the United States. Technical assistance and institution building also have high priority in AID. Development projects usually have time frames of three to five years and a budget of at least $1 million.

The Food and Agriculture Organization (FAO) of the United Nations invests primarily in relatively small-scale projects. For 1970-1980, Africa received 44% of FAO's money; Asia, 34%; Europe, 21%; and South America, 2%. FAO emphasizes providing technical assistance and training for natural resource surveys, land use planning, irrigation water management, fertilizers and plant protection, forestry, soil and water conservation, crop production, and animal disease control.

Evaluations of World Bank and AID projects generally show that none of them is an unqualified success or failure. However, if these two agencies and their dozens of sister agencies have actually played a significant role in agricultural growth in developing countries, it must be positive, because crop production is rising even in Africa (FAO, 1983).

India is an example of a newly independent (1947), poor country faced with what seemed the almost insurmountable handicaps of widespread poverty, poor transport and communication systems in rural areas, low literacy, and a fast-growing population. Progress has been slow, but in 1986 the agricultural problem Indian policy makers face is the happy one of how to deal with the storage of crop surpluses. AID can claim some credit for helping bring about the new state of affairs through its early and strong support of a strengthened teaching, research, and extension role for universities and ministries. It took about twenty years for that effort to bear fruit, which reinforces the need for a long-range view of development. The agricultural improvement has come about despite the occurrence of the usual droughts, locust attacks, floods, and other catastrophes.

AGRICULTURAL IMPROVEMENT

Increasing crop and livestock production to reduce the impact of drought requires much more than new technologies, however adapted and socially acceptable they may be. The first requirement is to provide incentives that the cultivator or pastoralist finds sufficiently attractive to justify the extra effort that must be expended to obtain higher production. Other requirements are roads, credit facilities, markets, readily available supplies, and transport vehicles. If higher yields are to be obtained through new technologies, there must also be effective research and extension programs as well as an education system that supplies the trained people needed to carry out the functions of public and private agencies.

International donor organizations have access to money and trained people; poor developing countries do not. Agricultural production and marketing systems are dependent on the basic infrastructure of the nation. Although donor organizations can and do invest in many segments of the society, three components of the socioeconomic system seem to be especially in need of strengthening in most developing countries: (1) education, at all levels; (2) transportation; and (3) agricultural research. All three require a long-term commitment by the government and donors.

The need for education should be self-evident. Illiteracy does not mean that improved practices will not be adopted, but it does mean that potential users will be severely handicapped.

The need for reasonably good transportation facilities may be less evident. During droughts, as experience in Ethiopia and other countries has demonstrated, relief efforts can be negated if roads are impassable. But transportation is essential all the time. The availability of seeds, fertilizers, pesticides, and veterinary services to farmers depends on transportation, usually by road. Sending surplus crops to cities and other regions is difficult or impossible if trucks are not available and roads are poor. Furthermore, the willingness of research and extension people, teachers, government officers, businessmen, and health workers to live outside the capital is heavily influenced by inaccessibility to political and economic centers. For these people, no roads or poor roads means a greater or lesser degree of isolation from family, good schools, health facilities, political and financial power centers, and many amenities.

The Western Sudan Agricultural Research Project in the Sudan, financed by the World Bank and AID, experienced some of the difficulties that remoteness causes for research development. The project was responsible for construction of an excellent research facility in one of the Sudan's best farming regions, near Kadugli in southern Kordofan Province. The opportunities to conduct research that would have scientific merit and important practical application seem almost limitless. Yet, staffing the station has been and is difficult. Professional people are unwilling to live in a small city where schools are deficient, health and public services are poor, air travel is unreliable, and the one "all-weather" road to Khartoum is closed from time to time by flood waters. The situation is the same in other developing countries.

A lack of proven and accepted agricultural practices that will increase yields is a major constraint in the poor developing countries. Extension services are unimportant if the extension personnel have nothing to promote, and that is the situation in all too many instances. Training research people is something that developed countries can do well. Ultimately, as in India, developing countries should train their own people. For some small countries, however, that may never be possible beyond the level of the bachelor's degree.

Brazil, the Sudan, and Niger are representative of countries needing three different kinds of research support. Several years ago, Brazil was a developing country in need of long-term and short-term training of academic and research staff and expatriate assistance in-country. Brazil now trains its own professionals; the country relies on other nations only for specialized training in certain advanced technologies. Brazil is a contributor to world agricultural science as well as a user. India, Nigeria, and Mexico are in a similar position. Extension services in these countries have many proven practices to promote.

The Sudan is representative of countries having a well-trained core of agricultural scientists that is severely handicapped by poor facilities and weak operational support. There is a continued need for graduate training of young professionals, but the principal deficiency is in research support. Expatriate scientists can play an important role if donor agencies provide funds to equip and operate new research facilities and then continue to support the facility after the expatriates have left. If donors support a facility and personnel for, say, five years and then terminate that support, the impact may be more harmful than beneficial. Short-term training in-country and overseas is of much less value than graduate education. Kenya and Ethiopia are two of a number of countries in this category. Extension services have good information for cash crop farmers, but not for food crop producers. The third group of countries is a large one, of which Niger is typical. Niger lacks trained people at all levels, needs much support for research facilities and research operations, requires short-term and long-term training at the undergraduate and graduate level, and would benefit from long-term expatriate assistance with research and university teaching. Most of the other Sahel countries, as well as many southern African countries, have similar problems. Research is badly needed to understand the nature of limitations on agricultural production and to produce a range of improved practices that the extension service can promote. When traditional sorghum varieties outyield "improved" varieties, it is difficult for farmers to have confidence in extension recommendations.

MINIMIZING DROUGHT IMPACT

Agricultural droughts are periods of below-average rainfall that adversely affect plant growth. They are a recurring phenomenon in dry climates. Although individual droughts cannot be anticipated, prudence calls for measures to be taken to prepare for them. Traditional agriculturists have devised ways to minimize the impact of drought: pastoralists increase their herds in good times to allow them to survive in bad times; cultivators store up grain for the same reason. Taking advantage of favorable years is essential to survival during unfavorable years. Planning for only the current year is not enough in the dry regions.

Research is the key to coping with agricultural drought. One of the most promising methods of reducing the problem of rainfall variability is the "response farming" procedure proposed by Stewart (1982). The response technique consists of an analysis of dates of onset of rains, followed by decisions of when to plant, the spacing to use, when and if fertilizers should be applied, and the plant thinning schedule to follow. As the cropping year unfolds, adjustments are made to maximize production or to minimize losses. Response farming is a refinement of what farmers in dry regions have always done. It requires a thorough understanding of crop, soil, water, and pest relations in each climatic zone.

Response farming is an example of the kind of long-range research that international organizations trying to cope with drought should support. There are no quick technological fixes available. Short-range attacks on the problem are wasteful of money and human resources. Donor agencies need to decide what they want to support and then stay with it through the early years, which are likely to seem unproductive in terms of an immediate impact.

DROUGHT-PROOFING AGRICULTURE

In principle, drought-proofing agriculture can be done by introducing irrigation. Risk reduction of that kind has been effective in minimizing or eliminating drought impact on crop production in the Great Plains area underlain by the Ogallala aquifer.

512

However, ground-water depletion has already led to the beginning of the end of that kind of drought proofing. And the same future awaits the pump-irrigated oases in the Libyan interior. Where surface water is the irrigation source, droughts still have an adverse impact. Drought in Ethiopia reduced crop production in the Sudan Gezira in 1984 because there are no major water storage dams on the Blue Nile. Lake Nasser shelters Egypt from the capricious variations in low and high flows in the Nile, but there is no similar protection for irrigators along the Niger River or many other rivers in the dry regions.

Expansion of irrigation in India and humid southeast Asia has wrought miracles in two short decades. Better rice cultivars and a package of practices that include irrigation have been responsible for greatly increased cereal yields. Asia has a long history of successful irrigation and was able to capitalize on the yield-increasing capabilities of improved cultivars of rice, wheat, corn, and sorghum. Sub-Saharan Africa has no such history of water management, and the dry regions have few perennial rivers and meager ground-water supplies. Irrigation in the dry regions has only a limited potential, and most of that is in small-scale pumping by individual farmers (Moris, et al., 1984). Reliance for crop production in the foreseeable future will have to be placed on dryland agriculture.

CONCLUSIONS

Coping with agricultural drought demands advance planning and the accumulation of excess food supplies in favorable years. For excesses to be available, cultivators must be able to respond to the opportunities presented by those favorable years: the drier and more drought-prone the area, the greater the need to capitalize on the good years. Research on soil-plant-climate relations and the application of that research to cultivators' fields is essential. Lack of proven acceptable practices in developing country dryland agriculture is a major handicap to achieving food security and preventing famines. Even more important, however, may be a poorly developed education system and inadequate transportation facilities, to say nothing of inappropriate government policies.

REFERENCES

Child, R. D.; H. F. Heady; W. C. Hickey; R. A. Peterson; and R. D. Pieper. 1984. Arid and Semiarid Lands. Winrock International, Morrilton, Arkansas.

Dregne, H. E. 1984. Evaluation of the implementation of the Plan of Action to Combat Desertification. United Nations Environment Programme, Nairobi, Kenya.

Dregne, H. E.; and W. O. Willis. 1983. Dryland Agriculture. American Society of Agronomy, Madison, Wisconsin.

FAO. 1983. FAO Production Yearbook. FAO, Rome.

Mellor, J. W.; and S. Gavian. 1987. Famine: Causes, prevention, and relief. Science 235:539-545.

Moris, J.; D. J. Thom; and R. Norman. 1984. Prospects for small-scale irrigation development in the Sahel. Utah State University, Logan.

Stewart, J. 1982. Impact of weather analysis on agricultural production and planning decisions for the semi-arid areas of Kenya. J. Applied Meteorol. 21:477-494.

UNEP. 1982. Compendium of projects and programmes of the United Nations system in the field of desertification. United Nations Environment Programme, Nairobi, Kenya.

Warrick, R. A. 1984. The possible impacts on wheat production of a recurrence of the 1930s drought in the U.S. Great Plains. Clim. Change 6:5-26.

CHAPTER 31
THE ROLE OF THE MEDIA IN IDENTIFYING AND PUBLICIZING DROUGHT

Clifford D. May

Almost exactly two years ago, the African famine suddenly loomed large in the consciousness of America and Western Europe.

It is at once remarkable that it took us so long to notice that this terrible tragedy was taking place and, as I will show, almost equally remarkable that we took note of it at all.

Famine is not new to Africa. There has not been a day that has passed in the last twenty years that some African child has not died of starvation or malnutrition.

But the Ethiopian famine was unique in several ways.

Ironically, Ethiopa had and still has in place an early warning system for drought and famine that is the most sophisticated and efficient in tropical Africa. This system was established shortly after the 1974 revolution, an event which came about in large measure as a response to Emperor Haile Selassie's indifference to a much more limited famine that erupted about that time.

In 1984, however, Ethiopia's rulers clearly felt that revelations of serious hardship in the countryside would diminish and distract from the festivities planned to celebrate the tenth anniversary of Ethiopia's "glorious socialist revolution."

Western journalists, long tightly restricted in their attempts to report on Ethiopia, were barred from traveling to areas where they could witness the devastation firsthand. Many Ethiopian-based relief workers were also reluctant to discuss the extent of the famine, for fear of running afoul of the government.

And of course, beyond concealing the fact of the famine, Ethiopian authorities and their main sponsor, the Soviet Union, made little effort to alleviate the situation. The result was an extraordinary migration of the hungry from the remote Ethiopian hinterlands—most Ethiopian peasants live more than a day's walk from any road—to a few central locations.

By the time Mohammed Amin—a Pakistani-born, Kenya-based British citizen and a freelance photographer on assignment for the BBC—arrived in the afflicted areas, thousands upon thousands of ragged, skeletal people had gathered to pose, as it were, for his cameras.

This is an important point. At the peak of the famine as many as 9 million Ethiopians teetered on the edge of starvation, an incredible number in absolute terms, but as a percentage of the overall population of Ethiopia—estimated at around 40 million—it is not actually so high. In many parts of Africa easily 30% of the population has been in such a state.

In those other areas, however, the hungry mostly hid themselves away in their huts in the bush. They were therefore difficult for the cameras to find, and they presented a less dramatic tableau when they were found.

What Mo Amin photographed looked like nothing ever before recorded, except perhaps for the Holocaust. This time, however, the camps had names like Korem and Makele rather than Dachau and Bergen-Belsen.

The footage set off a tidal wave of sympathy, and further press coverage. The Ethiopian government was surprised by the impact: money and food began to pour in from Western nations, who were quickly dubbed "the donor countries," a rather Orwellian linguistic ploy intended to disguise the fact that it was the capitalist/imperialist world that was now coming to the aid of socialist Ethiopia.

The Soviet Union did not seriously participate in the rescue effort but continued as the supplier of weapons for the Ethiopian military, which was and remains larger than any other in sub-Saharan Africa, South Africa not excluded.

From the Ethiopian government's point of view, this was a satisfactory situation, at least until the inevitable happened: the story, as the Western press reported it, began to shift slowly from the fact that millions were dying to the reasons why this had happened and the obstacles that stood in the way of a successful relief and development effort.

Few Western reporters were well-versed in such issues when they arrived in Ethiopia. And television, so powerful a medium for conveying the impact and immediacy of disaster, displayed serious limitations in attempting to probe beyond obvious results to far less visible causes.

But those journalists who expended time and effort soon caught on to another Orwellian twist: Ethiopian authorities always referred to the "drought" and the "drought-stricken compatriots." The word *famine* was meticulously avoided.

Drought and *famine* are not synonymous. Drought is rather one of several factors that, in combination, may produce famine and did indeed produce the Ethiopian famine.

Among the other factors were the government's economic and agricultural policies and diversion of national resources and income to the military sector, which was involved in internal conflicts, in particular against Eritrean separatists and Tigrean insurgents.

Whether the government could have concluded some sort of truce with the rebels—all of whom, by the way, also happen to be Marxists of various stripes—is open to question. That they made no serious attempt to do so is a matter of record.

The story of hunger in Africa has largely faded from the headlines over the past year. What controversy there has been has centered on the question of whether the relief and development movement should in the end be counted as a success or a failure.

To answer that, a distinction has to be made between relief and development. Relief is nothing more than filling empty bellies quickly, getting people through a crisis. In some cases the relief workers arrived too late or did too little, at times because they didn't want to jeopardize their relationship with the authorities. But by and large, I would argue, the relief effort saved millions of lives under very difficult conditions and so it should be counted a success.

Development, by contrast, means helping people to find ways to grow their own food, earn their own living, and in general win freedom from dependence on handouts.

Little or no progress has been made in this area in Ethiopia or in the other famine-prone countries of Africa.

Frankly, there is no science of development. The experts in this field, I would argue, are like art appreciation teachers: They know what it's all supposed to look like when it's finished but they can't produce it themselves.

In yet another twist worthy of Orwell, by the way, we have come to call the countries that are clearly not making progress toward development the "developing countries."

But while development is difficult to create it is nonetheless relatively easy to thwart. The obstacles that have been placed in the path of development in Ethiopia are instructive to examine and not entirely unique to that nation.

The government that took the land from the aristocracy after the revolution continues to hold it, with the peasants still reduced to the role of farm workers rather than farm owners. For peasants to try to improve the land under these conditions—for example, through the building of structures for rain water retention, the planting of trees as a barrier to erosion, the use of fertilizers—tends to be self-defeating. The farmers will tell you that if they do that, it just means the land will be taken away.

Other policies have added to the hunger as well:

The government has long maintained low, fixed prices on grain and other agricultural produce and that of course discourages farmers not only from investing but also from producing a surplus. In fact, the government has made the storing of grain—a traditional hedge against famine—a crime, terming it hoarding.

The government has embarked upon the collectivization of agriculture despite the poor performance of that mode of production over the past half century in the Soviet Union and the steady movement toward privatization of farming now taking place even in China and parts of Eastern Europe.

Agricultural investment, which has never been high in Ethiopia in any case, is mainly channeled to the unproductive collectivized sector.

Tangentially, an interesting and important point that has been generally overlooked is that in all the photographs and film of the Ethiopian famine, those seen going hungry were the farmers—that is, the food producers. The food consumers—the soldiers, the bureaucrats, the urban dwellers—have not been among the starving masses.

The government continues to see victory in its civil wars as its highest priority and it has demonstrated on many occasions that it views food as well as bullets as a useful weapon in the conflict.

Ethiopia's Relief and Rehabilitation Commission, an agency which long had the respect of all who dealt with it, has been increasingly criticized and emasculated. Its two top officials defected to the West this year, as have many Ethiopians of good conscience.

There are other factors that bode ill, too, notably an extraordinarily high birth rate—Africa's overall population growth is more rapid than Asia's or South America's—and extensive environmental destruction, which may now be having an impact on the climate.

It is not only during times of famine that Ethiopia does not produce enough food to feed its population. Even in the best years Ethiopians go hungry, as do many other Africans.

In fact, African food production per capita has been on the decline for a generation. Nowhere else in the world is this true.

Nor, by the way, is agriculture the only sector of the economy that is suffering. Throughout much of Africa now, factories are breaking down or closing, roads and railways are falling into disrepair, civil services are disintegrating, standards of living—never high—are declining alarmingly. Sixty percent of all Africans now live in poverty, according to the World Bank. A decade from now, that figure is projected to rise to eighty percent.

What's more, since most African countries have, like Ethiopia, fallen under the rule of dictatorial military regimes, the average African can neither change his situation nor even freely complain.

There has been rain in Ethiopia and other parts of Africa over the past year. That is the only one of the factors contributing to famine that has altered.

Unless other changes come about, it would appear inevitable that the next time there is a significant rainfall deficit—a drought—there will be another famine, perhaps one that will make the great famine of 1984-85 appear almost insignificant by comparison.

CHAPTER 32
DROUGHT CRISIS MANAGEMENT: THE CASE OF ETHIOPIA

Dawit Wolde Giorgis

Natural calamities and famine are recurring phenomena in Africa. Millions have perished and millions more have suffered, mainly because governments lack the capacity to detect and prevent catastrophes or mitigate their effects. Because of this, minor climatological irregularities and minor disruptions in production and supply systems severely affect most people. Initially, those living in marginal areas and under marginal conditions are affected; later on, the entire population is affected.

Ethiopia is one of the very few countries that has developed a disaster response mechanism since the 1974 famine. The Relief and Rehabilitation Commission (RRC) that a few colleagues and I established now has many years of experience and has become the largest and most efficient government agency in the country. Until very recently, it was a semiautonomous agency, operating outside the normal government bureaucracy and responsible only to the head of state. It had sweeping power to cut across government bureaucracies and mobilize available manpower and material resources in its mission to save lives affected by both natural and manmade calamities.

More than 200,000 people died as a result of the 1972-74 drought and famine, and more than 1 million people perished during the 1984-85 famine. In between these two major crises, an average of 2.5 million people each year have been victims of either drought or internal conflicts and have needed emergency assistance for survival. For these reasons, the Ethiopian experience provides a good example for analyzing the causes of recurring famine and the management of prolonged crises.

The recent Ethiopian famine moved the conscience of people to a degree that no other crisis in recent memory can match; as a result, international involvement was considerable. The affected population was close to 9 million, living mostly in inaccessible and rugged terrain. Five armed guerrilla movements operated mostly in the affected areas. The neighboring countries were hostile. The country's resources were limited. Ethiopia's relationship with the West was at its worst; its regime was Marxist, with a regular anti-Western rhetoric broadcast by the government-controlled media. My agency's appeal for assistance was directed mostly to the West. Thus the relief operation was huge, complex, and highly politicized.

To analyze how the crisis was managed, it is best to begin with the normal food supply situation. The three identified food supply systems in Ethiopia are crop dependent, market dependent, and livestock dependent, with some groups of people depending on more than one of these systems. The activities of the early warning system therefore focus on the major indicators that determine food availability in the three food supply systems. The early warning system monitors the performance of these indicators over time so that failure can be detected as early as possible. The chain of events that lead from production to consumption is central to the design and analysis of the early warning system. In the early days of its establishment, the RRC realized that its ability to act effectively during a natural disaster could be enhanced by prior knowledge of areas and numbers of people likely to be affected by food shortages and a corresponding buildup of food reserves from the major food-aid donors to cover all possible eventualities. In order to fulfill the former objectives, the early warning system was established in 1976 with the purpose of informing all its possible users, including the Ethiopian government and donor agencies, of impending food shortages following the primary and secondary rainy seasons.

The early warning system is designed to be useful for:

1. The early warning of impending food shortages.
2. The identification of both deficit and surplus-producing areas for market stabilization.
3. The management of regional food shortages.
4. The management of national food security.
5. The planning of sectoral and intersectoral regional development with regard to food supply.

These objectives are achieved by:

1. Establishing a regular system of crop monitoring.
2. Establishing a system for monitoring pastoral conditions and animal production in rangeland areas.
3. Establishing a system of monitoring prices and supplies.
4. Strengthening and extending meteorological reporting, with particular application to agricultural conditions.
5. Establishing a system for monitoring the status of community and family food stocks, dietary intakes, and nutrition of certain population groups.
6. Establishing a system for efficient data processing and intersectoral analysis.
7. Establishing a system of relaying the results of the data, collected in a clear, understandable form, to all agencies responsible for action.
8. Developing models to define the relationships that exist between the various aspects of determining food availability.

On the basis of the reports compiled by the early warning system, disaster area assessment teams move into action. During field visits, these teams assess the magnitude of the problem of food shortages through a series of indicators such as rainfall, pest and disease problems, crop performance, livestock status, market flows and prices, grain stock situation, food consumption, health and nutrition indicators, and a variety of social indicators. The conclusions of the disaster area assessment teams are immediately given to the head of state, concerned government agencies, RRC's emergency relief department, and the international donor community through regular RRC meetings or through an emergency session. These meetings are conducted under the chairmanship of the RRC commissioner three times a year under normal circumstances. In the case of the 1984-85 crisis, five early warning reports were issued and six meetings were held in one year. The early warning reports clearly indicated the failure of successive rainy seasons; the ecological imbalances and their impact on production; the areas that would be affected; and the number of people who would need assistance, region by region. The relief department outlined the kind of assistance and the immediate steps that had to be taken. While waiting for reactions from donor agencies, the RRC distributed whatever relief stock it had. RRC uses its logistics, transport, and air services to organize the movement of relief items from the ports and major warehouses to, or as near as possible to, the affected population. With the ruggedness of the terrain, poor road network, lack of transport facilities, and internal military conflicts (which impede free movement), this effort in itself becomes a major operation.

But speed is paramount to prevent the movement and dislocation of people and the establishment of shelters. It is best to assist people while they are on their land and in their villages. In this case, the sheer magnitude of the disaster and the lack of resources made it impossible to prevent what later become a totally unmanageable migration of people in all directions.

Generally, it takes four to five months between the time assistance is requested and the time it arrives where it is needed. To avoid unnecessary suffering of people during this time, the RRC had a food reserve project of 180,000 tons of grain. This figure was determined on the basis of a food ration of 400 g per person per day over a period of four months, to feed those persons estimated to be vulnerable to food shortage during a severe drought. The four-month period is the total lead time required for international donors to bring the needed supplies into the country. However, the food security reserve has always stood at less than 10% of the targeted figures because of our government's weakness and the unwillingness of donor governments to supply the required amount. In the case of the 1984-85 crisis, whatever we had as food security was consumed much earlier, and we were never in a position to replenish it.

Effective famine prevention or relief is inconceivable in the absence of an adequate food security reserve especially earmarked for emergency supply. If we had had 180,000 tons of reserve grain at the beginning of 1984, we could have easily avoided the deaths of thousands. We started sounding serious alarms in March 1984 through the regular donor conference held in Addis Ababa. I made a personal appeal through the United Nations in May. The first shipment (after our March appeal) arrived at our port five months later, in September. By then, hundreds of thousands had died and millions had been displaced. When we made our strongest appeal, in October of the same year, 7 million people were on the verge of death. It was during this month that the world started awakening to the realities of the Ethiopian situation. Even while the world expressed its concern and sympathy, not more than 2% of the total requirement of relief supplies arrived in the country from October through January. Thus we can say that no significant assistance came into the country between March 1984, when the disaster started taking heavy tolls, and January 1985, when larger amounts of assistance started arriving. This could easily have been avoided, partly by an adequate food security reserve and partly by an improved donor emergency response mechanism.

As I have tried to explain, the agency I was heading was semiautonomous and therefore was able to communicate directly with donors without interference from the party or government structure. But the crisis of 1984-85 occurred at a politically sensitive period. The regime was preparing to celebrate the tenth anniversary of the revolution. The entire government machinery and resources were mobilized toward what the government considered to be an important event. The media glorified the revolution, the ideology, and the regime's achievements. But the famine clearly showed the failure of the revolution. With rampant unemployment, poverty, destitution, civil war, and famine, the country was in a critical situation and was far from being able to celebrate any sort of achievement. Thus there was a clear contradiction between what the leadership of the government wanted to believe and the reality of the situation. Our efforts to publicize the famine and to inform the international community were seen as a deliberate attempt to embarrass the leadership, and the government media was making every conceivable effort to hide the famine.

While the tug of war between my agency and the hard-line elements at the top continued amid mutual recriminations, the famine in Ethiopia hit the headlines in Europe and America. Europe and America responded with unprecedented generosity, but the East's response remained pathetic. This presented another contradiction. The West in general gave more than 90% of the entire requirement, but the Ethiopian government refused to recognize this reality and continued its anti-Western rhetoric, while my agency continued to work with the forty-eight international voluntary agencies and more than thirty donor governments, most of which had representatives in Ethiopia. This created a problem for the RRC and particularly for me. It became increasingly difficult to reconcile the political interest of the government and the problems of the population. The famine was not the government's priority. Its priority was the celebration and the internal conflicts, and the regime did everything possible to make sure that the famine did not disrupt the order of its priorities. Had our own government acknowledged the existence of famine, fully implemented the recommendation of the RRC, and joined the efforts in appealing for assistance and coordinating the relief operation, then the crisis would have taken an entirely different direction.

With the relentless efforts of donor governments, voluntary agencies, and the RRC, the operation was successfully completed under difficult circumstances. The major problems were:

1. Coordination: The efforts of forty-eight voluntary organizations and eight agencies needed to be properly coordinated to promote efficiency, determine priorities, avoid duplication of efforts, and facilitate movement and implementation of relief projects. Bringing together these agencies, with their competing interests, diverse backgrounds, and differing areas of competence, was an immense responsibility. This important aspect of the relief operation was, remarkably, conducted by the RRC.

2. Port capacity: The capacity of two ports, Assab and Massawa, was 1.5 million tons annually. Massawa is in Eritrea and could not be used fully. Our annual relief requirement was 1.3 million tons of grain, in addition to other relief supplies.

3. Road communication: Ethiopia has the most backward road network. For a land of 1,224,000 km^2, there are only 3,595 km of asphalt roads, 7,460 km of gravel roads, and 2,470 km of seasonal roads. It has 11 km of roads for every 1,000 km^2.

4. Railways: There is only one railway line running between Djibouti and Addis Ababa. It covers 781 km and has an annual load capacity of 30,000 tons.

5. Transport facilities: At the peak of the crisis we had a thousand small and large trucks from different parts of the world; this created a serious problem with maintenance and availability of spare parts.

The initially limited number of airplanes (even though at one time we had fifty-one large aircraft, which served for six to ten months), the lack of medical personnel and nutritionists, and the lack of adequate warehouses were all problems that we had to cope with throughout the crisis period. But our most serious problem was the interference of party officials, who saw the situation entirely from the political point of view. It was indeed a very complex operation to save the lives of 9 million people scattered in thirteen provinces.

Between December 1984 and August 1985, when intense relief operations were conducted (258 feeding days), 624,580 tons of grain was distributed. An average of 6.2 million people (reaching, at peak time, 7.5 million) received the grain in the form of 53.3 million rations. The distribution of food was determined on the basis of an average per capita daily ration of 500 g and 150 g of grain and supplementary food, respectively. Out of the total distributed grain, the RRC handled 45.7%, and the remaining rations of food were handled by voluntary organizations.

Airplanes were used to reach otherwise inaccessible areas. Thus 114,000 tons of relief aid was airlifted from the ports directly to distribution centers. Planes were also used for airdrop operations. Air force detachments from the Royal Air Force, West Germany, Polish People's Republic, and Belgian Air Force undertook airdrop operations and in seven months delivered 12,000 tons of food.

A total of nearly 1 million tons of food was received and distributed during the period under review, the United States giving more than half of the entire requirement. The relief operation was conducted from 280 distribution centers, 150 feeding centers, and 45 shelters with 17,000 RRC employees and 500 expatriate relief workers. Almost 1 million people died (mostly before reaching our relief centers), 2 million people were displaced, and 200,000 children were either abandoned or orphaned, leaving a great deal to be done in the area of rehabilitation.

The crisis subsided in October 1985 after the fairly good small rains of March and the main rainy season of July and August. But the crisis of famine goes on in Ethiopia, not because there is drought, but because of the political system and the agricultural policy, which have proved to be unworkable in actual practice.

It is difficult to imagine how there could be food shortages in a country where 101.5 million m^3 of water flows annually. Out of this, 75% goes to Sudan, 15% to Kenya, 6% to Somalia, and 1% to the Red Sea; less than 3% is used in Ethiopia. Most of the valleys have abundant water for irrigation and drinking. Out of a potential 3 million ha of irrigable land, only 100,000 ha—less than 3%—has been developed.

With respect to animal resources, Ethiopia stands first in Africa and tenth in the world. On the Red Sea coast there are about 90,000 km^2 of potential fishing grounds with an estimated annual production potential of 66,000 tons. In addition, the rift valley lakes are estimated to have a production potential of 26,000 tons of fish a year. However, the annual fish catch of the country at present is between 600 and 1,000 tons.

The rapid rate of deforestation is also a cause for concern. One hundred years ago, 40% of the land mass was covered with forest. Today, forest covers less than 4% of the land area. Deforestation has contributed to soil erosion and recurring drought.

The immediate and root causes of the famine are many. It requires fundamental change in policy to avoid further catastrophes and bring Ethiopia to a level of self-sufficiency.

PART 9

Summary Address

CHAPTER 33
THE SYMPOSIUM IN PERSPECTIVE:
SUMMARY ADDRESS

Thomas D. Potter

My task here today is to try to summarize this very interesting conference on drought. In a way it's an impossible task, a little bit like trying to get a drink from a fire hose: it's simply not possible to summarize in a very short period of time all of the interesting papers we have heard. But let me try to point out the key problems in this field, in the context mentioned by the governor in his opening address on the drought problems that politicians face. These political problems are intertwined with the other kinds of problems associated with drought, which all of the speakers have brought out. I'll try to summarize these problems, which will be addressed by the workshop that immediately follows this symposium.

First of all, an observer at this symposium would be aware that we had some trouble defining drought. There are many concepts of drought—meteorological, agricultural, hydrological, socioeconomic; somebody also mentioned paper droughts during the past few days. Of course, it's very difficult to deal with a concept when we can't even agree on the definition. But at least we recognize that various types of drought exist and can attempt to use the appropriate definition for a given problem.

Now when we turn to what the meteorologists can do, our keynote speaker, Professor Hare, noted that the specific causes of drought are not well known at this time. There is some evidence that some of the causes are beginning to be known, at least the short-term ones. But, in general, we have to say at this stage that we still don't know exactly what causes drought, certainly not the long-term droughts in West Africa and other places. Turning to predictions, our keynote speaker very flatly said that we're not able to predict drought, and I believe that most people would agree with that. There are some prospects on the horizon, as noted by Dr. Eugene Rasmusson, that we may be able to predict short-term droughts fairly accurately within a few years. However, for the long-term droughts we simply don't have much of a clue about their causes at this time. Given the complexity of the climate system—not only the atmosphere but the oceans and the cryosphere (the ice fields) and all of the land surface processes, including the vegetation, *and* the interactions among all these components—my guess is that it's not likely that we are going to be able to predict long-term droughts from physical models before about the year 2000. Another way of making predictions of droughts is to use statistics. It's clear in most people's minds now that no useful cycles have been discovered yet for making predictions. To be sure, there are lots of cycles, but they're not very useful because they don't explain much of the total variance.

Another topic that was barely mentioned here is weather modification. Usually when a drought occurs, there are cries of "Why don't we use all the great technology that we have about rainmaking to break the droughts?" The answer is that, at this time, there is no credible evidence that rainmaking can be used operationally to break droughts. Certainly, there are some encouraging research aspects in this topic, but nothing we can use operationally now, let alone promise governments that it will be effective.

With respect to drought monitoring, the situation is a little bit better both from the standpoint of the ground networks that we've heard about and, in the longer run, in terms of satellites, which offer great potential (although they are extremely expensive). Though some operational products are beginning to emerge, many developing countries do not have access to these and probably won't in the near term because the cost is too high. To sum up, the meteorologists have good prospects in the near future for an explanation of the causes of droughts and for accurate prediction of short-term droughts. But in terms of what the users can apply right now, it's relatively limited.

Now, turning to the impact assessment situation, we're not much better off. The methodology of impact assessments is just now beginning to be developed. As a result, estimates or projections of climate impact made for governments are difficult to defend. The economic and social consequences of strategies implemented in response to these estimates could be significant if the events do not occur. One social scientist, unnamed, said that "drought is too important to be left to the meteorologists." I might add, "or to social scientists." Another one said that "improved early warning systems will not improve food security in Africa." An economist made a statement that said, in effect, "If you lay all of the economists end-to-end, you still won't come to a conclusion." But we have heard about several climate impact assessment techniques that are available now and others that are just beginning to be developed. Although there are promising developments in the area of climate impact assessment using traditional techniques and in the whole approach of using decision making, I think we still have a long way to go in the useful application of economic, social, and political impact assessments.

With respect to the technological and sociopolitical adaptations, we heard some very interesting presentations about activities in South Australia, India, Mali, and several other countries. These practically oriented techniques, it seems to me, offer a great potential to do something about drought now. That is, they can combine ideas from meteorologists and the impact assessment community in a systematic way to do some practical things *now*.

International organizations have a long way to go before they can provide effective support to nations that are attempting to respond to drought. A few things are being done now, but the results of the survey that Professor Dregne and others recently did for UNEP sums up the situation regarding desertification activities. Their general conclusion was that desertification is worse now than it was in 1977, despite the efforts of UNEP and other international organizations! This, of course, is not entirely the fault of international organizations, but they do have a role in this drama! The Economic Commission for Africa (ECA) and the WMO have proposed the African Center for Meteorological Applications for Development, which promises to be a focal point for drought monitoring and applications in Africa. The vice president of the World Bank made a very important statement that, along with all other organizations, the World Bank has not done a very good job of coping with the situation of drought in Africa partly because we have not adequately taken into account the facts of agrometeorology. Many of the donors feel that, although a few good things have been done, much more needs to be done before we can claim to have solved the problem of drought.

Turning, then, to the role of government, everyone agrees, of course, that drought response plans are a good idea. But, so far, as we have heard today and seen in the literature, there are very few good examples of drought plans that have been very effective, either here in the United States or in other countries. A problem mentioned by several people, starting with the governor, is that most people have little interest in drought after it abates and, hence, the politicians who respond to the needs of the people often ignore drought in the press of current problems. As a result, we face a very difficult problem in convincing the public and the political leaders first of all that drought does have a very great potential impact and, second, that we should develop effective plans, building on the bits and pieces of knowledge that we have. In one of the recent publications of the World Commission for Environment and Development, which is just now completing work on the effects of the environment on development in general, is a quote that says, "We know what to do but not how to do it." That's a fair statement to keep in mind for those of us concerned with drought as we proceed into the workshop that comes in the next day and a half. I believe that the statement by Mr. May should also be kept in mind: that there are no easy answers to the problems caused by drought, either with respect to early warning systems or the development of plans or even the involvement of the press.

This list of problems is a bit sobering, but we shouldn't be discouraged even though we realize that we've got a very big problem facing us. We need, in the workshop that is to follow this symposium, to define what data and information are needed, what techniques we have available now, how to implement these techniques, and how to evaluate them in terms of their usefulness. Professor Rosenberg, in his talk related to climatic change with respect to greenhouse gases and the effects on drought, gave us some very interesting challenges that we should keep in mind. He was talking in the context of the greenhouse gases and their effect on climate change and, hence, on droughts, but his statements could apply to the natural appearance of droughts as well. Meteorologists must improve both short-term and long-term predictions; there is a good prospect that short-term predictions will be improved in the next few years, although improvement of long-term predictions is probably fifteen years or more away. The biologists must try to understand the ecosystem effects of the actual situation in nature. More specifically, it seems to me the agrometeorologists should develop an effective way to estimate evapotranspiration. In dry areas, problems are evident in the use of the Palmer Index and the Penman calculation, which was designed for grassy fields in England. We simply don't have an effective way to estimate evapotranspiration, let alone the changes in it that might result from climatic changes. Rosenberg and his colleagues at the University of Nebraska are experts on evapotranspiration and I would certainly encourage them, from the standpoints of climate modeling and agrometeorology, to continue their work to develop effective methods of estimating evapotranspiration. Rosenberg also mentioned that governmental agencies have to stay alert to the developing body of scientific work about drought. Many of the government agencies and international agencies do try as best they can to keep up, but we need meetings like this to hear from people who are working on the front lines to develop practical programs needed to face drought. He made a very important point (which was illustrated by the Mali Pilot Project): we can do a lot more with the information we have right now. We don't need to sit on our hands and wait until we're able to better predict long-term drought; we can do something effective with what we have now. The Mali Project shows what can be done now, effectively and with relatively little cost. Finally, he mentioned that governments, despite all of these uncertainties and problems, shouldn't hide behind the uncertainties. We have enough information now to prepare intelligent contingency plans for drought and, most important, to develop effective ways to implement the plans so that they can provide the right kinds of information at the right time to the people who really need them.

Let me conclude, Mr. Chairman, by thanking the organizers for a splendid symposium on drought. They have put together a thorough look at all sides of the problem, including the essential aspect of policy response. All of us owe them a debt of gratitude. I'd like to close with a quote regarding drought from John Steinbeck's *The Grapes of Wrath*. All of us should keep this vivid picture in mind as we proceed to further study and implement plans with respect to drought.

The sun flared on the growing corn day after day until a line of brown spread along the edge of each grain bayonet. The clouds appeared and went away and in a while they did not try any more. The surface of the earth crusted a thin hard crust. In the water-cut gullies the earth dusted down in dry little streams. Every moving thing lifted the dust into the air.

PART 10

Workshop Summary

CHAPTER 34
INTRODUCTION

PURPOSE AND OBJECTIVES

The purpose of the workshop was to identify constraints on drought planning and to recommend viable actions and specific research that governments and international organizations might implement to lessen the impact of future droughts. The workshop was to be the culmination of discussions initiated during the symposium. The specific workshop objectives were:

1. To identify information needs and opportunities that might be used to improve national and international ability to assess and respond to droughts.
2. To develop an agenda of drought-related research priorities.
3. To recommend ways to stimulate national governments to develop drought assessment and response plans.
4. To suggest ways to involve international organizations in the planning process.

The ultimate goal of the workshop was to develop a "plan of action" for national governments and international organizations to follow in implementing drought planning activities.

ORGANIZATION

The workshop, like the symposium, was organized to approach drought as five separate but interrelated issues: (1) drought prediction; (2) detection, monitoring and early warning; (3) impact assessment; (4) adaptation; and (5) response. This approach closely parallels typical models of climate and society interaction and provides a convenient rationale for dividing the subject of drought.

Approximately sixty scientists and senior-level policy makers were selected in advance to participate in the workshop discussions (Appendix A). The list of workshop participants included a balance of scientists and policy makers as well as representative coverage of drought-prone regions. Representatives of twenty-one drought-prone countries were chosen to participate in the discussions.

Workshop participants were assigned to one of the five groups listed above. Participants were assigned according to expertise, with a fairly equal representation of policy-level officials in each group. Each group was assigned two discussion leaders and a recorder.

A primary goal in dividing participants among the five groups was to stimulate dialogue among scientists of different disciplines and between scientists and policy makers. Both a truly interdisciplinary and a science policy forum was sought because most of the issues concerning drought preparedness occur at the intersections of disciplines as well as the intersections of science and policy. The optimal drought policy should be based on scientific principles and technology. However, scientific research aimed at alleviating problems caused by drought should not be conducted without understanding the realities of policy development and implementation.

CHARGE TO WORKSHOP PARTICIPANTS

A position statement prepared by the organizers was provided to each workshop participant before the symposium. The complete text of the position statement is included in Appendix B. The purpose of the statement was to give participants a clearer understanding of the goals of the workshop and to update participants on recent "calls for action" for drought planning.

Each of the task groups was asked to discuss and provide a written response to a series of discussion questions. These questions were divided into two sets. The first set included three general questions common to each group: (1) What were the current impediments to drought planning? (2) How could these impediments be overcome? (3) How could international organizations (including donor organizations) facilitate drought planning activities?

The second set of questions was specific to each of the issues represented by the five task groups. The participants of each task group were asked to discuss these questions and to prepare written responses summarizing the key points.

A CHARGE TO THE READER

It is well recognized that a comprehensive topical and geographical approach to the planning of drought is not without liabilities. Within the limits of reason for a single initiative, it is not possible to tailor research and policy recommendations to every sociopolitical situation. Indeed, in discussing issues concerning drought planning in this report, some care has been taken to be as region *nonspecific* as possible in presenting the rudiments of effective drought planning.

The preferred approach in the workshop was, where possible, to reduce issues to common denominators that could be applicable in a variety of locations. That is, in most instances, region-specific issues were stripped away, leaving the bare mechanics of government and society as the instruments of drought policy. For example, rather than providing a detailed prescriptive analysis of a particular government's response to drought, predicated on the specific political ideology to which that government subscribed, the political inefficiencies common to most governments were discussed.

What follows in this report is the collective wisdom of persons who have distinguished themselves as experts in drought research, policy development, and implementation. Participants were encouraged to ponder the complexities of drought irrespective of their own institutional agendas or the agendas of sponsoring and participating agencies. The charge put to them was to devise a strategy that would address the elements common to all successful drought plans, be they national, subnational, or supernational.

The basic tools for drought planning are laid out for the reader to use with discretion. It is incumbent on the reader to adapt the specific recommendations listed here to his or her particular circumstances. Some recommendations may be relevant and helpful in specific instances, and some may not.

However, the recommendations of the workshop, if implemented, should lead to a more effective drought assessment and response strategy by government and international organizations. That, of course, is the goal of most of the research called for in this report.

CONSTRAINTS TO DROUGHT PLANNING

All task groups were asked to discuss and respond to the following questions:
1. What factors are considered to be constraints to the formulation and implementation of drought plans by state and national governments?
2. How can these constraints be overcome to facilitate the development of drought plans?
3. How can international organizations promote and facilitate drought planning activities?

The responses of the five task groups to these questions have been synthesized for presentation here. The responses to questions one and two, the identification of constraints and ways to overcome them, have been combined to facilitate the presentation of the issues raised by the task groups. The order in which these constraints appear is not intended to reflect the importance of one factor relative to another. The responses to question three are not included here but have been merged instead with the task group responses to specific questions.

Constraint #1. Inadequate understanding of drought

Drought is often viewed by policy makers and bureaucrats as an extreme event and, implicitly, rare and of random occurrence. Thus, drought may be viewed as an act of nature, something that is outside of government control. However, if drought continues to be perceived by policy makers as a quirk of nature—one for which there can be no planning—there will be no planning. A related constraint may be that if policy makers accept the challenge of planning for drought, they must also implicitly assume risk and responsibility for the negative effects of drought.

Policy makers and bureaucrats must learn that droughts, like floods, are a normal feature of climate. Their recurrence is inevitable. Drought is a problem that manifests itself in ways that span the jurisdiction of numerous bureaucratic organizations (e.g., agricultural, water resources, health, and so forth). Competing interests, institutional rivalry, and "turf protection" impede the development of concise drought assessment and response initiatives. This problem exists at both the national and international level.

To solve these problems, policy makers and bureaucrats, as well as the general populace, must be educated about the consequences of drought and the advantages of preparedness. Drought planning requires input by several disciplines. Decision makers must play an integral role in this process. Ideally, this process should be an interdisciplinary meshing of methodologies and perspectives; for the present, the process should be, at a minimum, multidisciplinary.

The development of a drought plan is a positive step that demonstrates governmental concern about the effects of a potentially hazardous and recurring phenomenon. Planning, if undertaken properly and implemented during nondrought periods, can improve governmental ability to respond in a timely and effective manner during periods of crisis. Thus, planning can mitigate and, in some cases, prevent some impacts while reducing physical and emotional hardship. This, in turn, could improve the constituents' image of governments. Planning should also be a dynamic process that reflects socioeconomic, agricultural, and political trends.

Constraint #2. Uncertainty about the economics of preparedness

Drought preparedness requires resources that are, at times, scarce. The costs of maintaining a high level of preparedness can be an impediment to the development of drought plans. It is difficult to determine the benefits of drought planning versus the costs of drought. Preparedness costs are fixed and occur now while drought costs are uncertain and will occur later. Further complicating this issue is the fact that the costs of drought are not solely economic. They must also be stated in terms of human suffering and the degradation of the physical environment, items whose values are inherently difficult to estimate.

Post-drought evaluations have generally shown previous governmental assessment and response efforts to be largely ineffective, poorly coordinated, untimely, and economically inefficient. For a discussion of the mid-1970s drought relief effort in the United States, see Wilhite, Chapter 25 in this volume. Unanticipated expenditures for drought relief programs can also be devastating to state and national budgets. Therefore, it is critical that both the human and the economic benefits of effective drought planning be emphasized when educating decision makers and policy officials.

It is essential that drought planning be integrated into existing institutional and political structures at appropriate levels of government and that the process be sufficiently coordinated to avoid duplication of effort. Specifically, drought plans should be incorporated into general natural disaster and/or water management plans wherever possible. This would reduce the costs of drought preparedness.

Constraint #3. The lack of skill in drought prediction

Drought prediction will always contain uncertainties. Some policy makers believe that because drought cannot be accurately predicted, drought planning is of limited value. As a result, many facets of drought response planning that are not necessarily dependent on the availability of accurate and timely predictions (e.g., food and/or water storage) are neglected as well. Drought contingency strategies put in place now would have added value as the ability to predict droughts becomes more reliable.

The solution to this problem requires an open dialogue between technical experts (e.g., meteorologists, remote sensing specialists, agronomists, engineers), prediction users, and decision makers in order to differentiate between what is desirable and what is feasible. These groups must continue to work together so that drought predictions, however uncertain, can be utilized to their fullest in the planning process.

It is important to realize, however, that while predictions may currently have limited utility in the planning process, predictive reliability is expected to improve. It seems only prudent to prepare response plans that can accommodate predictions as they do improve. It is also important to recognize that shorter-term weather forecasts, climate monitoring systems, and climatic probability statistics are available now and are all useful in the strategic planning and implementation process. Their utility must be clearly explained to policy makers.

Constraint #4. Variability in society's vulnerability to drought

There is great spatial and temporal variability in societal vulnerability to drought. For example, certain subnational regions are relatively more drought sensitive than others. As crop mixes change in an agricultural region over time because of factors such as economics (or climate), vulnerability to drought may also change. Superimposed on this spatial and temporal variability is the tendency to view drought as a subnational rather than a national problem, and unaffected areas are apt to be more hesitant to commit national resources for the benefit of affected regions.

The 1986 drought in the southeastern United States serves as a stark reminder of the vulnerability of all regions to the vagaries of climate. Certainly governments in this region were poorly prepared to assess and respond to this severe episode of drought in a timely and effective manner. Governments in the region have learned a valuable lesson and should be better prepared for the inevitable recurrence of drought in this region.

The traditional response by government to periods of severe drought has been to spread the costs throughout society (see Easterling and Riebsame, Chapter 14 in this volume). This approach, when undertaken reactively (i.e., by employing crisis management), usually has been inequitable and untimely. Good planning can reduce these costs by improving the efficiency of the assessment and response process and by lessening the direct and indirect impacts of drought. Planning should take place during noncrisis periods so that proper consideration can be given to the complex issues involved. For example, the Australian government, following criticism stemming from its response to the severe 1982-83 drought, established a task force to investigate the feasibility of formulating a national drought policy. After two years of study in which various alternatives and new programs (e.g., rainfall insurance) were evaluated, a national drought policy was adopted.

Constraint #5. Information gaps and insufficient human resources

A particularly troublesome problem, especially in developing countries, is the general lack of information necessary to provide the foundation for all components of a drought plan (i.e., prediction, monitoring, impact assessment, adaptation, and response). This information includes fundamental meteorological, agronomic, demographic, and economic data. A lack of other necessary resources (e.g., trained people) is also a problem.

This problem is compounded by insufficient historical data bases and the lack of systematic efforts to compile existing information into forms that can be compared with other data, readily analyzed and updated, and summarized for policy makers. For example, in many African countries there are multiple crop/climate/drought monitoring systems, all operating independently with little cross-checking of data or systematic comparison of methods, errors, and results. The information that does exist is not effectively transferred from the scientific community to the appropriate policy makers. Furthermore, the usefulness of such information in formulating policy is often not recognized or is challenged by policy makers.

Both current and comparative data are essential for prediction and evaluation. Historical data bases and existing reporting systems must be protected for that purpose. Remote sensing techniques that are useful in drought monitoring should be enhanced, as should the reporting of socioeconomic data. Some data acquisition systems could be developed by "piggy-backing" these on other "higher profile" programs, such as the International Geosphere-Biosphere Program. Also required are impact studies, the development of socioeconomic models to assess policy alternatives, and enhanced models to predict physical and biological processes.

Constraint #6. Inadequate scientific base for water management

Considerably more scientific knowledge is needed for appropriate and effective water management practices, particularly with respect to drought. Drought should be viewed in a comprehensive systems context that incorporates all water-dependent biophysical processes and human activities. For example, in the Climate Impacts, Perception and Adjustment Experiment (CLIMPAX), water management behavior in the California Water Project was found to be significantly influenced by climatic fluctuations, especially drought (see Easterling and Riebsame, Chapter 14 in this volume). More normative research is needed to increase water use efficiency, especially by existing technologies such as irrigation. Research in arid areas on the problems of salinization and soil erosion is also needed.

Water use efficiency could be improved by selecting crops and pastures that are better adapted to the environment and adopting agricultural practices, such as tillage methods and soil conservation practices, that improve water use efficiency.

<u>Constraint #7. Difficulties in identifying drought impact sensitivities and adaptations</u>

More knowledge is needed about the indirect impacts of drought as well as direct impacts. It is particularly important that methodologies be developed that allow establishment of credible linkages between moisture-deficient conditions and associated impacts. Moreover, equal effort should be given to identifying the possible range of adjustment and adaptations available to lessen the negative impacts of drought. This effort would include analyses of historic risks as well as an evaluation of the comparative experiences of drought-prone regions. Specifically, detailed risk assessments of previous droughts using natural or quasi-experimental methods could provide guidance for planning a response to future droughts. In addition, natural analogues to drought, such as persistent drawdown of slow-recharge aquifers in irrigation-dependent agricultural regions, provide opportunities to study drought-like impacts and human adjustments and responses.

SUMMARY

The identification of impediments to drought planning and the development of strategies to overcome these impediments is essential if governments and international organizations are to be better prepared for future episodes of severe drought. In this section of the report, seven constraints were identified that restrict the development of drought plans. In the task group reports that follow, greater attention will be directed to these constraints as the workshop participants consider the complexities of drought preparedness from an international perspective.

SCIENTIFIC AND TECHNOLOGICAL IMPEDIMENTS TO DROUGHT PREDICTION

Task Group 1 considered scientific and technological impediments to improving the reliability of monthly and seasonal drought forecasts. The group assessed the problem from three viewpoints: (1) predictability—what level of prediction skill is attainable? (2) understanding—what new knowledge must be acquired to achieve that level? and (3) data—what data deficiencies, actual or potential, are constraints to the development of needed predictive skills?

Inherent Predictability

Only a portion of the observed variability of monthly/seasonal averages is potentially predictable. The degree to which these fluctuations can be predicted varies with the parameter, season, geographic region, and climatic regime. Monthly climate forecasts are based primarily on the projected character of the general atmospheric circulation, and usually incorporate the skill existing in more accurate extended weather forecasts. Seasonal forecasts, on the other hand, are shaped by states of major heat sources and sinks. It now appears that the inherent predictability of seasonally averaged conditions is generally greatest in the low latitudes, where sea surface temperature exerts a strong influence on year-to-year variability. This is not necessarily true for the shorter time periods, such as months.

In the extratropical regions, accurate predictions of monthly means appear to be most achievable during winter. Existing skill is found mainly in forecasts of monthly mean temperatures; equivalent skill has not been obtained in the prediction of precipitation amounts. Accurate and reliable prediction of multiyear drought (onset, duration, intensity, and termination) is presently not possible.

Periodic occurrences of drought are identifiable in some data series, but in the absence of an adequate understanding of these fluctuations, there is always uncertainty as to timing and intensity, and the possibility that the cyclicity may be a transient feature. Predictions based on periodicities would seem to lack sufficient accuracy to justify their use in economic decision making. On the other hand, quasi-periodic lagged correlations that have predictive utility have been identified. Sequential events in phenomena such as the El Niño/Southern Oscillation (ENSO) offer such opportunities (see Rasmusson, Chapter 3 for a discussion of the ENSO phenomenom). Under those circumstances the occurrence of specified climatic conditions (e.g., anomalous sea surface temperatures) can be considered as a precursor of drought of a given probability within a specified area and time. The further understanding of such occurrences, the exploitation of these relationships, and the evaluation of the causative processes is warranted. Such relationships, being empirical, are not transferable.

Methodologies for using monthly and seasonal forecasts (with their current narrow applicability and marginal skill levels) are not well developed. For example, area or regional details of the seasonal or annual patterns are unlikely to be predictable. Predictions of monthly and seasonal precipitation are, therefore, of less potential value for individual farmers, or for estimates of hydrologic conditions over small watersheds, than they are for regional-scale planning. Furthermore, climate predictions are most useful for estimating average conditions over large regions, such as the entire southern Great Plains region of the United States. However, monthly and longer-period averages incorporate shorter-period extremes, at times of opposite sign, that can be of great importance in crop development and hydrological processes. That is, information is lost in the process of translating predicted meteorological parameters into predictions of agricultural or hydrological variables. On the other hand, since hydrological drought and economic consequences of drought follow meteorological drought, information gathered through climatological monitoring may make prediction of the latter more accurate.

Understanding

There have been significant advances in understanding systematic year-to-year climatic variability during the past decade. Particularly noteworthy is the improved understanding of variability within the tropics and its relationship to variations in the higher latitudes. This includes improved knowledge of interactions between the atmosphere and tropical oceans associated with the ENSO phenomenon. However, a far better understanding of the linkages and interactions between atmosphere, ocean, cryosphere, and land surface must be achieved to define more precisely the inherent predictability of monthly/seasonal means, and to exploit that knowledge in improved empirical/statistical and dynamical predictive models. The joint use of theoretical and empirical methods may improve the understanding of mechanisms and permit improved elaboration of physical prediction methods.

Data

Improved predictions are critically dependent on an adequate description of climatic conditions. At present, observing networks, and reports emanating from those networks, do not provide enough information for operational and research purposes. Some of the major concerns about the availability of adequate data are given below.

1. In some countries, conventional surface observation stations in global meteorological and hydrological (as well as national climatological) measurement networks are being downgraded or eliminated. A reason

commonly given for this action is the availability of satellite imagery. However, satellite-based systems should not be implemented at the expense of conventional observation systems where networks of the latter are clearly below a minimum acceptable level. Both are essential.

2. Elimination or downgrading of conventional observation systems disrupts or removes sources of benchmark data and time series that are urgently needed for improved monitoring and understanding of the climate system and for stochastic analysis and prediction. These data are also required to provide ground truth for satellite systems. Satellite systems must be calibrated and maintained to ensure accuracy and data homogeneity.

3. Improved methods are required for estimating precipitation by remote sensing, and new or improved methods for observing the upper ocean (temperature, currents, thermocline) and land surface conditions (net radiation balance, evapotranspiration, and vegetation coverage) are needed to develop a more complete understanding of the functioning of the climate system. This understanding could improve seasonal and longer-period predictive capabilities.

THE ROLE OF DROUGHT FORECASTS IN NATIONAL DROUGHT STRATEGIES

Task Group 1 also recommended ways in which drought forecasts could be incorporated into the development and implementation of national drought strategies, given current capabilities and constraints.

Predictions must be of demonstrable value if they are to be used. They must also be readily accessible, accurate, timely, and easy to understand and use. Otherwise, they are likely to be ignored.

Drought management responses can be based on at least four types of weather/climate information: (1) conventional weather forecasts; (2) climate predictions; (3) statistics used in forecasts; and (4) probability estimates of droughts of various duration and intensity, based on long-term climate records. Tactical decisions such as those concerning emergency water supplies and pasture allocation can benefit greatly from accurate five-day weather forecasts.

Monthly climate predictions have value in less immediate tactical decisions such as those concerning fertilizer applications, planting, forage (fodder) supplies, and water resources management. The combination of conventional predictions and statistics based on climatological records provides a useful means of evaluating possible future climates beyond the skill range of weather forecasts. Analyses of long-term climate records, used in association with knowledge of the agricultural and hydrological system, provide vital components of planning and design for sound water resources management at the farm level and for major land and water use and water transfer programs that form a major part of drought mitigation strategies. Although the products of these analyses are not predictions by meteorological convention, they warrant recognition. The incorporation of such climatological knowledge into drought mitigation planning programs is essential if these programs are expected to perform effectively over the life of the project.

544

SUMMARY

Clearly, drought prediction plays an important role in formulating a drought assessment and response strategy. The large geographic and temporal diversity of predictive skill underscores the need to continue focusing on research aimed at broadening the basic understanding of the physical mechanics of drought. However, many low latitude regions have enough predictive skill that such predictions may be useful in a comprehensive drought strategy.

Scientists and policy makers need a better understanding of how to incorporate the more skillful drought predictions into decision making. For example, the problem of linking drought predictions to efforts to detect and monitor drought should be considered a high priority. In the next section, this and other issues pertaining to drought detection, monitoring, and early warning are discussed.

TASK GROUP 2:
DROUGHT DETECTION, MONITORING, AND EARLY WARNING

INTRODUCTION

There is a general belief that information about the onset of drought conditions is a useful drought mitigation tool if provided to agricultural producers in a timely and reliable manner. The task group's view of the process or system for providing, receiving, and using such information is illustrated below.

The operation of such a system will vary considerably between different countries for geographical, developmental, and sociopolitical reasons. Nevertheless, several statements can be made about the status of existing systems, improvements to them, impediments to the introduction of additional systems, and the ultimate value placed on the systems by the end users. Implicit in all of the discussions that follow is a need for further research, since the systems and training programs are not perfect. Implementation of both systems and training programs is often limited by an inadequate number of trained people.

ASSESSING THE VALUE OF DETECTION AND MONITORING
TO DECISION MAKERS

Task group members were asked to consider whether information concerning the onset and severity of impending drought conditions was a useful drought mitigation tool for agricultural producers and others if it was provided in a timely and reliable man-

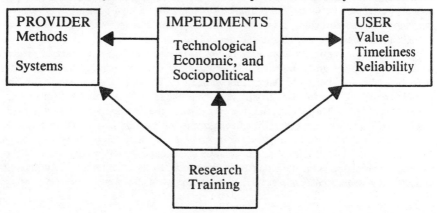

ner. The task group was also asked to consider whether information is currently incorporated into operational decisions and to suggest ways to improve the use of climate and climate-related information by decision makers at all levels.

It is assumed that a monitoring and early warning system is capable of providing reliable and timely information to users. The value of that information must be considered at four levels: (1) farm, (2) business and industrial, (3) governmental, and (4) international. For the agricultural producer, this information is valuable when making decisions at planting time (e.g., which variety or crop to plant, seeding rate or plant population/unit area, fertilization); during the growing season (e.g., fertilization, irrigation, use of various moisture conservation practices); harvest (e.g., when to harvest, storage requirements). Information needs for agriculture vary greatly over the crop season. Within business and industry this information may be helpful in the allocation of manpower and other resources and in estimates of supply and demand for a wide variety of commodities (e.g., energy). For government, this information is useful in planning and in making policy decisions relating to production estimates for import or export commitments, in declaration and revocation of drought disaster areas, and in implementation and discontinuation of assistance programs to farmers, municipalities, and others. At the international level, information about impending drought and its likely impacts assists donor countries and organizations as well as others in the timely implementation of a wide range of emergency aid responses.

By itself, climate and climate-related information has no discernible assessment value. Only when this information is reliable and provided to decision makers in a timely manner (and then only if users are properly educated or trained to apply this information in various strategic situations) does it assume real value. In the short run, the value of information derived from monitoring and early warning systems will be high if it helps users avoid making poor or incorrect decisions, particularly if these decisions are economically costly or may result in the loss of life or a reduction in the quality of life. The value of this information is also high if it reduces or lessens the physical (e.g., soil erosion) or socioeconomic (e.g., yield loss) impacts in the drought-affected area. Information about impending drought conditions could also help managers make timely decisions that would protect the environment, conserve scarce resources (e.g., water, herbicides, pesticides, fertilizer) and minimize disruption of normal societal activities. In the long run the information provided by these systems can increase the resiliency of drought-prone regions to environmental stress.

A multidisciplinary team established to interpret and advise users of critical decisions must place great emphasis on the reliability and timeliness of the data. Data must be collected at a sufficient spatial density to adequately represent impending drought conditions to many user groups, and it must be of sufficient quality to ensure accurate assessments. This is essential if the supplier of the data and information is to establish credibility with the user. Timeliness of the information is of equal importance. Unless data or data products are provided to users at critical decision points, they are of little or no value. These critical points must be determined for all primary users. Users must also participate in the development of products. Lines of communication must be established with all primary users and they must be open at all times.

EFFORTS TO DETECT AND MONITOR DROUGHT CONDITIONS:
CURRENT STATUS AND NEEDED IMPROVEMENTS

Task Group 2 was asked to consider if current efforts to detect and monitor drought conditions were reliable, timely, and easily understood by users. If they were not, the group was asked to suggest ways these monitoring systems and their products could be modified to enhance the ability to provide early warning of impending drought as part of a national strategy.

Existing drought monitoring and early warning systems are considered to be generally reliable and timely by some users. This statement simply reflects the complexity of the problem when viewed from the perspective of both the supplier of data and information and the user or consumer of such information. Most monitoring or early warning systems have been developed to provide data and information for broad geographical areas that are diverse in climate, water resources, soils, agricultural systems, culture, and so on. Thus, products from these monitoring systems must be well designed to accommodate this diversity in their output, and they must be appropriate to the needs of a wide variety of users.

Most current drought monitoring systems are based largely or entirely on meteorological data. Moreover, these data by themselves do not necessarily reflect the potential impact of weather events on agricultural systems, water availability and use, health, and so forth. For example, in the United States the Palmer Drought Severity Index (PDSI) is used by many to assess drought severity and the potential impact of drought, in spite of the fact that it has often been shown to be deficient and spatially inconsistent. And it is also frequently applied injudiciously with respect to the ecosystem being monitored. As a result, the PDSI can lead decision makers into inappropriate and excessive drought responses. Such a situation occurred in the United States during 1977, when more than two-thirds of the country was declared a drought disaster area (see Wilhite, Chapter 25 in this volume).

Although meteorologically based systems are subject to criticism, such systems are considered to be valuable as a first step or stage in the drought assessment process. Meteorological data can be used in conjunction with other data and information to estimate the probable impact of a particular weather event.

In developed countries, both meteorological and socioeconomic data and information on impending drought conditions is usually available on a timely basis. Examples include the U.S. Department of Agriculture and National Oceanic and Atmospheric Administration's Weekly Weather and Crop Bulletin, the Australian Bureau of Meteorology's Drought Review Bulletin, and Agriculture Canada's Prairie Provinces Water Supply Conditions report. Members of these organizations have early access to the information contained in the reports. However, information of this kind is not always disseminated to other users in a timely manner. Furthermore, once the information reaches many end-users or decision makers (e.g., farmer, manager, legislator, administrator), it may, for a number of reasons, be applied inappropriately. The user may not be trained to incorporate this information into a decision strategy. The product may also be poorly designed as a conveyor of information. Unfortunately, user needs are not always considered in product development or packaging.

In less-developed countries, the problems are understandably more pronounced. Often no monitoring system exists. This may be the result of many factors or combinations of factors, including (1) inadequate numbers of trained personnel; (2) limited financial resources; (3) lack of necessary historical climatic data sets and supplementary agronomic, hydrologic, and other information; and (4) lack of awareness of the potential benefits of this information. There is certainly a need to identify the most cost-effective minimum data set necessary to support a drought detection system in these instances.

Monitoring, detection, and reporting systems will be more effective if they are built on several independent data collection networks. Three main types of data collection networks exist for this purpose: (1) networks of surface-based instruments, including both *low-* (e.g., manual weather observation networks) and *high-technology* (e.g., automated weather observation networks) types; (2) satellite imagery; and (3) on-site inspections. Ironically, so-called low-technology methods of communication are not a feasible alternative for transmitting data and information in many developing countries because of deficiencies in basic infrastructure (e.g., a reliable telephone system). Automated data collection or high-technology systems that can transfer many kinds of data from meteorological and agronomic sensors through surface-based linkages or satellite linkages are becoming more affordable. There should be a concerted effort to develop strategic networks to provide data that supports drought detection and monitoring systems. However, no data collection system is complete unless it includes an efficient and effective means of communication from the observation point to the processing or analyzing point. Adequate quality control, regular instrument maintenance, efficient procedures, and communication channels for transmitting advice and warnings to users are also essential.

The outlook for satellite imagery appears good. However, the products from the various groups working on these techniques cannot yet provide unambiguous assessments of soil moisture, crop status, or estimates of yield. One explanation for this inability is the surface complexity of cropping systems in many parts of the world (e.g., China). It is likely that activities of the World Meteorological Organizations's World Climate Program (WCP), the International Geosphere-Biosphere Program (IGBP), and the International Satellite and Land Surface Climatology Program (ISLSCP) will lead to technological improvements in existing drought detection systems.

Finally, surface-instrument- and satellite-based monitoring systems should never replace on-site inspections of the distressed area. These inspections provide ground truth to calibrate the data from surface and satellite-based systems, and they also provide valuable data for the evaluation of probable impacts and adjustment mechanisms.

TECHNOLOGICAL, ECONOMIC, AND SOCIOPOLITICAL IMPEDIMENTS TO IMPROVING MONITORING AND EARLY WARNING SYSTEMS

The task group classified impediments to the effective operation and improvement of monitoring and early warning systems as *technological* and *economic and sociopolitical.*

Technological Impediments

Many national drought detection or monitoring networks operate without having explicitly defined user data and information needs. It is clear that the needs of agricultural producers, business managers, transportation officials, and government decision makers differ greatly. For example, while farmers are primarily concerned with soil moisture availability, industry and transportation officials are concerned with projected yields, which might affect sales and service demand. Governments, on the other hand, may monitor surface water supplies, feed stocks, and the production of commodities to determine when or if to implement emergency assistance programs. Therefore, network designers must consider user needs from the initial design phase for data collection networks through the development of dissemination systems. Coupled with this is the need to determine the primary target groups for the network products.

For monitoring systems to be successful in both the short and long run, communication channels between suppliers and users of information must always be open to spontaneous interaction both during and between drought periods, since perceptions can often be quite different. User needs and supplier capabilities are constantly changing, and interaction between the two groups facilitates this dynamic process. System managers must also formally solicit the opinions and suggestions of users on a periodic basis. These solicitations should include requests for opinions about and experiences related to the use of existing products and practices as well as ideas for future product development.

The tools for and techniques of monitoring impending drought conditions and the potential impact of drought on agriculture and other economic sectors are not yet adequately developed. In particular, further adaptation is needed to make these techniques more appropriate to the data and human resource constraints of less-developed countries. Nevertheless, it may be possible in some cases to operate a viable early warning system.

Substantial gaps often exist in basic data sets and in the ability to collect and disseminate such data to users in a timely manner in less-developed countries. Also, local extension networks are unlikely to be well established, and linkages between suppliers and users of information are poorly developed. The task of developing more widespread and efficient extension networks is critical to the dissemination process in these instances. Furthermore, without adequate education and training, farmers in less-developed countries cannot make use of information from an early warning system.

Economic and Sociopolitical Impediments

Task Group 2 generally concluded that drought early warning systems must be linked with attempts to monitor other trends that might contribute to the vulnerability of fragile ecosystems to drought, such as deforestation, soil erosion, and land use management. For example, the absence of an appropriate land use policy within less-developed countries may counter the utility of an early warning system.

It was also noted that government priorities for making decisions regarding resource allocation, particularly in less-developed countries, are not always firm. Fluctuating priorities make it difficult to ensure survival of a monitoring system whose success can be only evaluated in the long run.

The scarcity of financial resources in less-developed countries can lead to a number of obstacles, particularly the imbalance between high levels of funding for technology from international organizations and low levels of funding for national policy and implementation efforts. Governments need to be aware of this imbalance and clearly define a set of objectives attainable under existing internal conditions. The task group noted that the number and diversity of the political constituencies (e.g., national and local governments, regional organizations, nongovernmental organizations, and bilateral and multilateral donors) that fund early warning systems often give rise to conflicts among the groups involved.

In less-developed countries the low level of development, widespread illiteracy, relative isolation, and subsistence levels of many producers impedes the flow of information. This limits the utility of early warning systems about potentially limiting weather-related production factors, thereby restricting the number of realistic options available to producers. In these countries the flow of data and information about drought should not be separated but should be an extension of operational information services used to better manage rural production systems in normal and above-average years.

Government in drought-prone areas should have at its disposal a multidisciplinary team of experts to evaluate and synthesize available information concerning drought. The team of specialists must include a meteorologist and/or a climatologist, as well as experts in operational agriculture, hydrology, economics, and other disciplines that represent the major administrative regions and other interests that are, or are likely to be, affected significantly by the drought. Such a team would interact with drought planners and decision makers to ensure that all available information is harnessed in an effective and efficient manner in drought mitigation. The needs and languages of the decision makers should be understood by the team, knowledge transfer mechanisms should be established, and accountabilities should be clearly defined. Whatever the processes, it is of utmost importance that the activities of the specialists and decisions makers be closely coordinated.

A drought monitoring system incorporating meteorological and climatological information must be in place and its information made directly available to the team. The role of the meteorologist or climatologist is not to make decisions, but to provide information to those authorized to make decisions. To act effectively, the meteorologist or climatologist must be fully informed about drought mitigation plans and have full access to monitoring programs in order to acquire needed information. Presentations by the meteorologists to the team and to the decision makers will contain climate monitoring information, weather data and forecasts, climate predictions, climate risk statistics, and alternative climatic scenarios. The best available knowledge on the time and spatial variabilities of meteorological drought must be translated into relationships that are readily comprehended by other members of the team, decision makers, and those implementing action plans. For example, rainfall deficiencies should also be presented in terms of their likely effects on soil moisture, crop yields, water supply, runoff conditions, and so forth. The potential uses as well as the limitations of this information must be made clear by the meteorologist. Furthermore, the meteorologist must advise other members of the teams and/or decision makers of spurious climate predictions from other sources that might raise questions or unduly influence decision making.

Such interaction requires the involvement of a highly qualified and credible meteorologist or climatologist with broad disciplinary knowledge and an understanding of the other relevant disciplines. Effective interaction is unlikely to be attained immediately: the meteorologist may need years of experience to achieve credibility with decision makers and other users and to fully adapt climatological information to the needs of drought managers. Consideration should be given to allowing the advisory team to function continuously in association with resource monitoring and management persons and with crop insurance and similar programs in which weather and climate data and information are needed. The frequency of interactions can be greatly reduced in non-drought periods and intensified as circumstances require. Continuity will ensure that the appropriate skills and knowledge are maintained and available when required.

SUMMARY

Drought detection, monitoring, and early warning systems that provide timely and reliable information about the onset, spatial extent, and termination of drought conditions are a critical element of any national or provincial response strategy. The existence of a multidisciplinary team to interpret and disseminate this information is of equal importance to the success of such a strategy. Closely linked to this task is the calculation of likely impact. In the next section, issues surrounding the science of drought and impact assessment and, in a broader sense, climate impact assessment are considered.

TASK GROUP 3:
DROUGHT IMPACT ASSESSMENT

INTRODUCTION

Drought Impact Assessment within a Broader Context

Discussions thus far have been focused on drought and its impacts on society and the environment. It is crucial, however, that the drought phenomenon and its societal and environmental impacts be integrally related to broader considerations of climate variability, which also includes nondrought periods. Clearly, actions taken during nondrought periods often determine the level of vulnerability to drought. Conversely, the impacts of a drought on society and the environment often last years after the drought has passed. Thus, it is necessary to avoid the pitfall of focusing only on the impact of drought as an outlying climatic event. Many researchers, for example, agree that in less-developed countries there is a seasonal rhythm to rural poverty. Where there is malnutrition, some parts of the year are worse than others. The occurrence of drought in such situations exacerbates the underlying cause, thereby making a bad situation considerably worse.

The above example reinforces the view that climate information, including climate impact assessments, provides a decision maker with only one piece of information that he or she might need to make a prudent decision. The decision maker will need to take into account intervening political as well as socioeconomic factors. Assessments of past drought periods can provide information on how these factors should be weighted and used by decision makers.

Recent occurrences of widespread, severe drought have underscored the extreme vulnerability of both developed and developing societies to drought. Researchers, however, must not only focus their attention on situations in which drought-coping mechanisms worked and where societies exhibited resilience, but on those situations in which the coping mechanisms failed.

TECHNIQUES AND METHODS USEFUL
IN DROUGHT IMPACT ASSESSMENT

Before undertaking an evaluation of methods currently available for drought impact assessment, evaluation criteria should be established. The evaluation criteria should meet the users' requirements for drought impact assessments and determine the scientific credibility of the assessments themselves.

User requirements can be reduced to the need for (1) *accuracy* of the assessment, (2) an appropriate *spatial as well as temporal resolution* of the assessment, (3) *timing* of the assessment relative to specific decision-making needs, and (4) a comparison of the assessment to normal-run and past extremes.

Scientific credibility is determined by the *comprehensiveness* of the assessment: How well does the assessment identify important secondary impacts? How *useful* is the assessment for primary user groups? How *intelligible* is the assessment with respect to the target audience? Has the potential for misinterpretation of results been minimized?

<u>Types of Drought Impact Assessment</u>

Two broad categories of impact assessment can be identified. The first category concerns monitoring drought-related effects in "near-real time." The objective is to provide *timely* information for rapid and appropriate response. The second category includes assessments of past, present, and possible future droughts. The latter assessments are less concerned with timeliness than are the near-real time monitoring assessments. The second category is intended to document the full array of drought-related impacts to add to the general scientific understanding, to evaluate individual and societal (e.g., biophysical, economic, etc.) responses, and to make recommendations with regard to drought planning concerning improvements in those responses.

<u>Drought Impact Assessment Methods</u>

Three types of drought impact assessment methods are considered; descriptive empirical observations (documentation), simulation, and comparative experiences.

<u>Descriptive Empirical Observations.</u> Two approaches can be used for descriptive empirical observations. One approach is a field assessment of impacts in near-real time which monitors impacts of an ongoing drought situation at the site of the drought. The process can be either *data collection* initiatives (instrumental, visual, and other evidence collected by governments, private companies, and international organizations) or *subjective observations and analyses* (by citizens, missionaries and others), which is used principally as verification of data collected.

Highest priority is placed on rapid assimilation, transmission, and interpretation of information. One likely cost of increased speed of information transfer is reduction in the accuracy and reliability of the assessment. However, the longer the assessment system has been operational and the better developed it is, the greater will be the validity of the information being transmitted.

It is essential that these field assessments be integrated with or interpreted in conjunction with information derived from nonfield sources (e.g., standard economic indices, demographic factors, climatic analyses). Once integrated with other assessments, results should be immediately communicated to appropriate decision makers.

A second approach involves case studies of drought events, which are useful in identifying how societies might be affected by climate variability. In-depth, *post hoc* reviews of drought situations can often help to separate the impacts on society that might be attributed to drought from the impacts on society of other socioeconomic factors, including political decisions. Only with a proper understanding of what can really be attributed to drought can more effective methods be developed for mitigating the impacts of drought on society. It is important to note that the impacts of drought in different countries can be quite different, just as the impacts of two seemingly similar droughts in the same area but occurring at different times can also be different.

Simulation Assessments. Assessments using simulation are based on an understanding of the processes linking meteorological drought with biophysical processes and social and economic consequences. The models function by inputting climatic parameters (e.g., rainfall, temperature) into an expression of the socioenvironmental system (vegetation, soil, management) to arrive at an "objective" judgment of a situation.

Model levels can either be simple, in which case they usually give broad and/or site-specific answers, or complex, in which case they are likely to be deterministic and conceptually physical in nature and may incorporate expert systems (i.e., intelligent computer programs codifying the preprogrammed reasoning processes of experts in resolving specific problems).

The output of simulation models must be viewed with due consideration of model constraints. Errors in the input data are likely to be compounded in the output. This stresses the need for good data and for model validation procedures at each step (from environmental conditions to human impacts), especially in countries where data quality and availability are major problems.

Simulation models are generally of a single-output nature-for example, only one piece of information is generated from a simple model run. However, this is not true of plant process models. Models should have the capability to produce information at each step of their operation, which permits better linkages with other models that may only directly (but not less importantly) be concerned with drought impacts.

Models are frequently constrained by data restrictions such as too little data, unreliable data, and obsolete data. Changing technologies and economic forces may also affect the utility of outputs. Moreover, many simulation models are too specialized and too complex to use, regardless of where drought is occurring.

Comparative Assessments. Comparative assessments are based on the premise that lessons relevant to drought impacts can be learned by studying drought scenarios, or environmental situations that might in some way have effects that parallel those produced by droughts.

The *case-scenario approach* is based on the premise that we can learn about how society might better respond to drought episodes by reenacting previous drought situations. These reenactments involve asking experts what they would do now in the same situation, benefiting from hindsight. Such an approach might serve to uncover hidden constraints on the ability of society to respond in a timely and effective manner to the impacts of extended drought episodes.

No two droughts are the same, nor can we expect their impacts on society and the environment to be the same. However, it may be possible to identify appropriate *analogues of similar comparative situations* that could be used to suggest how both societies and individual citizens might respond more effectively to drought. For example, there may be situations in which gradual changes in the local or regional water balance may suggest agricultural responses that can be applied during d+rought situations.

IMPEDIMENTS TO IMPROVED RELIABILITY AND TIMELINESS
OF DROUGHT IMPACT ASSESSMENTS

The major impediments to improved reliability and timeliness of drought impact assessments stem not so much from a lack of scientific understanding as from inadequate logistical structures for implementing the assessments. These impediments fall into three categories: institutional, technological, and informational.

Institutional Impediments. Several facets of institutional impediments have been pointed out in previous sections. However, two factors deserve additional mention here. One is the tendency for institutions (governmental and nongovernmental) to hold on to information generated internally. Thus exchange of data and analyses (such as impact assessments) between institutions is hampered and often delayed. The second factor is that studies of the impacts of drought have seldom had the commitment of financial and human resources necessary to complete the intended task. This is a particularly difficult problem because it is necessary to assess drought impacts during the event as well as during the recovery period to gain a full appreciation of the lingering societal effects that may result.

Technological Impediments. Technological advancement is occurring at a rate that almost escapes the imagination. A problem accompanying this advancement is the increasing tendency to let technological capabilities dictate the kinds of research questions being posed. As new technologies are developed, research questions are subsequently devised to exploit the technological advances. This tends to stifle productive research. For example, in drought impacts research, the current and potential value of remote sensing technology is well recognized. However, letting this technology determine the research questions to be asked to the exclusion of other types of drought impact research is a serious mistake and can be viewed as an impediment to improving assessments.

Informational Impediments. As mentioned in earlier discussions of simulation impact assessment models, the lack of high-quality data is a major impediment to impact assessment, especially in less-developed countries. It is difficult to obtain adequate information on the condition of pastoralists because of their geographic isolation from population centers and, in many cases, their estrangement from their governments. The media may be helpful in these instances by publicizing the plight of these and other vulnerable population groups. Yet precisely because of this isolation and their lack of involvement with the state, pastoralists are at higher risk to the adverse consequences of drought. Without reliable data and communication systems, there is no effective way to monitor on a timely basis the plight of groups such as this.

IMPROVING DROUGHT AND CLIMATE IMPACT ASSESSMENT

Crucial to any impact assessment of drought is the nature of baseline and episodic data. Often the quality of this data is unknown and therefore frequently ignored. Sometimes the data are treated as probabilistic estimates of a population statistic, but these are of questionable value if based on sample surveys only, with little regard to basic flaws in the data network itself. The most obvious climate data required in drought assessment are rainfall amounts and their variance from some expected value. Station changes and data homogeneity must be documented in the assessment of long-term climate trends and climate norms. Although the climate and meteorological literature on station networks is extensive, few comparisons have been made between drought indices and the number of stations needed to accurately portray meteorological drought. This is a major concern since drought is rarely a spatially uniform phenomena. Analyses of the spatial reliability of such indices should be explored.

Assessing data quality is equally important for agricultural yields and socioeconomic survey data. For example, in Kenya, the four government yield survey methods each give different results, which have never been systematically compared. The data used in research should be scrupulously assessed, and data commonly used in operations should be subject to systematic reviews.

The data generated by a drought assessment needs to be made available in a variety of forms and on relevant time scales. It should also be tailored to the needs of the various users. Often the original input data have been manipulated in unknown ways and reported without due regard to the limitations of the original data, its management, and its analysis. Consistency and continuity of drought assessments should be a major goal and assessment products and data bases that are not well documented should be questioned. All assessments should be made available in a usable, readily understood form.

Investment to improve data quantity, documentation, quality, and communication could have widespread benefits for researchers and other data users. As a rule, data limitations and the problems of data quality should be identified and discussed in specific drought assessments where the particular techniques and methods employed require different approaches to data.

IMPROVEMENT IN METHODS

Improved climate and drought impact assessment methodology would achieve greater credibility and thereby greater utility. Current methods range from idiographic studies to highly quantitative deterministic models. In either case, regardless of quantitative elegance, these approaches tend to lack a convincing causality of atmospheric variability on the behavior of society and broad ecosystems; that is, they fail to separate objectively the "signal" of climate response from the "noise" caused by nonclimatic factors. To address this problem, more research is needed, using hindsight and climate fluctuation analogs.

Hindsight assessments provide the opportunity to evaluate the effects of naturally occurring climatic fluctuations and to impose signal-amplifying techniques (e.g., margins analysis) as well as noise-reducing techniques (e.g., case-control) to isolate climate-induced societal responses.

The results of processes that have effects similar to those produced by drought can be treated as analogues. These, too, can provide useful insight on the probable impact of drought. For example, reduction of the water level in the Ogallala Aquifer may elicit many of the same kinds of impacts on and social response to rainfed agriculture as might the impacts of a long-term decline in precipitation on rainfed agriculture.

More information is needed on the types of biophysical processes and human activities that are sensitive to climate fluctuation and the extent to which they are sensitive. What are the approximate (secondary and tertiary) effects of climate fluctuation as impacts trickle through social and economic systems? In addition, there is a need to identify "indicator activities" that reliably reflect the impacts induced by climate. These are key variables that act as precursors to the full impacts of the fluctuation.

Models must be tested for reliability and validity with test data. They should also be systematically compared to document their strengths and weaknesses. The use of a model is primarily to structure a certain relationship. Interpretation of a model must include an analysis of the error inherent in the model's structure and data. Complex models may be used to validate simple ones, which are more easily used and interpreted in operational programs.

There is also a need to test and evaluate various models in a wide range of situations to provide independent assessments of the value of the information that comes out of the models. Currently, many models are available for various tasks, but they are not used (often to the frustration of their developers) because the necessary (independent) assessments have not been made. Here, the potential exists for large gains for a fairly small investment of effort.

Integrated drought assessment by modeling techniques requires that several models (crop yield, production, economic, and social responses) be linked to document the nature and extent of drought impacts. Research into how these models may be linked, and into the interpretation of the output, would be useful. Several case studies of linked models could be prepared. Advantages of linking discrete models together include the capability to utilize sophisticated models for specific purposes and for ease of interpretation of the results by controlling model interactions.

SUMMARY

Just as it is difficult to distinguish drought monitoring from impact assessment, it is not clear how to delineate impacts of drought from adjustment and adaptation to drought. For example, forced migration out of a drought-plagued region would most likely be placed under the rubric of adjustment. However, to the people being forced to migrate, the move, undoubtedly, is simply another negative impact added to the host of drought impacts that forced the move in the first place.

Impact or adjustment? Regardless of the answer, human systems have exhibited remarkable ability to adjust and adapt to fluctuating environmental conditions such as drought. The next section discusses the tenets of effective adjustment and adaptation to drought.

558

TASK GROUP 4:
DROUGHT ADAPTATION AND ADJUSTMENT

VULNERABILITY TO DROUGHT

Task Group 4 considered, for various drought-prone regions, the proportion of agricultural producers that are well adapted or prepared to withstand the occurrence of short-term (seasonal) or longer-term (one or more years) drought. These were considered from the perspective of commercial versus subsistence agricultural producers.

In developed countries the proportion of commercial agricultural producers who can successfully withstand a short-term occurrence of drought is high, in terms of both business resilience and human welfare. The impact of short-term drought is significantly reduced because of irrigation and the availability of sufficient forage (fodder) and water for livestock. Even in the case of longer-term drought, the use of irrigation coupled with sufficient grain and forage storage facilities and a fully developed infrastructure can significantly lessen the impact on society and livestock. For example, in Australia, 40% of the farming community is not greatly affected by a drought.

For subsistence farmers, even short-term drought can be disastrous, especially for the peasant farmer whose only security is a small piece of land on which to grow his food and some cash crops. If seasonal rains fail, no alternative supply of water is available to sustain growth. The result is critical shortages of food, inadequacy of grazing land, suffering and possible loss of life for both human beings and livestock. The lack of an adequate infrastructure and the high price of grain from external markets impede governmental ability to rescue inhabitants of such distressed areas. Furthermore, the occurrence of a drought, short- or long-term, reduces the government's tax revenue and diminishes foreign exchange earnings from the export of cash crops.

However, governments should not dismiss the capability of local farmers to adapt to drought through the application of indigenous practices. Although these methods may not be widely known to organizations that have the responsibility for the development and implementation of monitoring systems, they have often enabled local farmers to withstand periods of severe environmental stress. Traditional societal responses include "fall back" sequences of responses at the family level, including risk/loss minimizing and management techniques such as cutting back on hired resources, on consumption, and on farm storage inventory depletion, and by the utilization of mixed cropping techniques.

The magnitude of drought impact is closely related to the intensity and duration of the drought. It is not necessarily the length of drought alone that determines its socioeconomic effects. For example, in some parts of Africa the intense drought of 1984 was quite short in duration but led to the destruction of much of the agricultural produce and livestock.

ENHANCEMENT OF THE ADAPTIVE PROCESS

The task group was asked to consider, under the presumption that a significant proportion of farmers in drought-prone regions are not optimally adapted to drought, how a national drought strategy might enhance the adaptive process. Recognizing that subsistence farmers are the least well adapted to drought, their case was used as the basis for a drought strategy. These farmers lack reserves of cash, grain, animals, or other assets for use in times of drought.

A national drought strategy for subsistence farmers in developing countries should have the following components: an information base, an institutional base, a developed infrastructure, and an impact assessment system. These components are discussed below in greater detail.

Compilation and Provision of Information

1. Historical risk analysis is needed to identify:
   - Frequency, duration, and amplitude of droughts using time-series data to estimate the probabilities of droughts and other exceptional climatic events.
   - Vulnerable areas (using the frequency and amplitude analysis noted above) to identify the geographical areas at greatest risk, so as to select the most appropriate sites for grain reserves and programs of public works.
   - Vulnerable populations (populations at greater risk including landless laborers, small landholders, and farmers without exchangeable assets such as animals) that need to be targeted as priority groups.
2. Crop monitoring reports are needed to provide short-term (ten-day period) assessments of the cropping season.
3. Long-term forecasts and sophisticated monitoring techniques, such as satellite imagery, would be used in conjunction with demographic information to project long-term trends, including desertification.

Development of Local Institutions

It was argued that the development of local political and economic institutions to assist farmers and others was necessary to provide effective drought planning and response. Such institutions would share information among affected groups and provide information to agencies at higher levels (for example, at the regional or national level); assess drought severity and other exceptional events; identify severely affected groups; and organize response, using local resources wherever possible.

Development of Infrastructures

The task group agreed that the development of infrastructures was the most important component of a national drought strategy. An infrastructure would be organized as follows:

1. Grain and other food reserves for relief would be prepared in advance of disasters, including the amount of reserves and conditions of their use. Provisions for livestock would be included.

2. Transportation system development would concentrate on ensuring access to the most isolated areas in the event of a drought emergency and on delivering relief provisions to such areas.

3. Organization of water resources would include the emergency provision of water for crops, people, and animals.

Analysis of Impact and the Effectiveness of Relief Measures

Effective provision of drought relief measures requires careful planning. Past and present relief efforts must be evaluated to arrive at improved methodologies. Such analysis would include assessment of the economic impact of drought, the economic effects of relief, and a technical evaluation of relief efforts (for example, an evaluation of the environmental effects of roads and dams built as part of public works programs).

TECHNOLOGICAL AND SOCIOECONOMIC IMPEDIMENTS TO DROUGHT ADAPTATION

Task Group 4 also considered possible technological and socioeconomic impediments to improving societal adaptation to drought.

Impediments to Drought Survival

Several factors that could impede drought survival as well as possible ways to overcome these impediments are discussed below.

1. Inadequate water supply. This might be overcome through the development of short-term or strategic irrigation by building wells, pipelines, canals, and runoff catchments for farm dams.

2. Low water use efficiency by crops and pastures. Water use efficiency could be improved by selecting crops and pastures that are better adapted to the environment, and by adopting water-conserving soil management practices.

3. Inadequate food for humans and animals. A solution to this problem requires the provision of adequate storage facilities for grain and forage, and an efficient distribution system.

4. Inadequate money. In some instances consideration should be given to implementing incentive programs such as a special bonds plan, which would allow farmers to purchase bonds in good years and redeem them in drought years, and to provide operating loans for potentially viable farmers.

5. Migration of farm population to the towns. Approval should be given to local projects which could be implemented to retard the flow of farmers from drought affected rural areas into urban areas (e.g., as in Brazil) during drought periods.

Impediments to the Social Adaptation to Drought

In general, Task Group 4 agreed that improvements in drought management should develop or enhance the capability of families to withstand drought and famine and develop a better system of collecting and disseminating information.

Additional issues that need to be considered when developing a general policy for societal improvement are:

1. The preparation of a comprehensive land use plan that incorporates factors such as climate, crop variety, and soil type.
2. The development of a land tenure system to give greater security to farmers.
3. The establishment of a formal communication system for local farmer groups (such as exists, for example, with soil conservation committees).
4. The establishment and publication of criteria for relief schemes, well in advance of drought.

SUMMARY

The foregoing discussion demonstrates some of the difficulties that may be encountered when attempting to cope with the impacts of drought. An issue that deserves further consideration, however, is the extent that a concerted drought response policy can facilitate the adjustment and adaptation process. The next section delves into this issue with the specific aim of integrating previous discussions into a set of principles for a drought response strategy.

TASK GROUP 5:
DROUGHT PLANNING AND RESPONSE

THE NEED FOR A DROUGHT POLICY

Task Group 5 was asked to consider whether or not state and/or national governments should have a drought policy to assess and respond to episodes of severe drought. If so, they were asked to identify the objectives of that policy.

The task group felt that national governments should establish a policy (or strategy) for the assessment of and response to drought. Droughts of both long and short return periods should be considered in developing plans. National policy should be based on expert identification of the existence and severity of drought, as well as on assessments by a designated government agency or agencies, of drought's current and possible future impacts. A national policy must also recognize the need for both coping with and responding to drought. National drought policy should stress the creation of an infrastructure to supply the basic data, analysis, and research needed for assessment and response. The infrastructure should be able to function independently of individual expertise, but it should be cognizant of the collective past experience of its members. A key part of national policy should be the development of a general plan to prepare for and respond to drought episodes. The general plan should be effectively integrated with state and area-wide plans.

USE OF IMPACT ASSESSMENT PRODUCTS

The task group considered the extent to which the products of current impact assessment efforts are used in the implementation of drought response strategies and how these products might be modified or adapted to best serve a national drought strategy. The group also addressed the question of whether or not the products of the assessment efforts could be easily interpreted by decision makers.

The task group felt that response to drought is always based on some type of assessment of the severity and duration of the event, its current and potential impacts, and the ability of government and/or other organizations to respond. Impact assessments are most effective when they concentrate on basic aspects of the economy for the affected area—e.g., food, health, housing. Methodologies should be developed that would assess the present and future state of the basic aspects of the economy in some standardized form while establishing an adequate and timely data base for input into these methodologies. Procedures are also needed to synthesize the results of these assessments for persons or organizations responsible for drought response. At the same time, more complete impact assessments should be made to indicate both short- and long-term effects of drought. These more complete assessments must be presented to advisors and planners for consideration in updating assessment and response criteria.

POST-DROUGHT EVALUATIONS OF ASSESSMENT AND RESPONSE EFFORTS

The task group was asked to consider how governments and international organizations could arrange for the conduct of *ex post facto* evaluations of drought assessment and response activities.

The best guide to the future is past experience and the lessons learned from it. This is true of drought occurrence, the physical and biological consequences of drought, and human response to it. It is important to register the experiences of each major drought so that the lessons learned can assist society in responding more effectively to future events.

Governments should conduct or commission evaluations of each major drought episode. These evaluations should include an analysis of the physical aspects of the drought; its impacts on soil, ground water, plants, and animals; its economic and social consequences; and the extent to which predrought planning was useful in mitigating impacts, in facilitating relief or assistance to stricken areas, and in post-drought recovery.

It is recommended that governments place the responsibility for evaluating drought and societal response to it in the hands of another agency to ensure an unbiased appraisal of actions taken. For example, the Food for Work Program of India is implemented by state governments but is assessed by an independent body, the Planning Commission. Evaluations carried out by volunteers and nongovernmental organizations (NGOs) can also be invaluable since they often see weaknesses that official agencies may miss or be reluctant to admit.

International agencies, both intergovernmental and nongovernmental, should realize the value of post-drought evaluations and be prepared to sponsor them in cases where the emergency extends beyond national boundaries, especially where internationally coordinated relief projects might have been mounted.

Because much of the talent needed for the conduct of post-drought evaluations lies in the world's universities, foundations, and public research funding organizations should be encouraged to fund university researchers willing and qualified to undertake these studies. In many countries there are also specialized agencies or corporations capable of analyzing climate impact. The human resources available within these agencies should be tapped, especially in relation to major events such as the Sahelian desiccation, where the scale of the problem might be too great for individual academic workers to contend with.

A post-drought evaluation should seek answers to the following questions:
1. Was the drought plan followed? If not, why not?
2. Were the actions taken and measures implemented effective in mitigating the impact of drought? Which actions and relief measures were effective and which were not?
3. Should other actions or assistance measures have been included in the plan?
4. Did aid reach all groups in the stricken area? If not, why not? How were the target groups for aid identified?

5. Were the measures timely in relation to the events of the drought-period?
6. Was it possible to correct errors during the emergency?
7. What financial and human resources were allocated to the relief effort? Where did the resources come from and how were they controlled?
8. How efficient was the logistical support and the available infrastructure? Were obstacles encountered that reduced the efficiency of the response? If so, what were they (for example, limitations of personnel and fuel, obstructions by customs officials)?
9. What was the level of cooperation between the agencies involved, both public and private? Did this hinder or help the flow of information or aid?
10. Was media coverage accurate and realistic in providing details of the event? What kinds of media were involved? What role did they play in the emergency?

Task Group 5 suggested that when conducting post-drought evaluation, extensive research is needed on the following topics:

1. The environmental and socioeconomic effects of prolonged rainfall deficiency or on various hydrological features such as the depletion of soil moisture and shallow ground water should be considered. Ground surveys and satellite monitoring could help in the assessment of these effects, which would have a bearing on future streamflow, water use, energy development, and agriculture.
2. The effects of the drought on land use, vegetation, and soil should be studied. The recovery of agriculture in badly affected areas would need to be watched since the recovery process would be highly relevant to future drought response.
3. *Ex post facto* evaluations should be conducted and their findings implemented. Sadly, just as interest wanes with distance from the spark of crisis, so does the urge to regroup and reorganize. Several strategies could be employed to counteract these natural tendencies. First, the implementation process will be made easier if evaluations contain specific and clearly articulated recommendations and rationales. Second, decision makers might be more easily persuaded to implement high-priority recommendations if they have been previously educated about the problem. Third, recommendations are more likely to be accepted if the planning process specifically calls for an evaluation and implementation sequence. Finally, incentives for implementation can be provided by scheduling various forums for the exchange of information and experiences by researchers, recipients of relief, and policy makers. Funding agencies should consider making implementation of the recommendations emanating from post-drought evaluations a requirement for participation in their programs.

SUSTAINING MOMENTUM FOR DROUGHT PLANNING

Task Group 5 members were asked to recommend courses of action to follow to ensure that the momentum for drought planning generated by this symposium and workshop will be translated into action by governments and international organizations. The following courses of action were recommended to sustain the momentum generated by the workshop:

1. Develop model drought plans for nations and states within nations:
   - Convene meetings of representatives of the United Nations, donor organizations, nongovernmental organizations, and national agencies to identify elements of a model drought plan and the data needed and available for implementation of the plan. This process should focus on specific regions and outline a procedure for developing, adopting, and sustaining a drought plan.
   - Develop training programs on drought planning and management.
   - Identify persons capable of serving as advisors to governments desiring to prepare drought plans.
   - Request that regional international organizations such as UNSO, SADAC, CILSS, and regional UN economic commissions assist governments in preparing drought plans, offer the model plan as a guide and suggest advisors to help governments prepare plans.

2. Develop a drought planning network by:
   - Establishing a roster of researchers and policy officials knowledgeable in drought planning.
   - Developing a newsletter that informs interested persons on events, publications, and other matters pertinent to drought planning and management.
   - Disseminating important informational materials on drought to appropriate government agencies and international organizations.

3. Publicize results of this drought planning conference:
   - Participants should inform colleagues and government officials of the outcome of the meeting and of the recommendations that can be considered in the development of country or institutional drought plans.
   - Organizers should brief agencies and organizations in the United States as well as state governors on the results, recommendations, and identified research priorities forthcoming from the symposium and workshop. The organizers are also urged to communicate the results to key persons and organizations in both developed and developing countries, as well as to nongovernmental organizations.

SUMMARY

Many of the recommendations that have appeared in this section are not possible without a continued research initiative focusing on all of the previously discussed aspects of drought. In the next chapter, a set of research priorities are proposed that will facilitate the formation of a national and international drought response policy.

CHAPTER 36
DROUGHT RESEARCH PRIORITIES

INTRODUCTION

In some instances, research is a key to resolving complex issues associated with improving the capacity of individual persons, governments, and international organizations to cope with drought. Each task group was asked to reflect on specific areas of research that would enhance the ability not only to predict, monitor, assess, adapt, and respond to drought, but also to identify those research activities that would facilitate the development of a national drought strategy. Three related issues addressed by the task groups were: (1) improving communication of research results to users, (2) narrowing the gap between research and user needs, and (3) identifying the research needed to support post-drought evaluations of assessment and response efforts. Resolution of these issues would increase society's understanding and awareness of the complex problems associated with drought as well as facilitate the development of drought strategies at various levels. The results of those discussions have been integrated and are presented below.

DROUGHT PREDICTION

The predictability of the climate system is inherently limited. The limits to predictability vary with region, season, and lead time. These variations have not been mapped adequately. Thus, an important task is diagnostic research to identify the "targets of opportunity": the regions, seasons, lead times, and predictands for which prediction seems most feasible.

Three components of climate research can be distinguished: (1) theory, (2) general circulation modeling, and (3) empirical analysis. All three components, as well as interaction between them, are essential for the diagnostic understanding of the climate system, which in turn is basic to the development of drought prediction. Empirically based climate prediction has made the most progress toward operational application, but future progress demands improved physical understanding so that further work on general circulation models (GCMs) and theory is imperative. Both empirically based and GCM-based predictions of climate anomalies are expected to possess intrinsic limitations. Further research into the accuracy of the predictability of both methods is needed. The verification of forecasts on an independent data set should also be included.

Predictive research priorities are determined primarily by the need to overcome important knowledge gaps that limit predictability. Tailoring the acquired prediction skills to applications is mainly the concern of scientists working directly with users. Integration of research activities from both groups can produce more appropriate products for users. Integration also facilitates innovative adaptation of technological spinoffs from research and informs the research groups of community and policy concerns. Integration is not easy and care must be taken not to weaken the efforts of each group. Much understanding and tolerance will be required on the part of research managers and others.

Increased interaction is needed between researchers and potential users of drought predictions to match what is desirable with what is feasible. In particular, such interaction is needed to determine the optimum forecast formulation in terms of predictand, lead time, and temporal and spatial resolution. Interdisciplinary teams need to examine such questions; the answers will, of course, be region specific.

User workshops and in-house assignments have greatly helped operational scientists to identify user requirements more clearly and to better design products and systems of information dissemination. However, users, researchers, and operational scientists should develop these products and systems jointly, since workshops alone may fail to influence research adequately. Once a workshop has been completed, users and researchers no longer have an effective means of communication, and insufficient communication usually results in misunderstanding and the dissemination of inappropriate information.

DROUGHT DETECTION, MONITORING, AND EARLY WARNING

The primary objective of monitoring systems is to provide information to a particular client or user group in a timely and reliable manner so that effective action can be taken to alleviate potential impact. Each user group has specific needs and the information derived from any monitoring system will need to be expressed in different formats to be useful to the various groups. Therefore it is essential that those who use the information be involved from the beginning in the design of the system and its products. Open lines of communication should be maintained in order to provide feedback critical for system modification.

Research on methodology and technique development in support of monitoring and early warning systems was considered a high priority. It is particularly important that these monitoring methodologies and techniques adequately take into account the data and human resource constraints that exist in developing countries. The use of satellite imagery offers tremendous opportunity for monitoring developing drought conditions. It is imperative that research on the application of this technology to the early detection of drought conditions be expanded. Extension networks in developing countries must also be augmented in order to facilitate the flow of information and advisories to the farm level, and educational programs should be implemented on the proper use of this information in farm management.

Greater attention must be given to extending our knowledge and understanding of the current application of climate and climate-related information by decision makers (e.g., government officials, farmers), especially during times of environmental stress (e.g., drought, insect infestations). Educational programs must be instituted that inform decision makers on how the timely application of this information, in conjunction with proper management alternatives, can mitigate some of the worst effects of drought.

A realistic land use policy should be established and monitoring programs should be implemented to observe long-term trends in environmental processes such as deforestation and desertification. These programs should operate in concert with programs designed to monitor environmental change that may occur in the short run due to natural phenomena such as drought. Only by monitoring both short- and long-term trends in environmental change will society be able to better understand the interrelationships that exist.

DROUGHT IMPACT ASSESSMENT

Many simple assessment techniques have been developed for which useful data are readily available in most locations. However, these techniques either have not been brought to the attention of potential users or they have not gained acceptance or credibility because they have not been tested or because they seem to lack sophistication. Perhaps it is this lack of sophistication that makes them applicable to broad-ranging environmental conditions.

Research is needed to assess how simple, easy-to-use techniques that could provide useful information can be applied with greater reliability, credibility, acceptance, and perhaps status. The potential exists to greatly improve impact assessments without a great deal of additional technical research and developmental work.

There is a need for an institutional arrangement that can put "reporters" in the field when a drought is imminent so that the local responses to the drought can be documented at the time of occurrence. Attempts to piece together the responses after the event are extremely difficult and often unreliable. However, if an accurate history of responses to drought in a region could be compiled, it should be possible to evaluate the kinds of data, indicators, and general information that would be the most valuable in assessing the potential impact of the next drought, as it develops.

Finally, the organization of research is important. As a result of the site-specificity of most data, the complexity of the research issues, and the need to interact with local experts and decision makers, the most fruitful research projects will be those undertaken in the targeted country, with an extended commitment to institution building. For most projects, five years is the minimum time required to complete the cycle from data collection through interpretation to dissemination and review. Research networks and international collaboration will be most useful if a viable, ongoing program is already under way in the targeted country.

DROUGHT ADAPTATION AND ADJUSTMENT

The following areas of research were identified as necessary for improving the ability of agricultural producers to adapt to and prepare for drought.

1. Collection of detailed weather information. Comprehensive weather information, particularly rainfall and temperature, and historical climate infor-

mation are important in determining the cropping system for a particular zone.

2. Agroecological zones. There is a need to divide regions and countries into agroecological zones using information such as effective rainfall, rainfall distribution, temperature, and soil type.

3. Water management. Water management research is critical since water is the major factor limiting productivity in the arid and semiarid zones. Two areas were identified as offering substantial opportunities for this research: appropriate tillage and water harvesting techniques.

Research on appropriate tillage practices directed toward improving moisture conservation and management has shown considerable promise for various crops in arid and semiarid environments. Appropriate water harvesting methodologies need to be developed so rain water can be harvested and used in crop production.

4. Genotypes. Research is needed to identify and test desirable genotypes for drought tolerance, early maturity, disease resistance, high yields, and adaptation to particular agroecological zones.

5. Climate-system interaction. Climate is the key factor that directly affects cropping patterns: it influences a farmer's decision to adopt a particular cropping system. There is a need to understand how cropping systems in given agroecological zones react to climate variations. Researchers also need to devise strategies that minimize the adverse effects of these variations on the productivity of different cropping systems.

6. Alternative crops and alternative uses of established crops. Alternative crops should be identified and promoted for each agroecological zone. Research on alternative uses of new or minor crops must be carried out in advance to guarantee a market for these crops.

7. Research on fertilizer use in cropping systems. Fertilizer use may help guard against drought by encouraging development of a root system, which will utilize soil water more efficiently. There is a need to identify the economic returns associated with different rates of fertilizer application for dryland cropping systems.

8. Alternative land use systems (agroforestry, silviculture, pasture). It is essential that alternative land use systems that are compatible with critical production factors (such as climate and soil) be identified for drought-prone regions.

DROUGHT PLANNING AND RESPONSE

Interaction between the scientific community and policy makers should be encouraged because scientists can have a strong influence on the decision-making process. Unfortunately, the scientific community usually has a poor understanding of this process and is apprehensive about the potential misuse of uncertain information. This is particularly true in the case of drought prediction and in estimates of potential drought impact. Strong and frank lines of communication must be developed via advocates who communicate effectively at the policy level. Improved communication lines will result in enhanced visibility and understanding of the capabilities of science. In addition, improved communication will also enhance feedback from policy makers, thereby leading to a more policy-oriented direction in research. Without adequate interaction between scientists and decision makers, the policy and planning community might disregard research and research products in the decision-making process.

The answer lies primarily in much stronger interaction between the scientist and user in both the research and the education process. A mechanism for establishing stronger interaction has been discussed by Task Group 1. However, this mechanism alone is insufficient. Participating agencies must have good internal communication and established priorities to ensure that their programs are responsive to any drought contingency plan. The redirection of agency funds and priorities is usually difficult to achieve, especially on short notice. If properly informed, politicians are in a particularly unique position to alter the priorities of government. However, planning, priority setting, and communication differ significantly according to political system and level of economic development.

Task Group 5 was asked to discuss research and information needs that would be valuable in facilitating post-drought evaluation of assessment and response actions implemented during drought. Five areas of research were identified: (1) hydrological impact, (2) recovery of agricultural activity, (3) economic impact, (4) decisions made during drought, and (5) social response to drought. These research areas are discussed briefly below.

Drought has a considerable impact on the hydrology of a stricken region. An assessment of this impact through ground surveys and satellite monitoring would be beneficial in future planning efforts, particularly with respect to water use, energy, and agricultural activity.

Depending on the duration, intensity, and spatial characteristics of drought, the agricultural recovery of an area could be handicapped despite average or better rainfall. Input requirements (e.g., seed, fertilizer, pesticides, implements, energy) could be determined on the basis of the magnitude of the drought impact. Assessments of this type would be helpful when drought recurs.

An assessment of losses in agricultural and agriculturally based industries should be made following each drought episode. This type of assessment in developing countries must include the condition of people and livestock and market prices of essential commodities. It is also important to assess the impact of relief measures on the various economic sectors and to determine if individual citizens, industries, municipalities, or others were affected substantially but were neglected by available assistance programs. What groups or individual persons should be targeted for assistance in the future? To what extent did assistance programs discriminate against women or female children or children in general?

Decisions made by governments during periods of drought are made for humanitarian and political reasons. It will be difficult, if not impossible, to change this reasoning. Therefore, it is important that evaluations of drought assessment and response efforts are carried out by an organization other than the one responsible for implementing program plans.

In many less-developed countries the occurrence and effects of natural disasters are considered inevitable and unavoidable. The general population considers these events and their effects to be unmanageable and out of the realm of governmental influence. A change in this outlook, based on scientific explanations and approaches, could help in mitigating the effects of events such as a drought. This change could be accomplished by organizing meetings, workshops, and symposia in developing countries where governmental leaders could explain the strategies to the people.

CHAPTER 37
DROUGHT POLICY: TOWARD A PLAN OF ACTION

Donald A. Wilhite and William E. Easterling

INTRODUCTION

From the preceding discussions it is clear that in most cases, governments and international organizations have been unable to respond effectively to drought. This inability to respond was recognized by workshop participants as a serious problem of global dimensions that can only be solved through interdisciplinary studies and cooperation between scientists and policy makers.

The workshop sought to identify information needs and opportunities, develop an agenda of drought-related research priorities, prepare recommendations on ways to stimulate the development of drought assessment and response plans by national governments, and suggest ways of involving international organizations in promoting the planning process. The ultimate goal of the workshop was to initiate a "plan of action" that would represent a first step in enhancing drought planning activities.

The suggestions that follow are the editors' distillation of the collective wisdom of workshop participants into a "plan of action." This "plan" could serve as a model for drought planning at various levels of government and in various socioeconomic and political settings.

BACKGROUND

In a recent comparative analysis of drought policy in the United States and Australia, Wilhite (1986a) separated the features of that policy into three components: (1) organization, (2) response, and (3) evaluation. Organizational components were considered to be planning activities that would provide timely and reliable assessments and function as a drought early warning system, and procedures for a coordinated and efficient response, such as drought declaration. Many of the organizational features could form the foundation of a drought plan, either at the national, subnational, or supernational level.

Response components refer to assistance measures and associated administrative procedures that are in place to assist individual citizens or businesses experiencing economic and physical hardship because of drought. In Australia, relief arrangements are included under the National Disaster Relief Arrangements (NDRA), a program whereby states are expected to meet a certain base level or threshold of expenditures for disaster relief from their own resources. Expenditures in excess of that base level are cost-shared by the federal government. A wide range of relief measures are included under the NDRA agreements.

Evaluation of organizational procedures and assistance or response measures implemented to mitigate some of the hardships of drought is the third component of drought policy. Post-drought evaluations should be initiated in the recovery period to determine if the instruments of drought policy were successful, and, if not, how policy and programs should be modified to ensure a more suitable response to the next episode of severe drought. Government response efforts seldom include an evaluation component. As a result, the mistakes of the past are often repeated.

The objectives of drought policy will, of course, vary between levels of government and from country to country. In the United States, for example, the objectives of a national drought policy might be:

1. To prepare an organizational structure for assessing and responding to drought-related problems and water shortages.
2. To develop standby legislation that adequately addresses the impacts of drought through relevant assistance measures.
3. To encourage and support basic and applied research leading to the development of appropriate management strategies for all drought-prone regions.
4. To foster and support water planning and management activities at both the state and regional level.

To be successful, whether in the United States or elsewhere, drought planning must be integrated within the national and state or provincial levels of government, involving existing regional (multistate) organizations as well as the private sector where applicable. At the national level in the United States, however, the diversity of impacts associated with drought and the multitude of federal agencies with responsibility for drought assessment and response make it difficult for a single federal agency to assume leadership in the development of a national drought assessment and response plan. The development of a national policy requires an interagency approach in these instances, under the leadership of a single agency. For this as well as other reasons, such as unique local water management problems, Wilhite, et al. (1986b) have suggested that where a complex federal bureaucratic structure exists, as it does in the United States, drought planning efforts may be most effective if first initiated at the state level. In other settings, such as in less-developed countries, the drought planning process may be coordinated more easily at the national level since the bureaucratic structure may be less formidable.

The objectives of drought policy at the state level will differ from those at the national level, reflecting the unique physical, environmental, socioeconomic, and political characteristics of a particular area. For example, drought policy objectives might be:

1. To develop a monitoring system that provides early warning of impending drought conditions and impacts.
2. To develop an organizational structure that enhances drought preparedness and response by linking levels of government.

The development of the organizational structure referred to in the second objective will provide the necessary integration with drought policies at the national level and should ensure adequate coordination between the two levels.

THE DROUGHT PLANNING PROCESS

In the discussion that follows, drought planning is presented as a process involving ten steps (Fig. 1). This process is intended to be flexible so that it can be easily adapted to many sociopolitical situations and levels of government. The first three steps actually involve mustering the necessary resources to initiate development of the plan. Continuous evaluation and updating for the procedures included within each step of the process is intended in order to keep the plan most responsive to the needs of the region.

Step 1

The process is initiated through the appointment of a task force to supervise and coordinate the development of the plan. This task force has the greatest impact if the members are selected by a high-ranking political official (or at his request by a senior-level policy official). The task force should include representatives from the relevant mission agencies within government and from nongovernmental organizations. At the national level the task force structure should also include representatives from selected drought-prone areas or states. At the state level, representatives of both state and federal levels must be included.

Step 2

As their first official action, the task force will develop a general statement of purpose and the specific objectives for the plan. A statement of purpose for a drought plan at the state or provincial level could call for the provision of an effective and systematic drought assessment and response protocol. Suggested objectives for the plan (Wilhite and Wood, 1985) are to:

1. Provide timely and systematic data collection, analysis, and dissemination of drought-related information.
2. Establish criteria for starting and ending various assessment and response activities by governmental agencies during drought emergencies.
3. Provide an organizational structure that assures information flow between and within levels of government and defines the duties and responsibilities of all agencies.
4. Maintain a current inventory of governmental agency responsibilities in assessing and responding to drought emergencies.
5. Provide a mechanism to improve the assessment of the impact of drought on agriculture, industry, municipalities, vulnerable population groups, and so forth.

Step 3

An inventory of natural and human resources, including the identification of financial constraints, should be initiated by the task force. This inventory would reveal

Appointment of
Drought Task Force
(STEP 1)

Statement of Purpose
and Objectives
(STEP 2)

Inventory of Natural and Human
Resources, Financial Constraints
(STEP 3)

Development of Drought Plan
(STEP 4)

Identification of Research Needs
and Institutional Gaps
(STEP 5)

Synthesis of Drought Management
Science and Policy
(STEP 6)

Identification of Response Options
(STEP 7)

Implementation of Drought Plan
(STEP 8)

Development of Educational
and Training Programs
(STEP 9)

Development of
System Evaluation Procedures
(STEP 10)

Figure 1. A ten-step drought planning process.

the assets and liabilities that might serve to enhance or inhibit fulfillment of the objectives of the planning process. A comprehensive assessment of available resources would provide the information necessary for further action by the task force.

Step 4

The task force would be the coordinating body for the development of a drought plan. Although the process would vary from one location to another, three primary organizational activities must be completed as part of this step. First, a moisture assessment committee must be established, or coordination achieved with existing mechanisms, to monitor current and estimate likely future moisture conditions (i.e., precipitation, soil moisture, surface water storage, ground water, and streamflow). Second, an impact assessment committee must be established to identify sectors most likely to be affected by drought. Third, a policy committee of senior-level officials should be established as a coordinating body to oversee the activities of the moisture and impact assessment committees.

Moisture Assessment Committee. The moisture assessment committee would have four primary objectives: (1) to inventory data quantity and quality from current observational networks, (2) to determine the needs of primary users, (3) to develop a drought monitoring system, and (4) to develop or modify current data and information delivery systems. The functions of this committee will necessitate close interaction with the impact assessment committee.

Membership of this committee should include representatives from agencies with responsibilities for forecasting and monitoring these features of the water balance. A climatologist should be an active member of the committee for interpretations of current climate conditions. The climatologist would also provide climatological probabilities for the onset, continuation, and termination of drought conditions.

Inventory current observation networks: The moisture assessment committee must also inventory current observational networks (e.g., meteorological, hydrological) and protect and enhance those networks where necessary. It must be recognized that most current drought monitoring systems are based largely or entirely on meteorological data. These data, by themselves, do not necessarily reflect the impact of weather events on agriculture, water availability and use, health, and so forth.

Data must be collected at a sufficient spatial density to adequately represent impending drought conditions to many user groups, and they must be of sufficient quality to ensure accurate assessments. Currently, many observational networks and reports emanating from those networks do not provide sufficient information for operational and research purposes. The committee must ensure that conventional surface observation stations in national and state measurement networks are protected from being downgraded or eliminated. These networks provide essential benchmark data and time series needed for improved monitoring of the climate system.

Determine needs of primary users: For monitoring systems to be successful in both the short and long run, network designers must consider user needs from the initial design phase for data collection networks through the development of dissemination systems. Coupled with this is the need to determine the primary target groups for the network products. Communication channels between suppliers and users of information must always be open to spontaneous feedback. Agencies and organizations responsible for maintaining drought monitoring or early warning systems must receive and use feedback from users at all levels to establish and modify needs and priorities. System managers must also formally solicit the opinions and suggestions of users on a periodic basis. These solicitations should include requests for opinions about and experiences related to the use of existing products and practices as well as ideas for future product development.

Development of a drought monitoring system: In developed countries, data and information on impending drought conditions is usually available, and available on a timely basis. In less developed countries, however, the problems of monitoring drought are understandably more basic than in developed countries. Often no monitoring system exists. This may be the result of many factors or combinations of factors (e.g., inadequate numbers of trained personnel, limited financial resources, and the lack of necessary historical climatic data sets and supplementary agronomic, hydrologic, and other information). There is certainly a need to identify the minimum data set necessary to support a drought detection system in these instances. The success of a drought monitoring system can only be evaluated in the long run, and thus support and funding for such a program must remain firm, a particular concern in developing countries.

Development of data and information delivery system: In both developed and developing countries, information is not always disseminated to users in a timely manner. Furthermore, once the information reaches the user or decision maker, it may, for a number of reasons, be applied ineffectively. For example, the user may not know how to incorporate this information into a decision strategy, or the product may be badly designed as a conveyor of information.

In less-developed countries the low level of development, widespread illiteracy, relative isolation, and subsistence levels of many producers impede the flow of information from early warning systems about potentially limiting weather-related production factors. This in turn restricts the number of realistic options available to producers. In these settings the flow of data and information about drought should not be separated from the need for information to better manage rural production systems in normal and above-average years. Also, governments should not dismiss the capability of local farmers to adapt to drought through the application of indigenous practices. Although these methods may not be widely known to organizations that have the responsibility for the development and implementation of monitoring systems, they have often stood the test of time and have enabled local farmers to withstand periods of severe environmental stress. On the other hand, subsistence farmers and pastoralists are also often the most vulnerable to drought. These farmers lack reserves of cash, grain, animals, or other assets for use in times of drought. Therefore, a national drought strategy in developing countries must include special provisions for these population groups.

In many less-developed countries, local extension networks are not well established and the linkages between suppliers and users of information are poorly developed. A goal of the moisture assessment committee, working in conjunction with the impact assessment committee, should be to develop more widespread and efficient extension networks. However, without adequate education and training, farmers will not be able to effectively use information from an early warning system.

Impact Assessment Committee. Because of the obvious overlap between the impact assessment committee and the moisture situation committee, frequent communication is essential. The impact assessment committee should be composed of an interinstitutional, interdisciplinary team of experts and planners. The team may contain decision makers or it may make evaluations or recommendations to decisions makers for appropriate action. Depending on the complexity of impacts associated with drought, subcommittees may need to be appointed to concentrate on particular impact sectors. The subcommittees would report directly to the committee. The committee's responsibility is not only to ascertain the impacts of drought but also to identify and muster available resources to mitigate those effects. The committee must then identify those government agencies and nongovernmental organizations that can provide some level of assistance in response to drought as well as the exact nature of that assistance. The committee must also determine the proper protocol for requesting assistance. Communication channels between the impact committee(s) and the agencies and organizations must be well developed to ensure the timely flow of information in both directions.

Policy Coordination Committee. The policy coordination committee, comprising senior-level officials, will serve as a coordinating body to oversee the activities of the moisture assessment committee and the impact assessment committee(s), keep political officials advised of the status of impacts in the distressed area, and make recommendations about further actions that need to be taken. This coordinating committee would have direct access to political leaders. The task force could evolve into this policy committee following completion of the plan, since the composition of the two groups is similar.

Step 5

Step 5 is to be carried out concurrently with Step 4. Its purpose is to identify research needed in support of the objectives of the drought plan and to recommend research projects to remove deficiencies that may exist. Early assessments of the likely impact of drought on crop yield, for example, may require the development of plant response models or the calibration of existing models.

Institutional deficiencies should be identified as part of Step 5. Agency responsibilities or missions may need to be modified to support activities to be performed under the rubric of the drought plan.

Step 6

An essential aspect of the planning process is the synthesis of the science and the policy of drought and drought management. Previous steps in the planning process have considered these issues separately, concentrating largely on assessing the status of the science or on the existing or necessary institutional arrangements to support the plan. It is clear from workshop discussions that communication and understanding between the science and policy community is poorly developed and must be enhanced if the planning process is to be successful. Direct and extensive contact is required between the two groups in order to distinguish what is feasible from what is desirable for a broad range of science and policy issues. Integration of science and policy during the planning process will also be useful in setting research priorities and synthesizing current understanding.

Crucial to this integration process is the provision of a structure to facilitate scientific information exchange once there is mutual agreement between scientists and policy makers that such information is useful. Since this is not their primary mission, it is unlikely that scientists will freely devote extensive attention to tailoring and otherwise making available research results on a frequent or continuous basis. Rather, a specific liasion person or group may be needed to facilitate this exchange.

Step 7

Reasonable response options must be determined for each of the principal impact sectors identified under Step 4 by the impact assessment committee. These options should examine appropriate drought mitigation measures on three timescales: (1) short-term (reactive) measures implemented during the occurrence of drought, (2) medium-term (recovery) measures implemented to reduce the length of the post-drought recovery period, and (3) long-term (proactive) measures or programs implemented in an attempt to reduce societial vulnerability to future drought. However, it should be noted that societal vulnerability to drought may be influenced substantially by non-drought-related actions taken or policies implemented during nondrought periods. Thus government must establish agricultural, environmental, and natural resource programs only after giving full consideration to their effects on the vulnerability of drought-prone regions.

Step 8

The drought plan should be implemented in such a way that it gives maximum visibility to the program and credit to the agencies and organizations that have a leadership or supporting role in its operation. All or a portion of the system should be tested under simulated drought conditions before it is implemented. It is also suggested that announcement and implementation occur just before the most drought-sensitive season to take advantage of inherent public interest. The media is essential to publicizing the plan and must be informed fully of its purpose, objectives, and organizational framework.

Step 9

Educational and training programs must be established to heighten public awareness of the drought problem and the long-term need for water conservation and environmental management. These programs must be long-term and directed at all age groups and economic sectors. If such programs are not developed, government and public interest in and support for drought planning will wane during long periods of nondrought conditions.

Step 10

The final step in the establishment of a drought plan is the creation of a detailed set of procedures to ensure adequate system evaluation. To maximize the effectiveness of the system, two modes of evaluation must be in place:

1. An ongoing or operational evaluation program that considers how new technology, the availability of new research results, legislative action, and changes in political leadership may affect the operation of the system.
2. A post-drought evaluation program that documents and critically analyzes the assessment and response actions of government and implements recommendations for improving the system.

As noted previously, drought planning must be a dynamic process. The operational evaluation program is proposed to keep the drought assessment and response system current and responsive to the needs of society.

Governments should conduct or commission a post-drought evaluation of the responses to each major drought episode. These evaluations should include an analysis of the physical aspects of the drought: its impacts on soil, ground water, plants, and animals; its economic and social consequences; and the extent to which predrought planning was useful in mitigating impacts, in facilitating relief or assistance to stricken areas, and in post-drought recovery. Attention must also be directed to situations in which drought coping mechanisms worked and where societies exhibited resilience; evaluations should not focus only on those situations in which coping mechanisms failed. Provisions must be made to implement the recommendations emanating from this evaluation process. Evaluations of previous responses to severe drought are recommended as a planning aid to determine those relief measures that have been most effective. Questions to be addressed by the post-drought evaluation review team as part of this evaluation process are included in the Task Group 5 report. To ensure an unbiased appraisal it is recommended that governments place the responsibility for evaluating drought and societal response to it in the hands of nongovernmental organizations such as universities and/or specialized agencies or corporations. Private foundations and research organizations should be encouraged to support post-drought evaluations.

International agencies, both intergovernmental and nongovernmental, should also realize the value of post-drought evaluations and be prepared to sponsor them when an emergency extends beyond national boundaries, especially when internationally coordinated relief projects might be mounted.

RECOMMENDATIONS

To stimulate and facilitate the development of drought plans by national and state (subnational) governments, two recommendations are offered. First, model drought plans should be developed. Drought plans have been developed by several countries and by states within countries. Although each drought plan must be unique, reflecting the special water problems and political and socioeconomic characteristics of regions, the development process is much the same. Indices used to monitor impending drought conditions and their potential impact can also often be shared, with minor modification. It is recommended that model drought plans be developed at the national and state level to facilitate the planning process.

To identify common elements of a model drought plan and the data needed for implementation of the plan, a meeting of representatives of the United Nations, donor organizations, nongovernmental organizations, and national agencies should be convened. Nations electing to prepare drought plans based on the elements identified at this meeting could modify or suggest modifications of these elements for implementation within their boundaries. An integral part of this identification process is the creation of training programs for drought planning and management, the identification of persons capable of serving as advisors to governments desiring to prepare drought plans, and the responses to requests from governments and international organizations for assistance in drought plan preparation.

Second, a drought planning information network should be developed. It is recommended that a roster of researchers and policy officials knowledgeable and interested in drought planning and management be established to encourage drought preparedness internationally. A newsletter would facilitate informing these persons and appropriate government agencies and international organizations of drought planning activities, publications, conferences and symposia, and so forth.

CONCLUSIONS

The workshop participants support the development of a drought assessment and response policy by national and state or provincial governments governments in drought-prone areas. A ten-step process has been proposed to facilitate drought preparedness. Droughts of both long-and short-return periods should be considered when developing these plans. This policy should rely on area-wide identification of the existence and severity of drought and assessments of drought's current and possible future impacts. A policy must also recognize the need for both coping with and responding to drought. It should stress the creation of an infrastructure to supply the basic data, analysis, and research needed for assessment and response. A key part of the national policy is the development of a general plan (one that is effectively integrated with area-wide plans) to prepare for and respond to drought episodes.

It is recognized that the impacts of drought on society and the environment often linger for years after the drought has passed. Conversely, actions taken during non-drought periods often determine the level of vulnerability to future drought episodes. Thus, it is necessary to avoid the pitfall of focusing only on the impacts of drought and ignoring the effects and interrelationships of decisions made and actions taken during nondrought periods. Governments must commit the financial and human resources necessary to complete evaluations of drought impact and drought recovery to gain a full appreciation of the lingering effects of drought on societies. Above all, drought planning must be viewed as a dynamic process requiring continuous evaluation and updating.

REFERENCES

Wilhite, D. A. and D. A. Wood. 1985. Planning for drought: The role of state government. Water Resources Bulletin 21(1):31-38.

Wilhite, D. A. 1986a. Drought policy in the U.S. and Australia: A Comparative Analysis. Water Resources Bulletin 22(3):425-438.

Wilhite, D. A., N. J. Rosenberg, and M. H. Glantz. 1986b. Improving federal response to drought. Journal of Climate and Applied Meteorology 25:332-342.

APPENDIX A:
WORKSHOP PARTICIPANTS

Task Group 1 Prediction	Task Group 2 Detection, Monitoring, Early Warning
N. Nicholls, Discussion Leader	M. Coughlan, Discussion Leader.
G. McKay, Discussion Leader	A. Shaikh, Discussion Leader
P. J. Lamb, Recorder	N. J. Rosenberg, Recorder
E. Rasmusson	K. G. Hubbard
V. Klemeš	S. Goward
H. Ren	A. Setzer
L. V. Tibig	N. Strommen
S. Hastenrath	T. Bekele
G. Stout	A. Maiga
E. M. Mussage	M. Sedrati
	M. O. Berry
	J. L. Domergue

Task Group 3
Impact Assessment

H. Farnham, Discussion Leader
A. R. Magalhães,
    Discussion Leader
W. E. Easterling, Recorder

M. Parry
T. Downing
C. Sakamoto
M. Glantz
A. Sollod
I. Cordery
E. G. O'Brien
R. P. Singh
R. Schulze
H. Hill

Task Group 4
Adaptation/Adjustment

R. French, Discussion Leader
J. McIntire, Discussion Leader
S. Sonka, Recorder

S. Tewungwa
J. Venkateswarlu
B. R. Khan
H. J. Bruins
G. Popov
C. Chiduza
M. Konate
X. Han

Task Group 5
Planning and Response

T. Potter, Discussion Leader
T. C. Moremi, Discussion Leader
H. Dregne, Recorder

D. A. Wilhite
D. M. Pessoa
S. K. Sinha
J. A. Rezio
N. Raun
F. K. Hare
M. Worsham
B. Singleton
J. Olsson
D. W. Giorgis
M. Yerg
W. Koellner

APPENDIX B:
WORKSHOP POSITION STATEMENT

The recent occurrence of widespread, severe drought has once again underscored the vulnerability of developed and developing societies. These events have emphasized the need for more research and information on the causes as well as the impacts of drought and the need for effective planning to help mitigate the possible worst effects of future droughts.

The traditional approach to drought management by individual citizens, governments, and international organizations has been one of reacting to droughts (i.e., crisis management) rather then preparing for them (i.e., risk management). In the last decade, the preparation of plans for alleviating some of the worst effects of drought has drawn increasing support from government officials and the scientific community.

The recommendations or "calls for action" on the issue of drought planning which appear in the recent literature are numerous. The U.S. National Science Foundation sponsored two workshops in the mid-1970s (reported in Yevjevich, et al., 1978; Rosenberg, 1980) in which ways to mitigate the worst effects of drought were identified. Participants concluded that planning was necessary to achieve this goal. Additionally, the U.S. General Accounting Office (GAO, 1979) reviewed federal relief efforts during the drought of 1976-77 and concluded that their efforts were largely ineffective, poorly coordinated, and untimely. The formulation of a national plan was recommended as a means of improving federal drought response efforts. At this writing no action on this recommendation by GAO has been taken.

Wilhite et al. (1986) have completed an evaluation of federal and state drought assessment and response efforts made in the United States during 1974-77. They recommend specific actions to improve drought assessment and response activities in the U.S. and elsewhere and suggest the development of drought plans at the state, federal, and regional levels as the best method to implement those actions. Several U.S. states have developed drought plans as a result of the mid-1970s and subsequent droughts. Certain of these plans have proven useful in dealing with drought-related water shortages (Wilhite and Wood, 1985).

Criticism and concern over the inefficiency and ineffectiveness of past drought response efforts by governmental and international organizations is not confined to the United States. Drought response efforts in many countries have been subject to criticism. During the mid-1970s, for example, response efforts in the United Kingdom, Canada, and Africa have drawn considerable attention. More recent responses to drought by governments and international organizations have been similarly criticized.

The criticism has generated considerable attention in the popular press and in the scientific literature.

Most recently, a report prepared by the U.S. Academy of Sciences (1986) and a memorandum from the World Meteorological Organization (1986) have emphasized the importance of improving drought assessment and response activities worldwide. The National Academy of Science report, a review of the programs of the National Climate Program Office, identified drought policy as a principal climate program policy issue and recommend that actions be taken now. Likewise, WMO has called for the development of national drought response plans in a recent memorandum to their permanent representatives. Further, U.S. Representative James Scheuer has drafted legislation (H.R. 4760) entitled the "African Drought Monitoring and Research Act of 1986." This legislation proposes to enhance current drought prediction and monitoring capability in order to improve our early warning of drought in Africa and elsewhere.

The arguments in favor of the preparation of drought plans and support for their development seem overwhelming to the organizers of the International Symposium and Workshop on Drought. Why then has so little action taken place? The purpose of this workshop is to identify the factors that constrain governments from undertaking systematic drought planning efforts and to identify ways to eliminate or overcome those constraints. Furthermore, we propose to develop an agenda of research priorities needed to support the development of more effective drought assessment and response systems. This will include the identification of potential funding sources. Finally, we propose to develop recommendations for an organizational structure to serve as the basis for the formulation of drought plans appropriate for developed and developing countries and a "plan of action" for implementing those recommendations.

Drought planning can be defined as actions taken by government, industry, individual citizens, and others in advance of drought for the purpose of mitigating some of the impacts associated with its occurrence. For purposes of this workshop, drought planning should include, but is not limited to, the following activities:

1. A monitoring/early warning system to provide decision makers at all levels with information about the onset, continuation, and termination of drought conditions and their severity;

2. Operational assessment programs to reliably determine the likely impact of the drought event;

3. An institutional structure for coordinating governmental actions, including information flow within and between levels of government, and drought declaration and revocation criteria and procedures;

4. Appropriate drought assistance programs with predetermined eligibility and implementation criteria;

5. Financial resources to maintain operational programs and to initiate research required to support drought assessment and response activities; and

6. Educational programs designed to promote the adoption of appropriate drought mitigation strategies among the various economic sectors most affected by drought.

REFERENCES CITED

GAO. 1979. Federal Response to the 1976-77 Drought: What Should Be Done Next? Report to the Comptroller General, Washington, D.C. 29 pp.

National Academy of Sciences. 1986. The National Climate Program: Early Achievement and Future Directions. Washington D.C.

Rosenberg, N. J., ed. 1980. Drought in the Great Plains: Research on Impacts and Strategies. Water Resources Publications, Littleton, Colorado.

Wilhite, D. A., N. J. Rosenberg, and M. H. Glantz. 1986. Improving Federal Response to Drought. Journal of Climate and Applied Meteorology 25:332-342.

Wilhite, D. A. and D. A. Wood. 1985. Planning for Drought: The Role of State Government. Water Resources Bulletin 21:31-38.

World Meteorological Organization. 1986. Model Drought Response Plan. Memo to Permanent Representatives of Members of WMO, May 14. Geneva, Switzerland.

Yevjevich, V., W. A. Hall, and J. D. Salas. 1978. Drought Research Needs. Water Resources Publications, Littleton, Colorado.

ABOUT THE CONTRIBUTORS

Teferi Bekele is an agricultural engineering expert for the Relief and Rehabilitation Commission in Addis Ababa, Ethiopia. He is involved in relief and rehabilitation project planning (drought prediction, priority setting, planning, project preparation, and monitoring) for drought-prone areas of Ethiopia. He is a member of the Ethiopian Engineering Association.

Timothy R. Carter is a research scholar at the International Institute for Applied Systems Analysis (IIASA), Laxenburg, Austria. He is working on a IIASA/United Nations Environment Program (UNEP) project, Integrated Approaches to Climatic Impacts: The Vulnerability of Food Production in Marginal Areas. He is a member of the Institute of British Geographers and the Association of British Climatologists, and a fellow of the Royal Meteorological Society.

Ian Cordery is an associate professor of civil engineering at the University of New South Wales, Australia, where he teaches surface water hydrology. He has specialized in flood hydrology for many years and has had considerable professional involvement in formulating philosophy for the estimation of flood magnitudes for design. In the last five years, he has become interested in drought, particularly the possibilities of forecasting drought.

Michael J. Coughlan is the head of the Climate Analysis Section of the Australian National Climate Centre, Australian Bureau of Meteorology, with responsibilities for broad-scale climate monitoring activities and operation of the Australian Drought Watch System. He is chairman of the Australian National Committee for the World Climate Program, honorary treasurer of the Australian Branch of the Royal Meteorological Society, and a member of the WMO Commission for Climatology.

Thomas E. Downing is a consultant at the Center for Technology, Environment and Development, and a graduate student in the Graduate School of Geography at Clark University, Worcester, Massachusetts. He spent four years in Kenya working on environmental management and climate impact assessment and is currently coediting a volume of papers, Drought in Kenya: Lessons from 1984. He is a member of the Association of American Geographers.

Mary Downton is an associate scientist in the Environmental and Societal Impacts Group at the National Center for Atmospheric Research, Boulder, Colorado. As a statistician and computer programmer, she has participated in studies on a broad range of topics related to the interactions between climate and society. She is currently studying the impacts of temperature change on the citrus industry in Florida.

Harold E. Dregne is Horn Distinguished Professor of Soil Science at Texas Tech University in Lubbock. His special interests are arid land development and conservation of natural resources. His publications include books dealing with arid lands, irrigation water salinity, soils, dryland agriculture, and desertification. He is a fellow of the American Society of Agronomy, the Soil Science Society of America, and the American Association for the Advancement of Science, and he is a member of Sigma Xi and Phi Kappa Phi.

William E. Easterling is an associate professional scientist in the Climate and Meteorology Section of the Illinois State Water Survey. He is also an adjunct assistant professor in the Geography Department at the University of Illinois. His research involves the interaction of climate and society and the application of climate information in decision making. He is a member of the American Meteorological Society, the Regional Science Association, and the Association of American Geographers.

Reginald J. French is the chief soil agronomist in the Department of Agriculture, Adelaide, South Australia. He has carried out field studies on land use, soil conservation, soil fertility and plant nutrition, and the effect of climatic factors on the phenology and water use efficiency of crops and pastures, and he is studying multifactor systems that can help farmers reach the potential yield of crops and pastures under dryland farming. He is a fellow of the Australian Institute of Agriculture Science.

Dawit Wolde Giorgis is a visiting fellow at the Center of International Studies at Princeton University, Princeton, New Jersey. He is the former chief commissioner of the Relief and Rehabilitation Commission (RRC) of Ethiopia, which administered international aid during the recent famine in Ethiopia. Giorgis helped establish the RRC in 1975, the only agency of its kind in Africa. He was also chief government/political representative in Eritrea and deputy foreign minister of Ethiopia.

Michael H. Glantz is the head of the Environmental and Societal Impacts Group and senior scientist at the National Center for Atmospheric Research. He is interested in the effects of climate on society and the effects of society on climate, especially the interaction between climate anomalies and human activities and its effects on quality of life. He has edited several books and is the author of numerous articles on issues related to climate, environment, and policy.

Samuel N. Goward is a faculty member of the geography department of the University of Maryland. His primary research interest is extraction of land physical measurements from remotely sensed observations. He is currently principal investigator for cooperative research between the University of Maryland's geography department and the Earth Resources Branch of NASA/Goddard Space Flight Center.

F. Kenneth Hare is commissioner of the Ontario Nuclear Safety Review. He recently retired from the University of Toronto, where he was a university professor in geography and provost of Trinity College. He is by training a geographer and climatologist, and he is interested in the interdisciplinary study of the human environment. Recently he has been involved in some major controversial environmental issues, including climatic change, acid deposition, and lead in the environment.

Stefan L. Hastenrath is a professor in the Department of Meteorology at the University of Wisconsin-Madison. His publications include studies of climate and circulation of the tropics; drought in Northeast Brazil; and climatic and heat budget atlases of the tropical Atlantic, eastern Pacific, and Indian oceans. He is a member of the American Meteorological Society, the American Geophysical Union, the Meteorological Society of Japan, and the Royal Meteorological Society.

Kenneth G. Hubbard is an associate professor of the Center for Agricultural Meteorology and Climatology at the University of Nebraska-Lincoln and director of the High Plains Regional Climate Center. His areas of interest are automated weather monitoring, physical processes in the boundary layer, and climatology. He is a member of the American Meteorological Society, the American Society of Agronomy, Gamma Sigma Delta, and the AMS Committee on Agricultural and Forest Meteorology.

Vit Klemeš is a senior scientist at the National Hydrology Research Institute of Environment Canada. He has held research positions at the Czechoslovak Academy of Sciences and the University of Toronto, taught at the Universities of Toronto and Ottawa, and was a visiting professor at several universities in Europe, the United States, and Australia. His main research interests are in hydrology and water resource systems, in which areas he has published extensively.

Mama Konaté is chief of the Agrometeorology Division in the National Meteorology Directorate, Bamako, Mali. He also is chief of the World Meteorological Organization pilot project in agrometeorology, which he initiated. His research interests involve general agroclimatology and operational agrometeorological assistance. He is Mali's principal delegate to the WMO Commission for Agricultural Meteorology and is a member of the advisory working group of that Commission.

Clifford D. May is a correspondent in the Washington, D.C., Bureau of the New York Times. From 1983 to 1985 he was a Times correspondent in Africa and the West Africa Bureau Chief. In that capacity, he covered stories in more than two dozen African nations, with a particular emphasis on questions of economic development. In late 1984 and 1985, Mr. May covered the catastrophic famine in Ethiopia and several other countries.

John McIntire is a principal economist with the International Livestock Centre for Africa (ILCA) in Addis Ababa. He was the principal economist with the International Crops Research Institute for the Semi-Arid Tropics (ICRISAT) from 1980 to 1984. His principal area of interest is the economics of technical change in African agriculture.

Tswelopele C. Moremi is the coordinator of rural development for the Ministry of Finance and Development Planning in Gaborone, Botswana. She is responsible for the overall coordination of rural development projects and programs within the government of Botswana. She is also the executive secretary of the Rural Development Council (RDC), which makes policy recommendations to Botswana's Cabinet on all rural development matters.

Raymond P. Motha is a supervising agricultural meteorologist at the Joint Agricultural Weather Facility of the U.S. Department of Agriculture's World Agricultural Outlook Board. He is responsible for global agricultural weather monitoring and determining the impact of anomalous weather on the crop yield potential. Dr. Motha is a member of the American Society of Agronomy and the American Meteorological Society.

K. Kailasanathan is an agrometeorologist at the Water Technology Centre, Indian Agricultural Research Institute, New Delhi. He has written numerous articles for national and international journals, including several popular articles on biometeorology and agricultural meteorology.

Neville Nicholls is a principal research scientist with the Bureau of Meteorology Research Centre, Melbourne, Australia. His publications include papers on long-range weather forecasting and the causes and impacts of the El Nino/Southern Oscillation phenomenon. He is a member of the American Meteorological Society's Committee on the Southern Hemisphere and is on the editorial board of the Journal of Climatology.

Martin L. Parry is a senior lecturer in geography and the coordinator of the Atmospheric Impacts Research (AIR) Group at the University of Birmingham, England. He is also a project leader of the Climate Impacts Project of the International Institute for Applied Systems Analysis (IIASA), Laxenburg, Austria.

Dirceu M. Pessoa is an economist and social researcher in the Department of Economics at the Social Research Institute of the Fundacao Joaquim Nabuco, Recife, Brazil. He specializes in studies on rural development related to economic development on regional and national levels. His publications have dealt with agricultural problems in Northeast Brazil and drought planning and management. He is a member of the Brazilian Federal Economic Council and the American Economic Association.

Thomas D. Potter is the director of the World Climate Programme Department in the World Meteorological Organization, Geneva, Switzerland. He is responsible for overall coordination of the international World Climate Programme. Dr. Potter is a former director of the Environmental Data and Information Service and the National Climatic Center. He is a fellow of the American Meteorological Society and a member of Sigma Xi.

Eugene M. Rasmusson is a faculty research associate at the Cooperative Institute for Climate Studies, Department of Meteorology, University of Maryland. His research centers on climate variability problems, and he has analyzed the El Niño/Southern Oscillation phenomenon extensively. He is a fellow of the American Meteorological Society and a member of the American Geophysical Union and the American Association for the Advancement of Science.

William E. Riebsame is the director of the Natural Hazards Center at the University of Colorado in Boulder. He teaches hazards and natural resources management, and his research interests include people-environment relationships, especially in the Great Plains and mountain West. He is a member of the American Association of Geographers, the American Meteorological Society, and the American Association for the Advancement of Science.

Norman J. Rosenberg, former director of the Center for Agricultural Meteorology and Climatology, University of Nebraska—Lincoln, is director of the Climate Resources Program of Resources for the Future, Washington, D.C. He specializes in microclimatology; other research interests include carbon dioxide sources and sinks in agricultural fields. Rosenberg is a fellow of the American Society of Agronomy, the American Meteorological Society, and the American Association for the Advancement of Science.

Clarence M. Sakamoto is chief of the Models Branch of NOAA's Assessment and Information Services Center. He is also professor of Atmospheric Sciences at the University of Missouri-Columbia. His research emphasizes the transfer of agroclimate technology to developing countries. Dr. Sakamoto is a certified consulting meteorologist with the American Meteorological Society. He is a member of the International Society of Biometeorology and Sigma Xi.

Roland E. Schulze is a professor of agricultural engineering at the University of Natal, Pietermaritzburg, South Africa. At the time of the Symposium, he was a visiting professor at the Utah Water Research Laboratory, Utah State University, Logan.

Suresh K. Sinha is a professor of plant physiology at the Water Technology Centre of the Indian Agricultural Research Institute in New Delhi. His main research interest is crop productivity, particularly with limited irrigation under drought. He is a fellow of the Indian National Science Academy and the Indian Academy of Sciences. He is also a member of the Scientific Advisory Committee on the Climate Impact Programme of IIASA/UNEP.

Steven T. Sonka is a professor of management in the Department of Agricultural Economics at the University of Illinois at Urbana–Champaign. He is also a principal scientist at the Illinois State Water Survey. His research centers on decision making by agricultural decision makers, climate's impact on decision making, computer-assisted decision making, and the changing structure of agriculture.

Thomas R. Stewart is a psychologist with the Center for Research on Judgment and Policy at the University of Colorado. He specializes in the study of human judgment and decision making and has conducted research on visual air quality, expert judgment in weather forecasting, and the decision processes involved in the use of weather forecasts by fruit growers.

Louis T. Steyaert is the program manager for the NOAA Assessment and Information Services Center's program on drought early warning. His area of specialization includes development of tools for using satellite data to assess the impact of weather variability on crop production in developing countries. He is a member of the American Meteorological Society, International Society of Biometeorology, and Sigma Xi.

Norton D. Strommen is chief meteorologist of the World Agricultural Outlook Board of the U.S. Department of Agriculture. He coordinates weather and climate activities for USDA. He is a fellow of the American Meteorological Society and a member of the American Association for the Advancement of Science, Sigma Xi, the International Society of Biometeorology, and the American Society of Agronomy.

Jonathan Taylor is an assistant professor of geography and recreation at the University of Wyoming, Laramie. In 1985 he researched Great Plains farmers' perceptions of drought, general climate, and aquifer conditions in a study supported by the Environmental and Societal Impacts Group, National Center for Atmospheric Research. This study provided the data on which the paper in this volume is based.

K. Traoré is chief of the Research and Development Section of the Agrometeorology Division at the National Service of Meteorology, Bamako, Mali. His research involves the use of climate and weather data in operational assistance to agriculture, and he is coauthor of several reports and publications on that subject. He is also involved in the monitoring of weather impact on crops and food production for Mali's Early Warning System.

Compton J. Tucker is a research scientist with the Laboratory for Terrestrial Physics, NASA/Goddard Space Flight Center, in Greenbelt, Maryland.

A. K. Vasistha is an economist in the Division of Agricultural Economics at the International Research Institute in New Delhi. He is presently visiting the International Rice Research Institute in the Philippines to study advanced techniques in agricultural economics.

Jagarlapudi Venkateswarlu is the head of the Division of Resource Management, Central Research Institute for Dryland Agriculture, in Hyderabad, India. He is responsible for coordinating and supervising research on dryland farming at national and regional levels. His research activities include crop production under semiarid conditions in Alfisols. He is the technical editor of the Journal of the Indian Society of Soil Science.

Donald A. Wilhite is an associate professor of agricultural climatology at the Center for Agricultural Meteorology and Climatology at the University of Nebraska-Lincoln. He also has an adjunct appointment with the National Center for Atmospheric Research. He specializes in studies of the impact of climate on society, particularly climate's effects on agriculture. He is the author of numerous papers on drought management and planning, his primary area of research activity. He is a member of the American Meteorological Society, the American Association for the Advancement of Science, and Sigma Xi.